The beasts of the field and forest had a Lion as their king. He was neither
wrathful, cruel nor tyrannical, but just and gentle as a king could be.
During his reign he made a royal proclamation for a general assembly
of all the birds and beasts, and drew up conditions for a universal league,
in which the Wolf and the Lamb, the Panther and the Kid, the Tiger and
the Stag, the Dog and the Hare, should live together in perfect peace
and amity. The Hare said, 'Oh, how I have longed to see this day, in which
the weak shall take their place with impunity by the side of the strong'.
And after the Hare said this, he ran for his life.

Aesop

Es regierte einmal ein Löwe über die Tiere des Feldes und des Waldes.
Er war weder aufbrausend noch grausam oder tyrannisch, sondern so
gerecht und sanftmütig, wie ein König nur sein konnte. Eines Tages berief
er eine Vollversammlung seiner Untertanen ein und verkündete neue
Regeln für einen Universalbund, in dem der Wolf und das Lamm, der Leo-
pard und das Zicklein, der Tiger und der Hirsch, der Hund und der Hase
in vollkommener Harmonie und Freundschaft miteinander leben sollten.
Da sprach der Hase: „Oh, wie habe ich diesen Tag herbeigesehnt, an dem
die Schwachen ihren sicheren Platz an der Seite der Starken einnehmen
werden." Und kaum hatte er dies gesagt, rannte er um sein Leben.

Äsop

Of Lions and Lambs

Benita Suchodrev

KEHRER

Texts by / Texte von

Matthias Harder
Curator, Helmut Newton Foundation /
Kurator, Helmut Newton Stiftung

[12] *Blackpool 2.0*

Benita Suchodrev
Photographer / Fotografin

[182] *Of Lions and Lambs /
Von Löwen und Lämmern*

Mark Gisbourne
Art historian, Critic, Curator /
Kunsthistoriker, Kritiker, Kurator

[312] *From Bathos to Pathos /
Vom Bathos zum Pathos*

There's no place like this place,
anywhere near this place, so this must be the place.

Seen on a wall in Blackpool

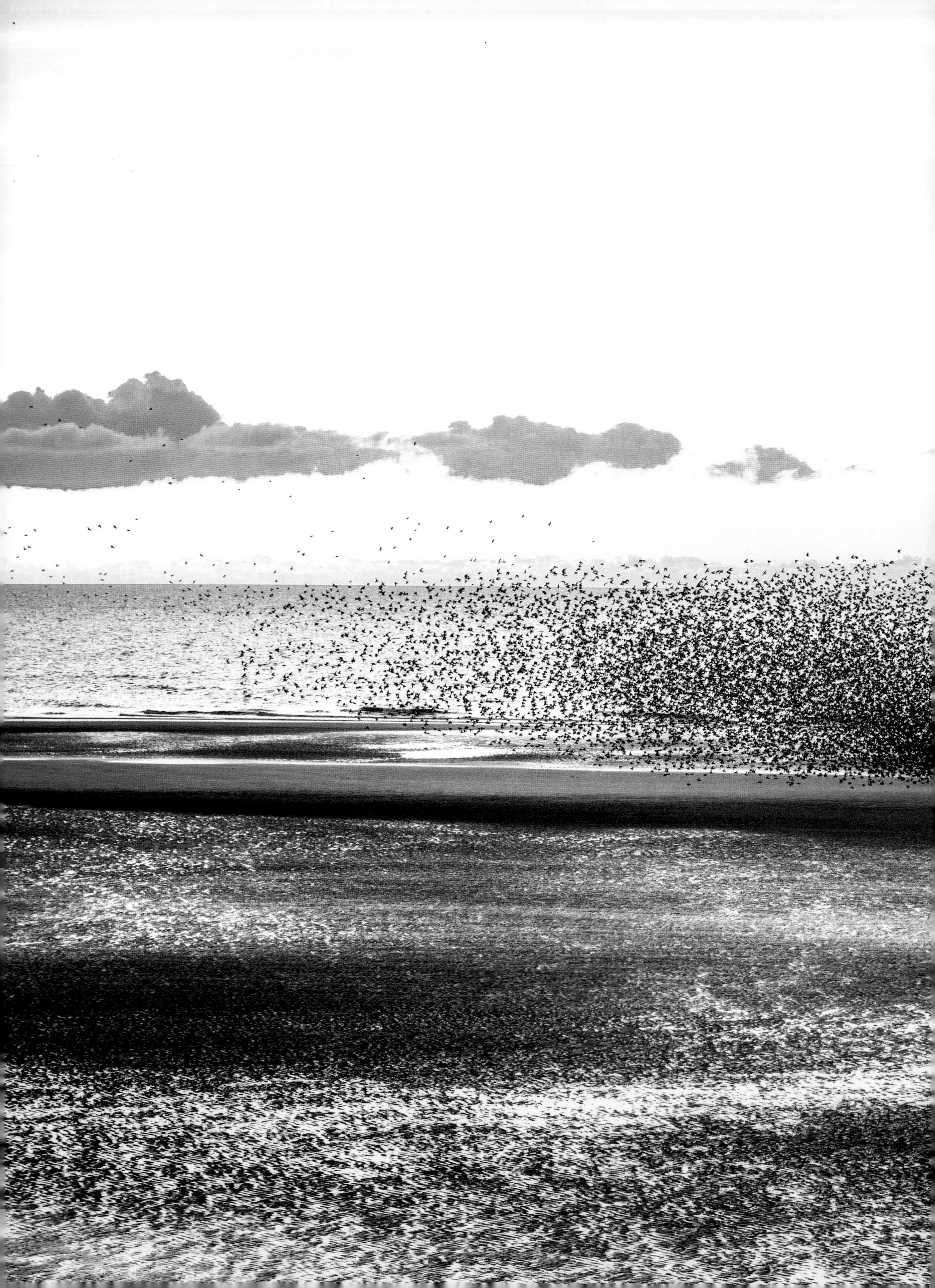

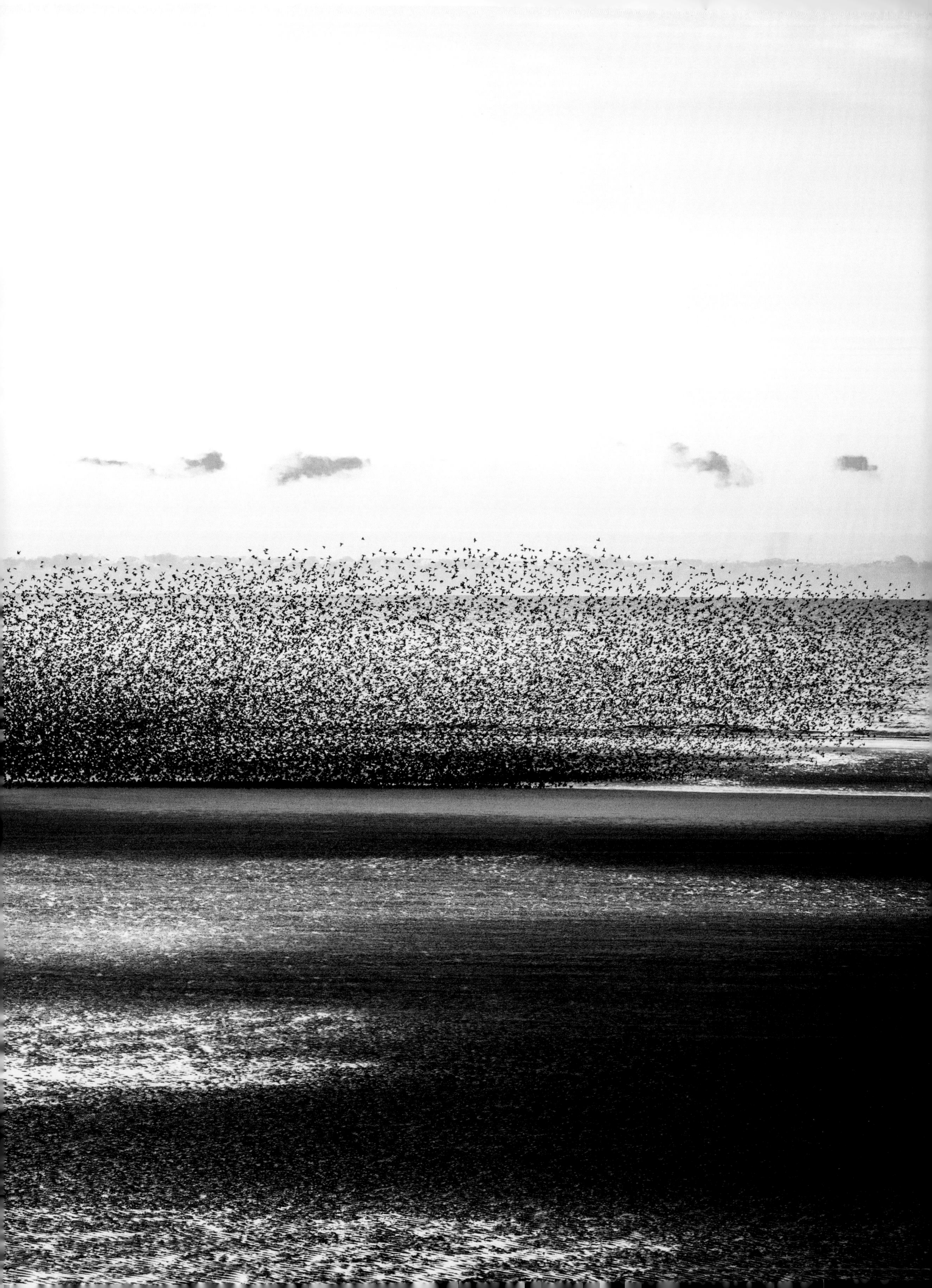

Matthias Harder
Curator, Helmut Newton Foundation /
Kurator, Helmut Newton Stiftung

Blackpool 2.0

When we visit a relatively unglamorous place for a second time — a place we first came upon by accident but nevertheless found of interest — it suddenly seems familiar. Ideally, we now want to experience more, see more and know more. The earlier visit creates a layer of visual experience and emotional memory that we now want to enhance. In the case of Benita Suchodrev, who is already much travelled, this place is called Blackpool. It is certainly not the United Kingdom's top destination, especially not on the eve of Brexit. Every year, some 40 million tourists visit from all over the world, most of them travelling to London, only a very few to Blackpool. Translated into pictures — or perhaps rather into a picture essay — the place, with its substantial tourist history, has now become a metaphor for unimaginative, cheap entertainment, as we could see and feel above all in Benita Suchodrev's first photo series, *48 Hours Blackpool*. In this second publication, once again Suchodrev applies a magnifying glass, as it were, to the coastal town on the Irish Sea. The tattered Union Jack flapping in the wind appears at the end of the book as a symbol of gradual decline. But equally, a glimmer of hope, especially a sense of cohesion between people, shines through again and again. Of course, the narrative time does not correspond to real time; the whole series could also be a daydream-like film told through stills, not unlike the style of Jim Jarmusch.

Consciously choosing February to travel along the English coast, as Benita Suchodrev has now done two years after her first trip, presents a certain amount of risk and makes wild beach parties unlikely — in our expectation of the images as well. And so, once again, we see no Blackpool visitors bathing, lying on the sand and in the sun or riding on carousels, no children larking about on the beach, no posing teenagers. Unlike in summer, this time life plays out not just outdoors, but also in the pubs full of retro charm and in more exclusive venues. Heavy drinking goes on everywhere, albeit a little more stylishly at the parties. It

is primarily the locals whom Suchodrev has portrayed here almost as quickly and intuitively as in her first Blackpool series: in 2017, it was mainly British tourists going over the top as they enjoyed stag parties on the street or perhaps indulged their gambling addiction just for the weekend, as Blackpool has countless amusement arcades.

During her first trip to Blackpool, Benita Suchodrev hardly ever looked through the camera viewfinder or at the screen while she took photos, unlike most of her colleagues who aim to create perfect compositions. And on this occasion, too, she would react spontaneously to a situation, and so not all her pictures are squeezed into a geometric grid. Nevertheless, a balanced composition is important to Suchodrev, and it can arise with or without looking through the viewfinder, as can be seen in the book. Suchodrev continues to take an interest in the individual and in people's intense gaze, in emotions, including the rifts in society. She remains true to herself and to the high-contrast translation of harsh life into sombre, sometimes mysterious black-and-white images, even when the light of February's much shorter days was completely different when compared to the summer images of the first project. Spectacular cloud formations with huge flocks of birds appear in the sky and the winter sea is very rough — the Berlin photographer captures both of these in pictures. Another new feature is the extensive depiction of a masked ball. Here we encounter men in dinner jackets and bird masks, others wearing the traditional three-piece suit along with a Batman mask, the women in furs or strapless evening dresses with feather-trimmed hats, while the 'Welcome to Blackpool' sign on desolate Barton Avenue one rainy night emphasises the contrast between two diametrically opposed worlds. In other night shots, she lets us in on the capitalist system's dark side, for example in the lives of homeless people and beggars looking for a makeshift bed for the night, while all the shops are closed and a milky, hazy light created by stores' neon signs hangs over the town.

Alongside the people and their portraits Benita Suchodrev also includes animals, such as seagulls and pigeons, dogs and sheep, elephants and monkeys. She encountered some of them on the street, on the loose to an extent, others in the zoo. Animals are, both directly and figuratively, a new and important aspect in Suchodrev's visualisation of Blackpool. Neither the people with their addictions nor the caged animals, linked here by a bridge that is both visual and thematic, can escape their fate. They have come to terms with it; they have given up the fight. And where there are sheep, there are also lambs — which find their way into the book's title, *Of Lions and Lambs*. The proud, titular lions appear twice in this publication: as a close-up portrait pressed against the bars of a cage — a particularly sad sight — and in the form of a bronze, snarling version with its paw on the globe. But the UK's once hegemonic, indeed global pretensions now seem — at least from Blackpool's perspective — somewhat absurd. This is emphasized all the more as on the next double page Suchodrev follows up with an equally threatening animal, namely a carnivorous dinosaur in attack mode. But this one is made of mere plastic, provoking fear or respect only in little children, if at all. Benita Suchodrev returns time and again to the now half-empty promenades and drag bars, where once more she finds interesting themes and earns the trust of local drunks. Within the entire series of images, Suchodrev gives the appropriate space to short sequences, following, for example, a drag queen and taking multiple portraits of her on the street. These surprising narratives come to an end just as quickly, dissolving into the next scene. Suchodrev leaves lots of room for imagination, and in this way shows a similarity with Arthur Schnitzler's *Dream Story*: visual clues suffice, nothing is elaborated; rather, the tension is maintained at its peak and unbroken as we pursue our own understanding of the story.

In *Of Lions and Lambs*, Suchodrev plunges once again into the microcosm of this town of 140,000 souls, revealing visually something that surely remains hidden to most visitors on their short trips to the west coast of England. She shows us the patina of the ageing house façades and funfair rides; she looks empathetically and with keen powers of observation upon outsiders and ordinary people. The heart of her visual interest remains the human being in all his or her facets. And so, as we leaf through the book, we accompany the photographer from one encounter to the next and *en passant* — beyond her subjective approach — learn a few things about this town, such as the merciless clash between rich and poor, the existence of a Jewish cemetery, numerous old people's homes and soup kitchens. We are walking with Suchodrev around dark streets, accompanying her to a golf club, looking at the window displays of household goods' stores and antiques shops where Princess Diana still smiles on decorative plates, following her into supermarkets with overflowing shelves, into hoarders' houses and church vestibules with illuminated crosses. Suchodrev addresses and scrutinizes many of the clichés that Continental Europeans would surely often mention in connection with the UK, although her raw, poetic images offer an in-depth depiction of the atmosphere of a specific place that most of us do not know personally. In doing so, she picks up where she left off in *48 Hours Blackpool* and spins another thread into her story, one that incorporates religion: on a sign with white lettering in an otherwise dark church, we read verses about the Lion and the Lamb as God — hung up so that the congregation can sing along. The two animals represent the greatest possible dualism and, at the same time, God or two different approaches to religion — one can hardly imagine a greater contrast. What is intoxicating and authentic about Suchodrev's stories — in her first as well as her second Blackpool book — is both her method and her use of style. And we should bear the tension within these fascinating, disturbing images until, on our first visit to Blackpool, we can compare them with our own.

Blackpool 2.0

Wenn wir einen relativ unspektakulären Ort ein zweites Mal besuchen, an den wir zunächst zufällig gereist sind, dort aber etwas Interessantes vorgefunden haben, kommt er uns plötzlich vertraut vor: Im Idealfall wollen wir jetzt mehr erfahren, mehr sehen und kennenlernen. Der frühere Besuch bildet eine Schicht aus visueller Erfahrung und emotionaler Erinnerung, die wir nun erweitern wollen. Im Fall von Benita Suchodrev, die schon viel gereist ist, heißt dieser Ort Blackpool. Es ist wahrlich nicht die Top-Destination im Vereinigten Königreich, insbesondere nicht am Vorabend des Brexits. Es kommen jedes Jahr etwa 40 Millionen Touristen aus der ganzen Welt, die meisten von ihnen reisen nach London, nur sehr wenige nach Blackpool. In Bilder — oder vielleicht besser: in einen Bildessay — übersetzt, ist der Ort mit seiner durchaus bedeutenden touristischen Historie inzwischen eine Metapher für unreflektiert-billiges Entertainment, was wir vor allem in der ersten Werkreihe *48 Hours Blackpool* von Benita Suchodrev sehen und spüren konnten. Mit dieser zweiten Publikation wird die Küstenstadt an der Irischen See von der Künstlerin erneut wie unter ein Brennglas gelegt. Der zerfetzte Union Jack, der im Wind flattert, taucht als Symbol des schleichenden Untergangs am Ende des Buches auf. Doch auch Hoffnung, insbesondere im zwischenmenschlichen Zusammenhalt, blitzt immer wieder durch. Die erzählte Zeit entspricht natürlich nicht der Realzeit, das Ganze könnte ebenso ein tagtraumhafter Film sein, der in Standbildern erzählt wird, dem Stil Jim Jarmuschs nicht unähnlich.

Die englische Küste bewusst im Februar zu bereisen, wie es Benita Suchodrev nun zwei Jahre nach ihrem ersten Abstecher erneut unternahm, ist ein gewisses Wagnis und lässt auch für die Rezeption der Bilder keine ausgelassenen Strandpartys erwarten. Und so sehen wir wiederum keine badenden, im Sand und in der Sonne liegenden oder Karussell fahrenden Blackpool-Besucher, keine am Strand herumtobenden Kinder oder posierenden Jugendlichen. Das Leben spielt sich diesmal — anders als im Sommer — nicht nur draußen ab, sondern ebenso in den Pubs voller Retrocharme und in exklusiveren Sälen. Heftig getrunken wird überall, auf den Partys nur etwas stilvoller. Es sind in erster Linie die Einheimischen, die Suchodrev hier porträtiert hat, und das beinahe ebenso schnell und intuitiv wie in der ersten Blackpool-Serie: 2017 waren es zumeist britische Touristen, die auf den Straßen recht exzessiv Junggesellenabschiede feierten oder vielleicht nur ein Wochenende lang der Spielsucht frönten, denn Spielhallen gibt es in Blackpool unzählige.

Benita Suchodrev schaute während ihrer ersten Blackpool-Reise nur selten durch den Kamerasucher oder auf das Display, während sie fotografierte — anders als die meisten ihrer Kollegen, die auf perfekte Bildkompositionen bedacht sind. Auch dieses Mal reagierte sie spontan auf Situationen, und so ist nicht jedes ihrer Bilder in ein geometrisches Raster gepresst. Gleichwohl ist der Fotografin eine ausbalancierte Komposition wichtig, und die kann mit oder ohne Kamerasucherblick entstehen, wie im Buch zu sehen ist. Suchodrev interessiert sich weiterhin für das Individuelle und für intensive Blicke der Menschen, für Emotionen inklusive gesellschaftlicher Abgründe. Sie bleibt sich und der kontrastreichen Übersetzung des echten Lebens in düstere, mitunter mysteriöse Schwarz-Weiß-Bilder treu, selbst wenn im Vergleich zu den Sommerbildern des ersten Projekts im Februar mit weitaus kürzeren Tagen eine völlig veränderte Lichtsituation herrschte. Der Himmel zeigt spektakuläre Wolkenkonstellationen mit riesigen Vogelschwärmen und das Meer ist im Winter sehr unruhig — beides hielt die Berliner Fotografin in Bildern fest. Neu ist ebenso die groß angelegte Situationsschilderung eines Maskenballs. Hier begegnen wir Männern im Smoking und mit Vogelmaske, andere erscheinen im traditionellen Dreiteiler mit Batman-Maske, die Frauen im Pelz oder in schulterfreien Abendkleidern mit gefederten Hüten, während das Schild „Welcome to Blackpool" an der trostlosen Barton Avenue in einer regnerischen Nacht den Kontrast zwischen zwei diametralen Welten betont. In anderen Nachtaufnahmen lässt sie uns teilhaben an den Schattenseiten des kapitalistischen Systems, etwa am Leben der Obdachlosen und Bettler, die sich ein provisorisches Nachtlager suchen, während alle Läden geschlossen sind und sich ein milchig-diesiges Licht über die Stadt legt, das sich aus den Leuchtreklamen der Geschäfte speist.

Neben die Menschen und ihre Porträts stellt Benita Suchodrev auch Tiere, etwa Möwen und Tauben, Hunde und Schafe, Elefanten und Affen. Einigen von ihnen begegnete sie auf der Straße, also gewissermaßen in Freiheit, anderen im Zoo. Das Tier ist — unmittelbar und im übertragenen Sinn — ein neuer, wichtiger Aspekt in Suchodrevs Visualisierung von Blackpool. Weder die Menschen in ihren Abhängigkeiten noch die Käfigtiere, zwischen denen hier eine visuelle und inhaltliche Brücke geschlagen wird, können ihrem Schicksal entfliehen. Sie haben sich arrangiert, sie haben aufgegeben, Widerstand zu leisten. Und wo Schafe sind, da sind auch Lämmer — die in den Buchtitel hineinfinden: *Of Lions and Lambs*. Die dort genannten stolzen Löwen tauchen in dieser Publikation zweimal auf: als nahansichtiges Porträt an Gitterstäbe gepresst, ein besonders trauriger Anblick, und in Form einer bronzenen, zähnefletschenden Version mit der Tatze auf der Weltkugel. Doch dieser frühere hegemoniale, ja globale Anspruch Großbritanniens wirkt — zumindest von Blackpool aus betrachtet — inzwischen etwas absurd. Das gilt umso mehr, als die Fotografin ein ebenso bedrohliches Tier auf der nächsten Doppelseite folgen lässt, nämlich einen fleischfressenden Dinosaurier im Angriffsmodus, der jedoch nur aus Kunststoff gefertigt ist und Schrecken oder Respekt wohl allenfalls bei Kleinkindern auslöst. Benita Suchodrev kehrt immer wieder in die nun halbleeren Flaniermeilen und Travestiebars zurück, wo sie erneut interessante Motive findet und Vertrauen zu den bürgerlichen Trinkern. Die Fotografin gibt kleinen Sequenzen innerhalb der gesamten Bildabfolge den entsprechenden Raum, so folgt sie beispielsweise einer Dragqueen und porträtiert sie mehrfach auf der Straße. Solche überraschenden Narrationen brechen alsbald wieder ab und blenden zur nächsten Szene über. Suchodrev lässt unserer Fantasie viel Freiraum, und so ist es ähnlich wie in Arthur Schnitzlers *Traumnovelle*: Visuelle Andeutungen genügen, nichts wird ausformuliert, die Spannung vielmehr auf einem Höhepunkt gehalten und nicht aufgelöst, während wir in der Rezeption die Geschichte individuell weiterdenken.

Die Fotografin dringt mit *Of Lions and Lambs* erneut ein in den Mikrokosmos dieser 140.000-Einwohner-Stadt und legt visuell etwas frei, das den meisten Besuchern auf ihren Kurztrips an die englische Westküste mit Sicherheit verborgen bleibt. Sie zeigt uns die Patina der in die Jahre gekommenen Hausfassaden und Fahrgeschäfte, sie trifft mit empathischem Blick und einer scharfen Beobachtungsgabe auf Außenseiter und Normalbürger. Im Mittelpunkt ihres visuellen Interesses steht weiterhin der Mensch in all seinen Facetten. Und so begleiten wir die Fotografin beim Blättern im Buch von einer Begegnung zur nächsten und lernen — jenseits des subjektiven Ansatzes — en passant einiges über diese Stadt, etwa über das unbarmherzige Aufeinanderprallen von Arm und Reich, über die Existenz eines jüdischen Friedhofs, zahlreiche Altersheime und Suppenküchen. Wir wandern mit ihr gleichsam herum auf dunklen Straßen, begleiten sie zu einem Golfclub und blicken mit ihr in die Auslagen von Haushaltsgeschäften und Antiquitätenläden, wo noch immer Prinzessin Diana von Schmucktellern lächelt. Wir folgen ihr in Supermärkte mit überquellenden Regalen, in Messiewohnungen oder Kirchenvorräume mit illuminierten Kreuzen. Suchodrev bedient und hinterfragt viele Klischees, die Kontinentaleuropäer mit Blick auf Großbritannien wohl häufig nennen würden, wobei ihre poetisch-rauen Aufnahmen intensiv die Atmosphäre eines konkreten Ortes nachzeichnen, den die meisten von uns wohl nicht persönlich kennen. Dabei knüpft sie da an, wo sie mit *48 Hours Blackpool* aufgehört hat und spinnt einen weiteren Faden in ihre Erzählung ein, hin zur Religion: Auf einem Schild mit weißen Lettern in einer ansonsten dunklen Kirche lesen wir Verse vom Löwen und vom Lamm als Gott — aufgehängt für die Gemeinde zum Mitsingen. Beide Tiere stehen hier für einen größtmöglichen Dualismus und zugleich für Gott oder zwei Religionsansätze — stärker kann man sich Kontraste kaum vorstellen. Das Rauschhafte und Authentische in Suchodrevs Erzählungen — im ersten wie im zweiten Buch über Blackpool — ist Methode und Stilmittel zugleich. Und die Spannung dieser faszinierend-verstörenden Bilder sollten wir aushalten, bis wir sie beim ersten Besuch von Blackpool mit den eigenen Eindrücken vor Ort abgleichen können.

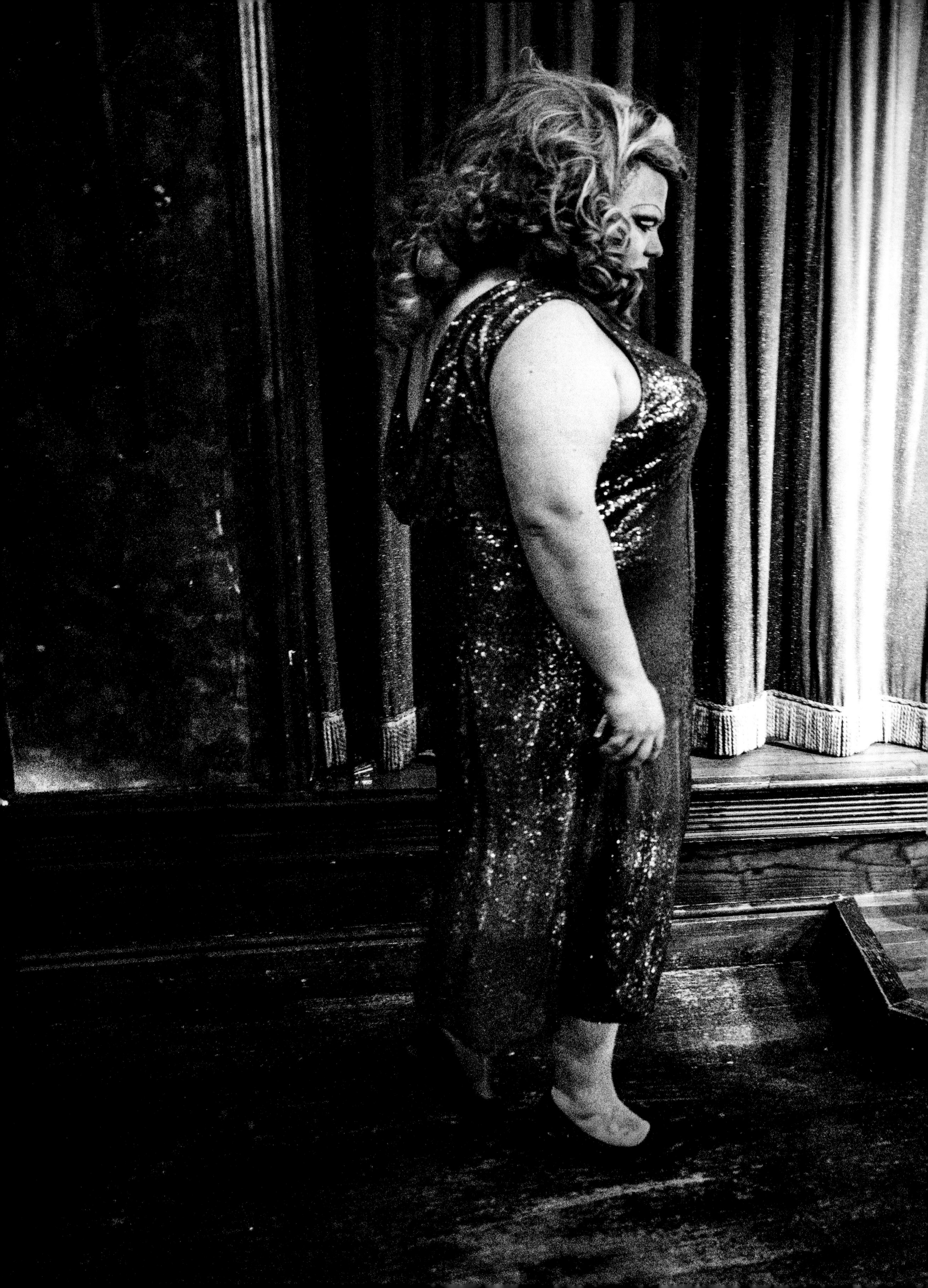

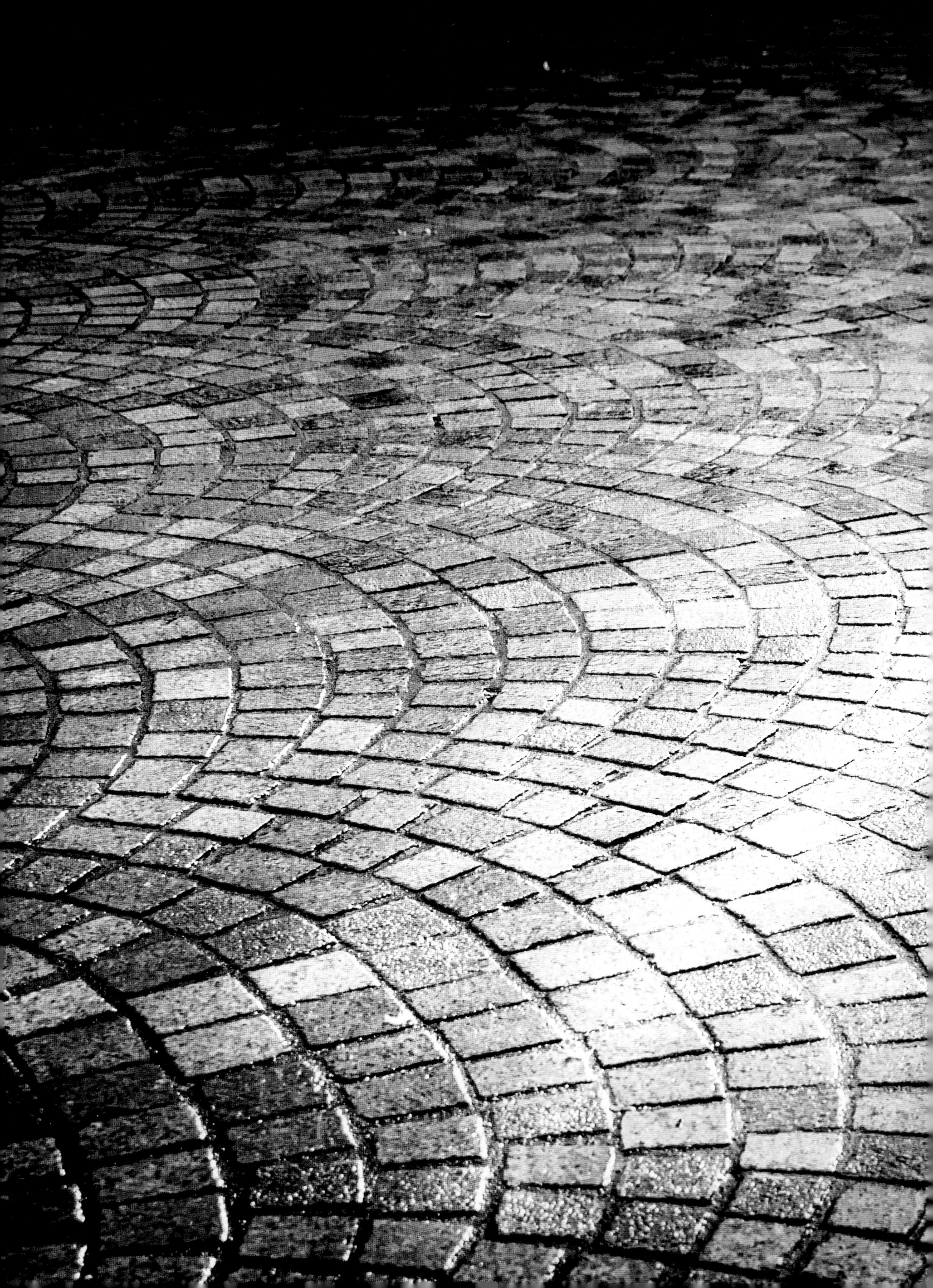

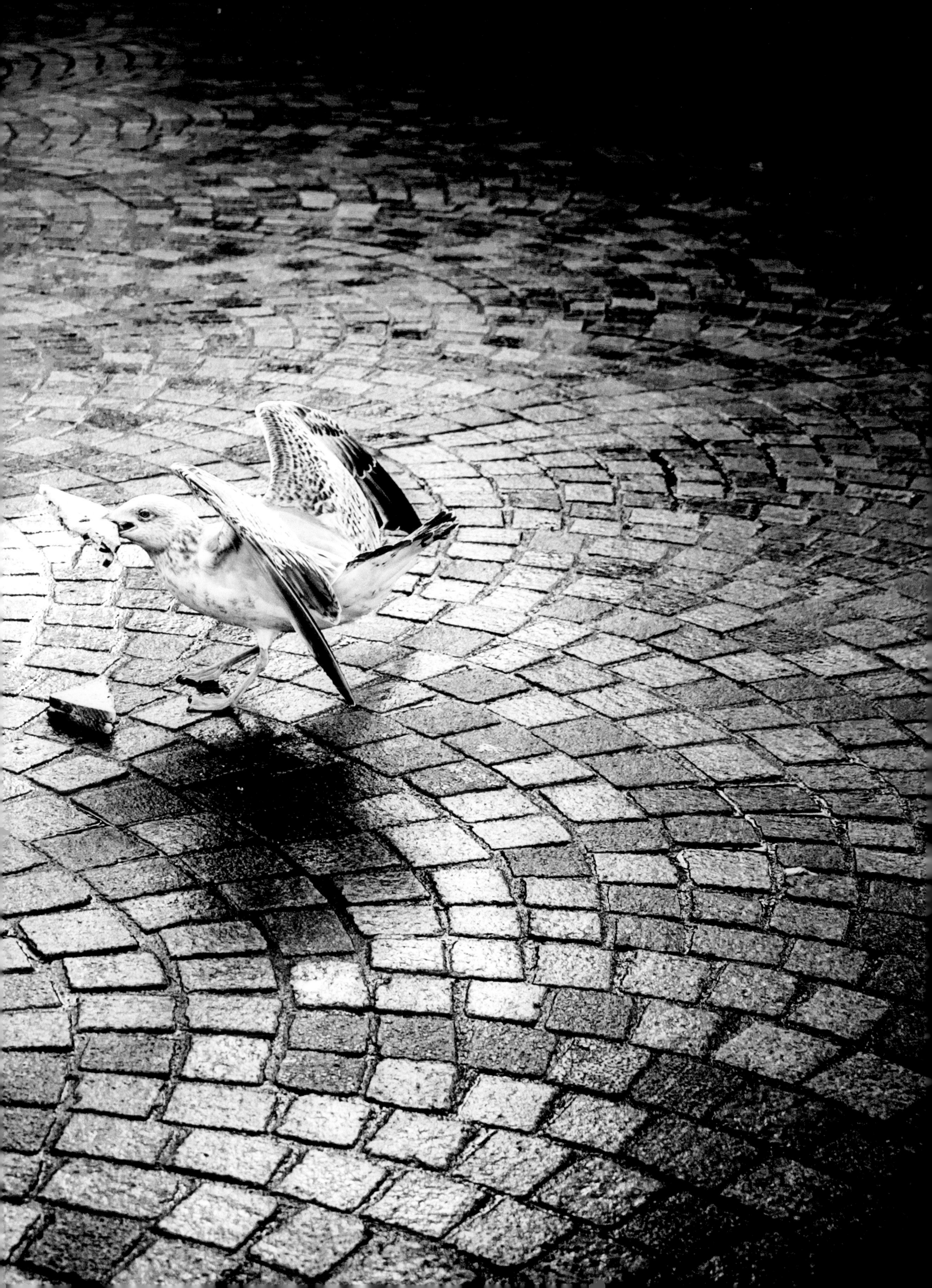

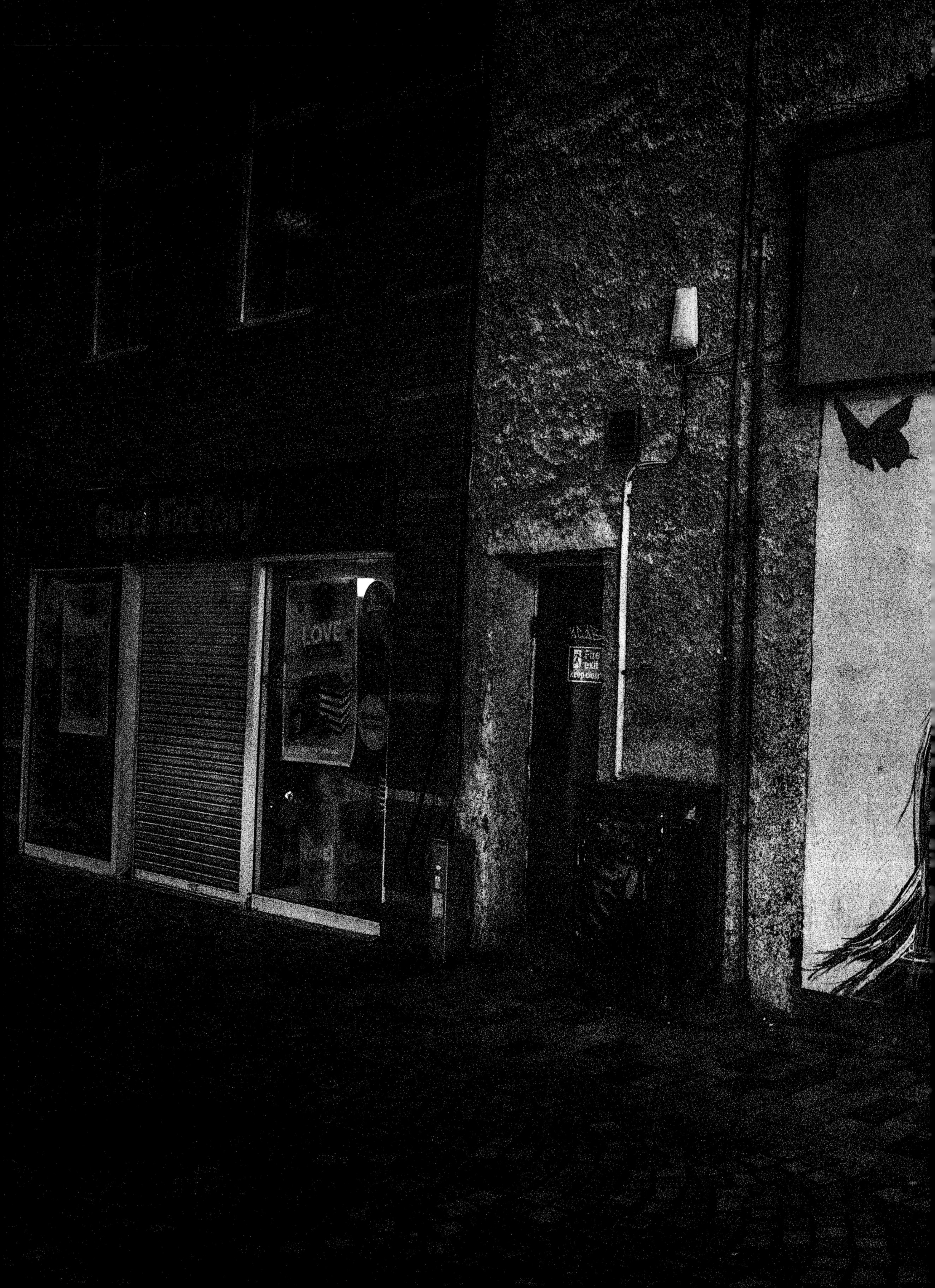
LOVE
Fire
exit
keep clear

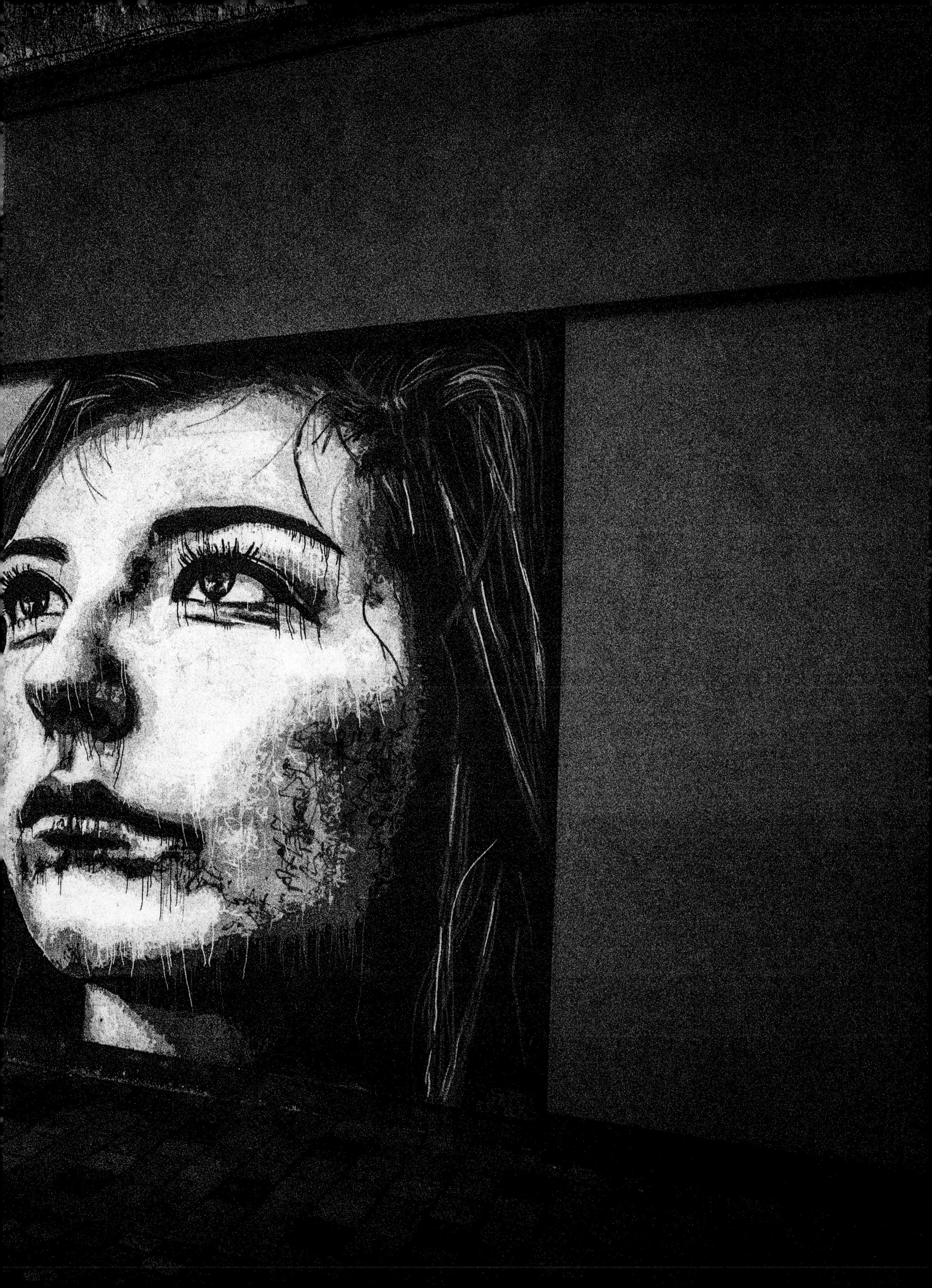

stern

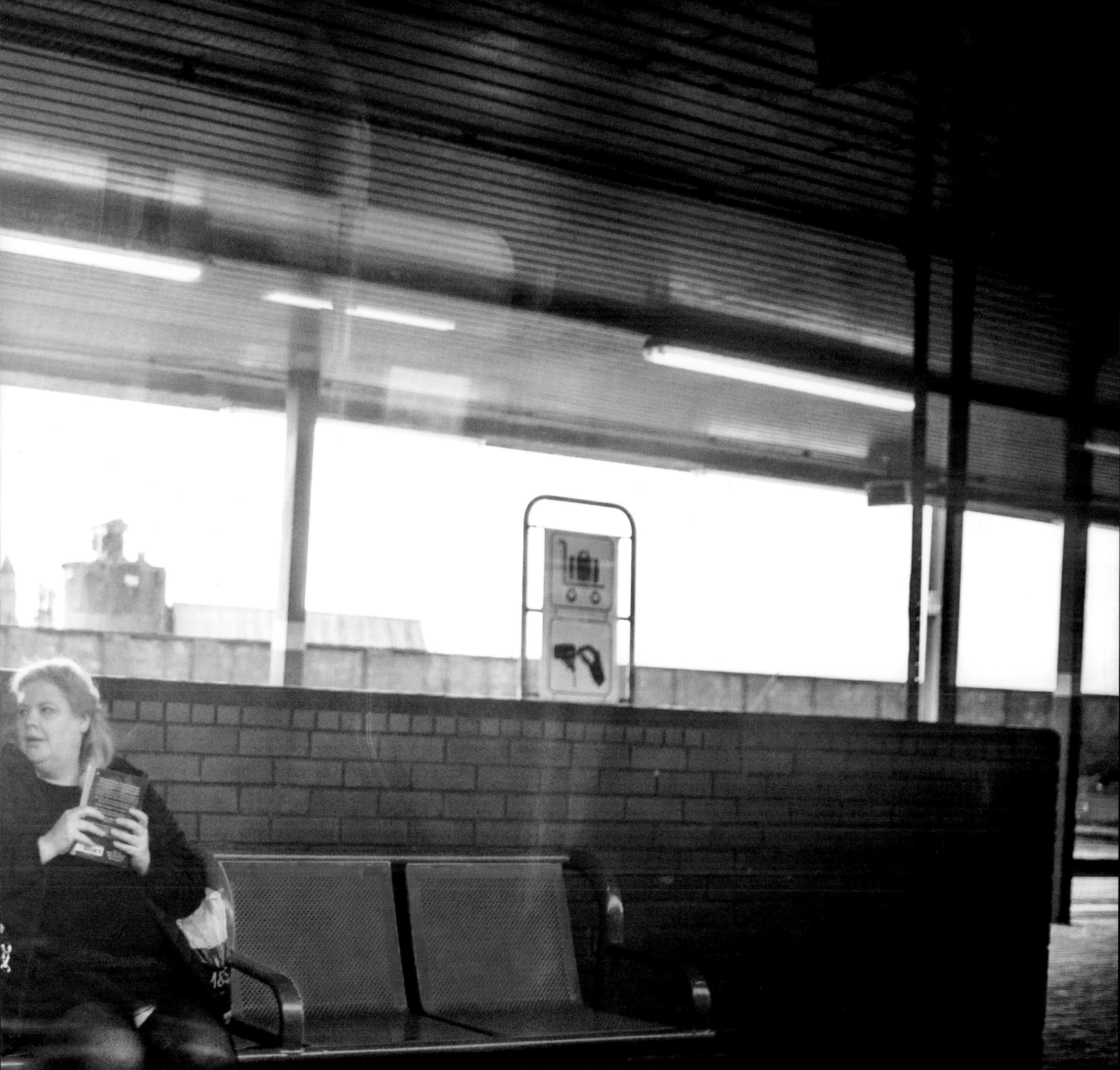

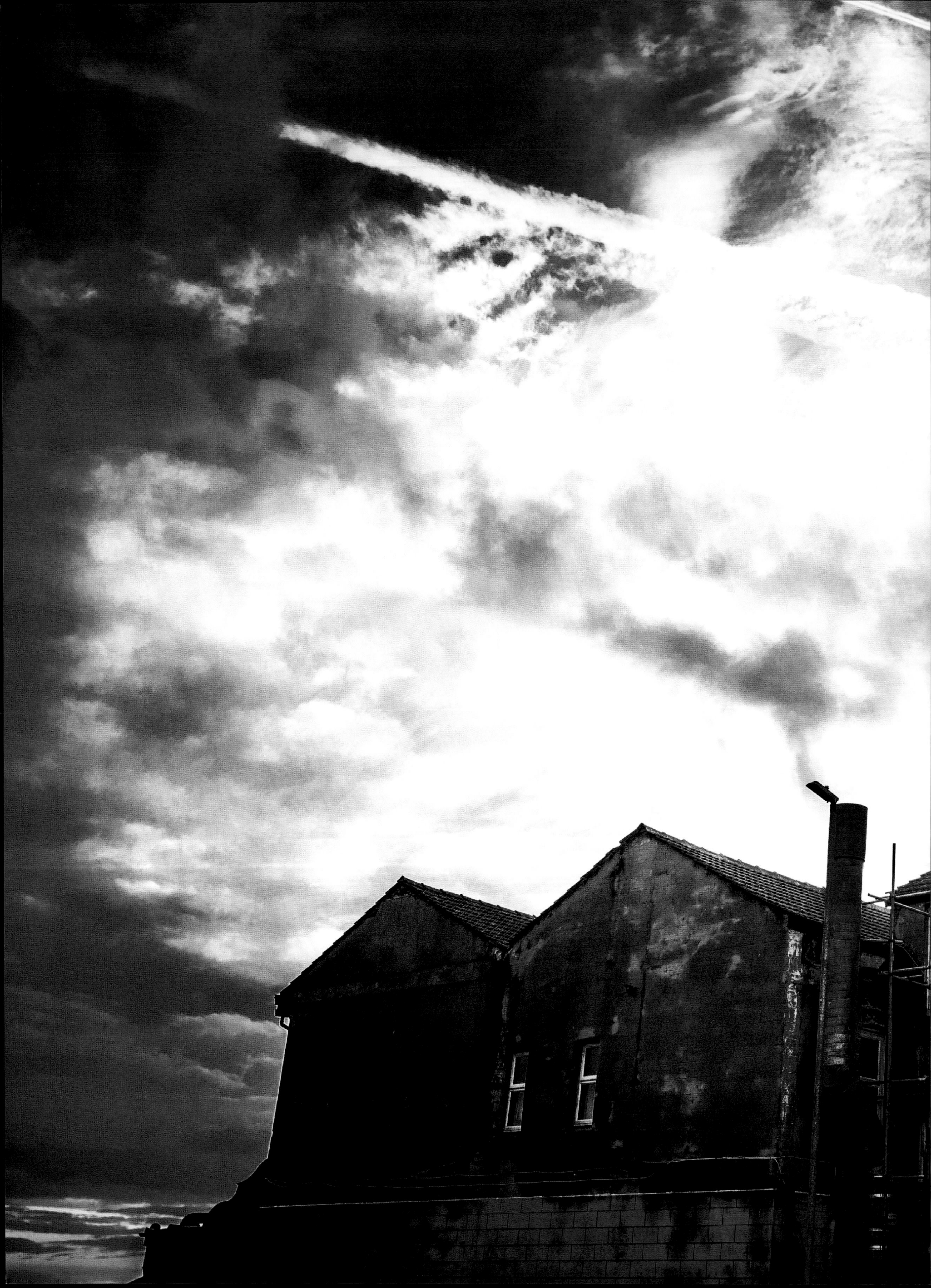

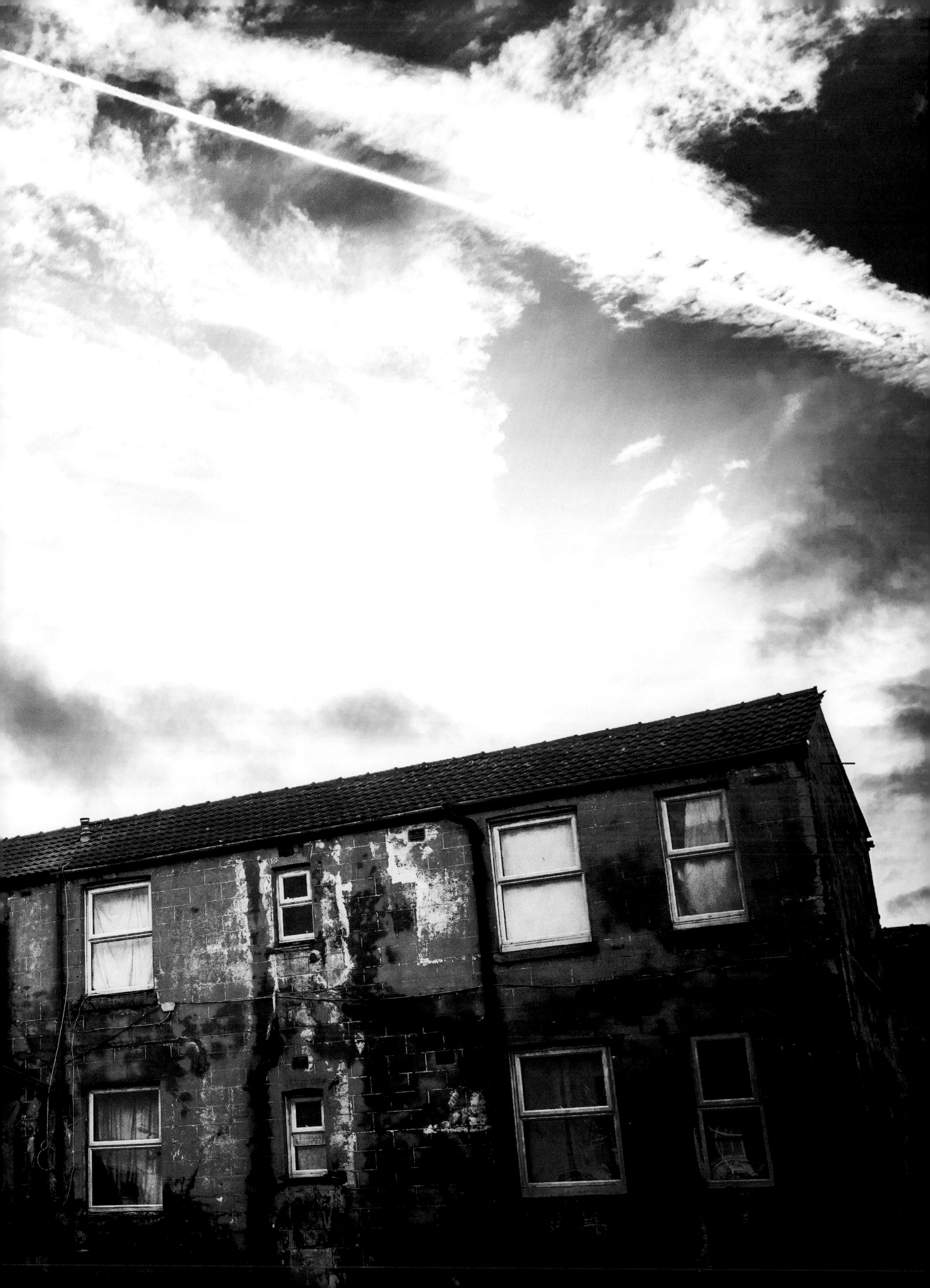

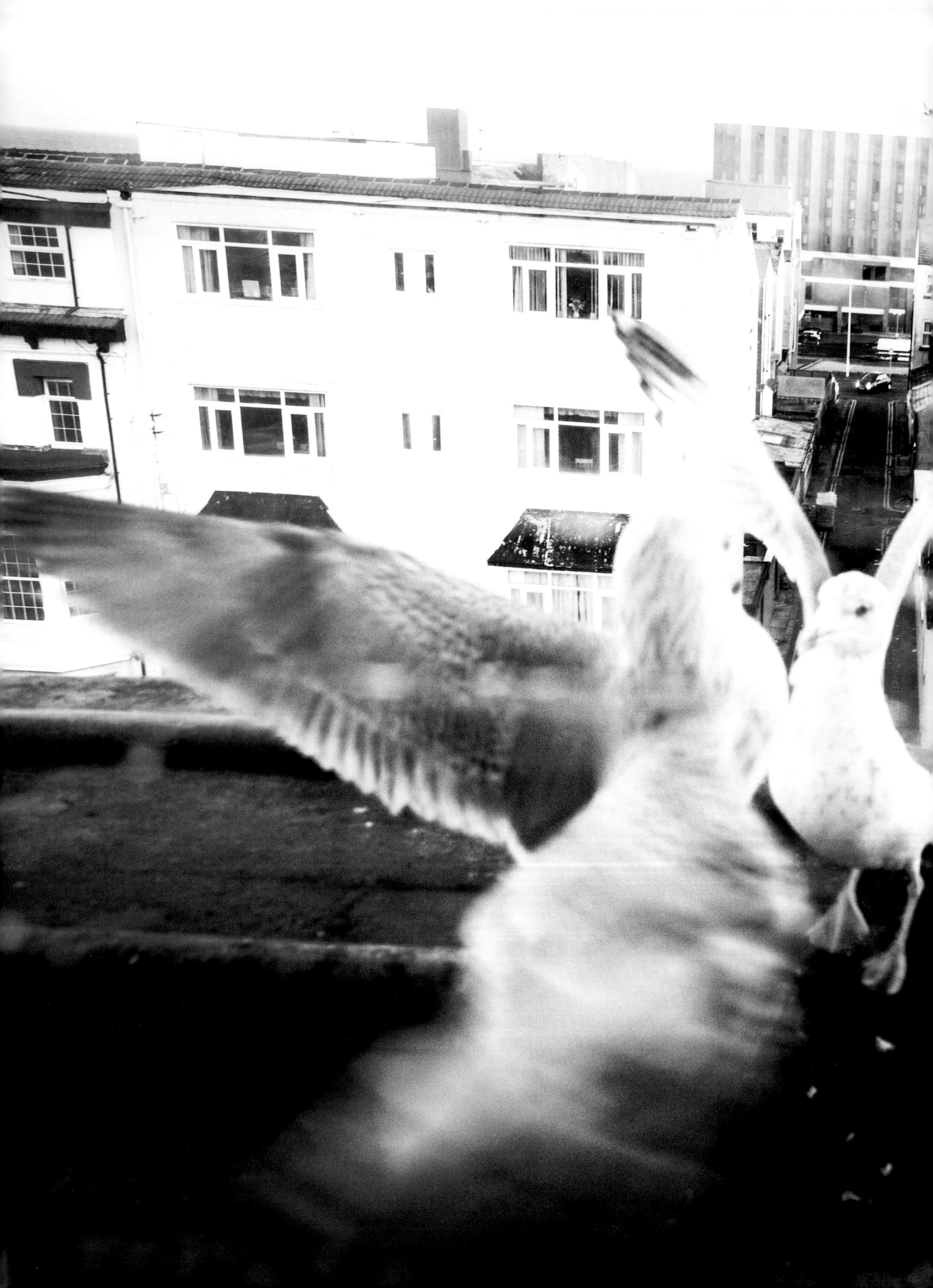

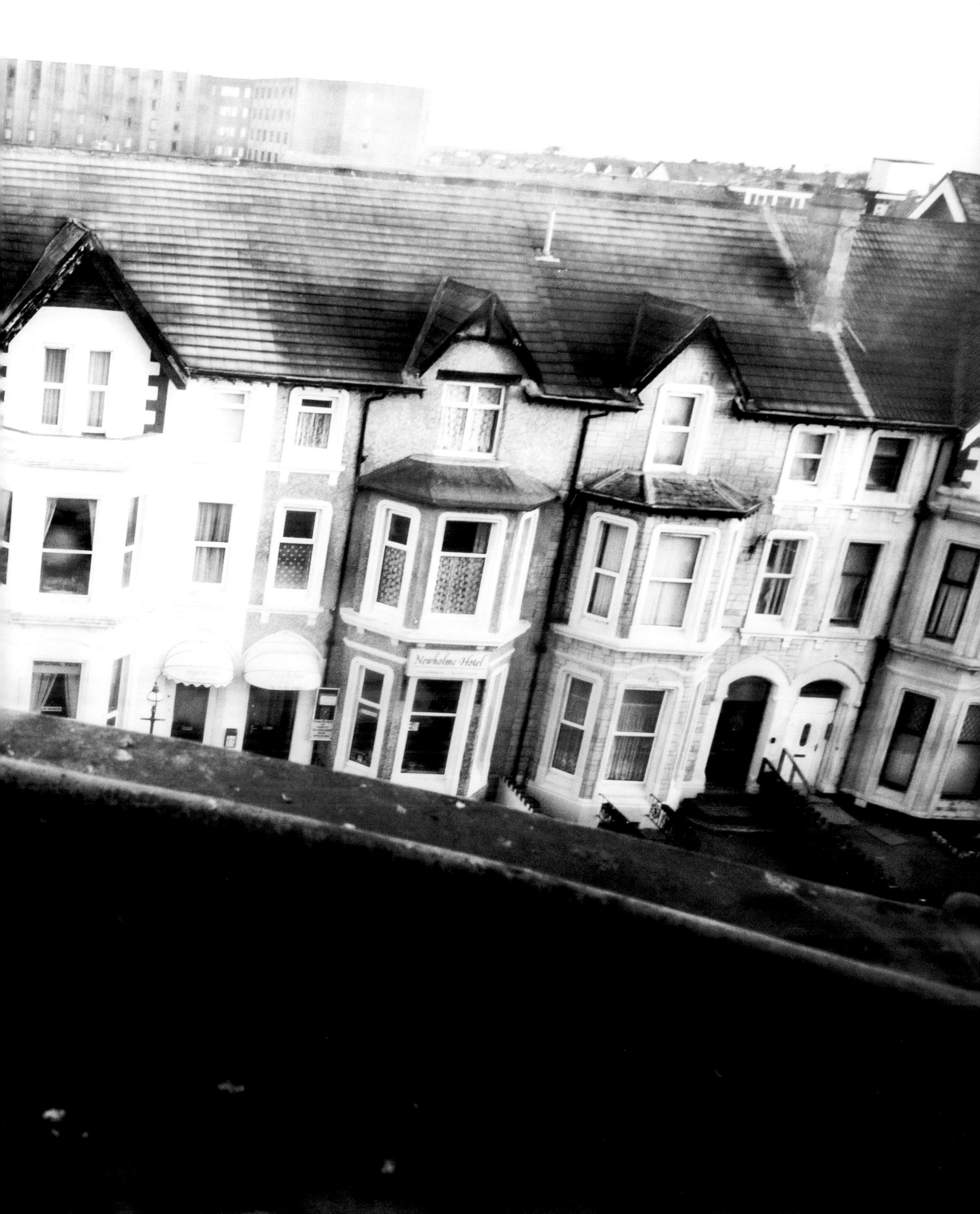
Newholme Hotel

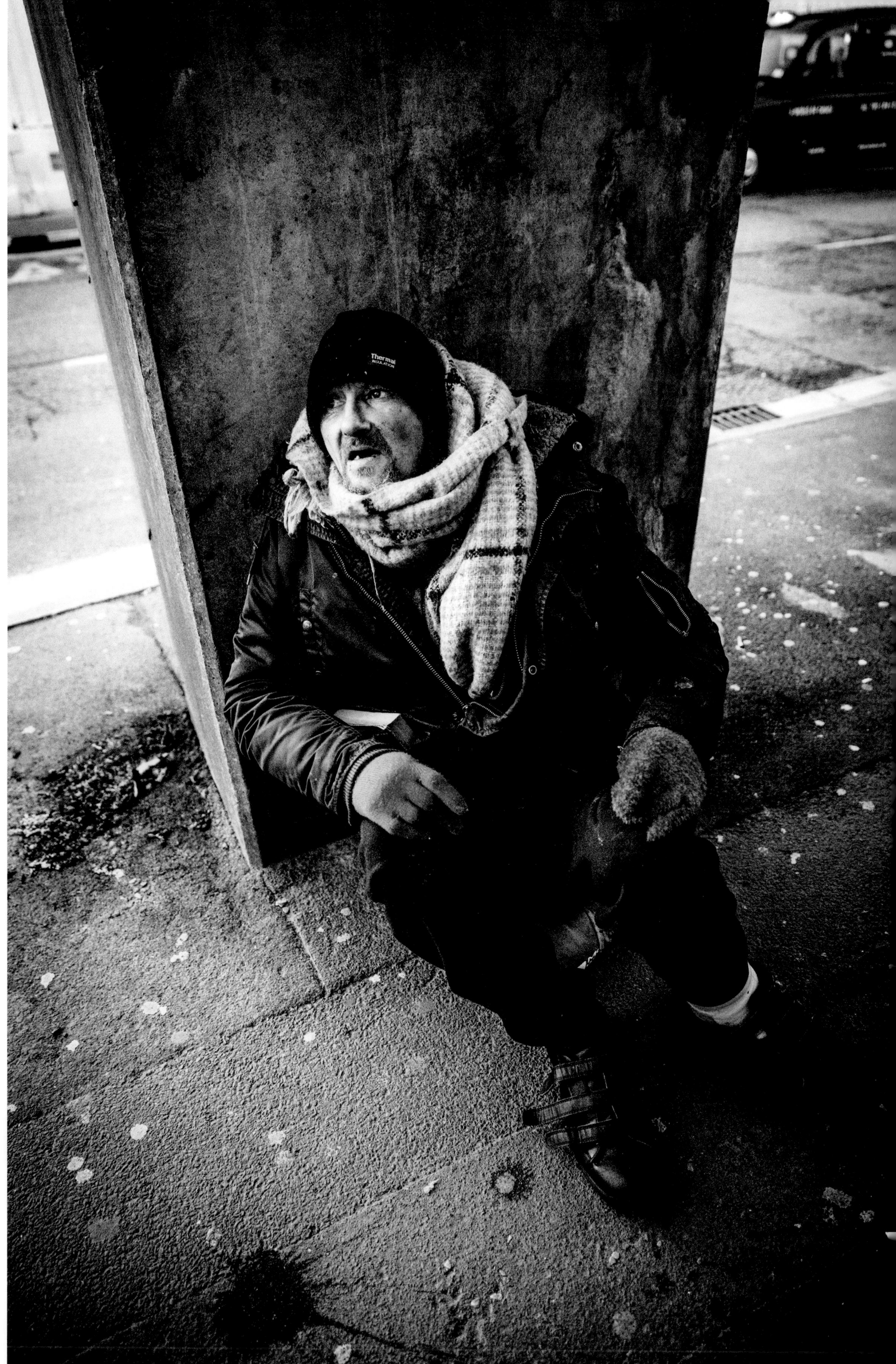

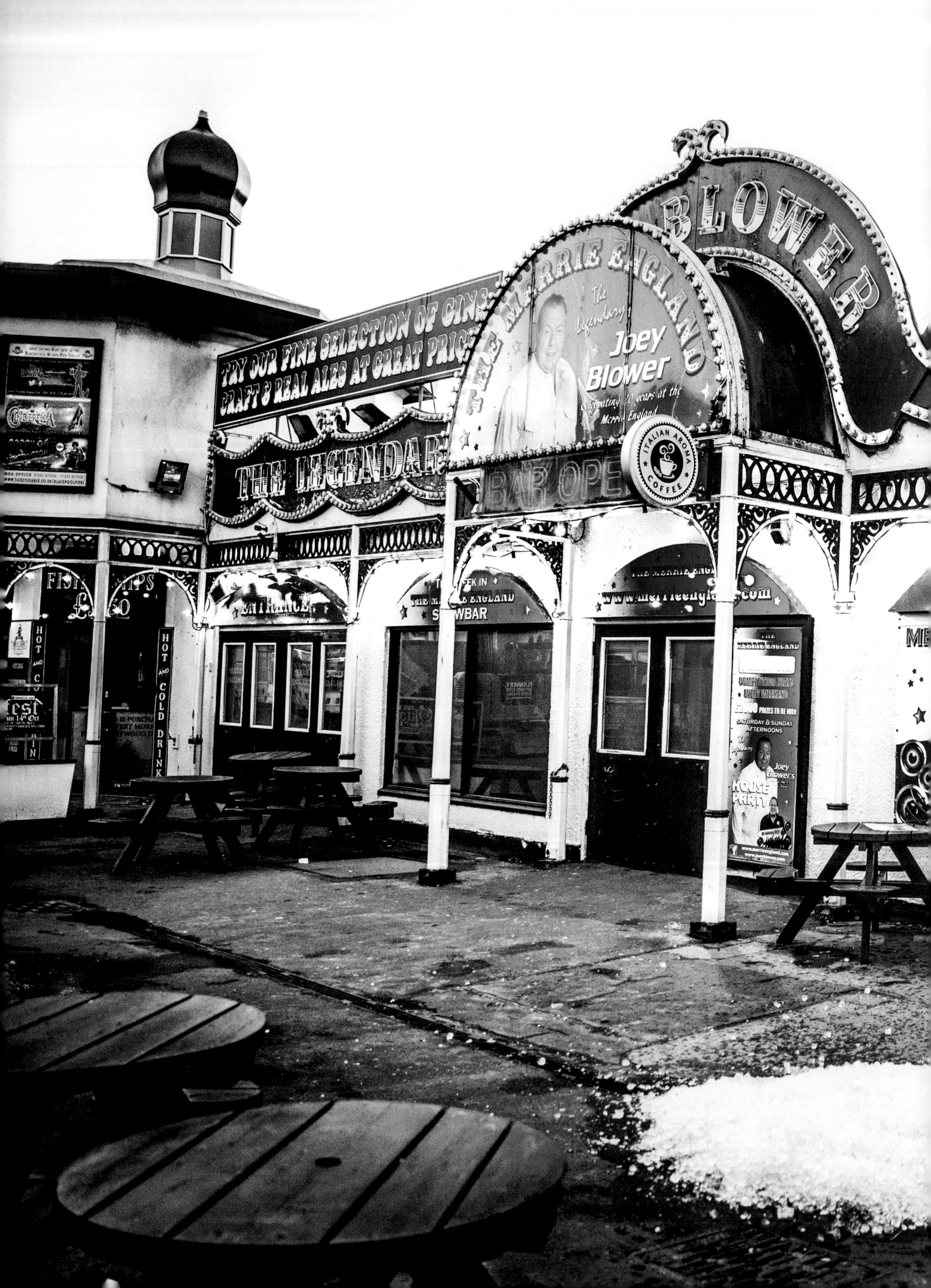
BLOWER
THE MERRIE ENGLAND
The Legendary
Joey
Blower
ITALIAN AROMA COFFEE
BAR OPEN
TRY OUR FINE SELECTION OF GINS
CRAFT & REAL ALES AT GREAT PRICES
THE LEGENDARY
FISH & CHIPS
£5.60
HOT DOG
HOT AND COLD DRINKS
ENTRANCE
THIS WEEK IN
THE MERRIE ENGLAND
SHOWBAR
www.merrieengland.com
COMPETITION HEATS
EVERY WEEKEND
£2,000 PRIZES TO BE WON
SATURDAY & SUNDAY
AFTERNOONS
Joey Blower's
HOUSE
PARTY
CINDERELLA

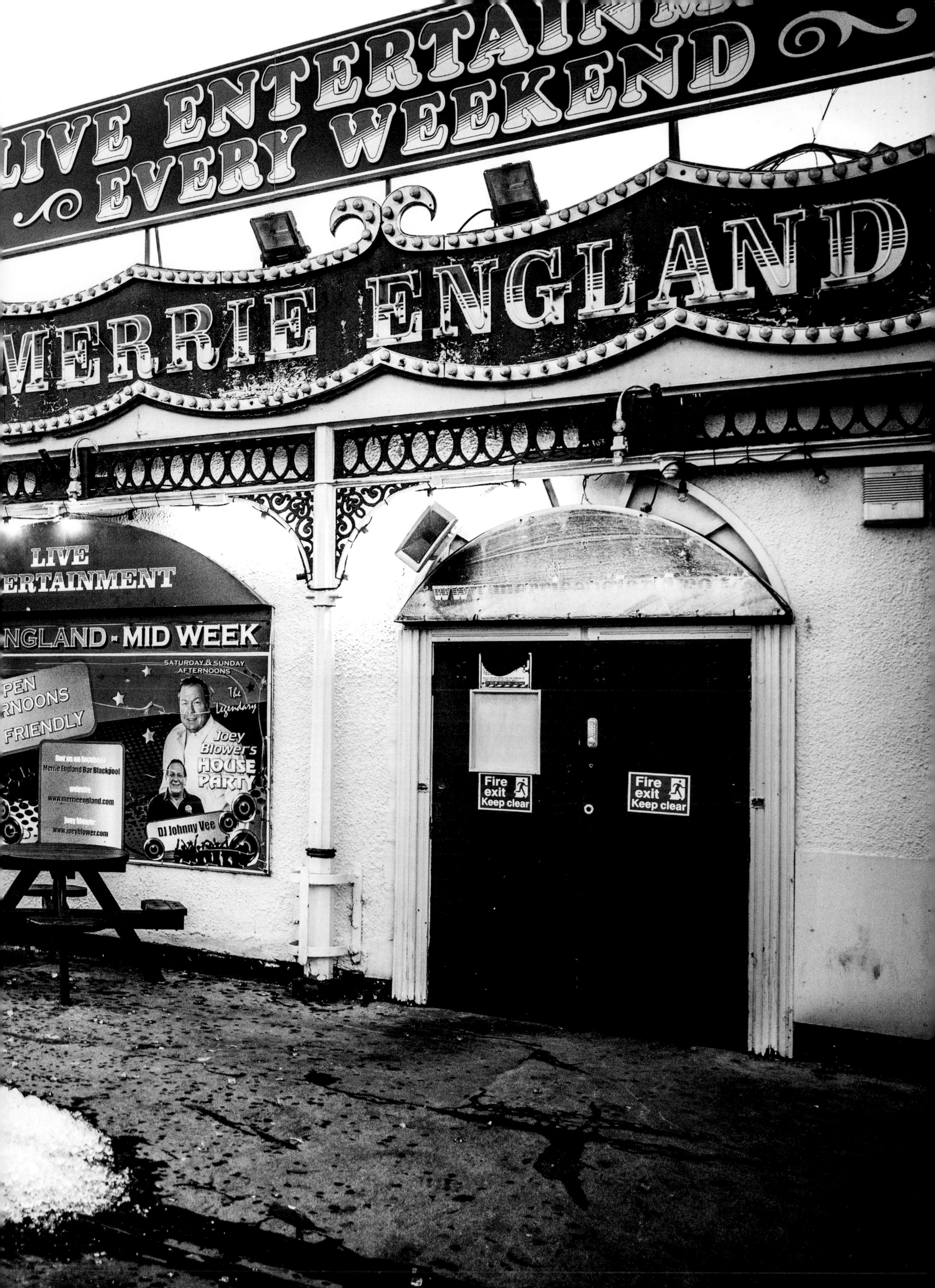

LIVE ENTERTAINMENT
EVERY WEEKEND
MERRIE ENGLAND
LIVE ENTERTAINMENT
ENGLAND · MID WEEK
SATURDAY & SUNDAY AFTERNOONS
The Legendary
Joey Blower's HOUSE PARTY
OPEN AFTERNOONS
FRIENDLY
find me on facebook
Merrie England Bar Blackpool
website:
www.merrieengland.com
Joey Blower:
www.joeyblower.com
DJ Johnny Vee
Fire exit Keep clear
Fire exit Keep clear

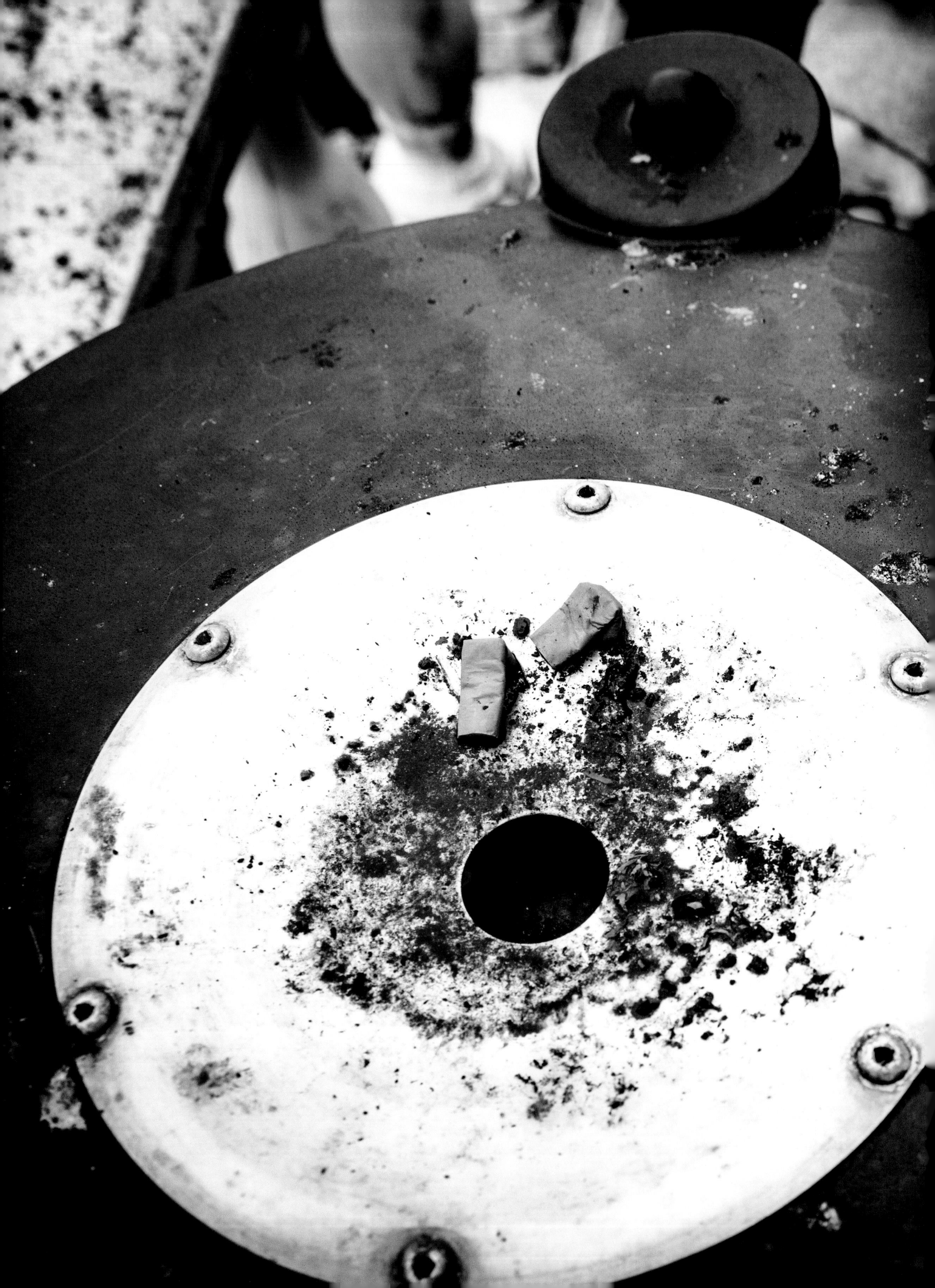

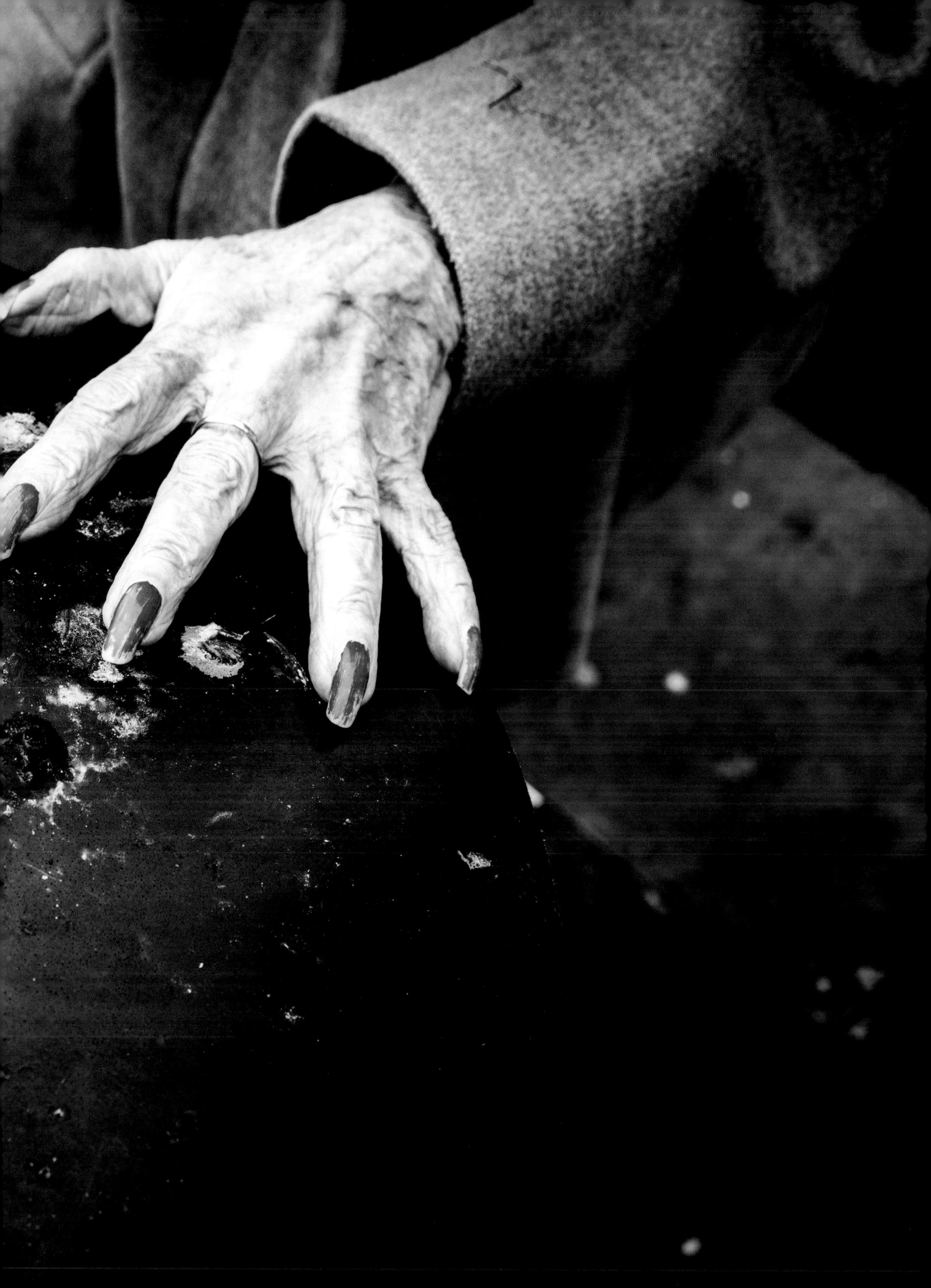

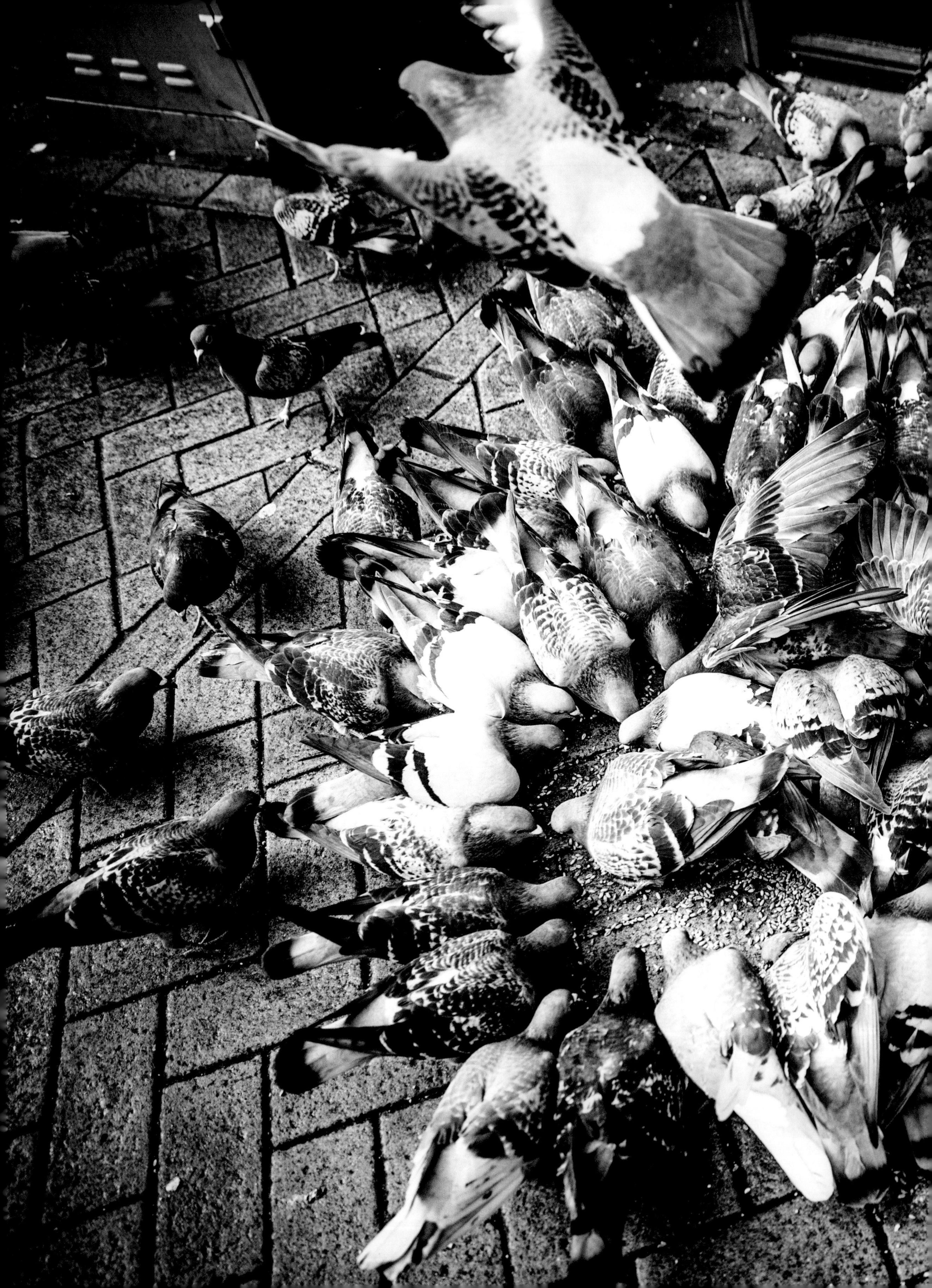

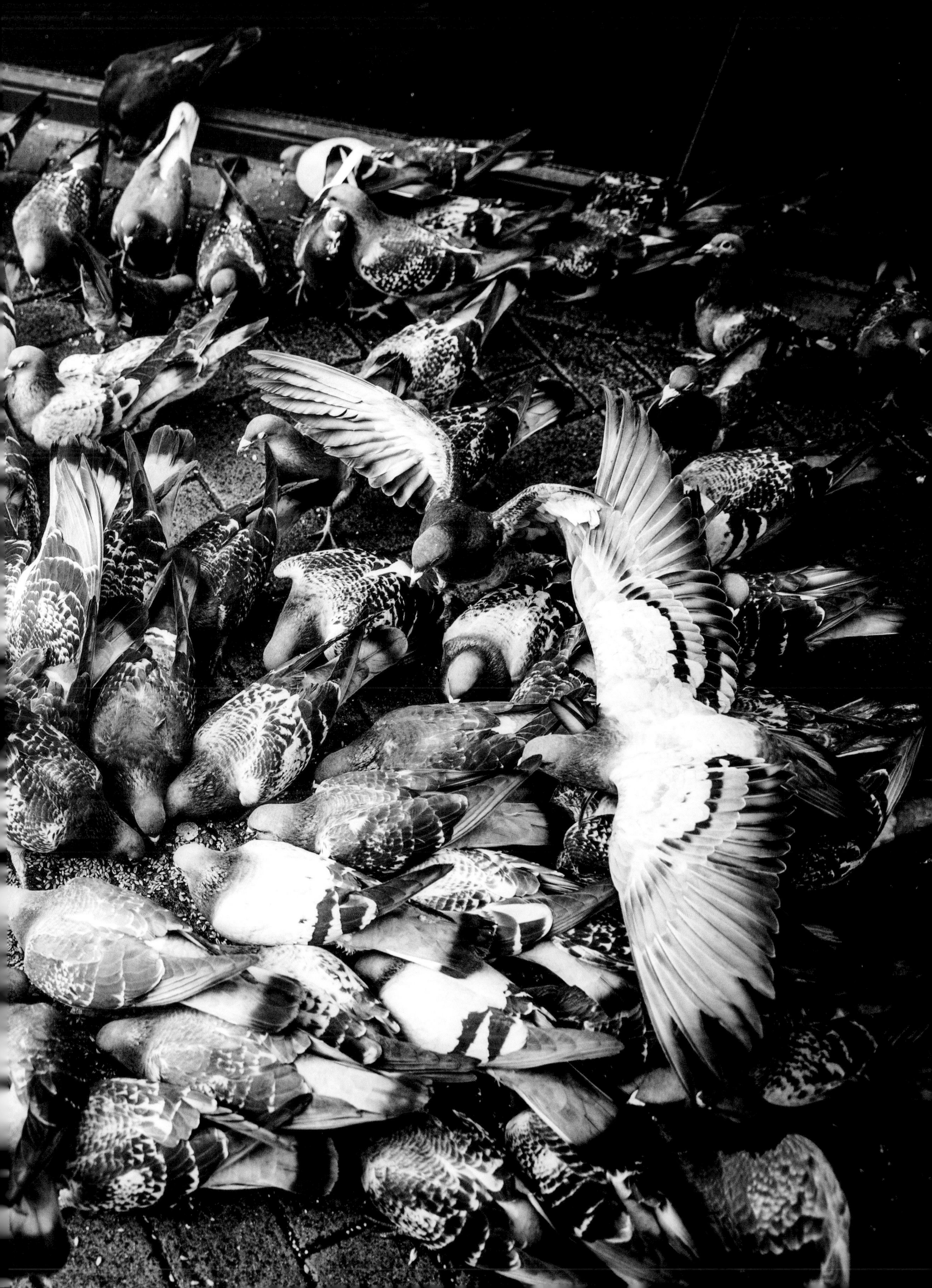

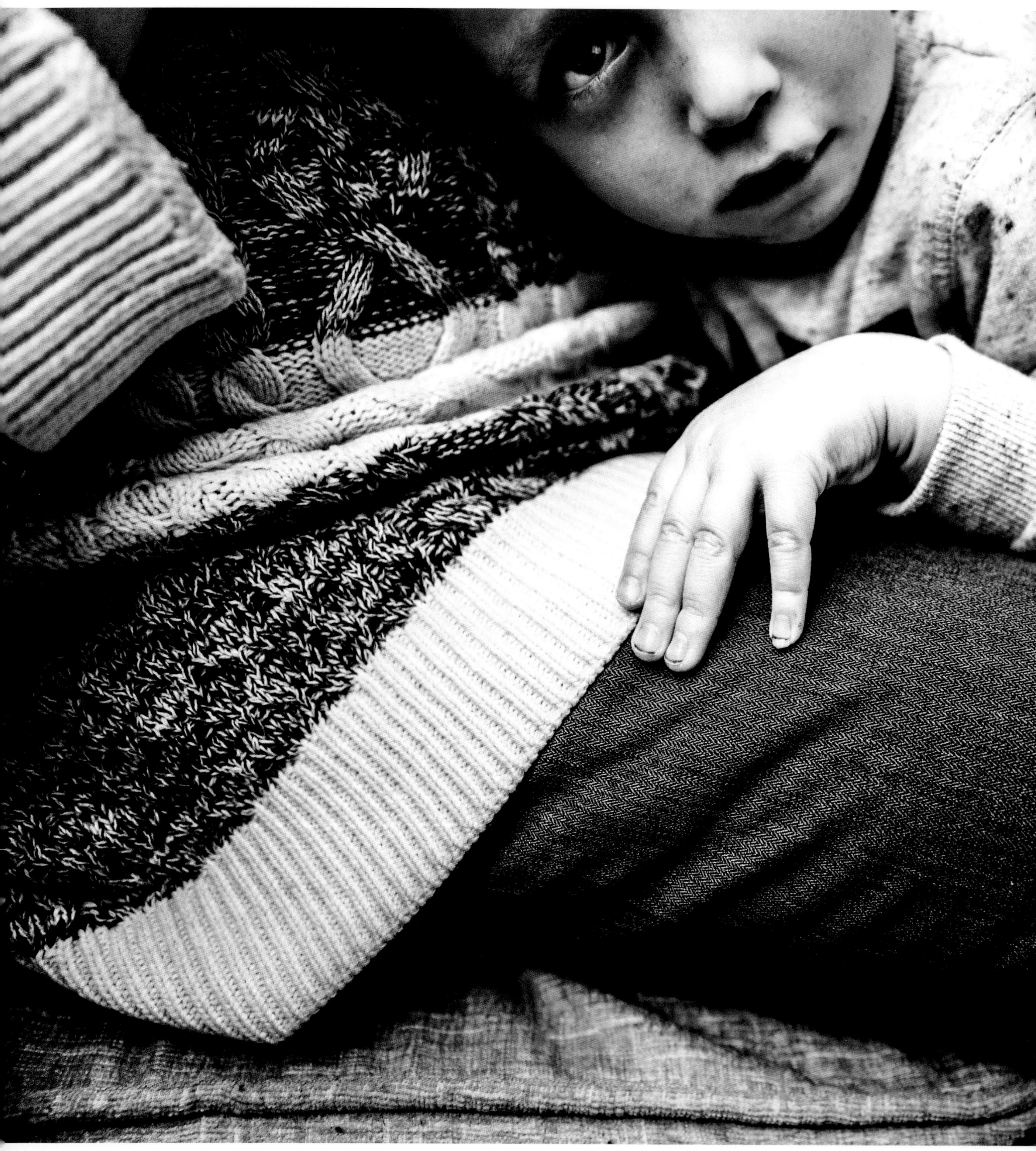

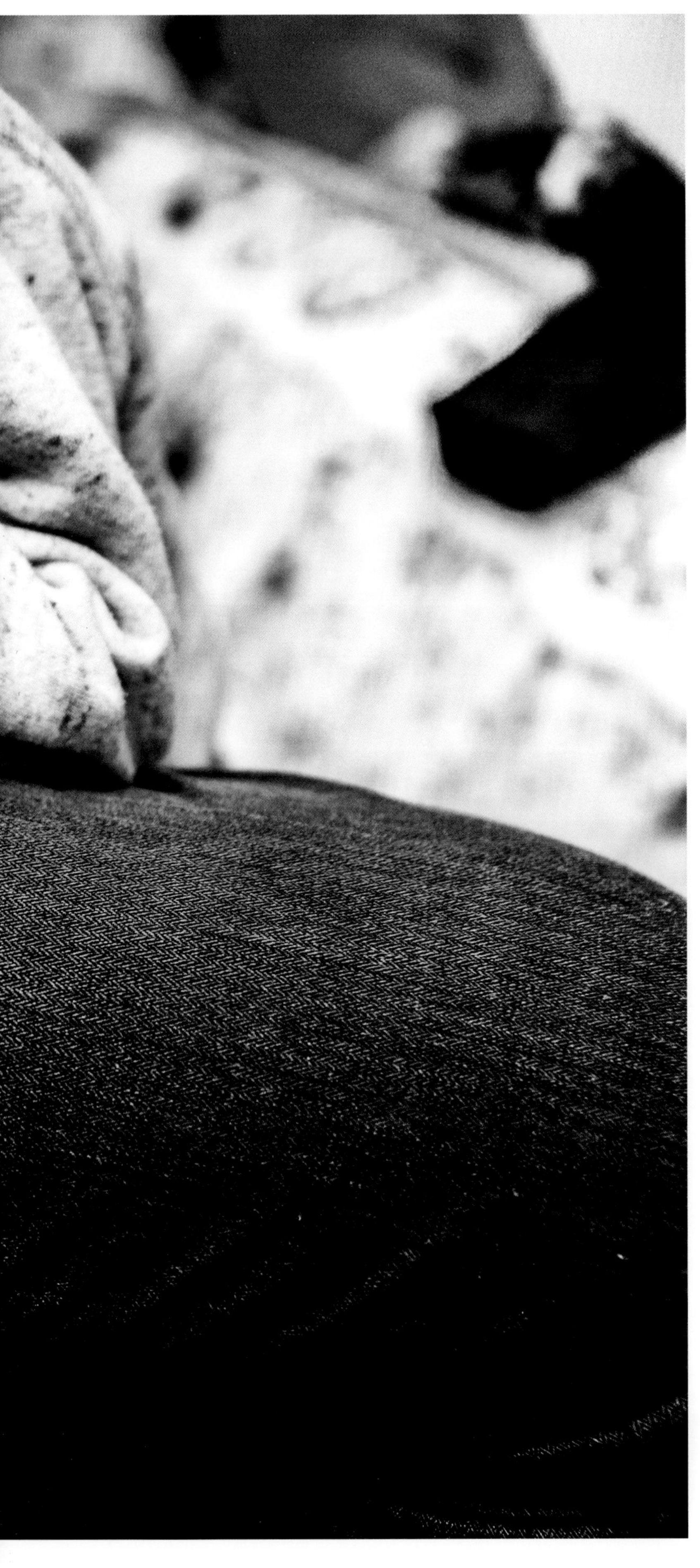

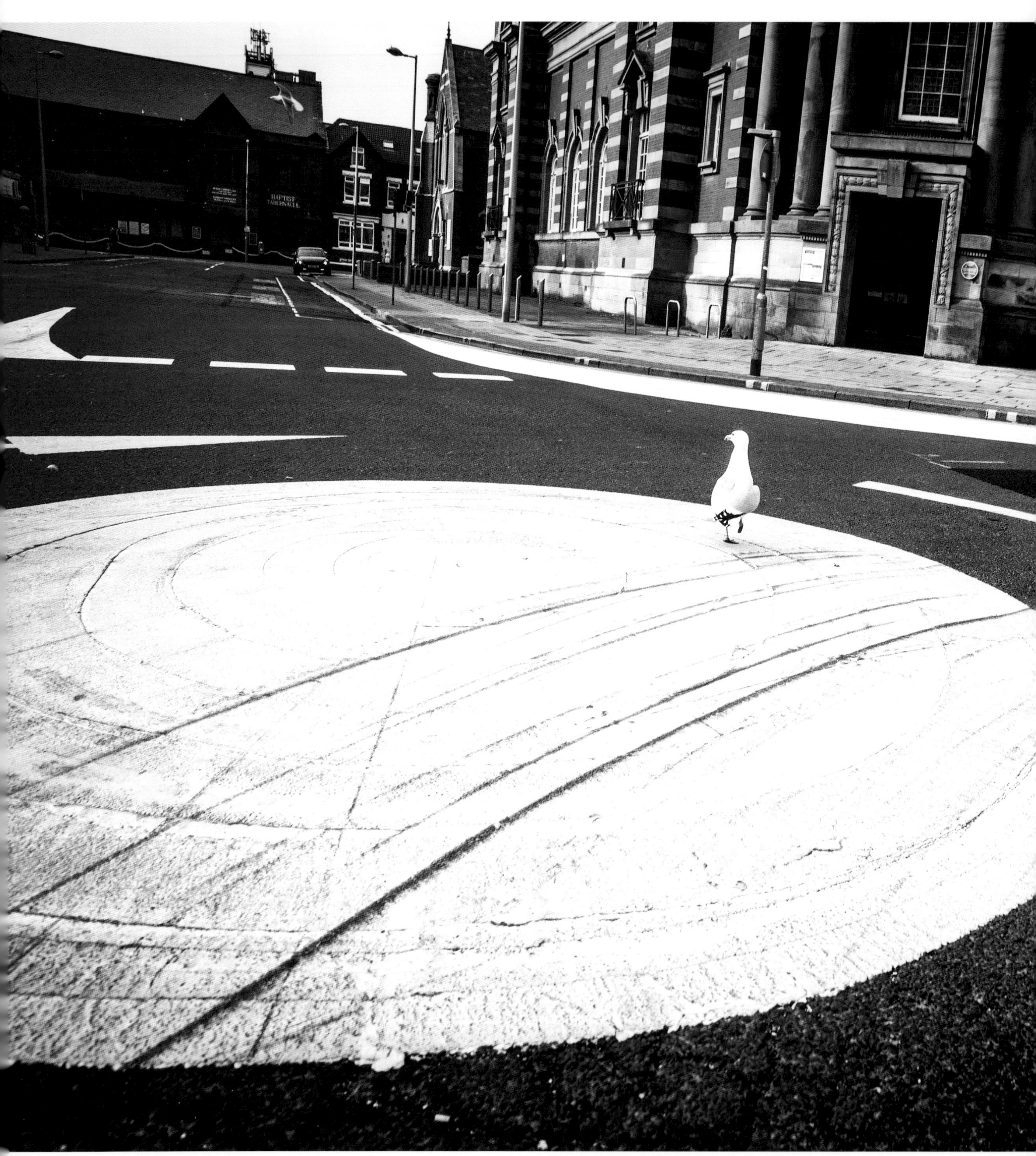

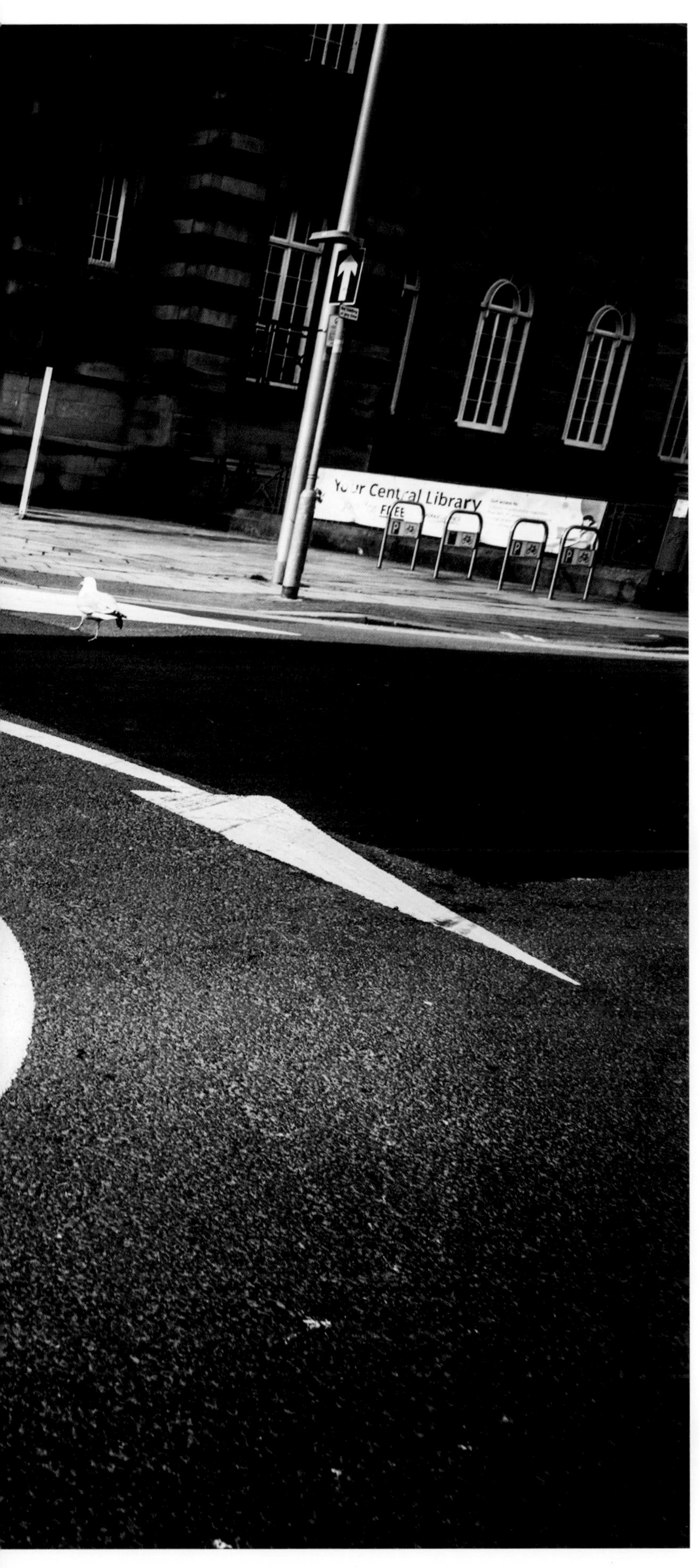
Your Central Library
FREE

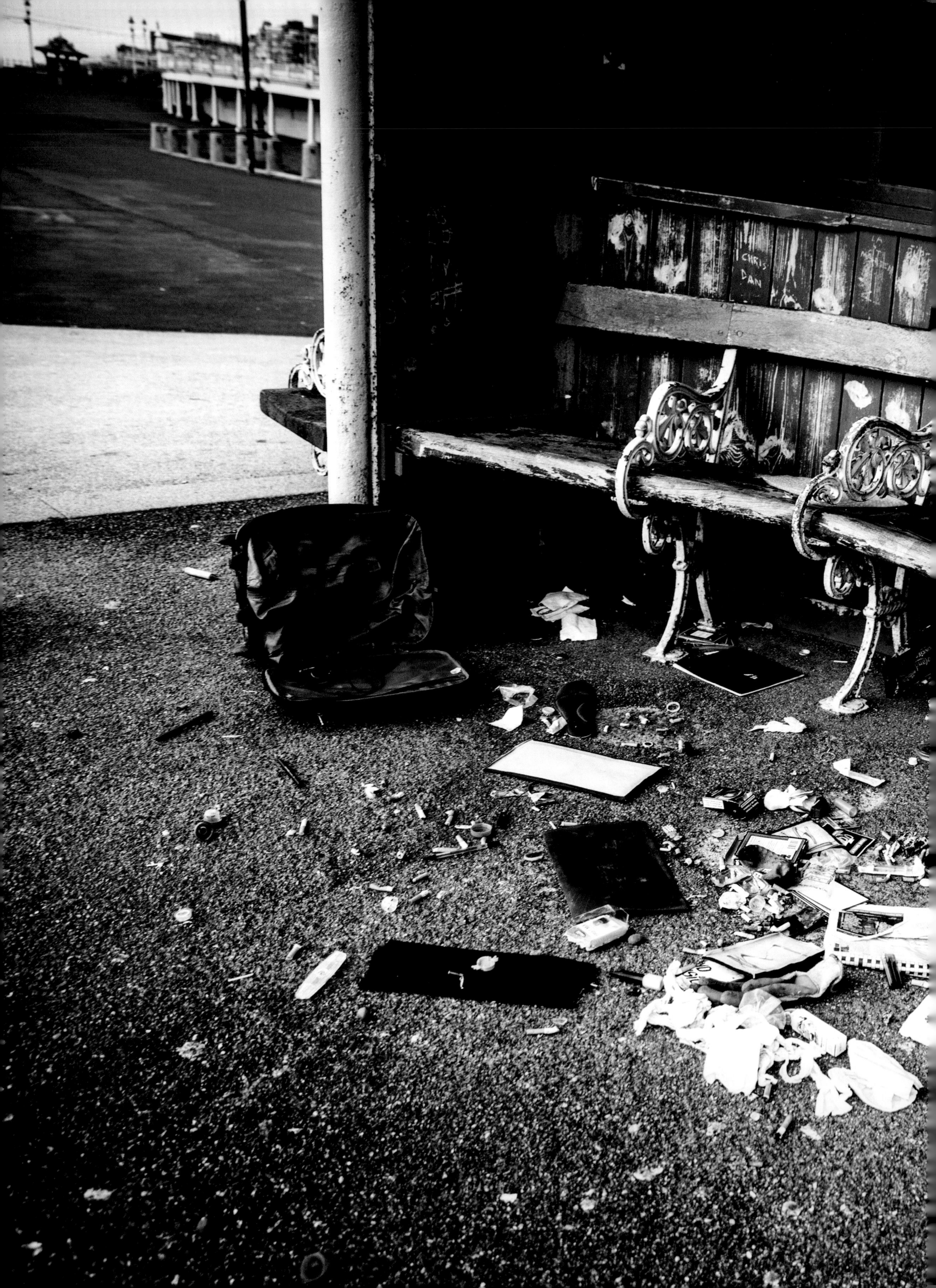

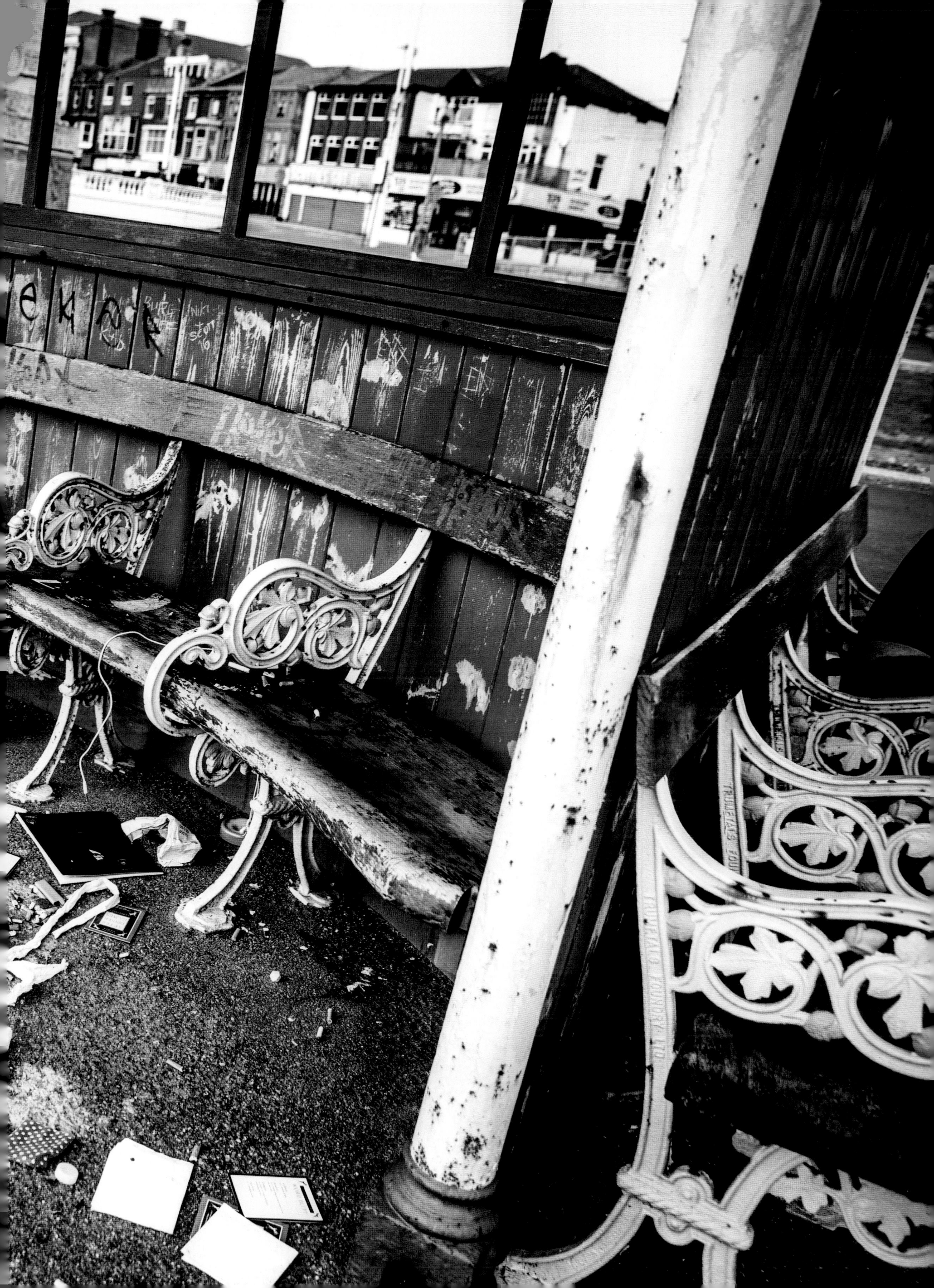

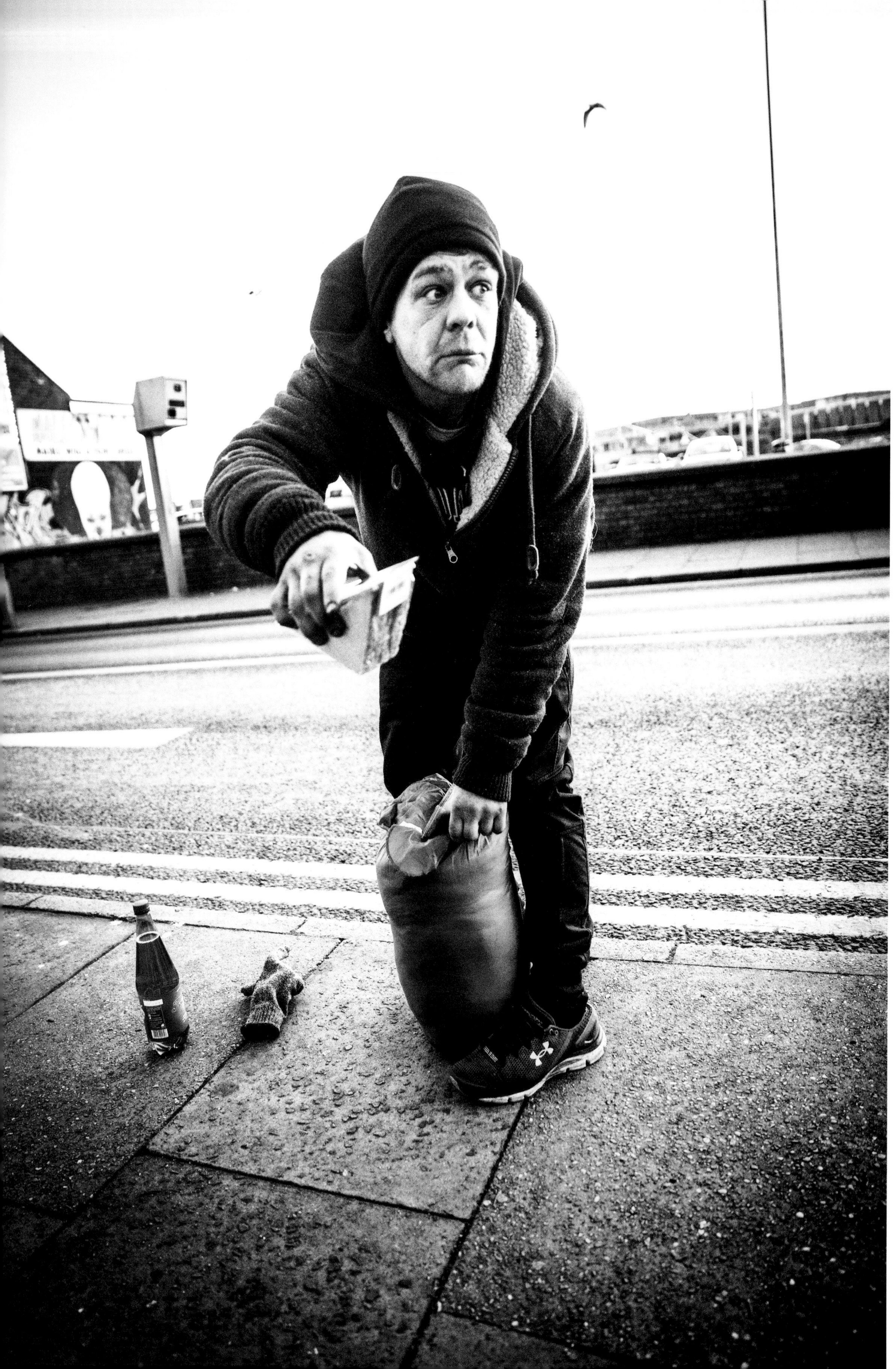

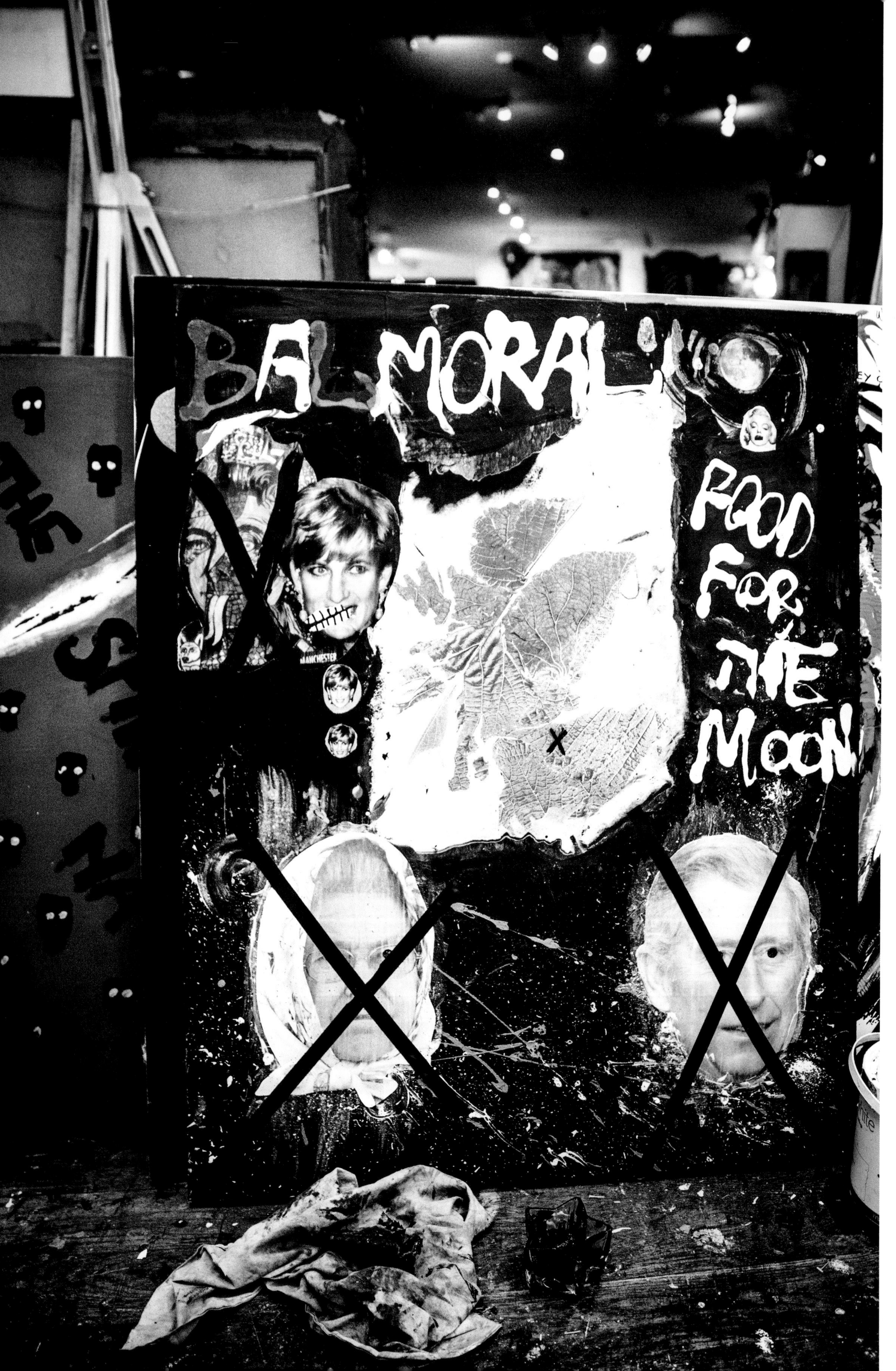

BALMORAL
FOOD FOR THE MOON
THE SM
MANCHESTER

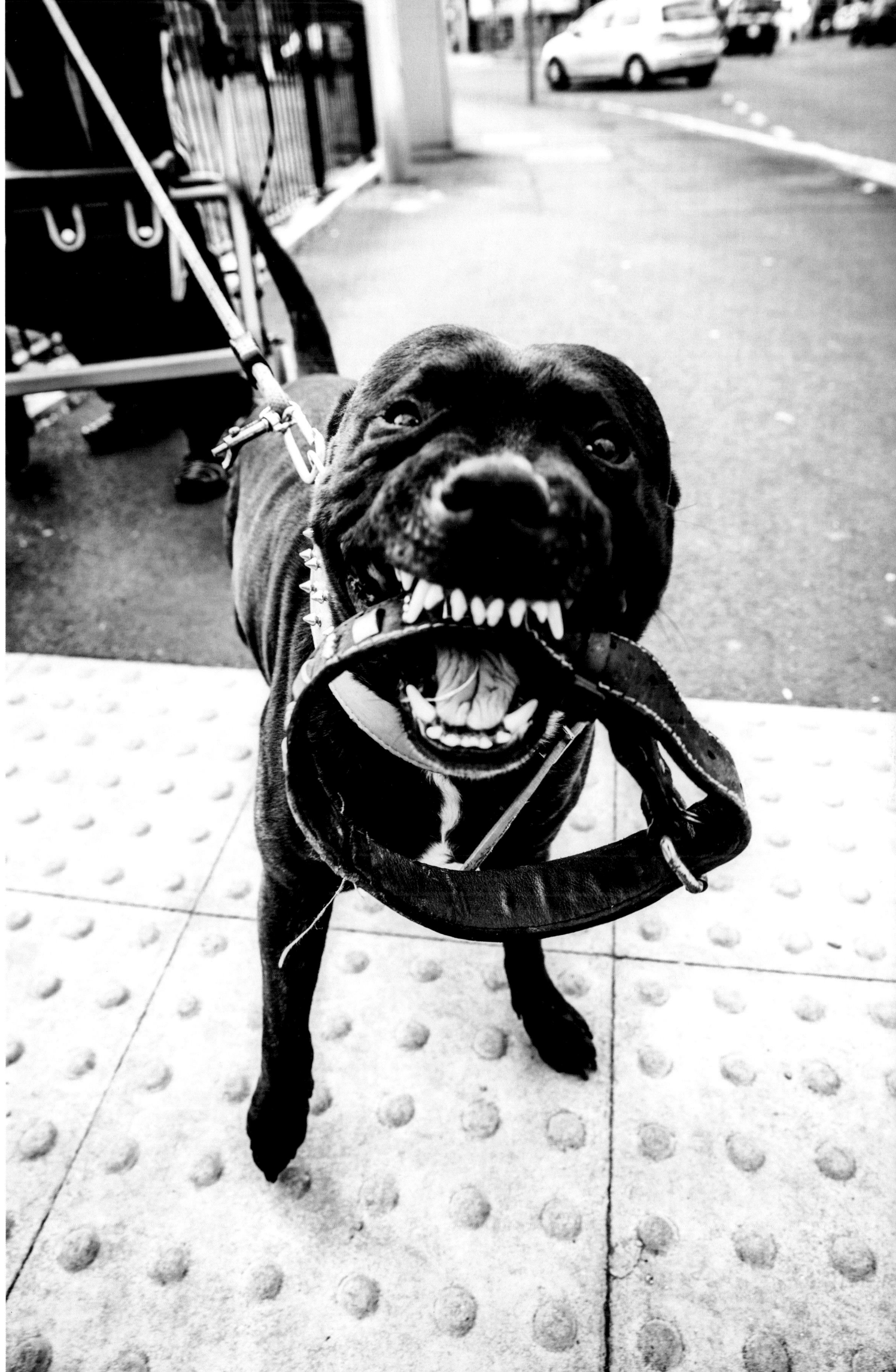

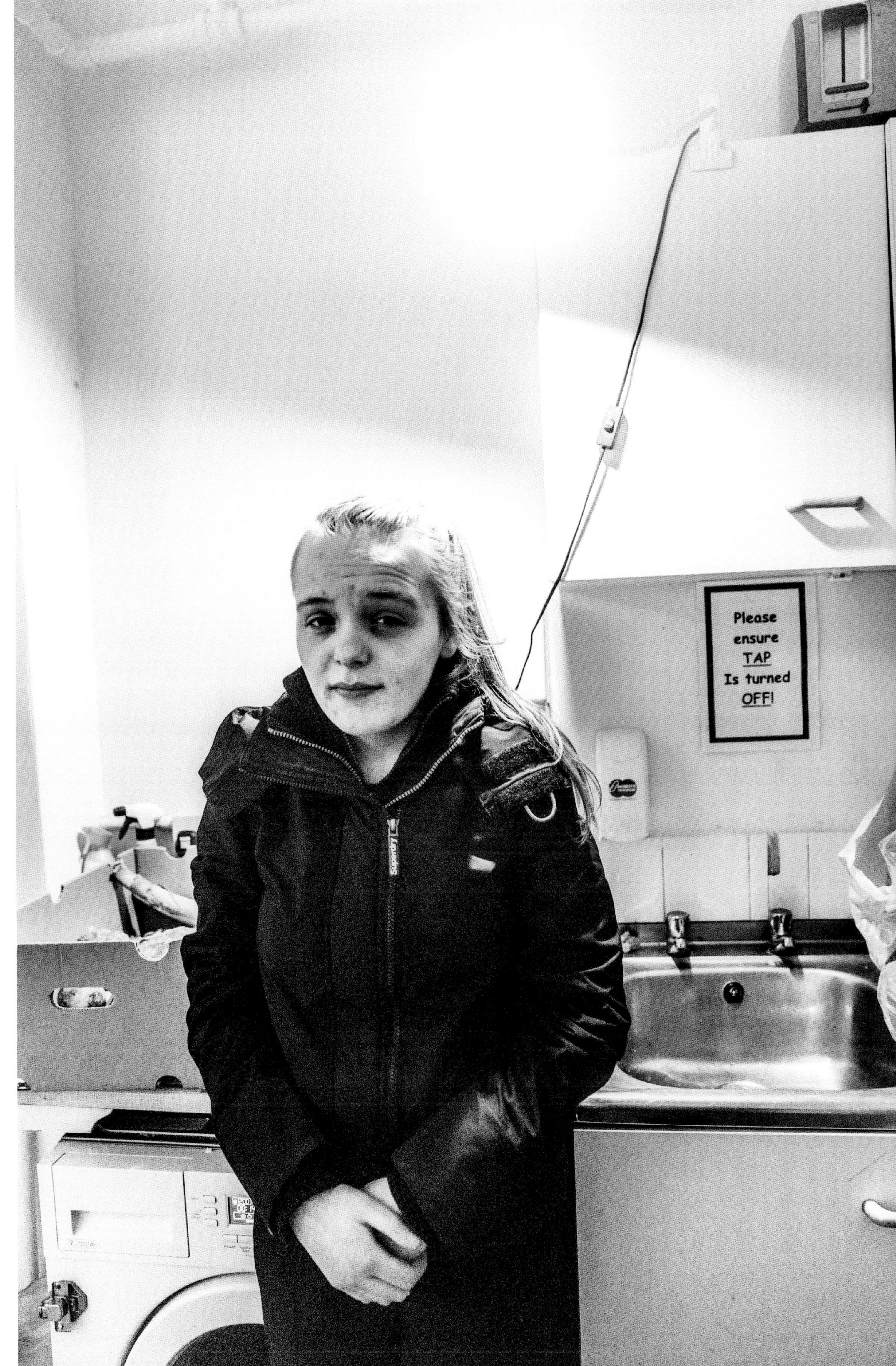
Please
ensure
TAP
Is turned
OFF!

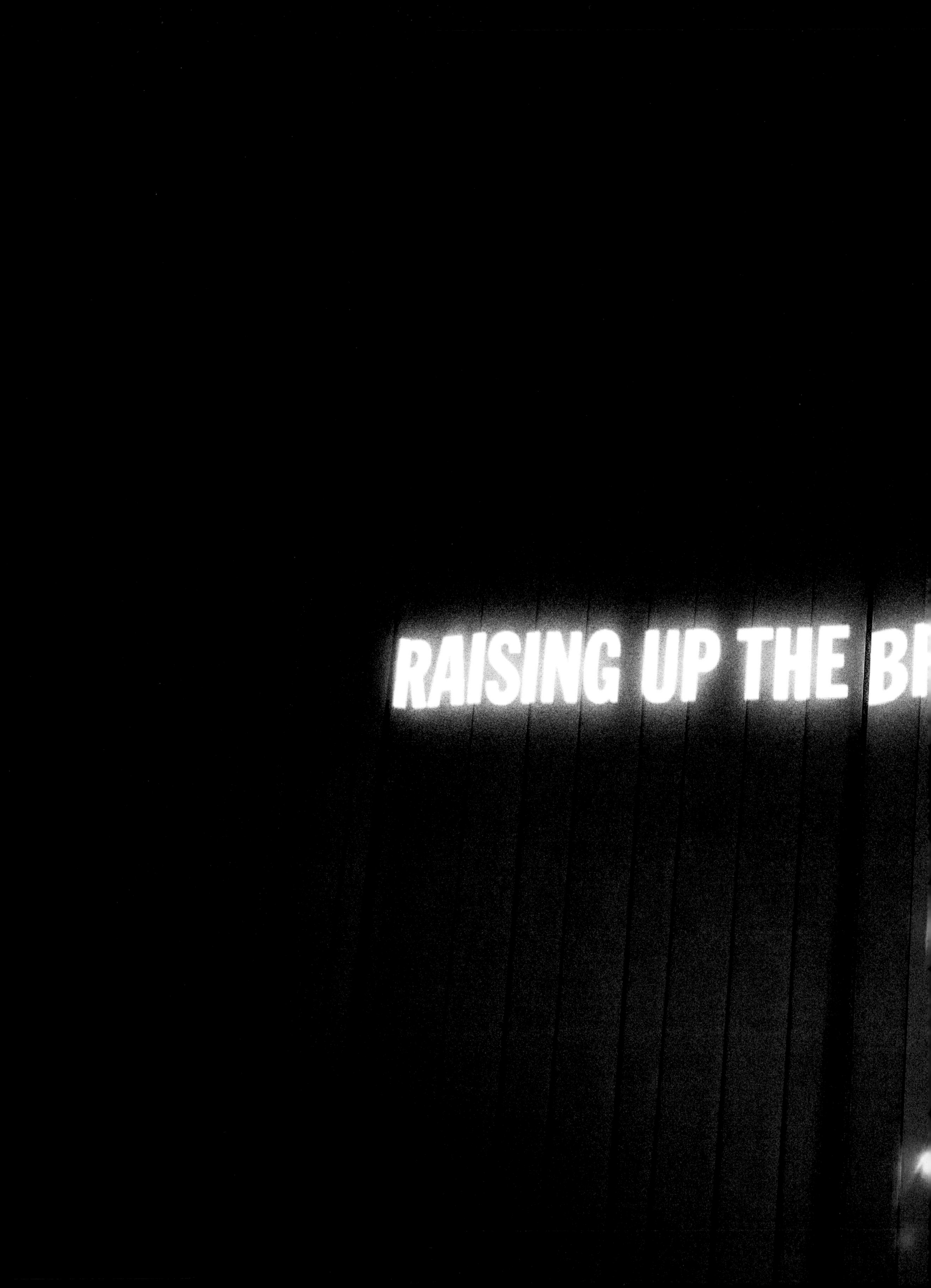

RAISING UP THE BR

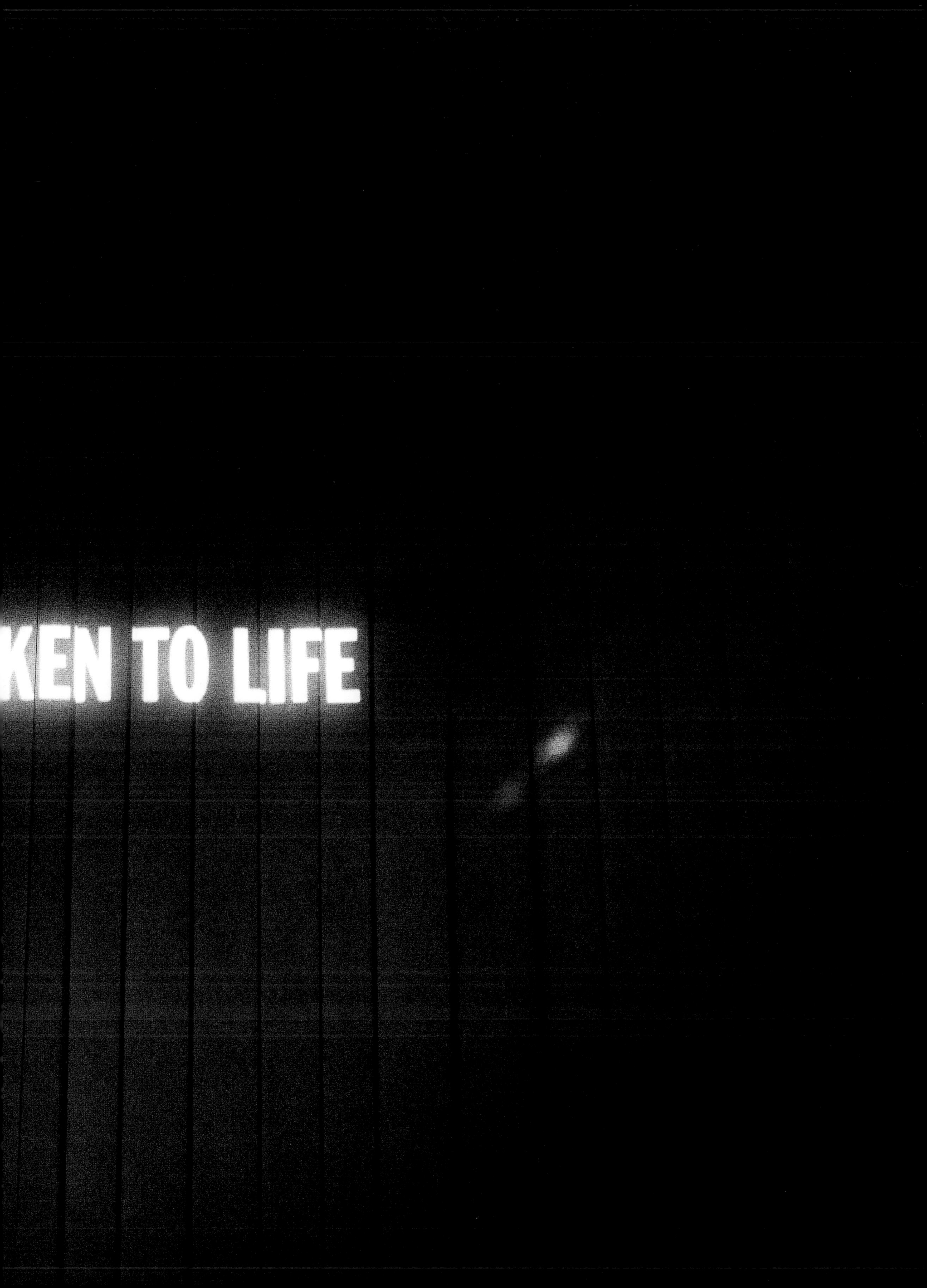

KEN TO LIFE

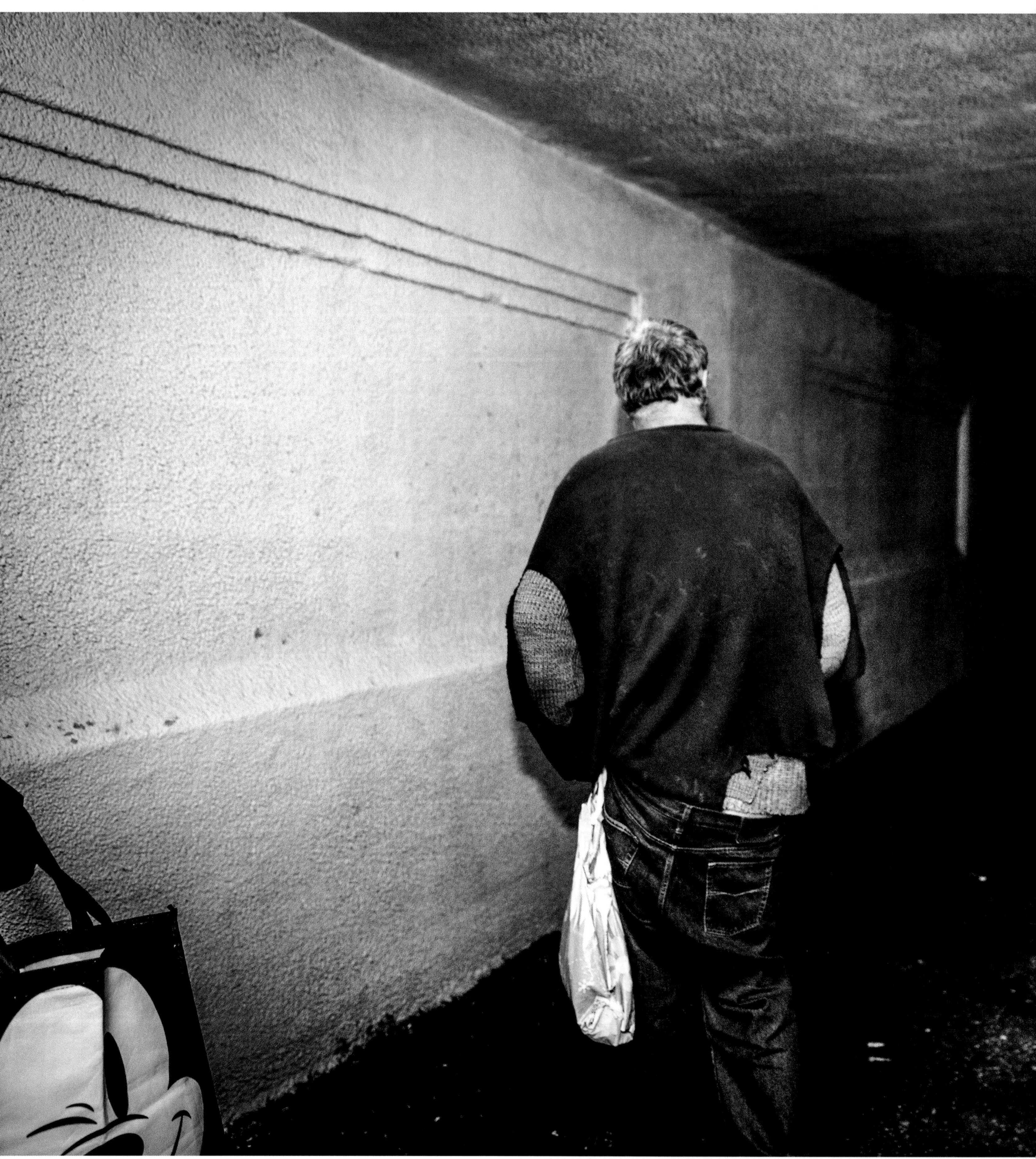

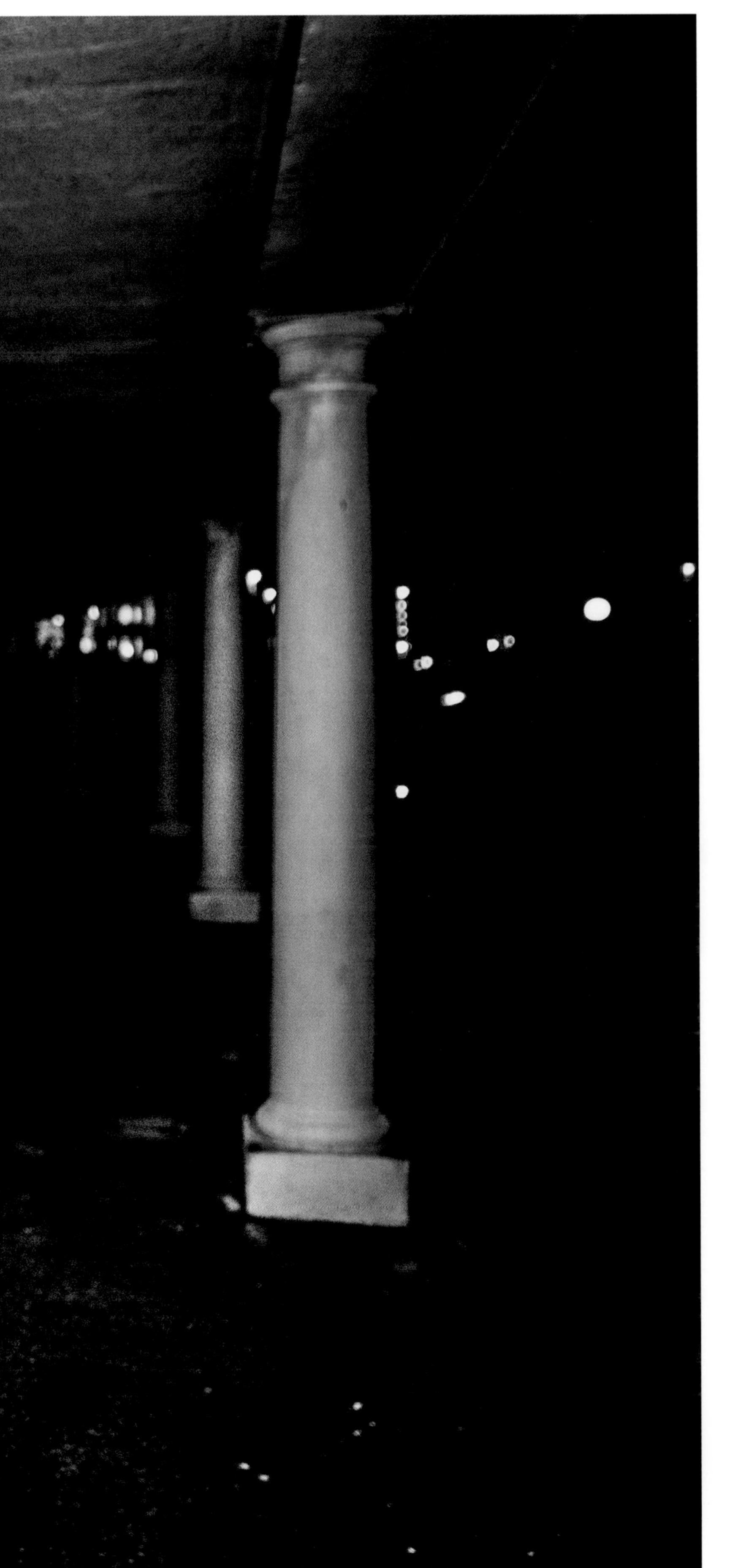

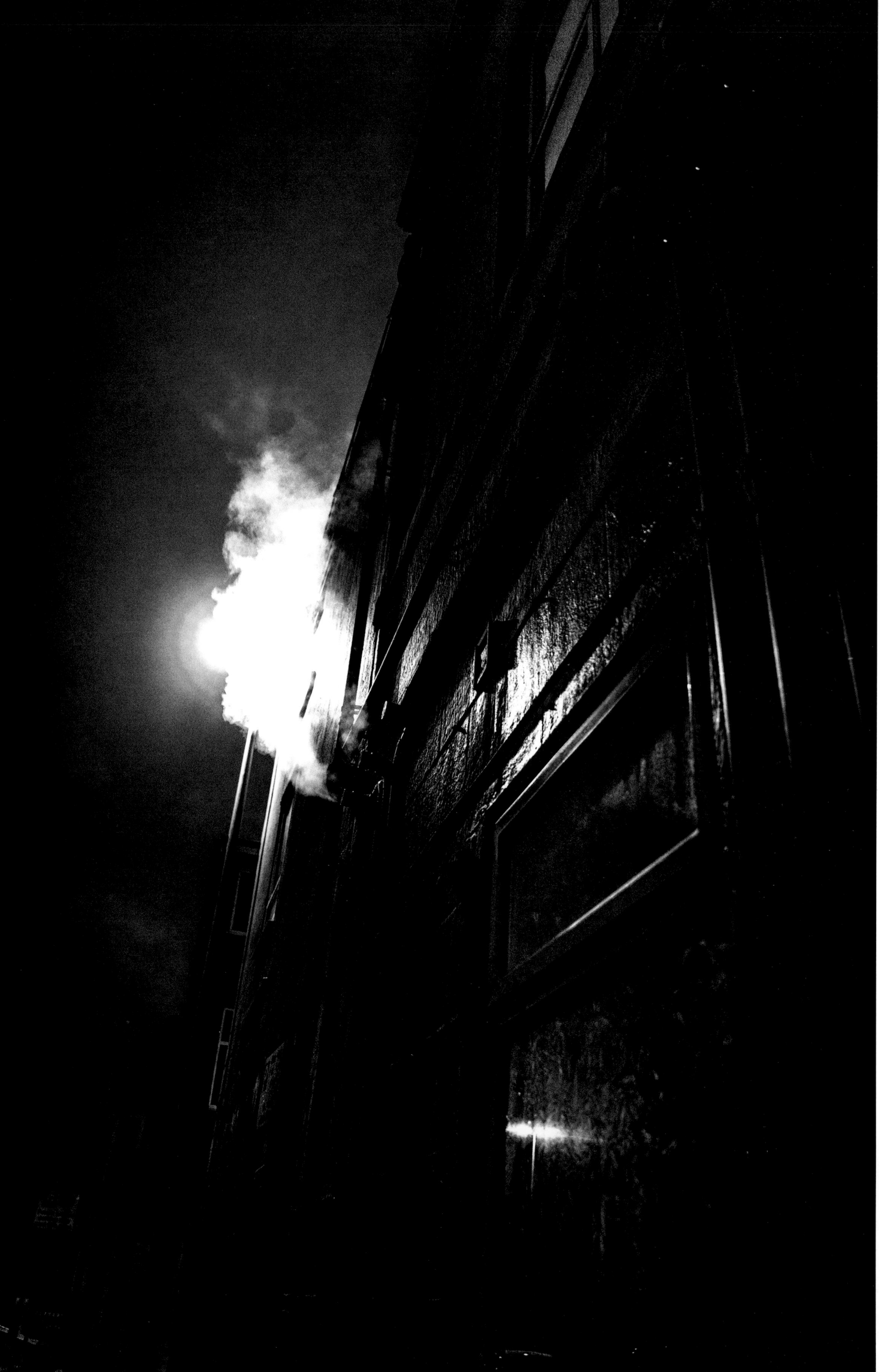

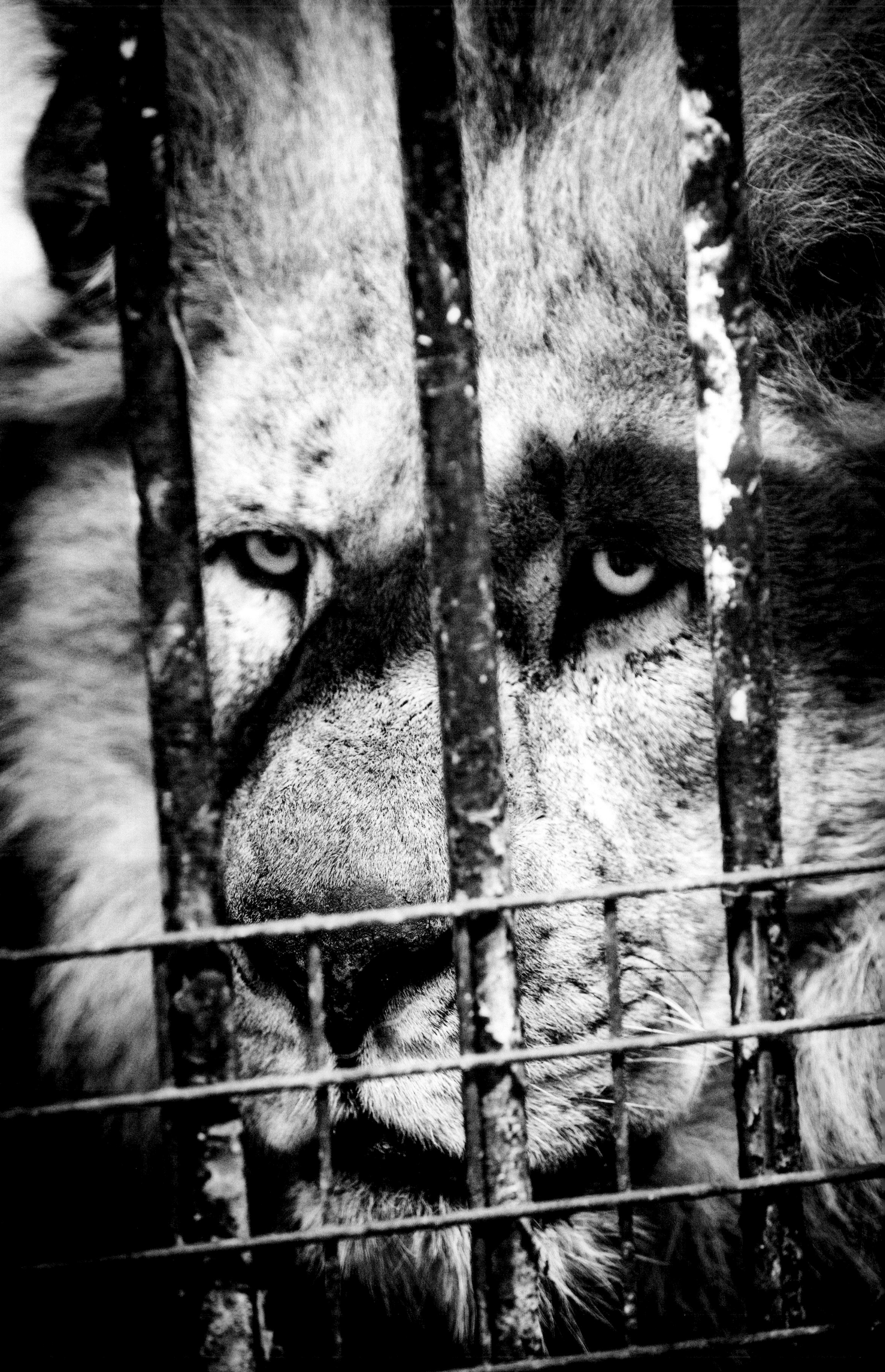

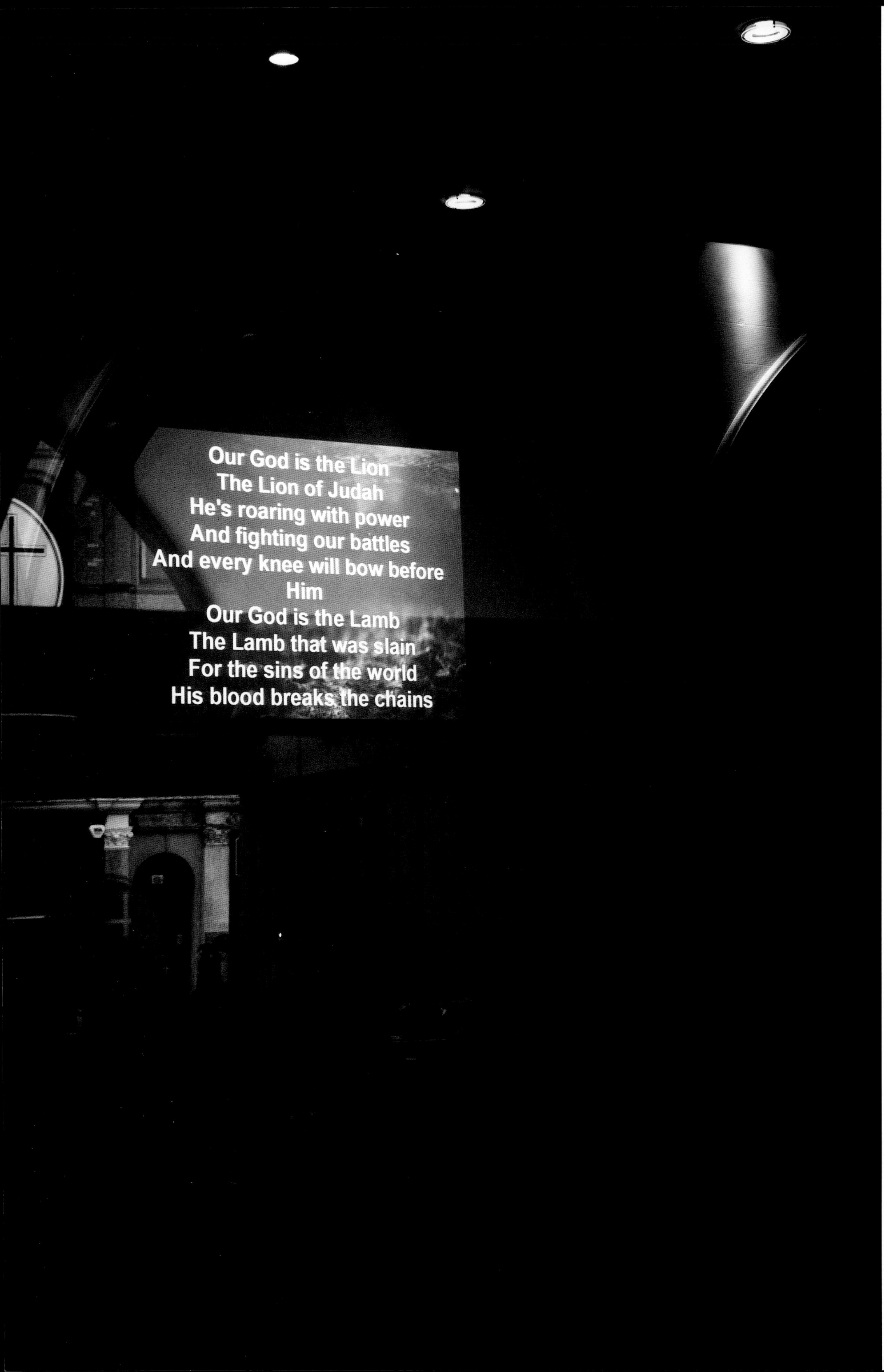

Our God is the Lion
The Lion of Judah
He's roaring with power
And fighting our battles
And every knee will bow before
Him
Our God is the Lamb
The Lamb that was slain
For the sins of the world
His blood breaks the chains

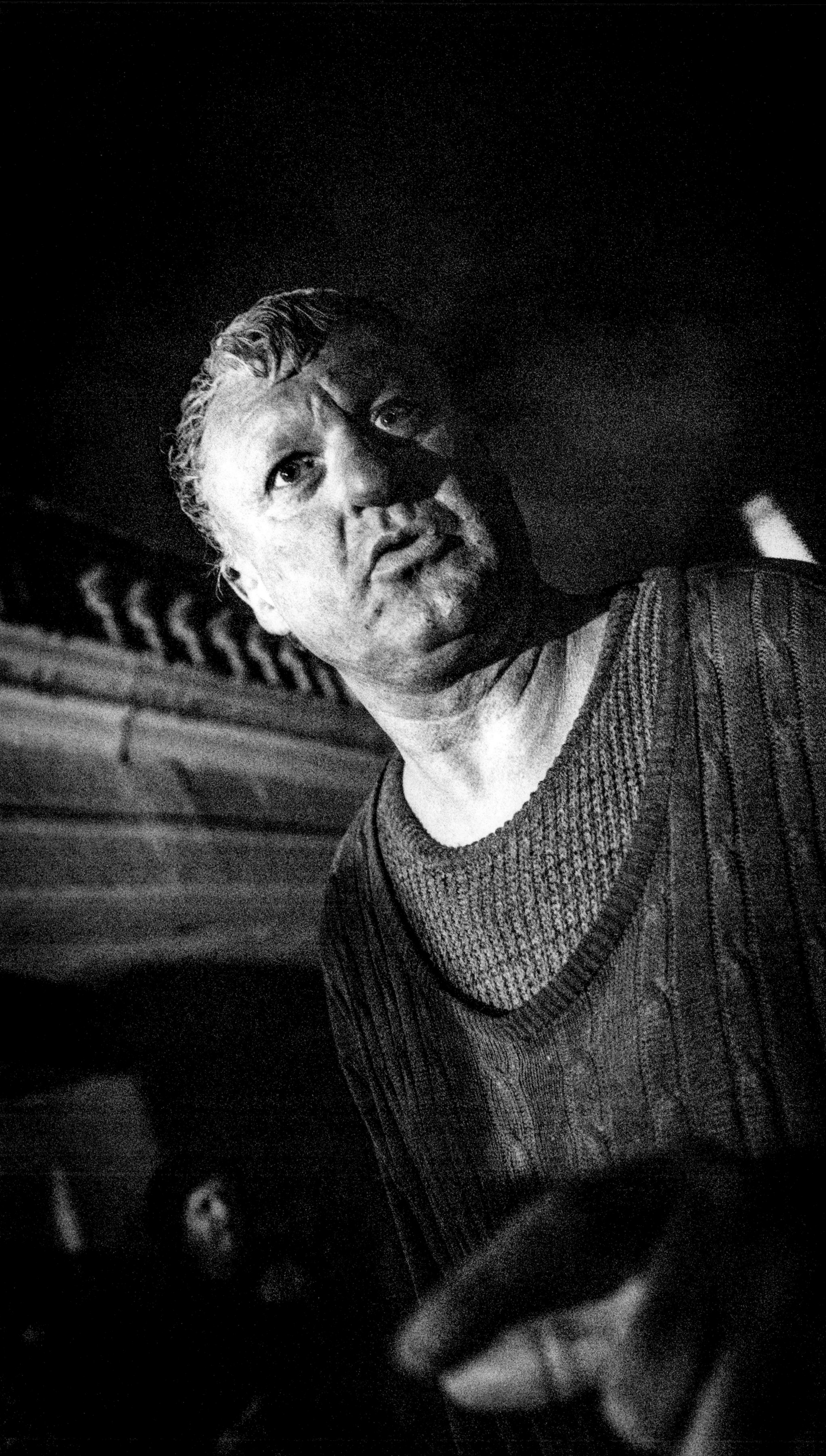

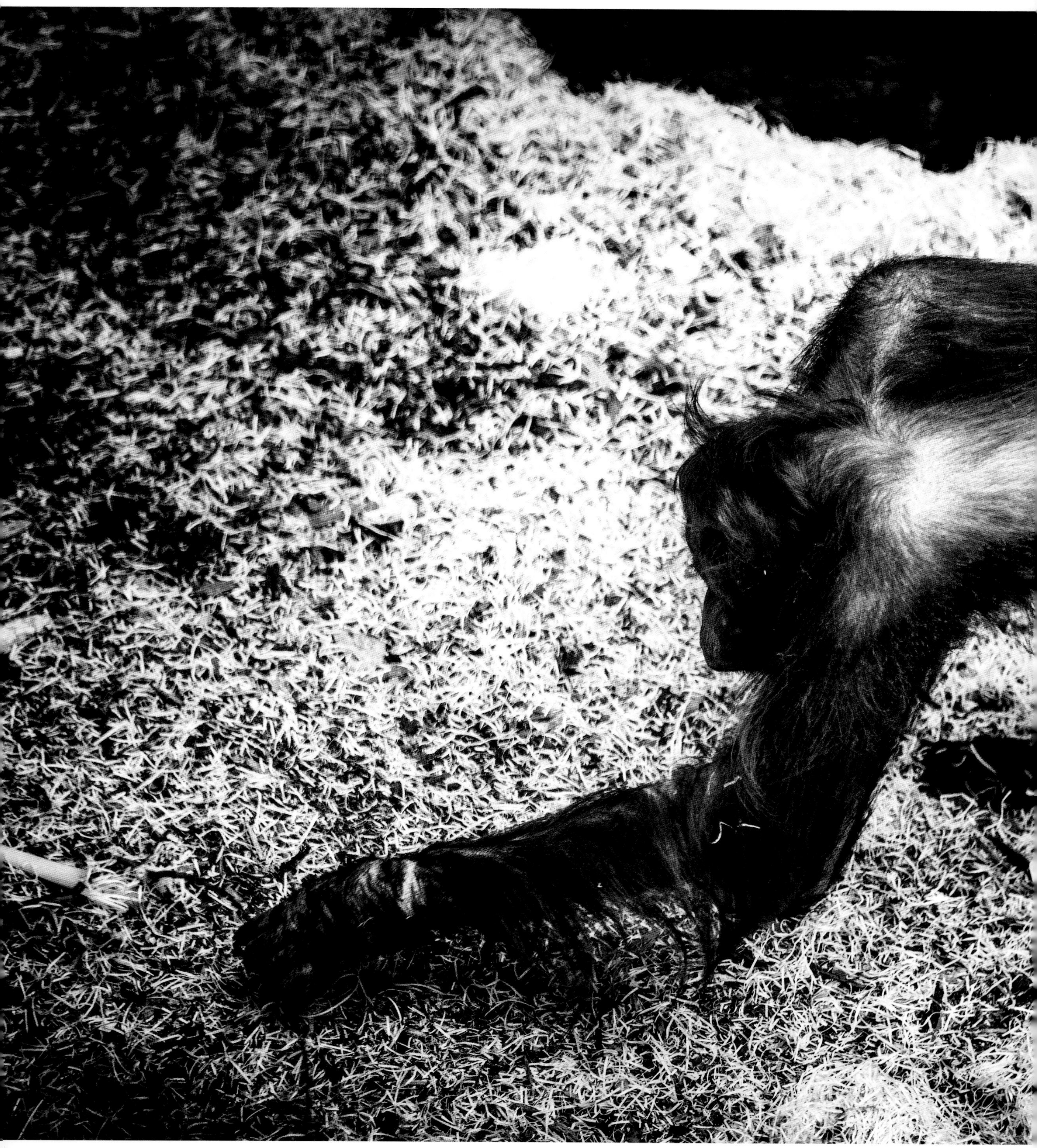

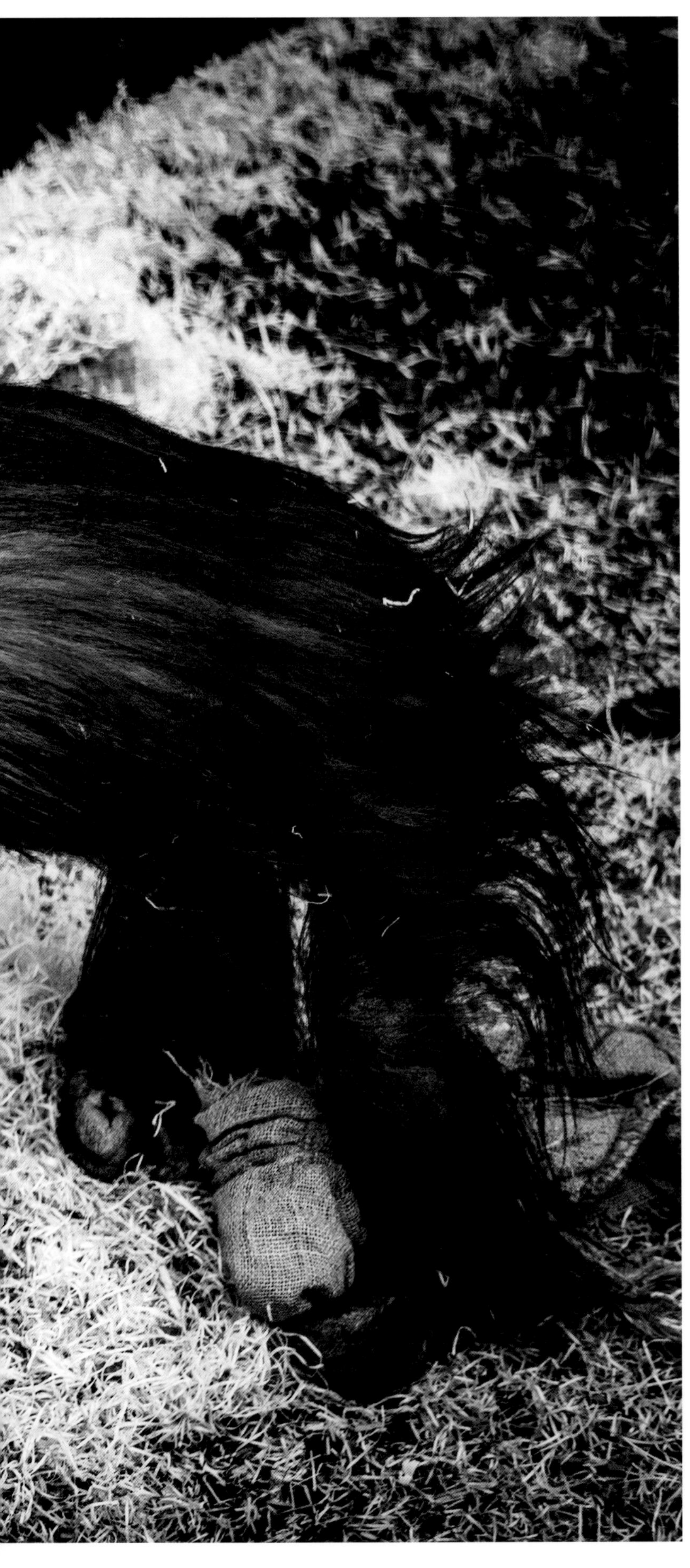

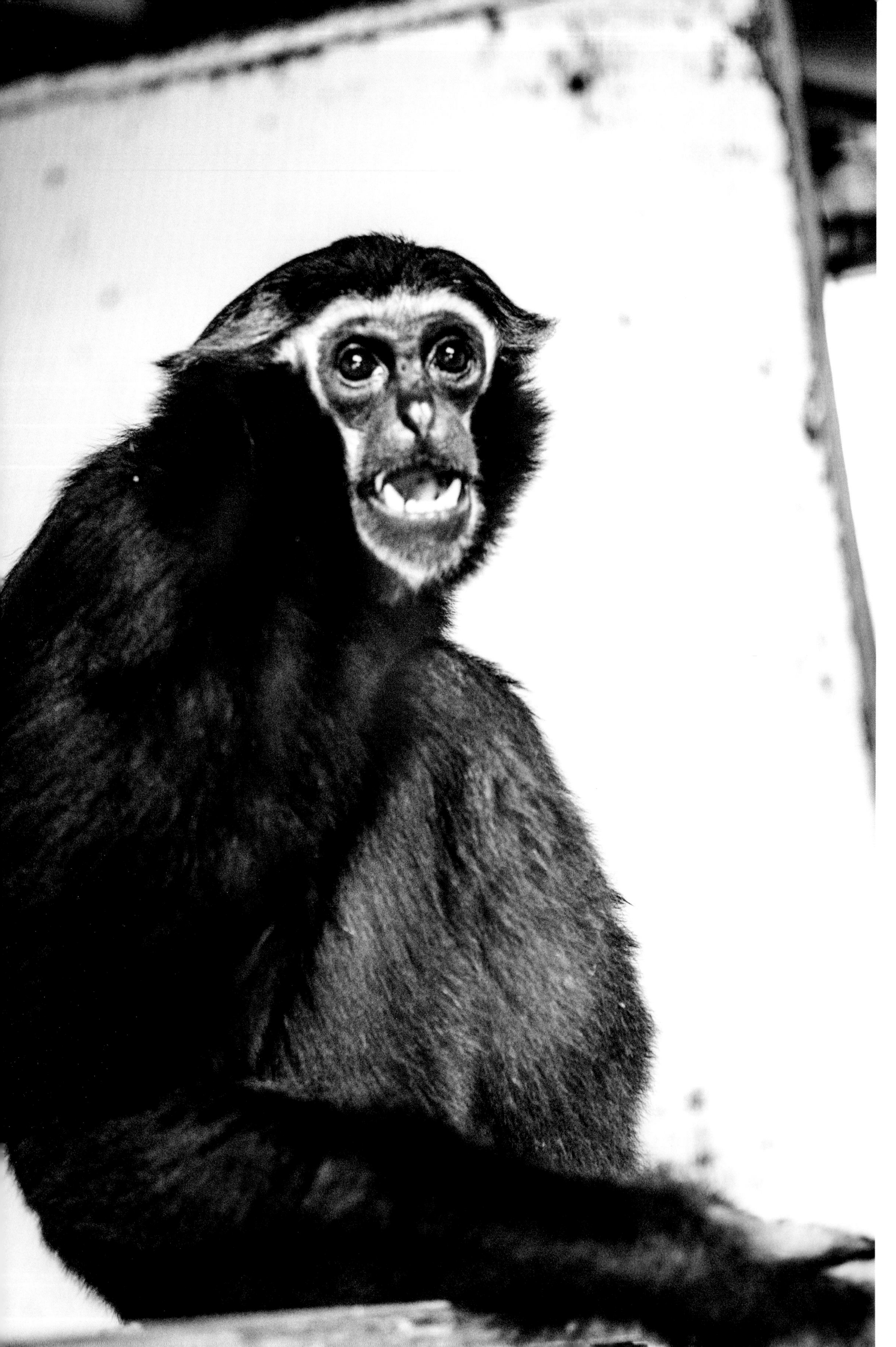

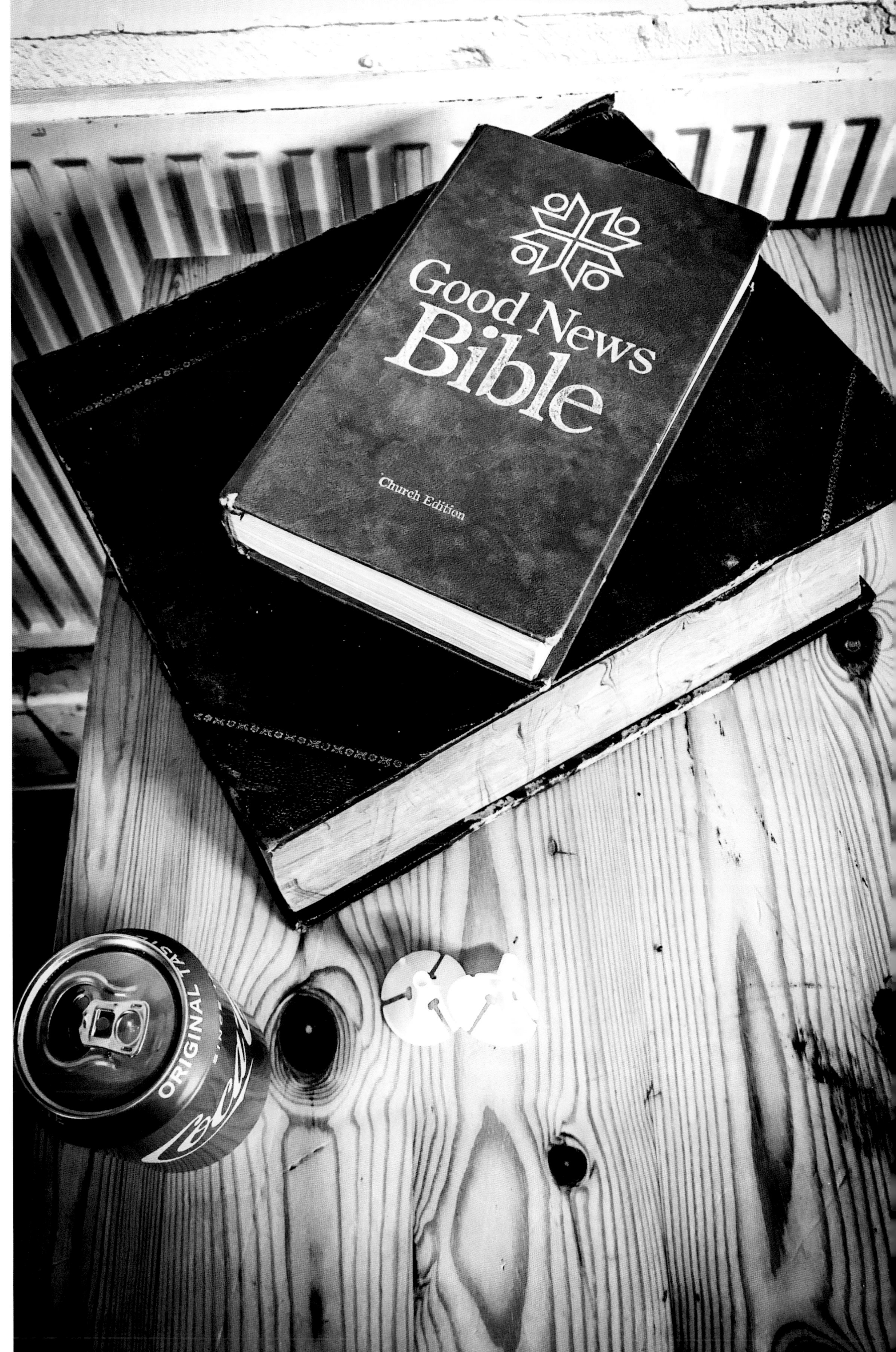
Good News
Bible
Church Edition

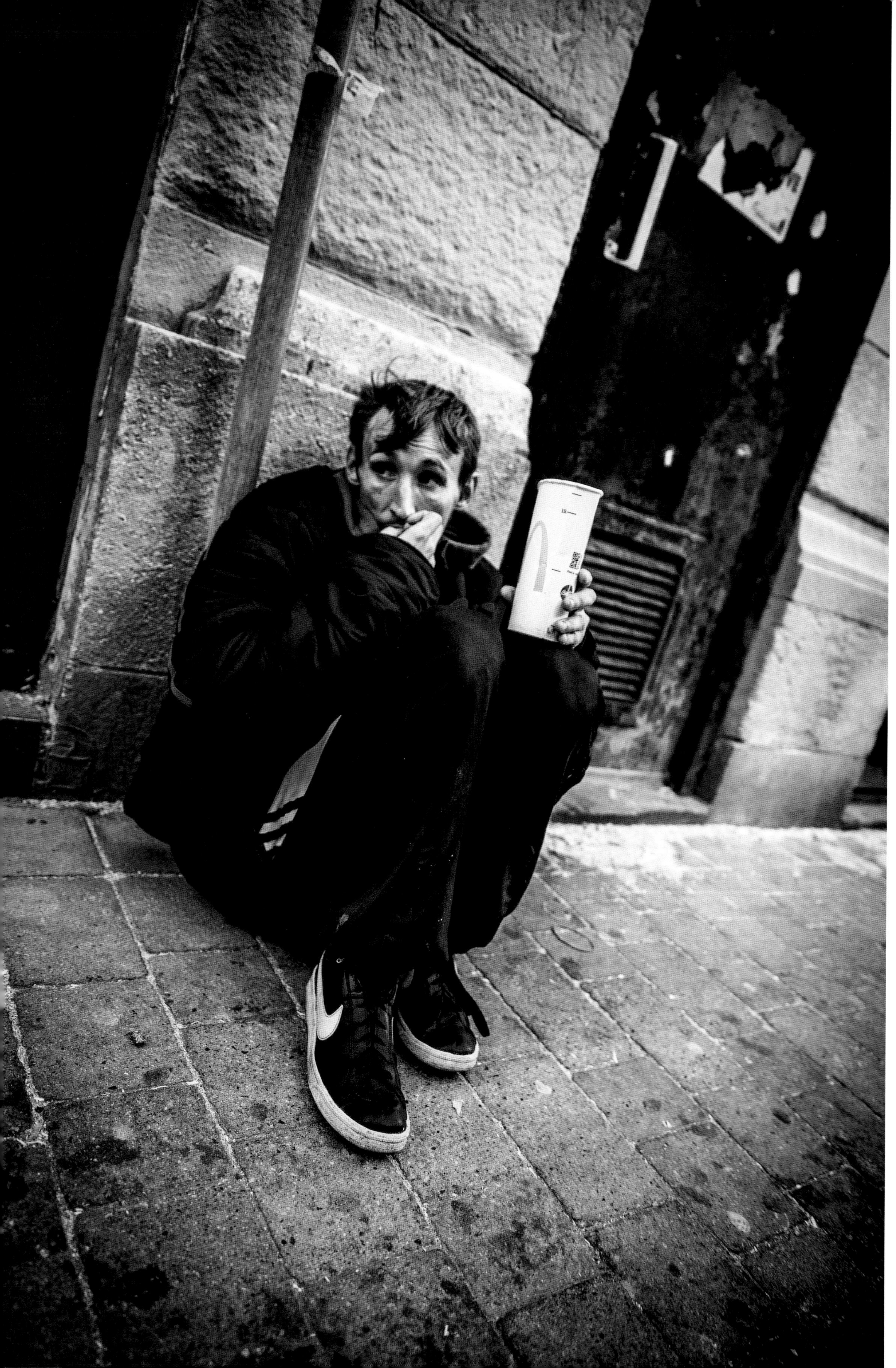

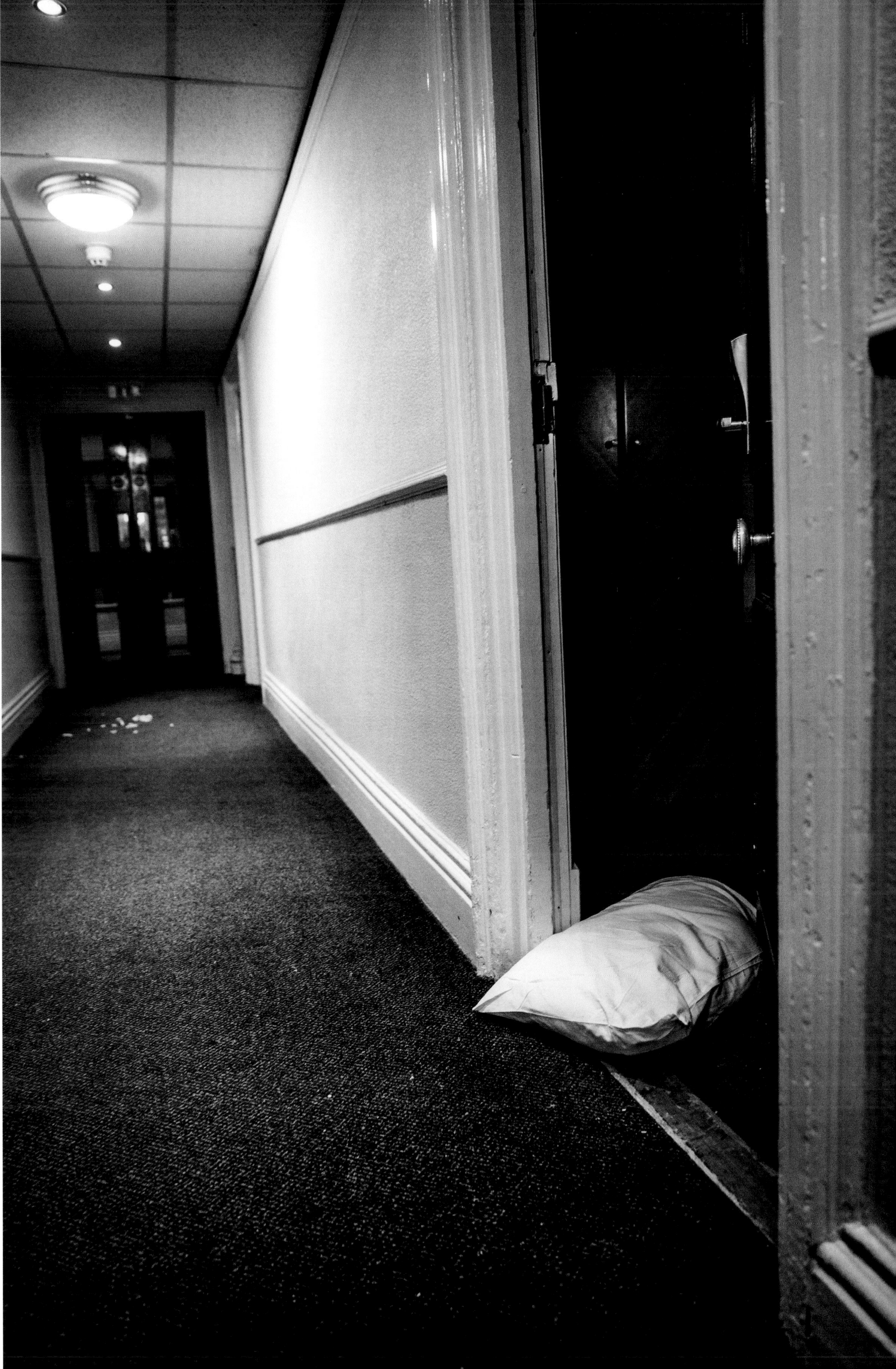

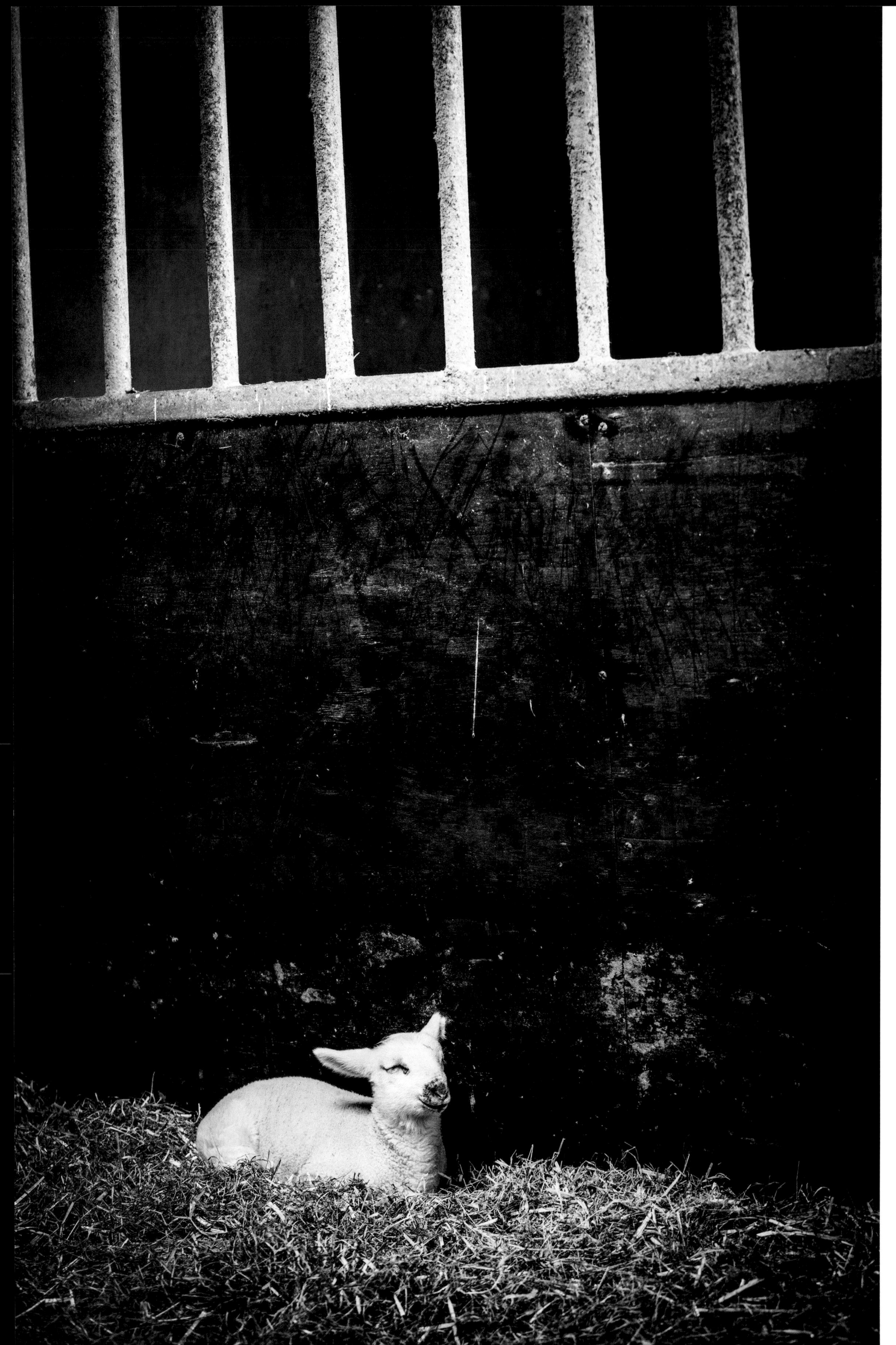

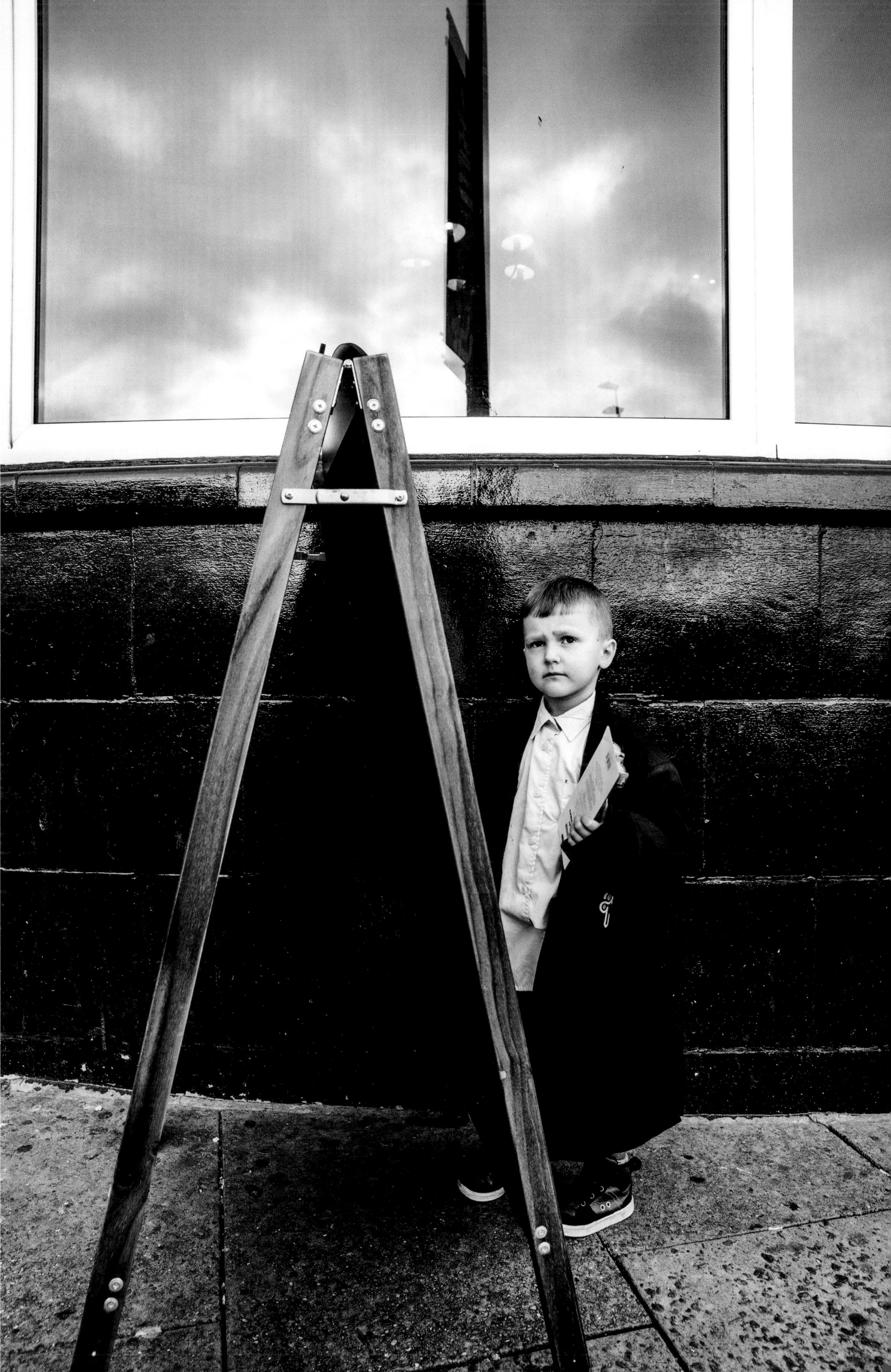

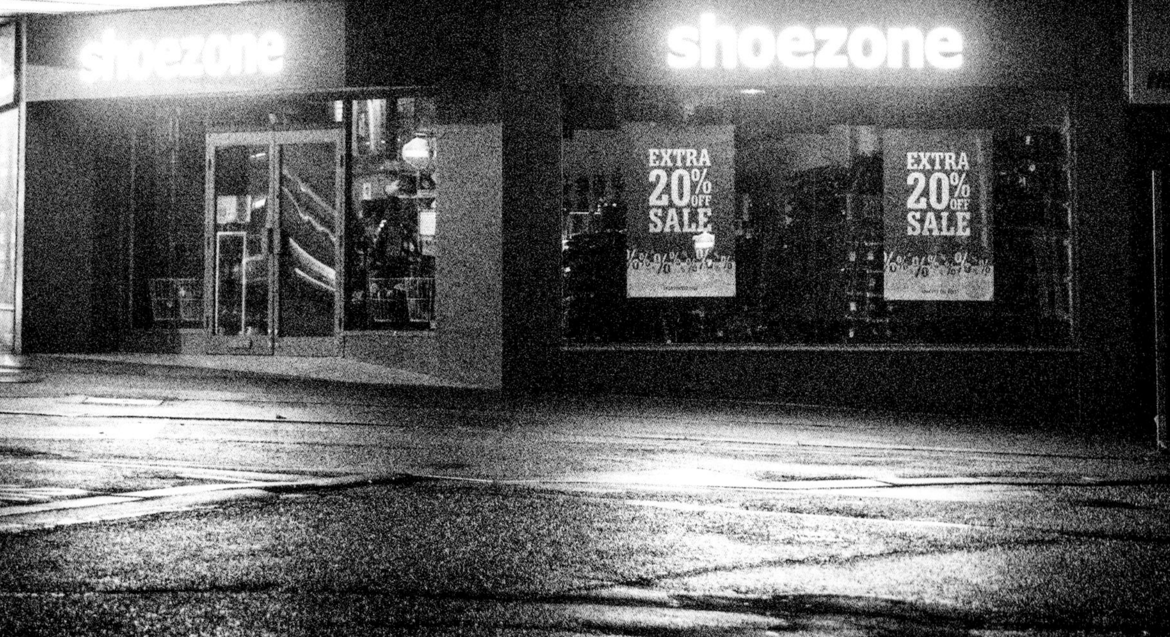

CENTRAL
METHODIST CHURCH
JESUS
THE
LIGHT
OF THE
WORLD
shoezone
shoezone
EXTRA
20% OFF
SALE
EXTRA
20% OFF
SALE

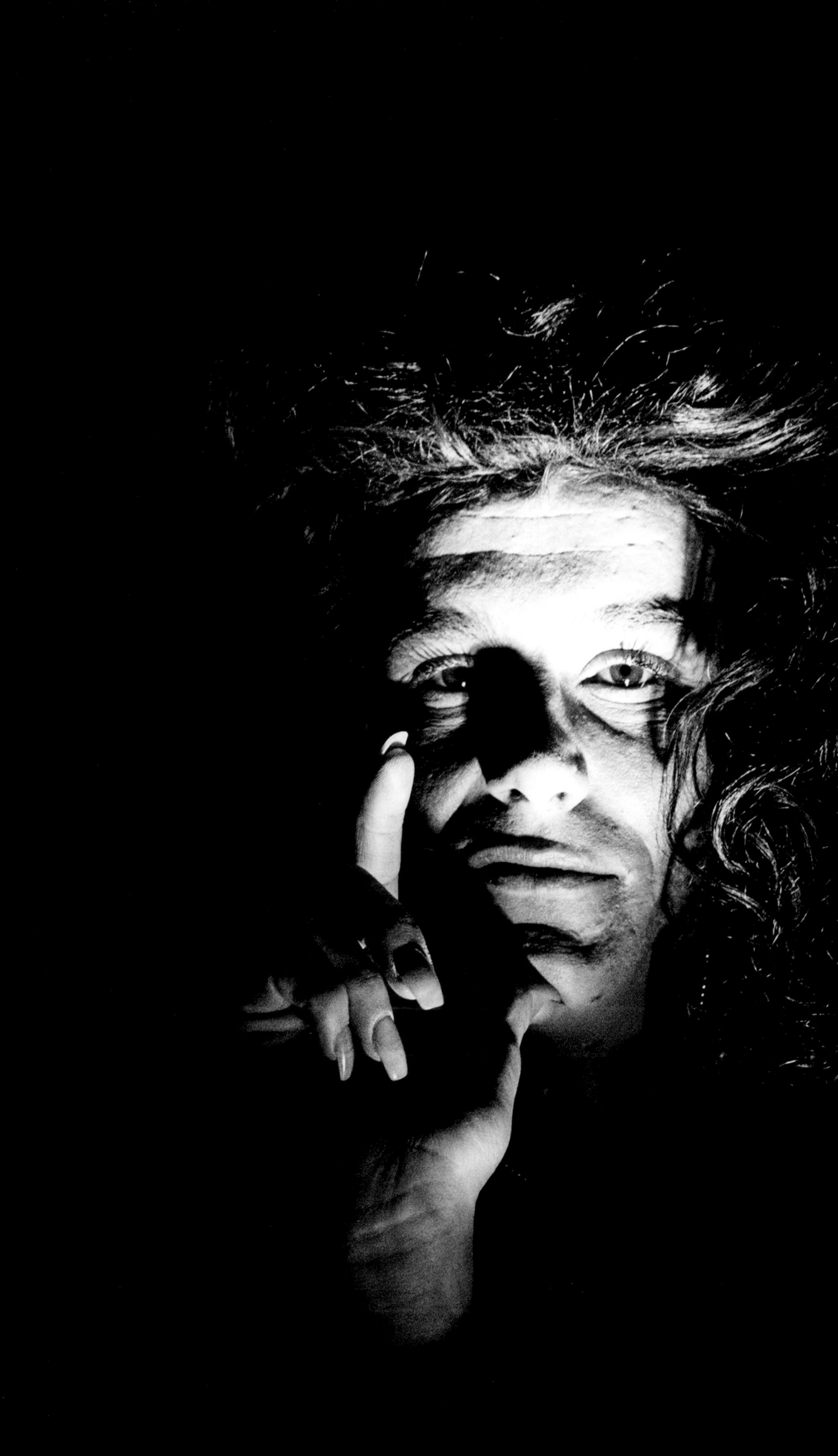

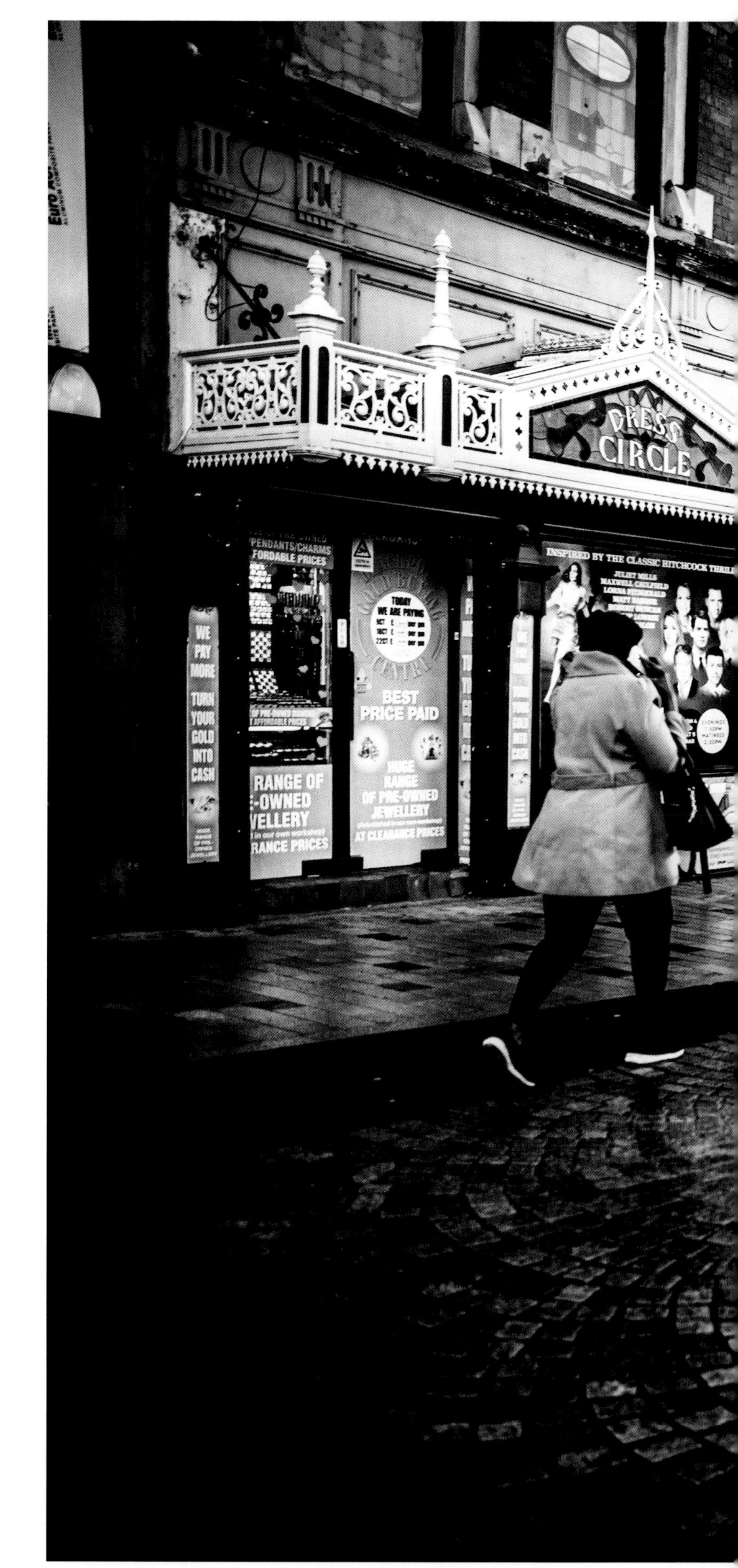

DRESS
CIRCLE
INSPIRED BY THE CLASSIC HITCHCOCK THRILLER
JULIET MILLS
MAXWELL CAULFIELD
LORNA FITZGERALD
PENDANTS/CHARMS
FORDABLE PRICES
WE PAY MORE
TURN YOUR GOLD INTO CASH
BEST PRICE PAID
RANGE OF PRE-OWNED JEWELLERY
FRANCE PRICES
HUGE RANGE OF PRE-OWNED JEWELLERY
AT CLEARANCE PRICES
TODAY WE ARE PAYING

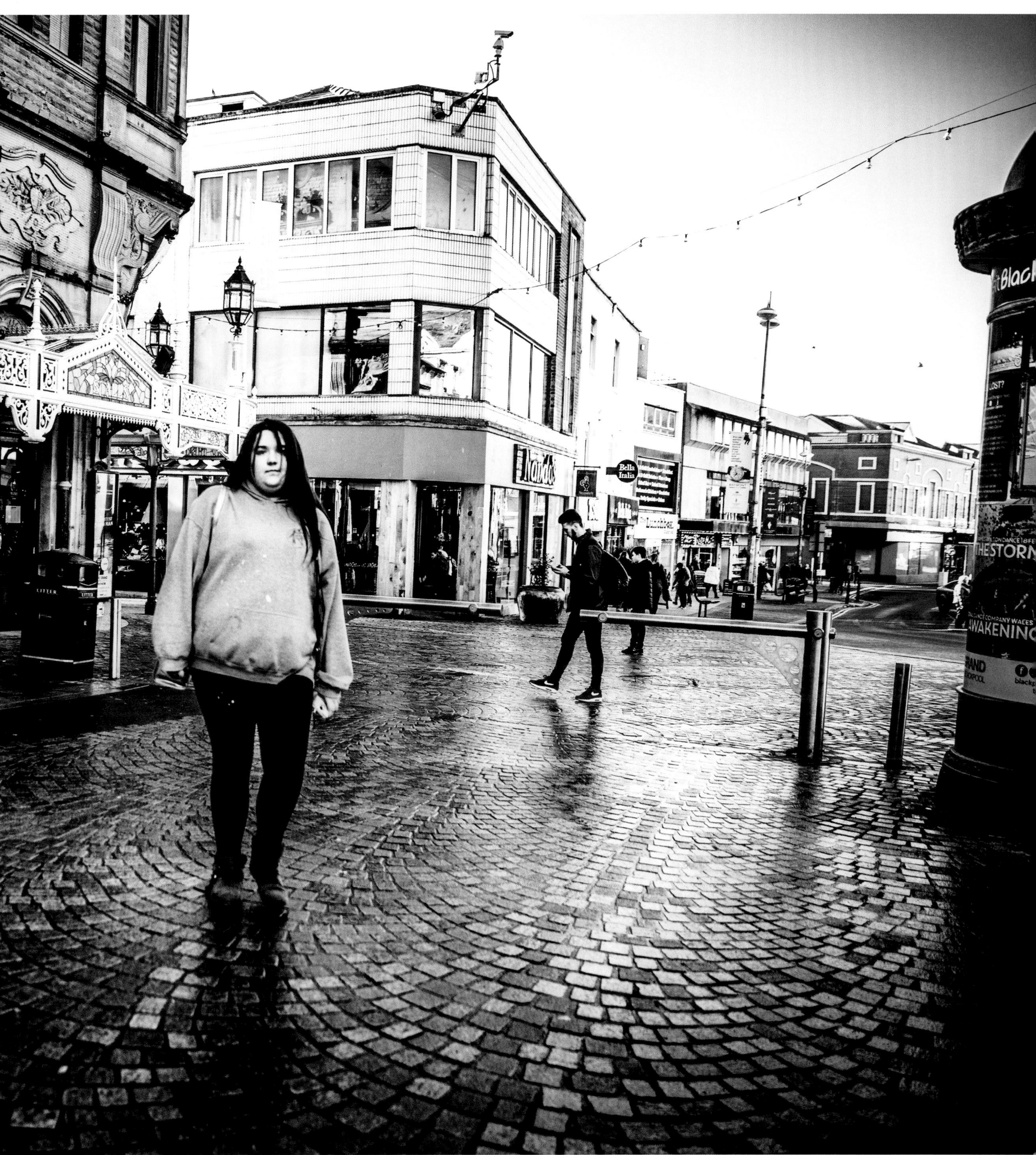

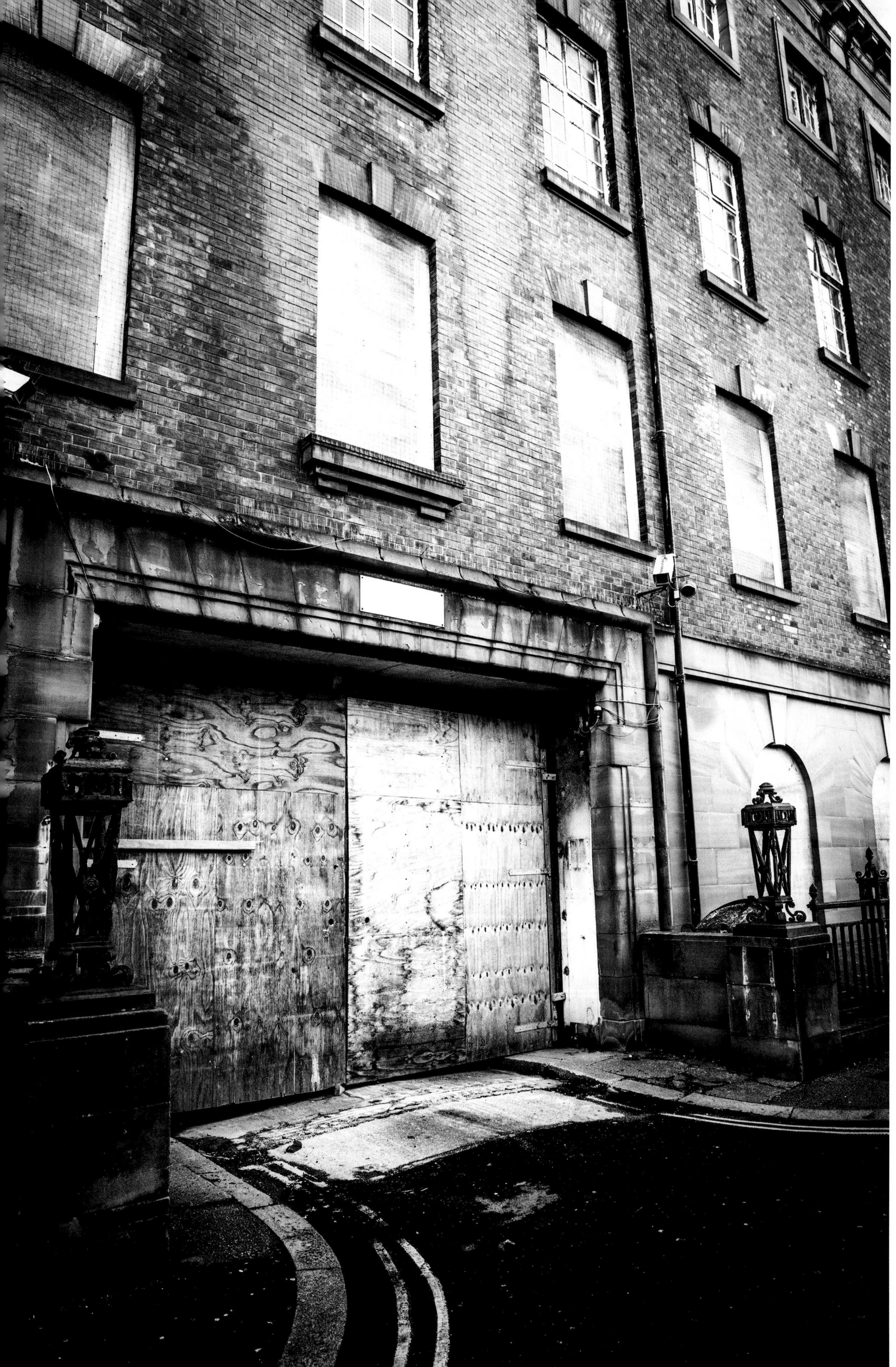

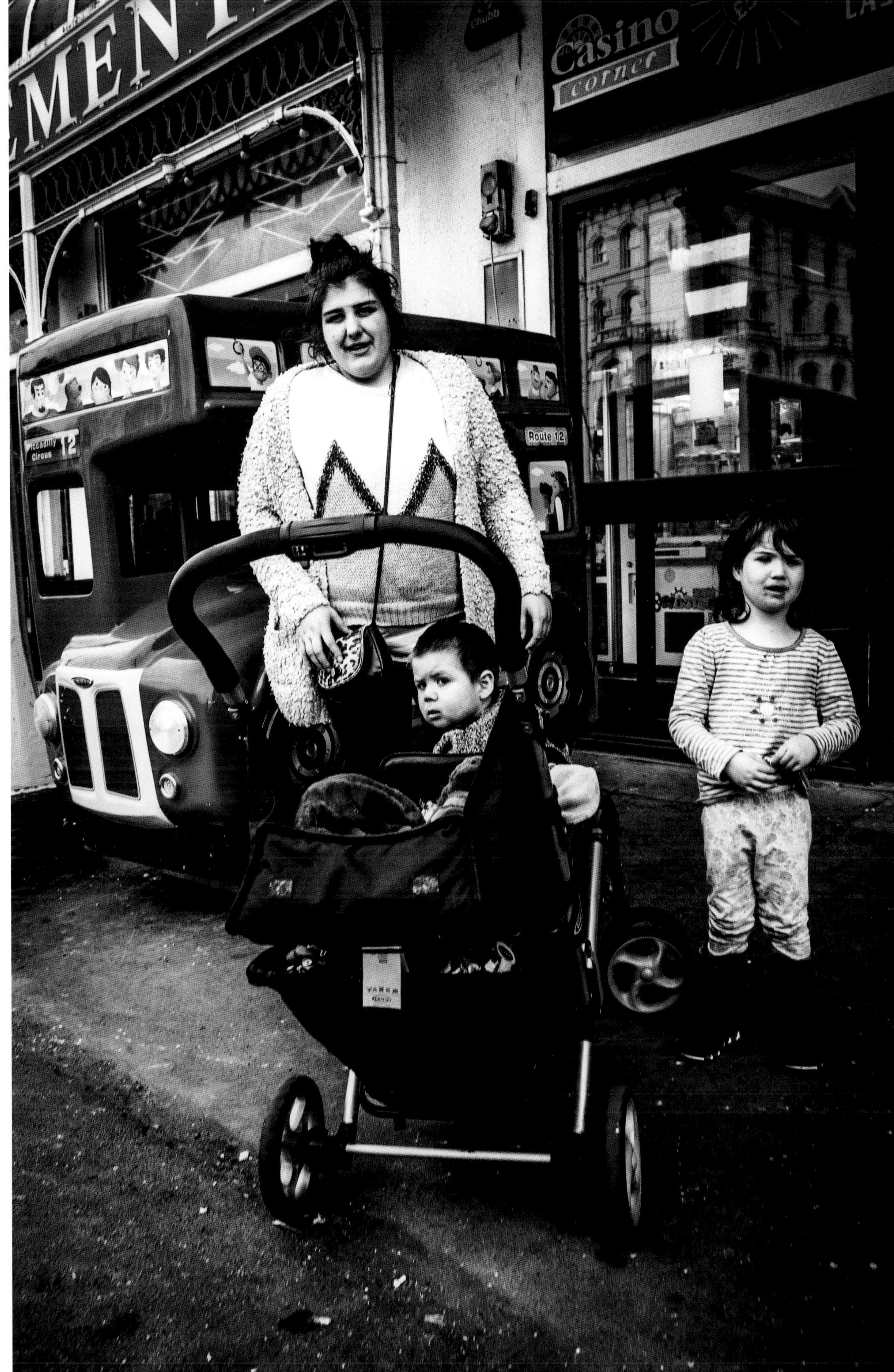

MENT
Casino corner
Chubb
Piccadilly Circus 12
Route 12

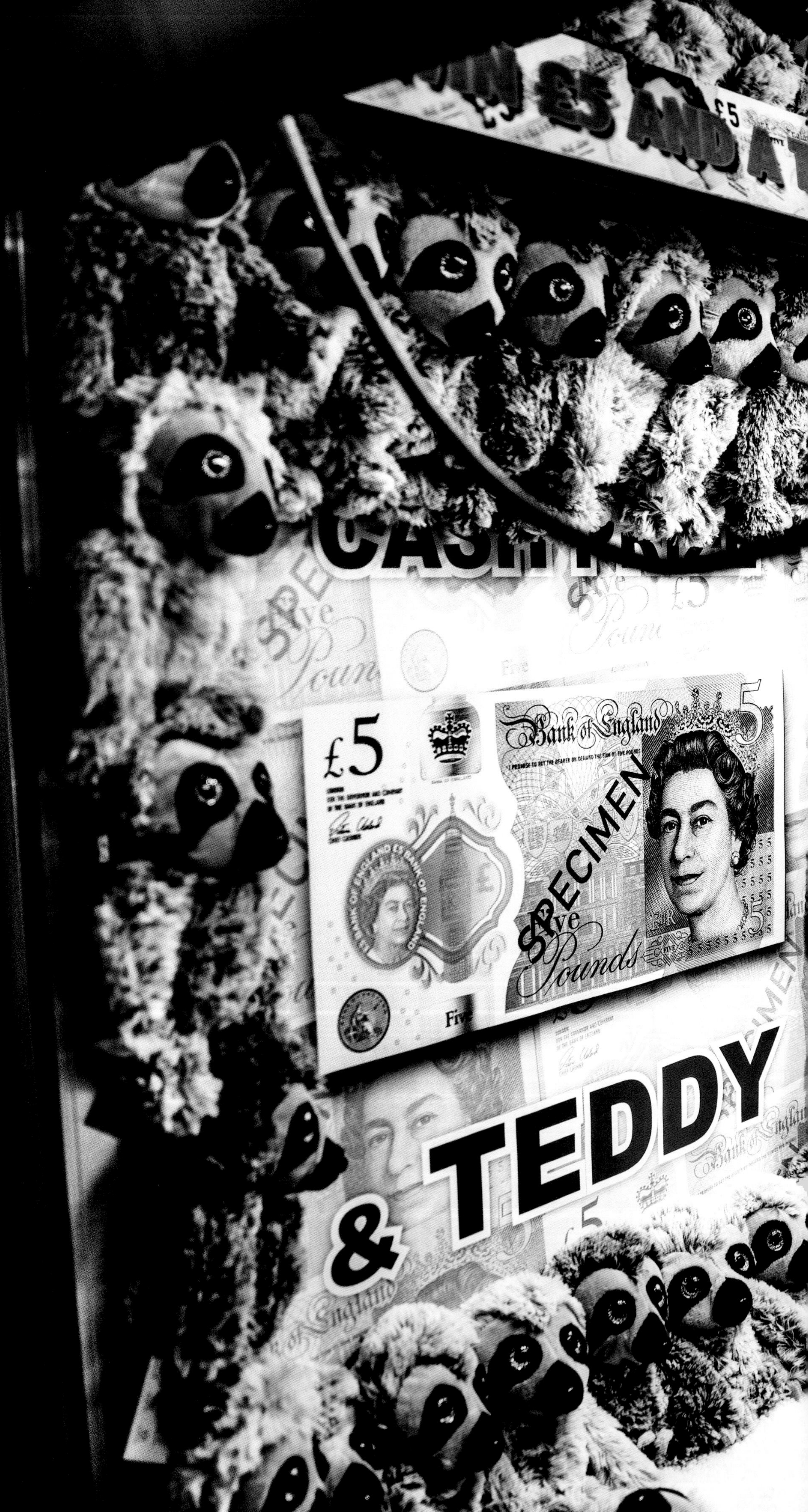
CASH
£5
TEDDY
&
Bank of England
£5
SPECIMEN
Five Pounds
Five Pounds

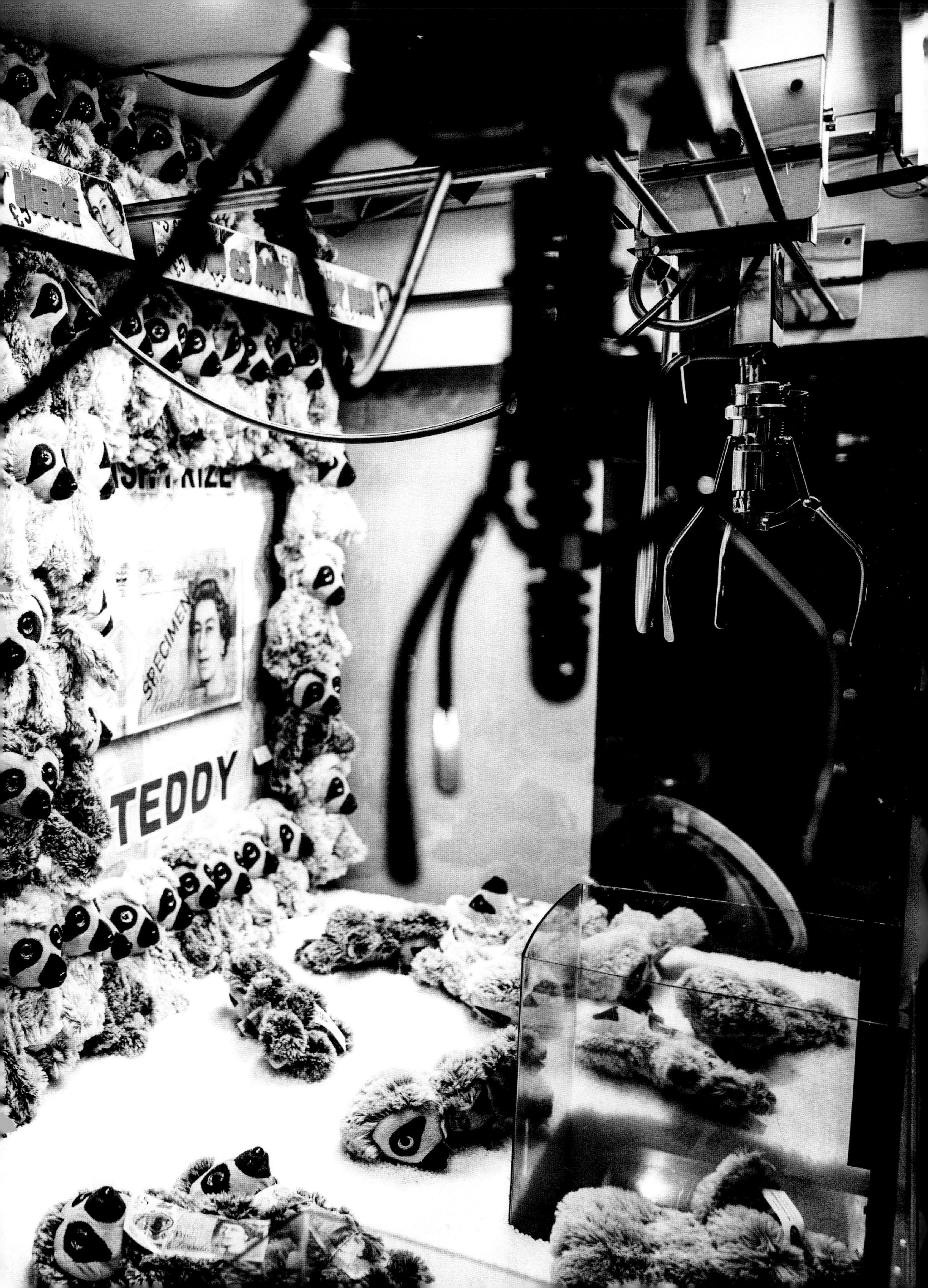

HERE
£5
SPECIMEN
TEDDY

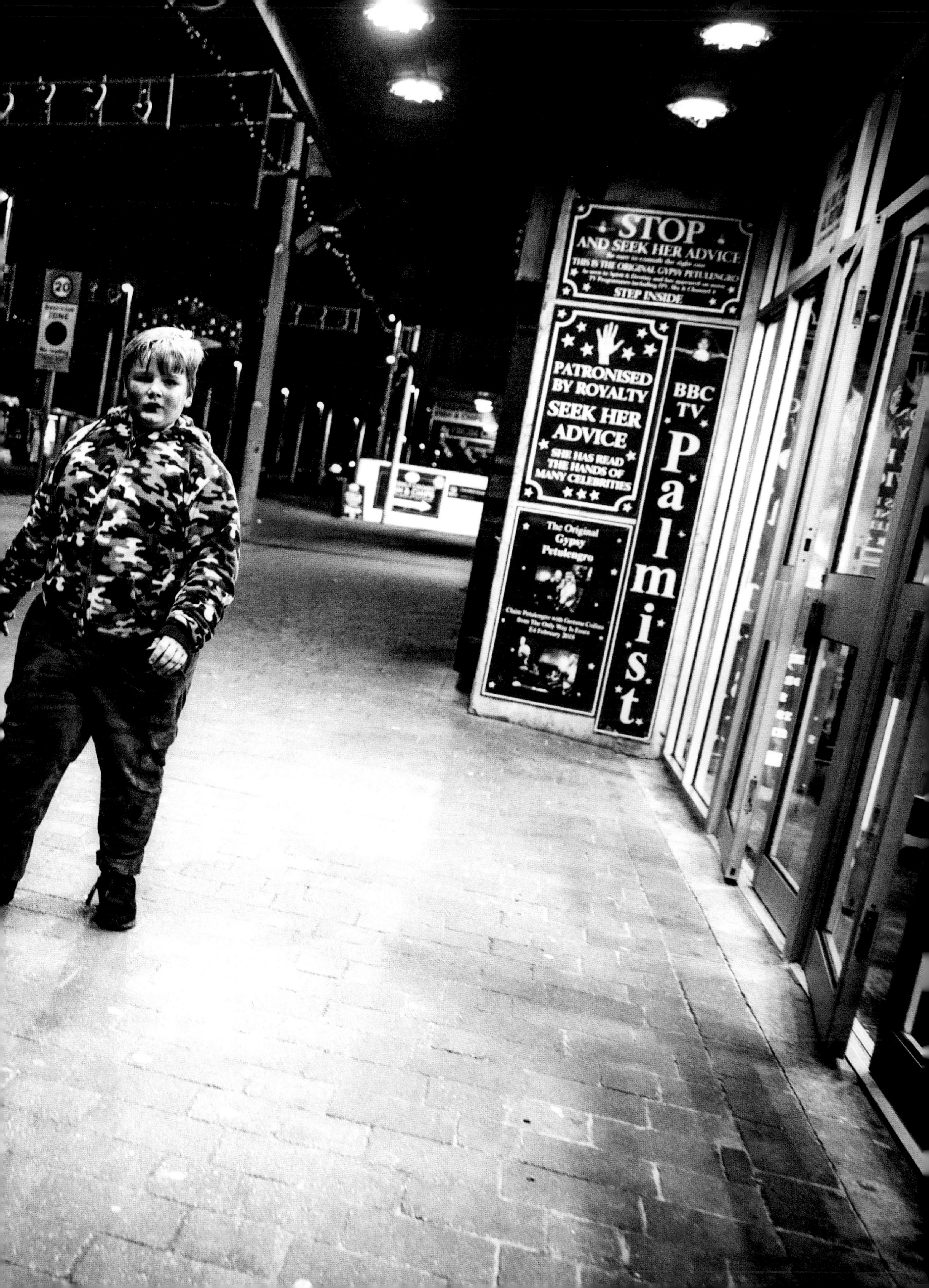
STOP
AND SEEK HER ADVICE
THIS IS THE ORIGINAL GYPSY PETULENGRO
STEP INSIDE
PATRONISED BY ROYALTY
SEEK HER ADVICE
SHE HAS READ THE HANDS OF MANY CELEBRITIES
BBC TV
Palmist
The Original Gypsy Petulengro

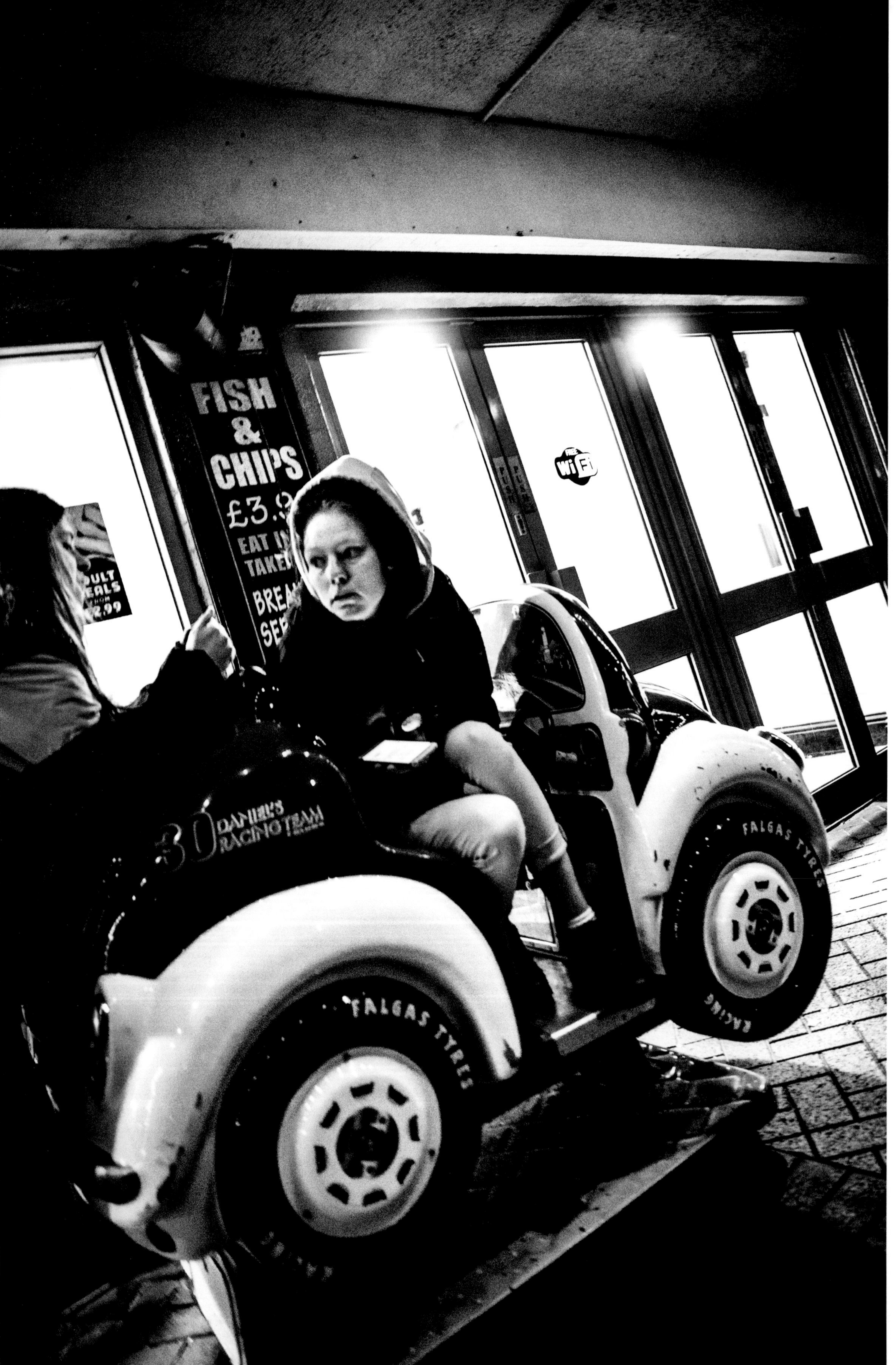

FISH
&
CHIPS
£3.9
EAT IN
TAKE
BREA
SEE
WiFi
30 DANIEL'S RACING TEAM
FALGAS TYRES
FALGAS TYRES
RACING

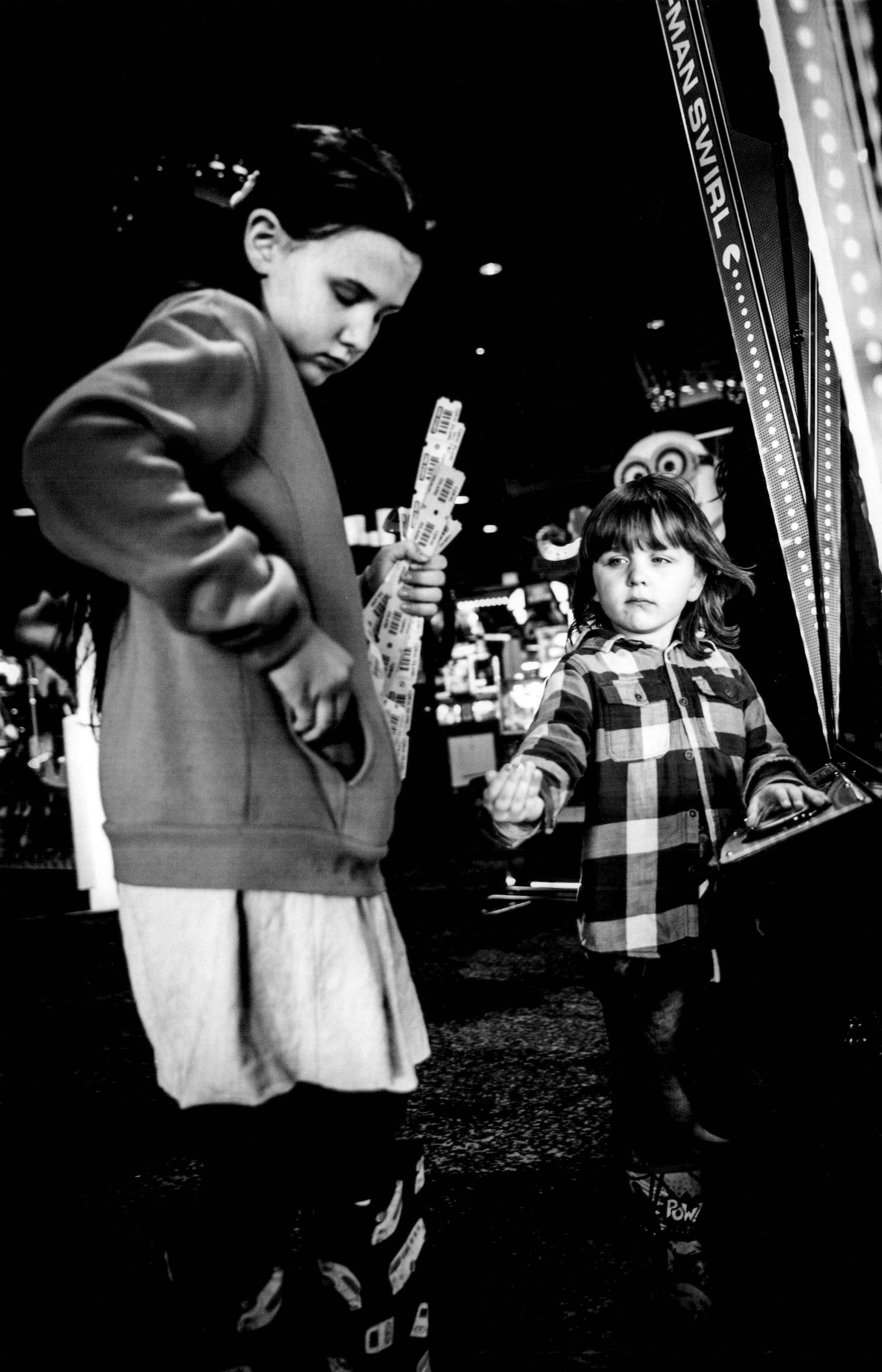
MAN SWIRL

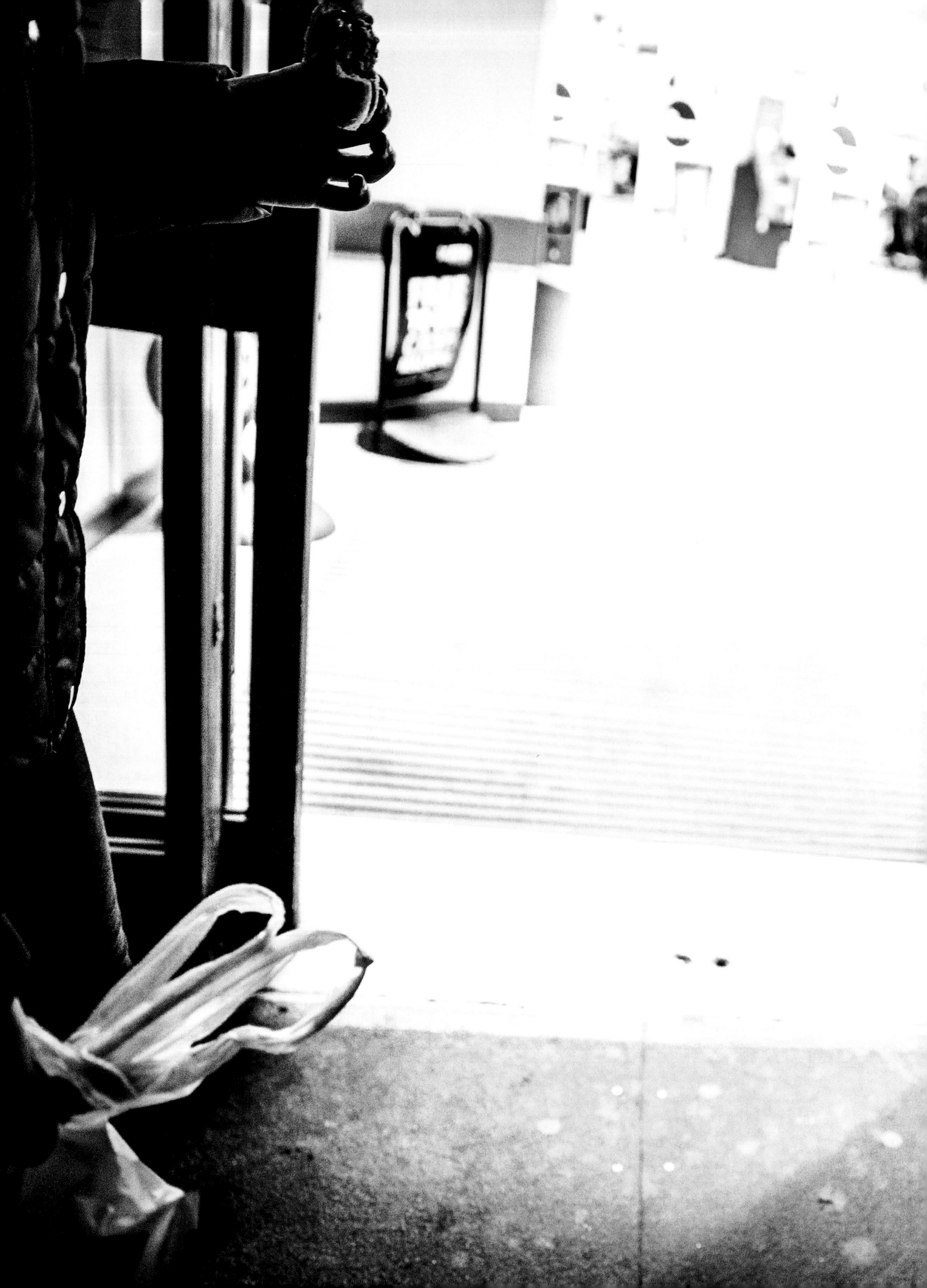

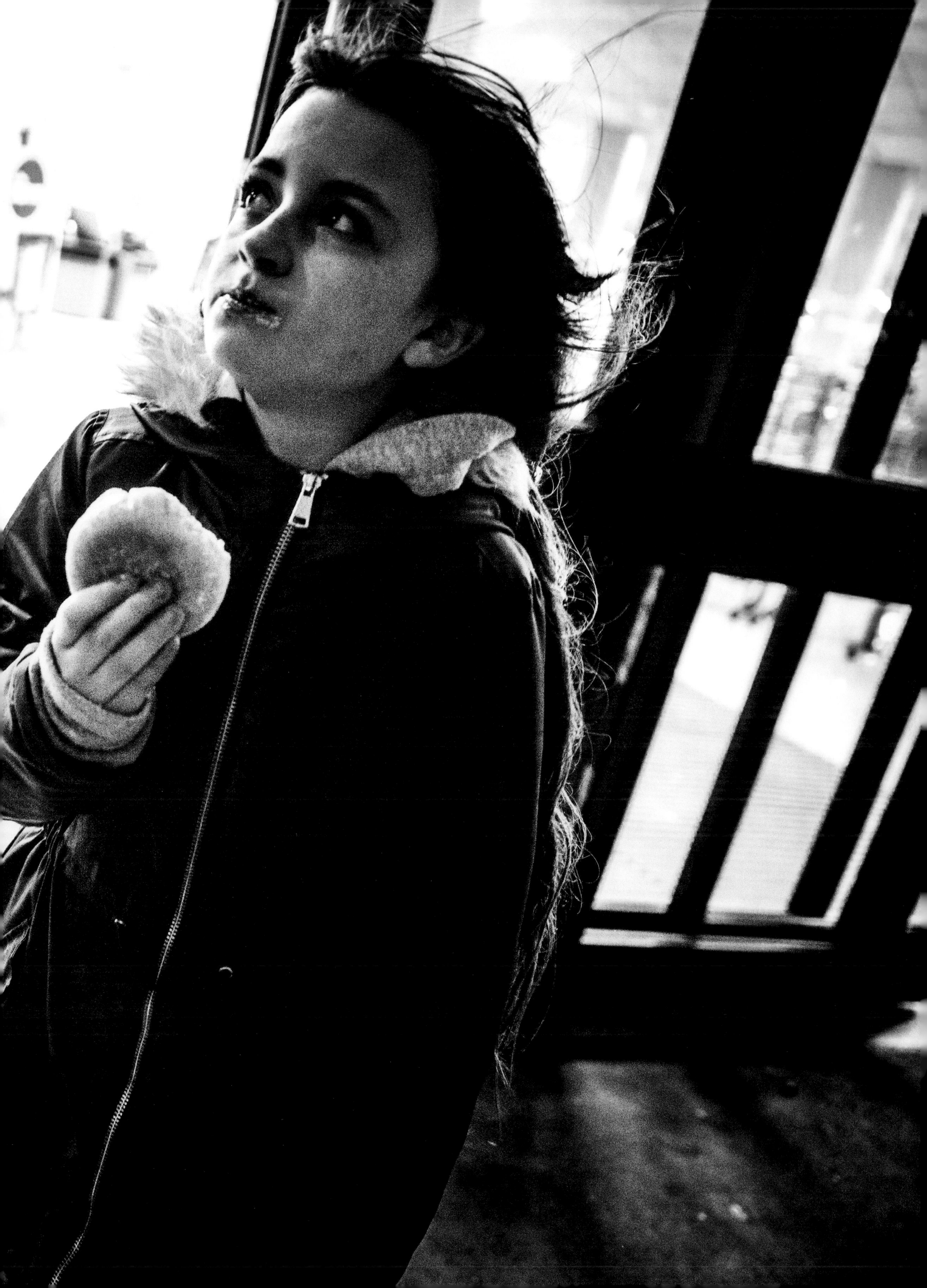

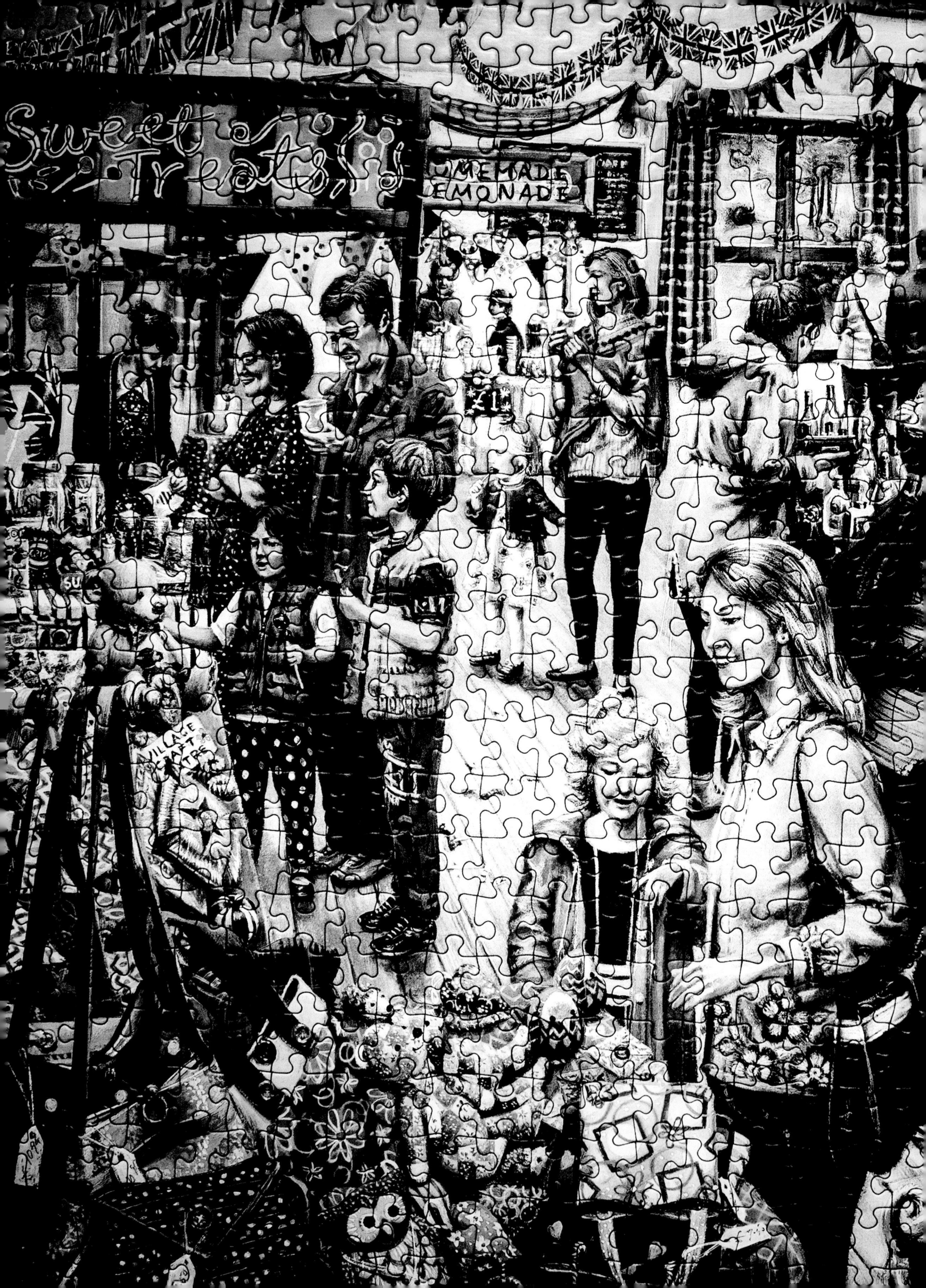

Sweet Treats
HOMEMADE LEMONADE

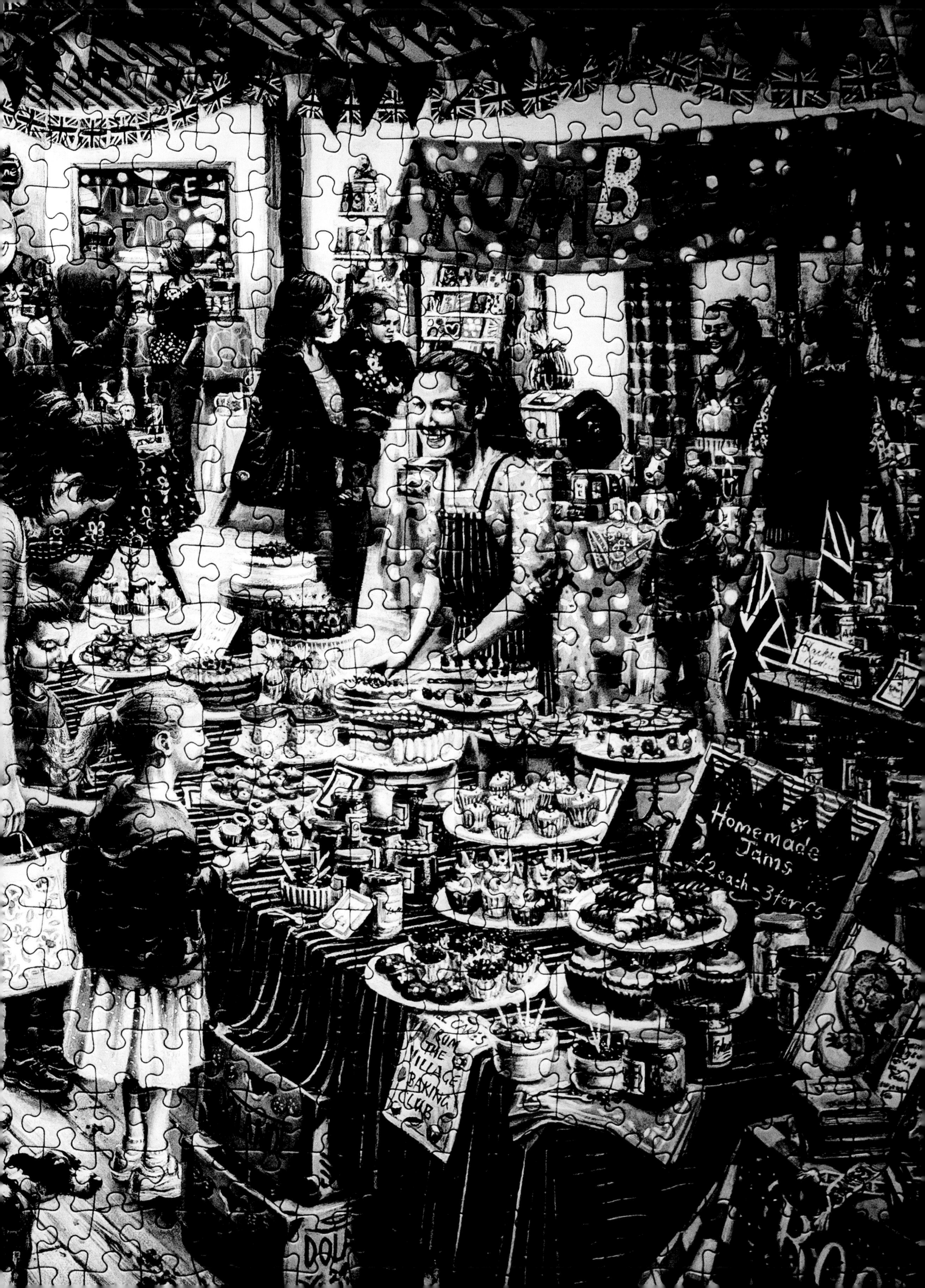

VILLAGE FAIR
Homemade
Jams
£2 each - 3 for £5
FROM THE
VILLAGE
BAKING
CLUB

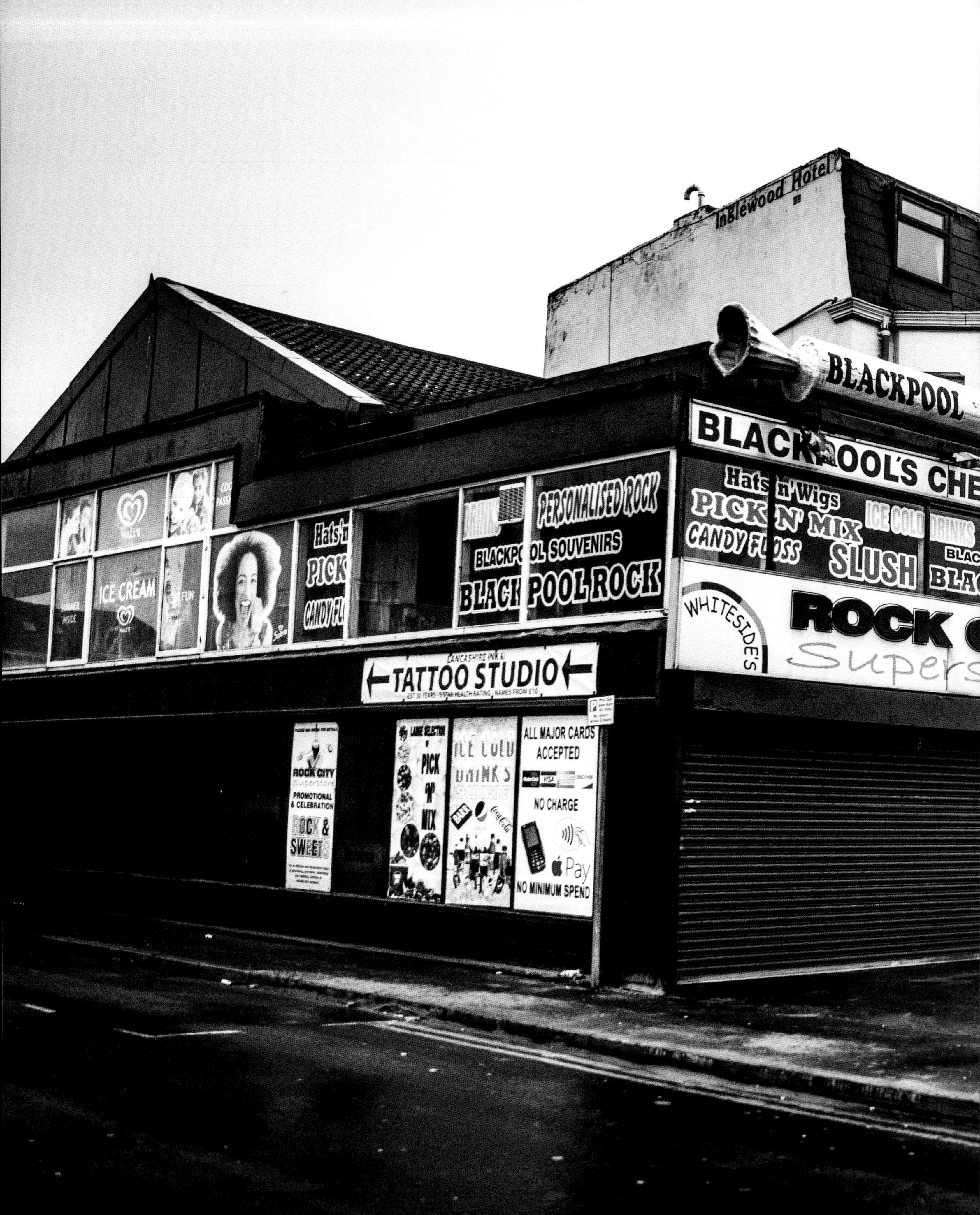
Inglewood Hotel
BLACKPOOL
BLACKPOOL'S CHE
Hats 'n' Wigs
PICK N' MIX
ICE COLD
CANDY FLOSS
SLUSH
DRINKS
BLAC
WHITESIDE'S
ROCK C
Supers
WALL'S
ICE CREAM
SUMMER INSIDE
FUN
Hats 'n
PICK
CANDY FL
DRINKS
PERSONALISED ROCK
BLACKPOOL SOUVENIRS
BLACK POOL ROCK
LANCASHIRE INK
←TATTOO STUDIO←
EST 30 YEARS · 5 STAR HEALTH RATING · NAMES FROM £10
ROCK CITY
Superstore
PROMOTIONAL
& CELEBRATION
ROCK & SWEETS
LARGE SELECTION
PICK 'N' MIX
ICE COLD DRINKS
SOLD INSIDE
ALL MAJOR CARDS
ACCEPTED
MasterCard
VISA
DISCOVER
NO CHARGE
Pay
NO MINIMUM SPEND

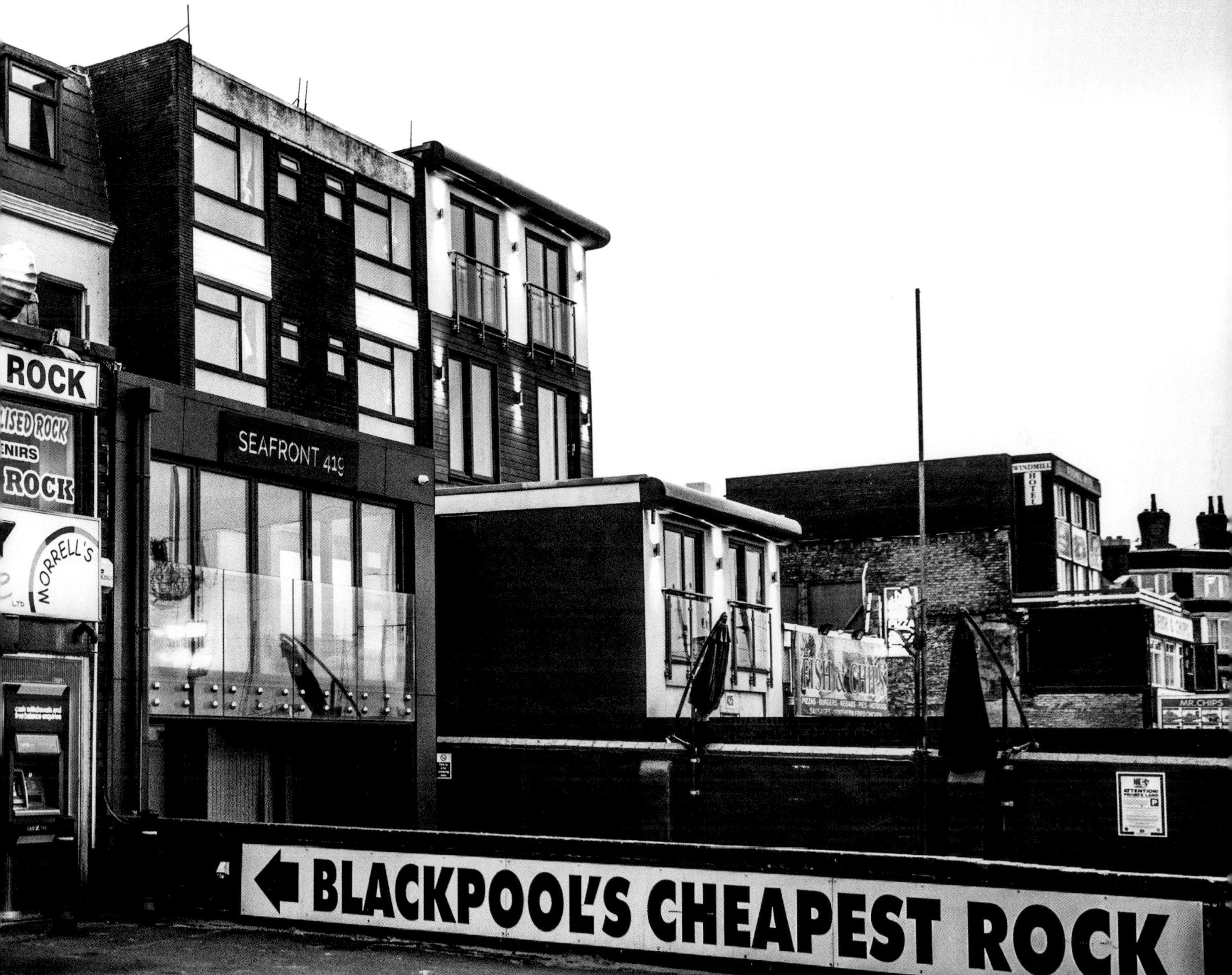

ROCK
ISED ROCK
ENIRS
ROCK
MORRELL'S
LTD
SEAFRONT 419
WINDMILL HOTEL
FISH & CHIPS
PIZZAS · BURGERS · KEBABS · PIES · HOTDOGS
SAUSAGES · SOUTHERN FRIED CHICKEN
MR. CHIPS
← BLACKPOOL'S CHEAPEST ROCK

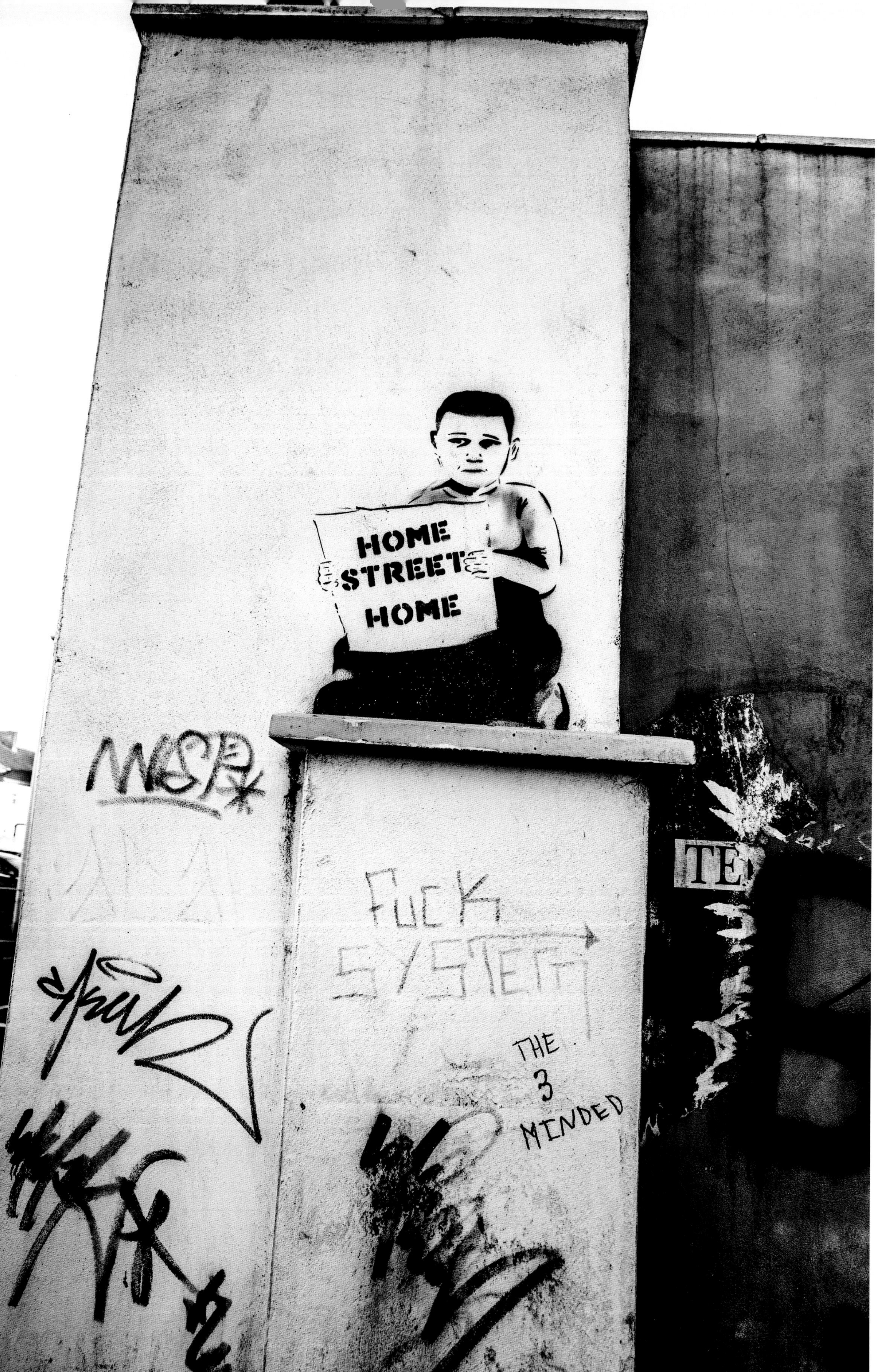

HOME
STREET
HOME
FUCK
SYSTEM
THE
3
MINDED
TE

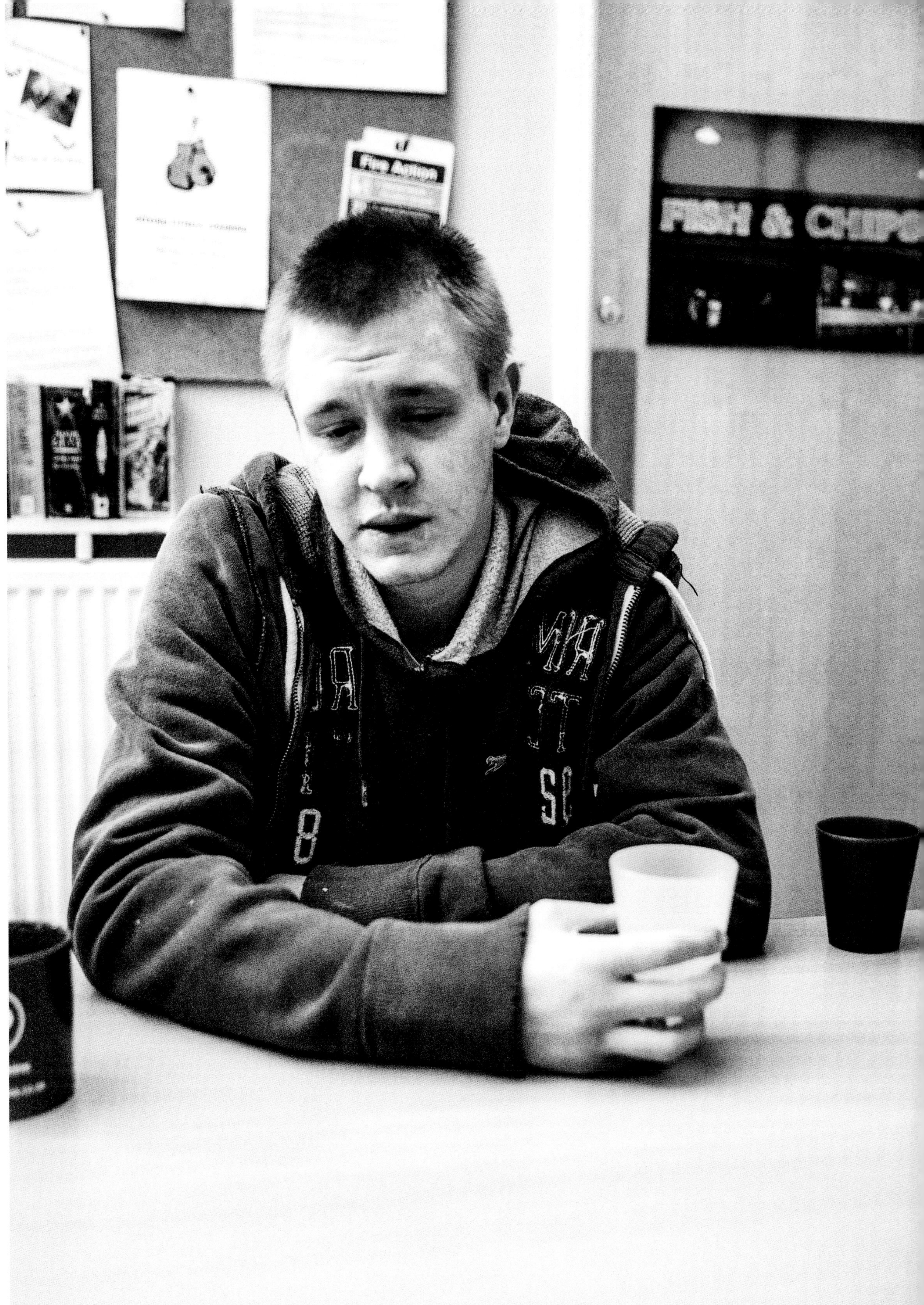

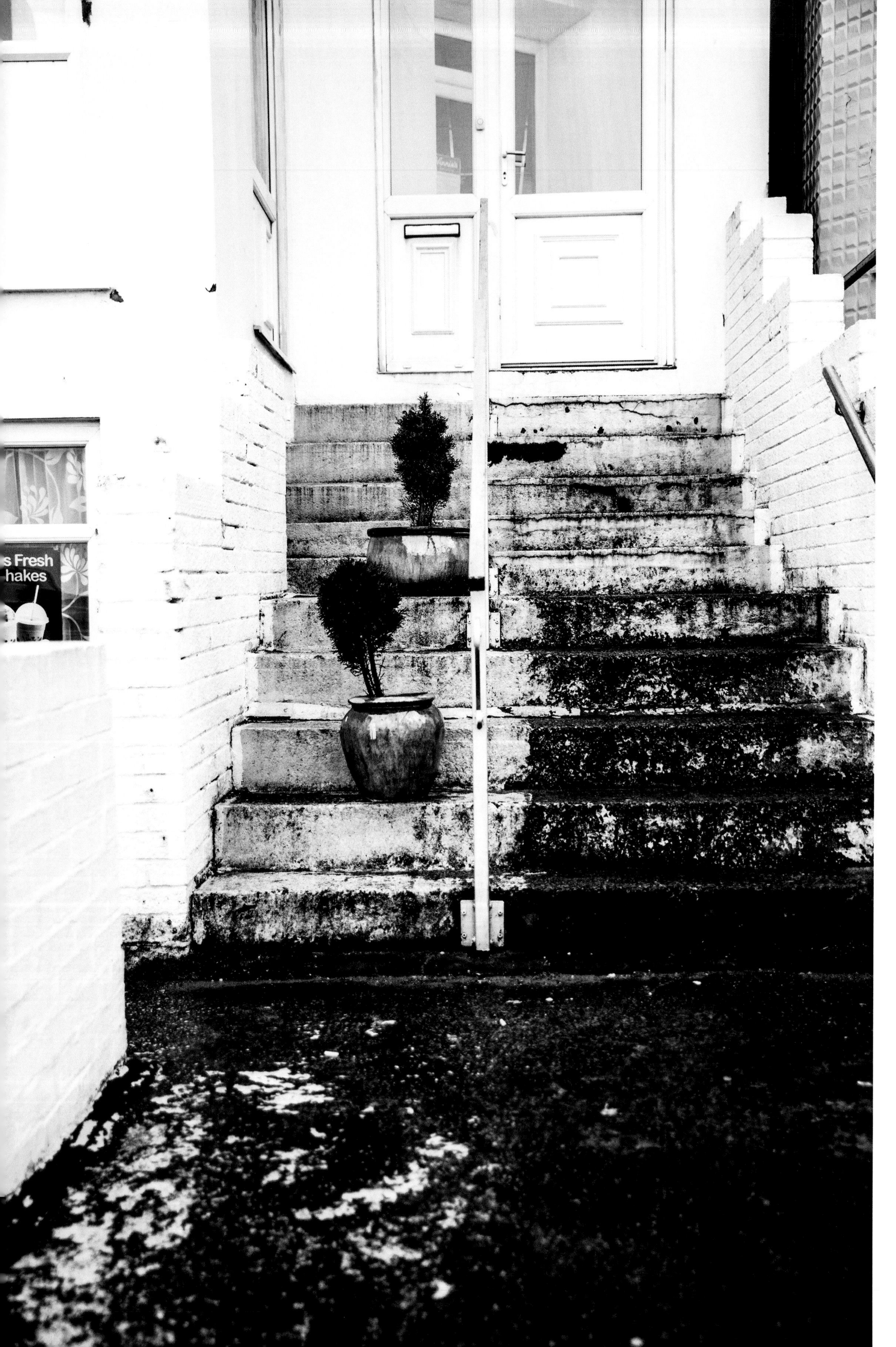
s Fresh
hakes

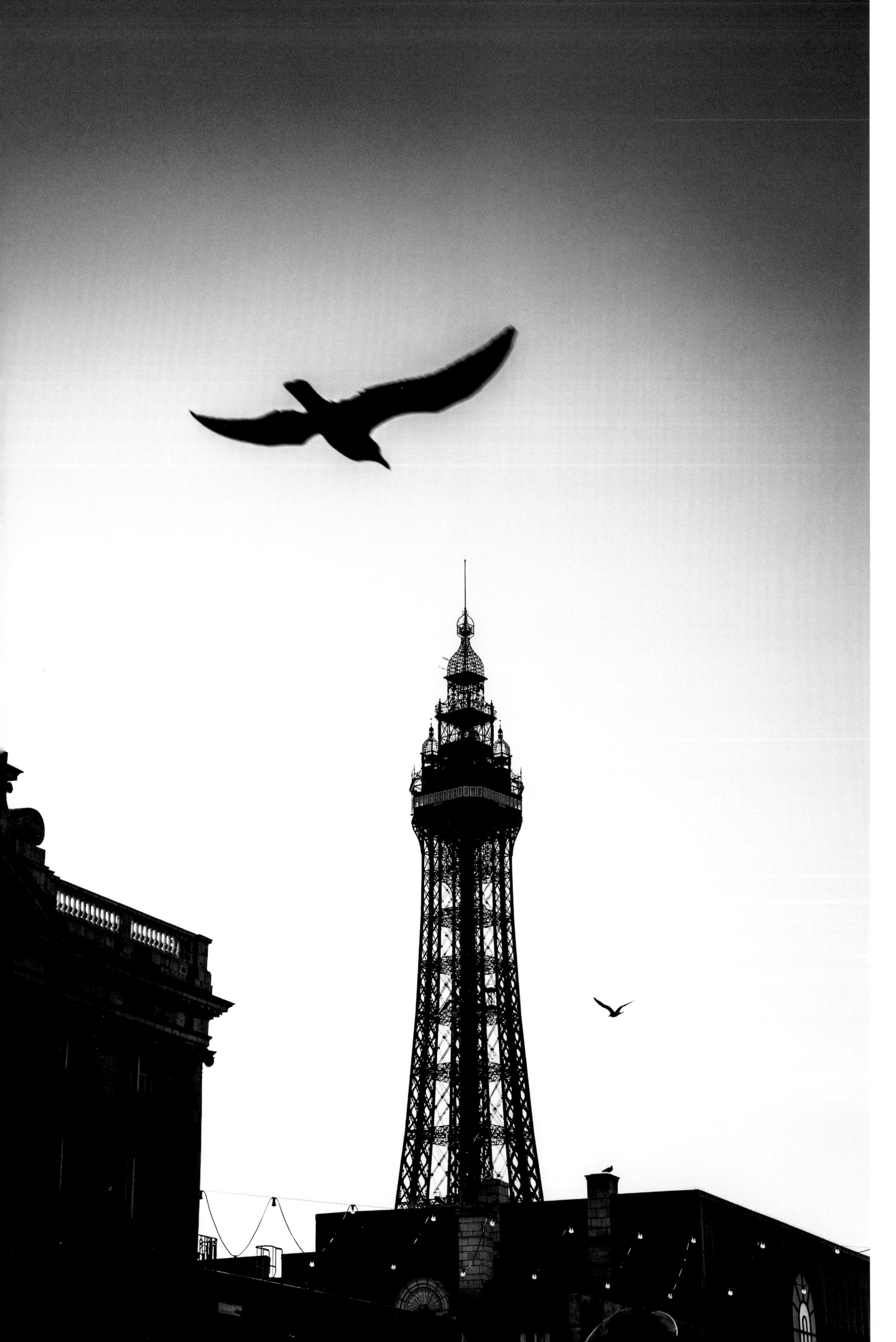

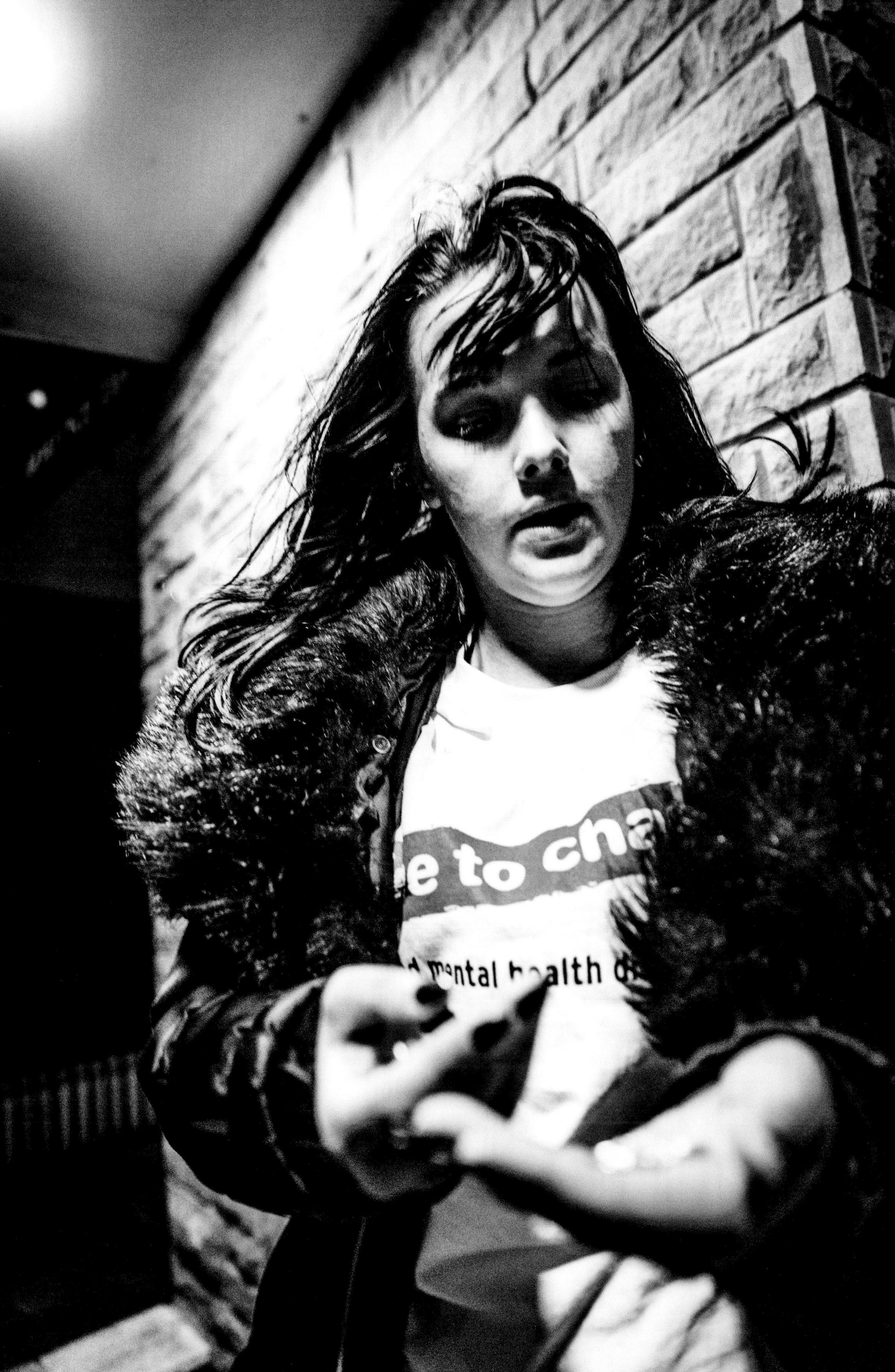

e to cha
mental health d

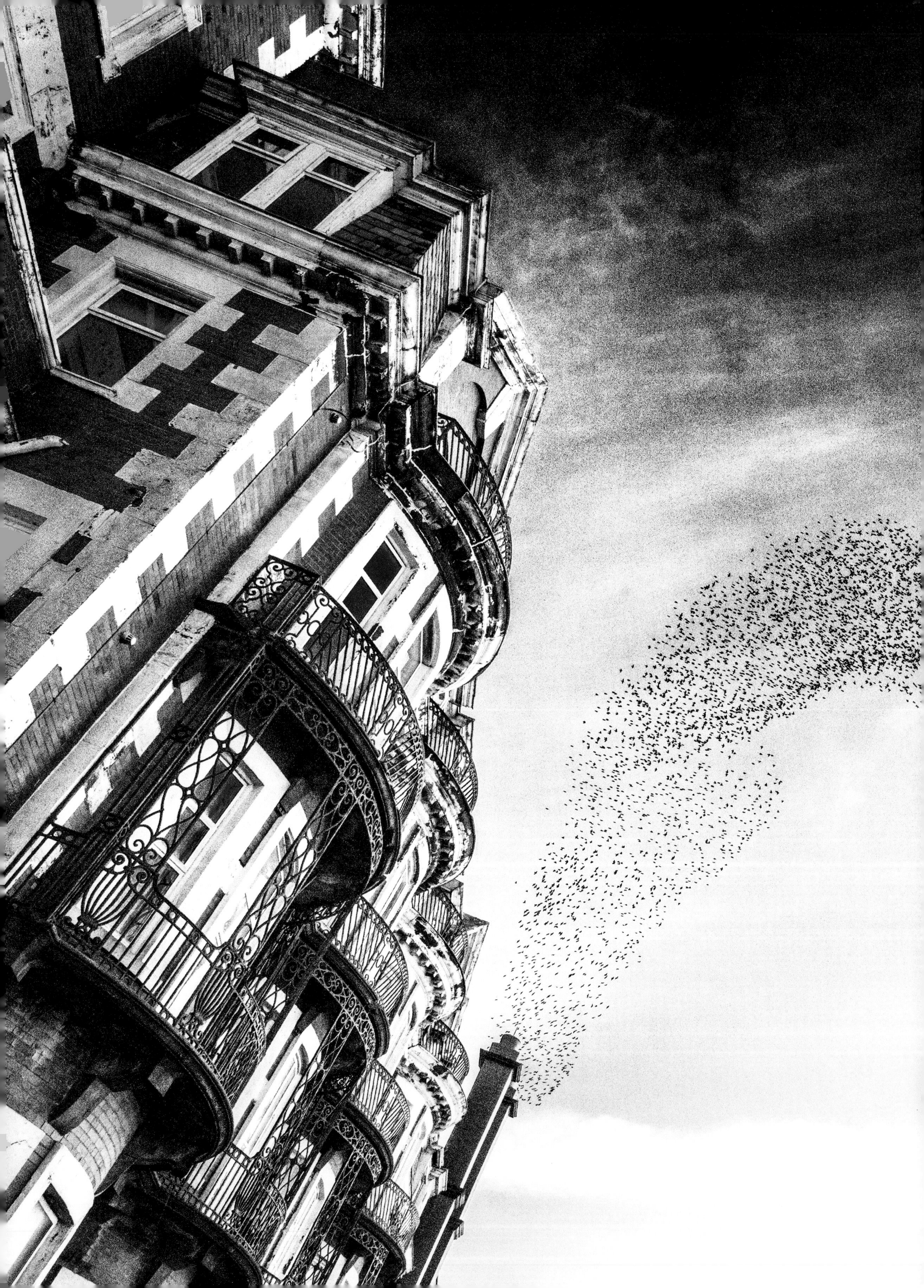

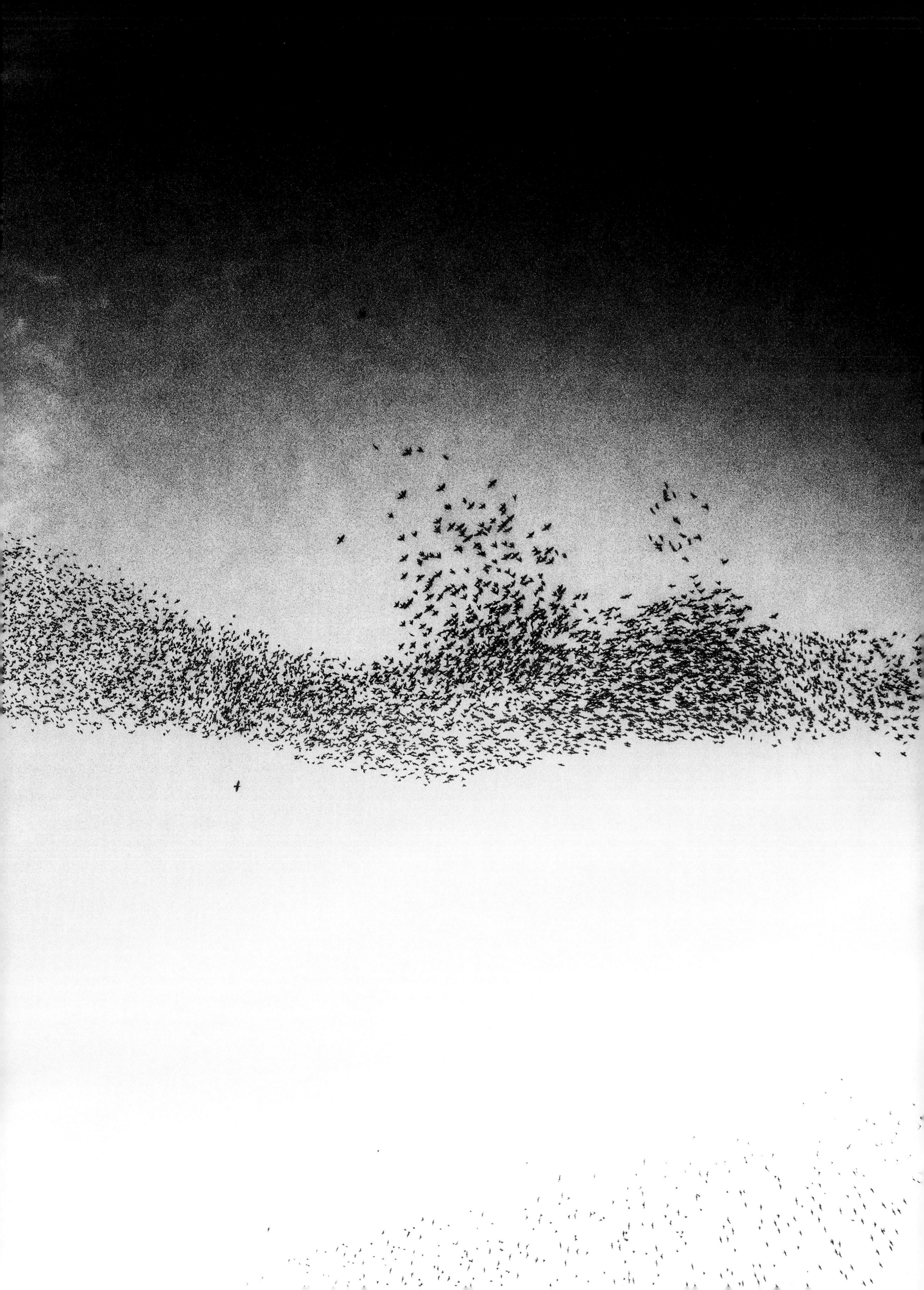

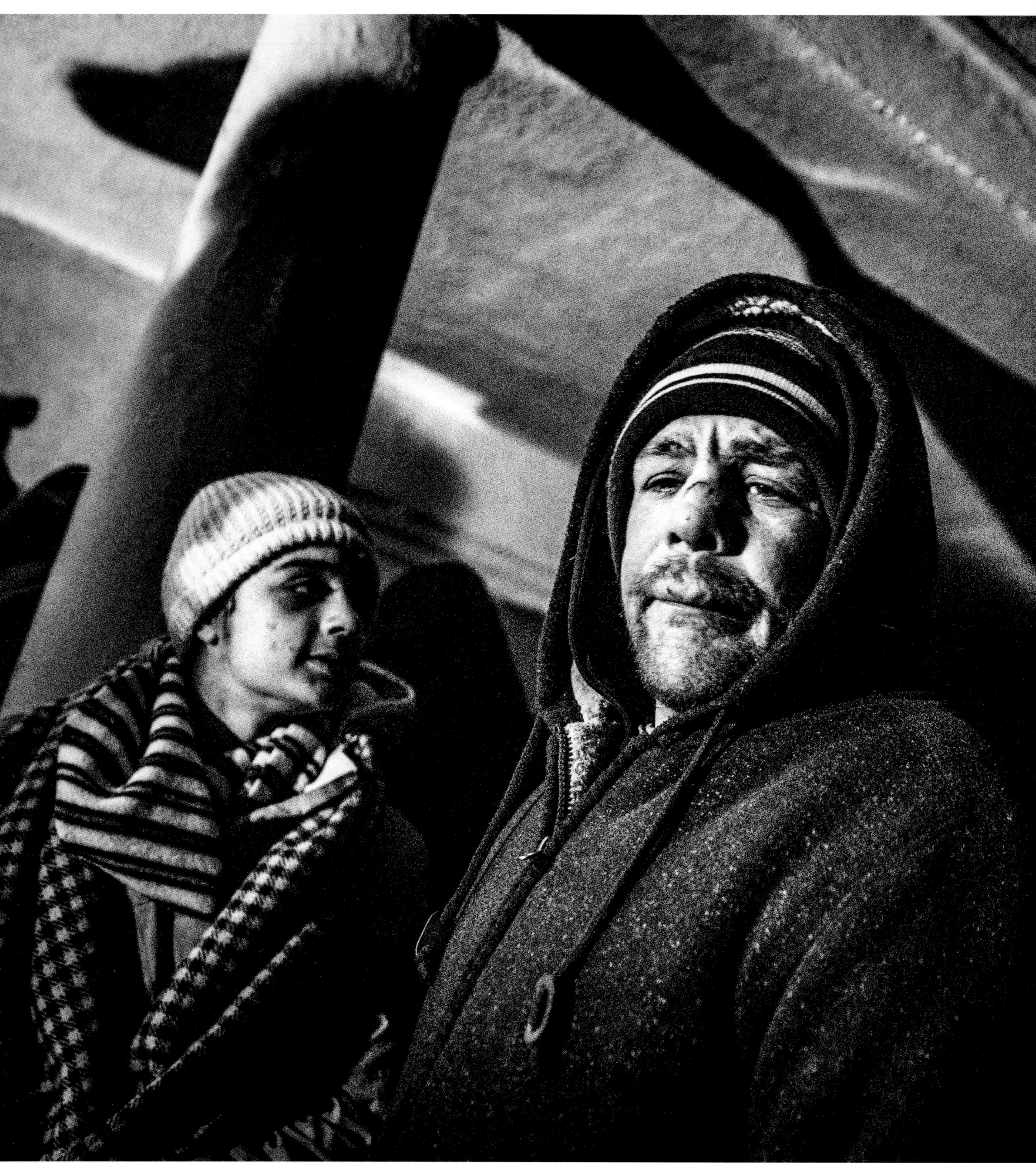

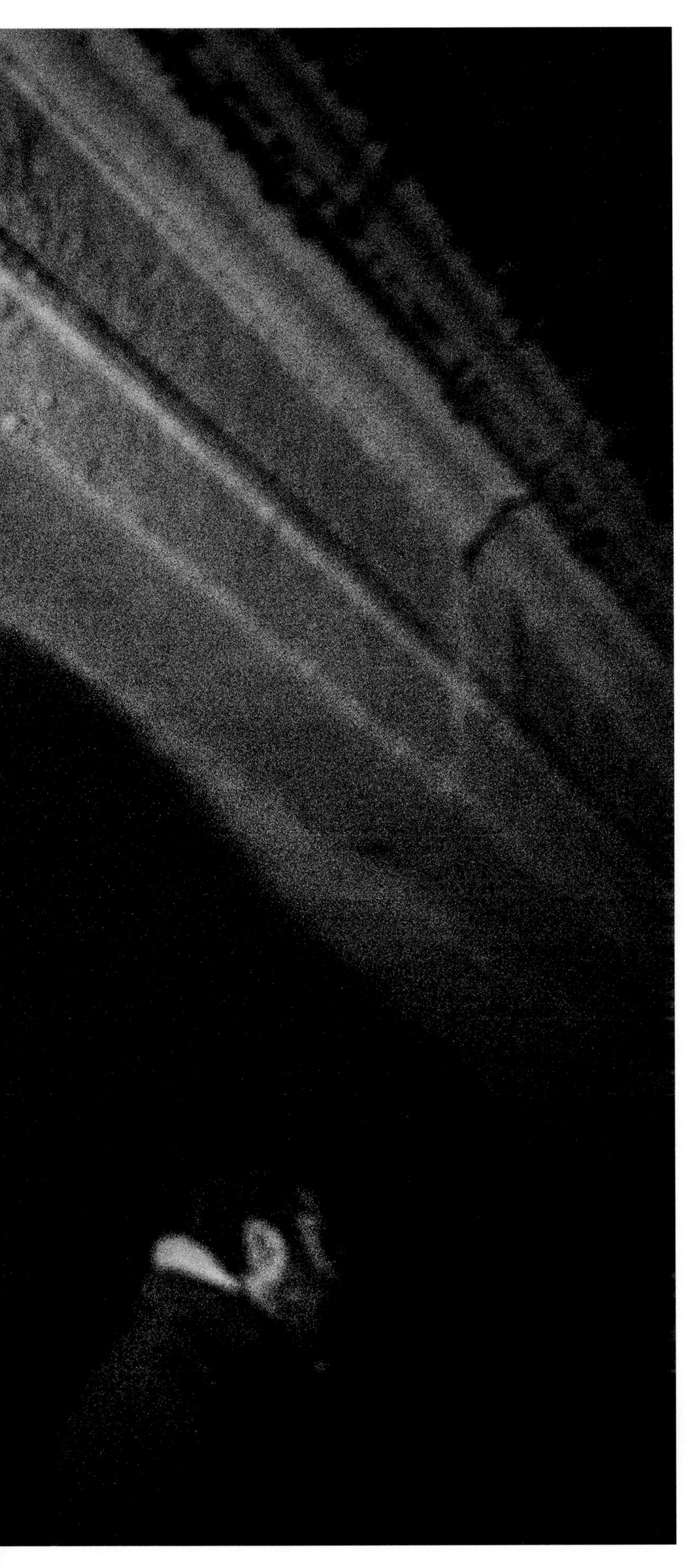

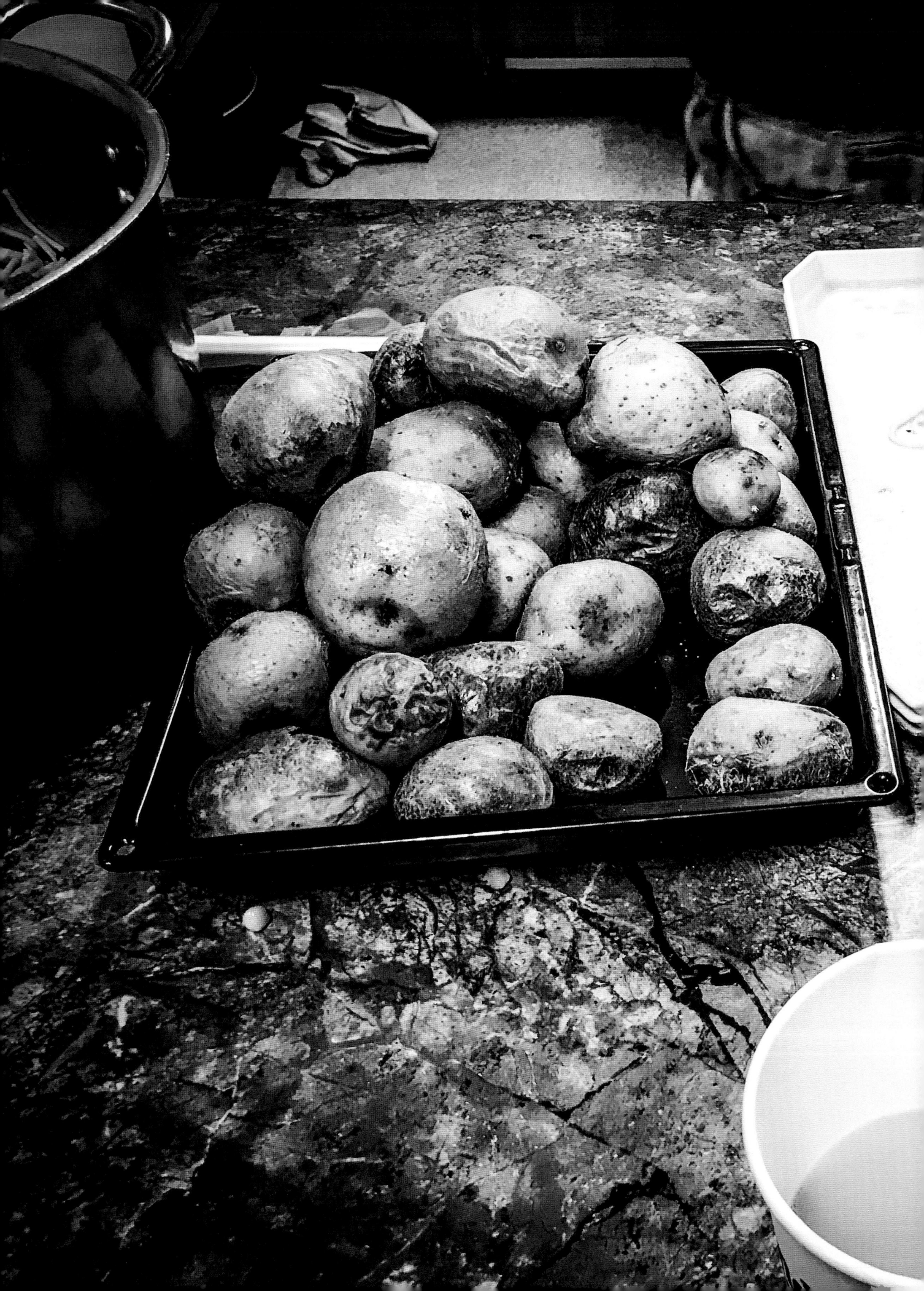

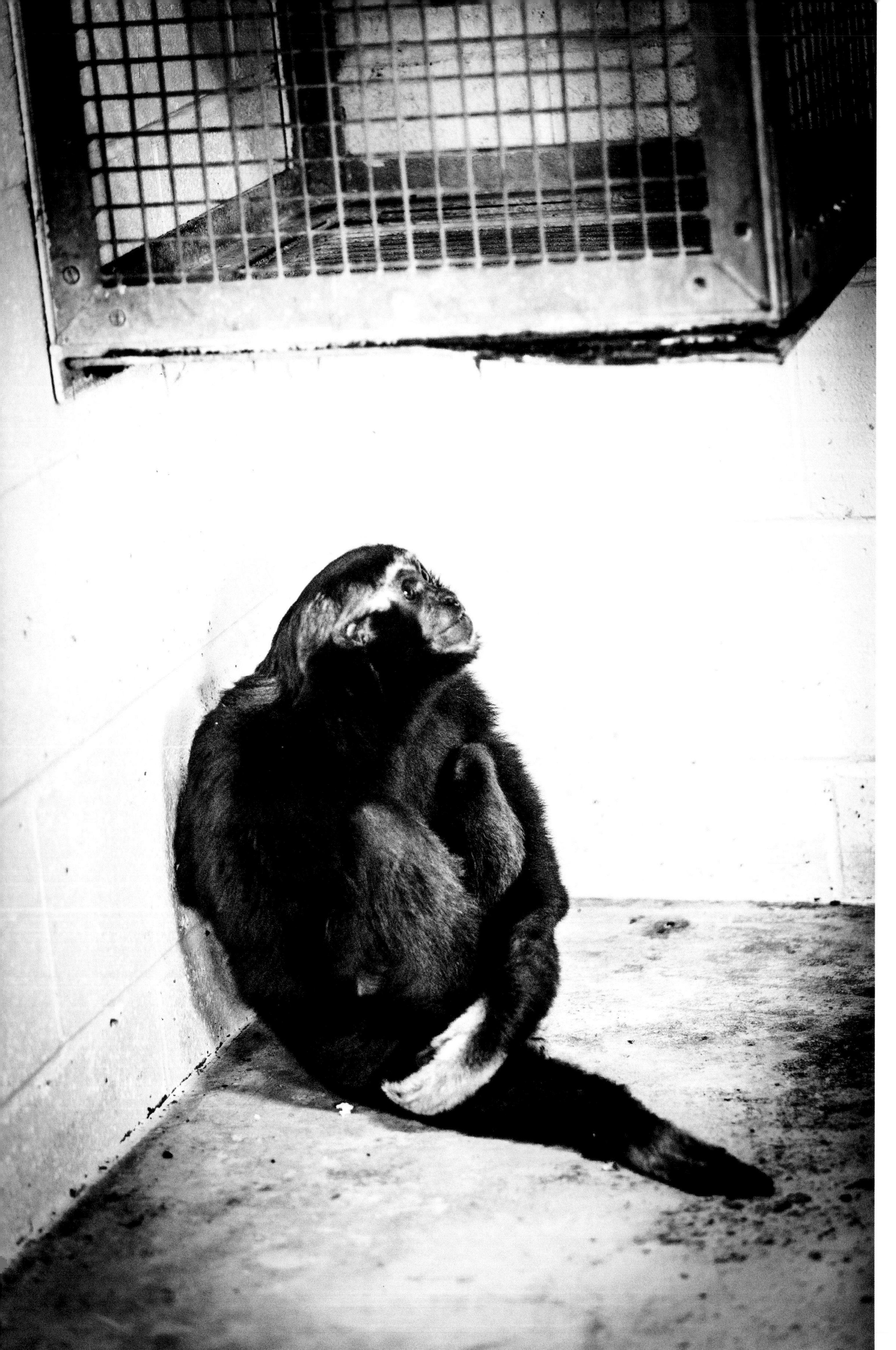

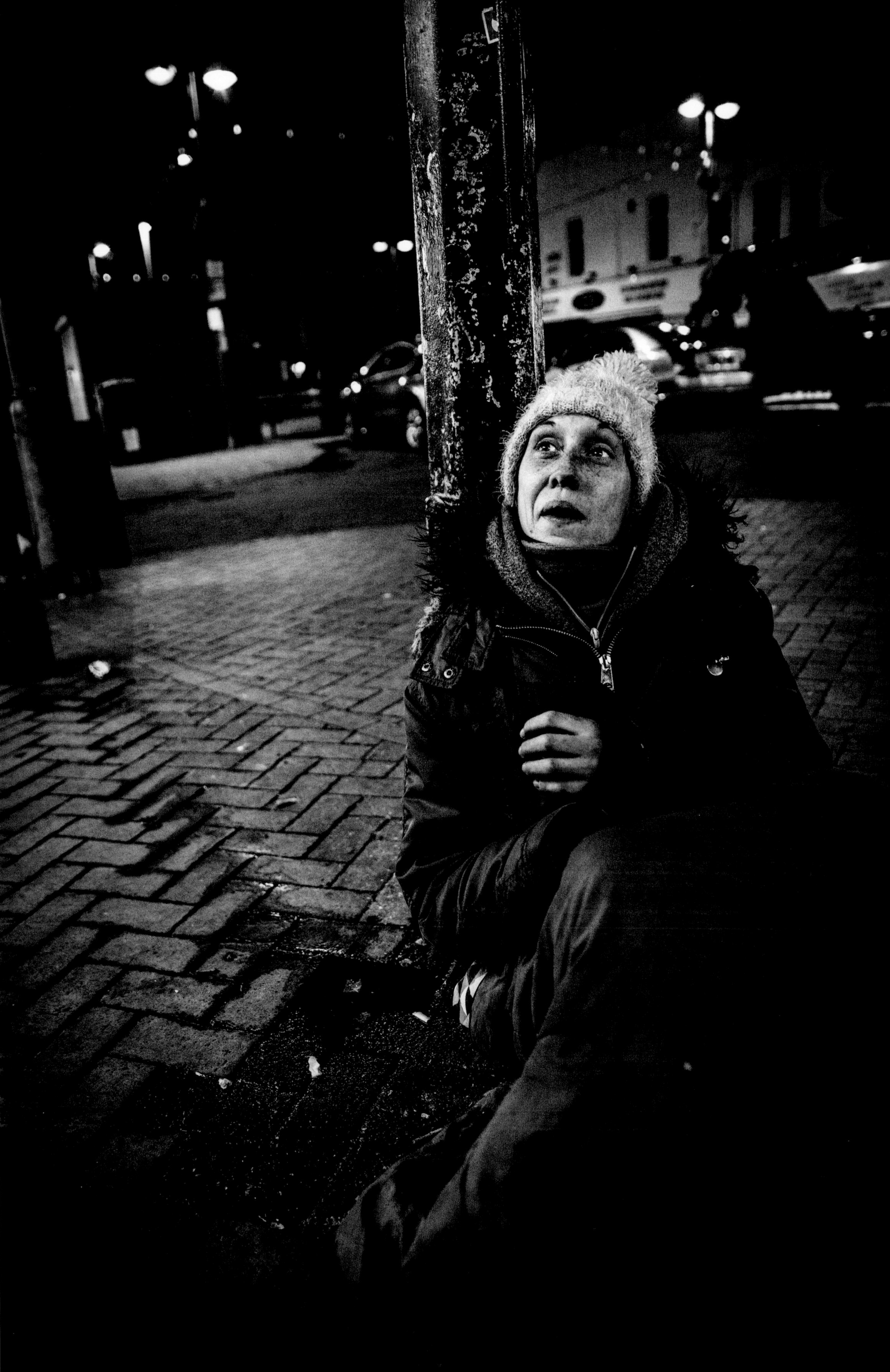

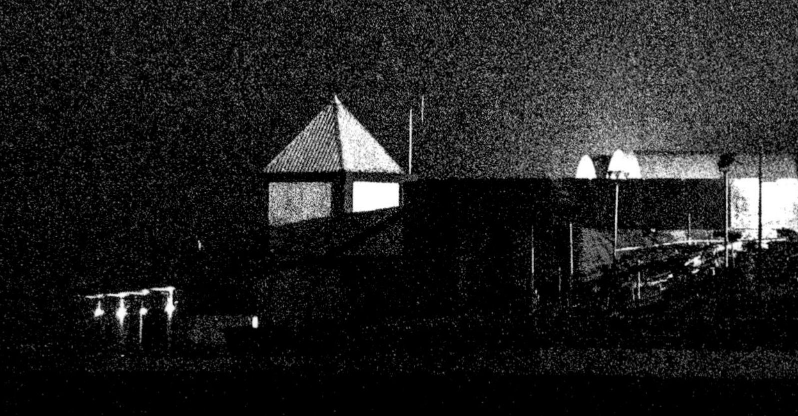

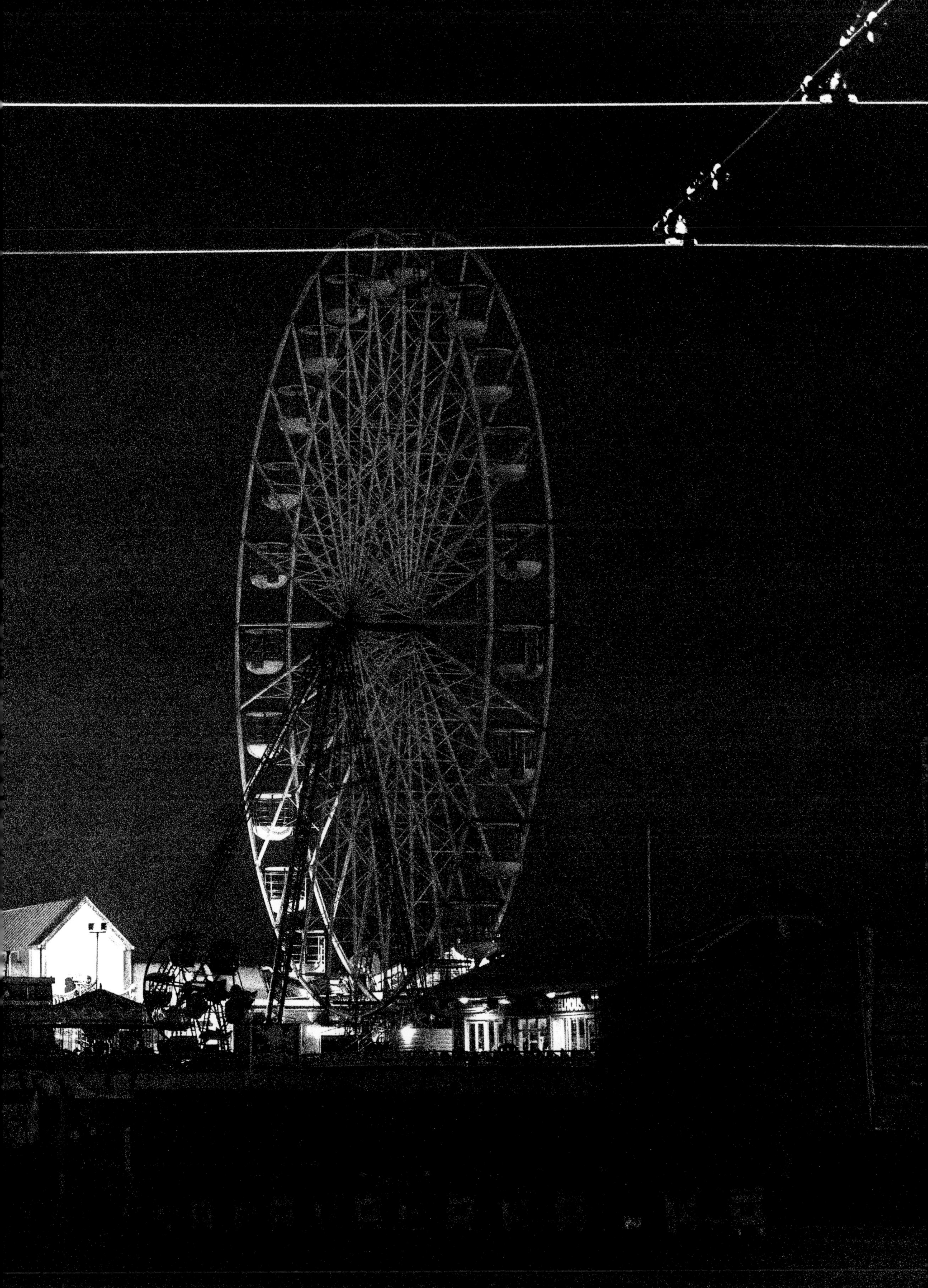
ELHOUSE

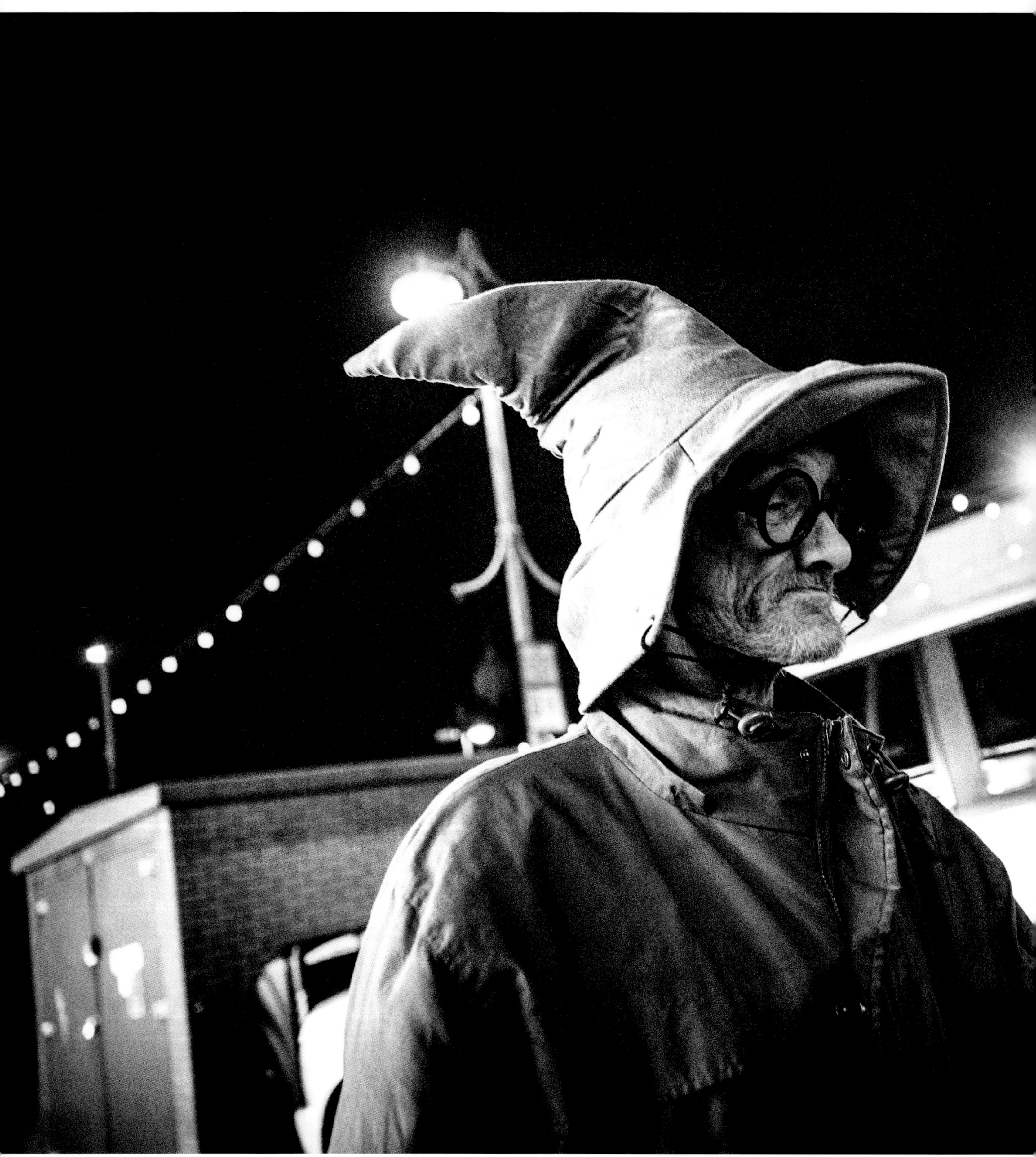

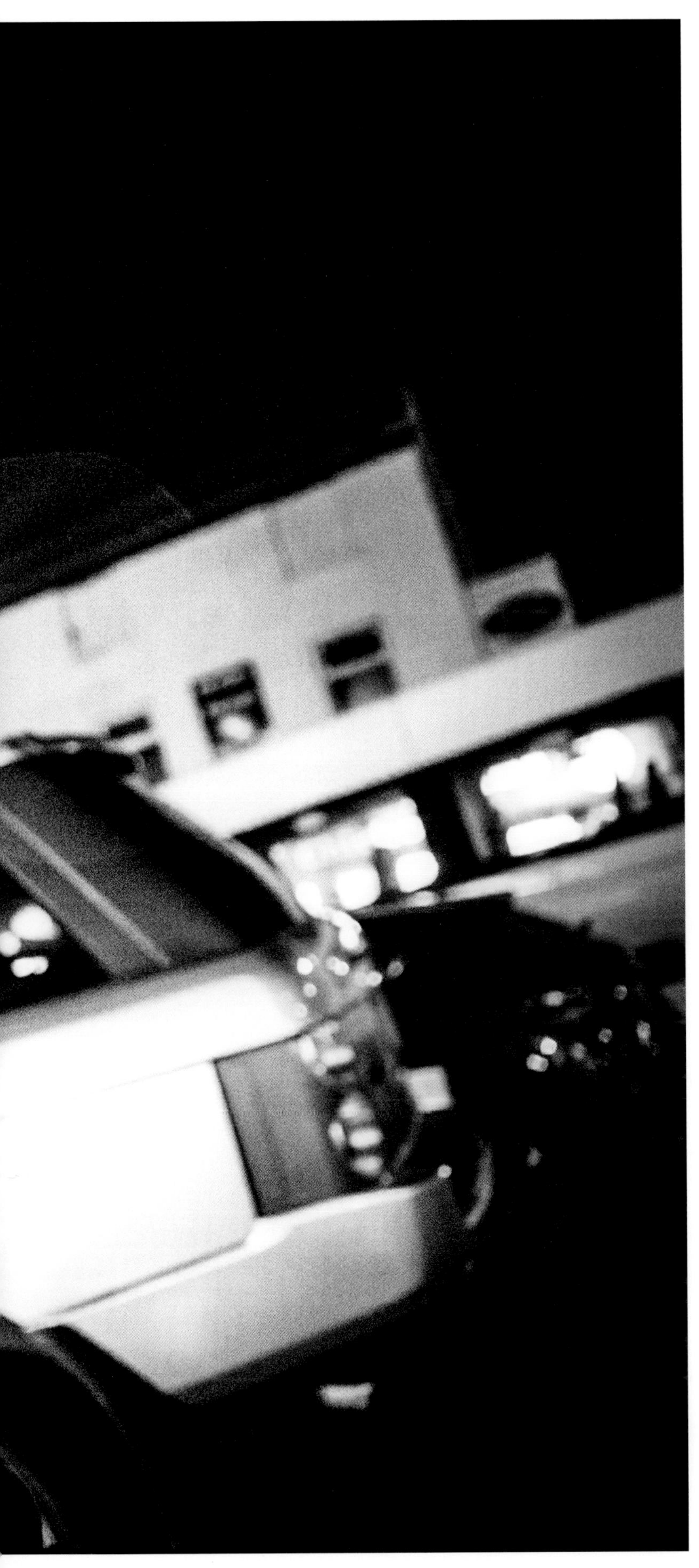

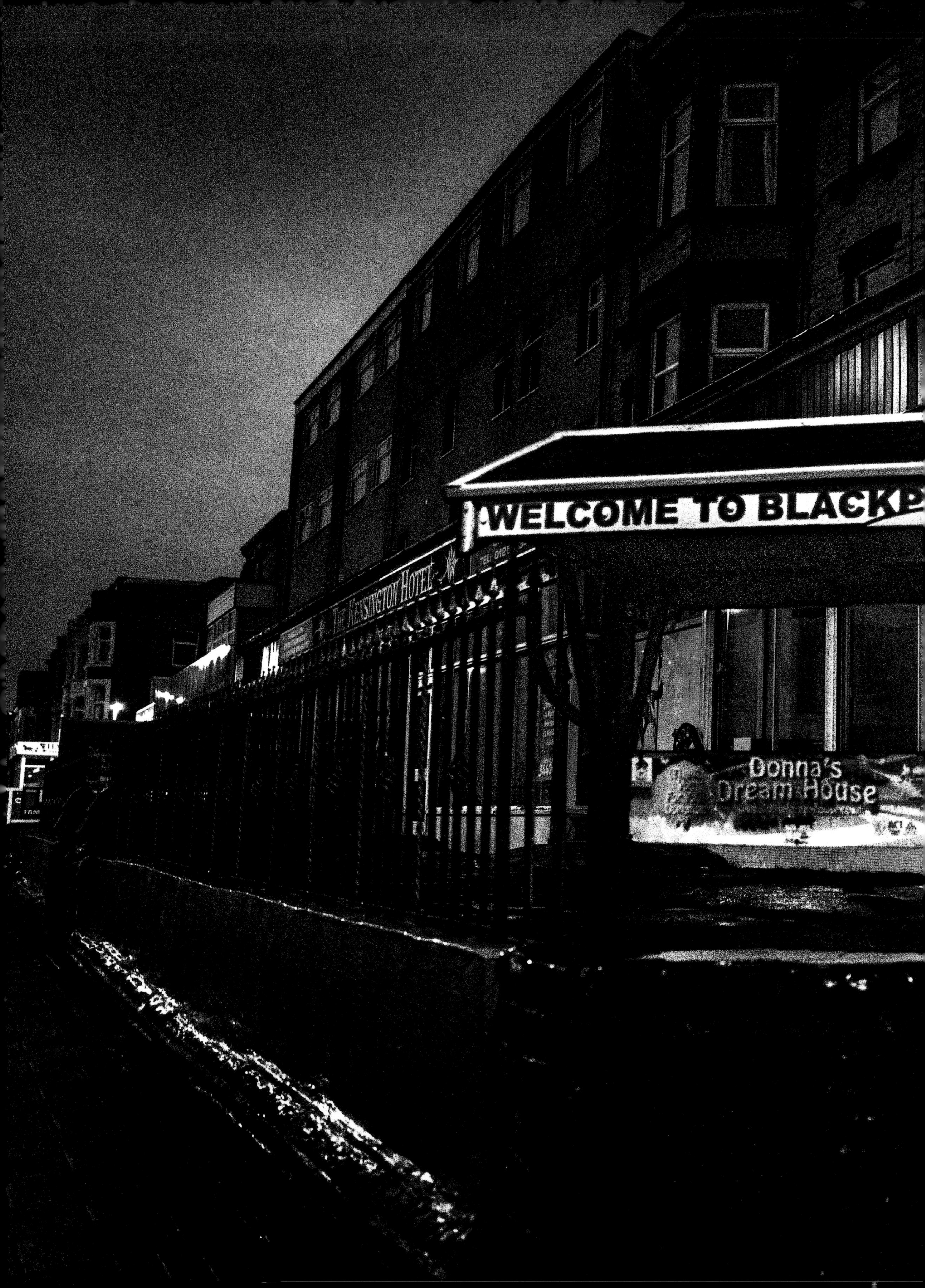

WELCOME TO BLACKP
THE KENSINGTON HOTEL
TEL: 0125
Donna's
Dream House

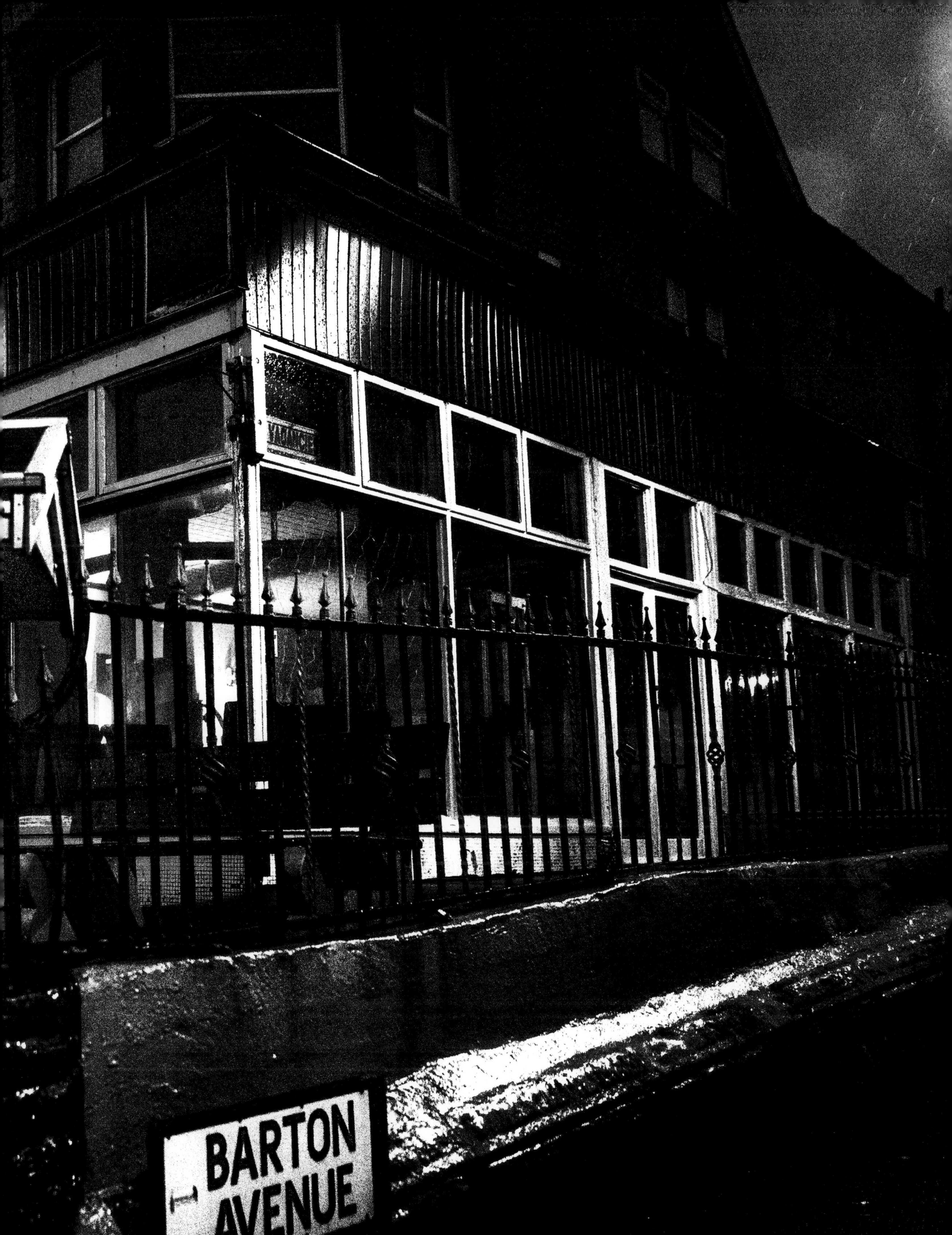

BARTON
AVENUE

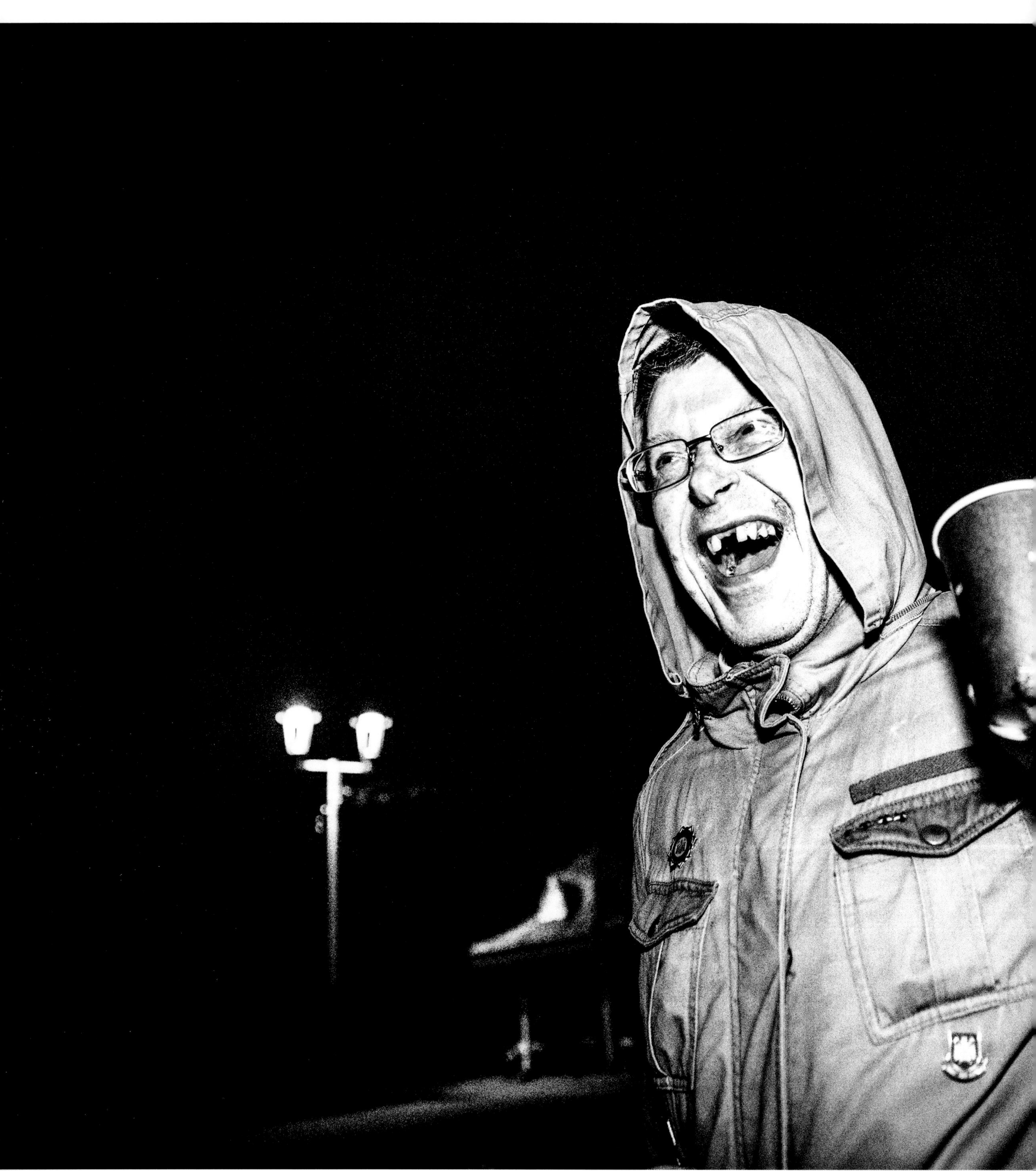

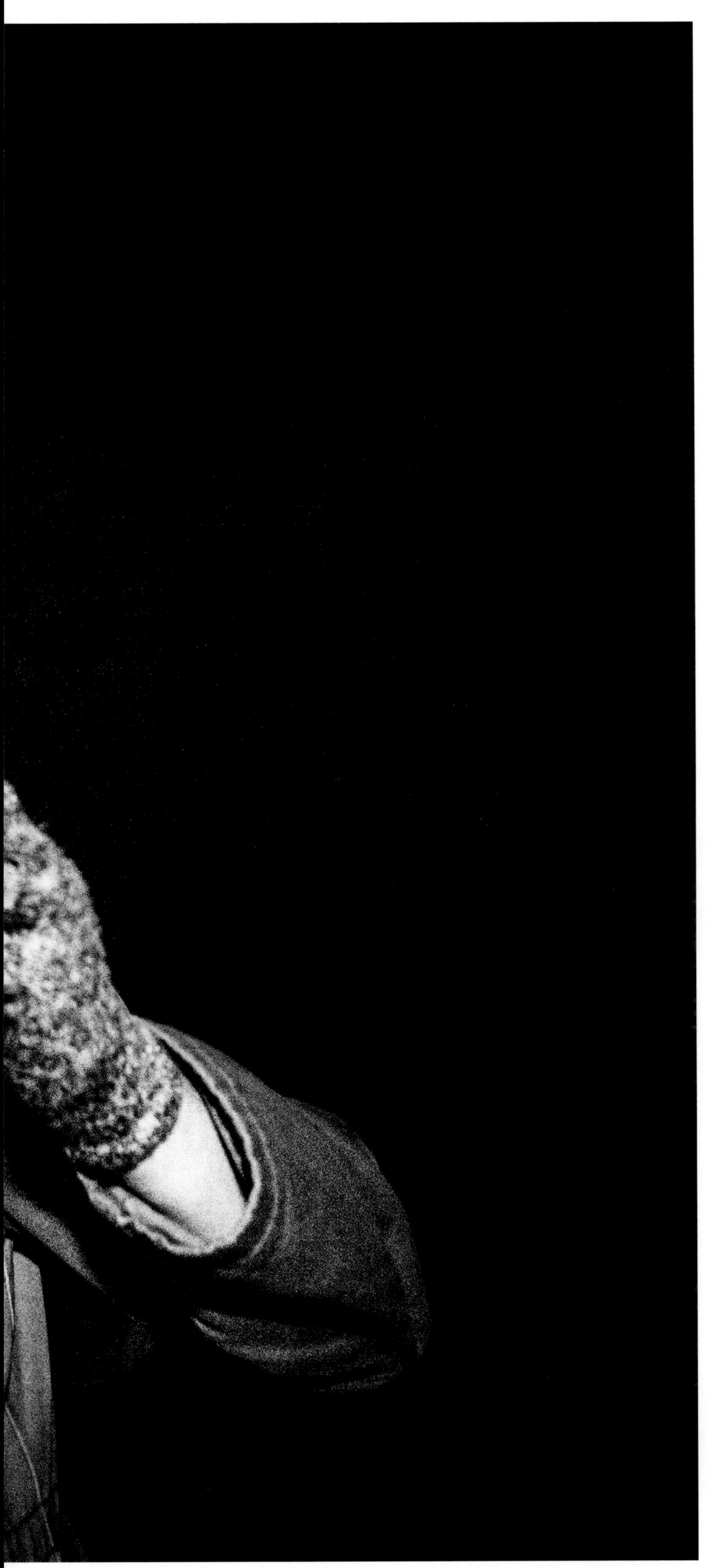

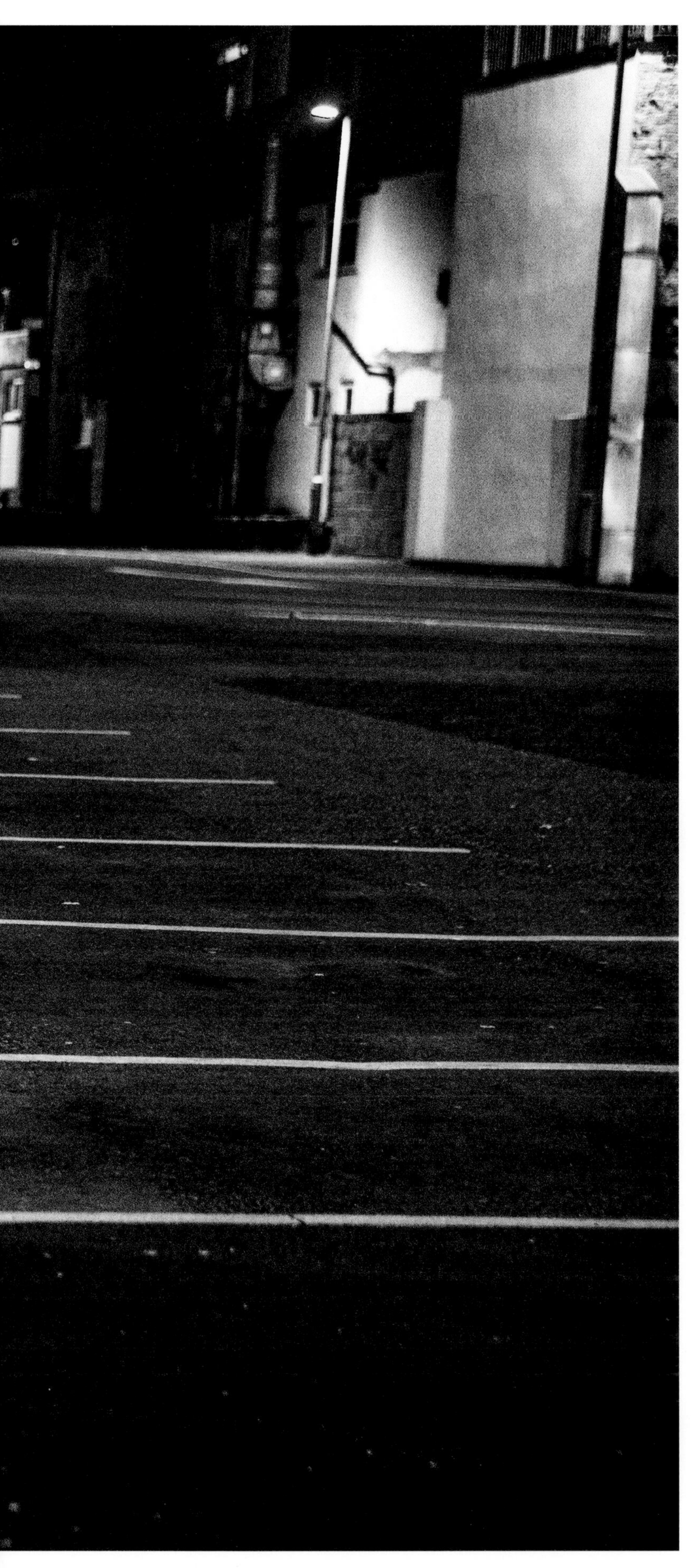

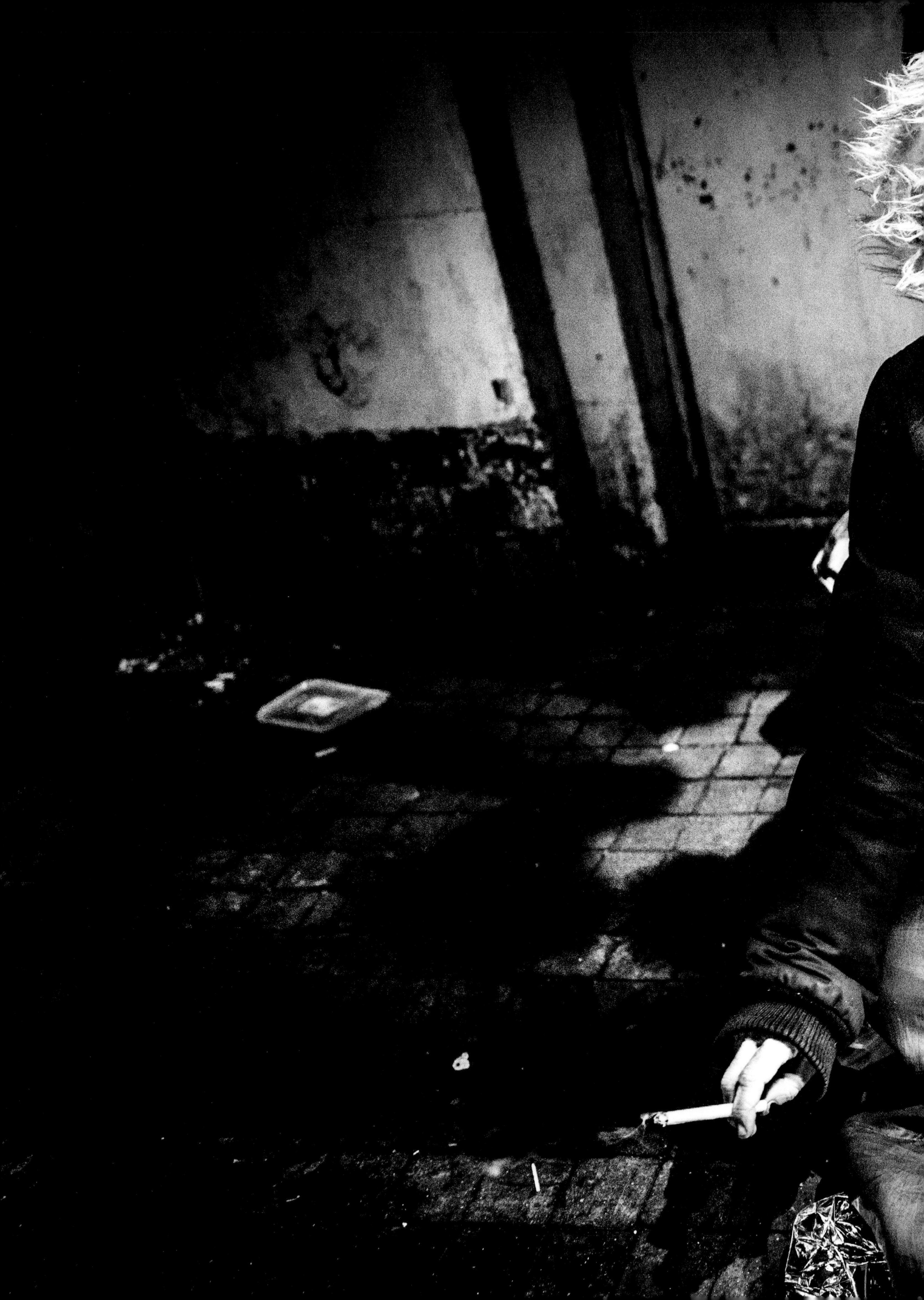

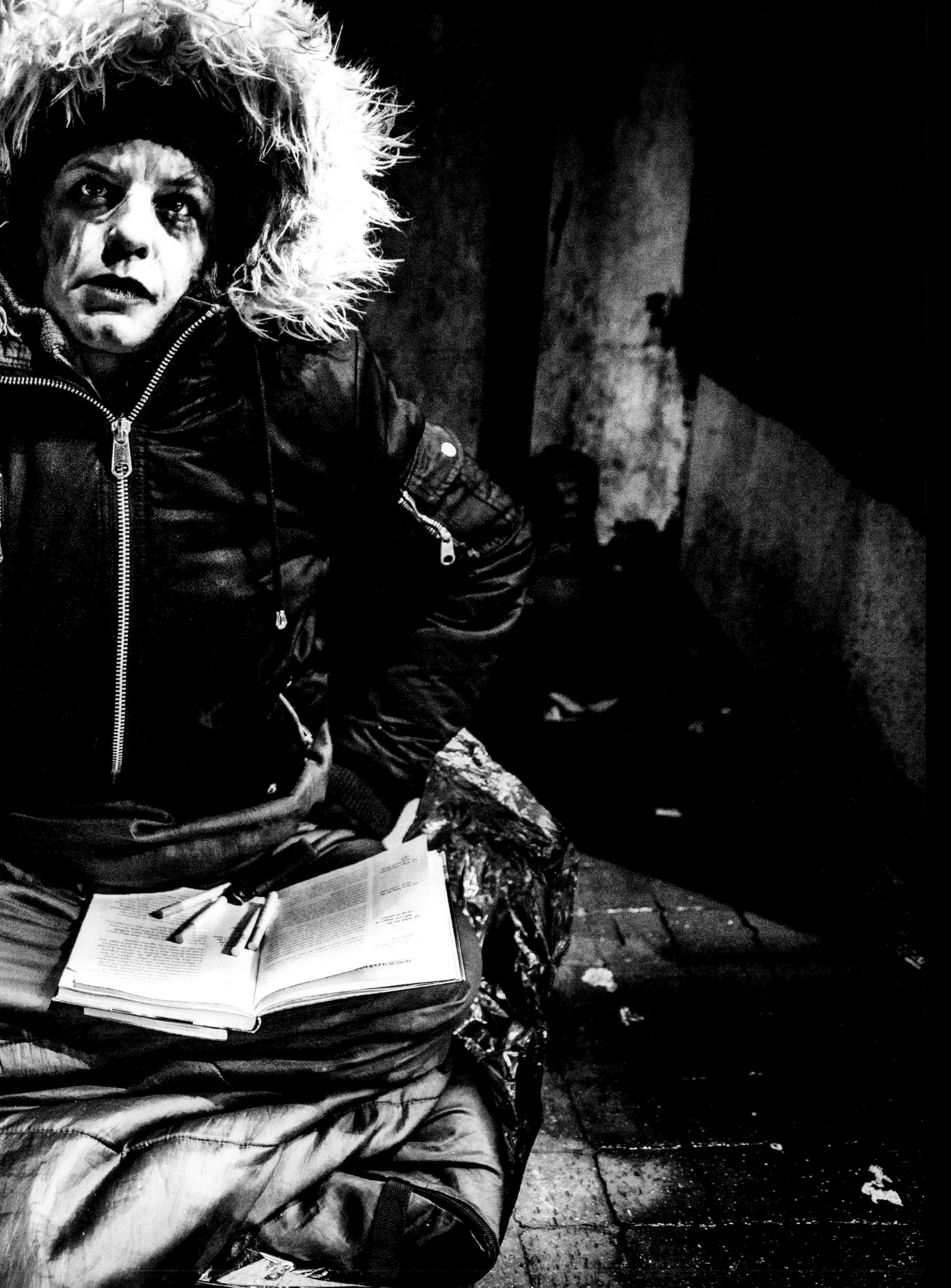

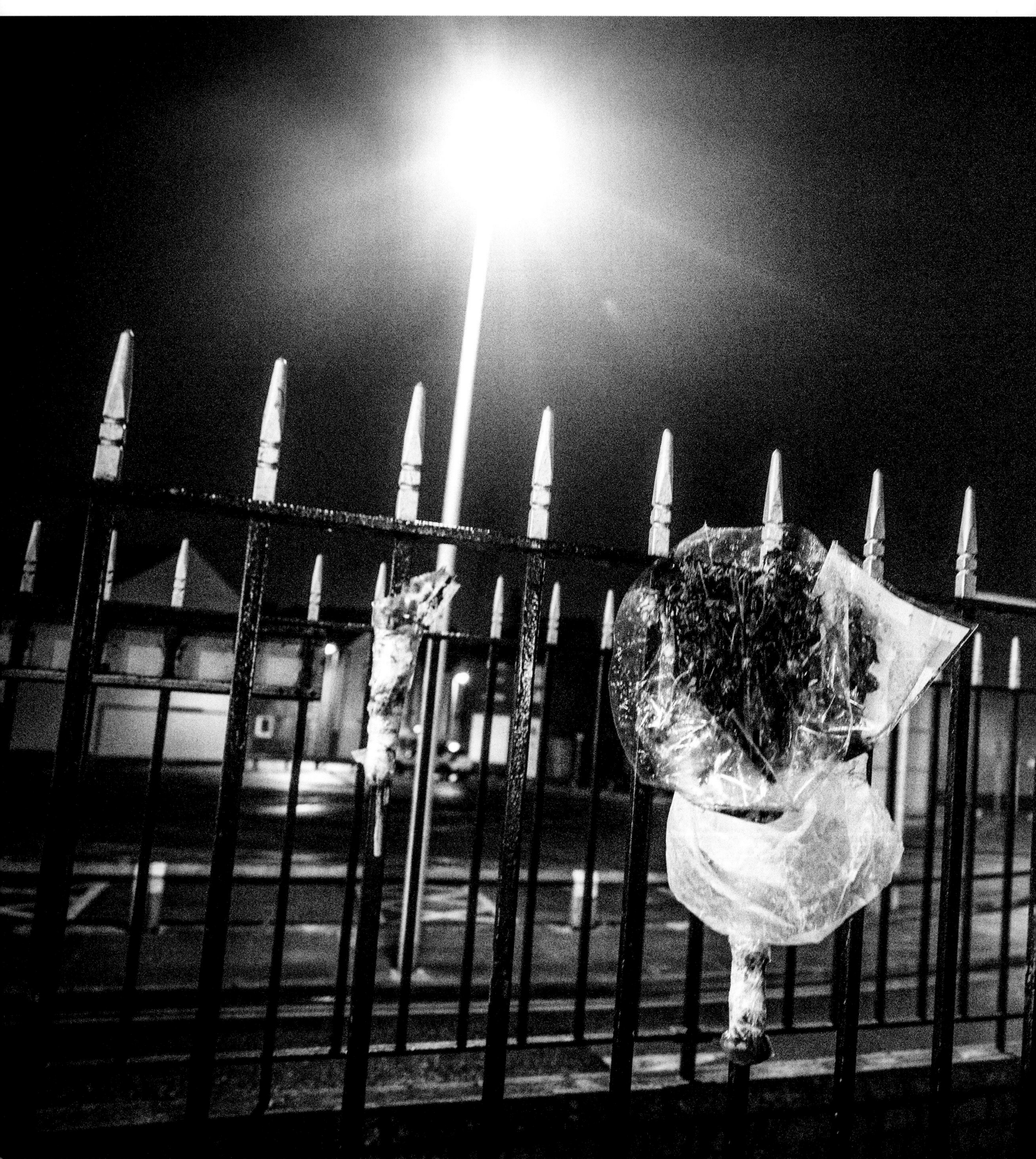

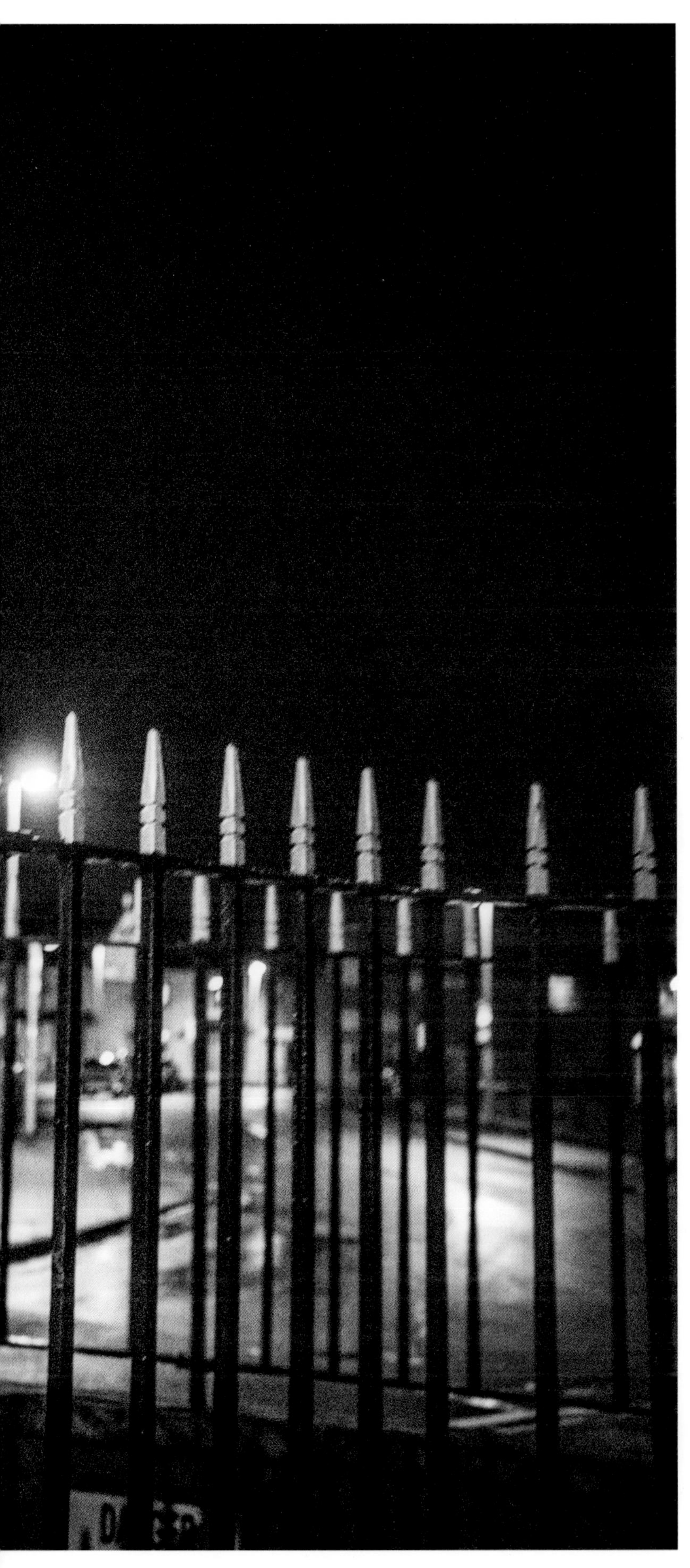

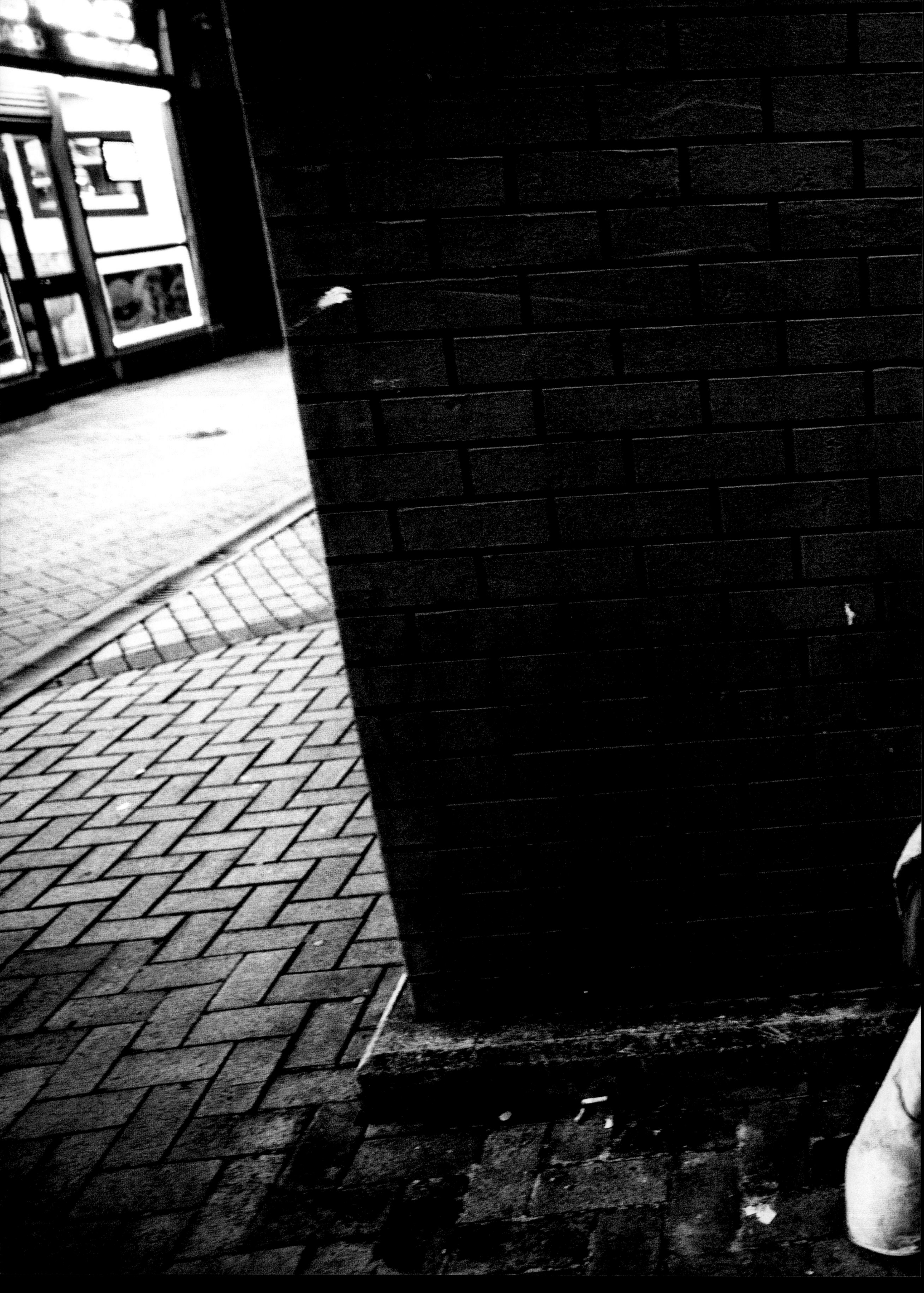

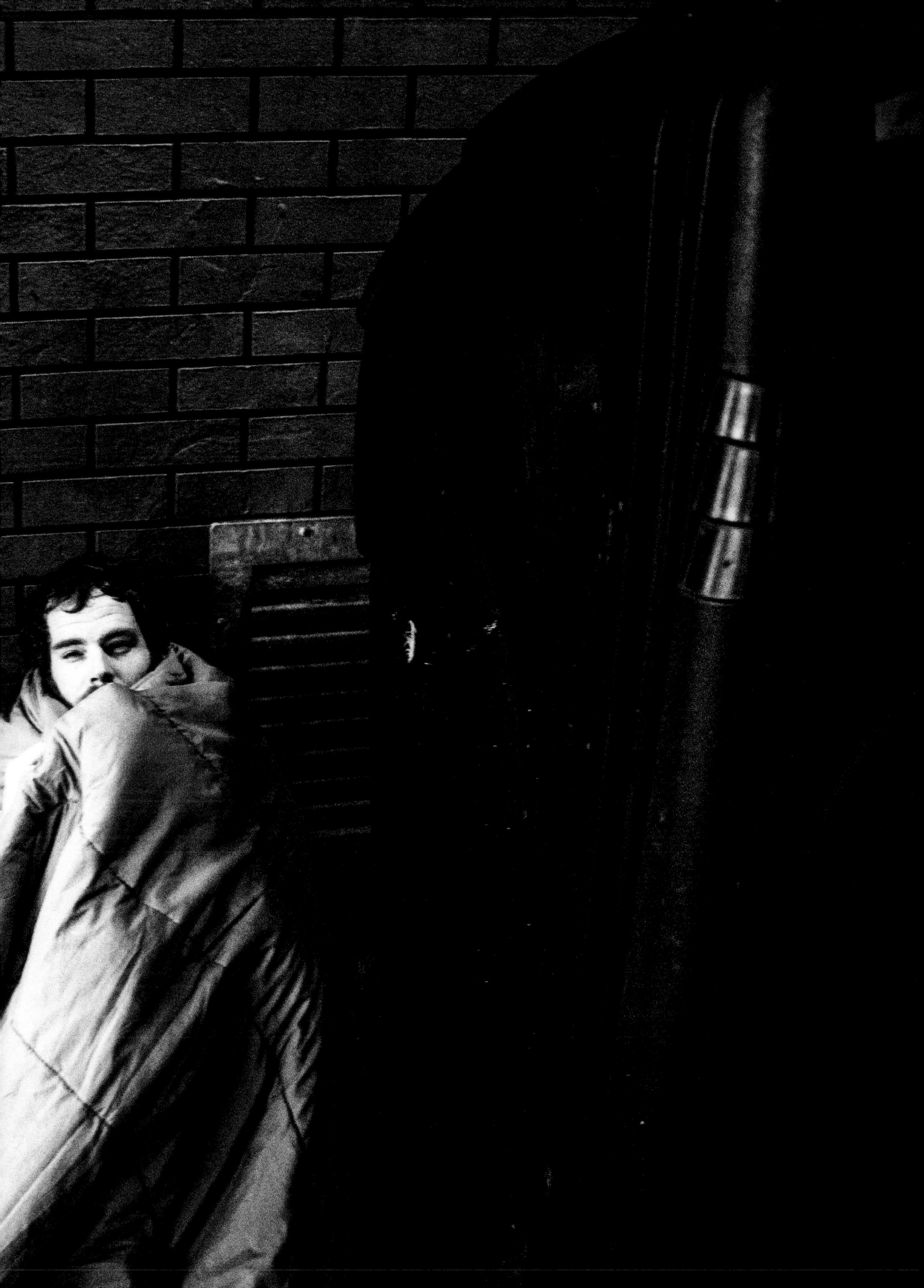

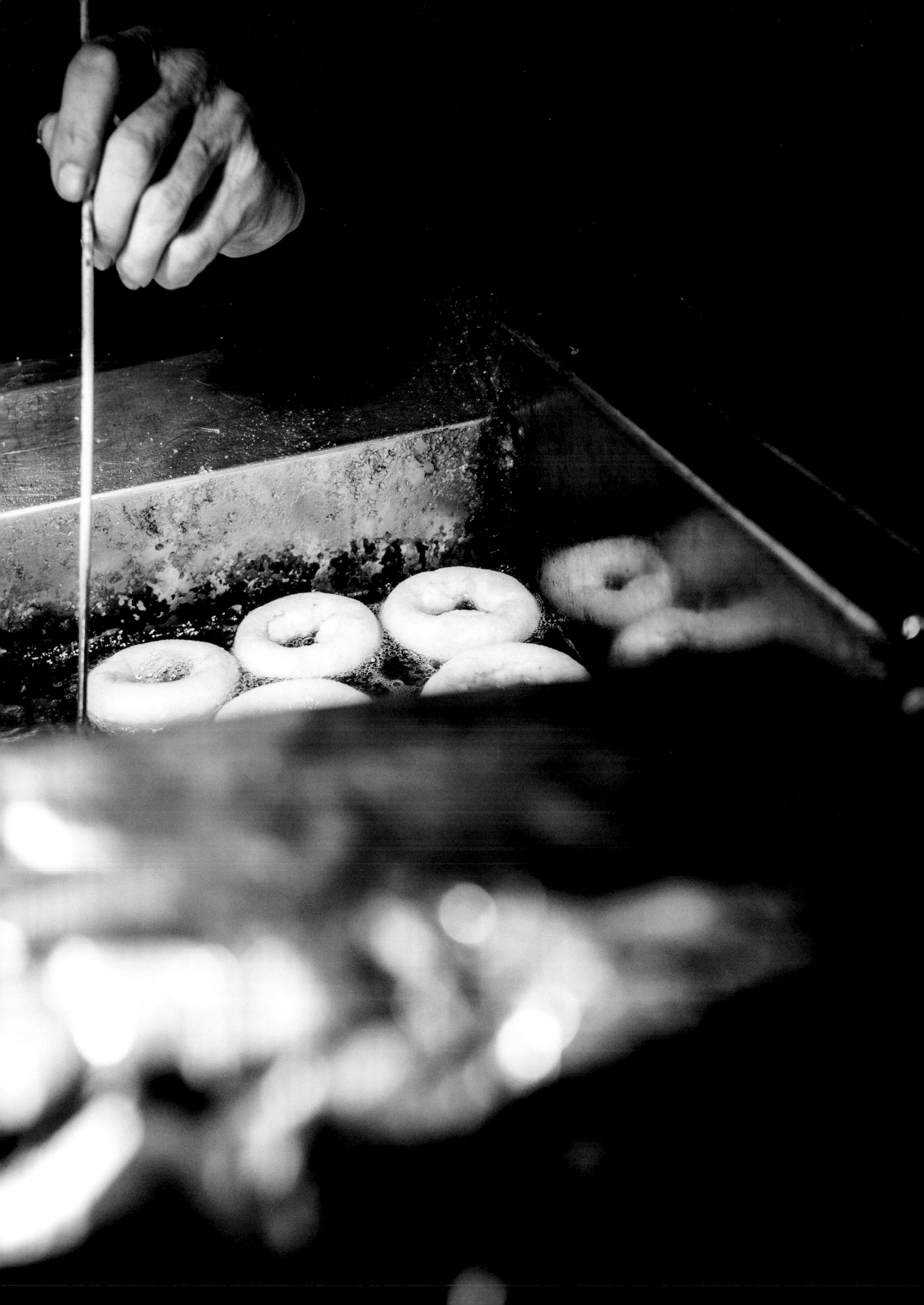

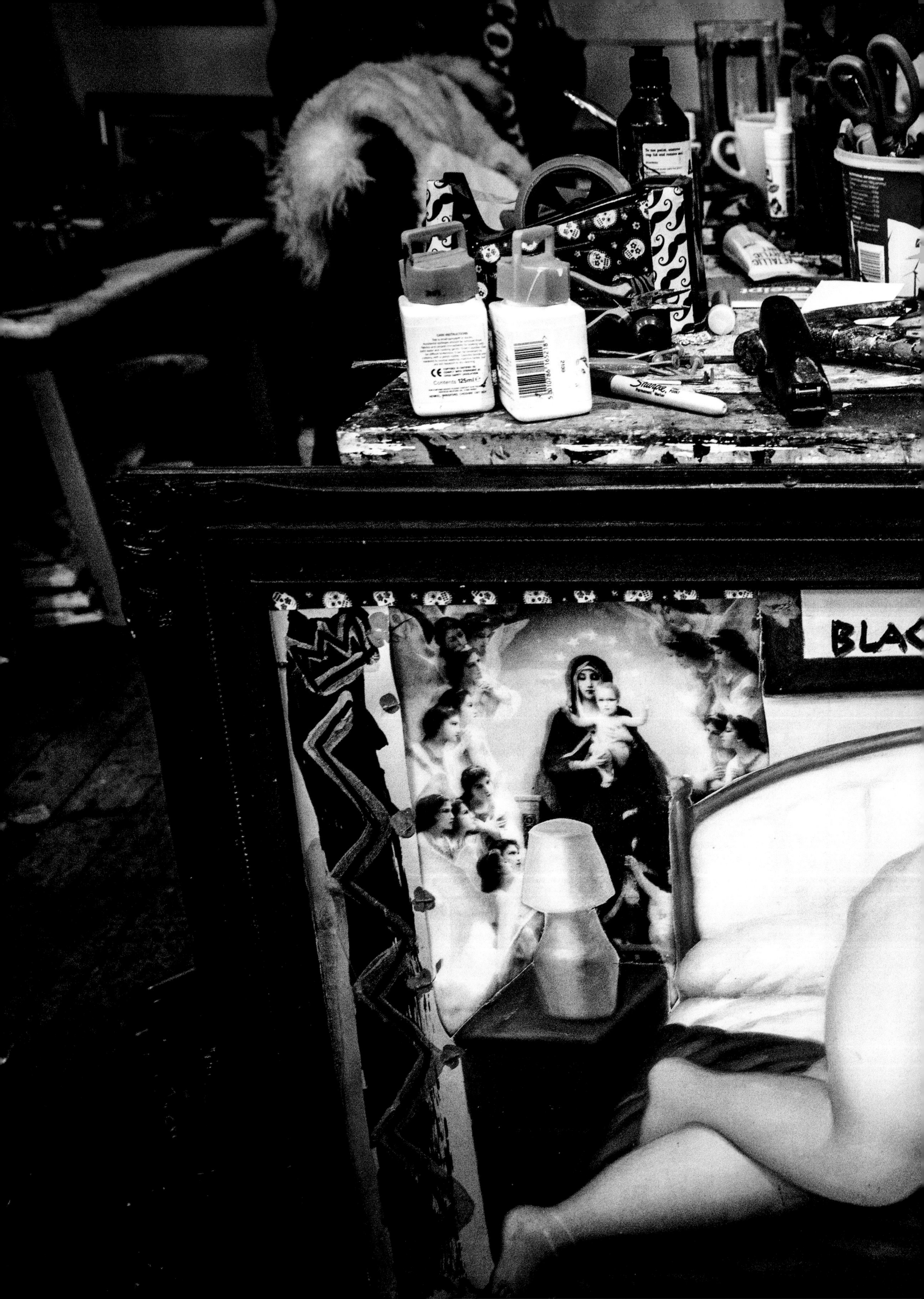
BLAC

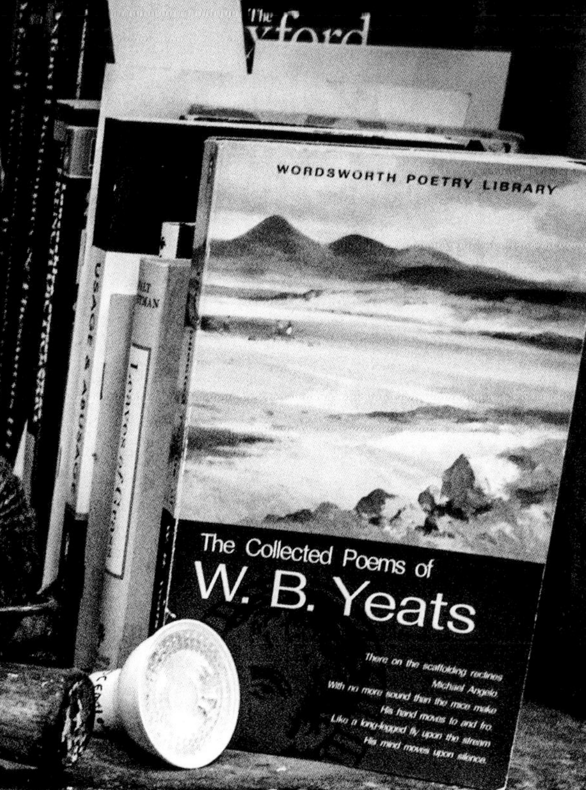
WORDSWORTH POETRY LIBRARY
The Collected Poems of
W. B. Yeats

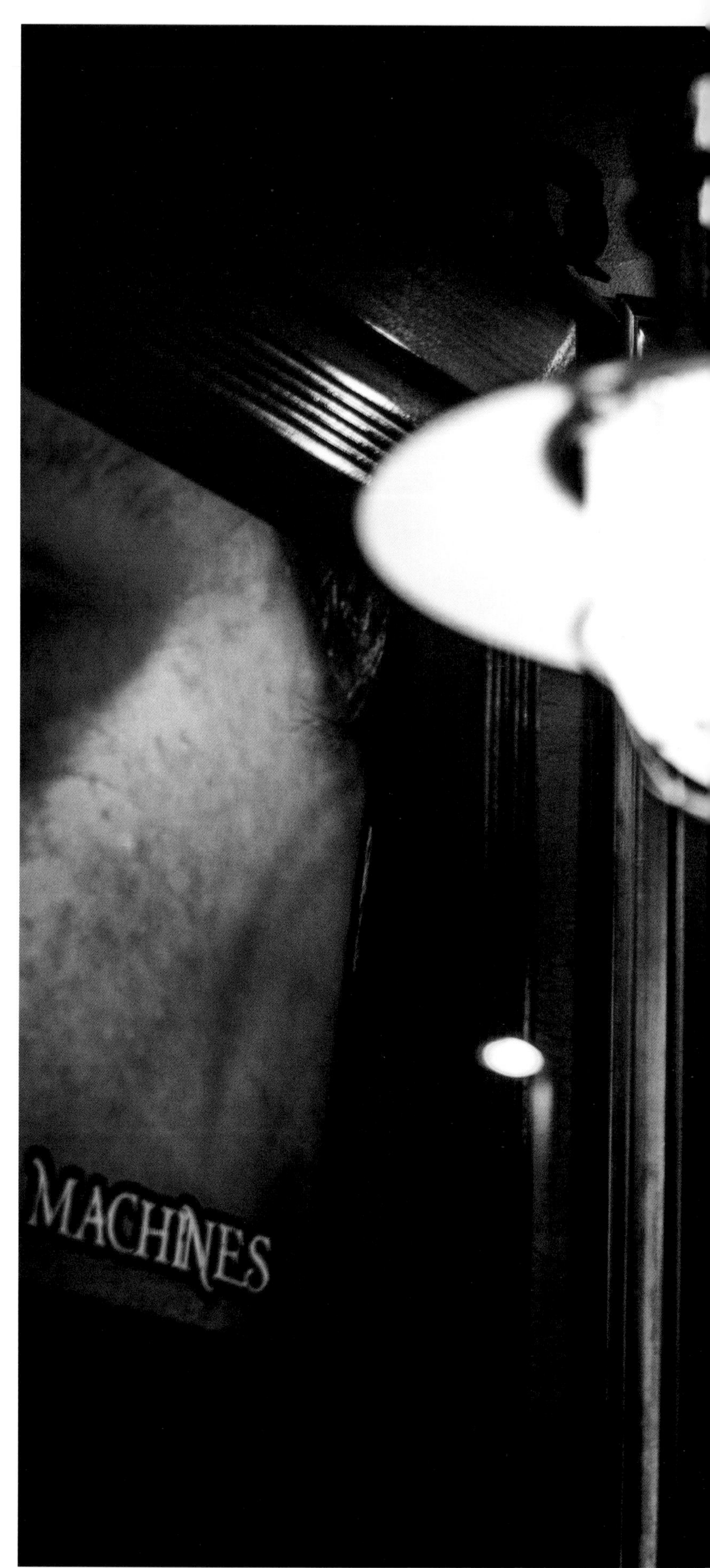
MACHINES

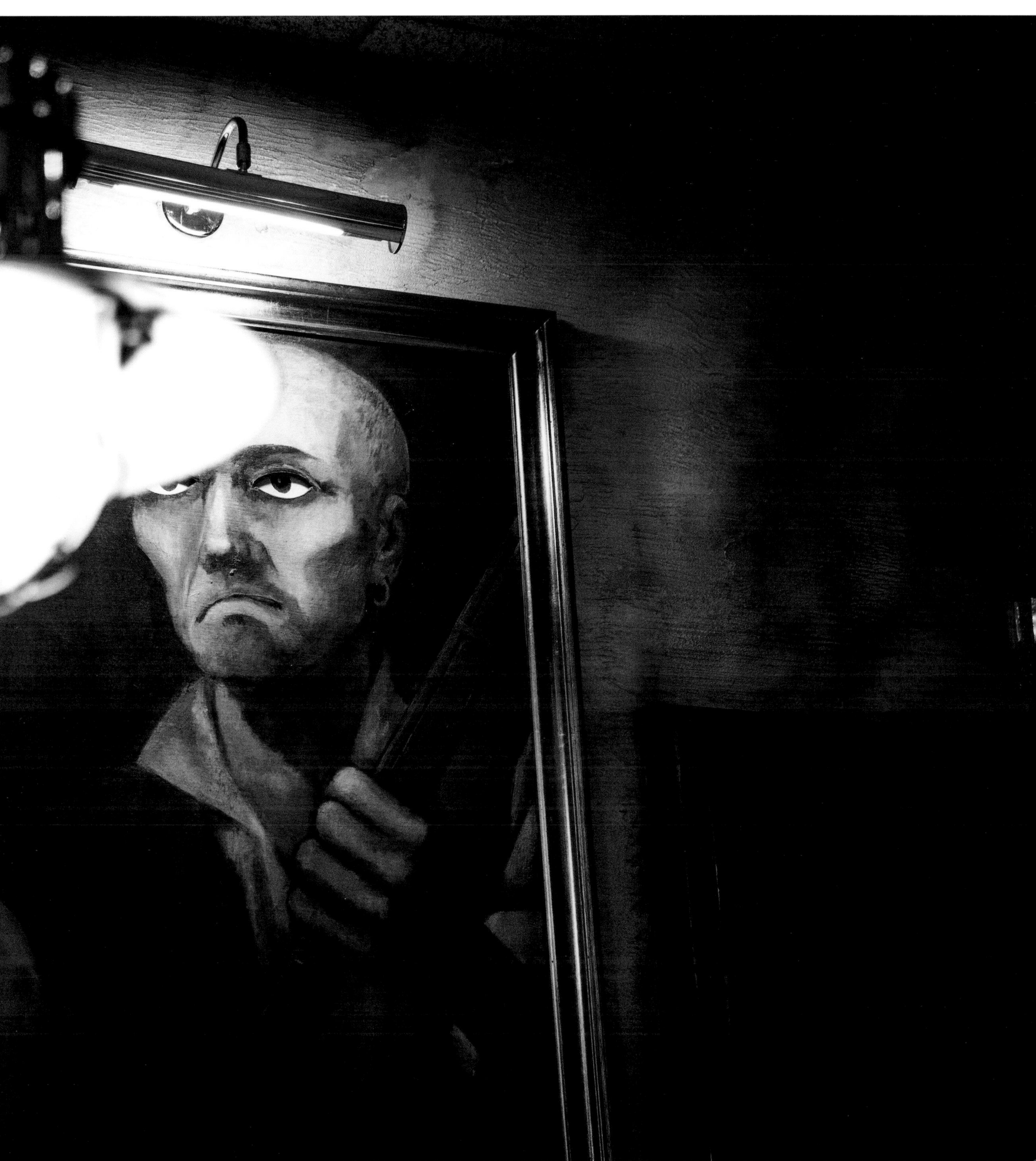

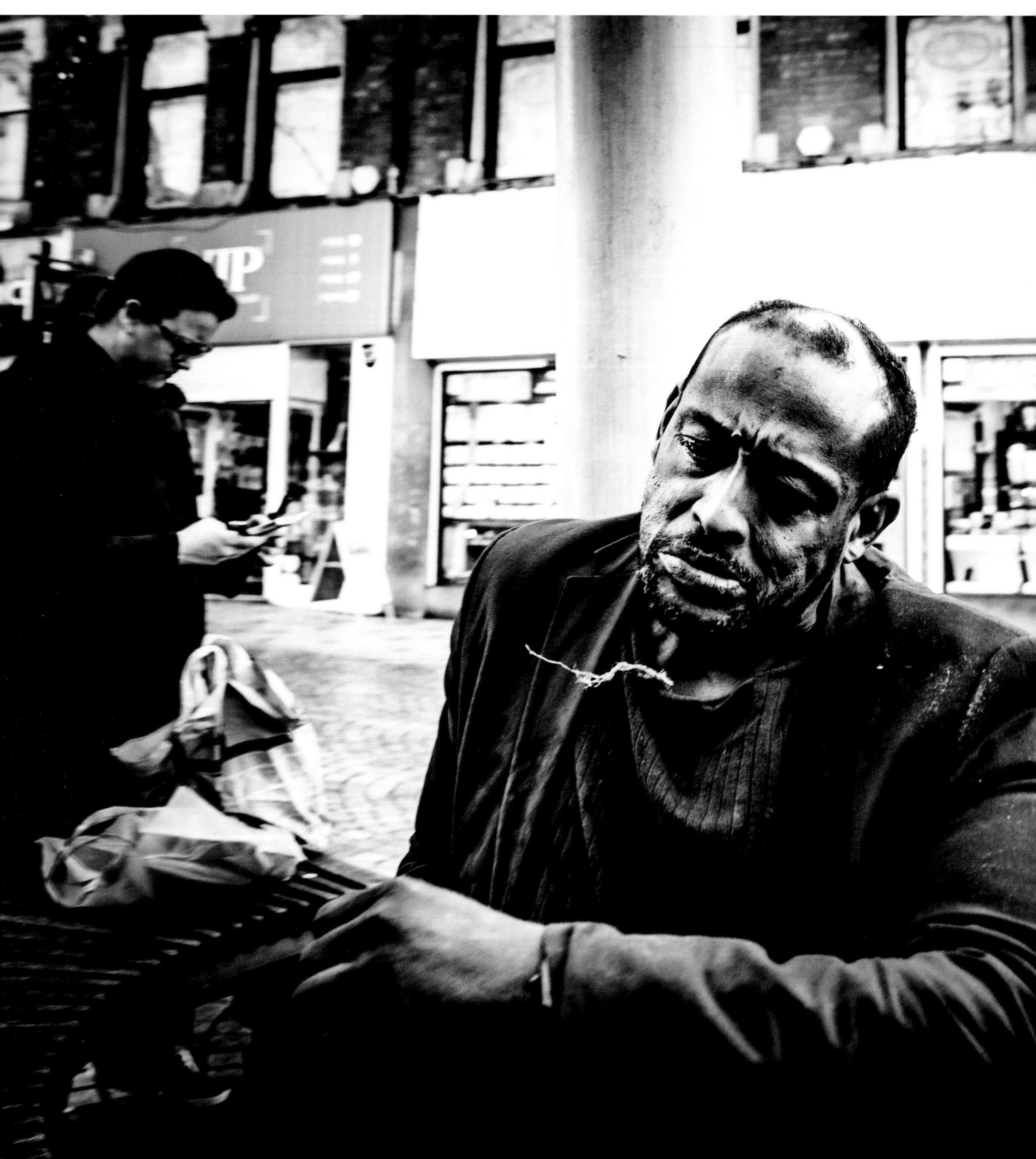

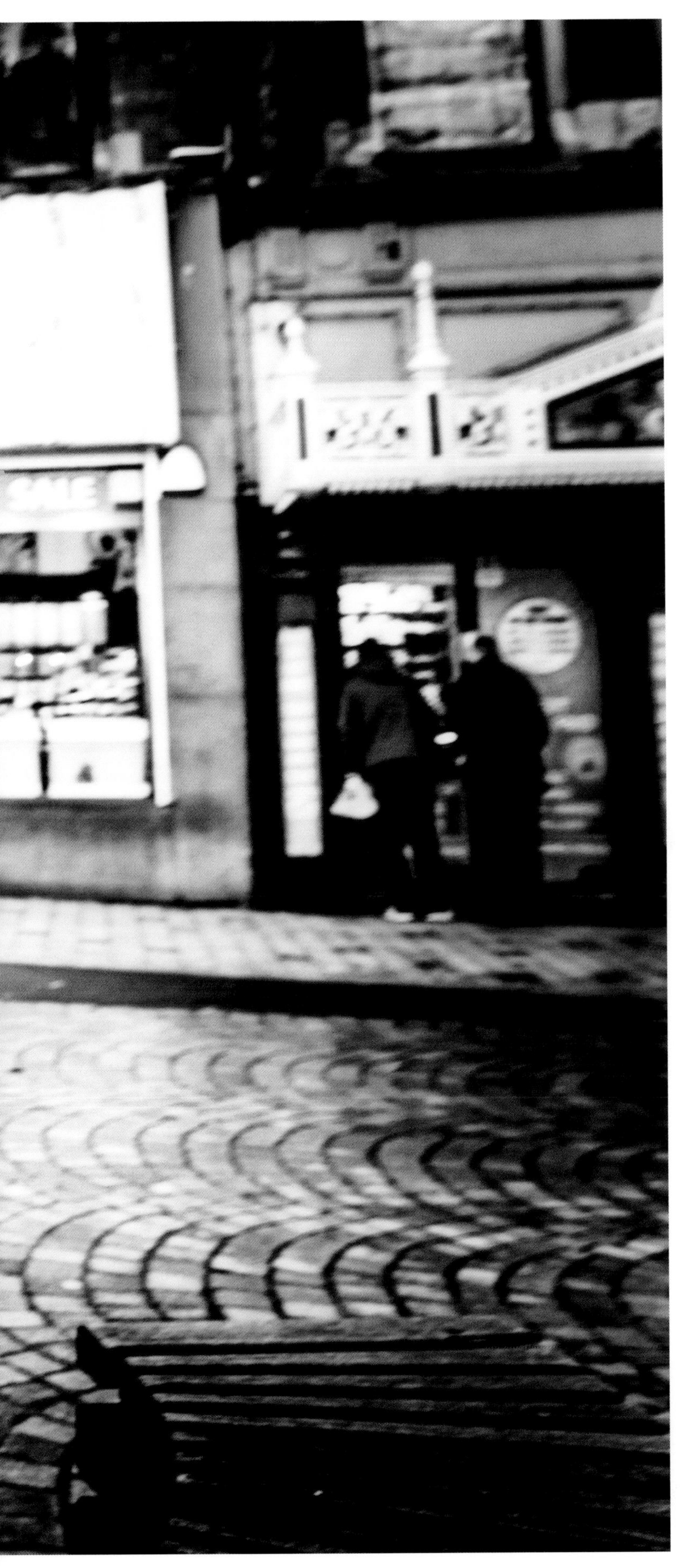

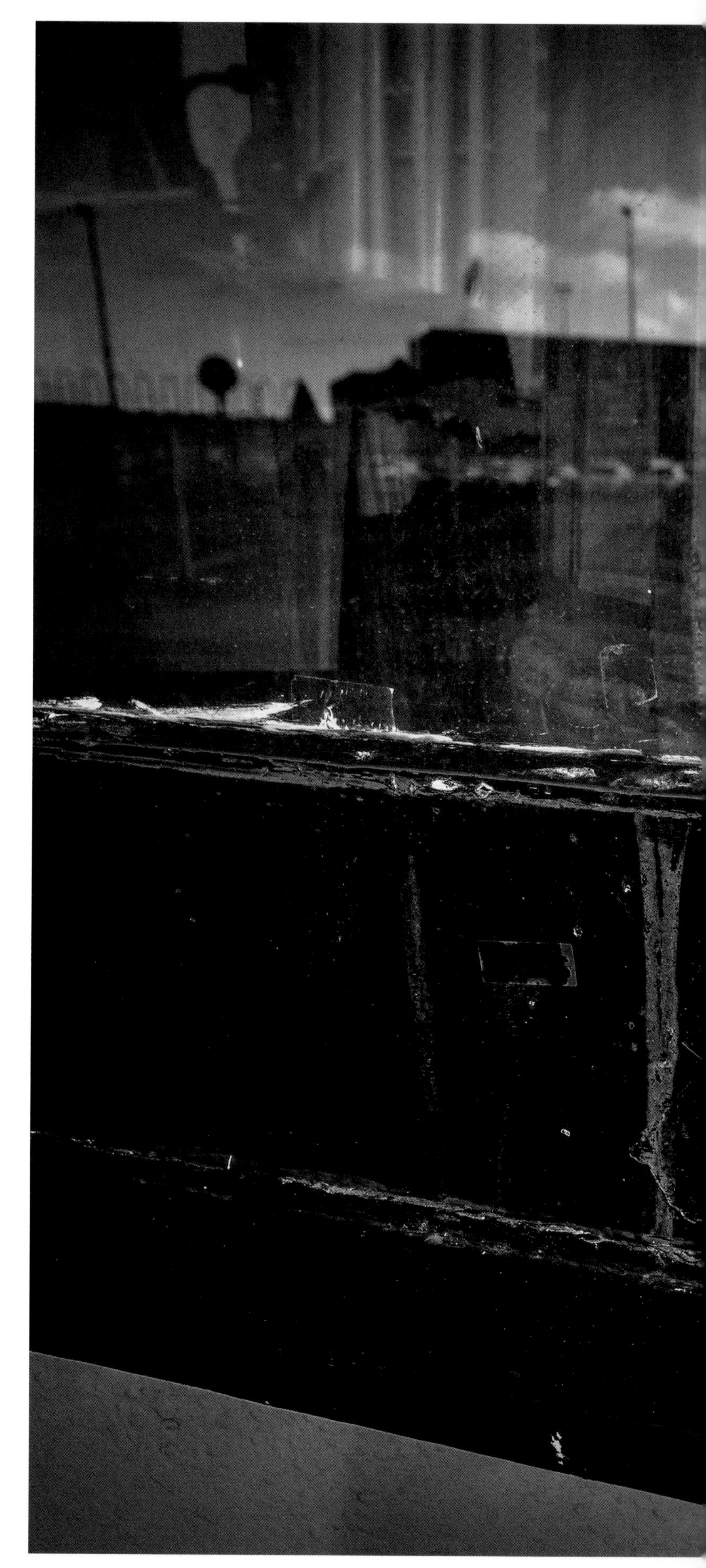

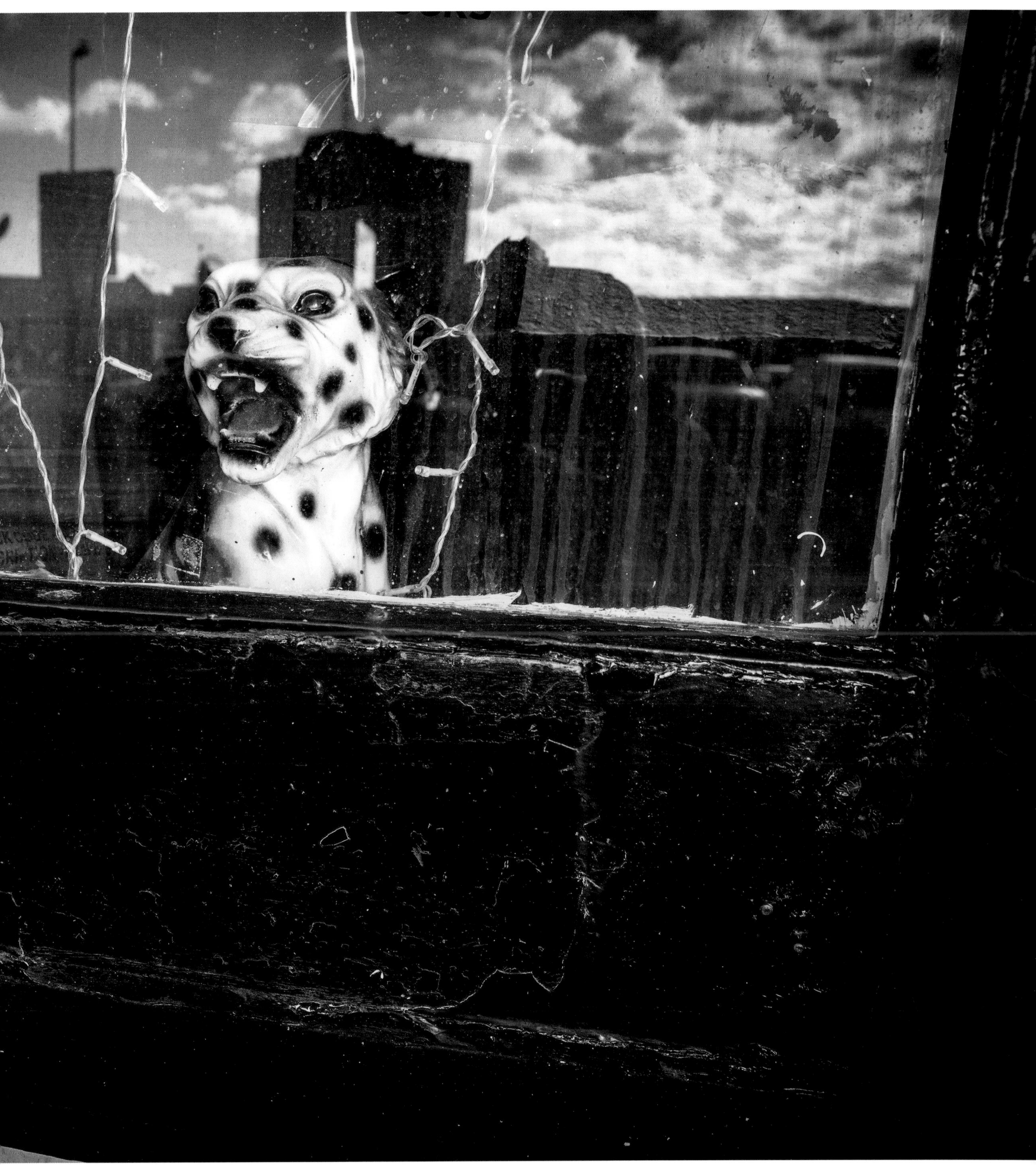

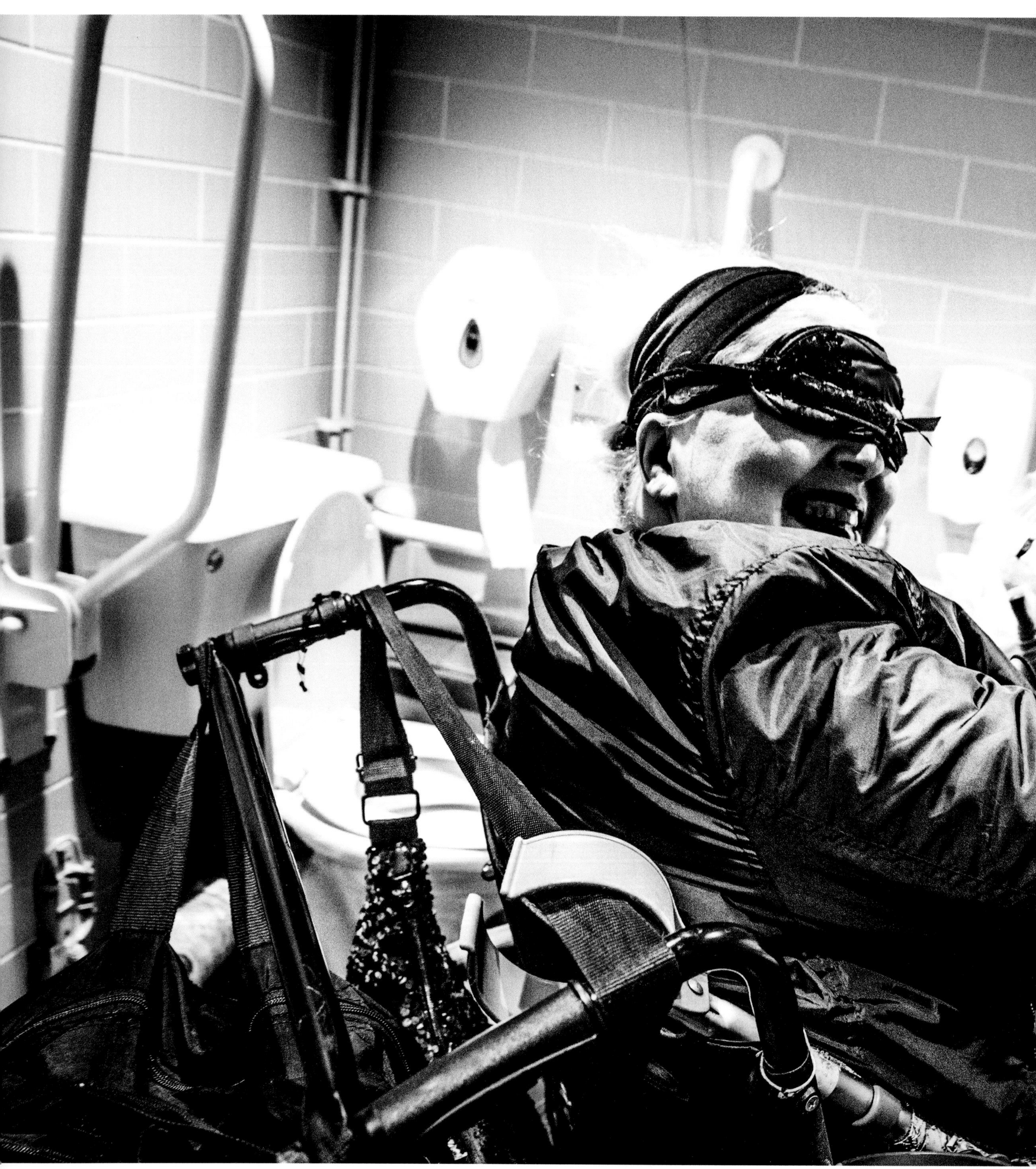

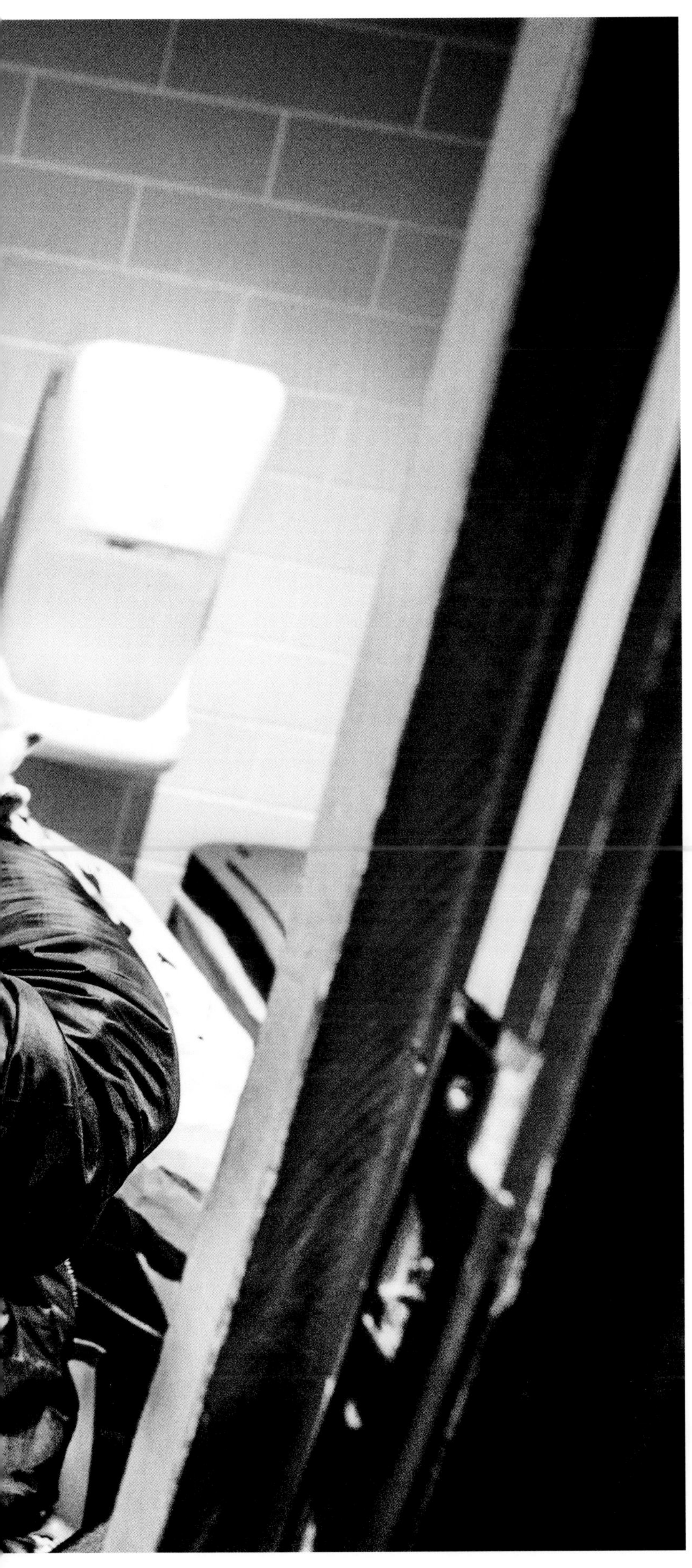

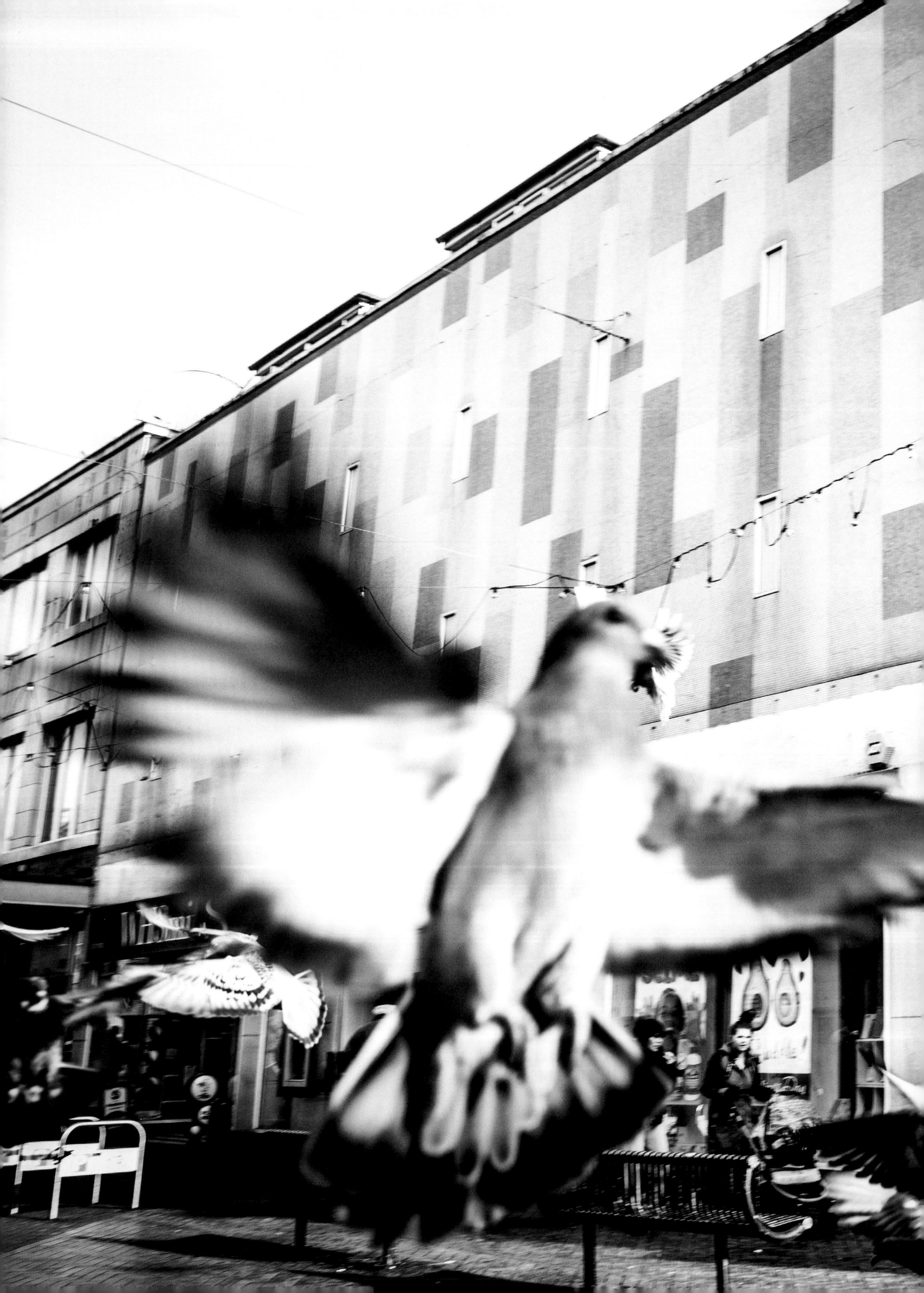

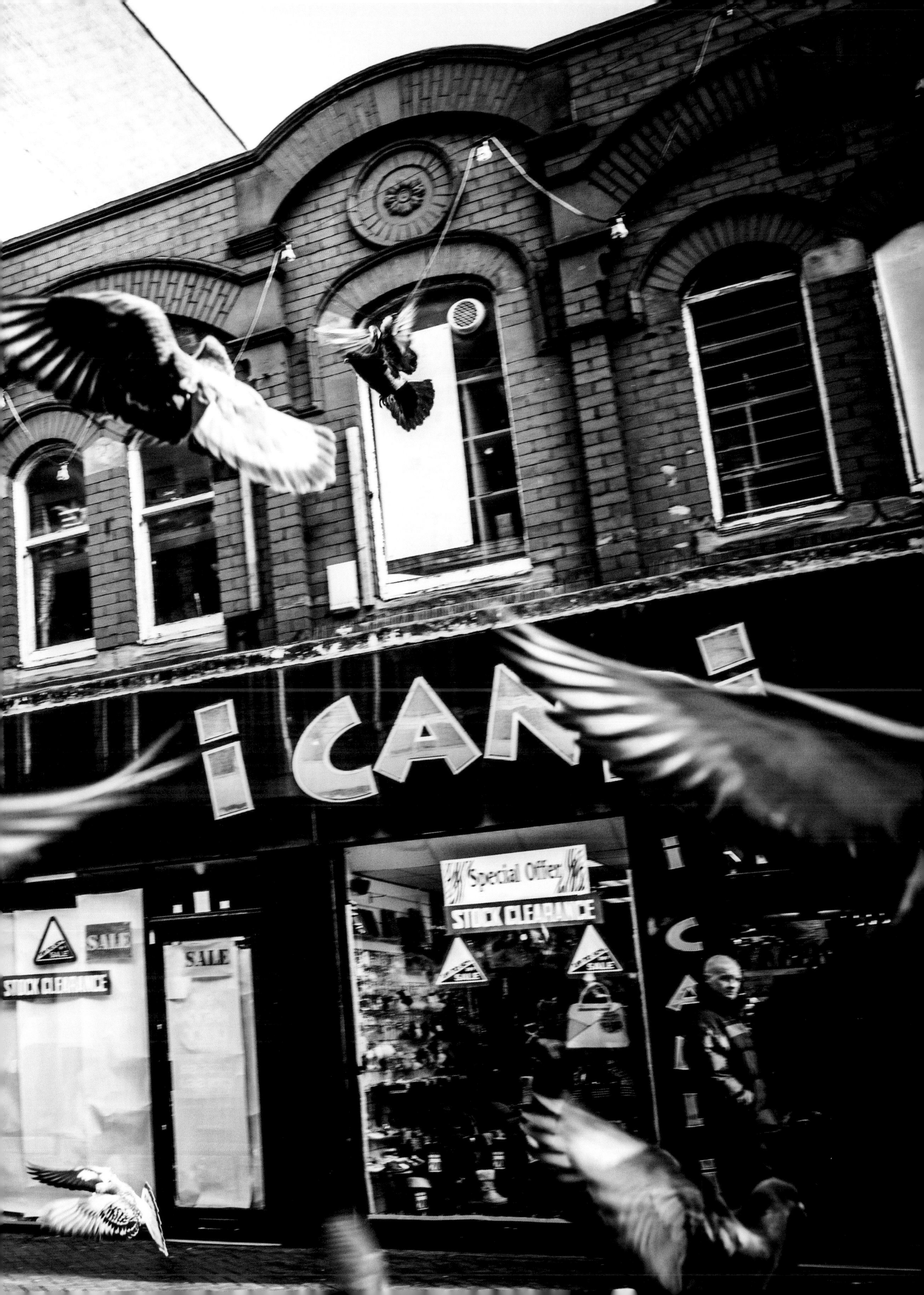
i CAN
Special Offer
STOCK CLEARANCE
SALE
SALE
STOCK CLEARANCE

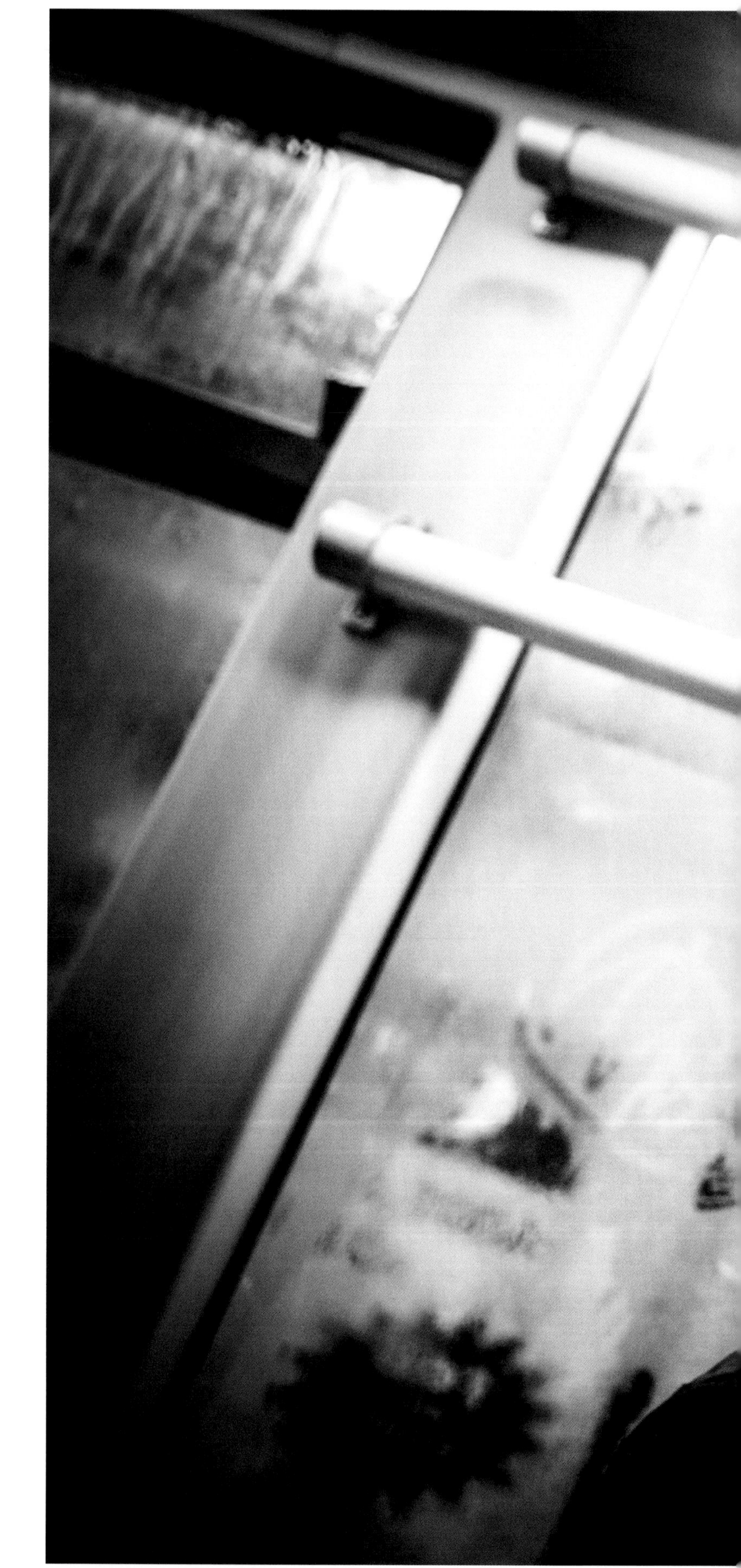

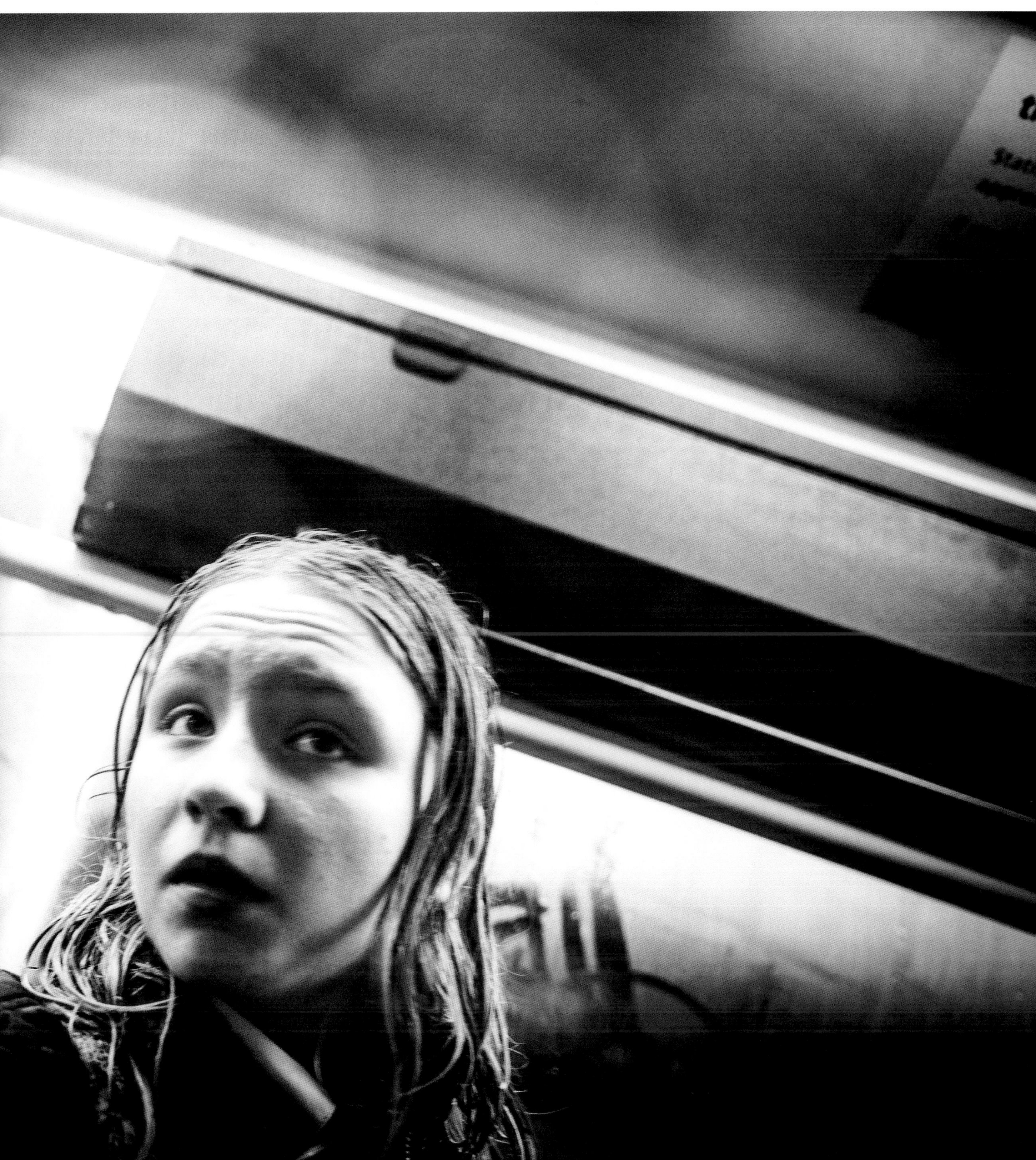

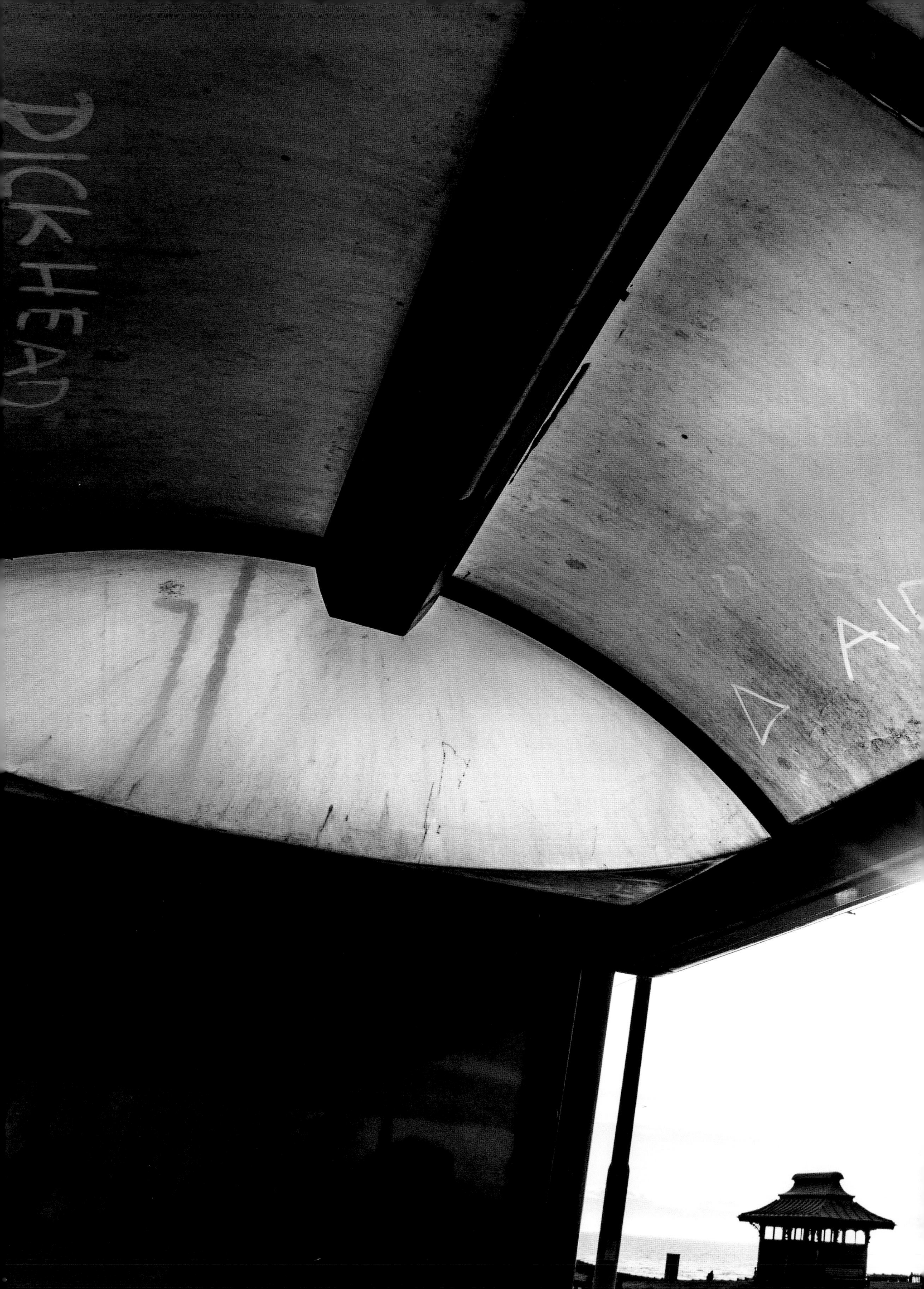

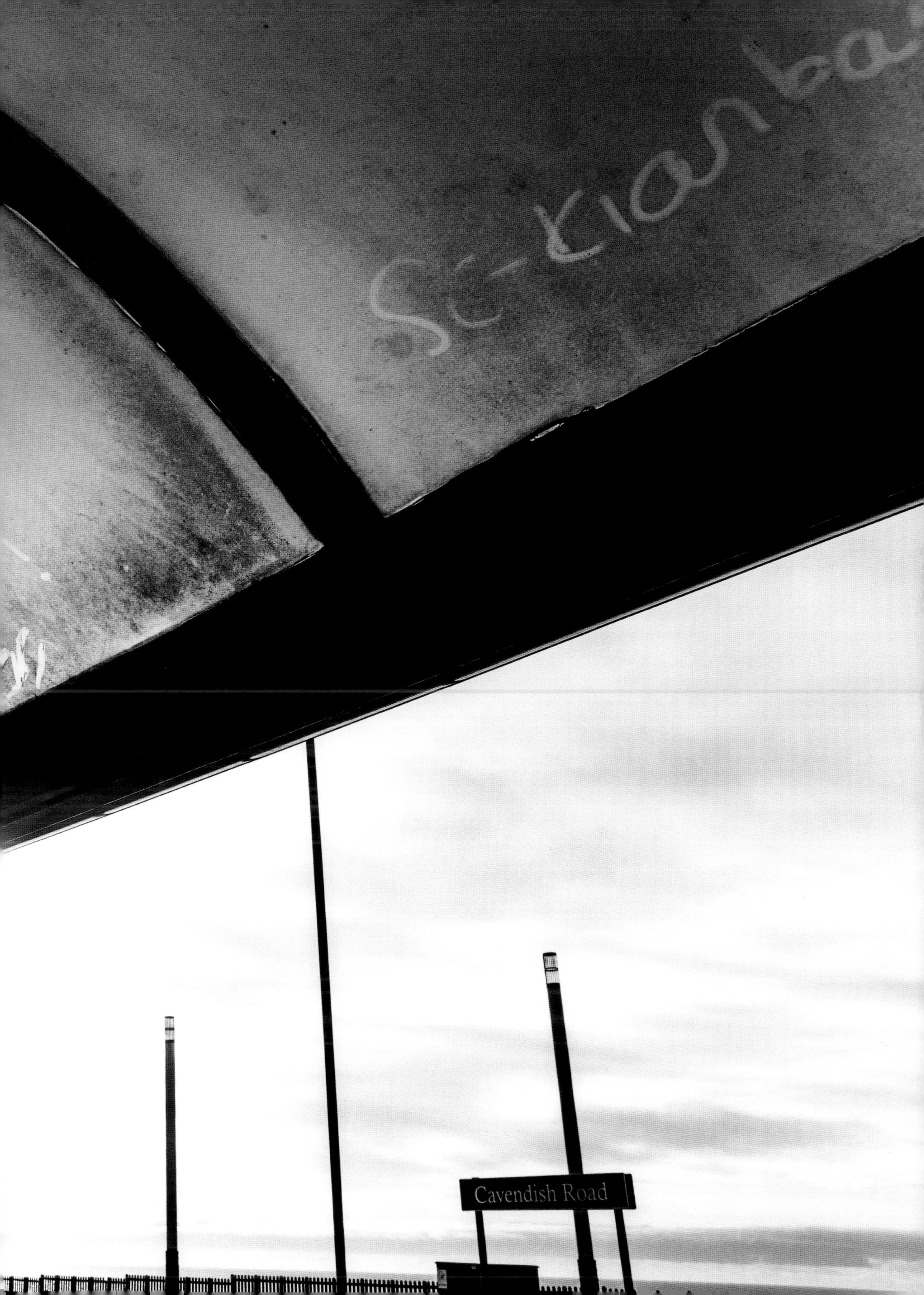

Cavendish Road

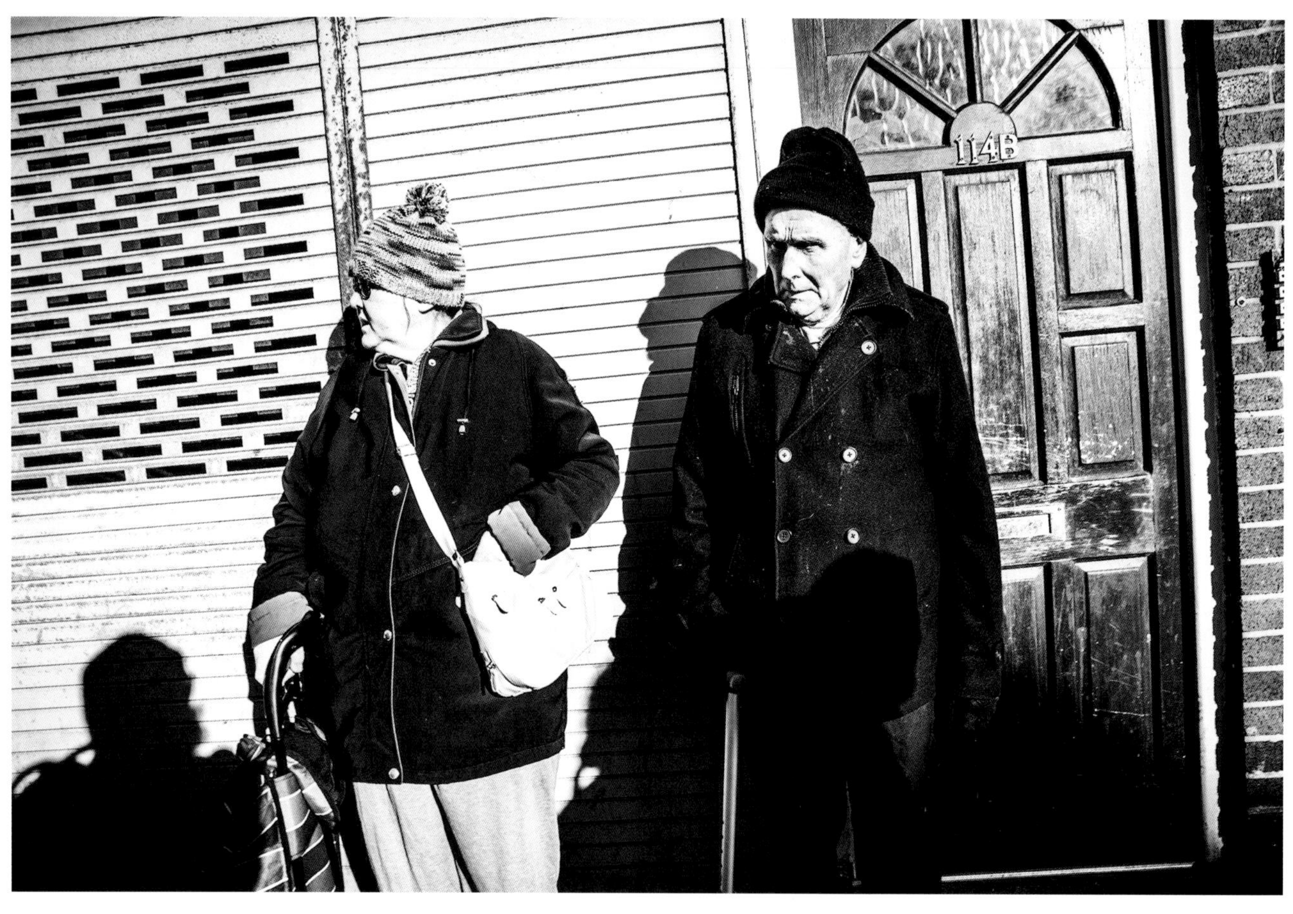

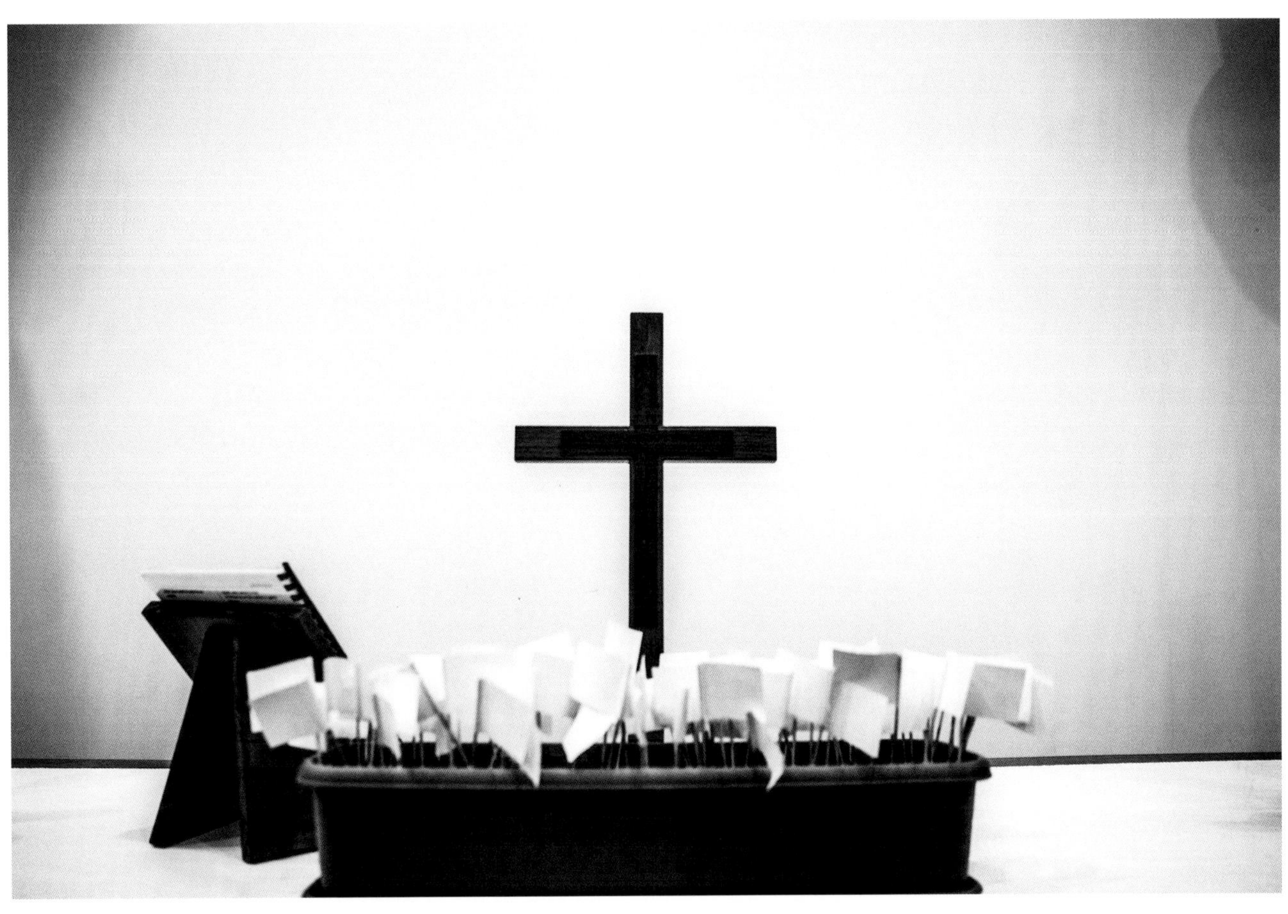

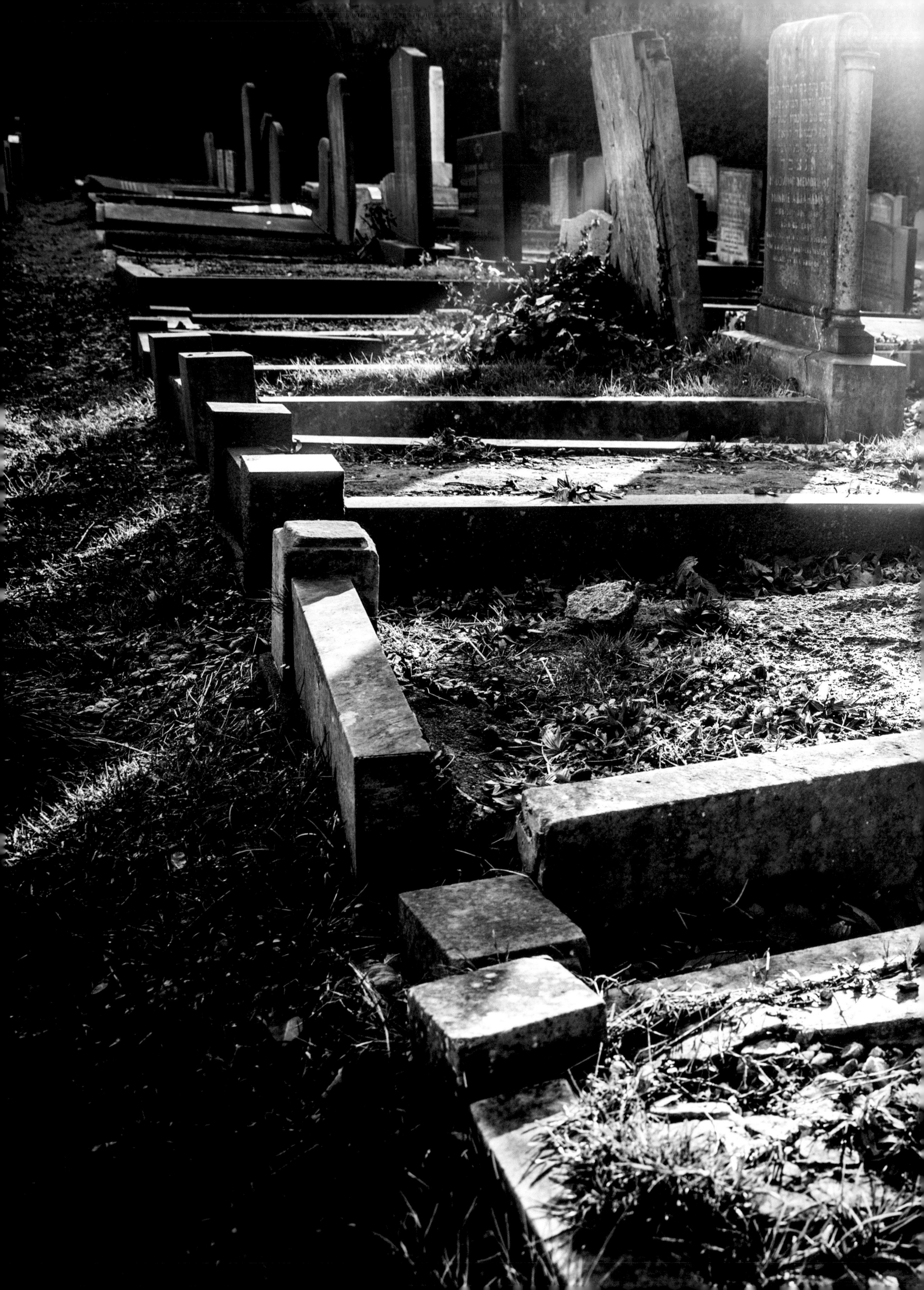

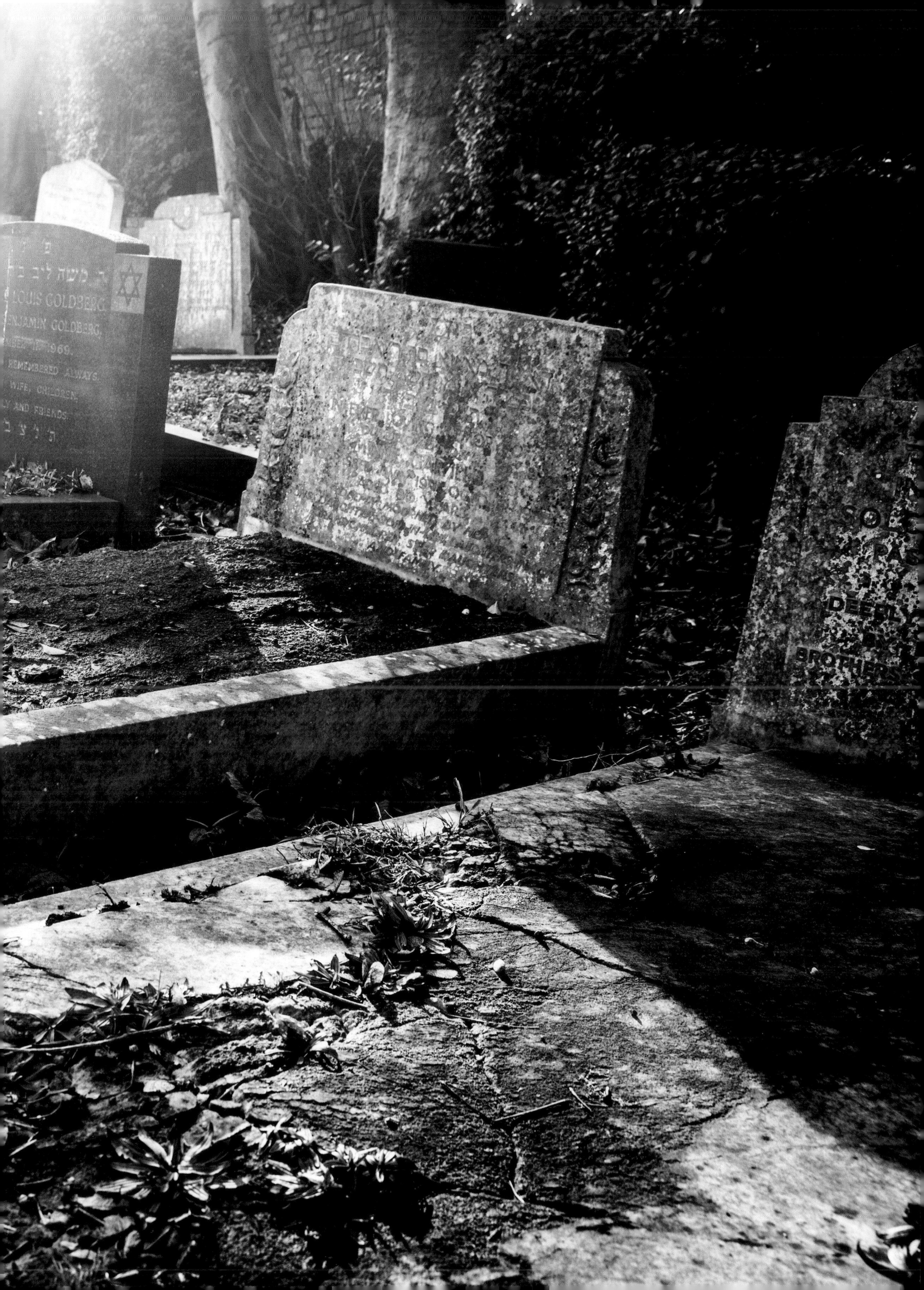

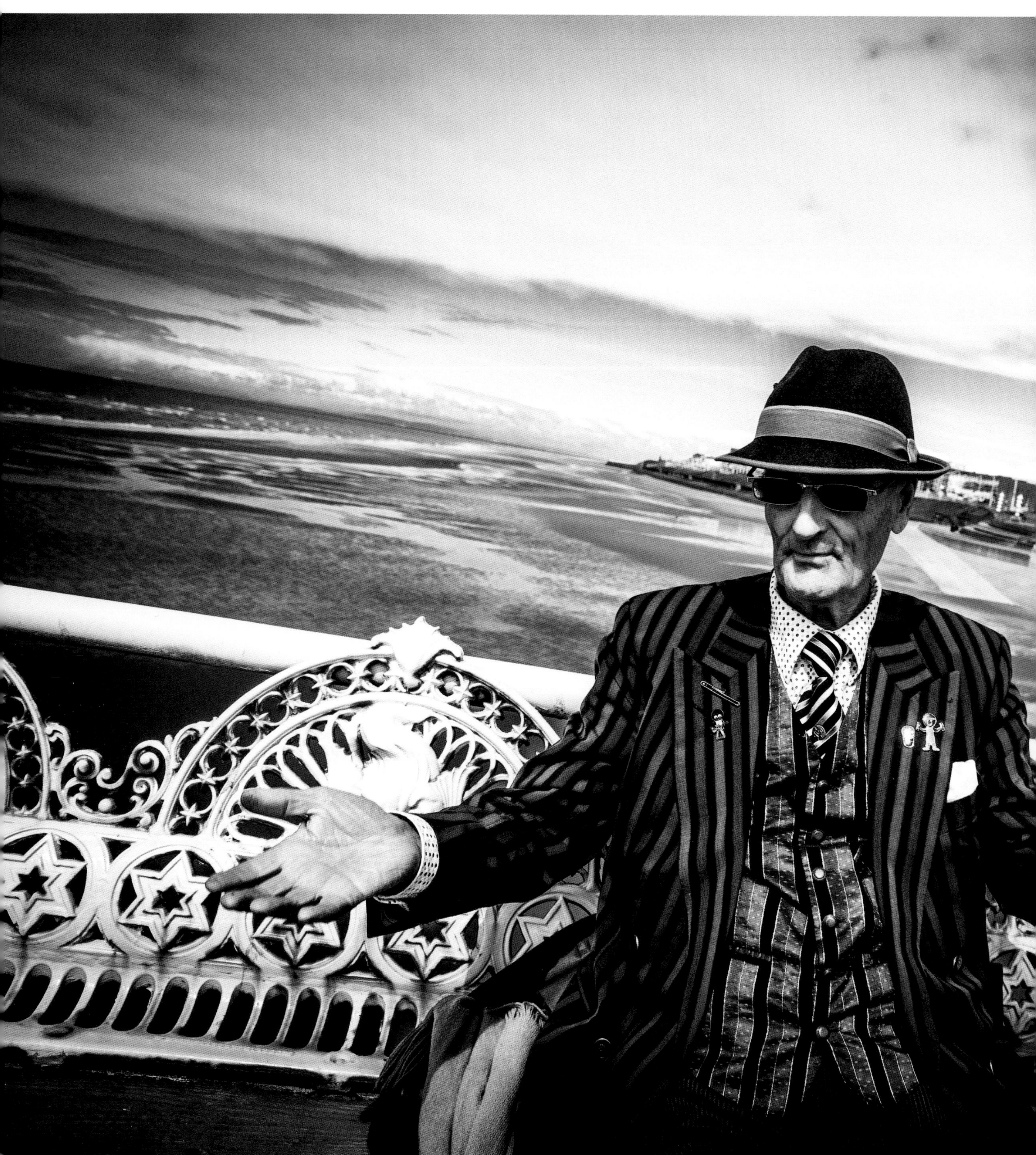

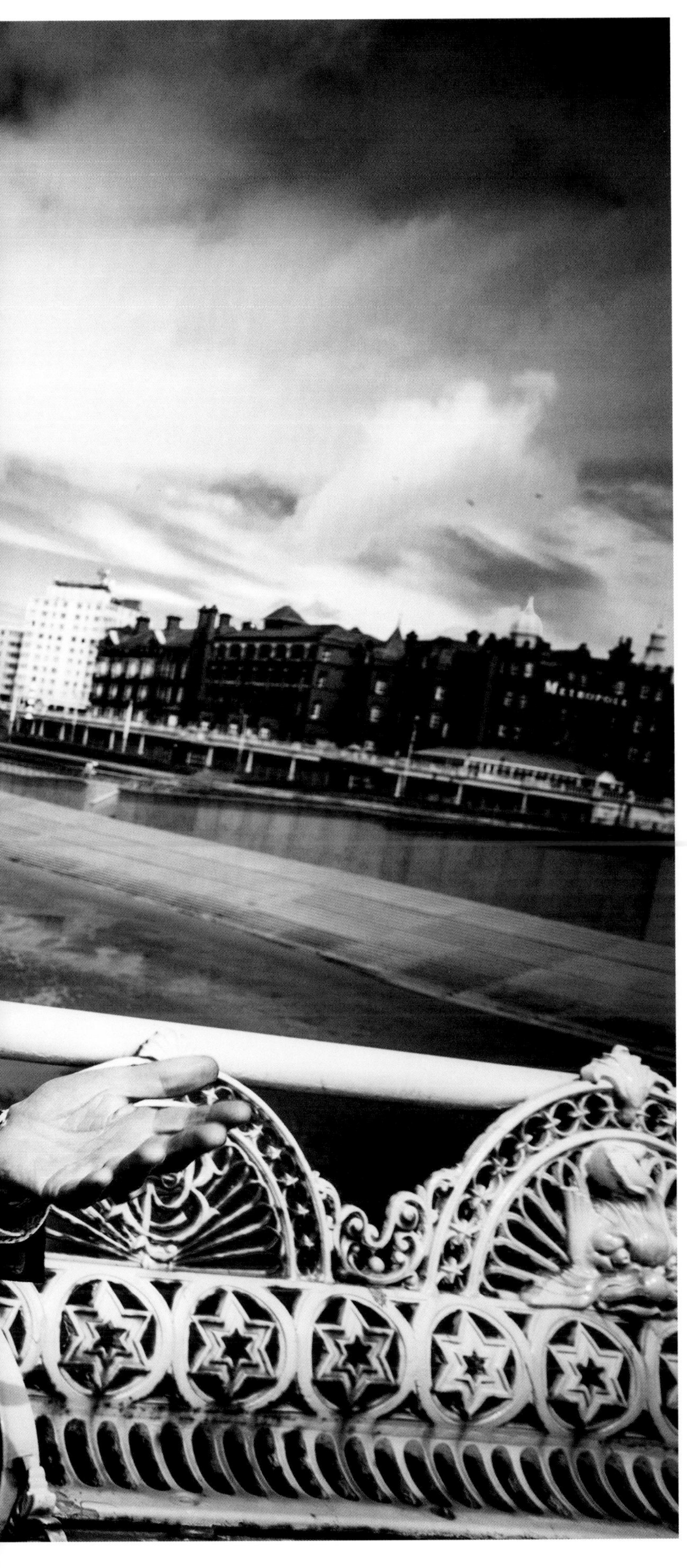

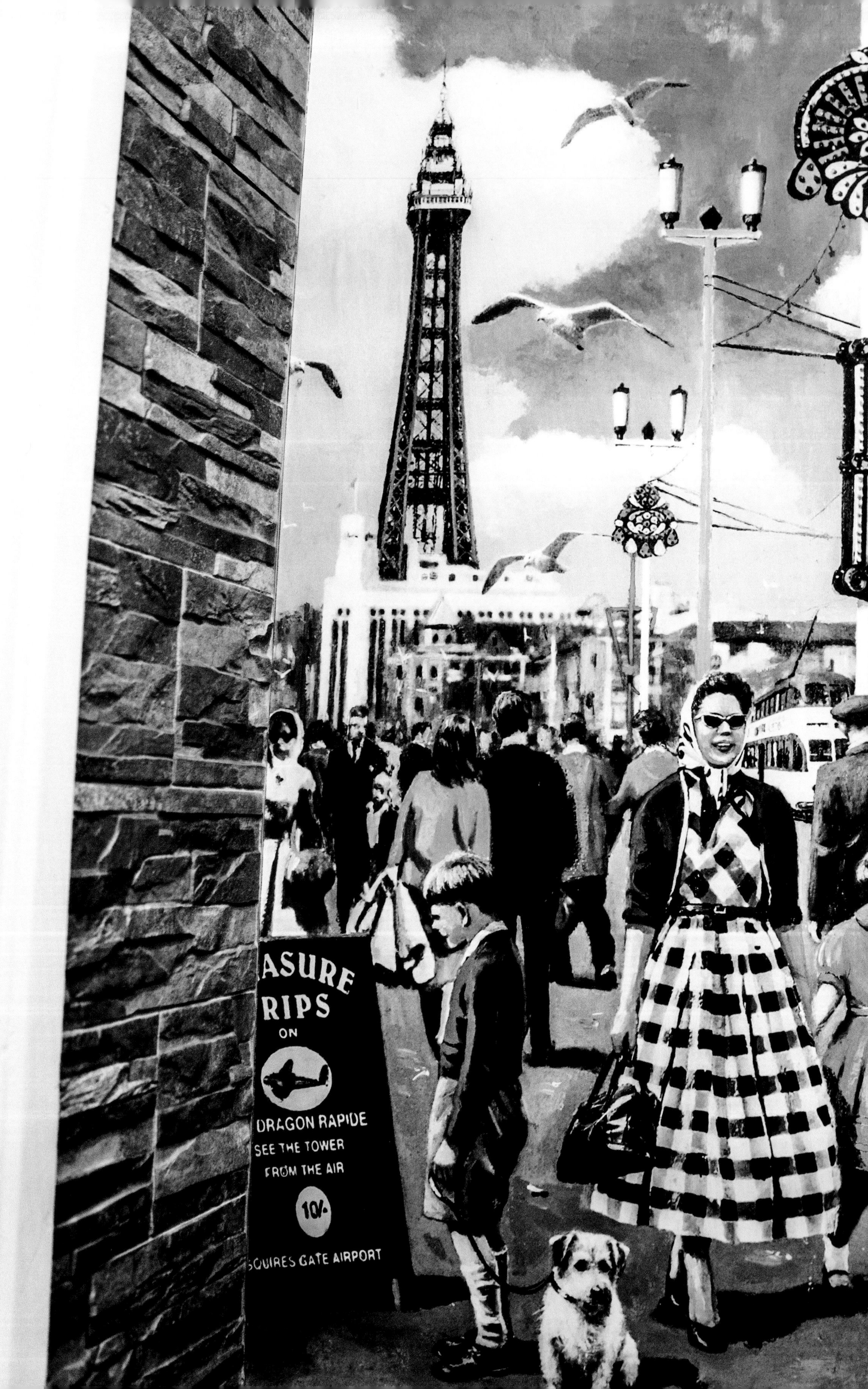
ASURE
RIPS
ON
DRAGON RAPIDE
SEE THE TOWER
FROM THE AIR
10/-
SQUIRES GATE AIRPORT

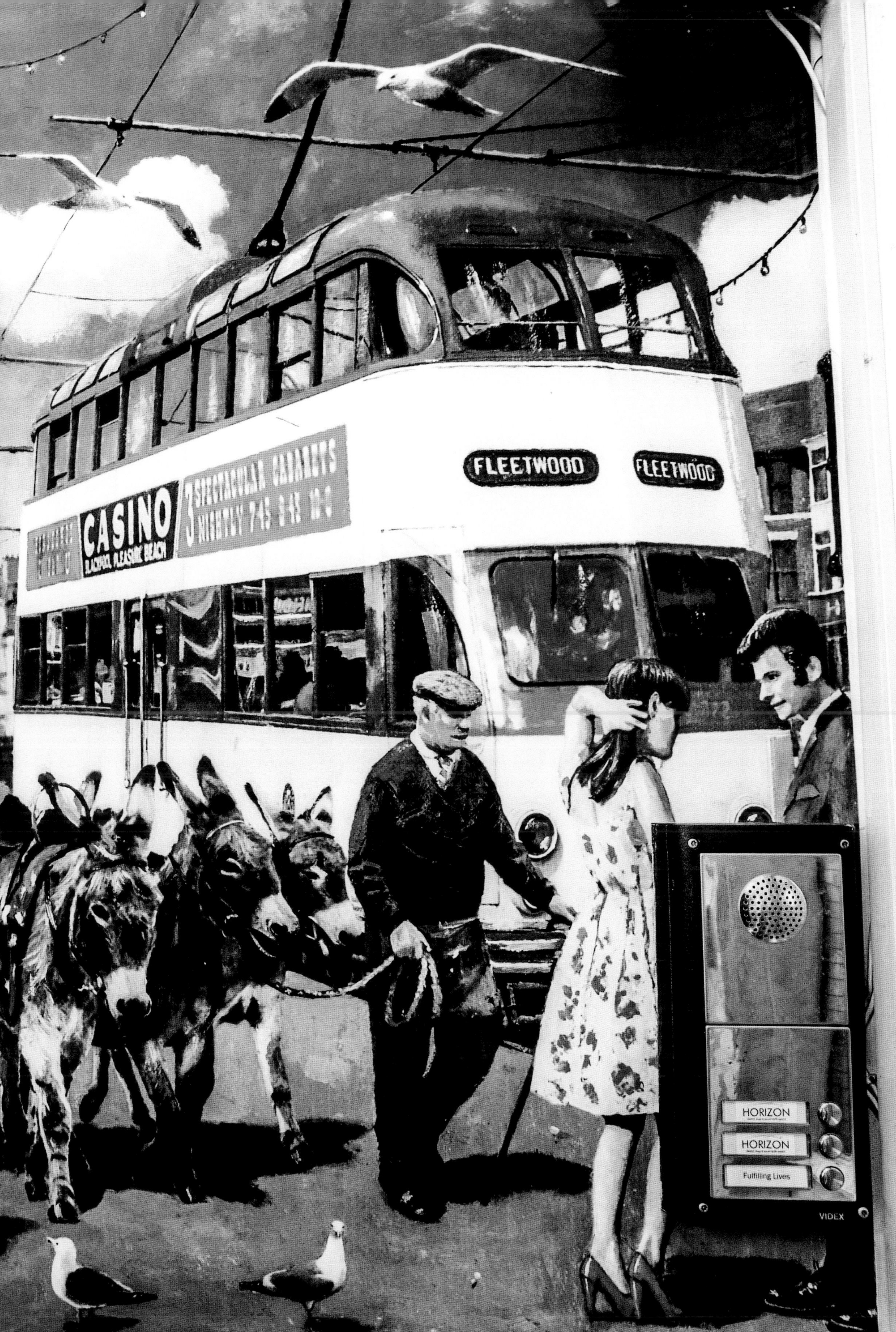
FLEETWOOD
FLEETWOOD
CASINO
BLACKPOOL PLEASURE BEACH
3 SPECTACULAR CABARETS NIGHTLY 7-45 9-15 10-0
HORIZON
HORIZON
Fulfilling Lives
VIDEX

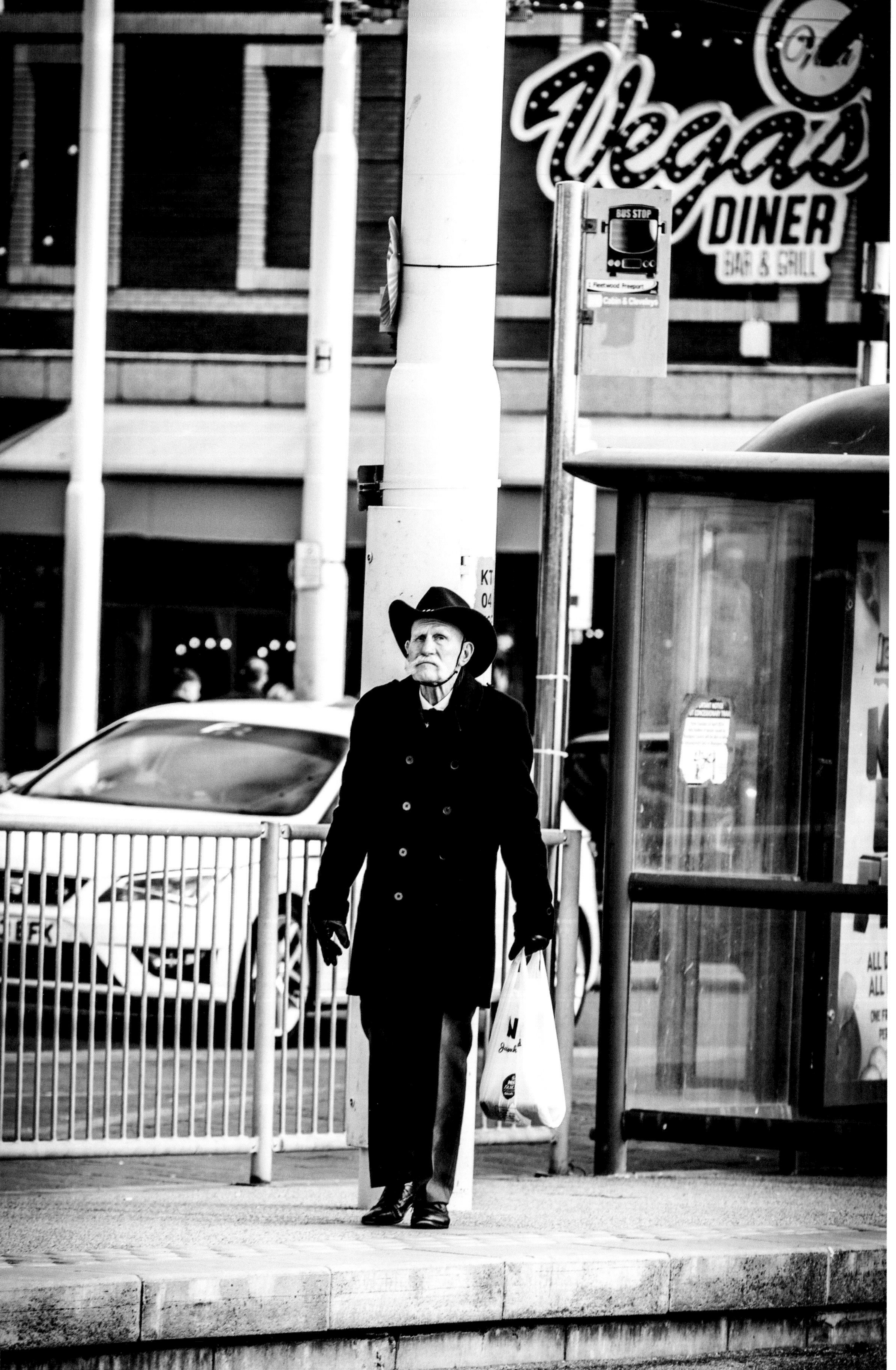
Vegas
DINER
BAR & GRILL
BUS STOP
Fleetwood Freeport
Cabin & Chestays
KT
04

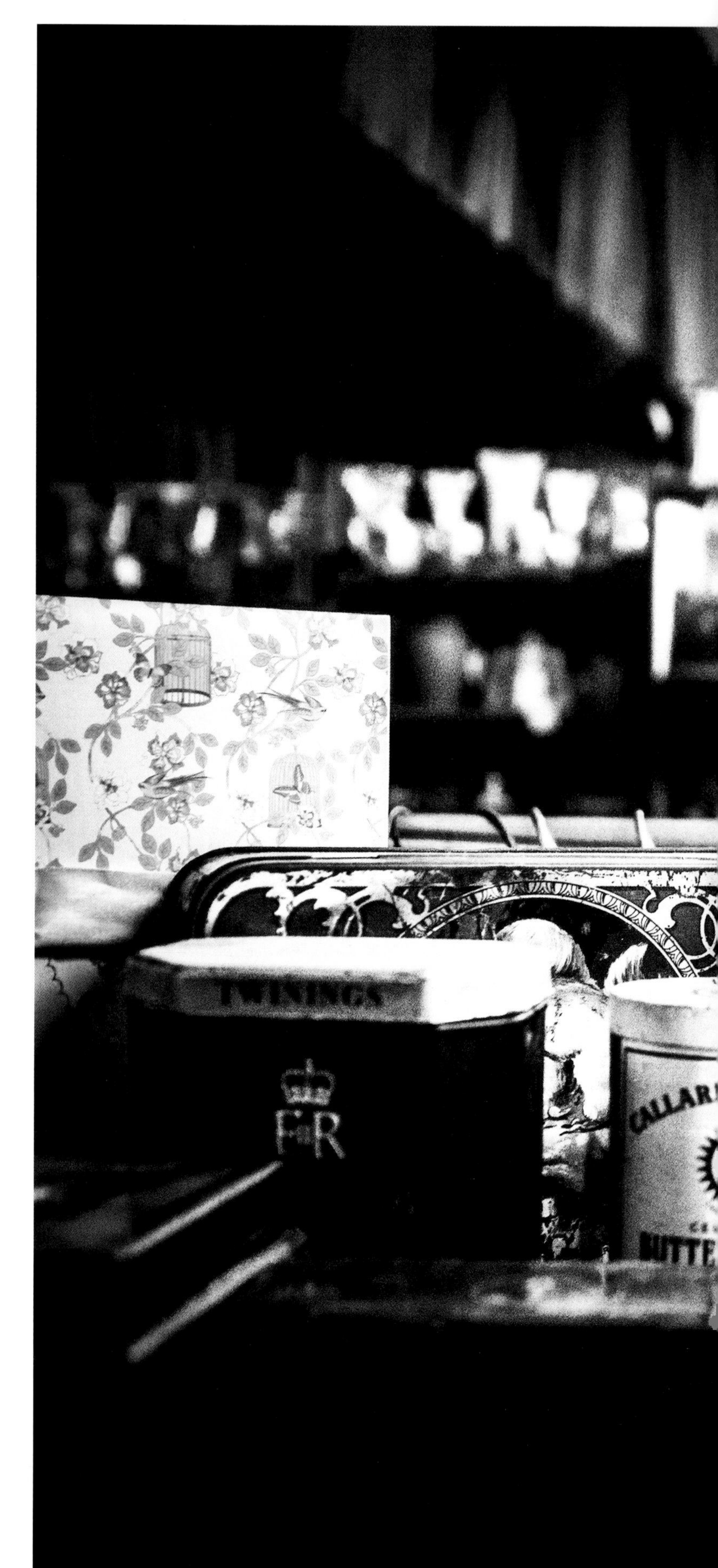

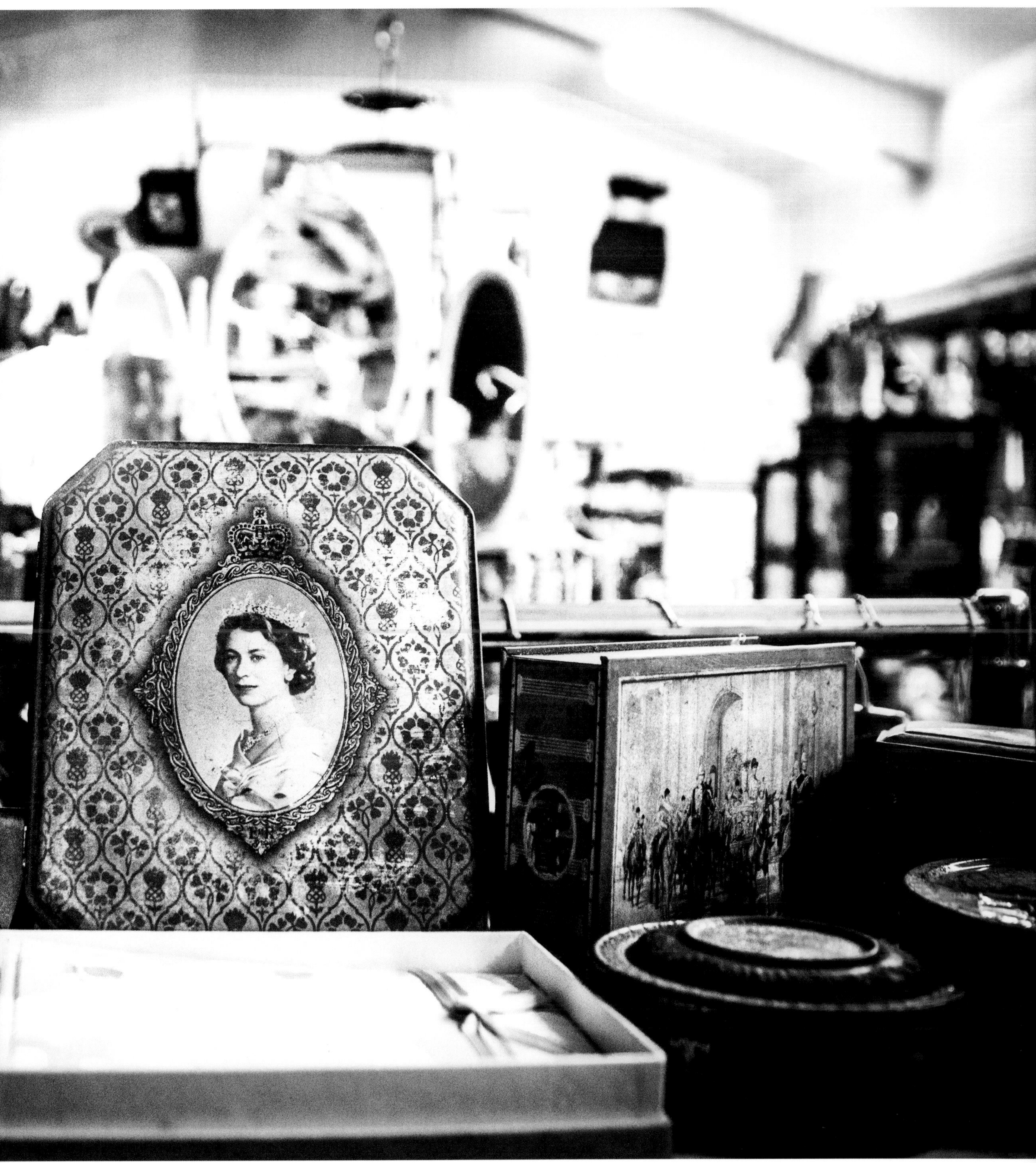

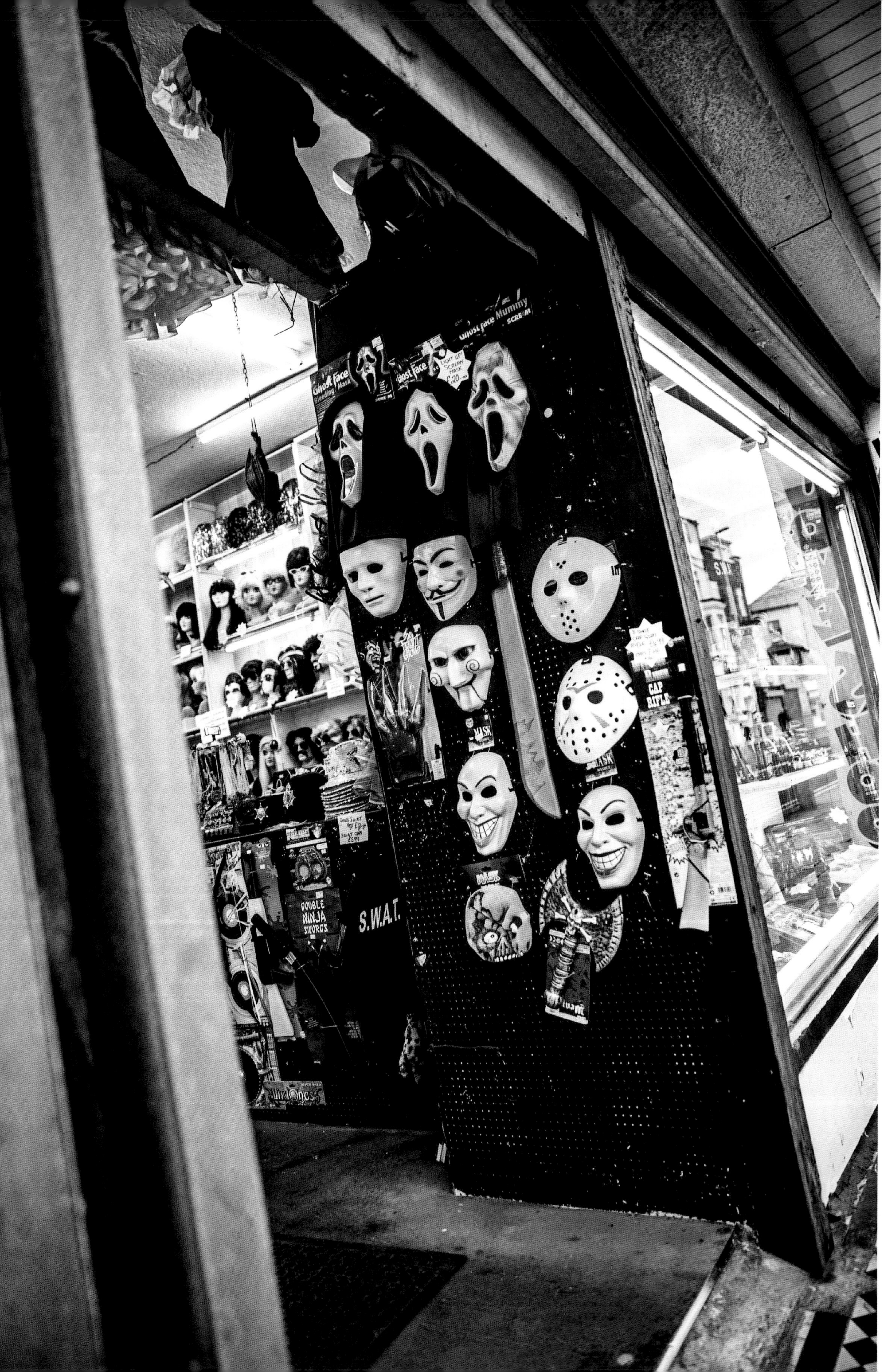

Ghost face Mummy
SCREAM
Ghost Face
Bleeding Mask
Ghost face
LIGHT UP!
SCREAM
MASK
MASK
MASK
GAP RIFLE
DOUBLE NINJA SWORDS
S.W.A.T.

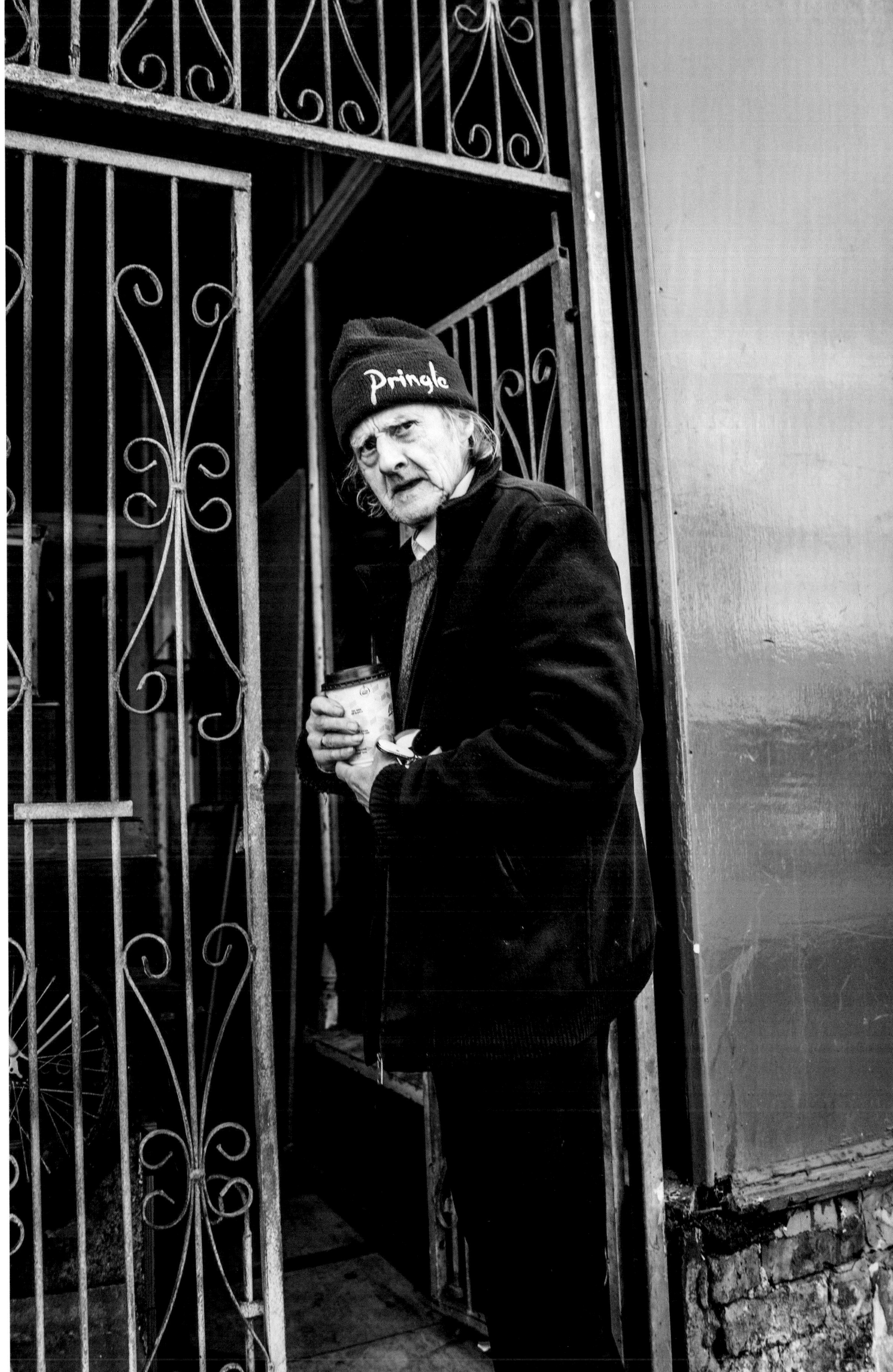
Pringle

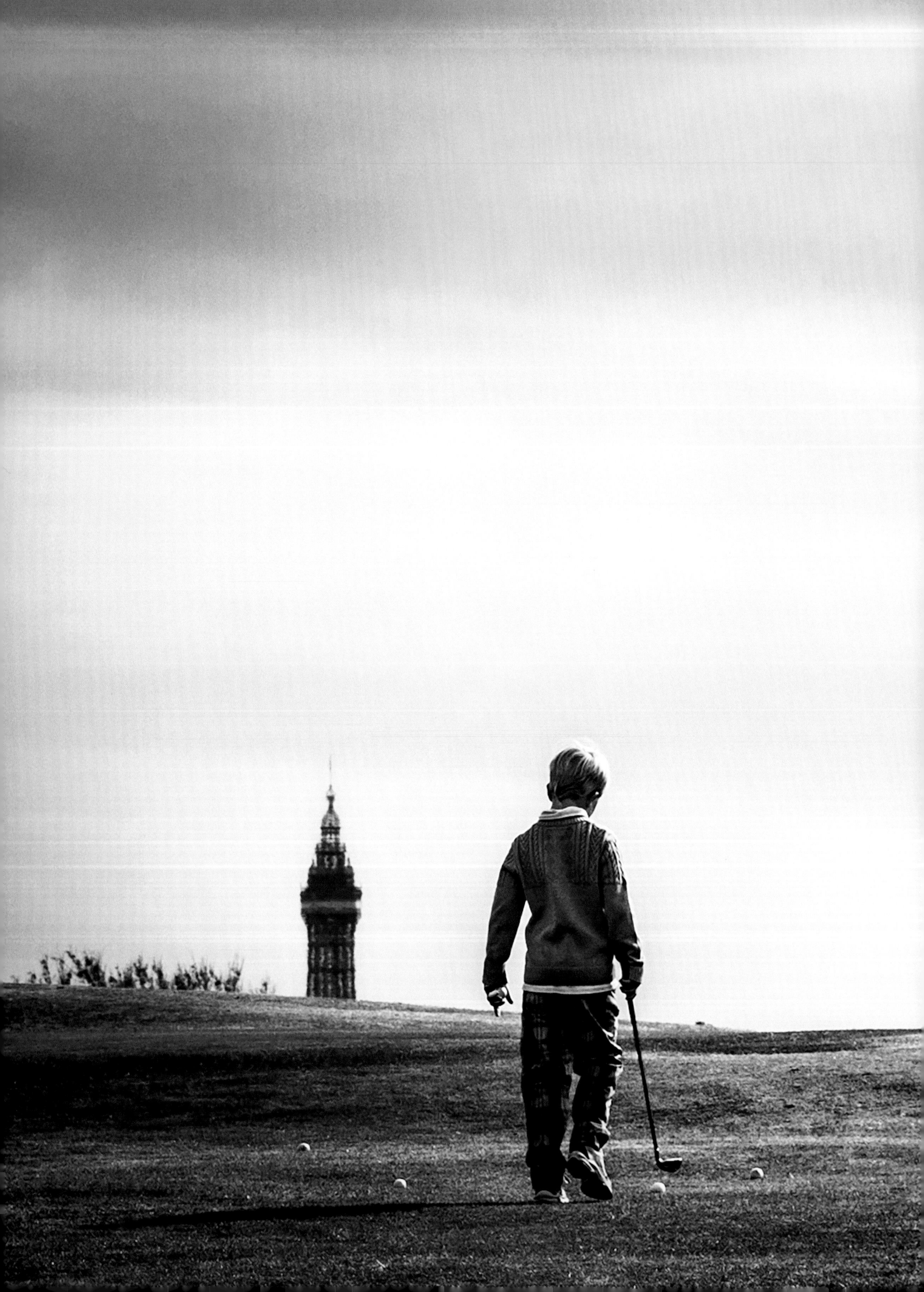

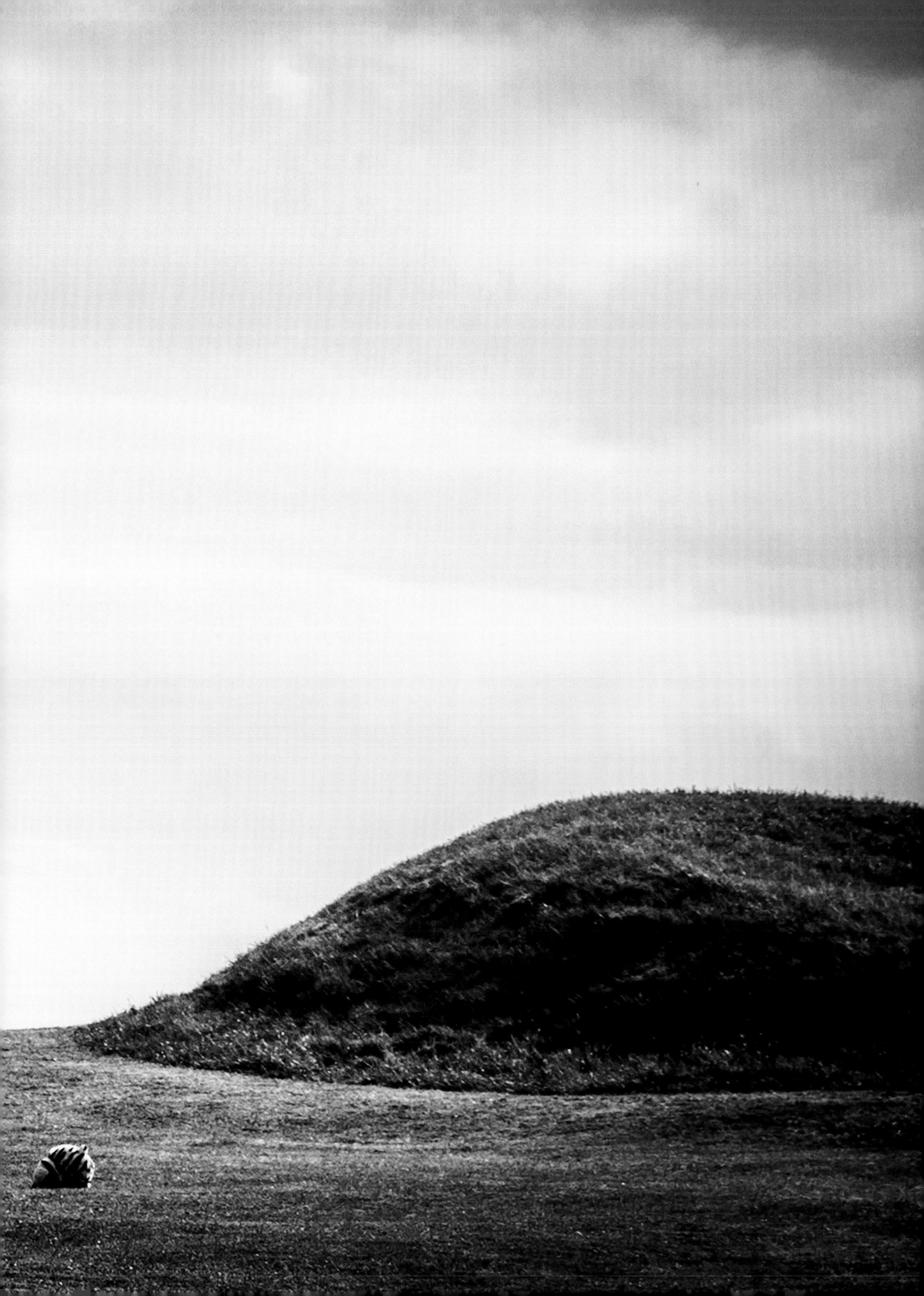

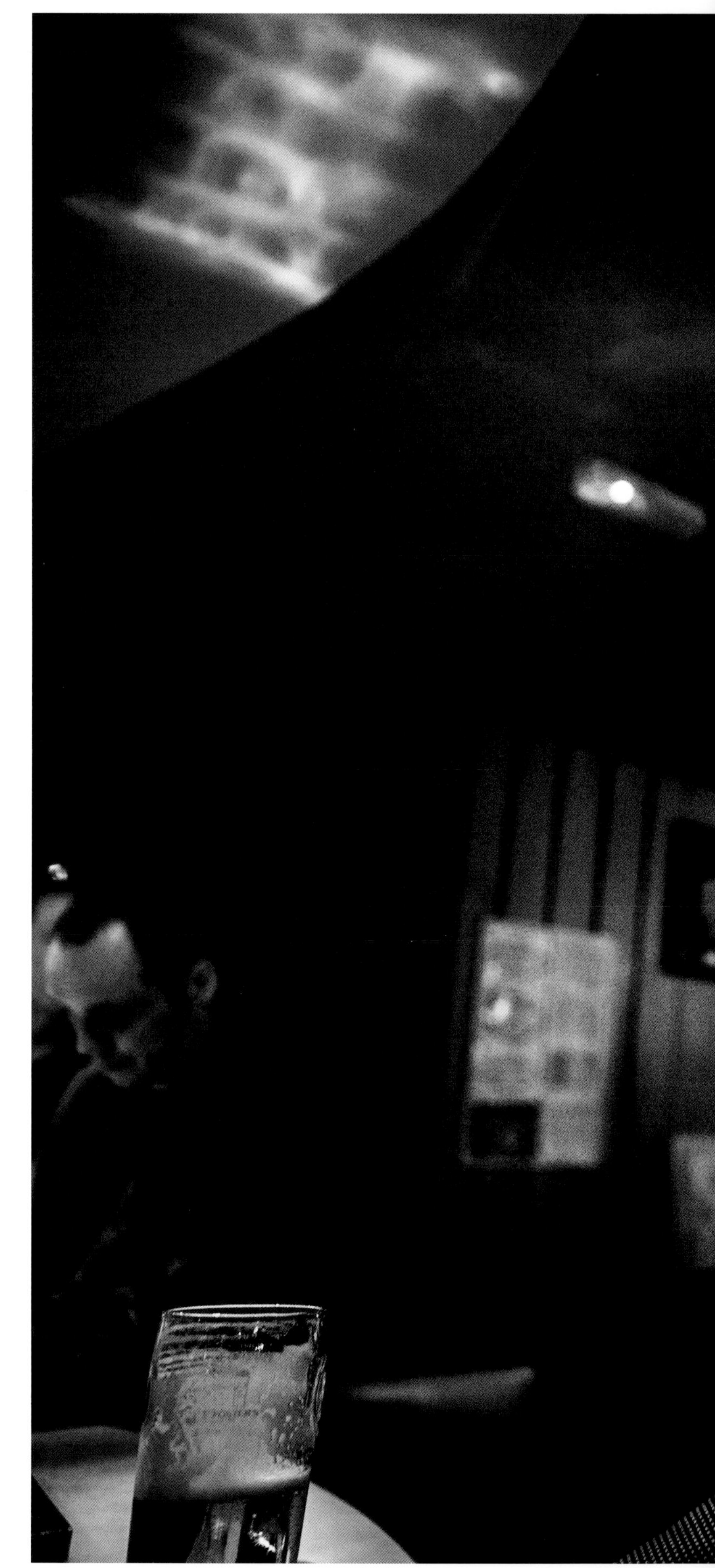

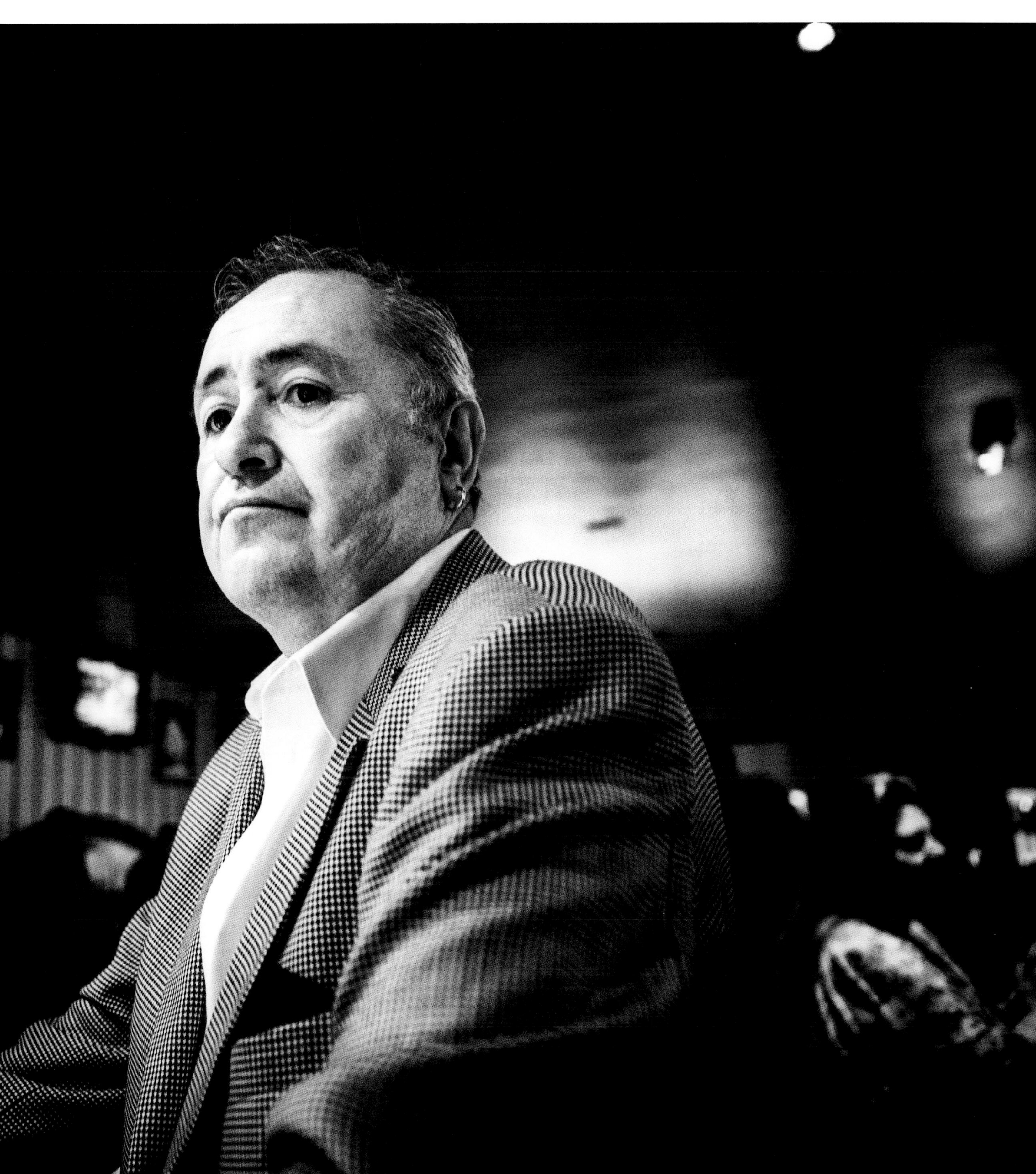

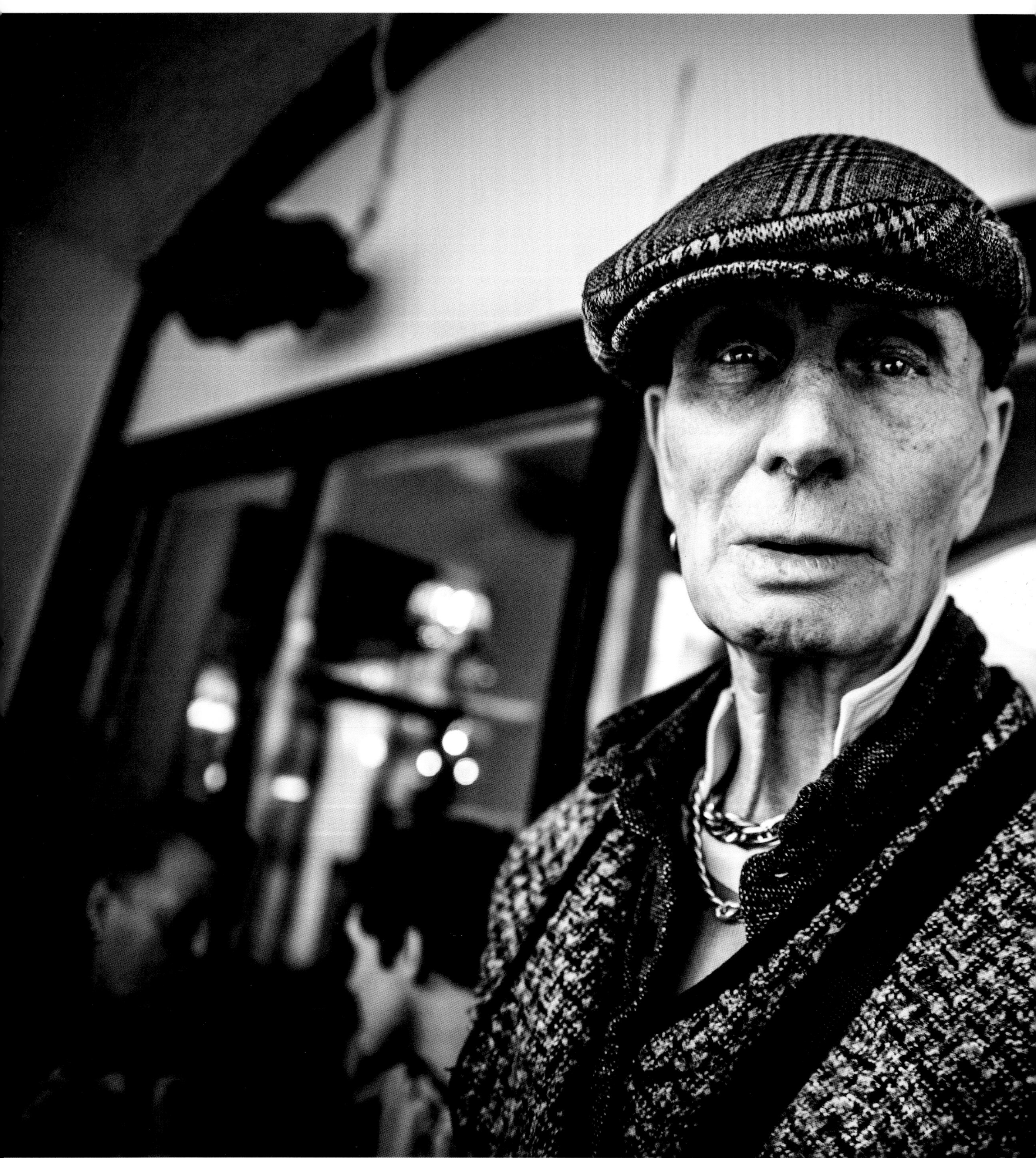

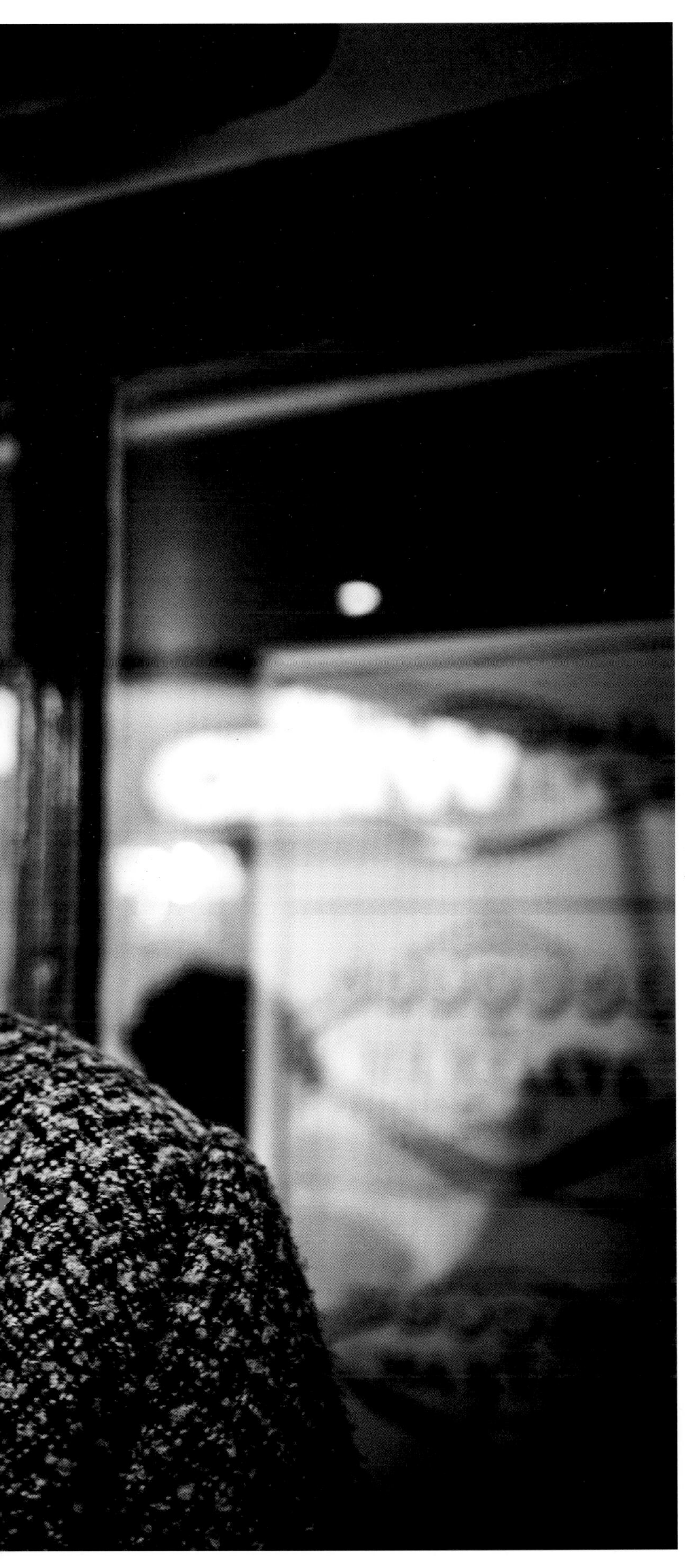

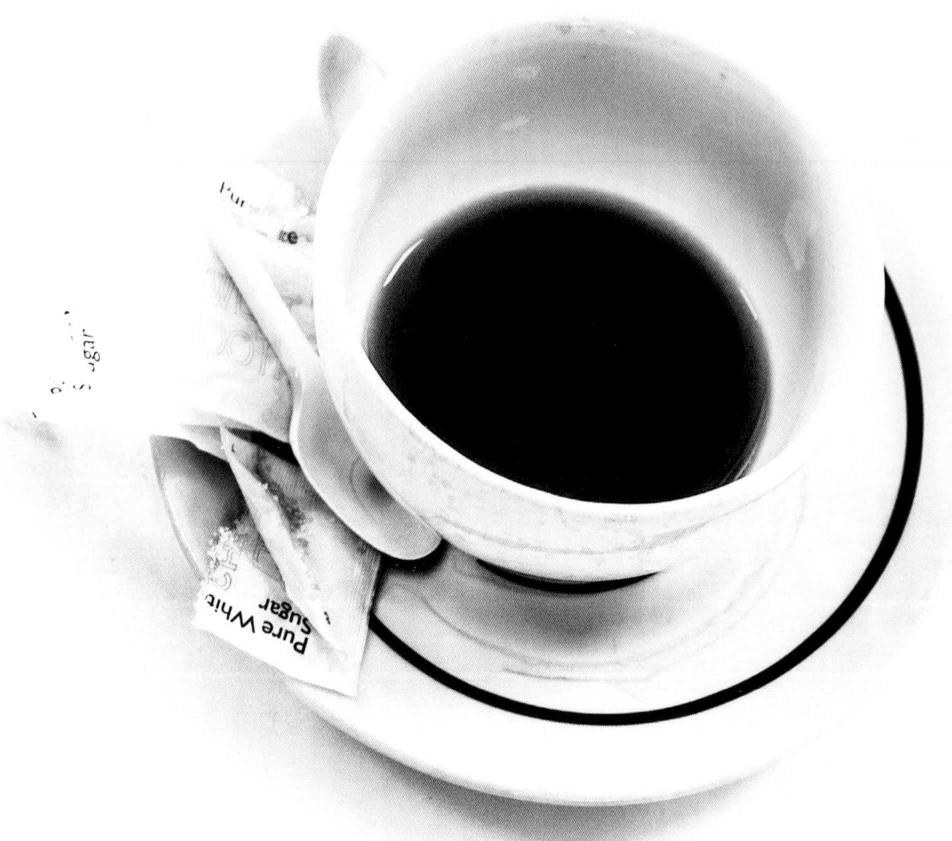
Sugar
Pure White
Sugar

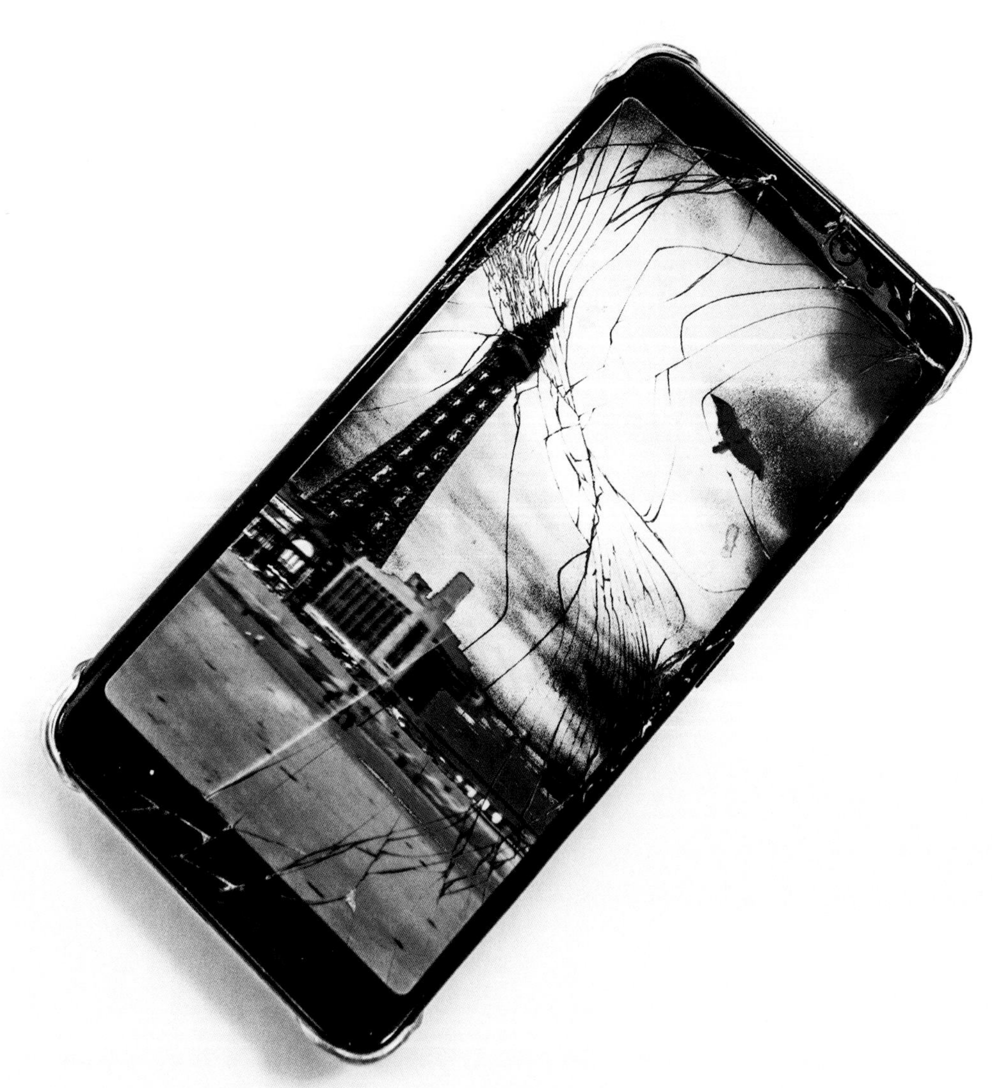

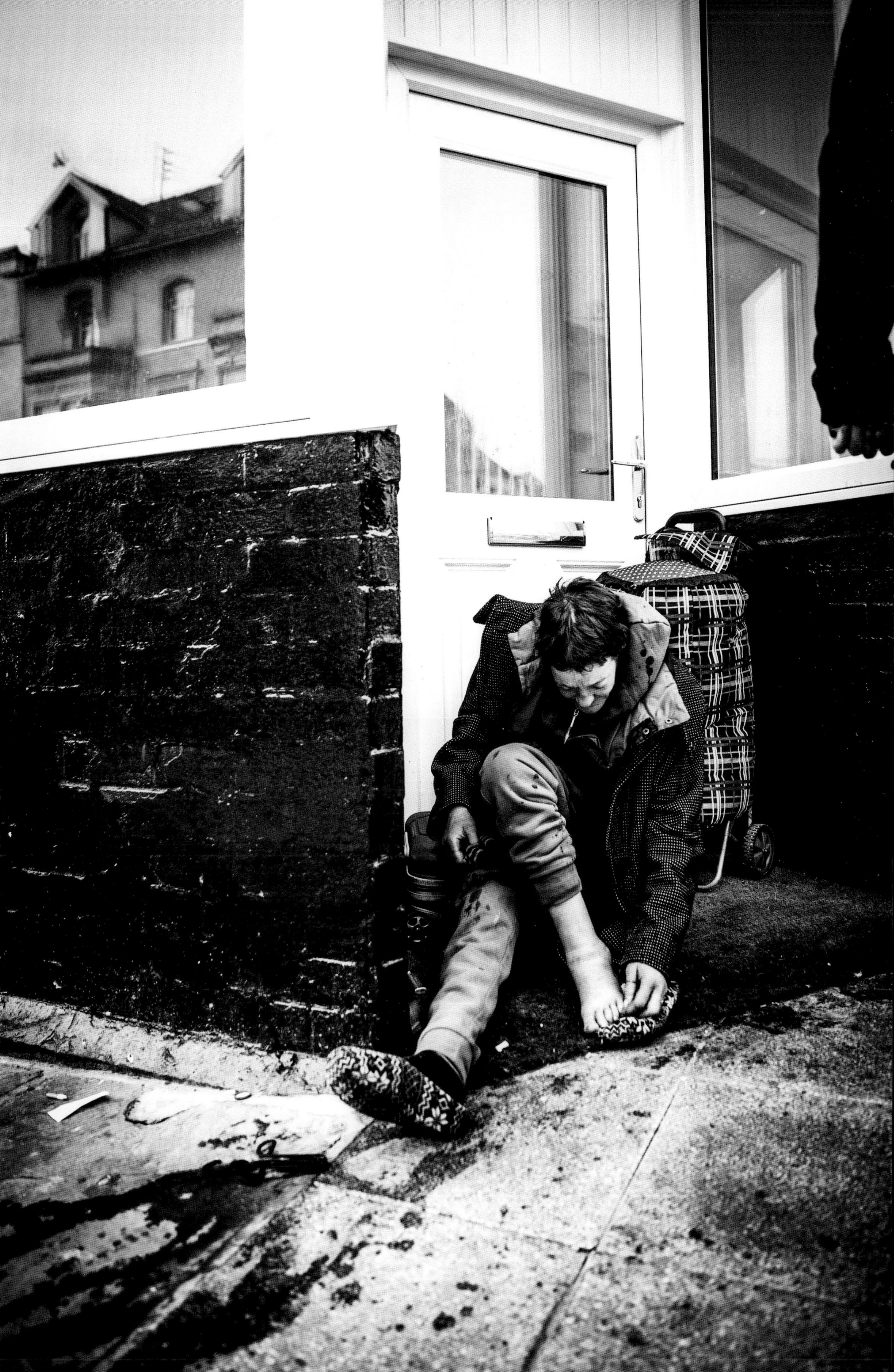

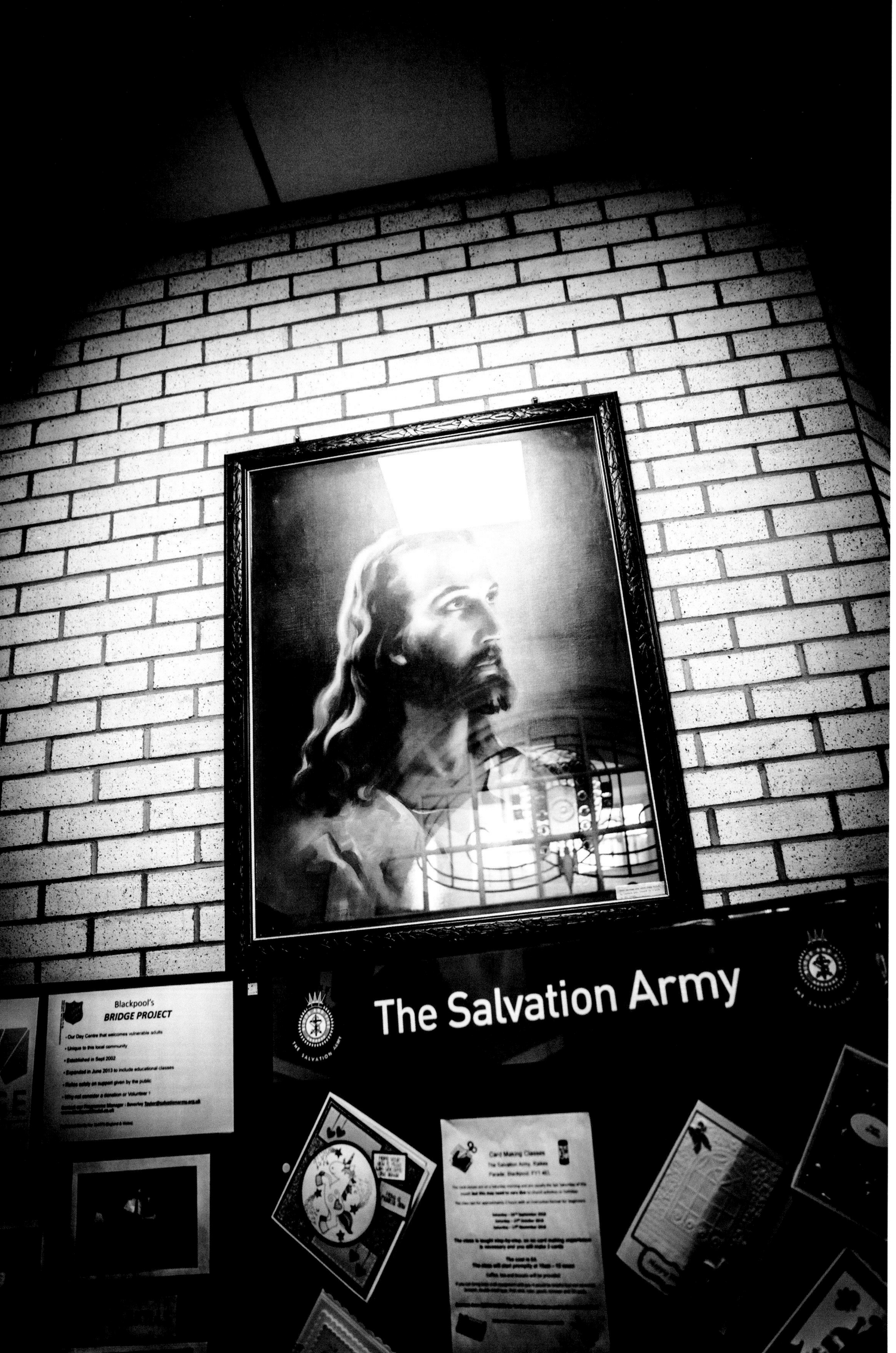

Blackpool's
BRIDGE PROJECT
The Salvation Army
Card Making Classes

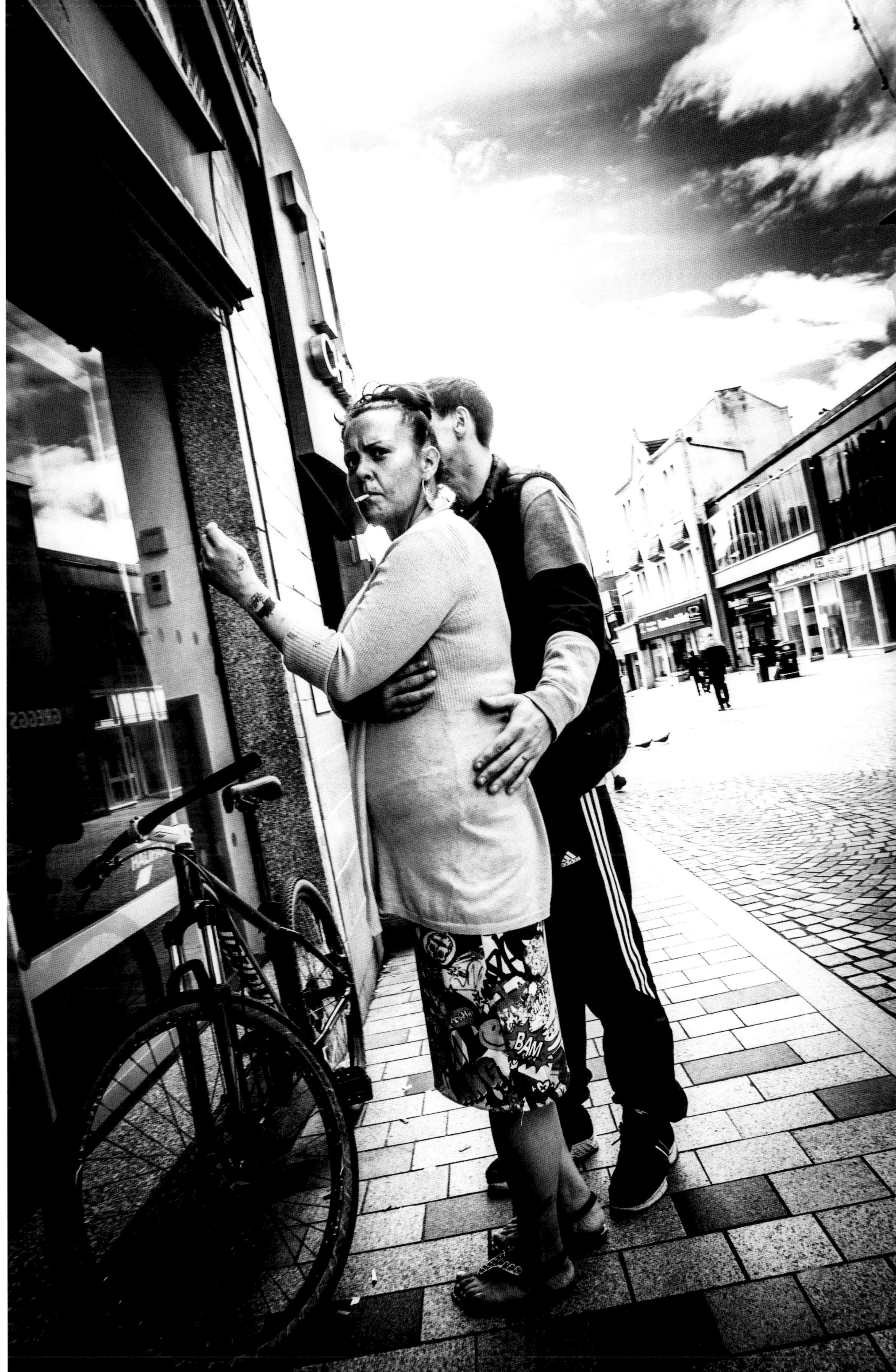

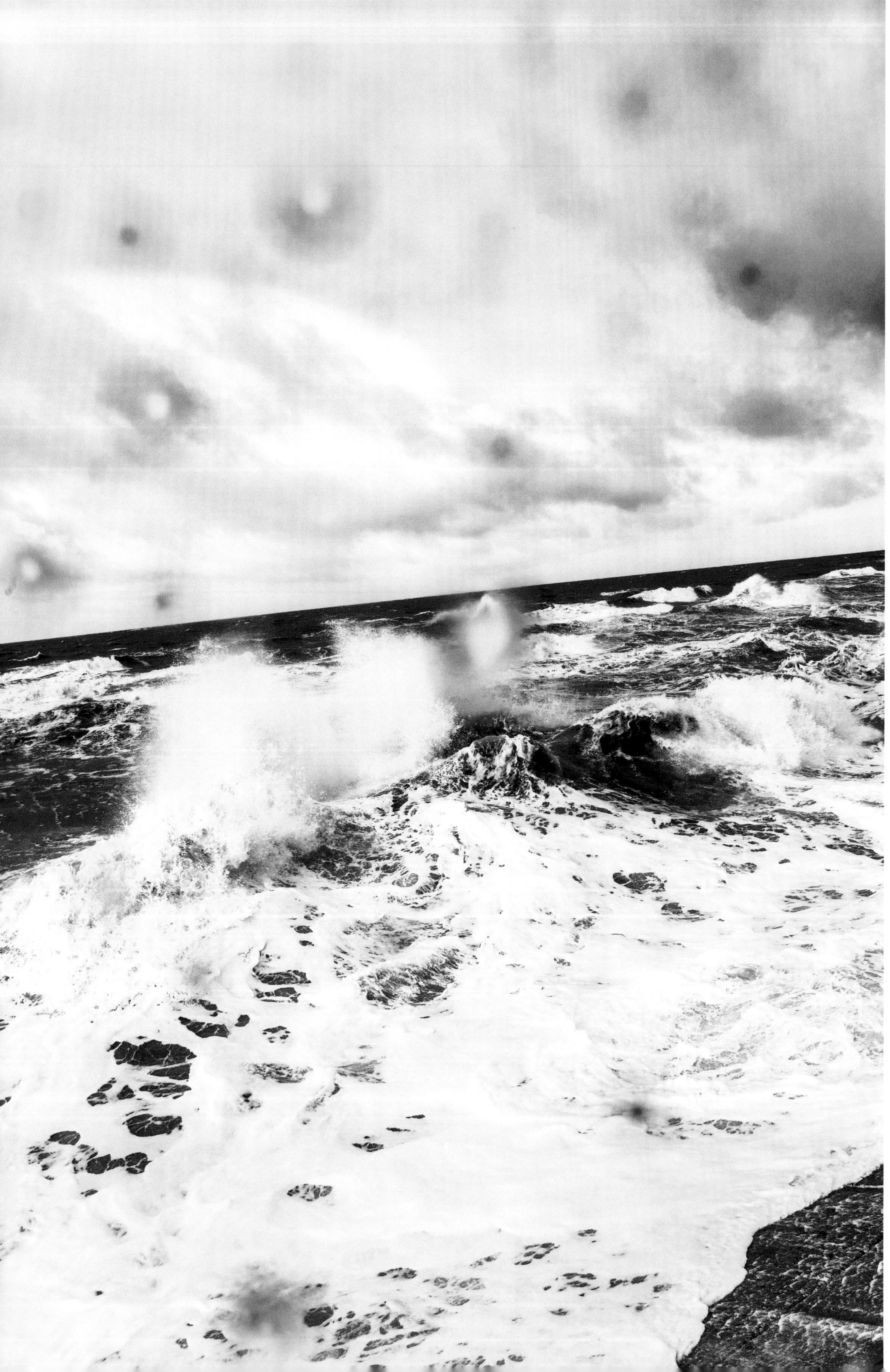

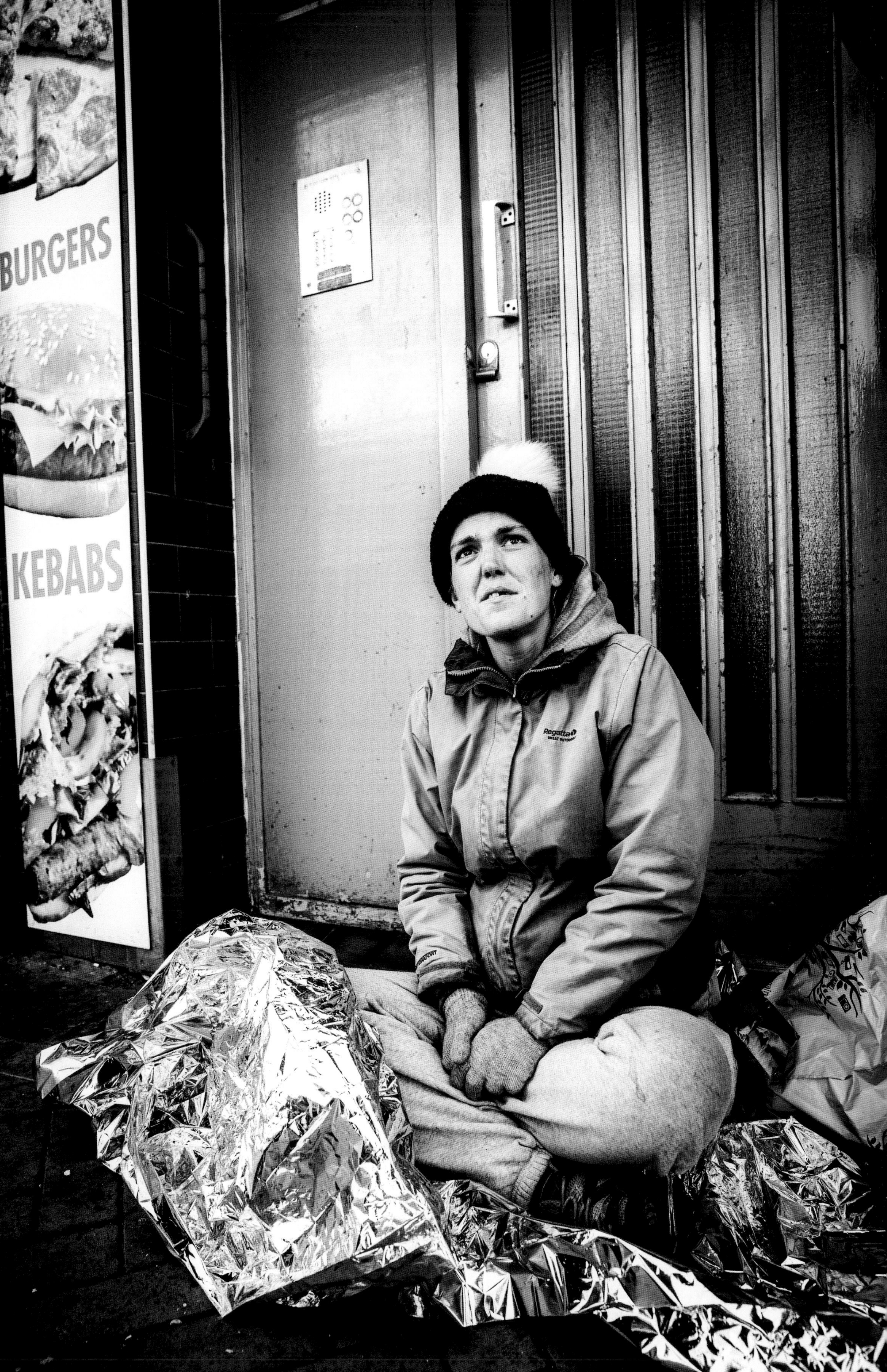

BURGERS
KEBABS
Regatta
GREAT OUTDOORS

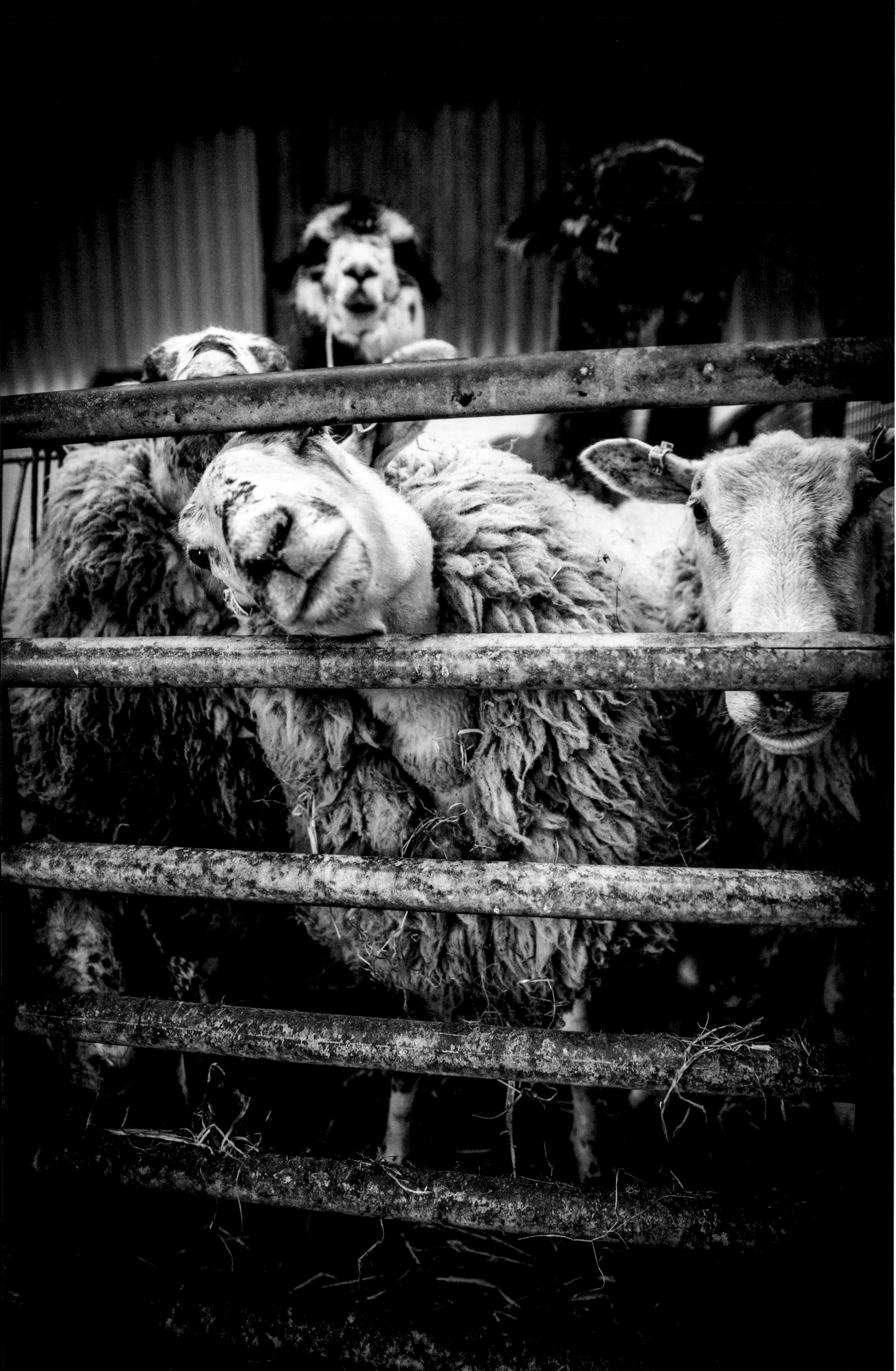

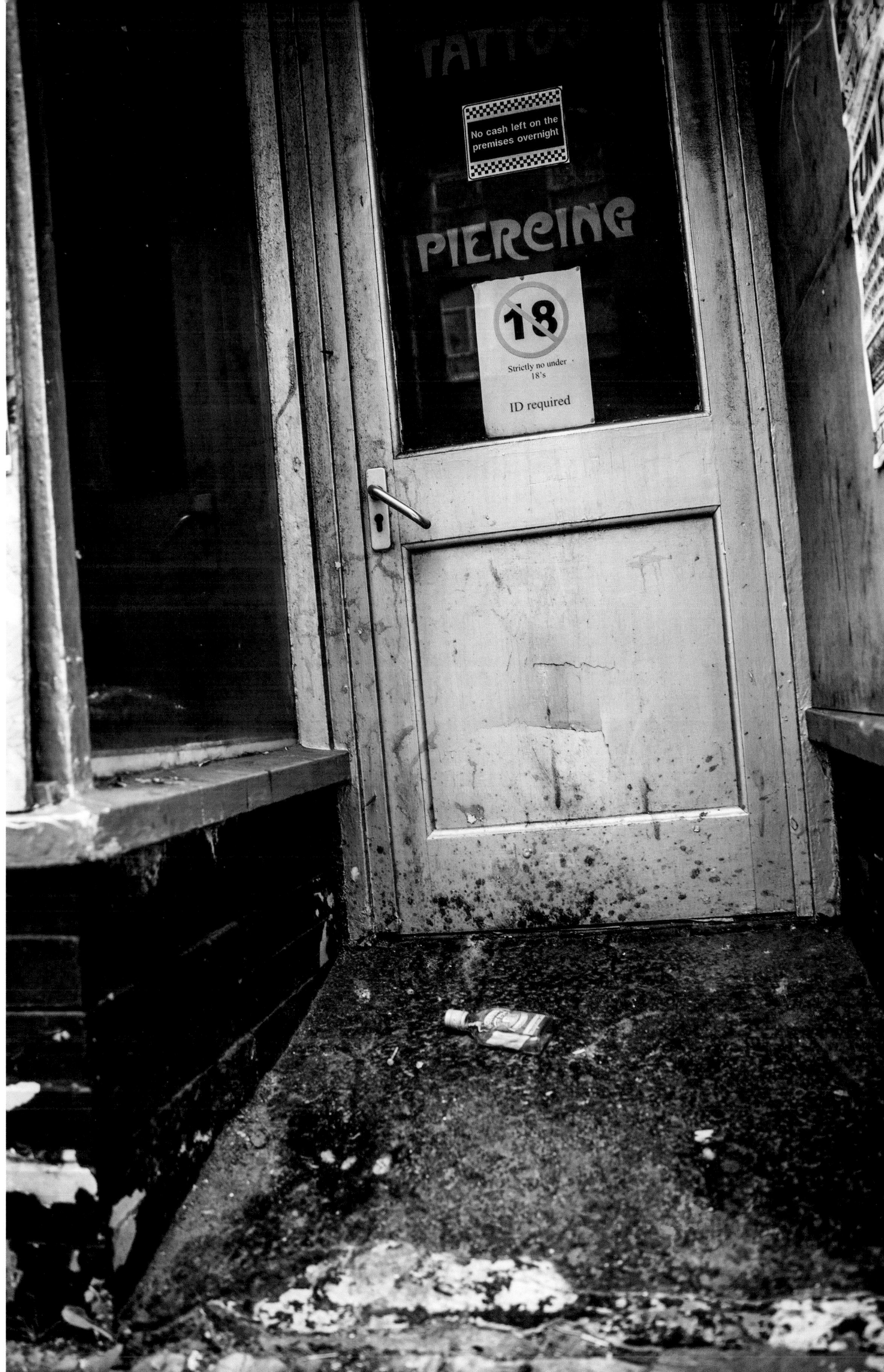
TATTOO
No cash left on the
premises overnight
PIERCING
18
Strictly no under
18's
ID required

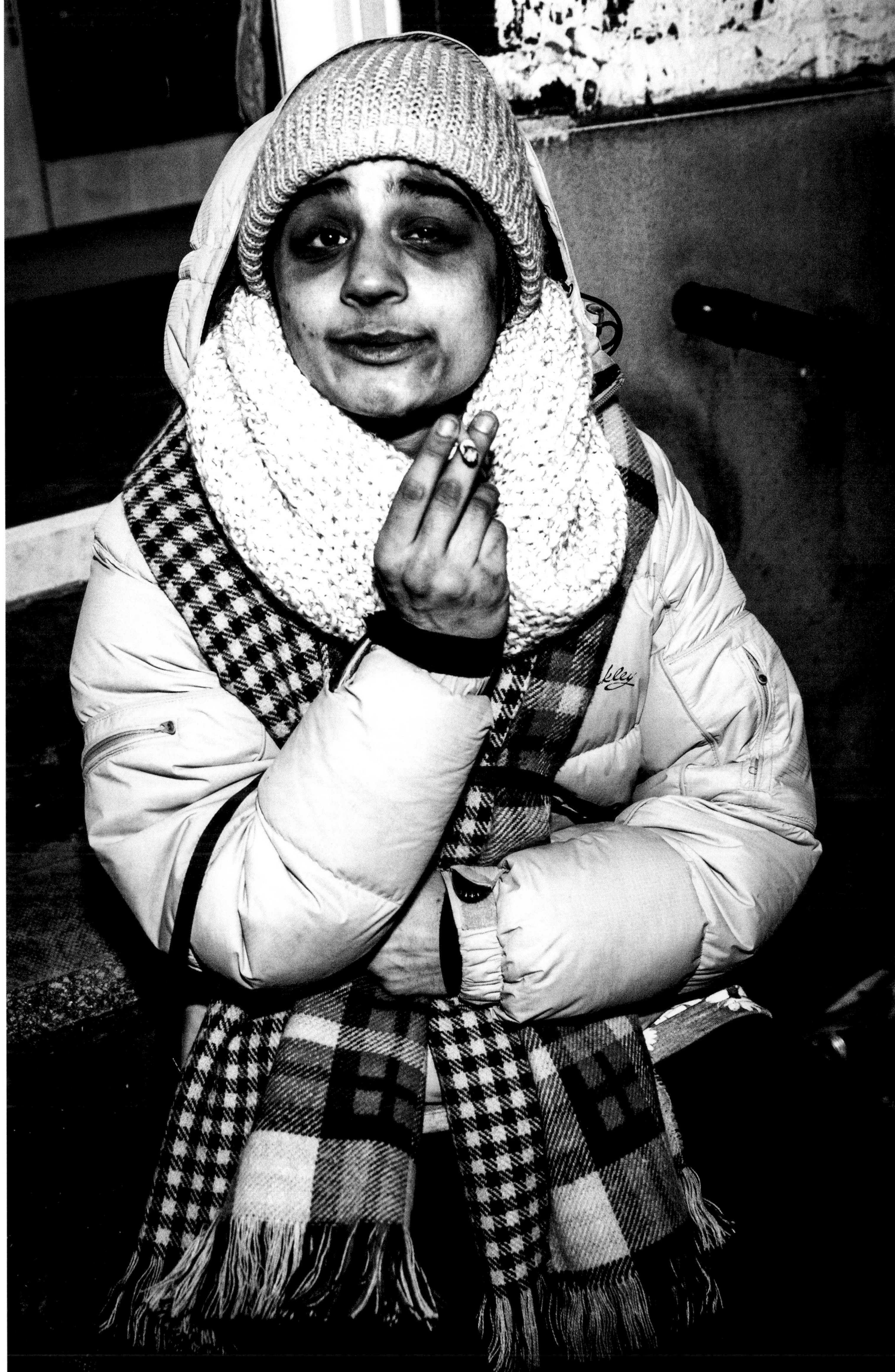

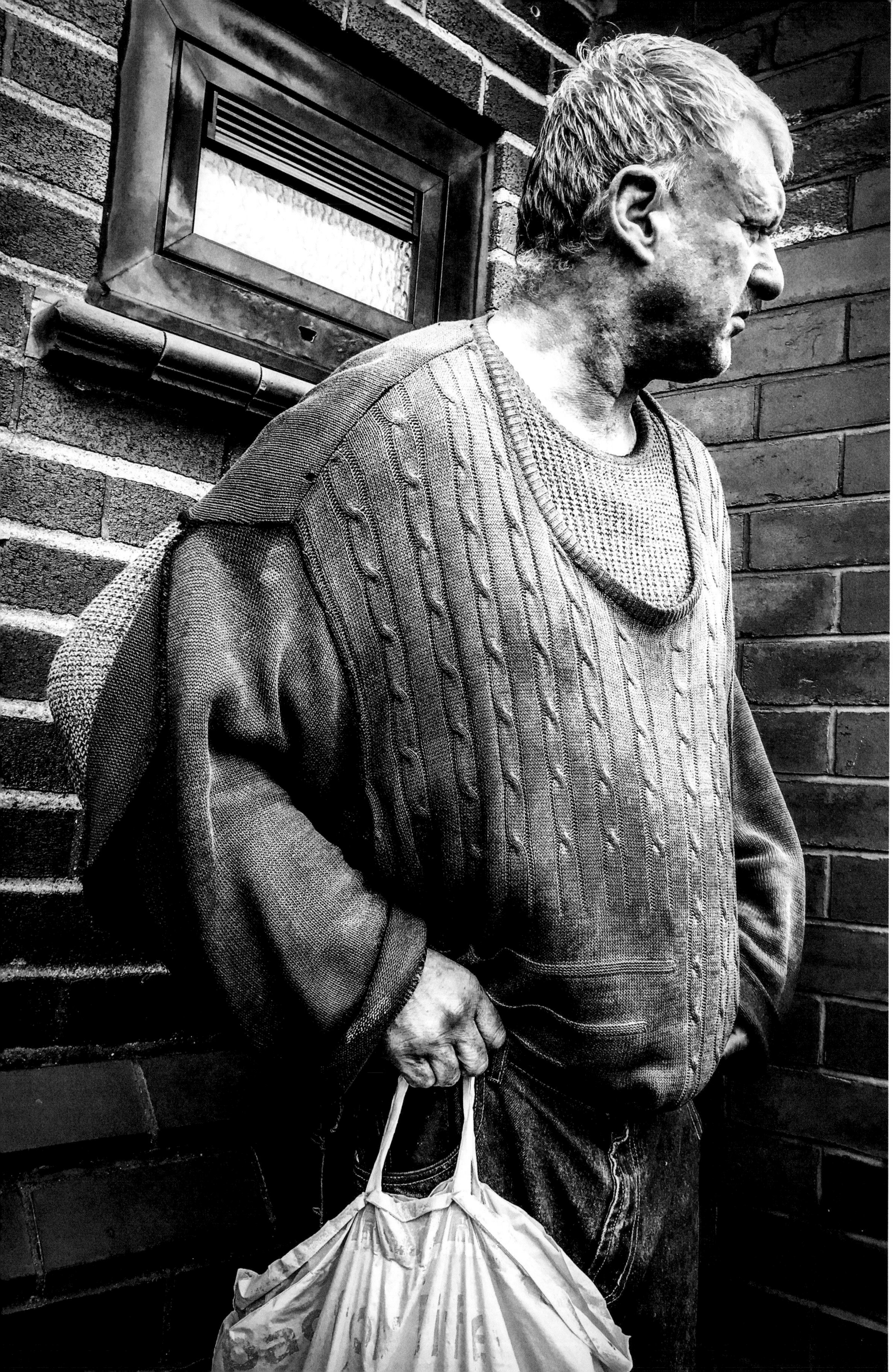

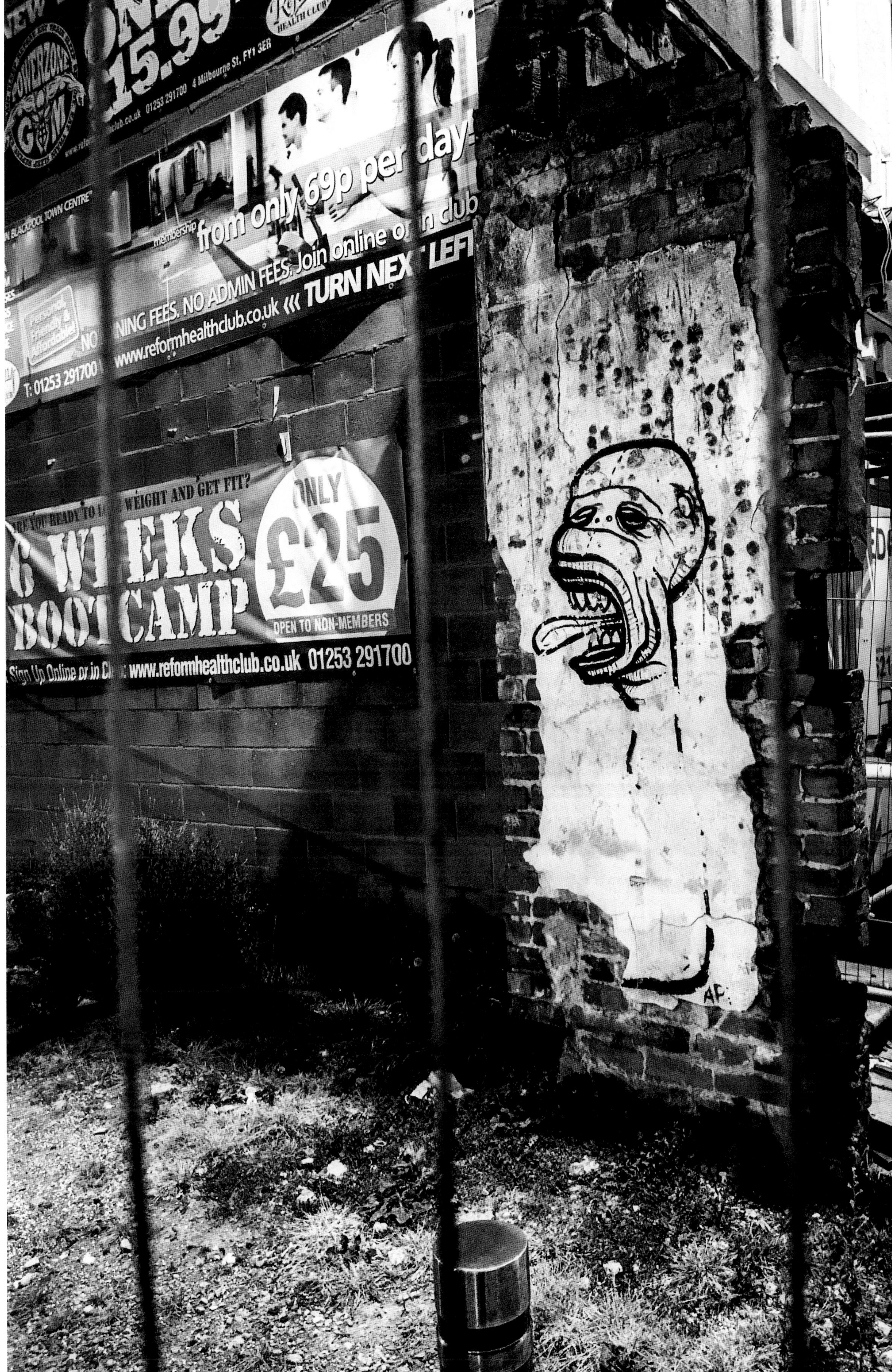
POWERZONE GYM
ONLY 15.99
Reform HEALTH CLUB
4 Milbourne St, FY1 3ER
0253 291700
.co.uk
BLACKPOOL TOWN CENTRE
membership from only 69p per day!
NO JOINING FEES. NO ADMIN FEES. Join online or in club
Personal, Friendly & Affordable!
www.reformhealthclub.co.uk <<< TURN NEXT LEFT
T: 01253 291700
ARE YOU READY TO LOSE WEIGHT AND GET FIT?
6 WEEKS BOOT CAMP
ONLY £25
OPEN TO NON-MEMBERS
Sign Up Online or in Club www.reformhealthclub.co.uk 01253 291700

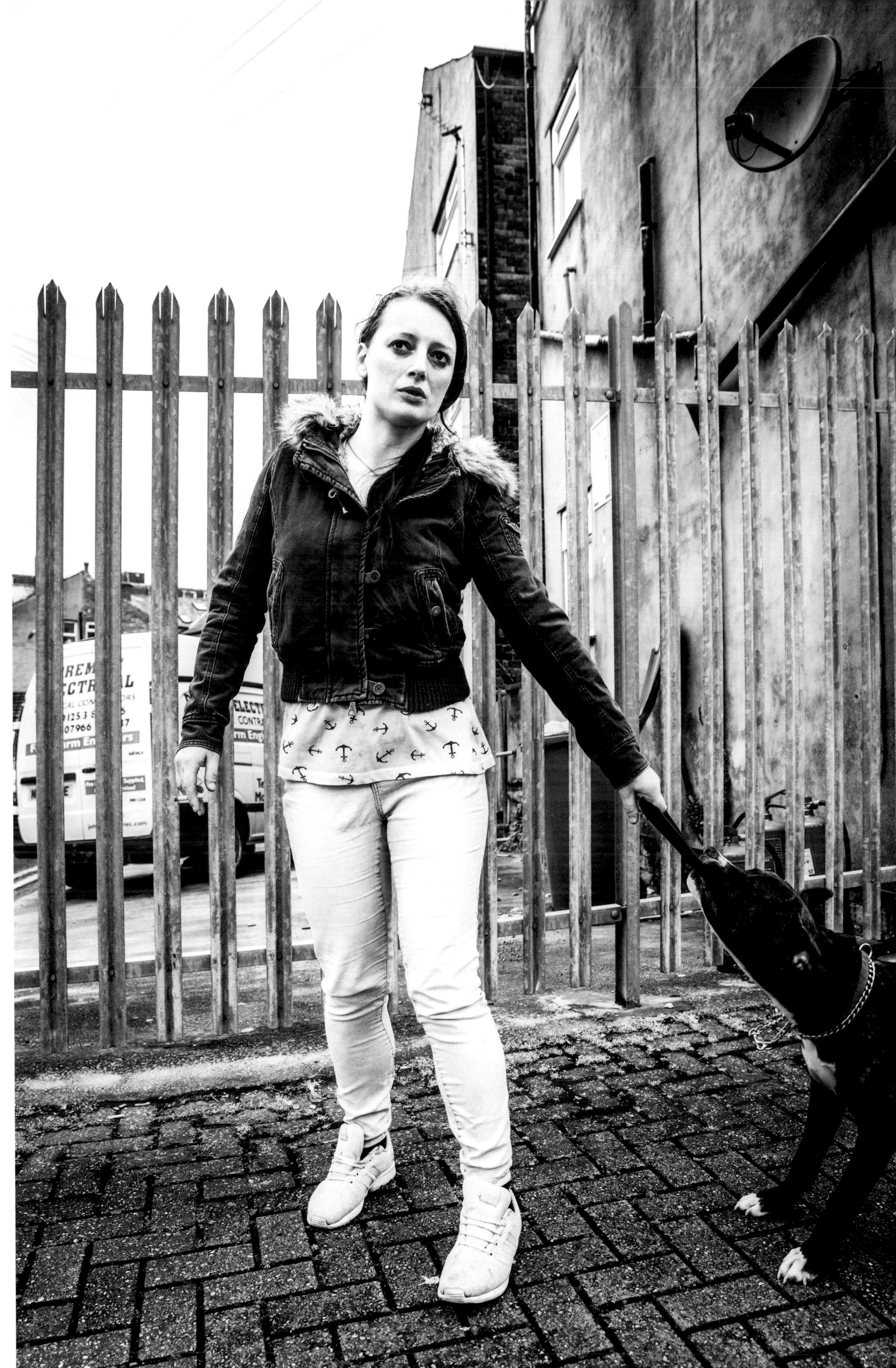

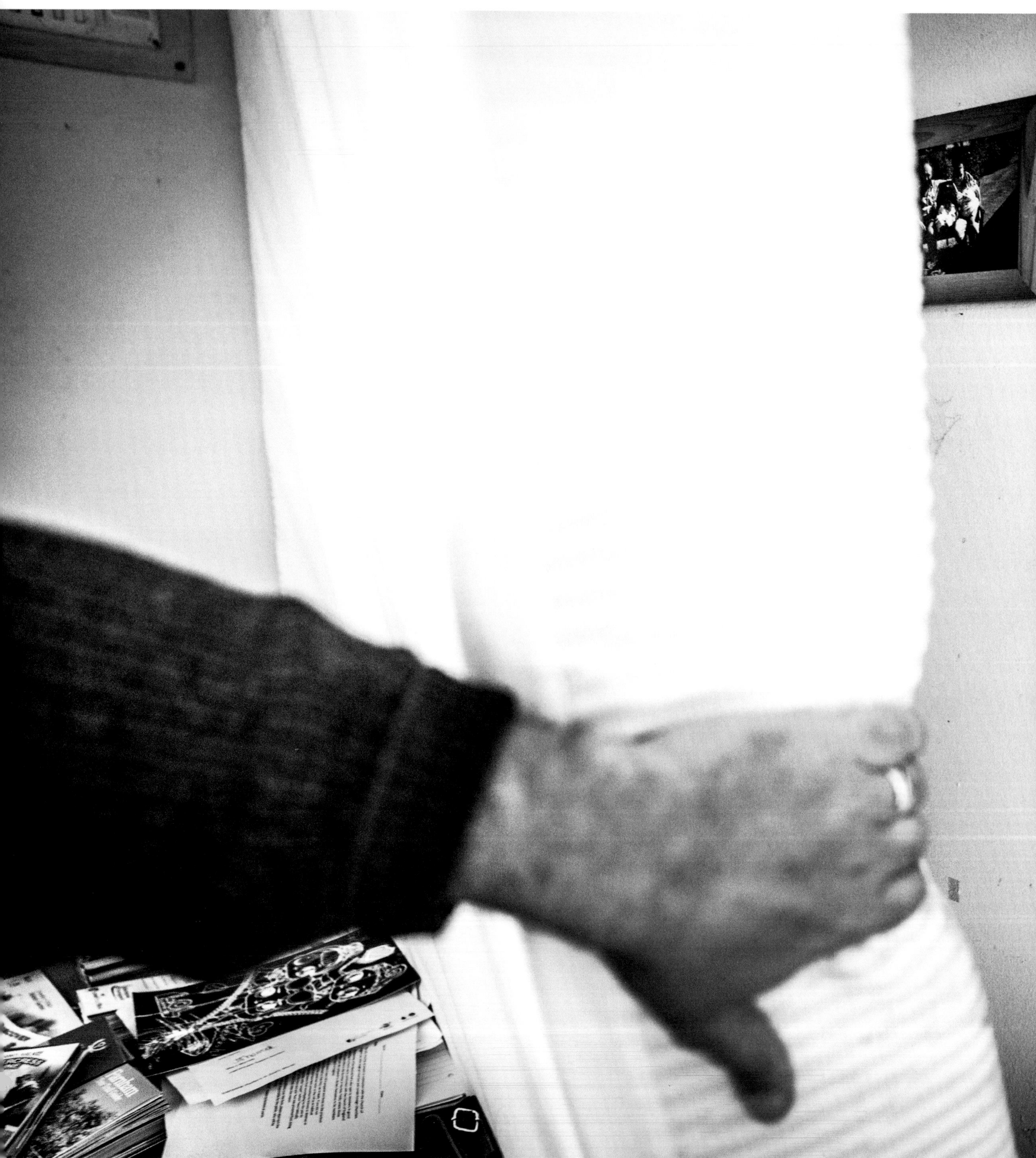

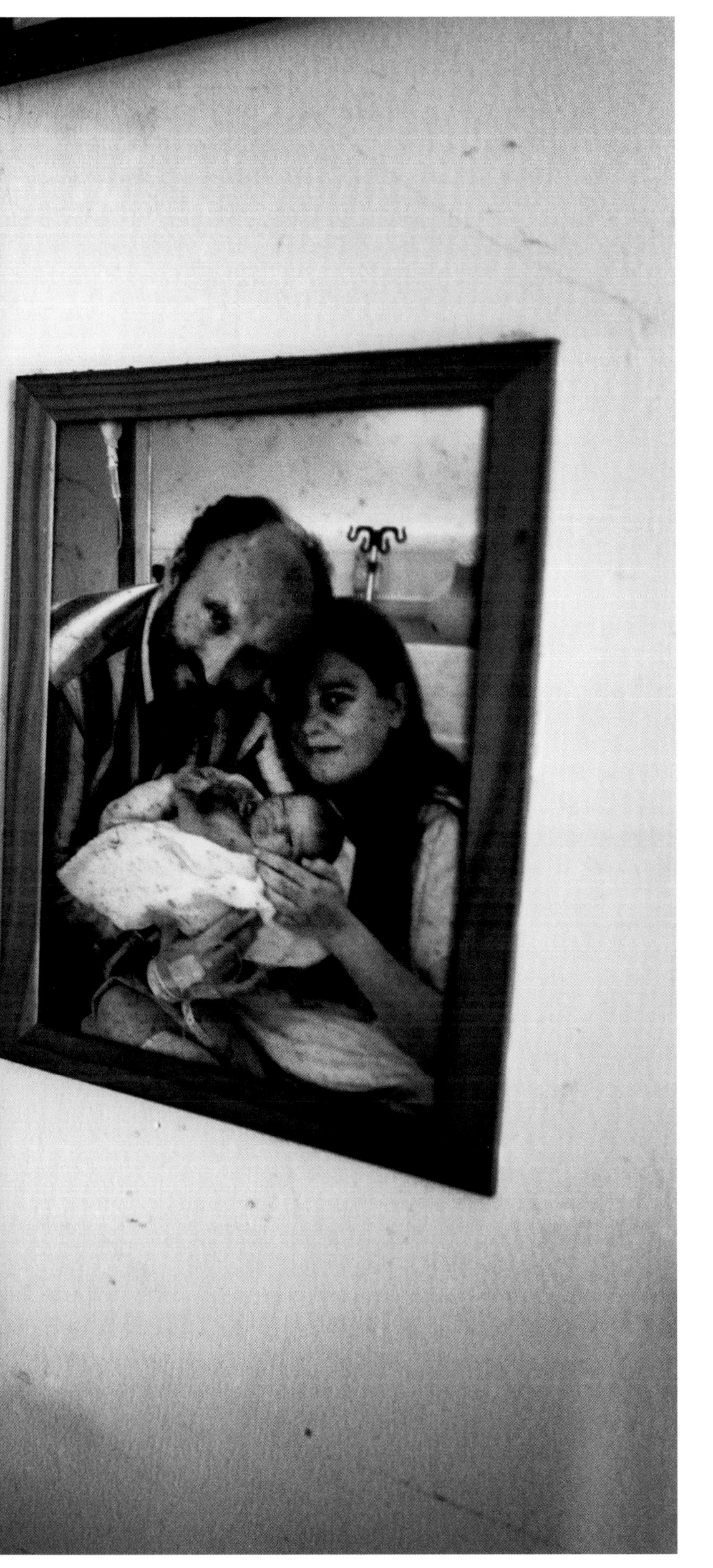

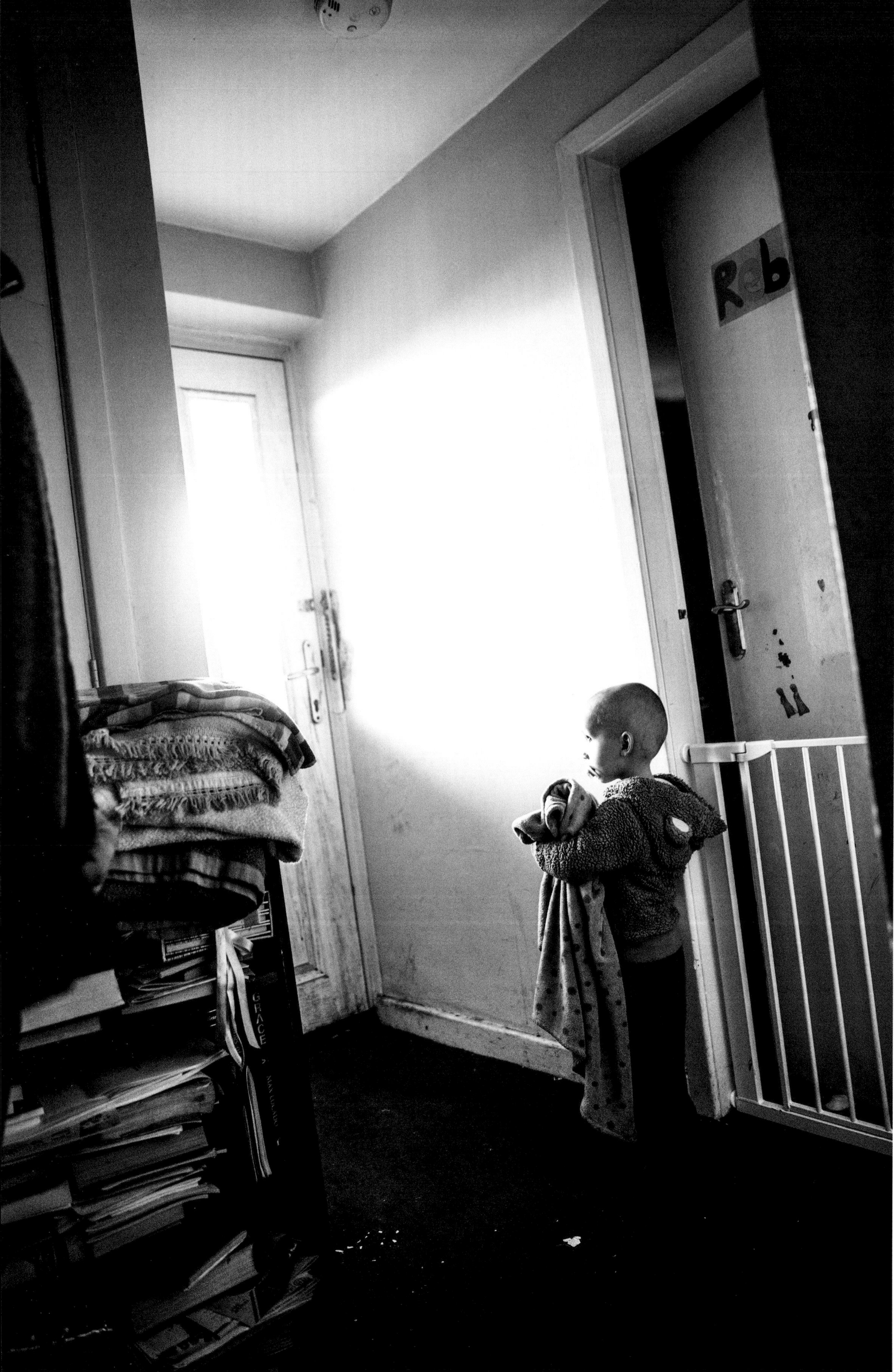

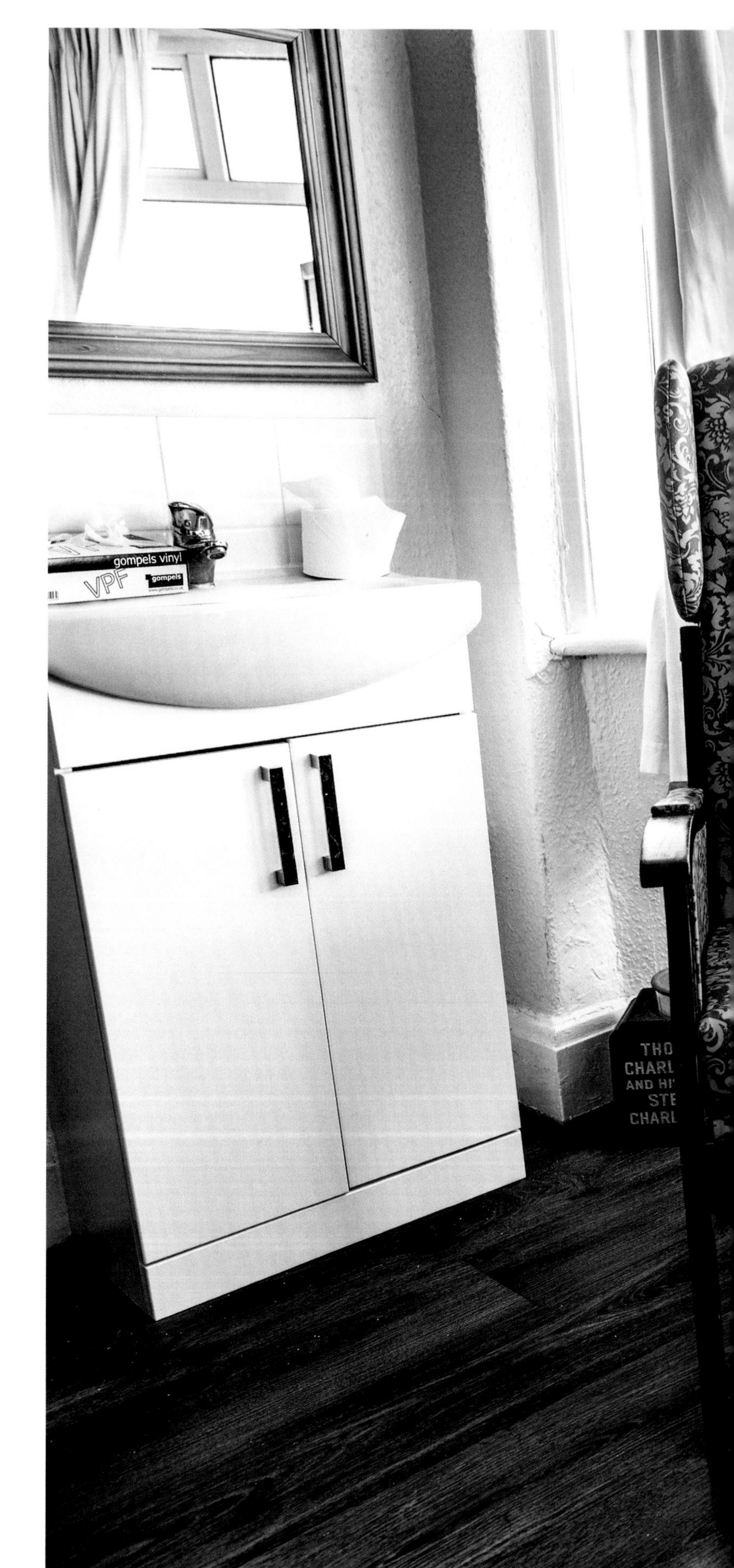
gompels vinyl
VPF
gompels
THO
CHARL
AND H
STE
CHARL

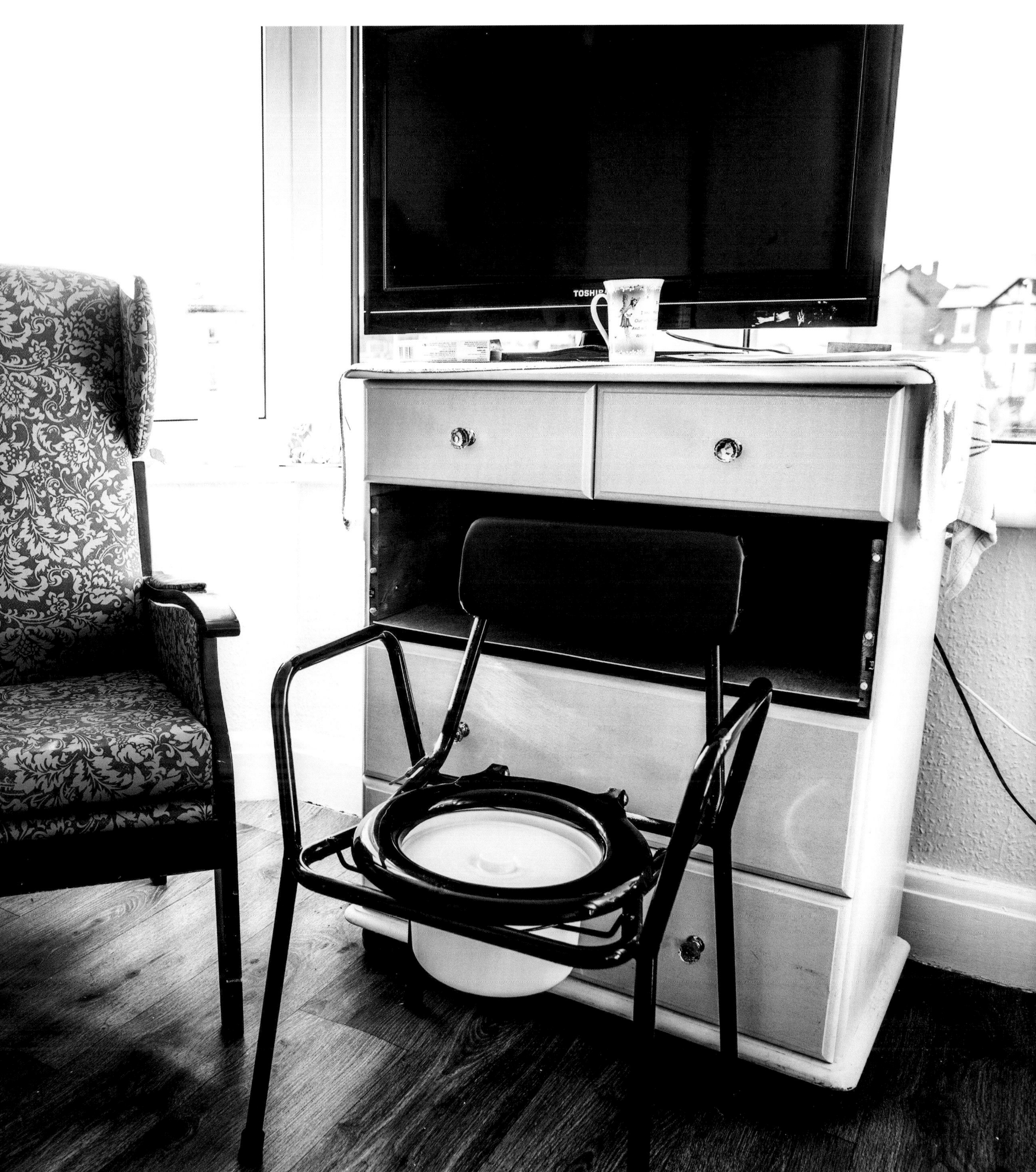

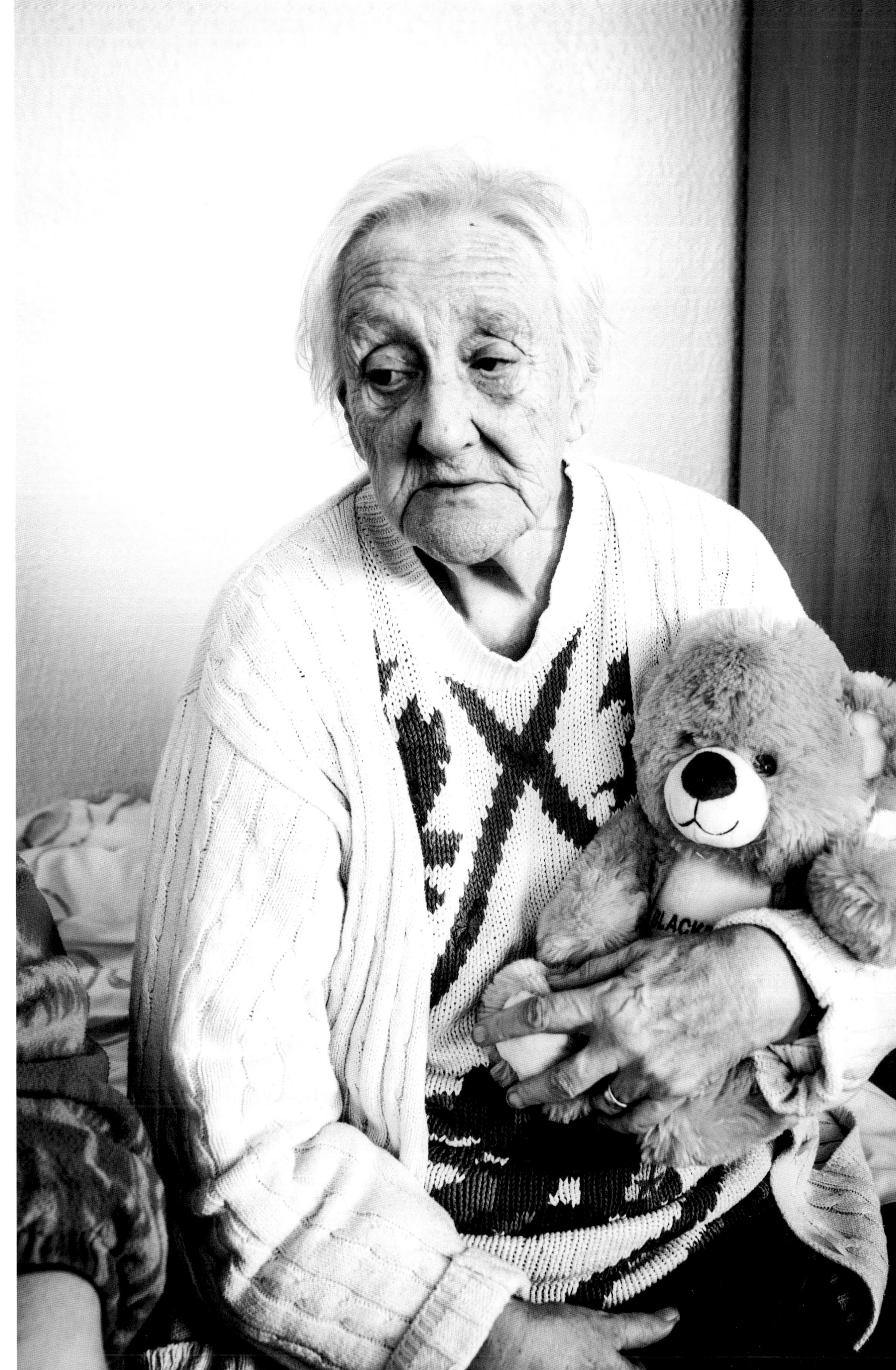

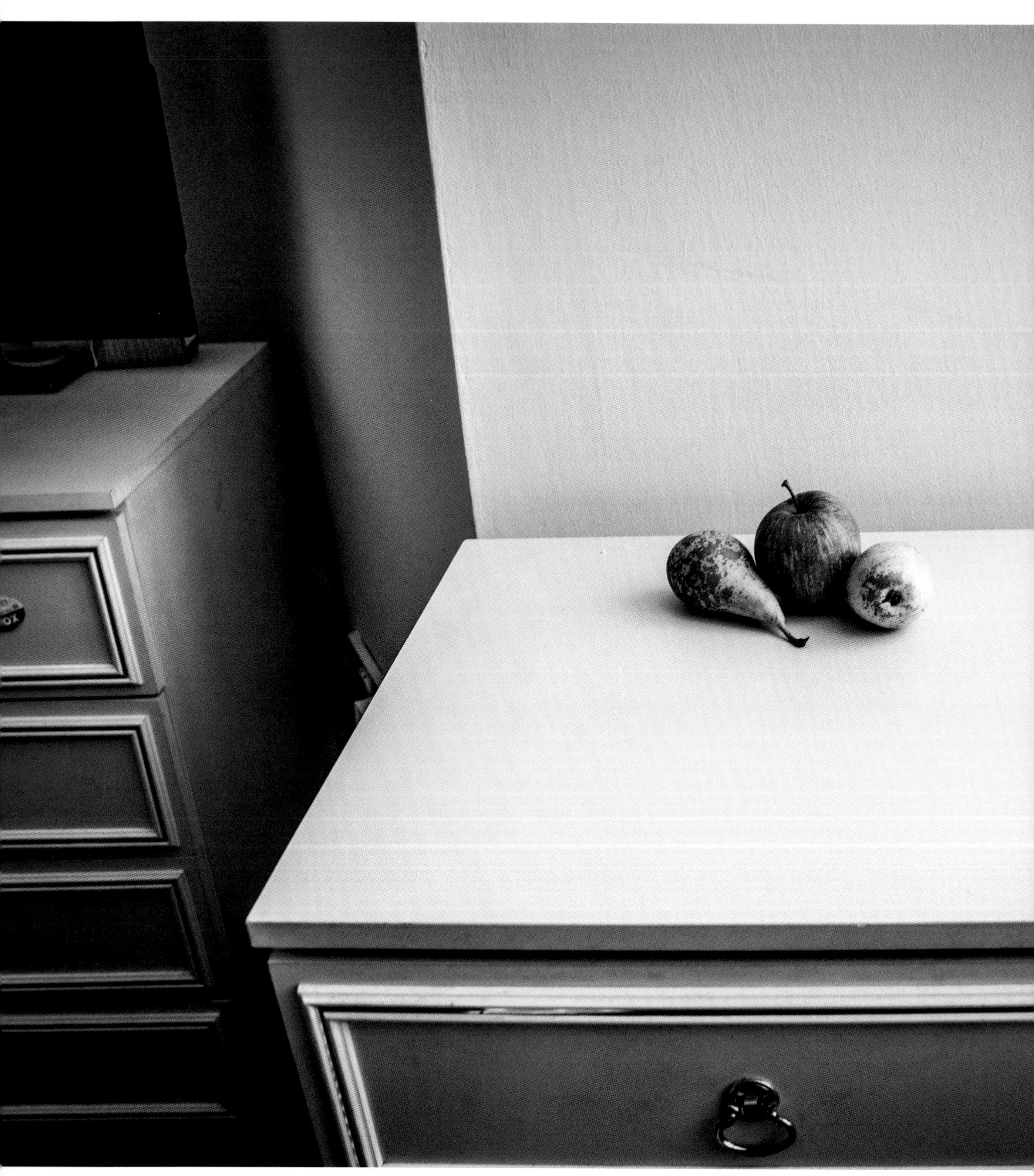

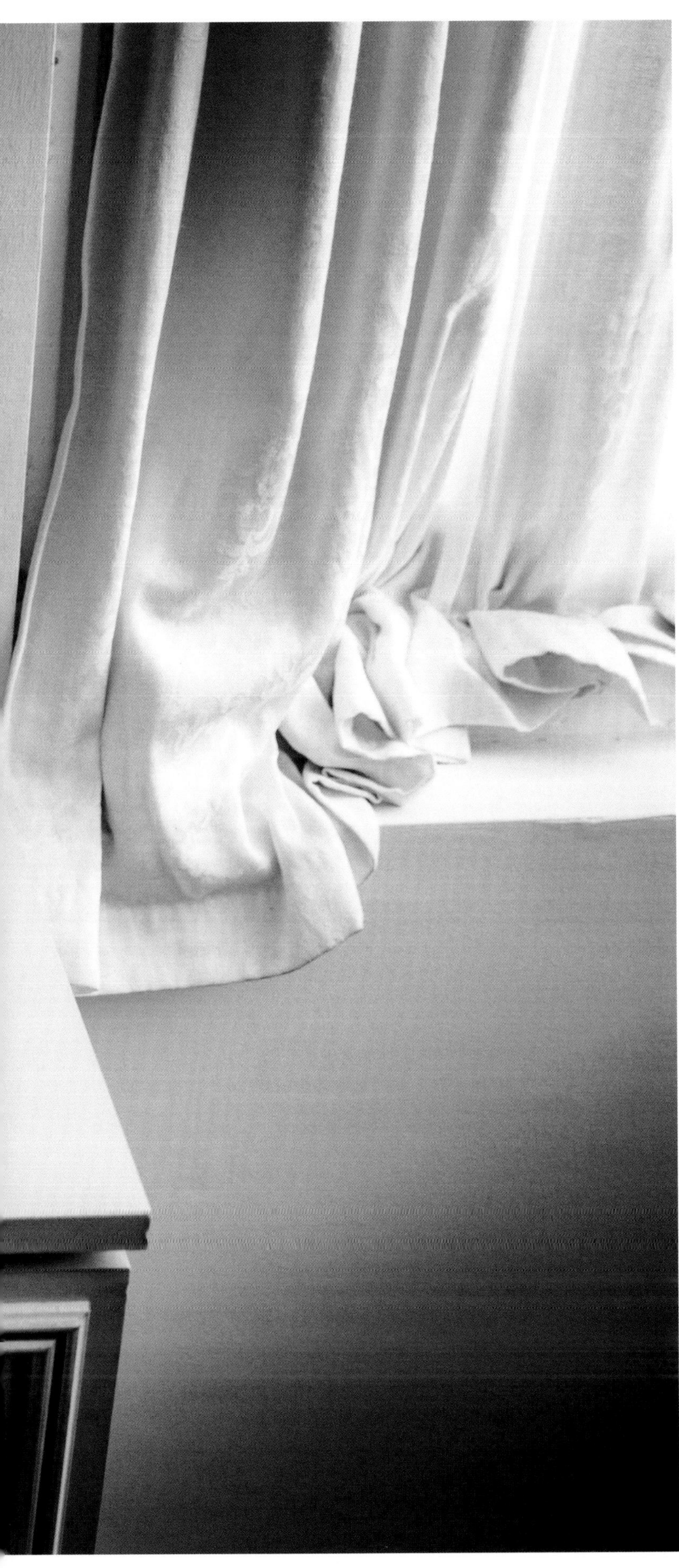

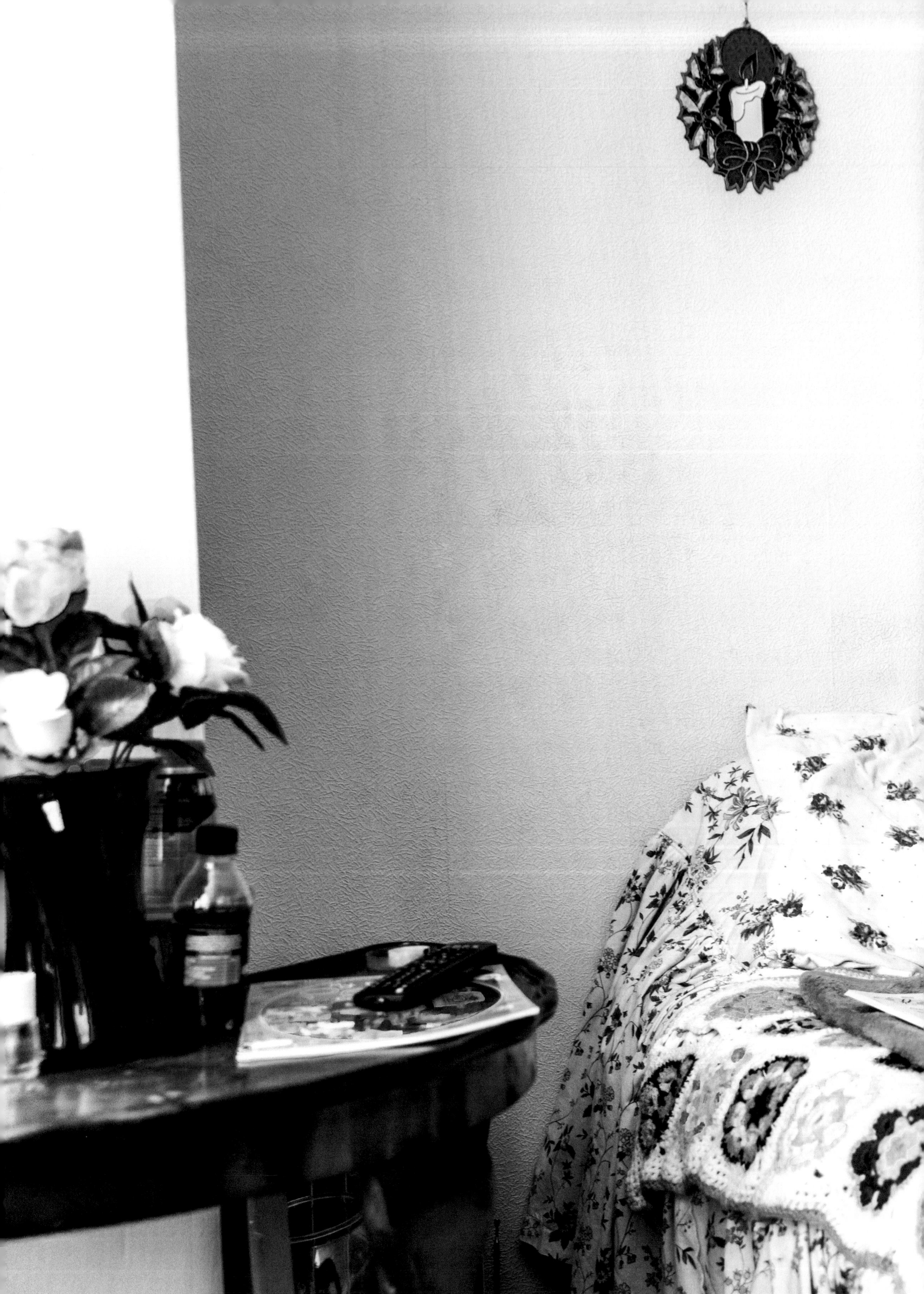

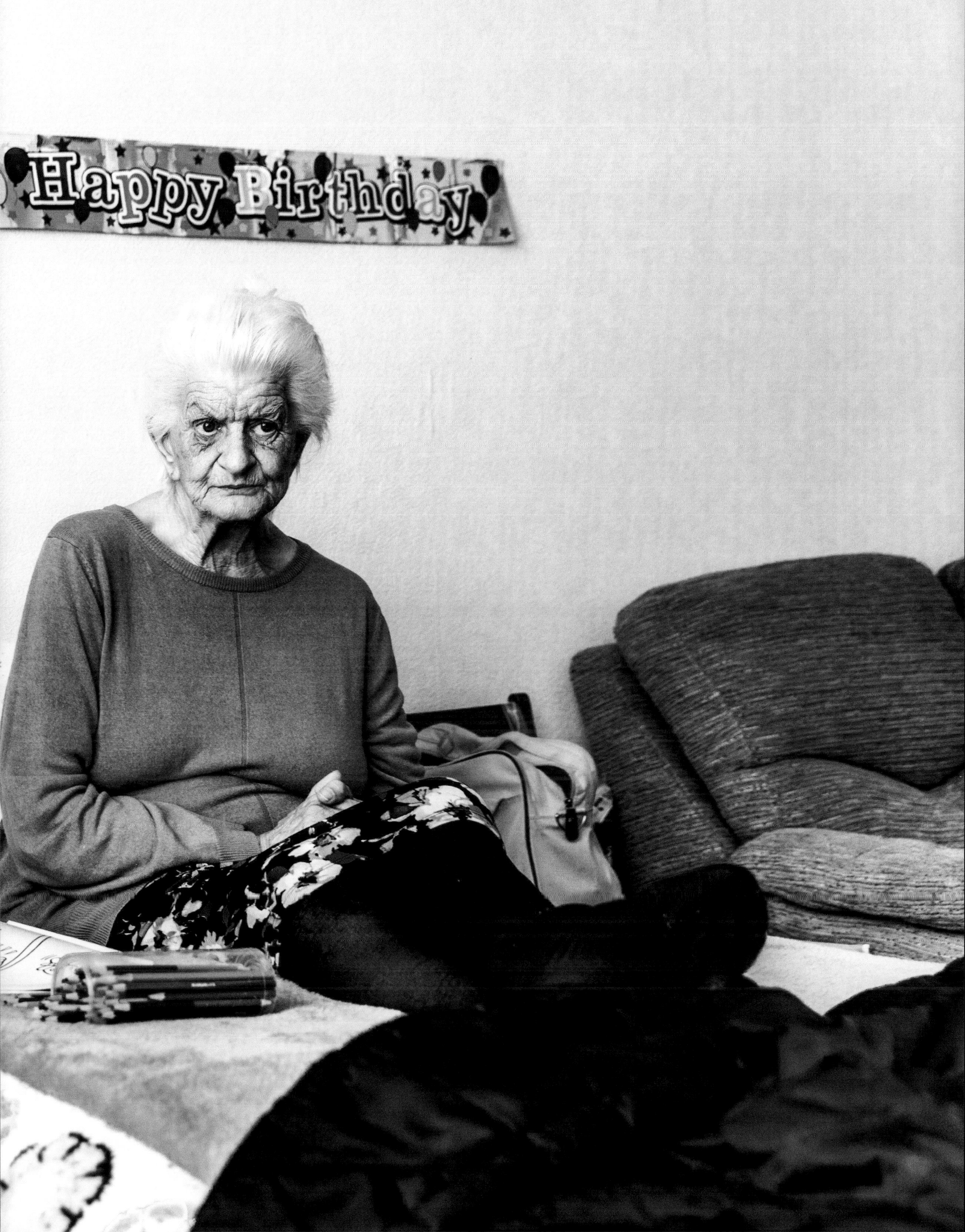

Happy Birthday

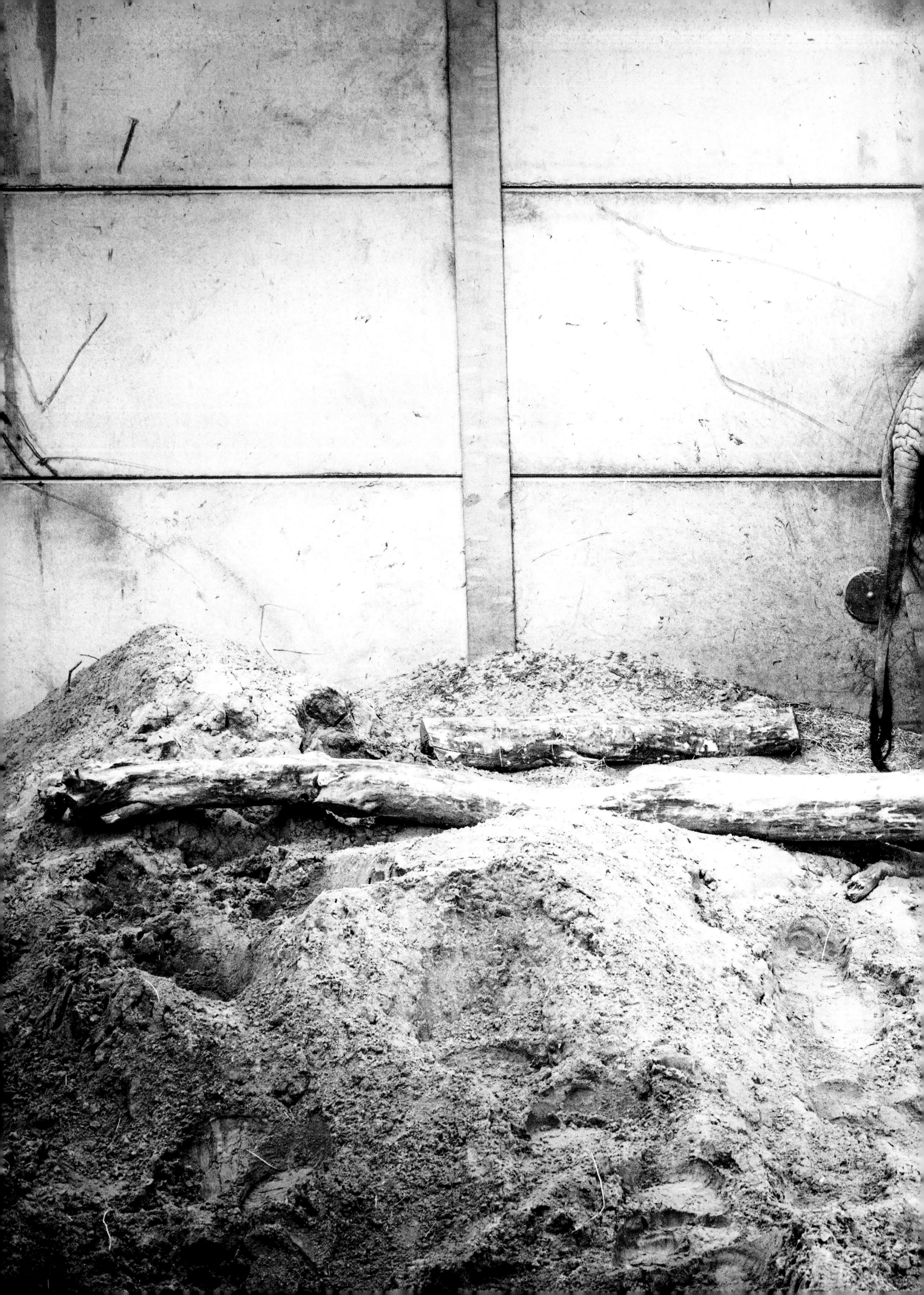

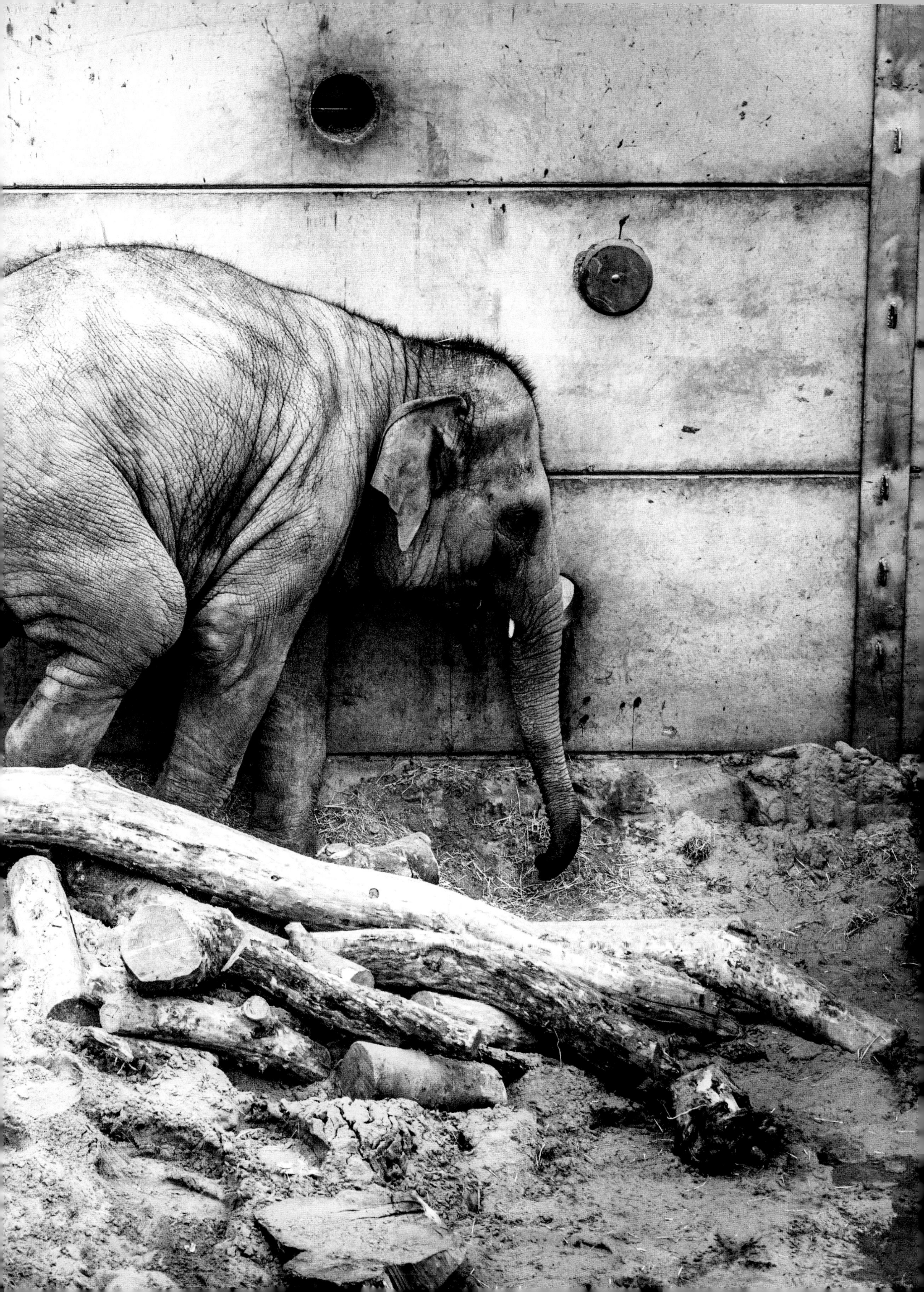

Benita Suchodrev
Photographer / Fotografin

Of Lions and Lambs

In early January 2019, I received an email from a man I had never met, a fan of my work who had just purchased a copy of my book, *48 Hours Blackpool*. He claimed to have stumbled upon an old newspaper article about this coastal town and thought that given my interest in the subject I might like to read it. Apologetically he explained that the scanner in his flat was out of order, which was why he resorted to the 'old-fashioned' means of photographing the individual paragraphs and sending them as sequenced attachments. Surprised and moved by the thoughtful gesture, I read the twelve paragraphs in one breath on that late afternoon and, as the sun set on that evening, it dawned on me that my story about Blackpool, contrary to what I believed, was far from over. One might ask at this point what was so special about that article that had led me to this conclusion and inspired my subsequent trip to Blackpool in a few weeks' time to resume my documentation. Though well written, the article offered but a few brief accounts by local residents confirming Blackpool's reputation as the most deprived English seaside town. And yet it was this article that compelled me to take a closer look at the silhouettes cowering in the doorways of rundown houses, at the men and women whose voices are stifled by the clatter of slot machines and the bustle of tourists on the promenade during high season; the noises that I was also deafened by on my first brief visit two years earlier. During the off-season, when the promenade is deserted and the town falls silent, there is no one around to hear these voices, and the pictures that shine so bright and full of contrast in the high summer sun fall flat and grow dull beneath the overcast sky.

When I returned to Blackpool in February, I found a cold and dreary town with empty shops, locked piers and new tram rails under construction blocking the streets. Murmuring flocks of starlings circled above the raging sea and solitary seagulls fought over breadcrumbs near the shops surrounding the town centre. I had to gasp; there was nobody to photograph. But I was already there and by choice. I surrendered myself to fate. There was a church in the town square that I remembered from my last visit. I shot one of my favourite photographs near that church and thought the town square might be a good starting point and a good spot to feed the last remains of my tuna sandwich to the seagulls. That's where I met Alan, aka 'the birdman', who resembled a fairy-tale character with his bushy hair, funny ears and skinny stature. Kind-hearted, principled and impoverished, Alan travelled every day into town with his broken trolley in tow to spend his last pounds on birdseed. He did not like feeding the seagulls because they were cruel to their young and instead fed the pigeons that the locals referred to as 'vermin'. Since feeding birds is forbidden by the city council, he also paid his share of fines. Casually disgruntled, smoking his electronic cigarette, he kept going on and on about the faults of the town and the whole country and offered to show me the heated indoor market where I made an attempt to buy him a cup of coffee, which he sovereignly refused, claiming that he did not accept charity. So I bought some bread rolls for his birds. Our paths were to cross frequently in the coming days. But in the meantime we parted and I headed to the church where I hoped to meet someone who might point me in the right direction. That's where I bumped into a stout, biblical-looking man with anti-establishment views and an easy-going, no-questions-asked attitude who handed me a list of all the soup kitchens in town and invited me to Sunday service where I met a young girl, a struggling drug addict in whose company I visited my first soup kitchen. The plot thickened with each day. I soon found myself in a retirement home eating bananas with a lovely old lady I remembered from my previous visit, a time when she could still walk; then met colourful locals at a community centre and later in an apartment in Grange Park. I spent an evening at an overnight youth shelter listening to the story of a young man who tried to end his life by plunging off the pier (as so many in Blackpool do) after learning that his mother, his last living relative whom he hasn't spoken to in years, just died of a brain aneurysm. And on a rainy day, over lunch at an empty restaurant, I was approached by a twitchy yet very articulate homosexual man with a degree in Japanese and origami who claimed to have come from a wealthy clan of shipbuilders and was suspected of stabbing his partner to death with a samurai sword; he presented me with the mouldy newspaper article and gave me two origami birds he had made out of sweet wrappers. I donated clothing, drank hot chocolate with homeless kids and underage mothers, offered a comforting ear to a toothless woman stabbed by her belligerent neighbour, and visited the studio of an eccentric local artist obsessed with Basquiat. I took pictures of a charismatic middle-aged prostitute in her shabby apartment, a former cowboy from Arizona with a heart full of passion for karaoke and a belly full of ale, strangers on train platforms, drag queens, wasted youths in a club, deserted alleys on a rainy night, closed shopfronts and hermits in torn rags feasting on ham sandwiches and coffee under a dark overpass near the water. Somewhere between old posters of showgirls plastered on historic hotels and tacky porcelain statues behind cracked B&B windows, I photographed beggars, wet schoolkids on a bus, the Irish sea during a storm, deserted cemeteries, caged animals, wild birds and finally, on my last night, a masquerade ball in the lobby of a posh hotel. This final image of the moneyed British class seemed like a mirage to me. My mind was brimming with the loners and drifters with blistered feet seeking refuge for the soul and protection from the rain in the corroded Victorian shelters by the promenade at dawn, and with the faces I encountered every morning when I left my hotel room: elderly, emaciated couples with parchment skin and missing teeth sitting next to rubbish containers, coughing and smoking in tandem with trembling hands, looking as though they want to die but can't, not yet, so they slowly and systematically kill themselves with tobacco and alcohol. And now, the glitzy young women in satin dresses that kept appearing like fantastical mermaids and fairies before my eyes, hiding their gazes behind the plumage of their masks while sipping champagne, seemed like a figment of my imagination, worlds removed from the overweight twenty-somethings in wheelchairs, rolling around town with a bottle of booze and a basket of chips on their lap. Their slick, tuxedo-clad boyfriends would not be sitting with broken noses in a puddle of urine and beer in some pub doorway at night. And the silver-haired dames attending the party with their kilted beaux could hardly fathom the notion of falling asleep on a second-hand mattress in a mouldy apartment with peeling wallpaper, let alone seeing their daughters as impoverished teen mothers pushing children in dirty buggies with another child on the way. These guests seemed to be anything but an embodiment of the misery and hardship of human existence scrutinized for centuries by philosophers and world literature, and yet it was my impression that not a single person in that room genuinely enjoyed or valued their privileged status and surroundings. The mix of bitterness and self-indulgence struck me as odd, even offensive, and the contrast felt sharper that evening than ever before; perhaps because in a town so small where the level of destitution is so high, such opulence or festivity seemed sorely inappropriate.

By contrast with my first book, *48 Hours Blackpool*, whose swift, brutally honest depictions of British tourists rushing along the amusement mile inadvertently lived up to the popular notion of Blackpool as a 'playground for the British working class', this book is more about Blackpool as a dying ground for those whose class does not matter. For the most part, it's about those who live in a contemporary Western society and, for a reason that may or may not exist, seem to carry on their shoulders every conceivable physical, mental and emotional burden, including the burden of guilt for their own demise, which they cannot hinder or control simply due to the weakness inherent in their human nature. Many of those who end up in Blackpool are fuelled by the false assumption or hope that their distant past will rub off on their present; that the memories of those carefree childhood days when they frolicked along the promenade in the company of their parents and siblings can help them turn the page to a happier chapter. But the page won't turn. They arrive in Blackpool out of desperation and grow more desperate with time. The concentration of poverty, sickness, depression, the sense of hopelessness, loss and lack of purpose that hover as a black cloud over this historic coastal town can hardly be summed up in a few pictures. They are the fibre of a progressive disease that targets the weakest and turns them into something like the 'walking dead'. If only in death all are finally equal, then is death the one ray of hope? I am not a religious person, but in this context I can't help think of lambs that are sacrificed again and again, continuously slaughtered to die many deaths and be reborn only to die again, even while living. Their children are the tenderest of lambs that are served on dinner plates following inauguration speeches. And the rest of us … well, the rest of us are either lambs who believe they are lions or lions that life turns into lambs.

Von Löwen und Lämmern

Anfang Januar 2019 erhielt ich eine E-Mail von einem Mann, dem ich nie begegnet war, einem Fan meiner Arbeit, der gerade mein Buch *48 Hours Blackpool* gekauft hatte. Er sei auf einen alten Zeitungsartikel über diese Küstenstadt gestoßen, schrieb er, und da mich das Thema offensichtlich interessiere, wolle ich ihn vielleicht lesen. Entschuldigend fügte er hinzu, dass sein Scanner defekt sei, weshalb er auf die „altmodische" Methode zurückgegriffen habe, die einzelnen Absätze zu fotografieren und als E-Mail-Anhänge zu schicken. Überrascht und gerührt von der aufmerksamen Geste, las ich die zwölf Absätze an jenem Spätnachmittag in einem Atemzug durch, und als am Abend die Sonne unterging, wurde mir allmählich bewusst, dass meine Geschichte über Blackpool, anders als ich geglaubt hatte, noch lange nicht zu Ende war. Man könnte an dieser Stelle fragen, was an dem Artikel so besonders war, dass ich zu diesem Schluss kam und ein paar Wochen später nach Blackpool aufbrach, um meine Dokumentation fortzusetzen. Obwohl gut geschrieben, enthielt der Text nur wenige kurze Berichte von Einheimischen, die den Ruf Blackpools als sozial am stärksten benachteiligte Seestadt Englands bestätigten. Und doch war es dieser Artikel, der mich zwang, mir die Figuren näher anzusehen, die in den Eingängen baufälliger Häuser kauerten, die Männer und Frauen, deren Stimmen während der Hochsaison vom Geklapper der Spiel-automaten und vom Touristengewühl auf der Promenade erstickt werden — denselben Geräuschen, die auch mich bei meinem ersten Kurzbesuch vor zwei Jahren taub gemacht hatten. In der Nebensaison, wenn die Promenade verödet und die Stadt verstummt, ist niemand da, der diese Stimmen hört, und die Bilder, die in der Hochsommersonne so hell und kontrastreich strahlen, werden unter dem bedeckten Himmel eintönig und trist.

Als ich im Februar nach Blackpool zurückkam, fand ich eine kalte und trostlose Stadt vor, mit leeren Geschäften, gesperrten Seebrücken und neuen Gleisbaustellen für die Straßenbahn, die die Durchfahrt blockierten. Schwärme von Staren kreisten murmelnd über der tosenden See, während sich vor den Geschäften rund um die Innenstadt einzelne Möwen um Brotkrümel stritten. Ich musste schlucken; es war niemand zum Fotografieren da. Nur ich war schon da, und das mit Absicht. Also ergab ich mich dem Schicksal.

Auf dem Marktplatz stand eine Kirche, die ich von meinem letzten Besuch noch in Erinnerung hatte. In der Nähe dieser Kirche schoss ich eines meiner Lieblingsfotos und dachte, der Platz könnte ein günstiger Ausgangspunkt und ein guter Ort sein, um die letzten Reste meines Thunfischsandwichs an die Möwen zu verfüttern. Dabei lernte ich Alan kennen, auch bekannt als „der Vogelmann", der mit seinem buschigen Haar, den lustigen Ohren und der hageren Statur einer Märchenfigur glich. Gutherzig, prinzipientreu und arm wie eine Kirchenmaus kam Alan jeden Tag mit seinem kaputten Rollkoffer im Schlepptau in die Stadt, um seine letzten Pfunde für Vogelfutter auszugeben. Die Möwen fütterte er ungern, weil sie ihre Jungen grausam behandeln; stattdessen widmete er sich den Tauben, die von den Einheimischen als „Ungeziefer" bezeichnet werden. Weil der Stadtrat das Vogelfüttern verboten hatte, zahlte Alan auch seinen Teil an Bußgeldern. Bisweilen zog er verärgert an seiner E-Zigarette, redete in einem fort über die Schwächen der Stadt und des ganzen Landes und erbot sich, mir die beheizte Markthalle zu zeigen, wo ich versuchte, ihm einen Kaffee zu kaufen, was er mit der Begründung, er nehme keine Almosen an, unumschränkt ablehnte. Also kaufte ich ein paar Brötchen für seine Vögel. Unsere Wege sollten sich in den kommenden Tagen des Öfteren kreuzen. Einstweilen aber trennten wir uns, und ich steuerte auf die Kirche zu, wo ich jemanden zu treffen hoffte, der mir ein paar hilfreiche Tipps geben konnte. Dort lief ich einem stämmigen, biblisch aussehenden Mann mit nonkonformistischen Ansichten und einer entspannten, keine Fragen stellenden Grundhaltung in die Arme, der mir eine Liste aller Suppenküchen in der Stadt

überreichte und mich zum Sonntagsgottesdienst einlud,
wo ich eine junge Frau kennenlernte, eine ums Überleben
kämpfende Drogenabhängige, in deren Begleitung ich
meine erste Suppenküche besuchte.

Die Handlung wurde mit jedem Tag dichter. Bald fand ich
mich in einem Altenheim wieder, wo ich Bananen mit einer
bezaubernden alten Dame aß, die ich noch von meinem
letzten Besuch kannte — damals konnte sie noch gehen;
anschließend traf ich einige schillernde Ortsansässige in
einem Bürgerhaus und später in einer Wohnung in Grange
Park. Ich verbrachte einen Abend in einem Nachtasyl für
Jugendliche und lauschte der Geschichte eines jungen
Mannes, der sich (wie so viele in Blackpool) mit einem
Sprung von der Seebrücke umbringen wollte, nachdem er
erfahren hatte, dass seine Mutter, seine letzte lebende
Verwandte, mit der er seit Jahren nicht gesprochen hatte,
gerade an einem Hirnaneurysma gestorben war. An einem
regnerischen Tag sprach mich beim Mittagessen in einem
leeren Restaurant ein nervöser, aber sehr redegewandter
Homosexueller mit einem Abschluss in Japanisch und Origami an, der behauptete, er stamme aus einem wohlha-
benden Schiffbauerclan und werde verdächtigt, seinen
Lebensgefährten mit einem Samuraischwert erstochen zu
haben; er zeigte mir den angeschimmelten Zeitungsaus-
schnitt und schenkte mir zwei Origamivögel, die er aus
Bonbonpapier gefaltet hatte. Ich spendete Kleidung, trank
heißen Kakao mit obdachlosen Jugendlichen und minder-
jährigen Müttern, schenkte einer zahnlosen Frau, die von
ihrem streitsüchtigen Nachbarn niedergestochen worden
war, ein tröstendes Ohr und besuchte das Atelier eines
exzentrischen einheimischen Künstlers, der von Basquiat
besessen war. Ich machte Fotos von einer charismatischen
Prostituierten mittleren Alters in ihrer heruntergekom-
menen Wohnung, einem ehemaligen Cowboy aus Arizona
mit einem Herz voller Leidenschaft für Karaoke und einem
Bauch voller Bier, von Fremden auf Bahnsteigen, Dragqueens, betrunkenen Jugendlichen in einer Disco, men-
schenleeren Gassen in einer Regennacht, verrammelten
Ladenfronten und Einsiedlern in zerrissenen Lumpen, die
sich unter einer dunklen Überführung am Wasser an
Schinkensandwiches und Kaffee gütlich taten. Irgendwo
zwischen alten Revuegirl-Plakaten, die an den Fassaden
historischer Hotels klebten, und kitschigen Porzellanfigu-
ren hinter gesprungenen Pensionsfenstern fotografierte
ich Bettler, durchnässte Schulkinder in einem Bus, die Iri-
sche See im Sturm, einsame Friedhöfe, eingesperrte Tiere,
wilde Vögel und schließlich, an meinem letzten Abend,
einen Maskenball in der Halle eines Nobelhotels.

Dieses letzte Bild vom britischen Geldadel erschien mir
wie ein Phantom. Mein Kopf war voll von den Außensei-
tern und Landstreichern mit Blasen an den Füßen, die bei
Tagesanbruch in den rostigen viktorianischen Unterstän-
den an der Promenade Zuflucht für die Seele und Schutz
vor dem Regen suchten, und von den Gesichtern, die mir
jeden Morgen begegneten, wenn ich mein Hotelzimmer
verließ: ältere, ausgemergelte Paare mit Pergament-
haut und Zahnlücken, die neben Müllcontainern saßen, mit
zittrigen Händen zugleich husteten und rauchten und
dabei aussahen, als wollten sie sterben, aber könnten es
nicht, noch nicht, sodass sie sich langsam und systematisch
mit Tabak und Alkohol zugrunde richteten. Und jetzt tauch-
ten, eine nach der anderen, wie sagenhafte Meerjungfrauen
und Feen diese glitzrigen jungen Frauen in Satinkleidern
vor mir auf, die ihre Blicke hinter dem Federschmuck ihrer
Masken verbargen, während sie Champagner schlürften,
und kamen mir vor wie Ausgeburten meiner Fantasie,
Welten entfernt von den übergewichtigen Twens in ihren
Rollstühlen, die mit einer Flasche Schnaps und einer Schale
Pommes auf dem Schoß durch die Stadt zuckelten. Ihre
schneidigen Freunde im Smoking saßen nachts nicht mit
gebrochenen Nasen in einer Pfütze aus Urin und Bier vor
irgendeiner Kneipentür. Und die silberhaarigen Damen, die
mit ihren Kilt tragenden Beaus den Ball besuchten, konnten sich kaum ausmalen, in einer feuchten, muffigen Wohnung mit abblätternden Tapeten auf einer gebrauchten
Matratze einzuschlafen, geschweige denn, sich ihre Töch-
ter als verarmte Teenagermütter vorstellen, die Babys in
schmutzigen Wagen durch die Gegend schieben, während
das nächste Kind schon unterwegs ist. Diese Gäste schie-
nen alles andere zu verkörpern als die Not und das Elend
des menschlichen Daseins, wie Philosophen und die Welt-
literatur es seit Jahrhunderten erforschen, und doch hatte
ich den Eindruck, dass nicht ein Mensch in diesem Raum
seine privilegierte Stellung und Umgebung wirklich genoss
oder wertschätzte. Die Mischung aus Verbitterung und
Maßlosigkeit kam mir seltsam, ja abstoßend vor, und der
Kontrast fühlte sich an diesem Abend schärfer an als jemals
zuvor — vielleicht weil in einer so kleinen Stadt, in der das
Armutsniveau derart hoch ist, eine solche Opulenz oder
Festlichkeit arg unangebracht erschien.

Im Gegensatz zu meinem ersten Buch *48 Hours Blackpool*,
dessen schnelle, schonungslos ehrliche Aufnahmen von
über die Vergnügungsmeile hetzenden britischen Touristen unbeabsichtigt dem verbreiteten Bild von Blackpool
als „Spielplatz der britischen Arbeiterklasse" entsprachen,
handelt dieses Buch eher von Blackpool als Sterbeplatz für

diejenigen, deren Klasse keine Rolle spielt. Es dreht sich
im Wesentlichen um Menschen, die in einer modernen
westlichen Gesellschaft leben und aus Gründen, die exis-
tieren mögen oder nicht, jede nur denkbare körperliche,
seelische und emotionale Last auf ihren Schultern tragen,
einschließlich der Last des selbst verschuldeten Nieder-
gangs, den sie wegen der angeborenen Schwäche ihrer
menschlichen Natur einfach nicht aufhalten oder kontrol-
lieren können. Viele von denen, die in Blackpool landen,
treibt die falsche Annahme oder Hoffnung an, dass ihre
entfernte Vergangenheit auf ihre Gegenwart abfärbt; dass
die Erinnerung an die sorgenfreien Tage ihrer Kindheit,
als sie in Begleitung ihrer Eltern und Geschwister die Promenade entlangtollten, ihnen hilft, ein glücklicheres Kapi-
tel in ihrem Leben aufzuschlagen. Doch die Seite schlägt
nicht um. Sie kommen aus Verzweiflung nach Blackpool
und verzweifeln mit der Zeit nur noch mehr. Die Ballung
von Armut, Krankheit, Depression, Hoffnungslosigkeit,
Verlustgefühlen und mangelnder Sinnhaftigkeit, die wie
eine dunkle Wolke über dieser historischen Küstenstadt
schwebt, lässt sich kaum in ein paar Fotos zusammenfas-
sen. Sie bildet das Gewebe einer fortschreitenden Krankheit, die auf die Schwächsten zielt und sie in so etwas wie
„lebende Tote" verwandelt. Wenn nur im Tod alle Menschen endlich gleich sind, ist dann der Tod der einzige
Hoffnungsschimmer? Ich bin kein religiöser Mensch, aber
in diesem Kontext muss ich unwillkürlich an Lämmer den-
ken, die wieder und wieder geopfert, die kontinuierlich
geschlachtet werden, um viele Tode zu sterben und bloß
wiedergeboren zu werden, um erneut zu sterben, selbst im
Leben. Ihre Kinder sind die zartesten Lämmchen, die nach
politischen Sonntagsreden auf großen Tellern serviert
werden. Und wir anderen … nun, wir anderen sind entwe-
der Lämmer, die glauben, sie seien Löwen, oder Löwen, die
das Leben zu Lämmern macht.

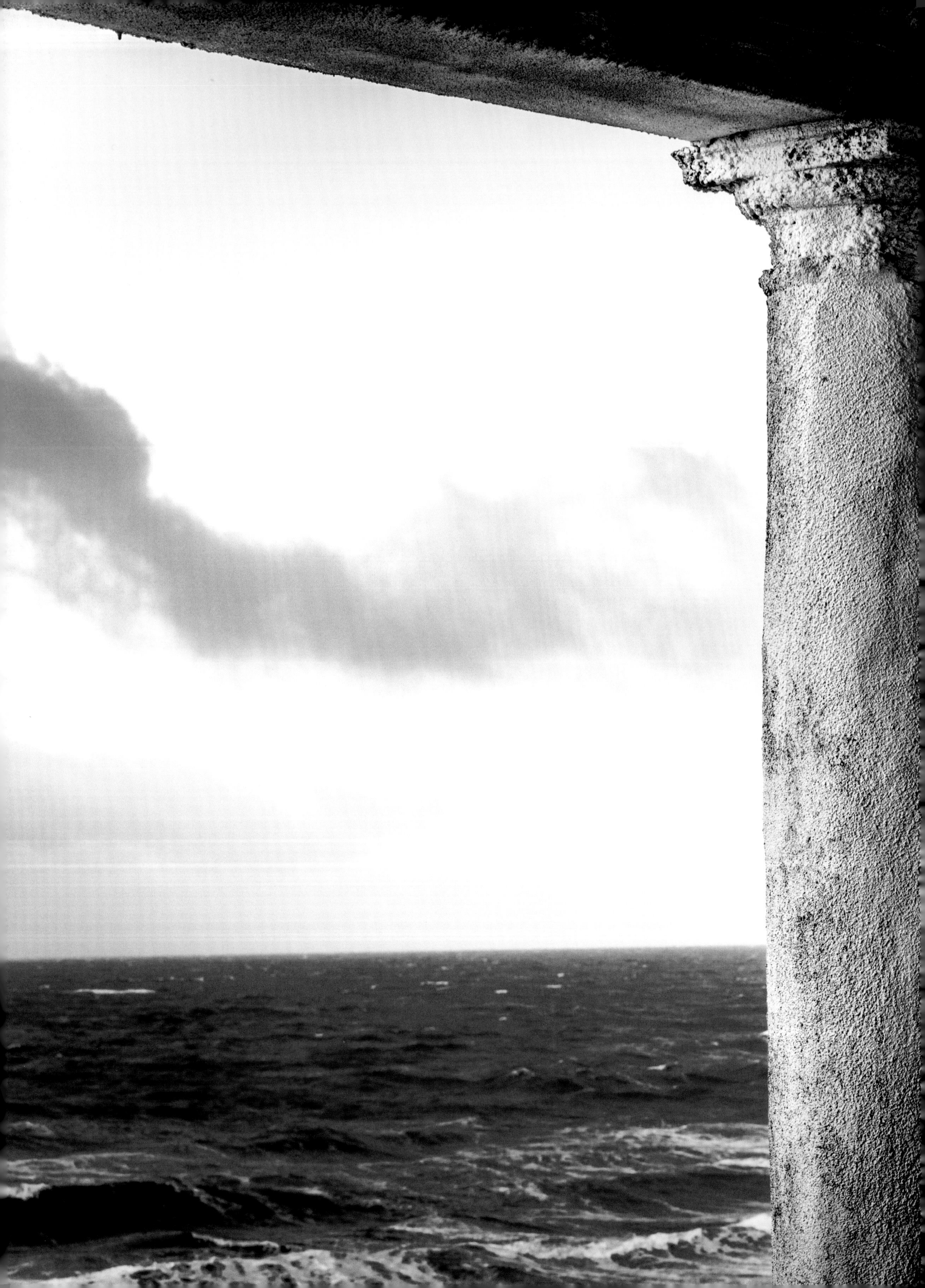

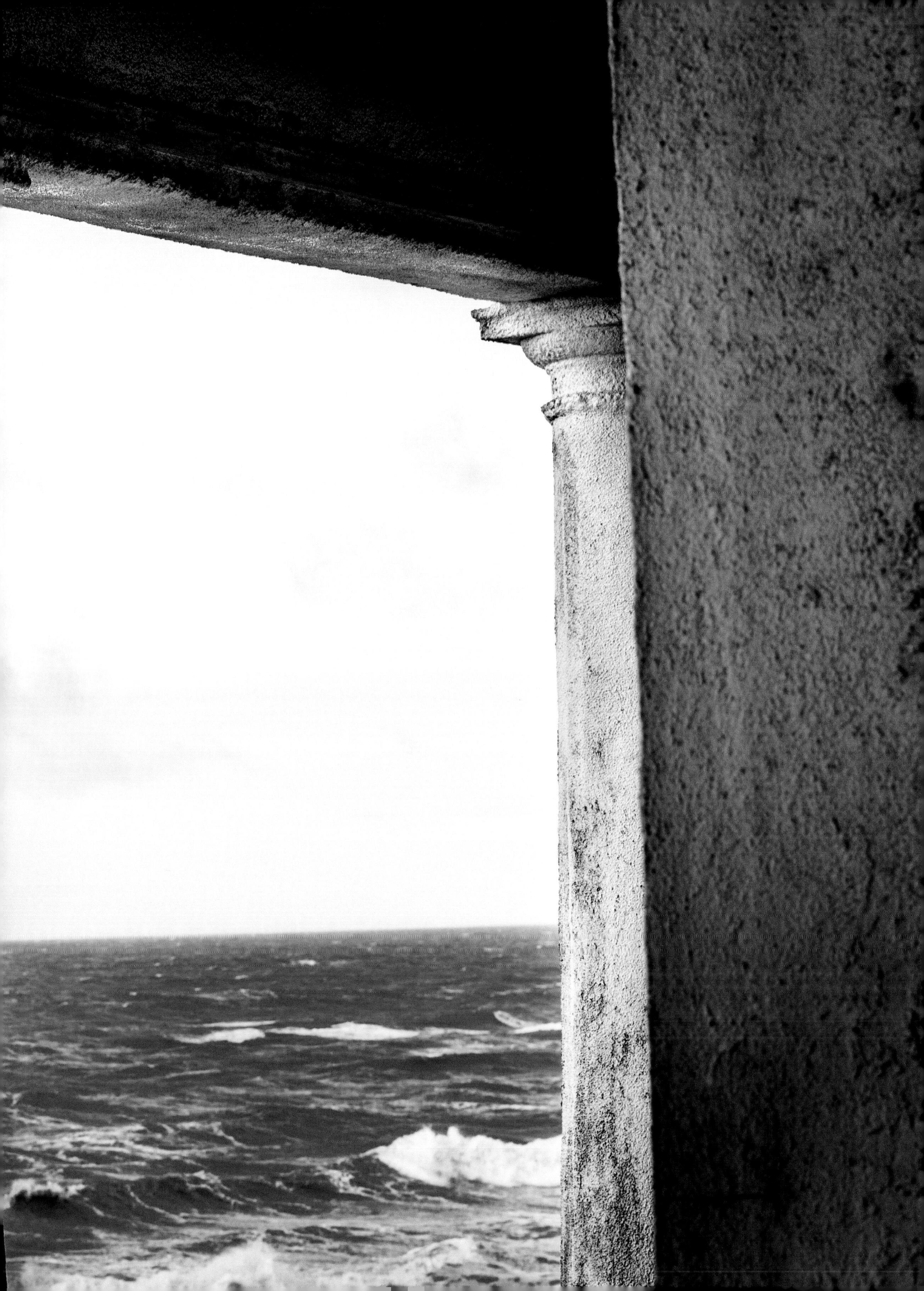

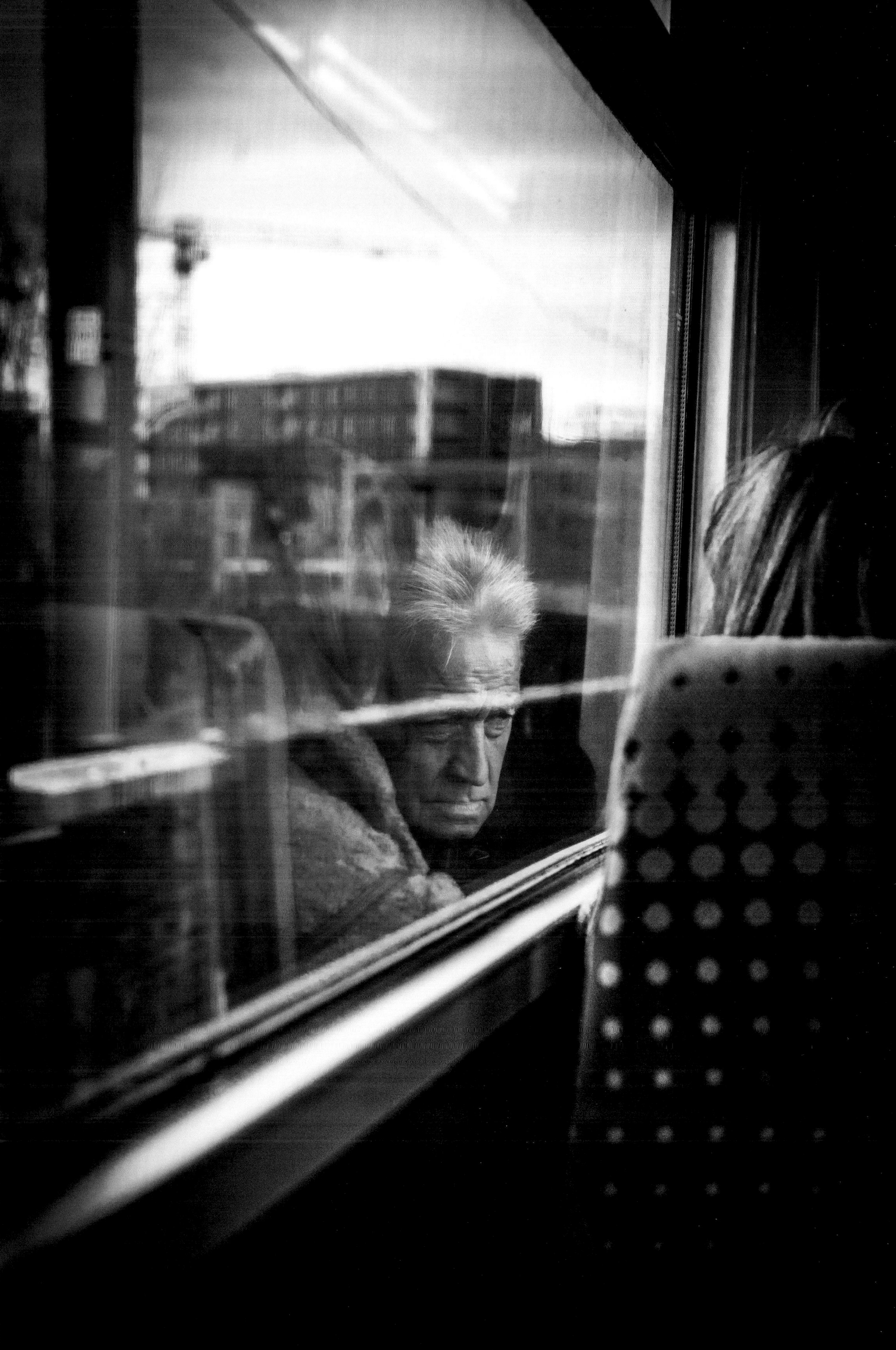

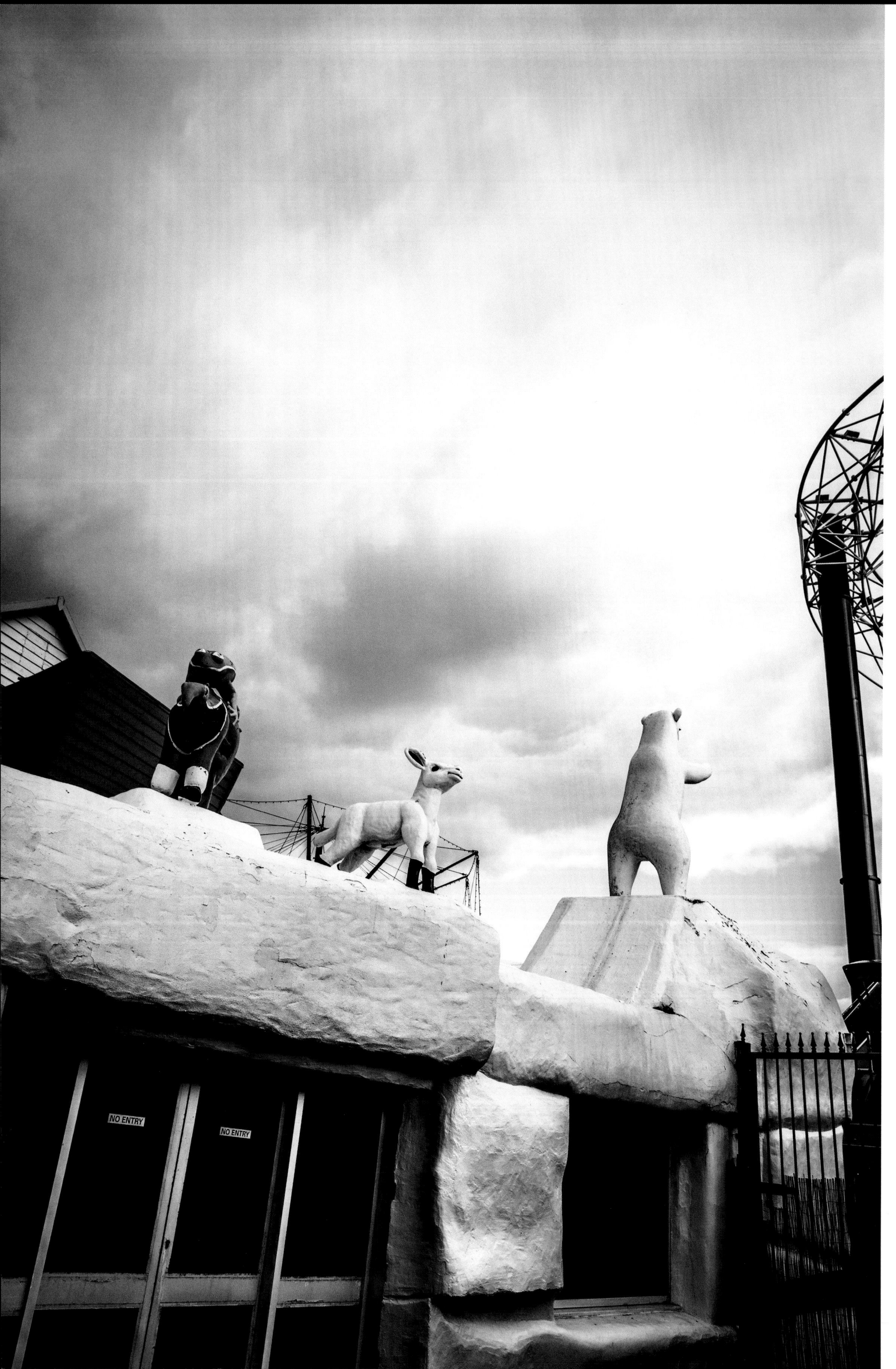

NO ENTRY
NO ENTRY

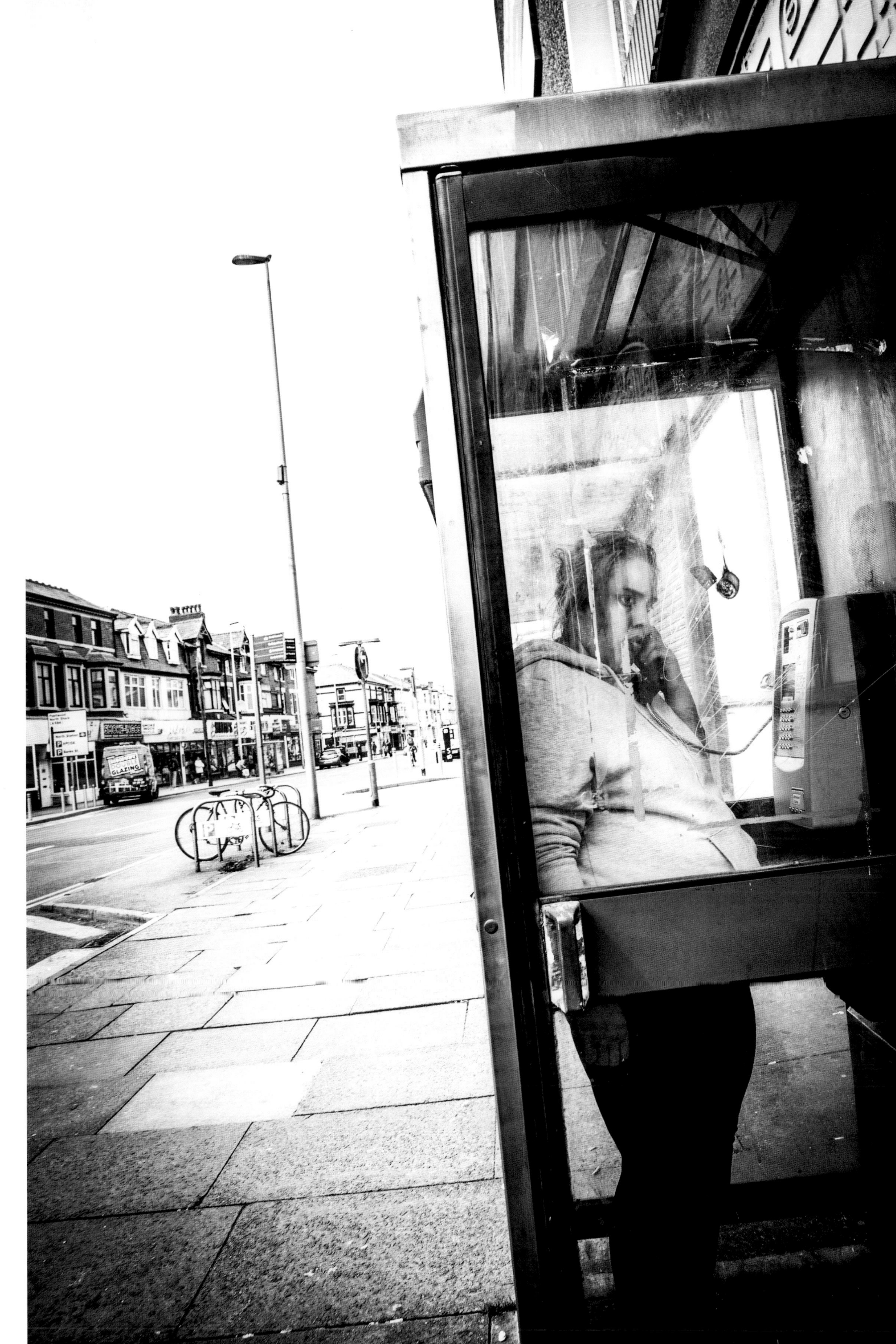

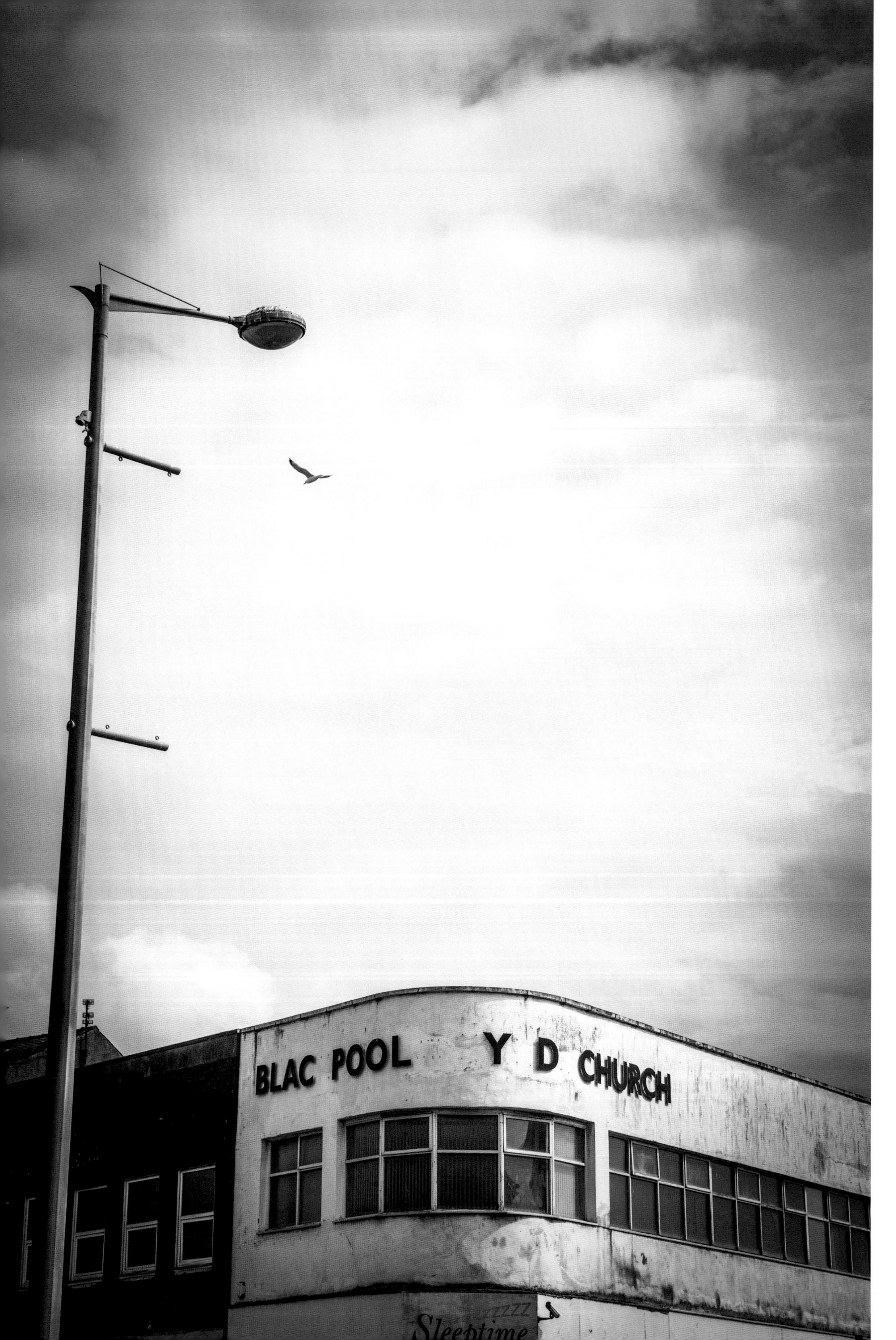

BLAC POOL   Y D CHURCH
Sleeptime

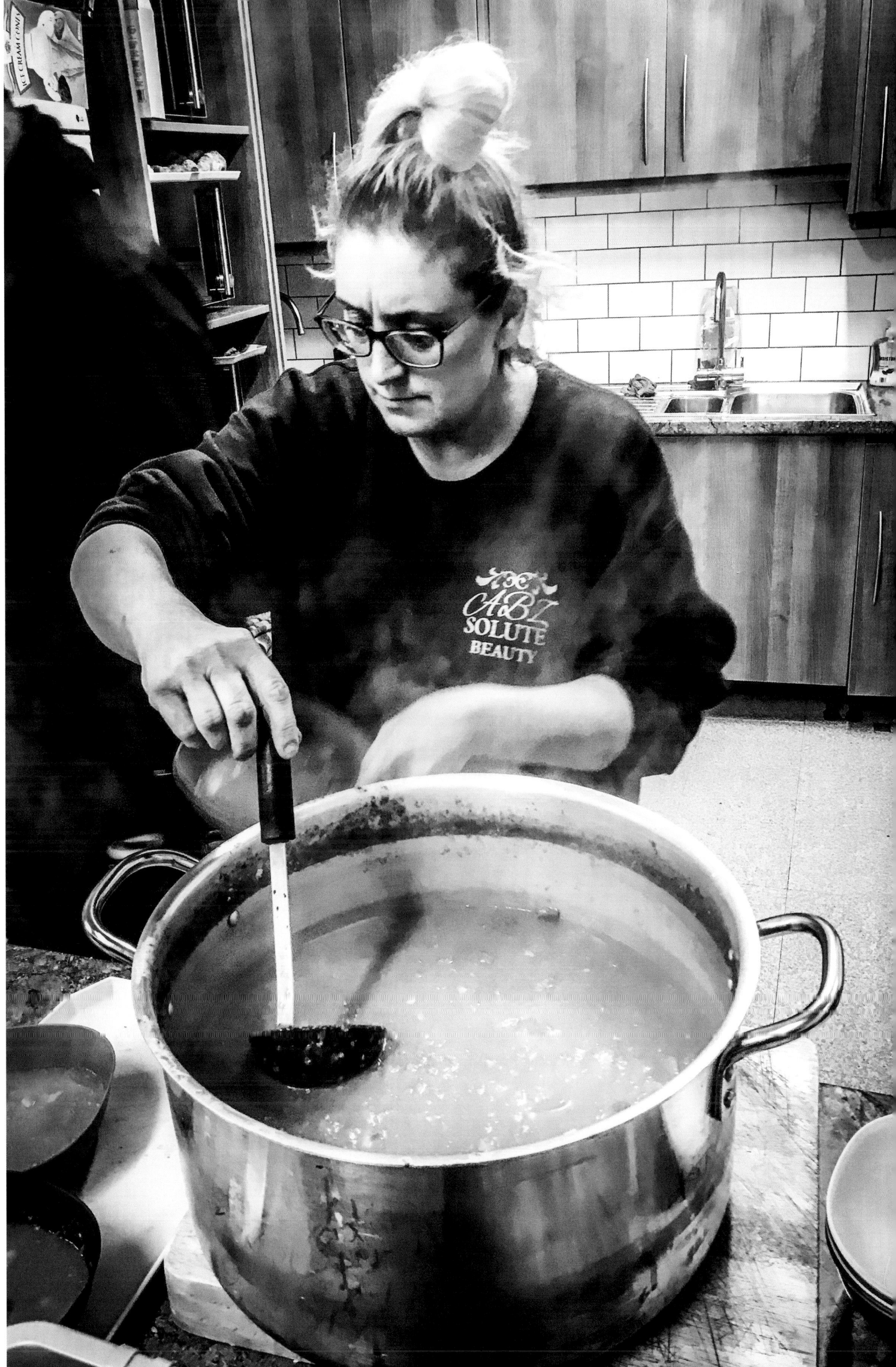

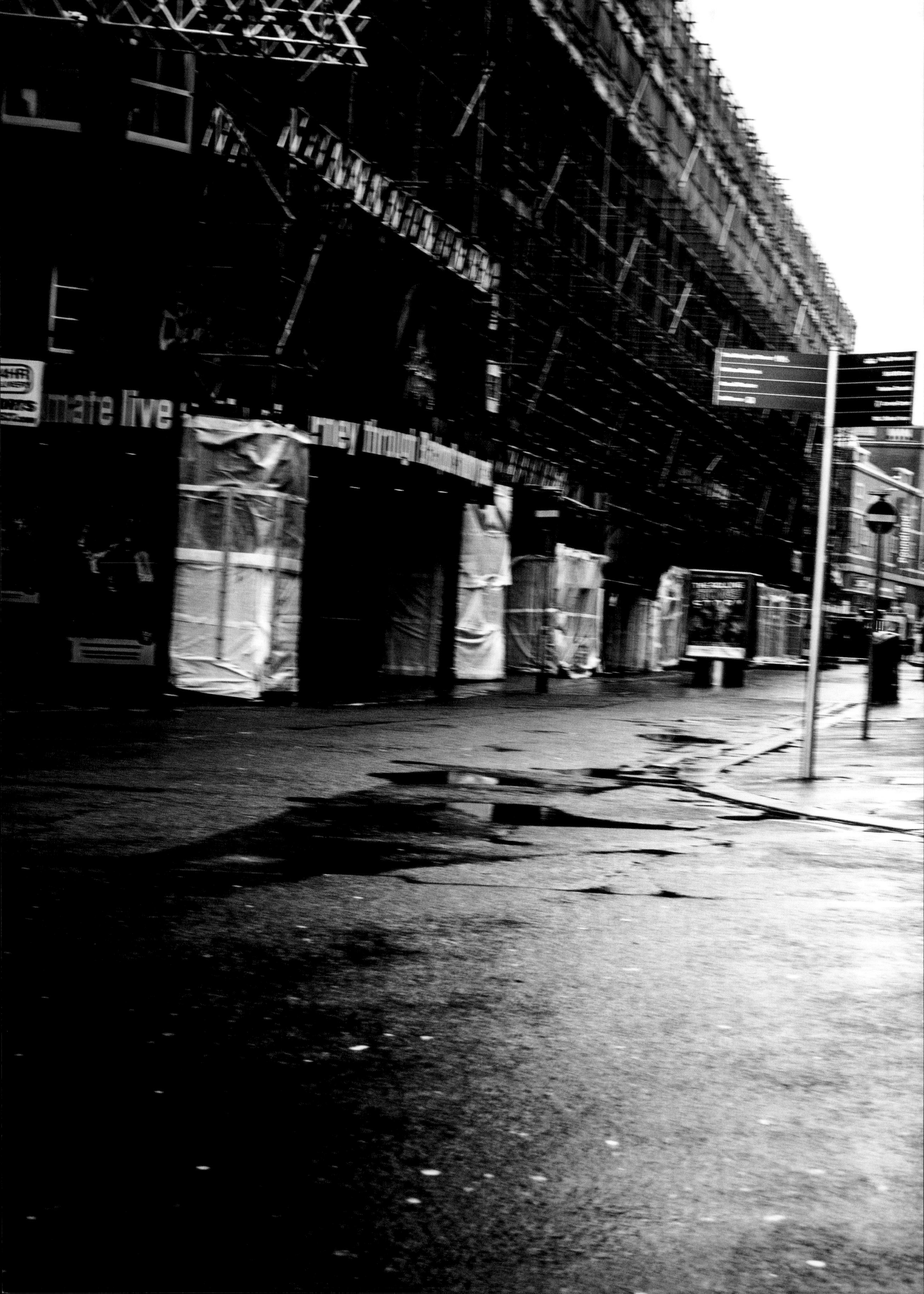
mate live

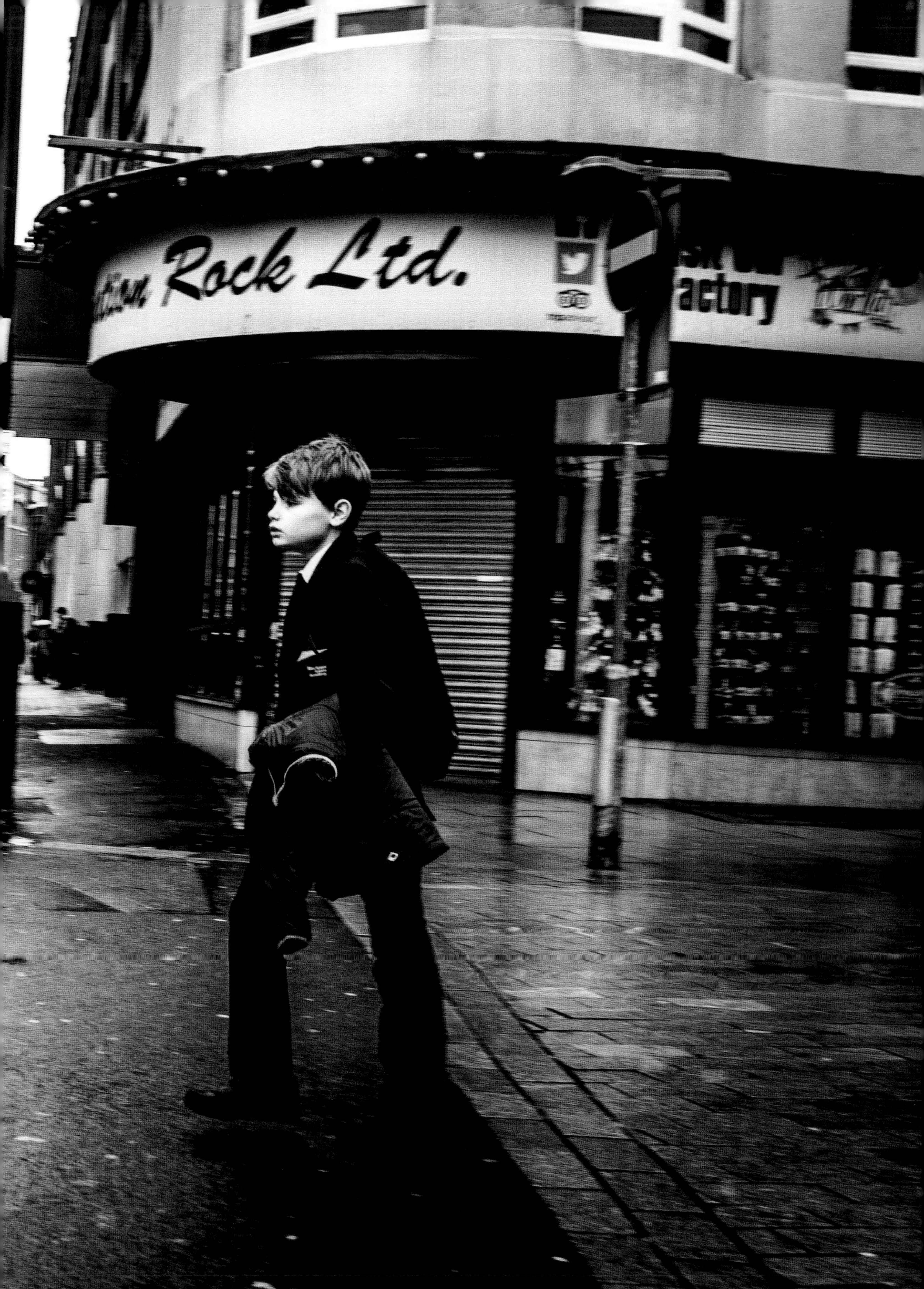
Rock Ltd.
Factory

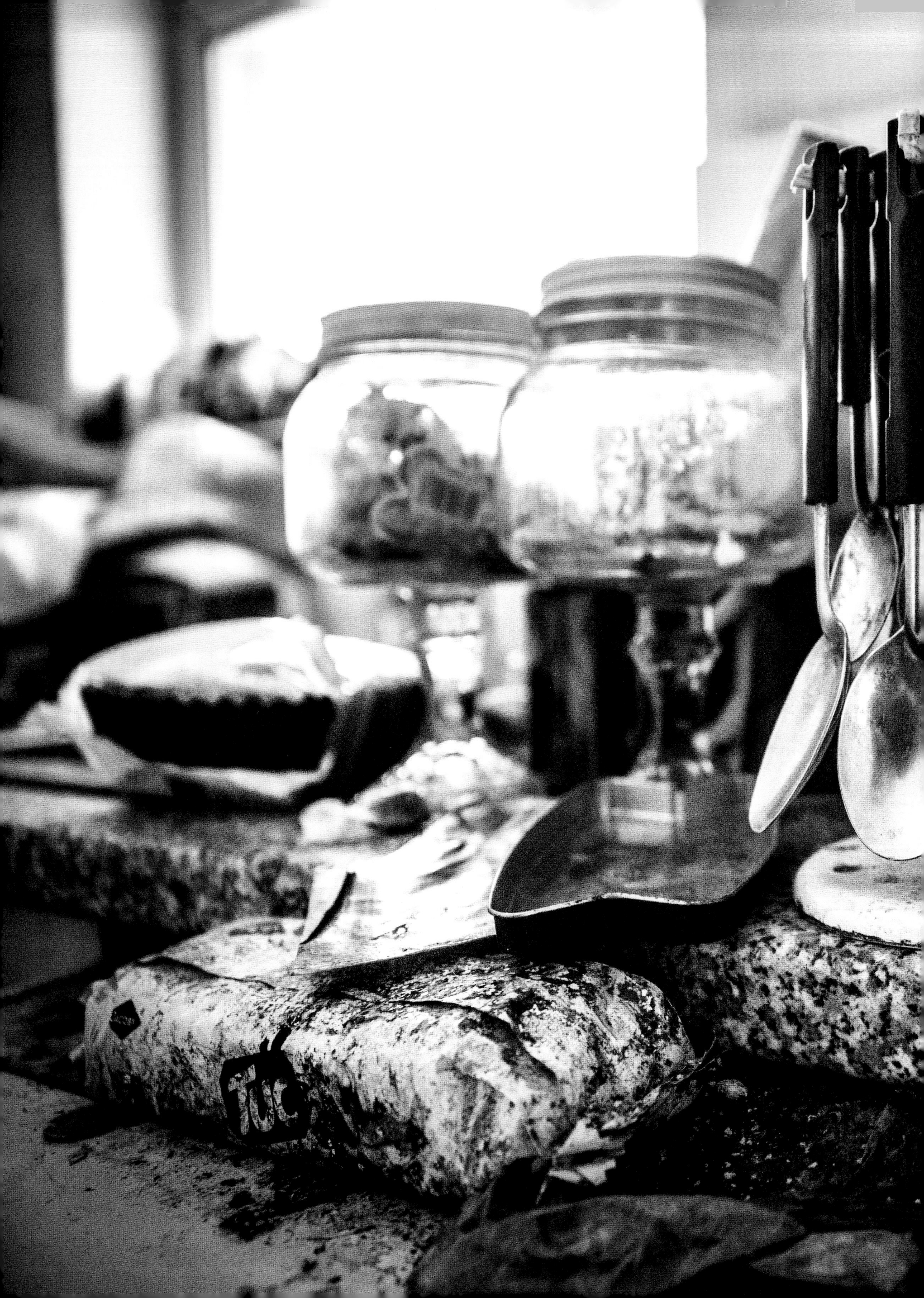

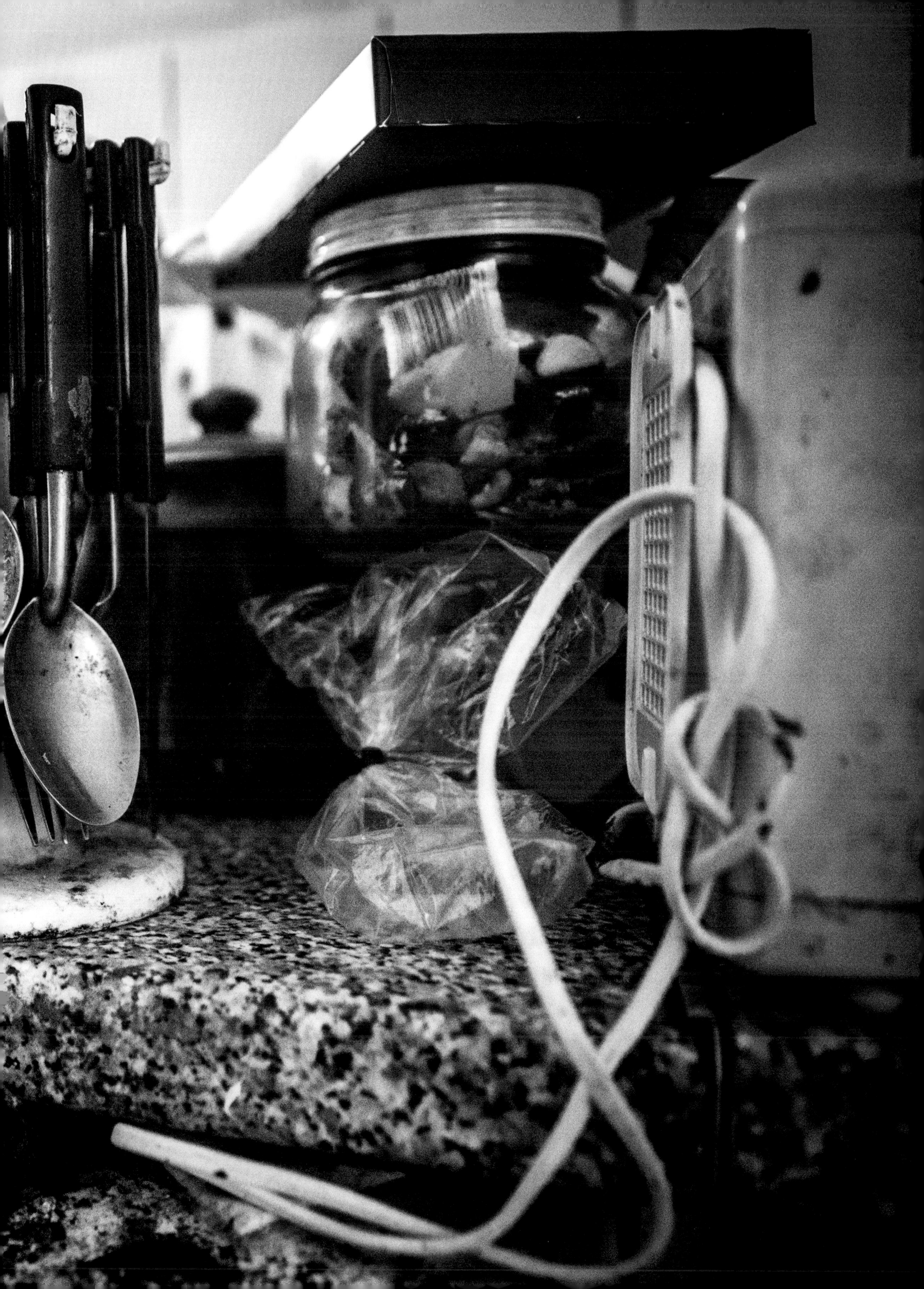

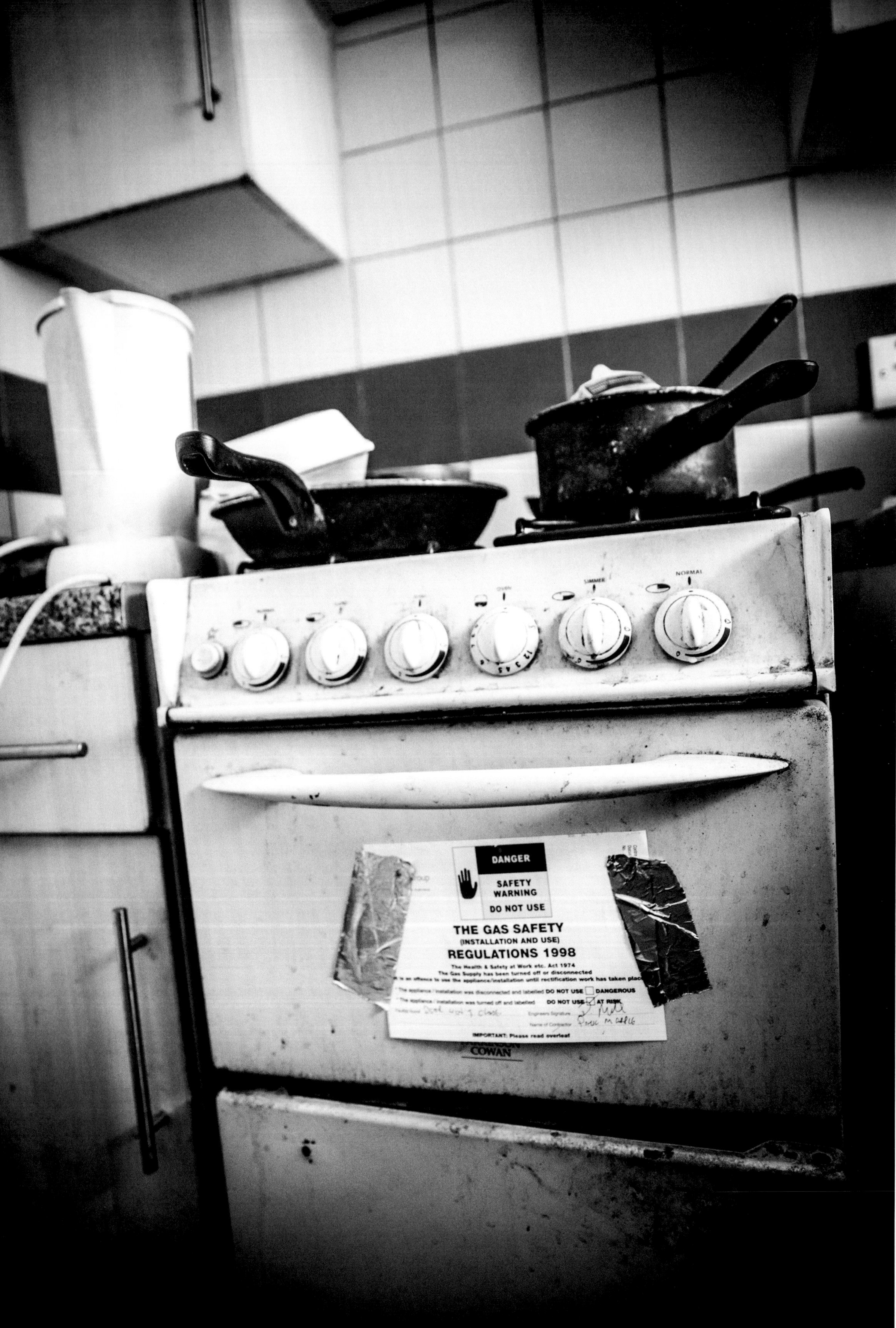
DANGER
SAFETY
WARNING
DO NOT USE
THE GAS SAFETY
(INSTALLATION AND USE)
REGULATIONS 1998
The Health & Safety at Work etc. Act 1974
The Gas Supply has been turned off or disconnected
It is an offence to use the appliance/installation until rectification work has taken place
The appliance/installation was disconnected and labelled DO NOT USE DANGEROUS
The appliance/installation was turned off and labelled DO NOT USE AT RISK
Engineers Signature
Name of Contractor
IMPORTANT: Please read overleaf
COWAN

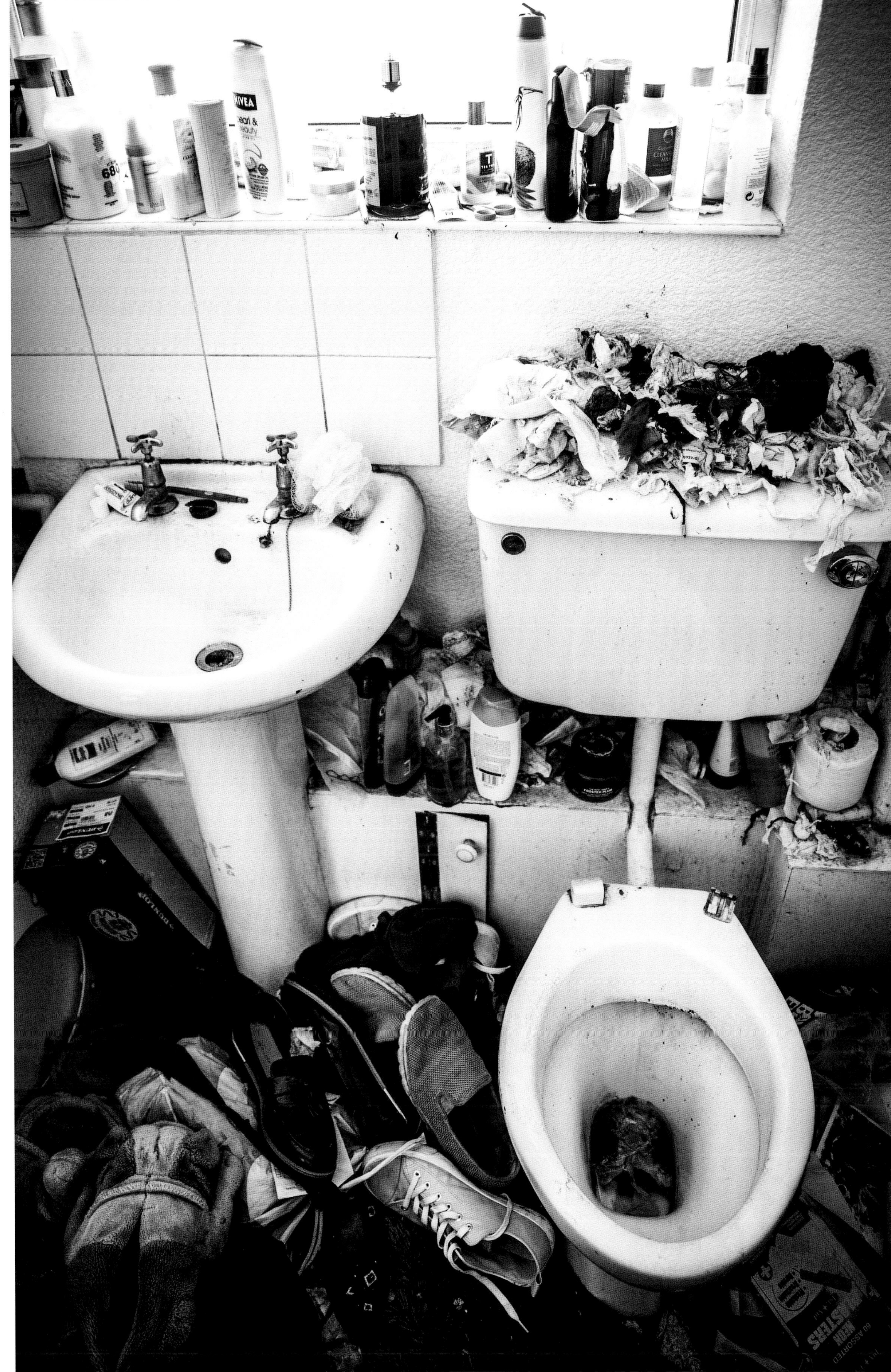

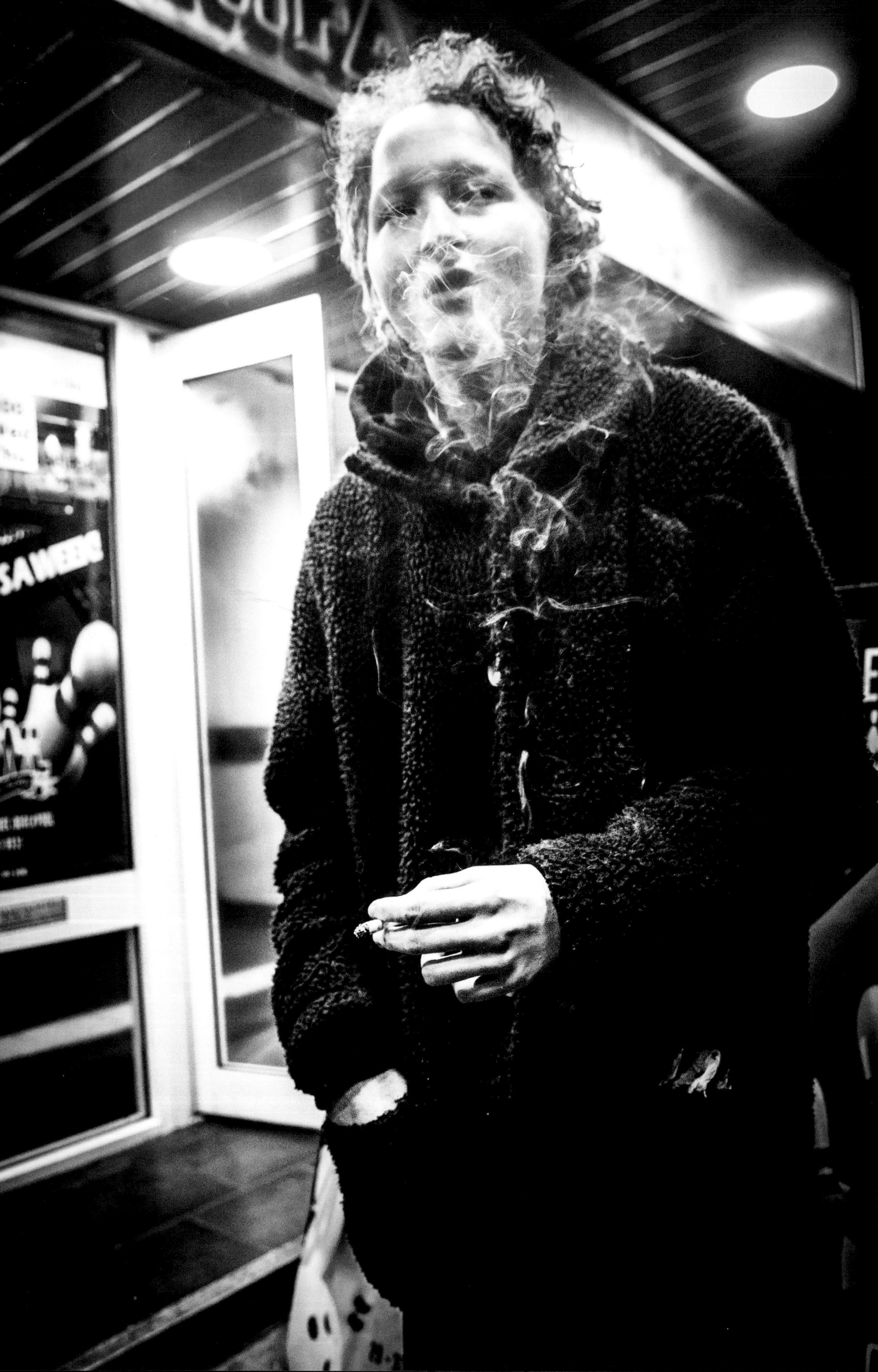

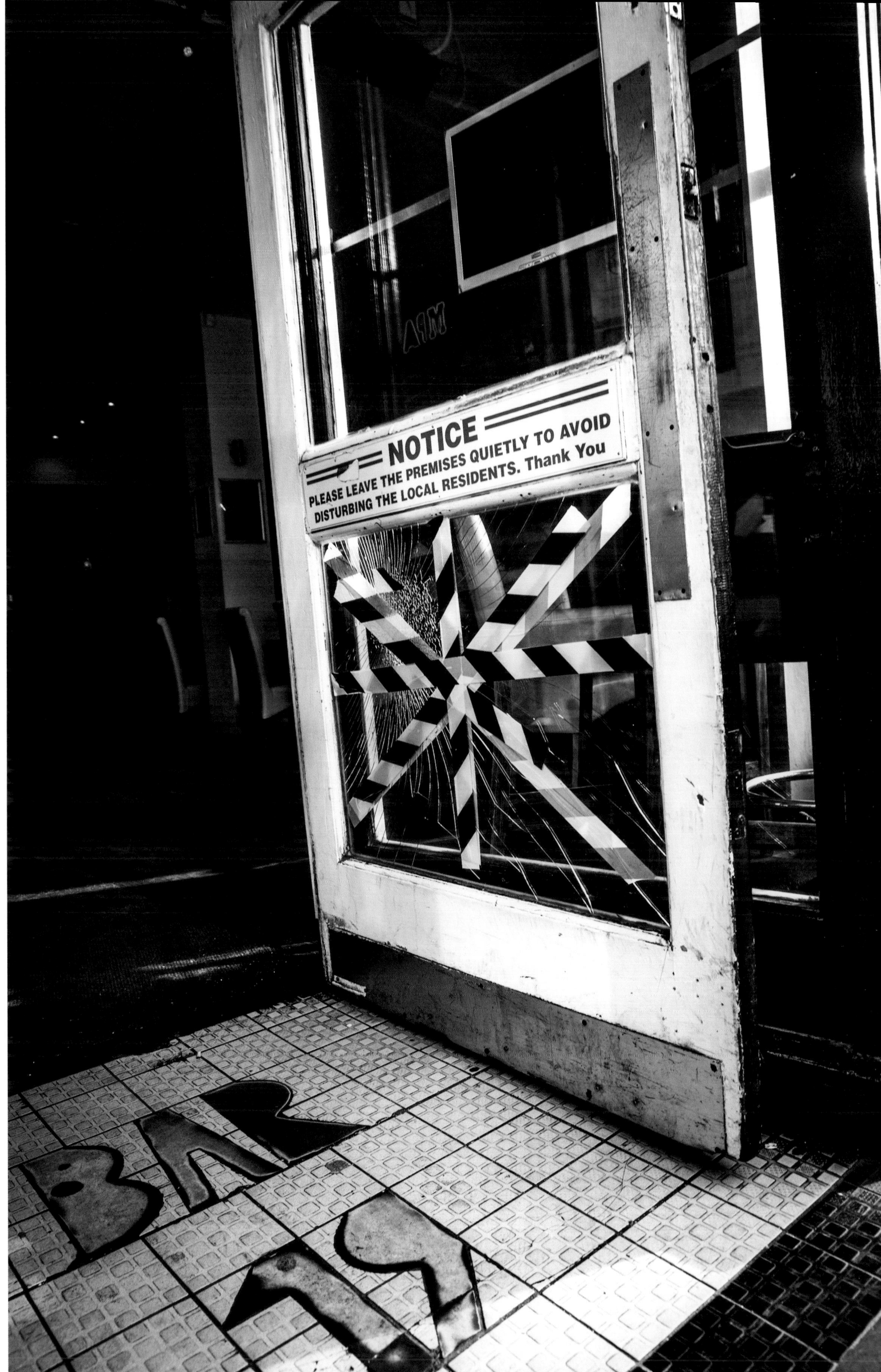

NOTICE
PLEASE LEAVE THE PREMISES QUIETLY TO AVOID
DISTURBING THE LOCAL RESIDENTS. Thank You

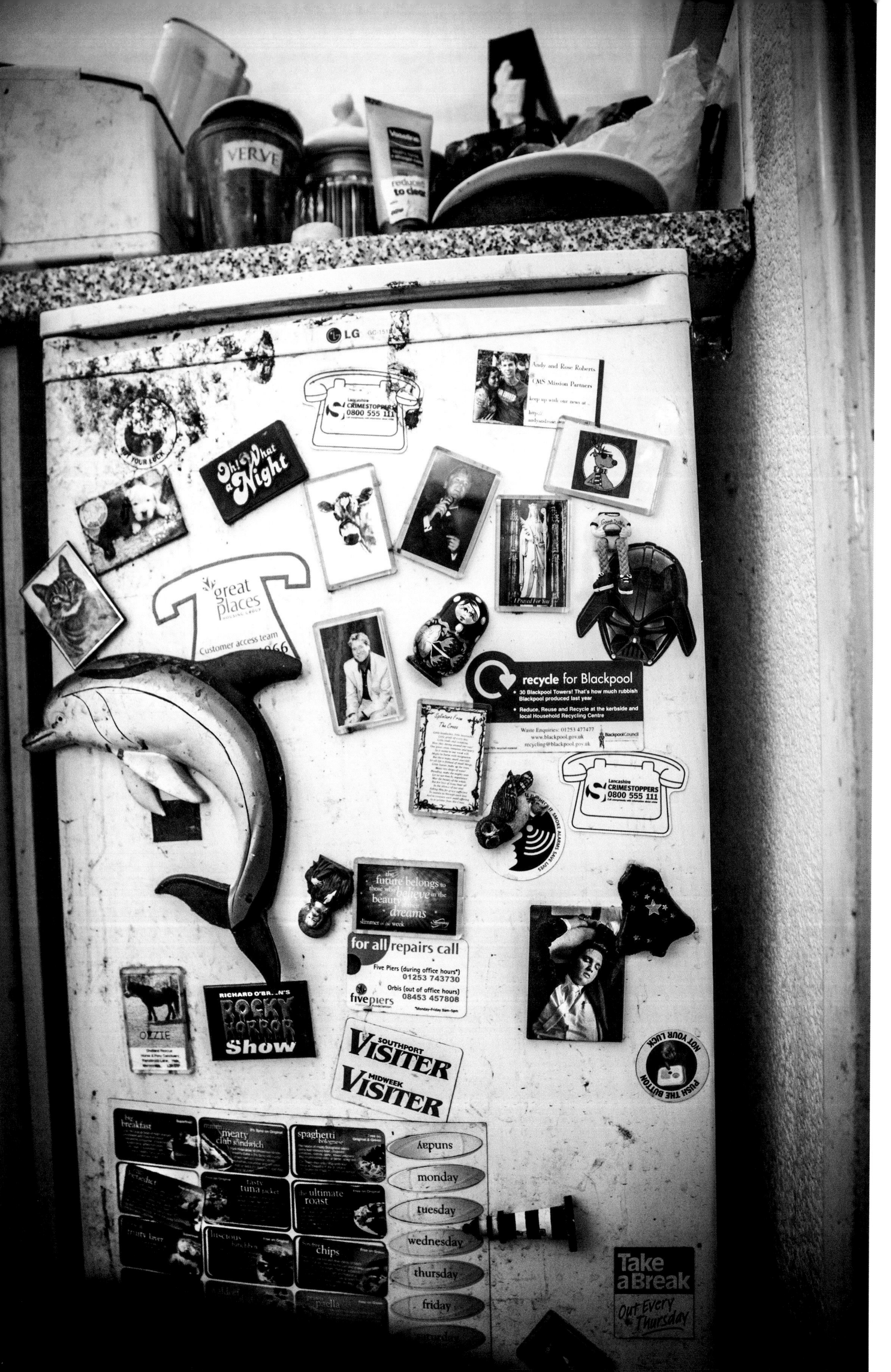

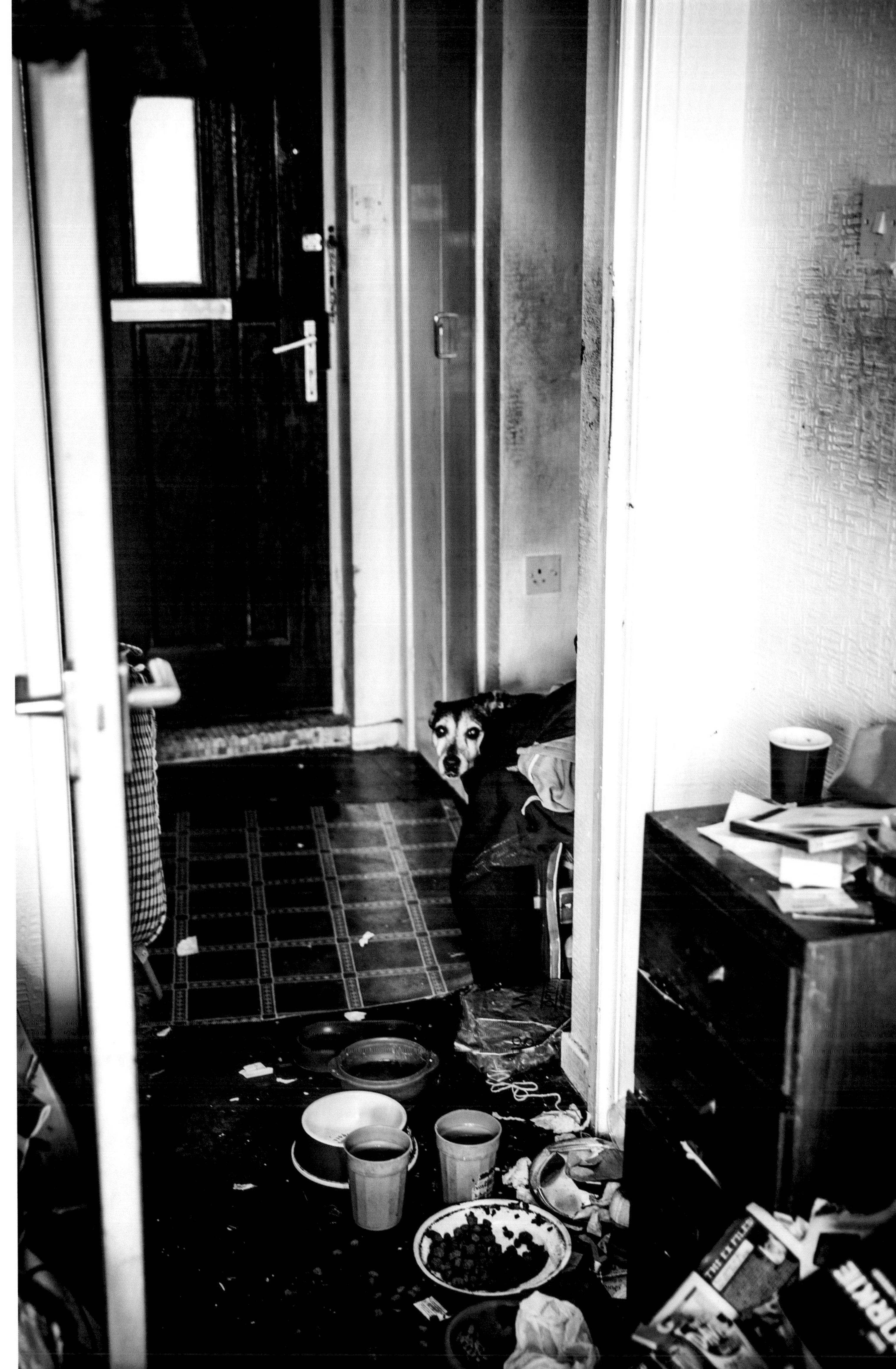

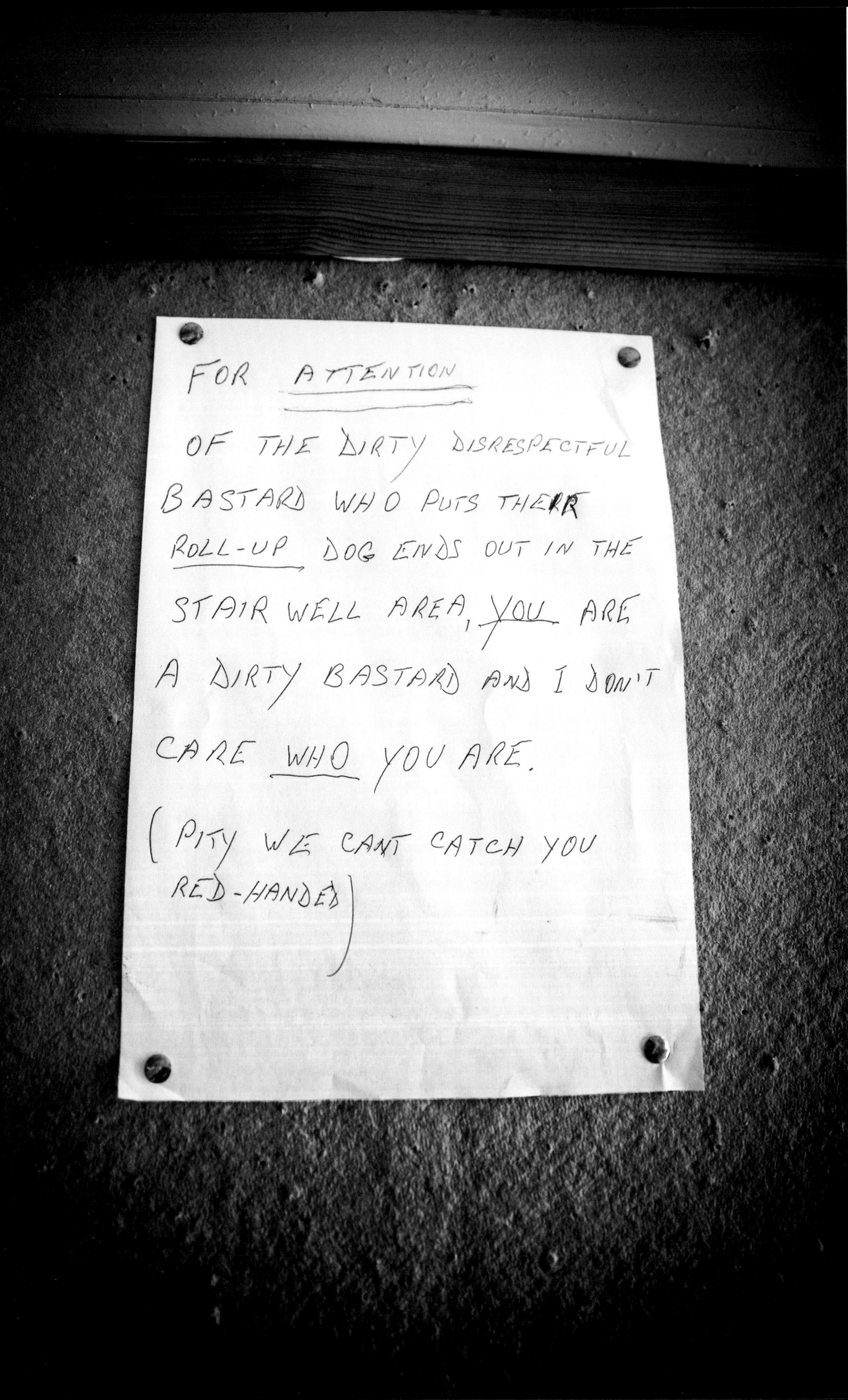

FOR ATTENTION

OF THE DIRTY DISRESPECTFUL
BASTARD WHO PUTS THEIR
ROLL-UP DOG ENDS OUT IN THE
STAIR WELL AREA, YOU ARE
A DIRTY BASTARD AND I DON'T
CARE WHO YOU ARE.
(PITY WE CANT CATCH YOU
RED-HANDED)

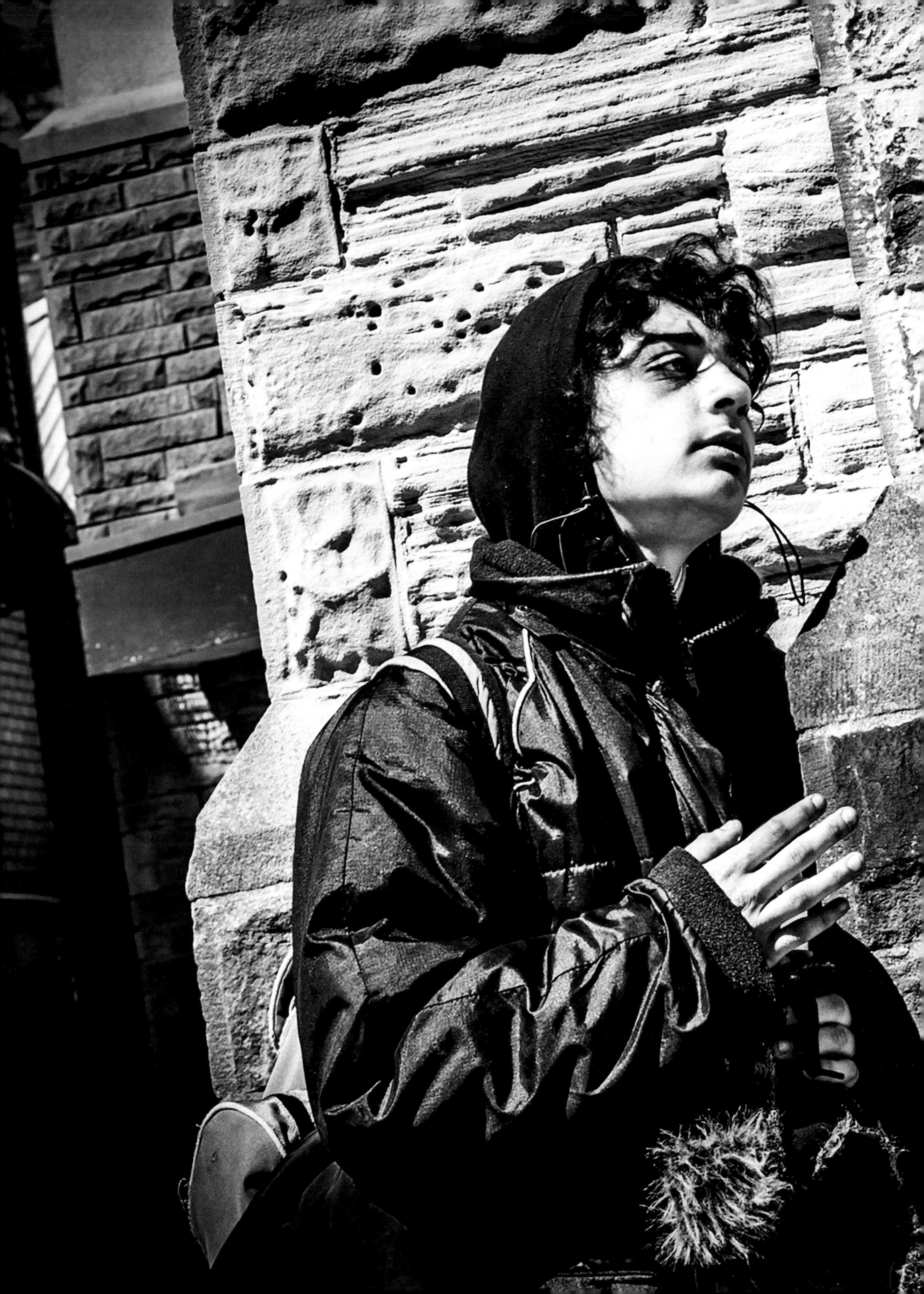

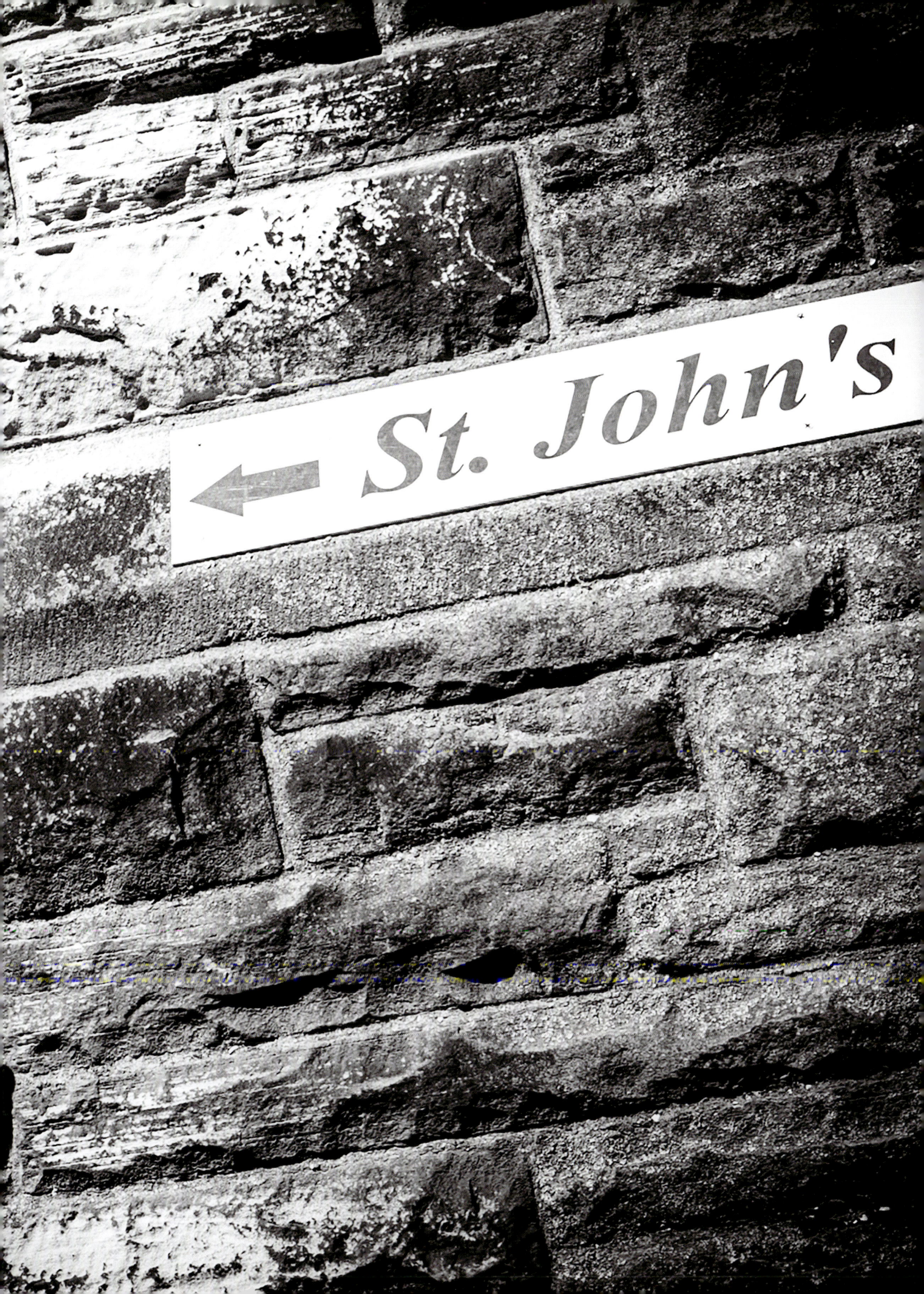
St. John's

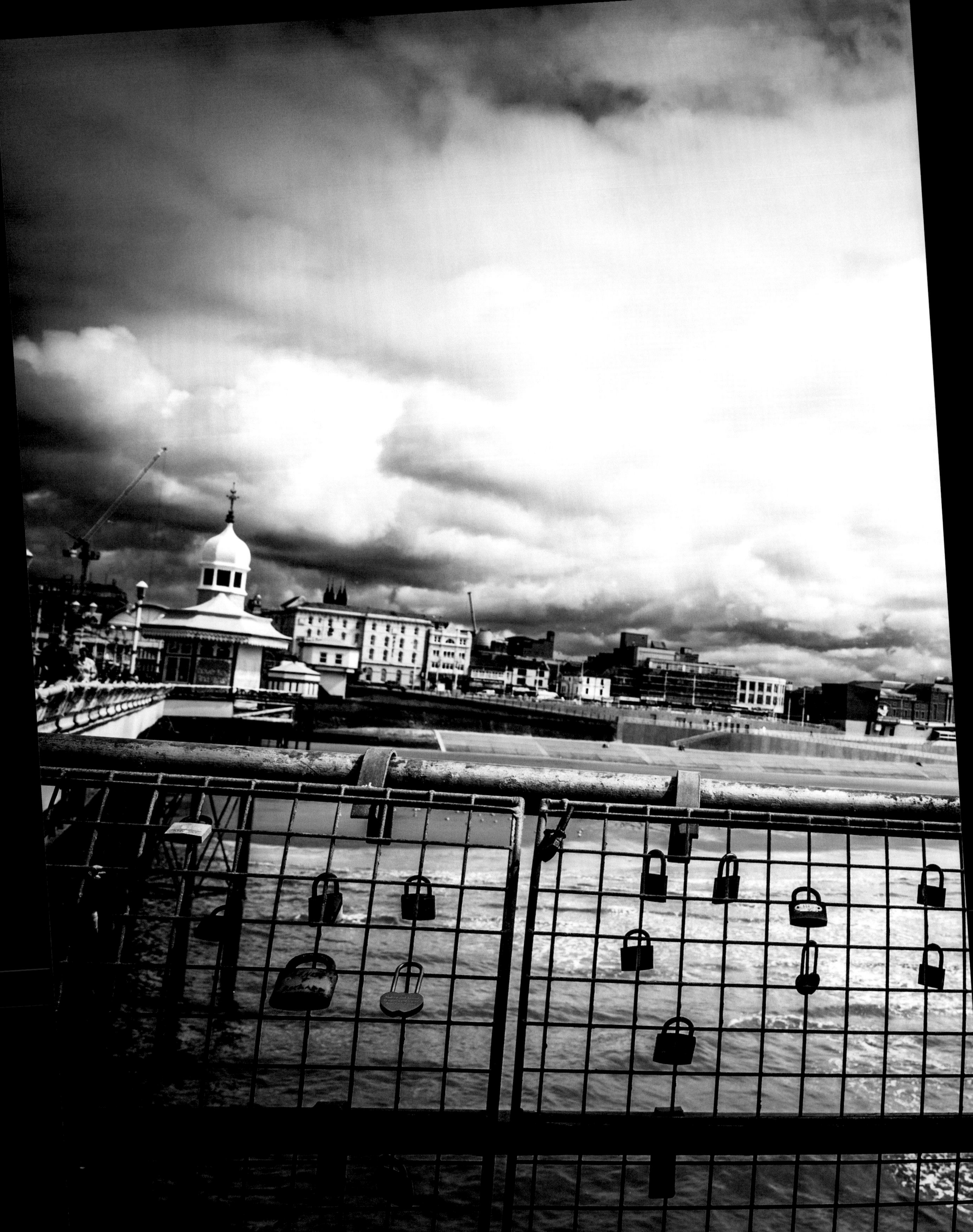

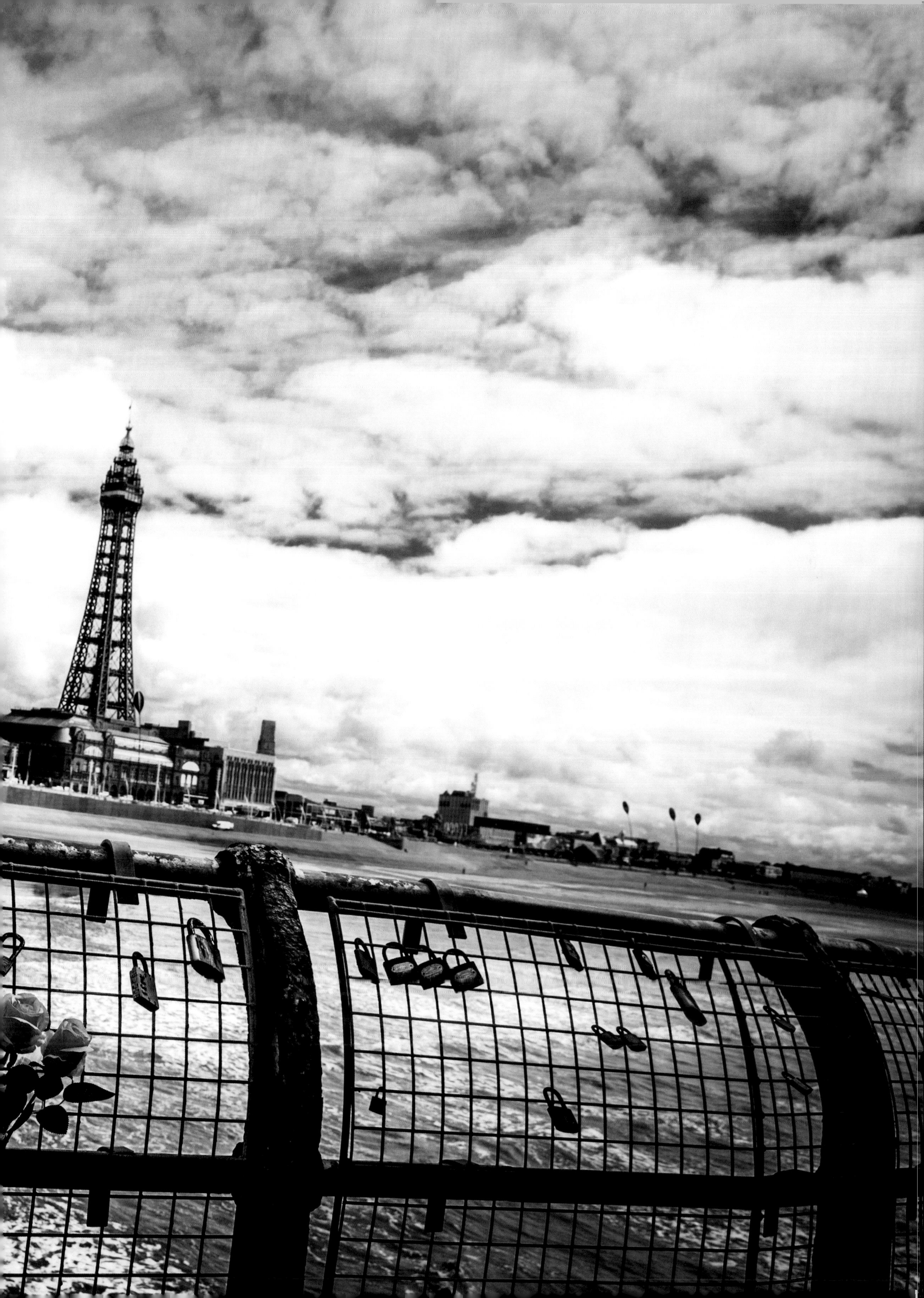

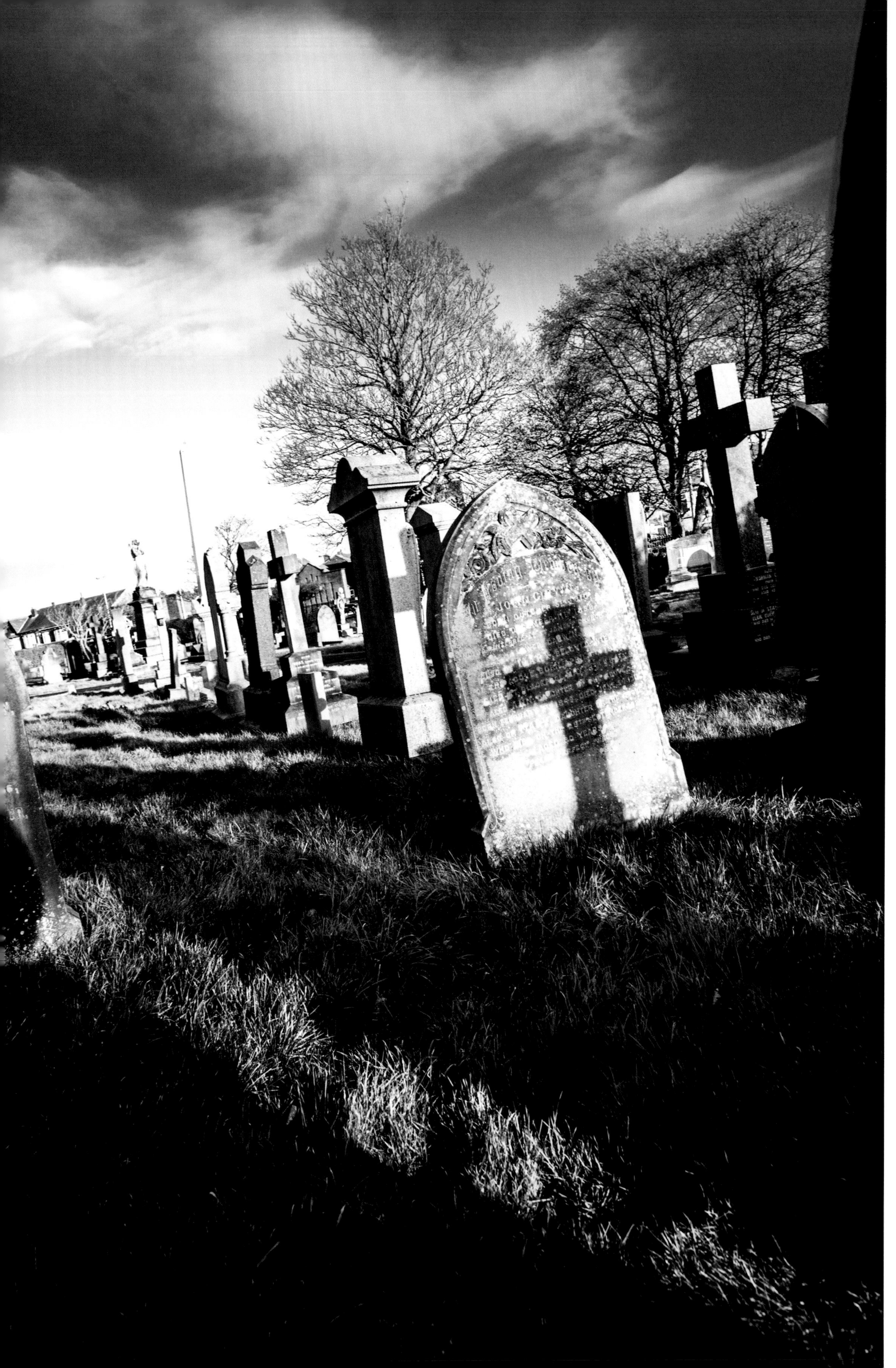

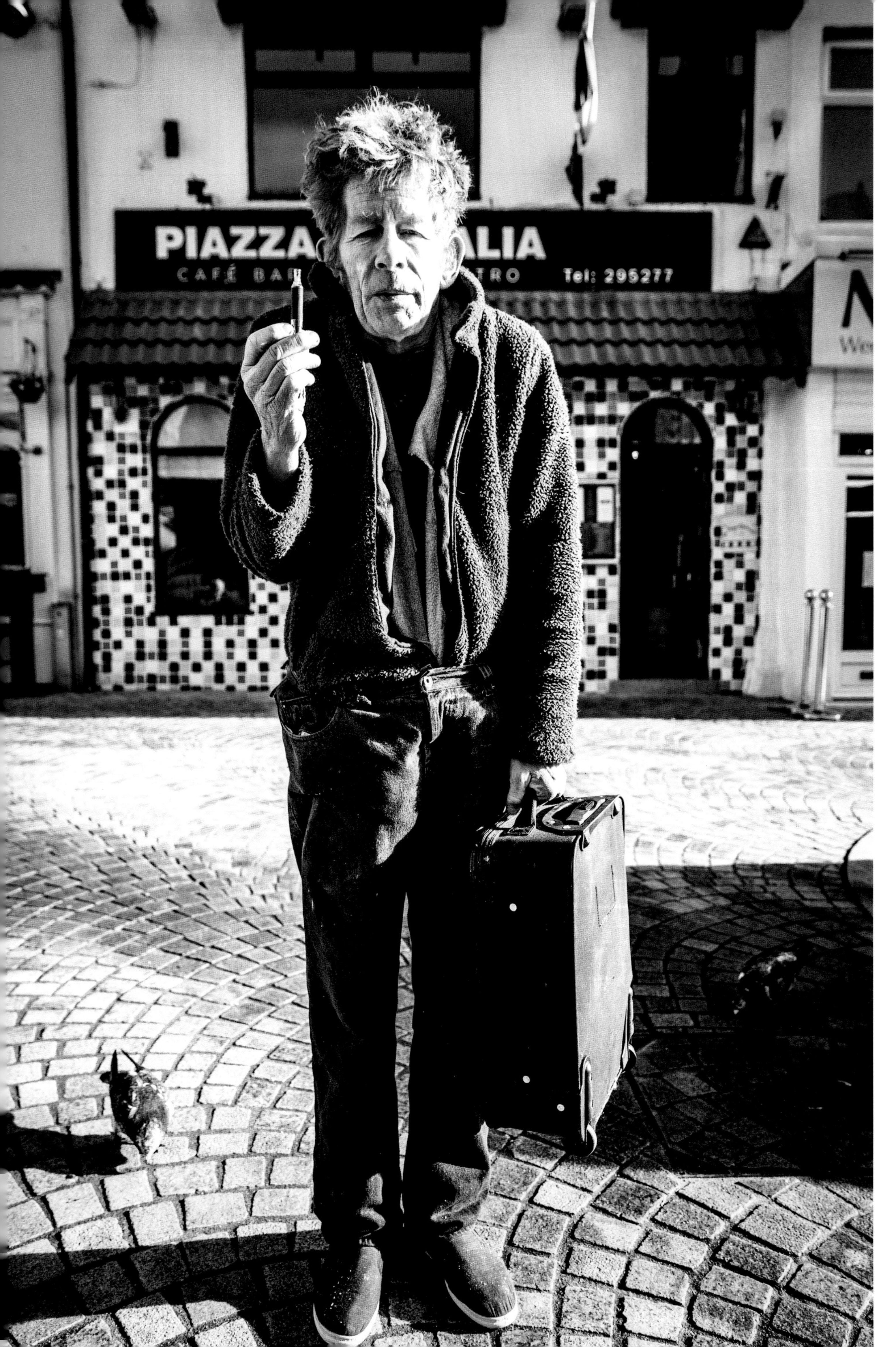

PIAZZA   ALIA
CAFÉ BAR   TRO   Tel: 295277

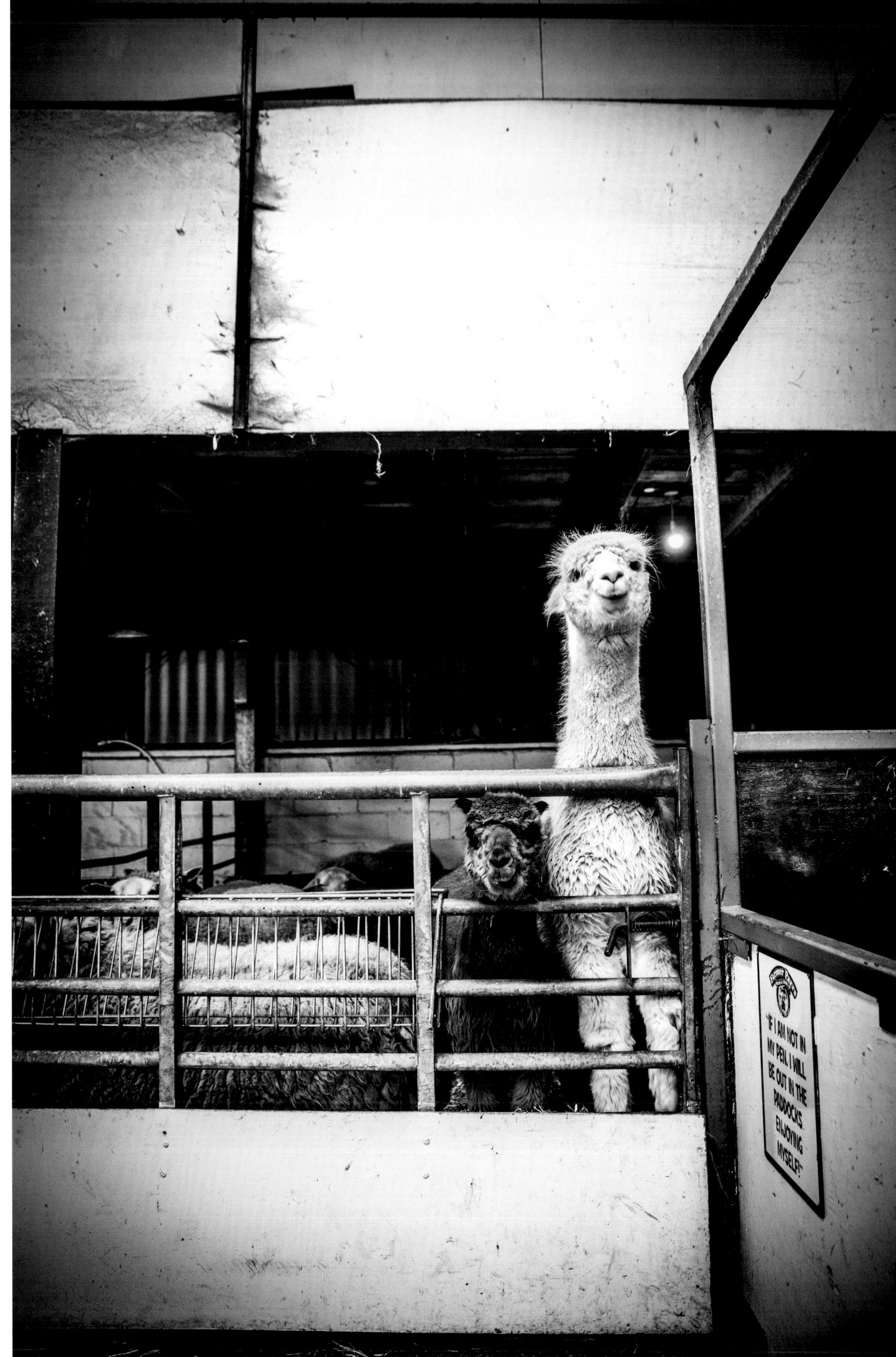
"IF I AM NOT IN
MY PEN, I WILL
BE OUT IN THE
PADDOCKS
ENJOYING
MYSELF"

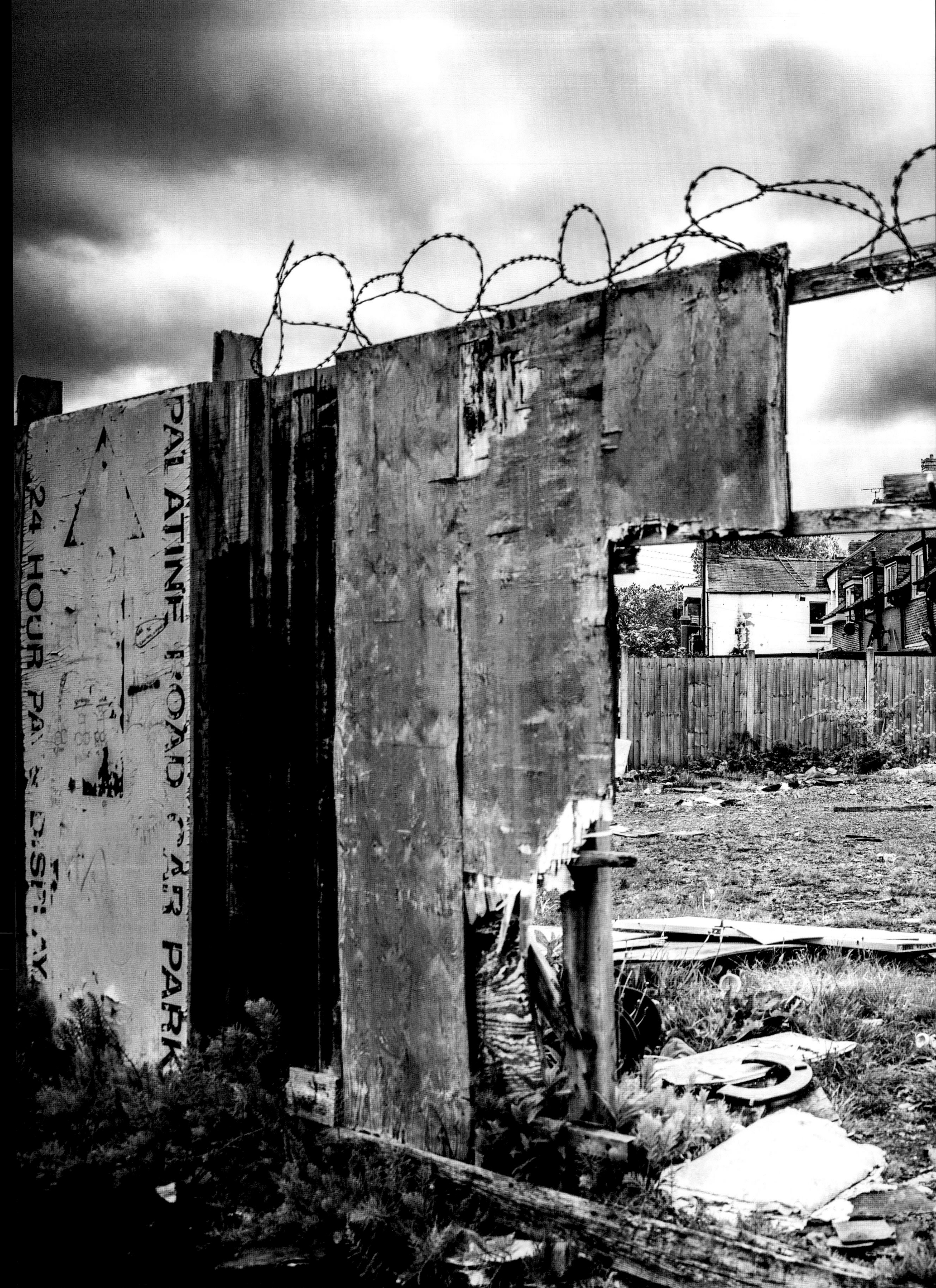

PALATINE ROAD CAR PARK
24 HOUR PAY & DISPLAY

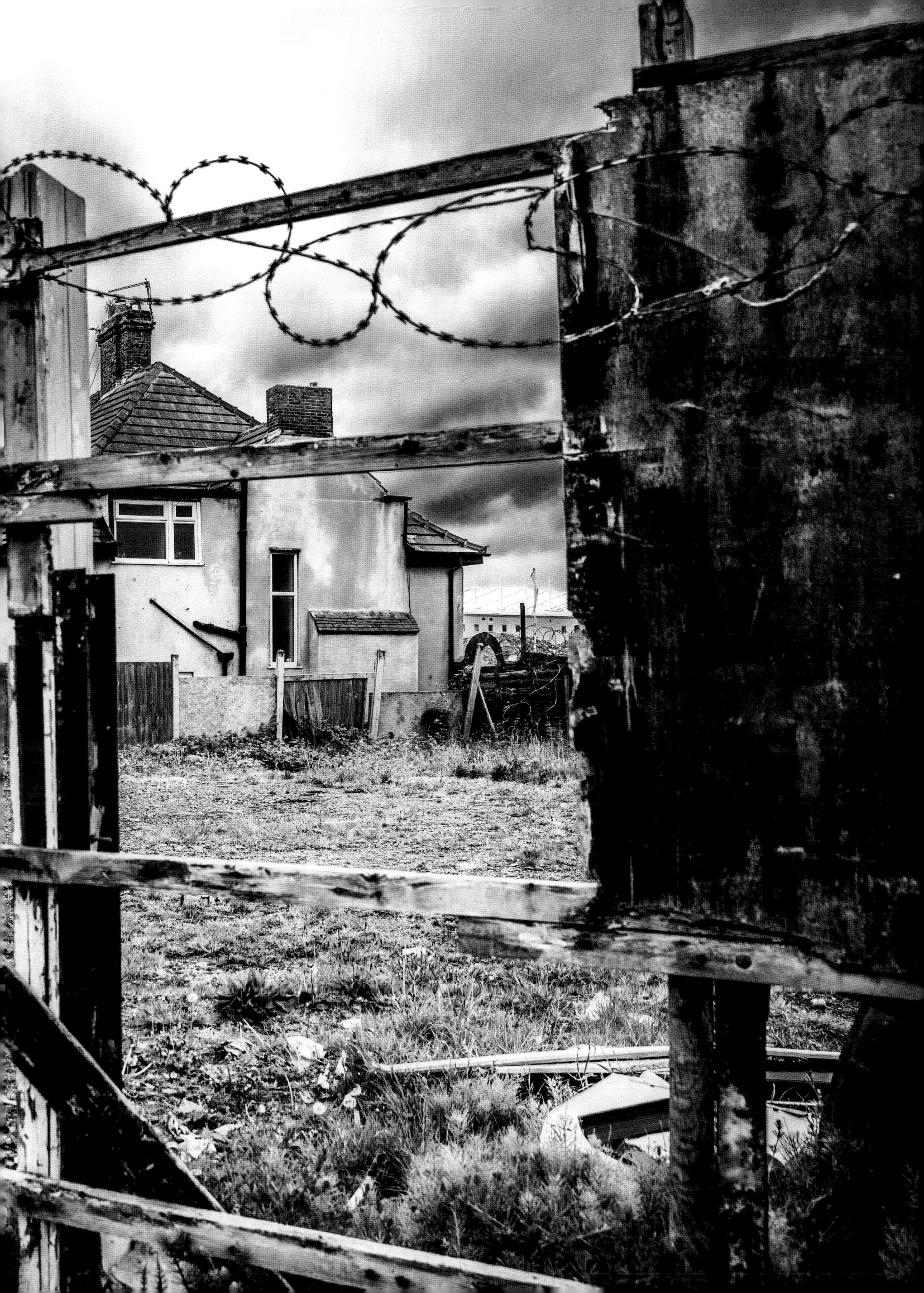

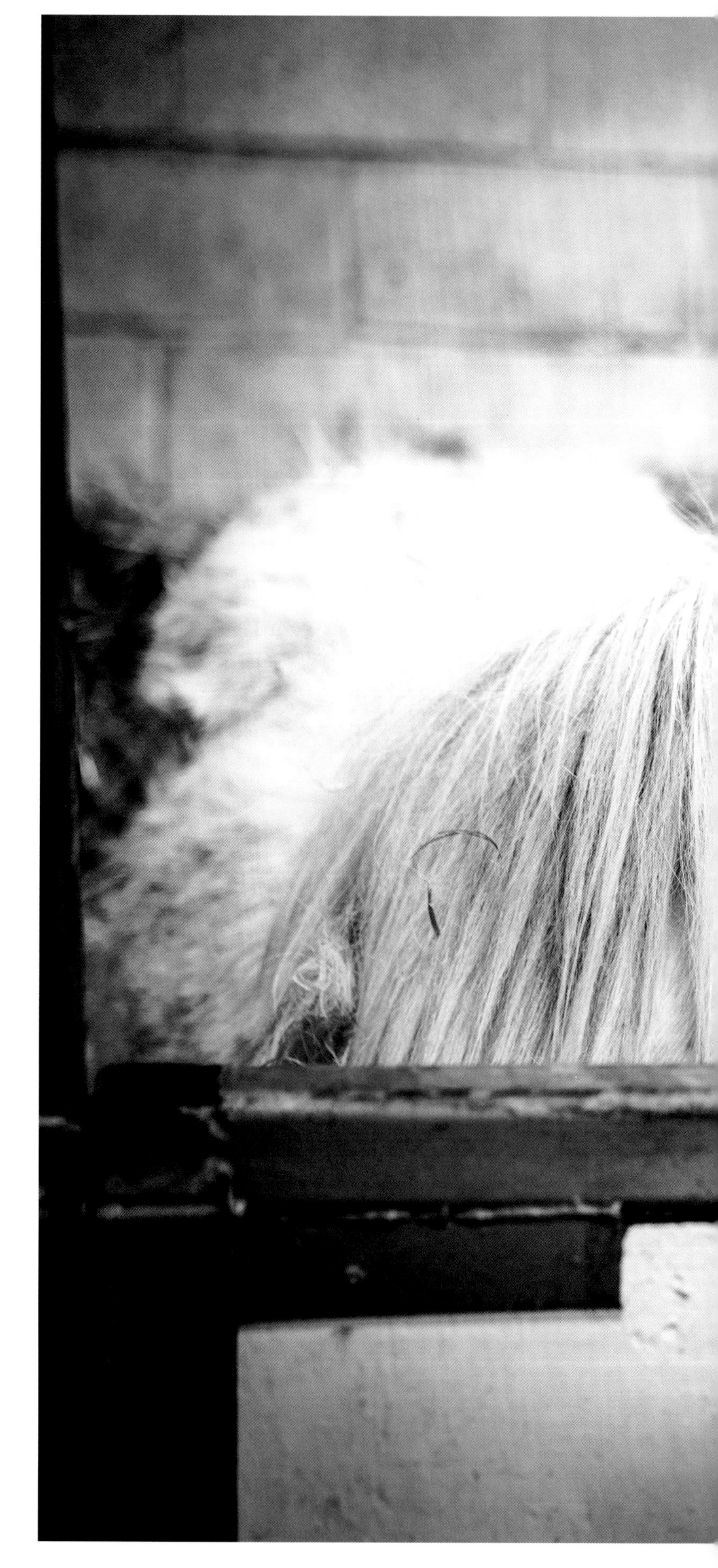

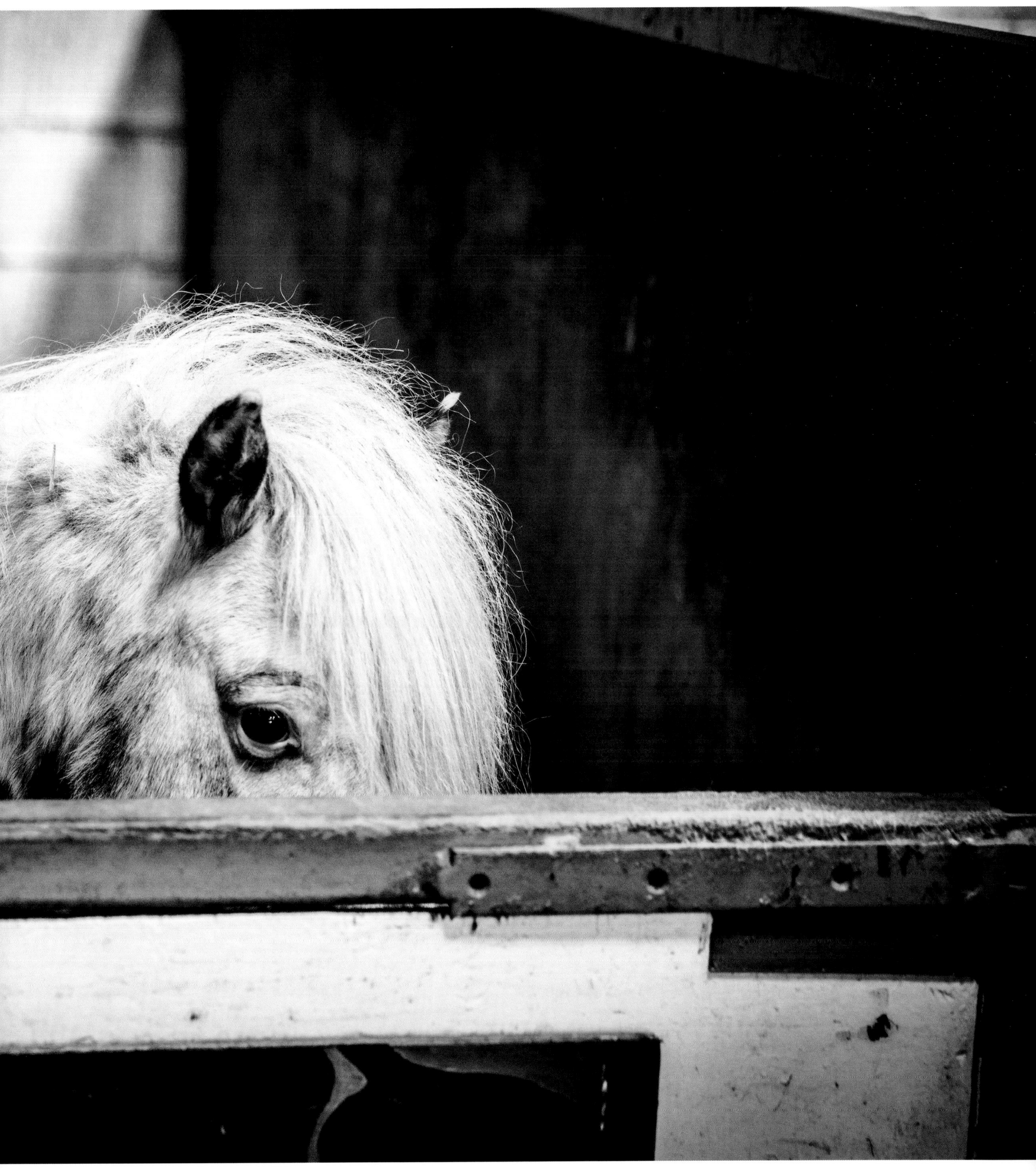

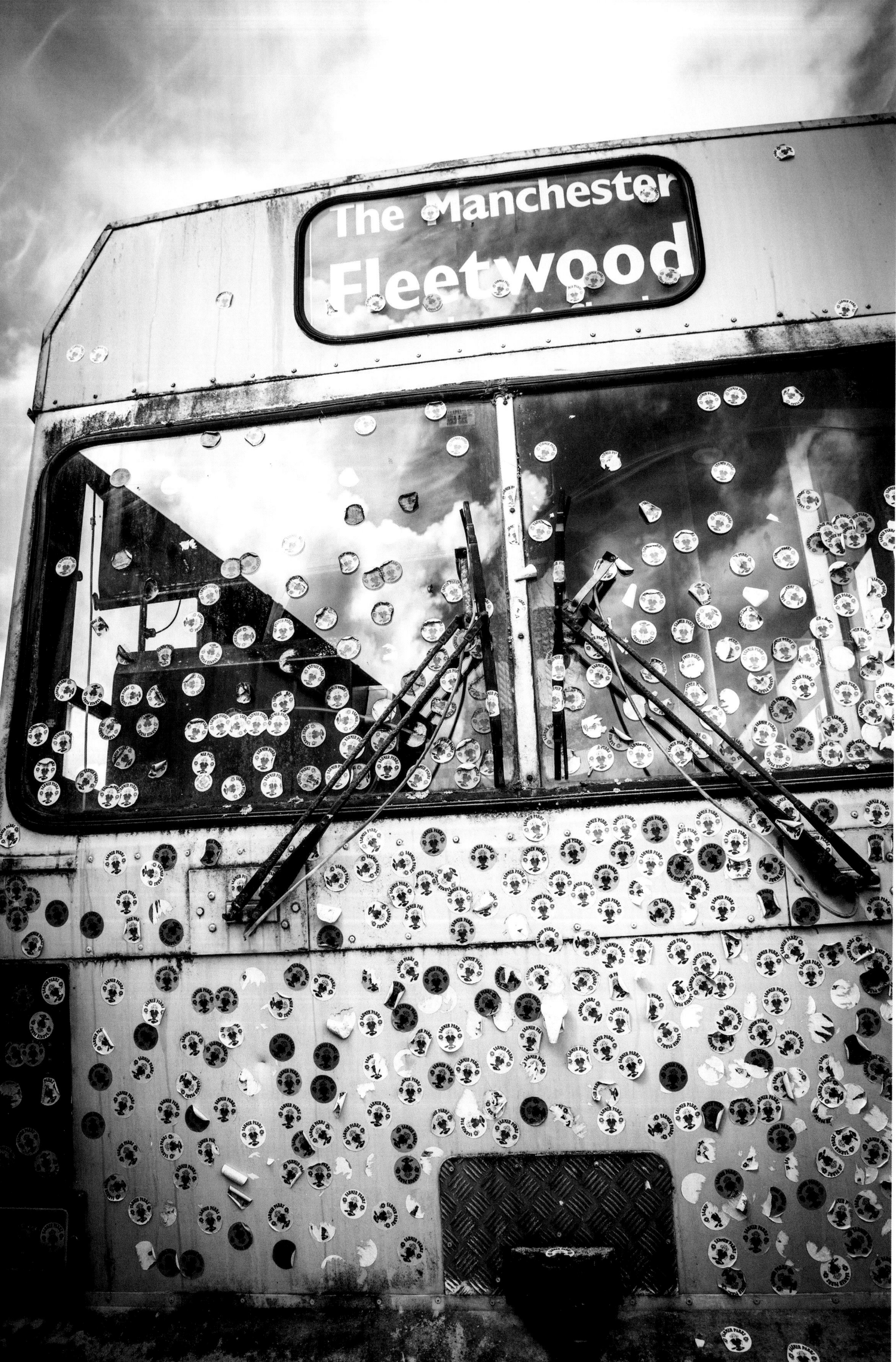

The Manchester
Fleetwood

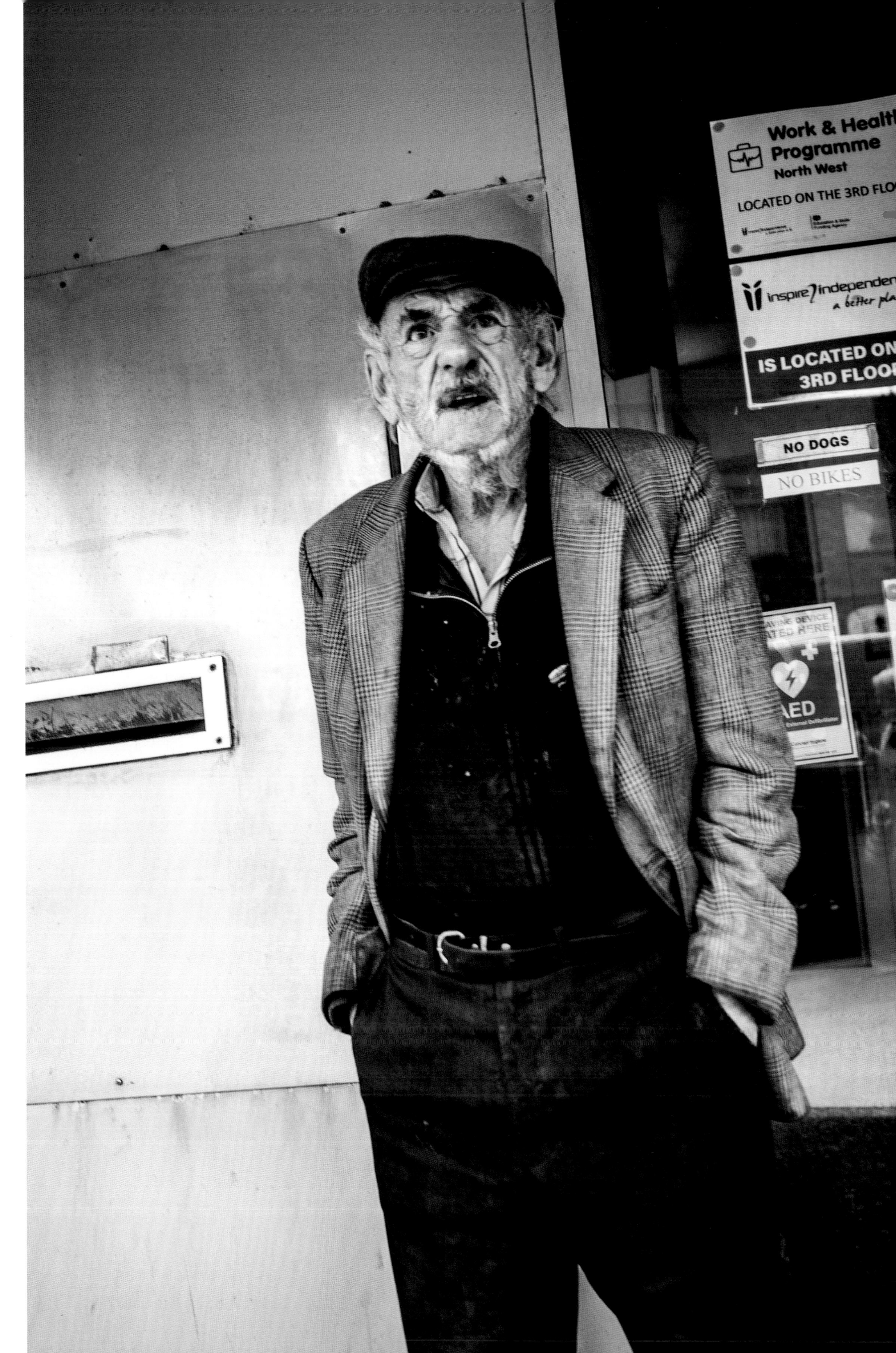

Work & Health
Programme
North West
LOCATED ON THE 3RD FLOOR
inspire independenc
a better place
IS LOCATED ON
3RD FLOOR
NO DOGS
NO BIKES
AED

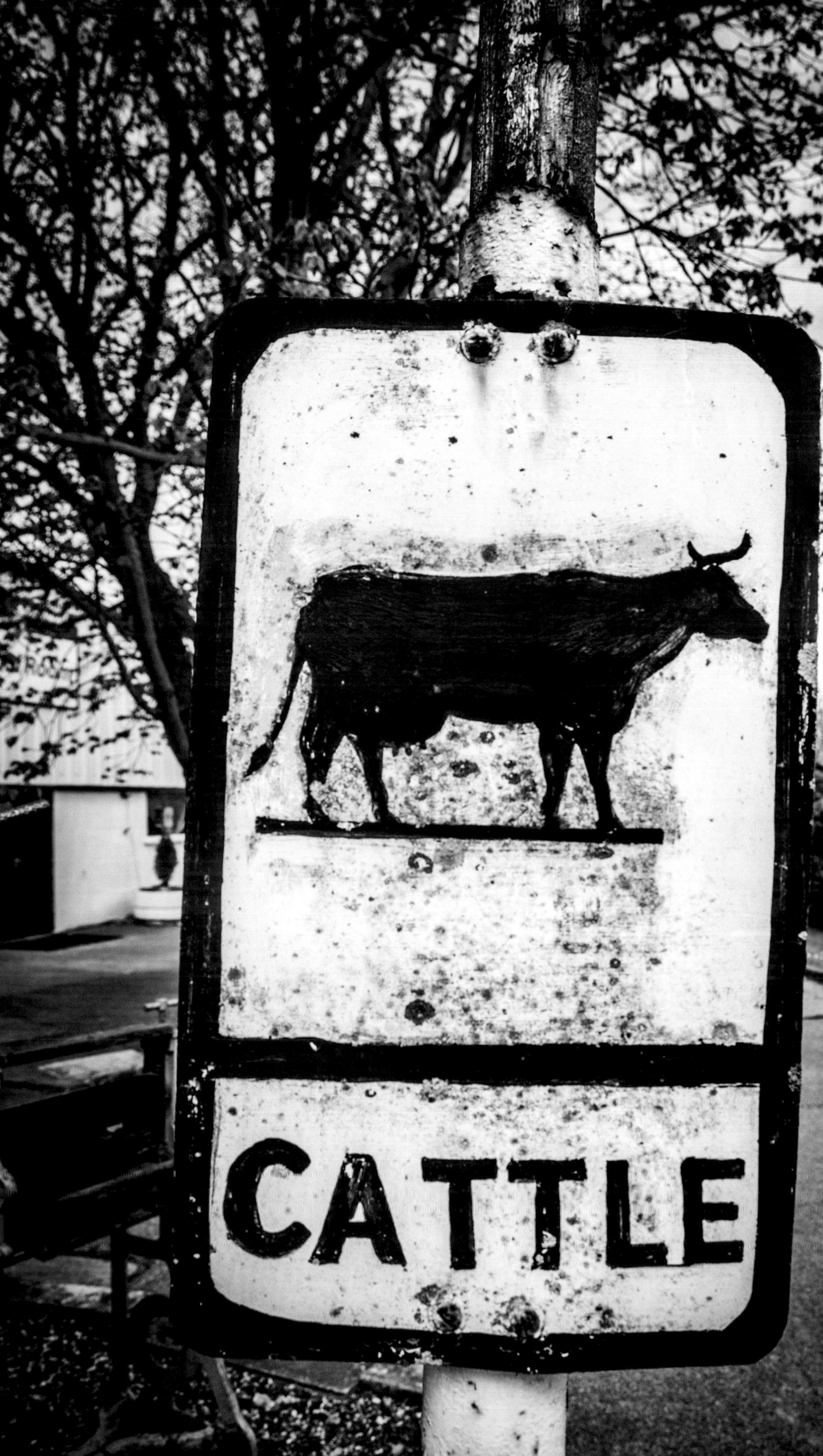

CATTLE

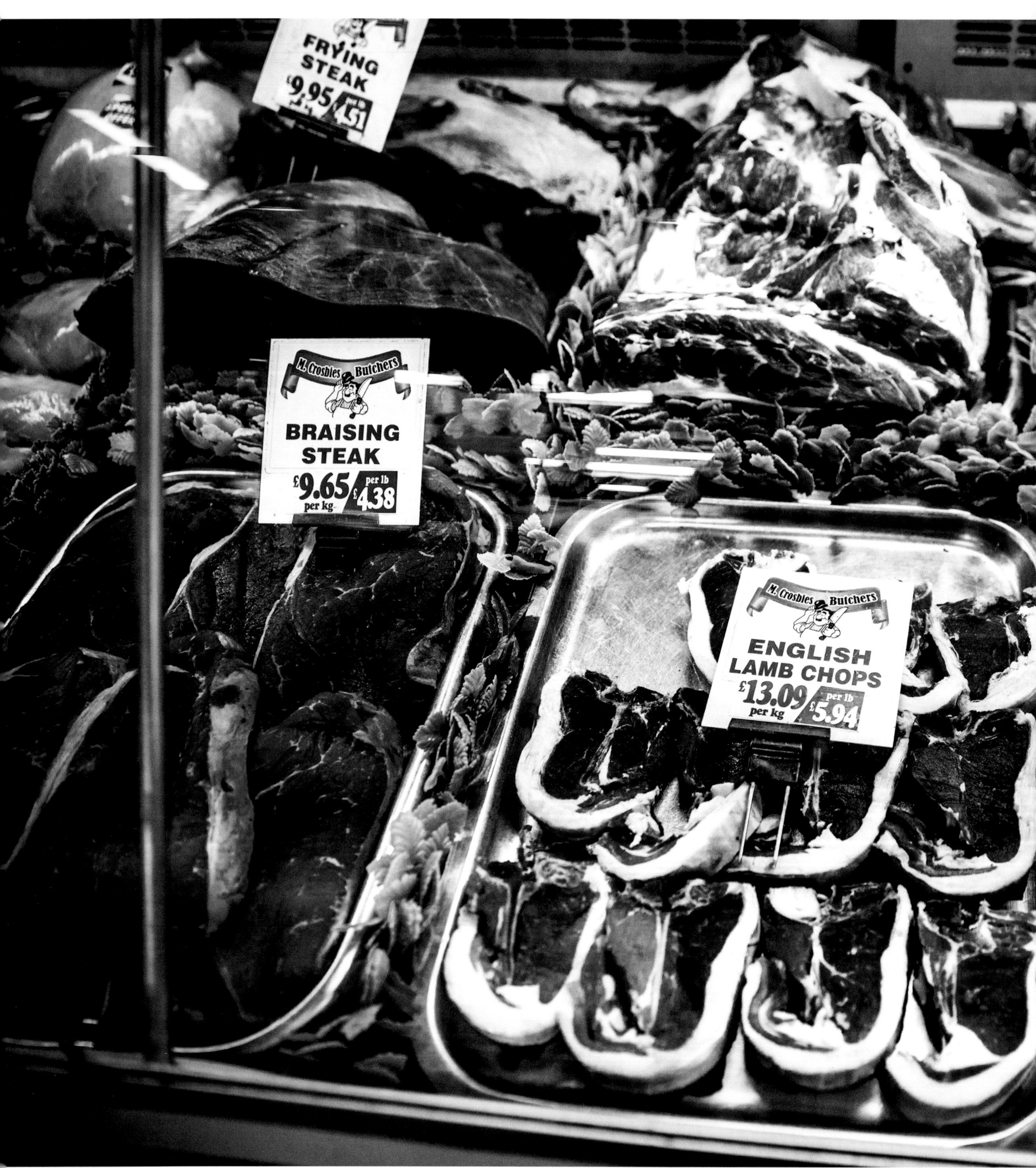
FRYING
STEAK
£9.95
M. Crosbies Butchers
BRAISING
STEAK
£9.65
per kg
per lb
£4.38
M. Crosbies Butchers
ENGLISH
LAMB CHOPS
£13.09
per kg
per lb
£5.94

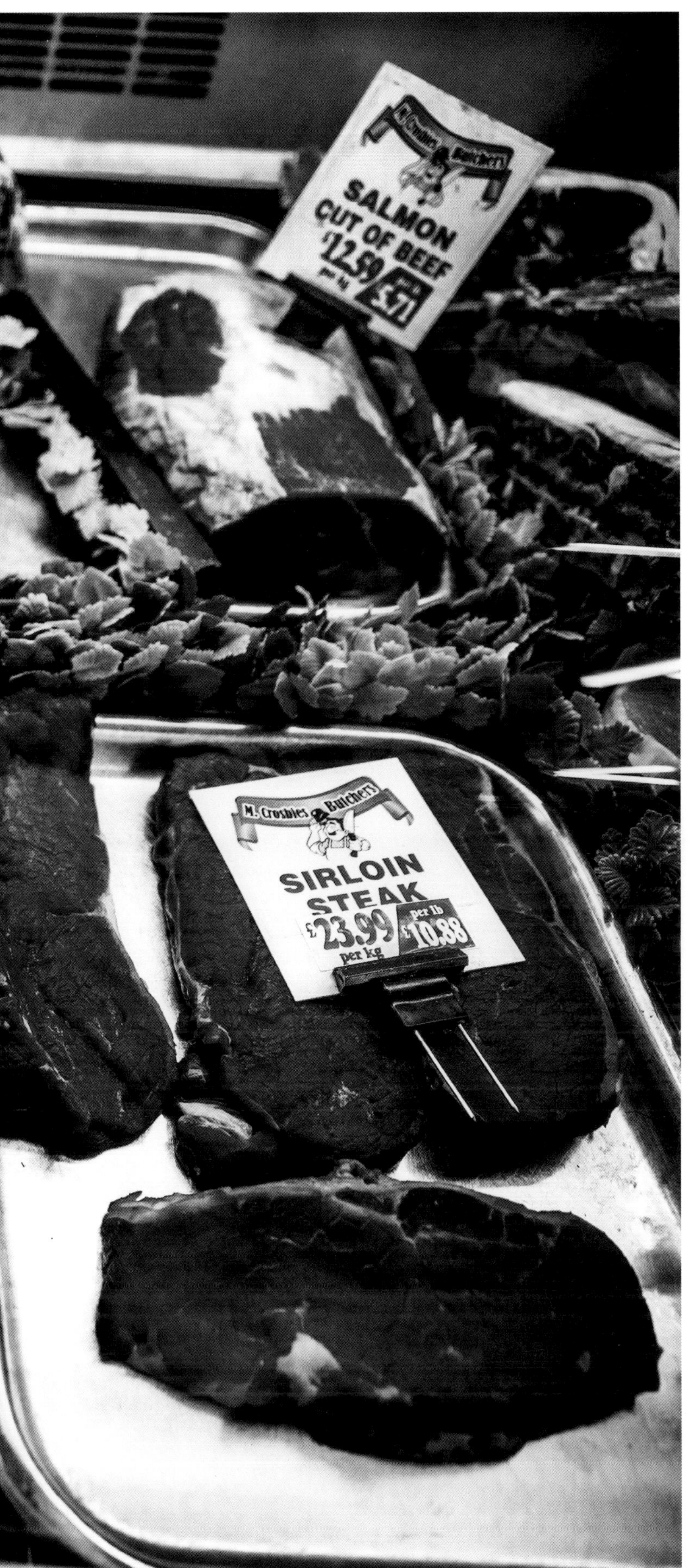
M. Crosbies Butchers
SALMON
CUT OF BEEF
£12.59
per k
M. Crosbies Butchers
SIRLOIN
STEAK
£23.99
per kg
per lb
£10.88

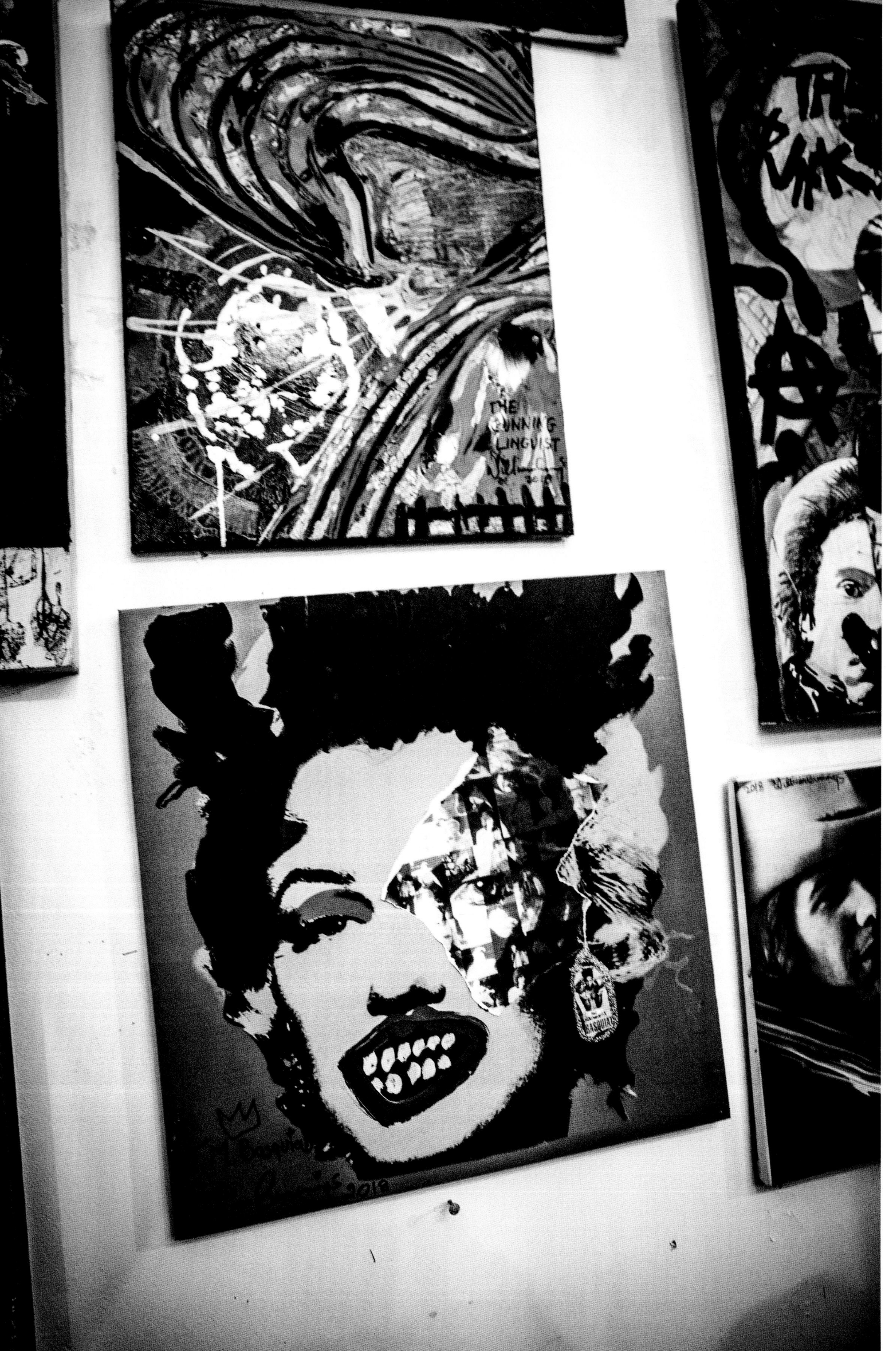
THE
CUNNING
LINGUIST

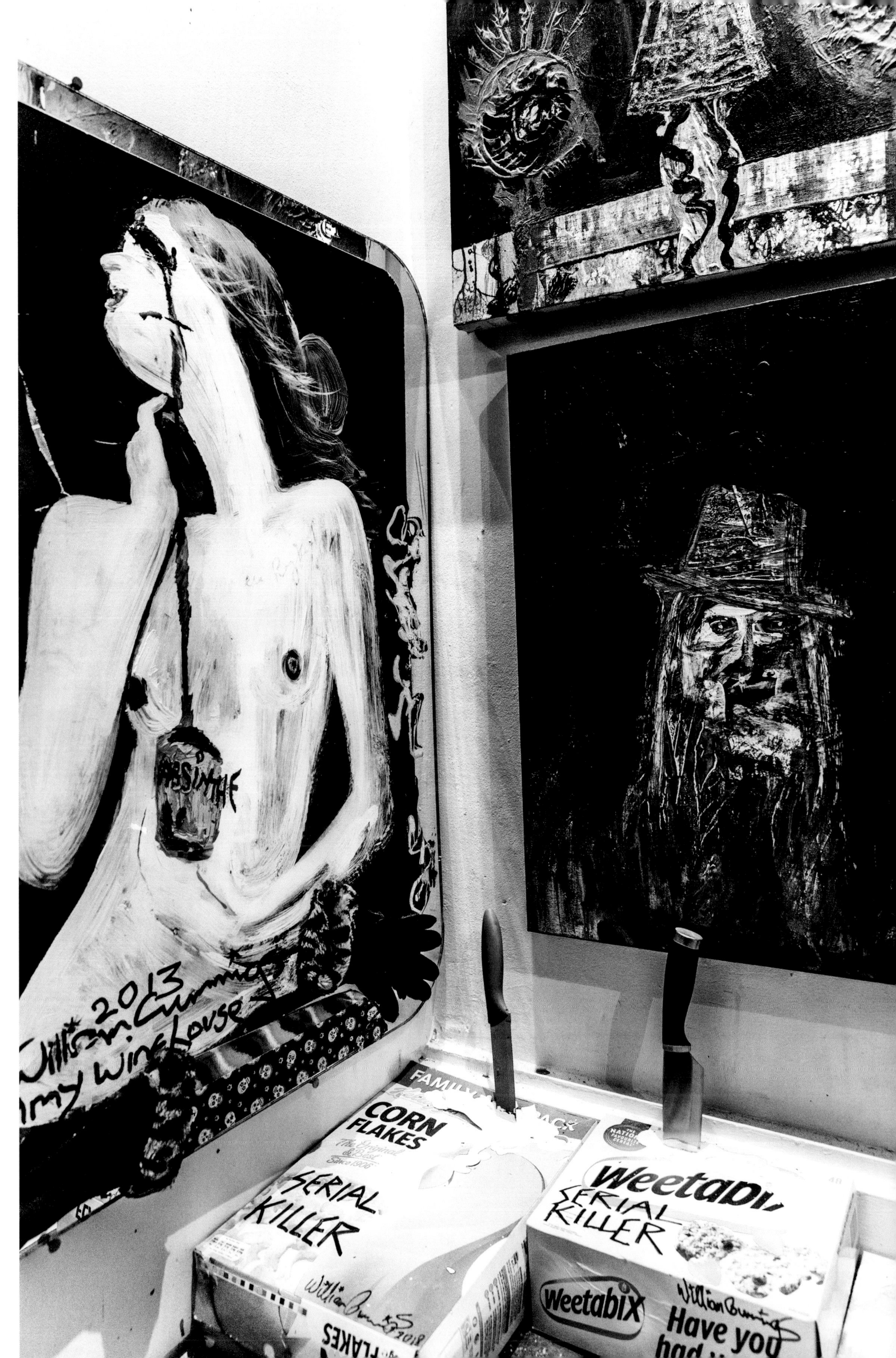
ASSINTHE
2013
William Cunning
Amy Winehouse
FAMILY
CORN
FLAKES
The Original
& Best
Since 1906
SERIAL
KILLER
William Cunning
FLAKES
THE
NATION
Weetabix
SERIAL
KILLER
Weetabix
William Cunning
Have you
had ...

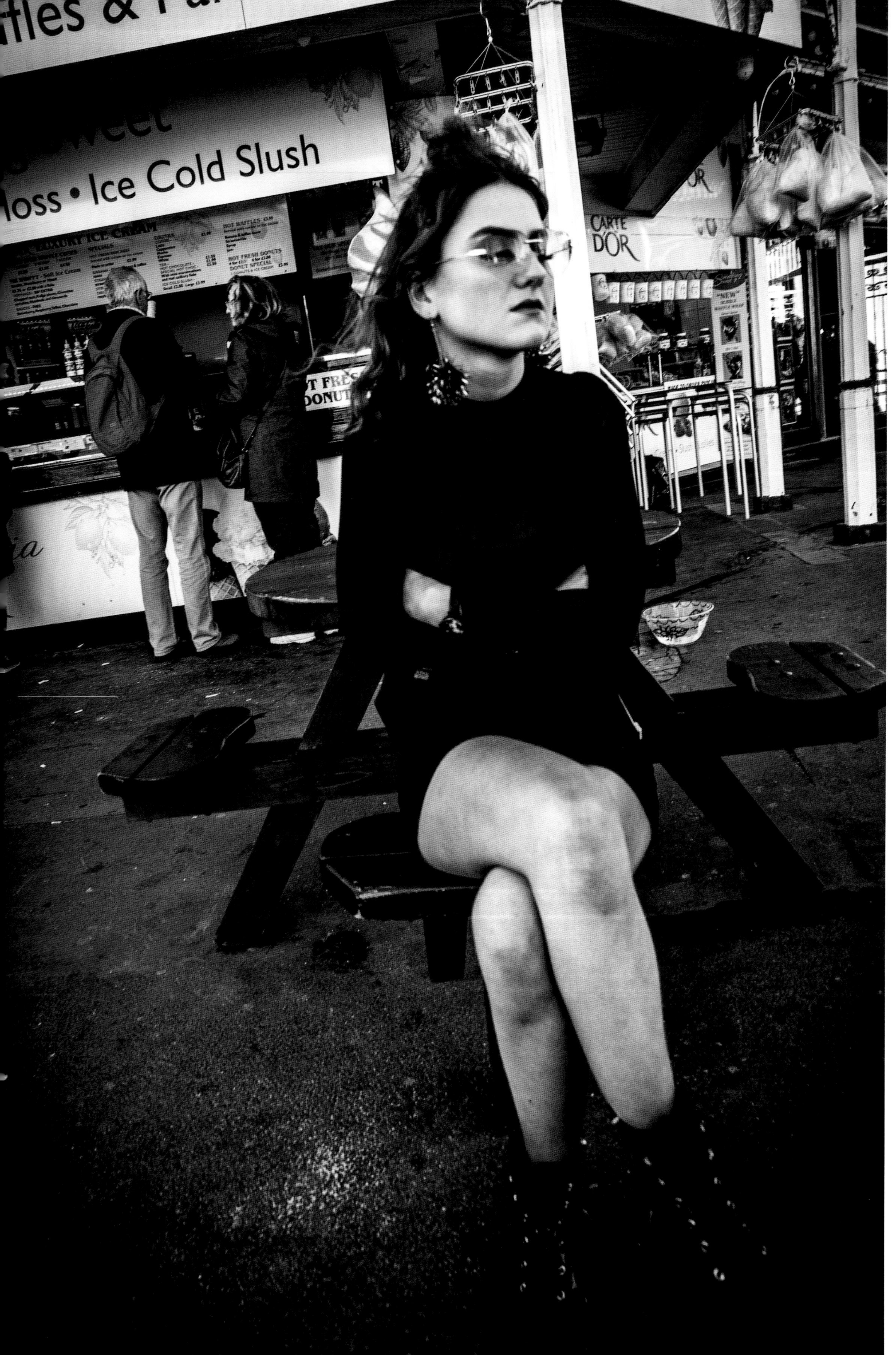

ffles & Pa
weet
oss • Ice Cold Slush
LUXURY ICE CREAM
HOT WAFFLES
HOT FRESH DONUTS
CARTE D'OR
NEW

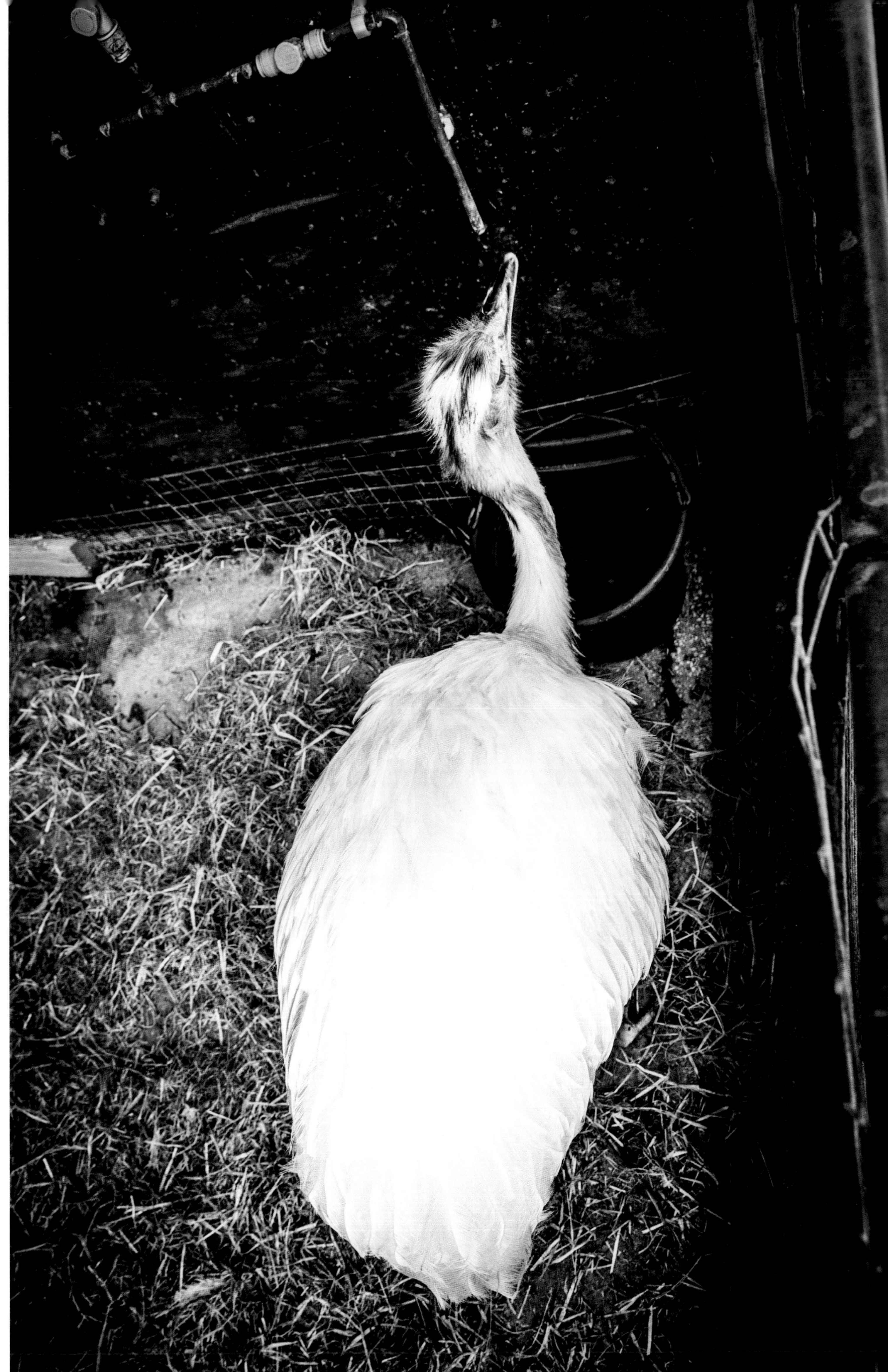

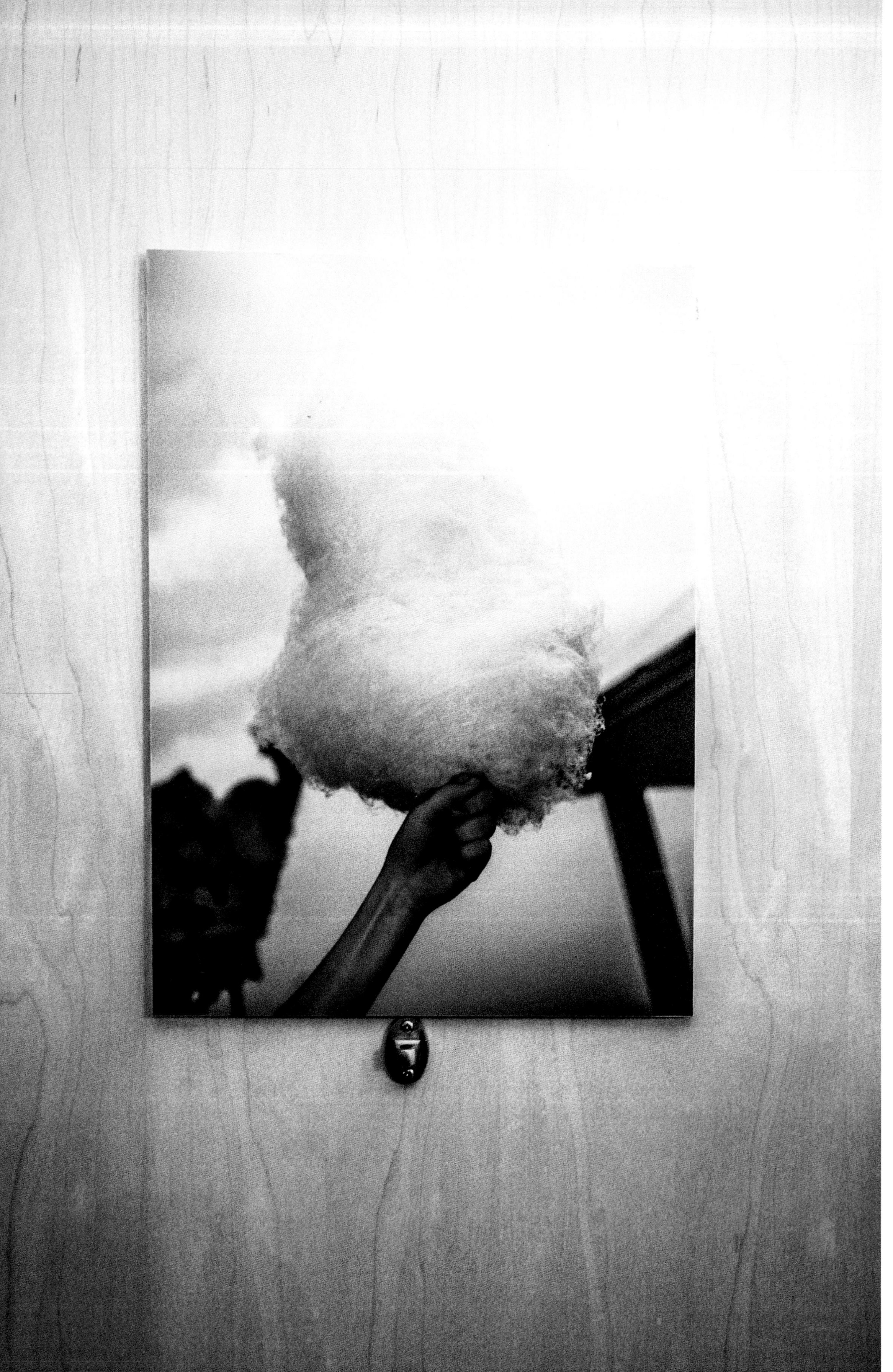

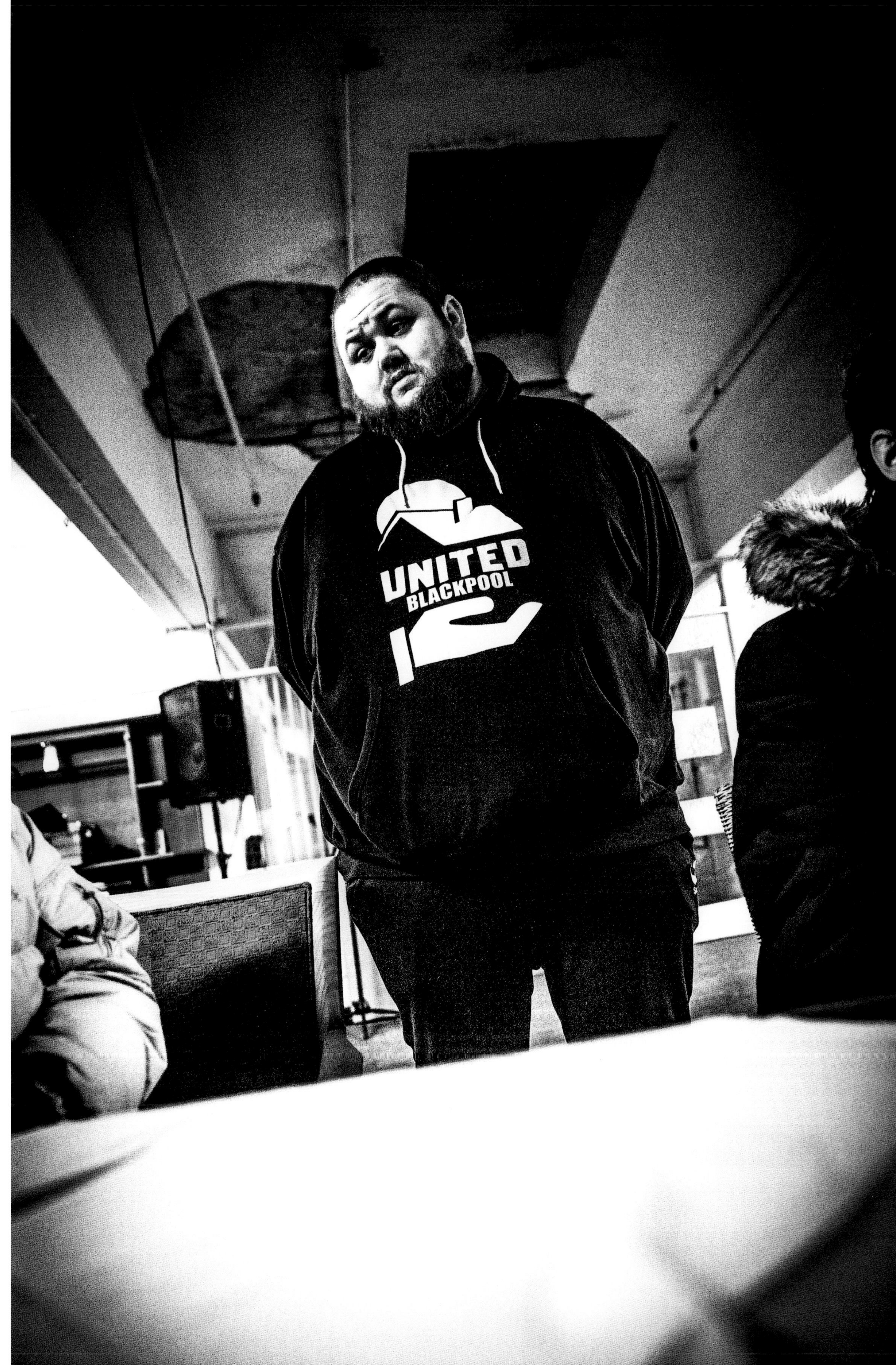

UNITED
BLACKPOOL

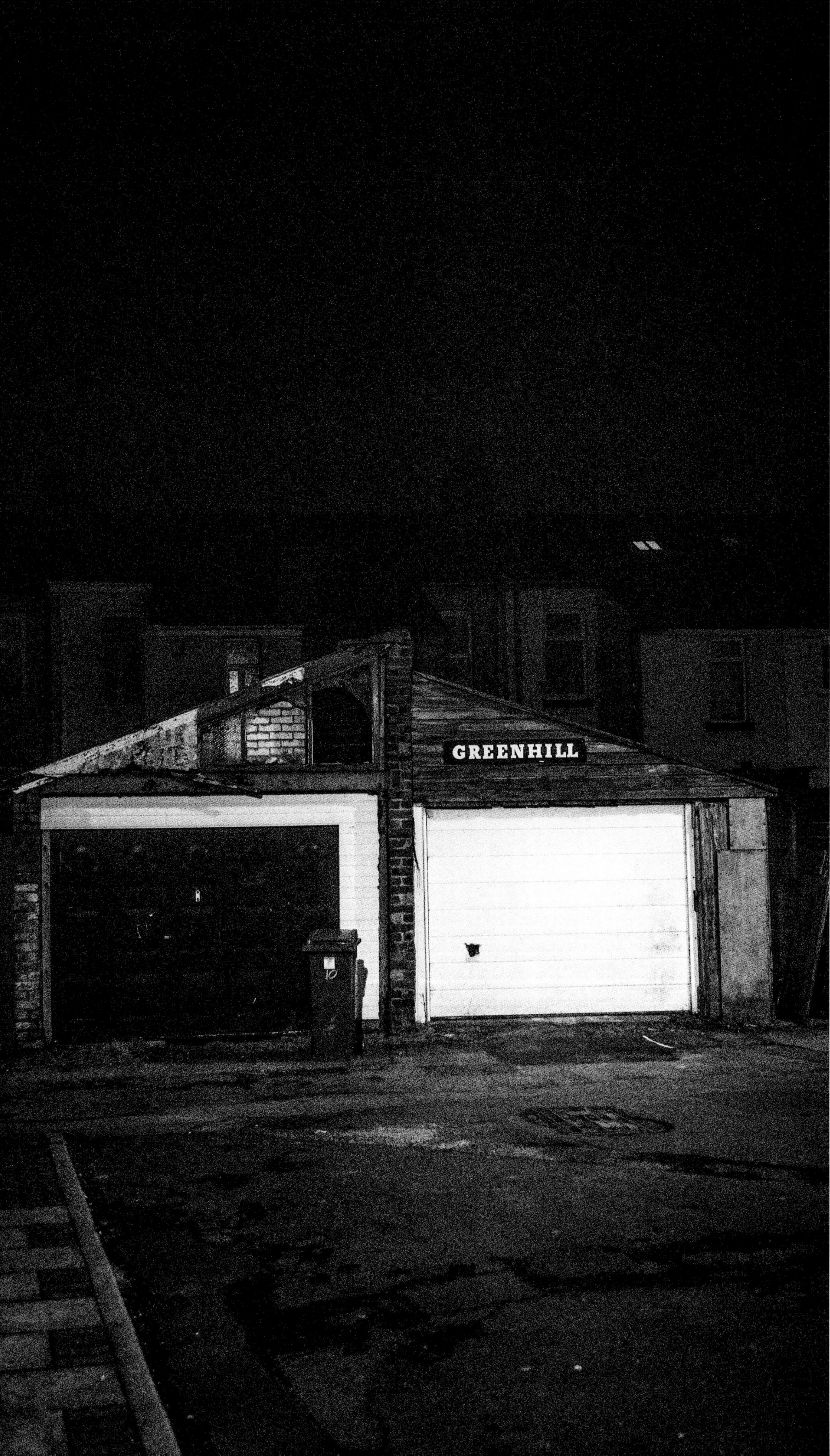
GREENHILL

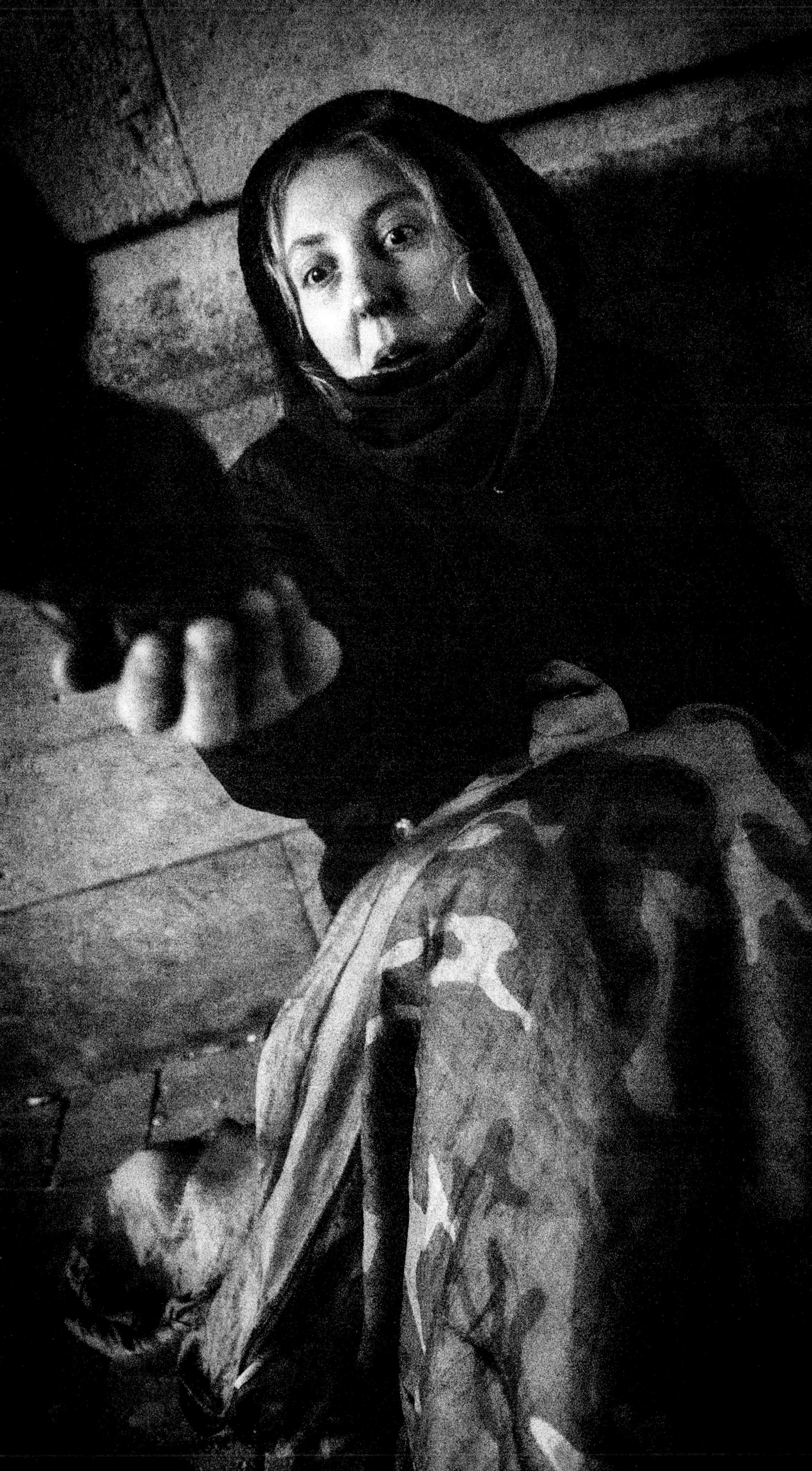

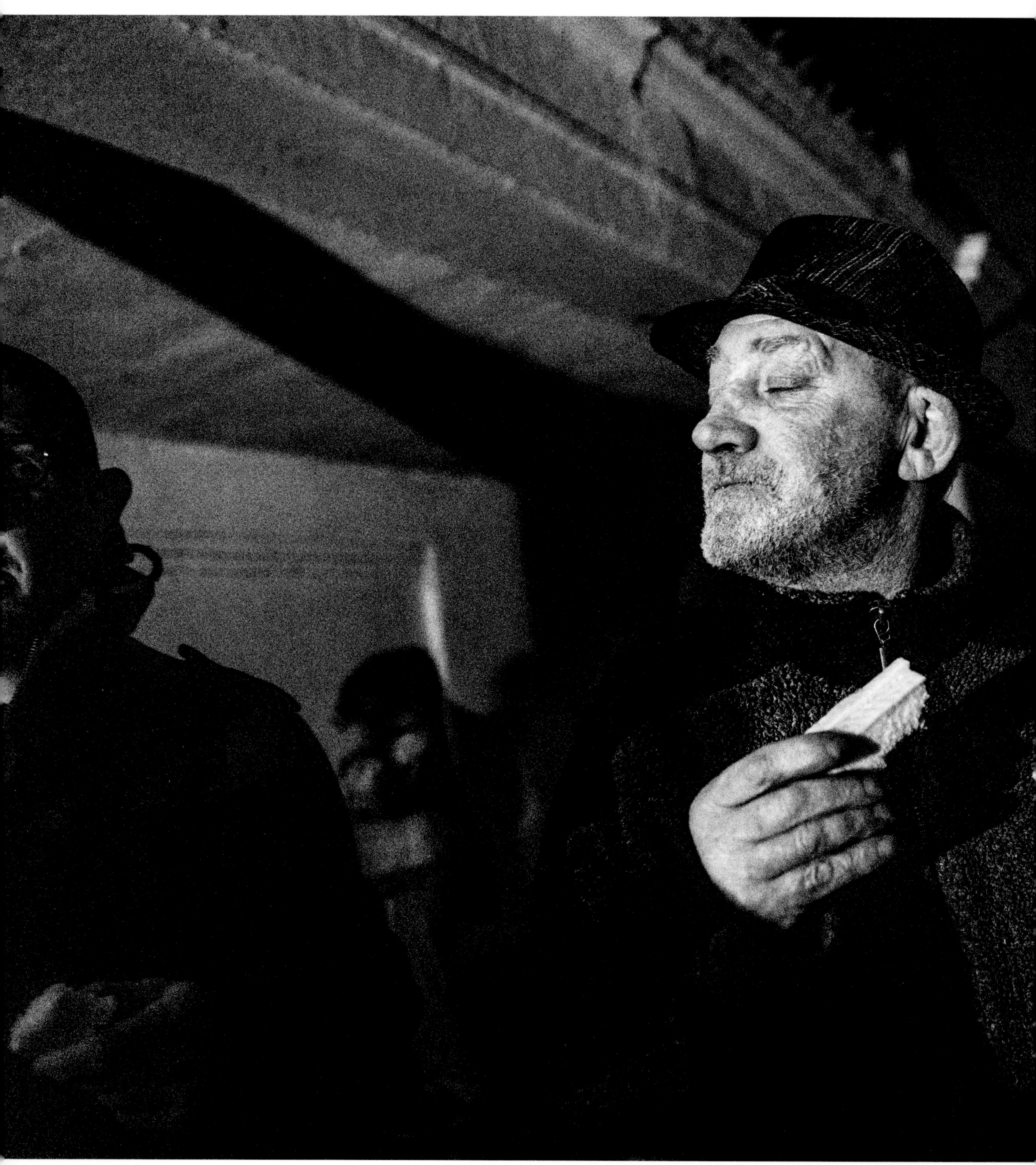

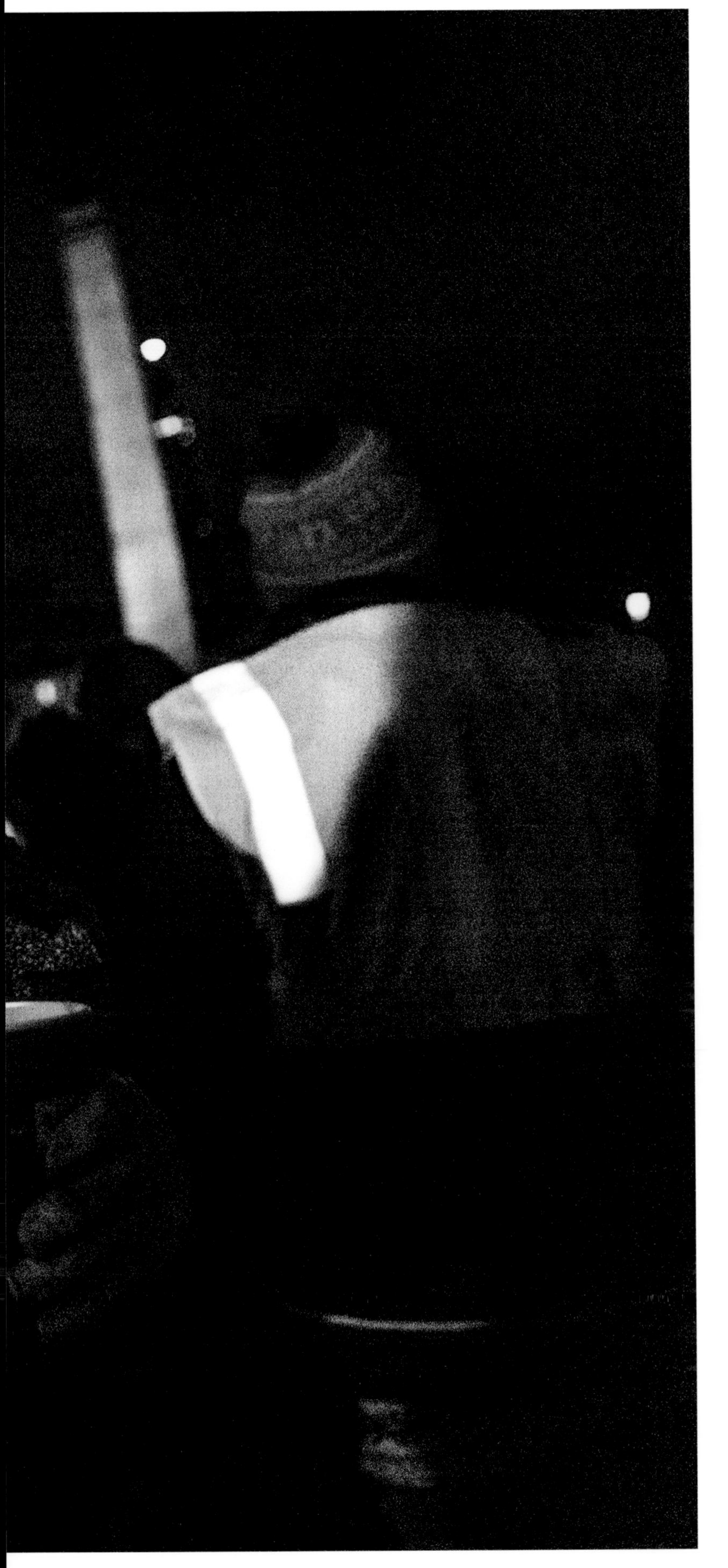

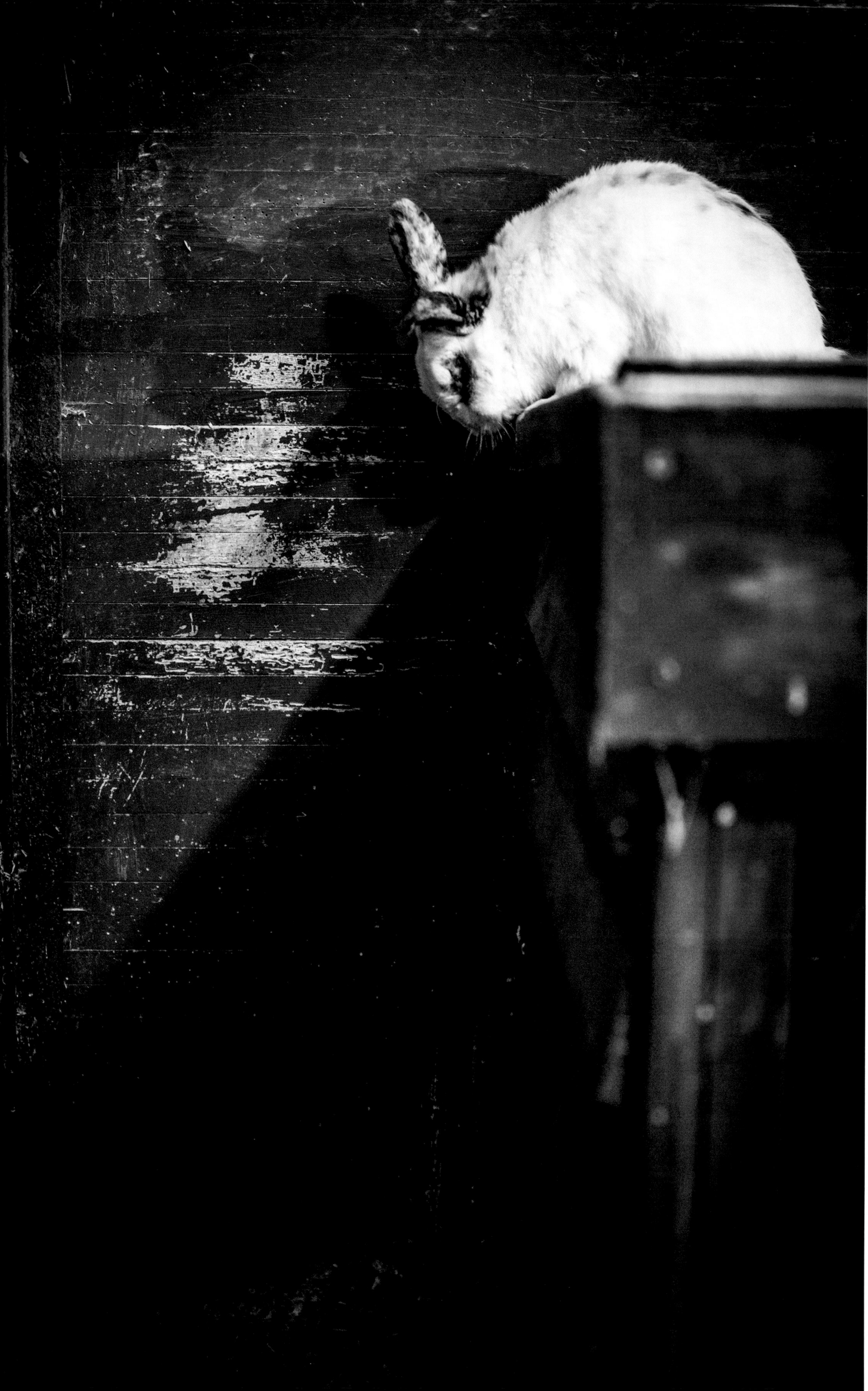

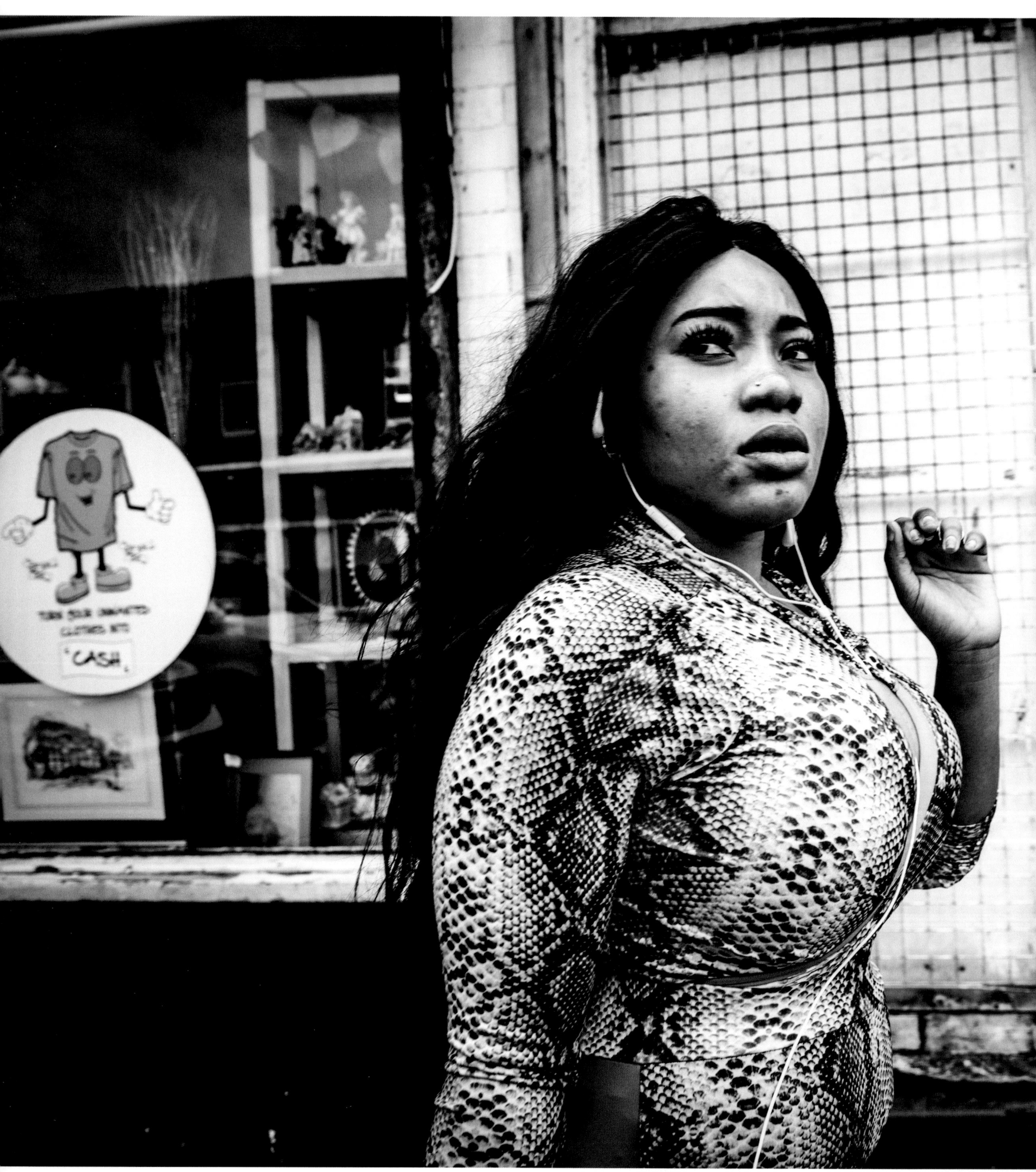

TURN YOUR UNWANTED
CLOTHES INTO
'CASH'

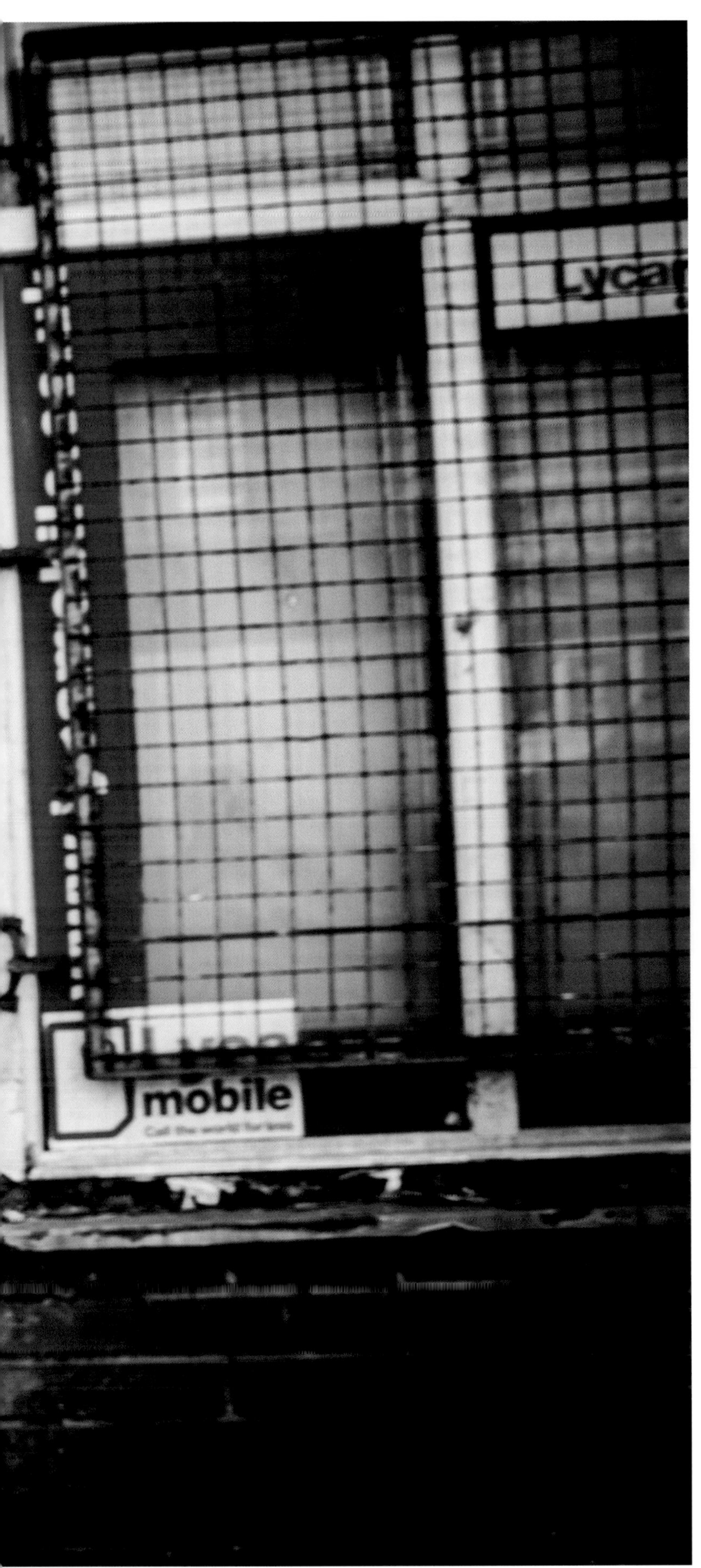

Lyca
mobile

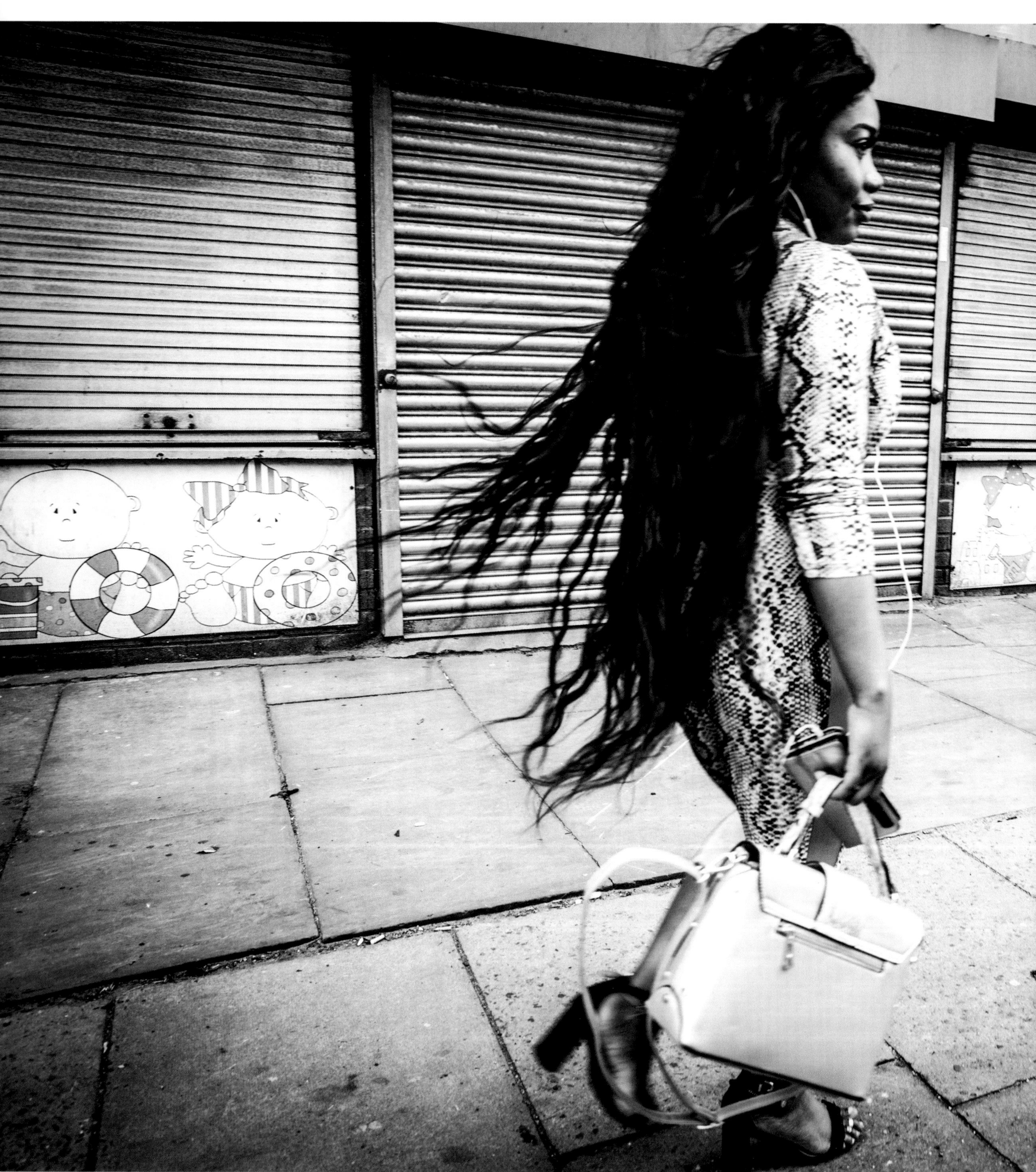

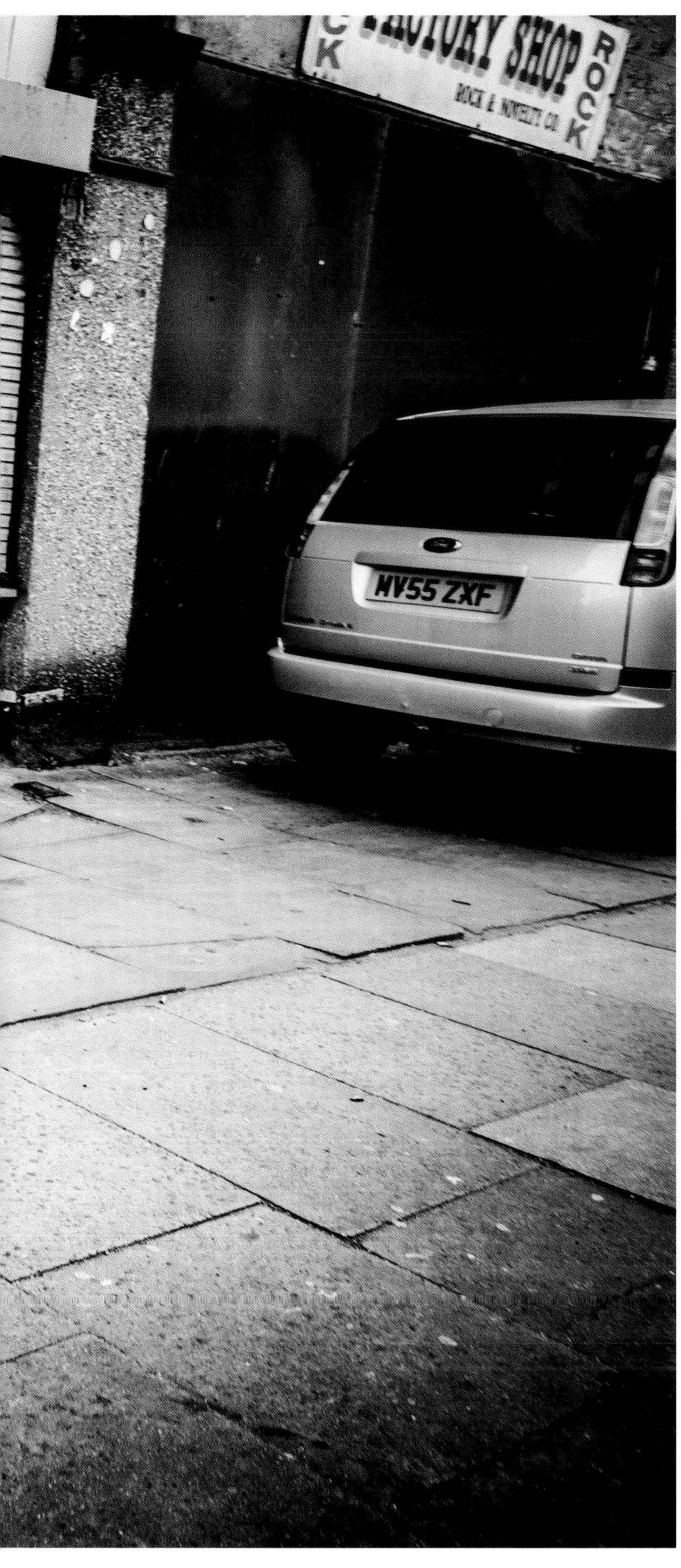
FACTORY SHOP
ROCK
ROCK
ROCK & NOVELTY CO.
HV55 ZXF

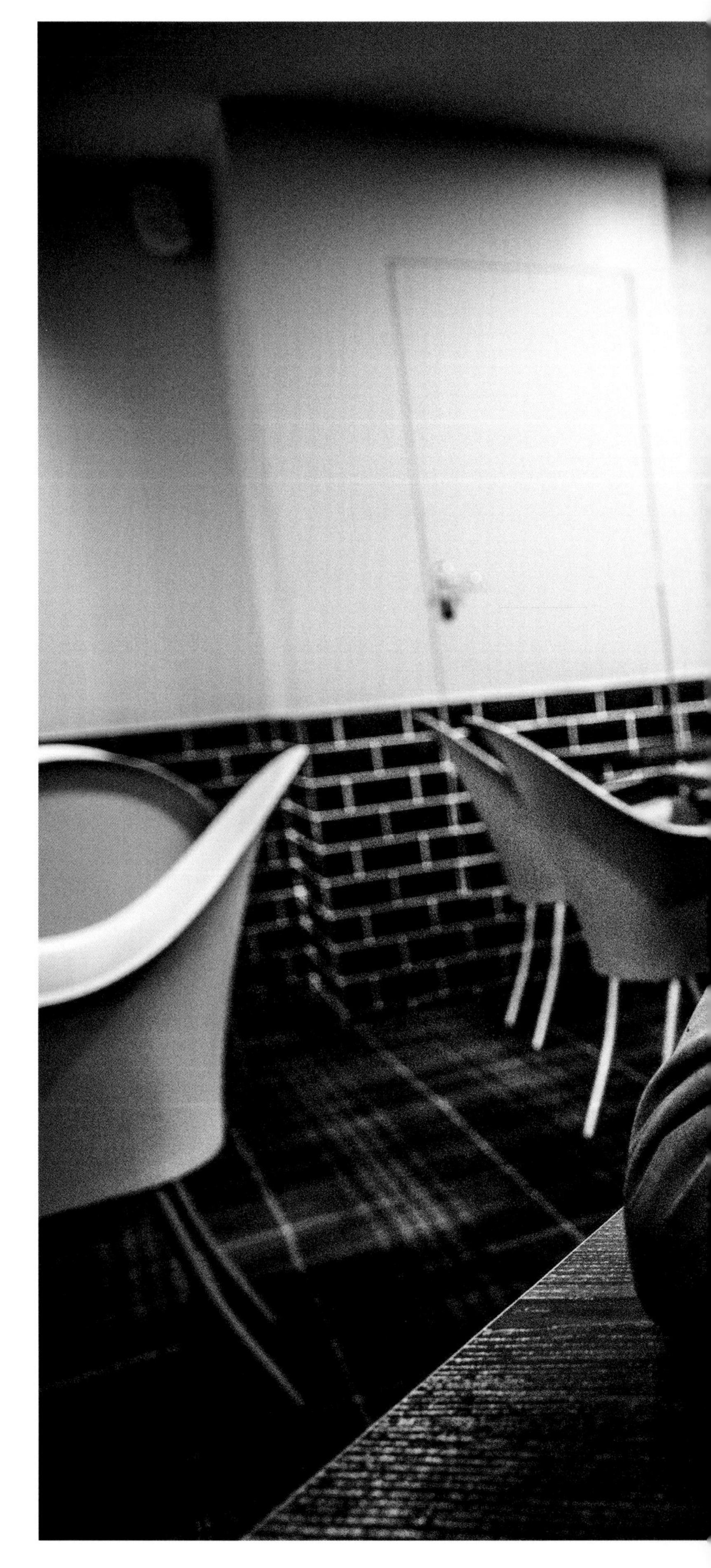

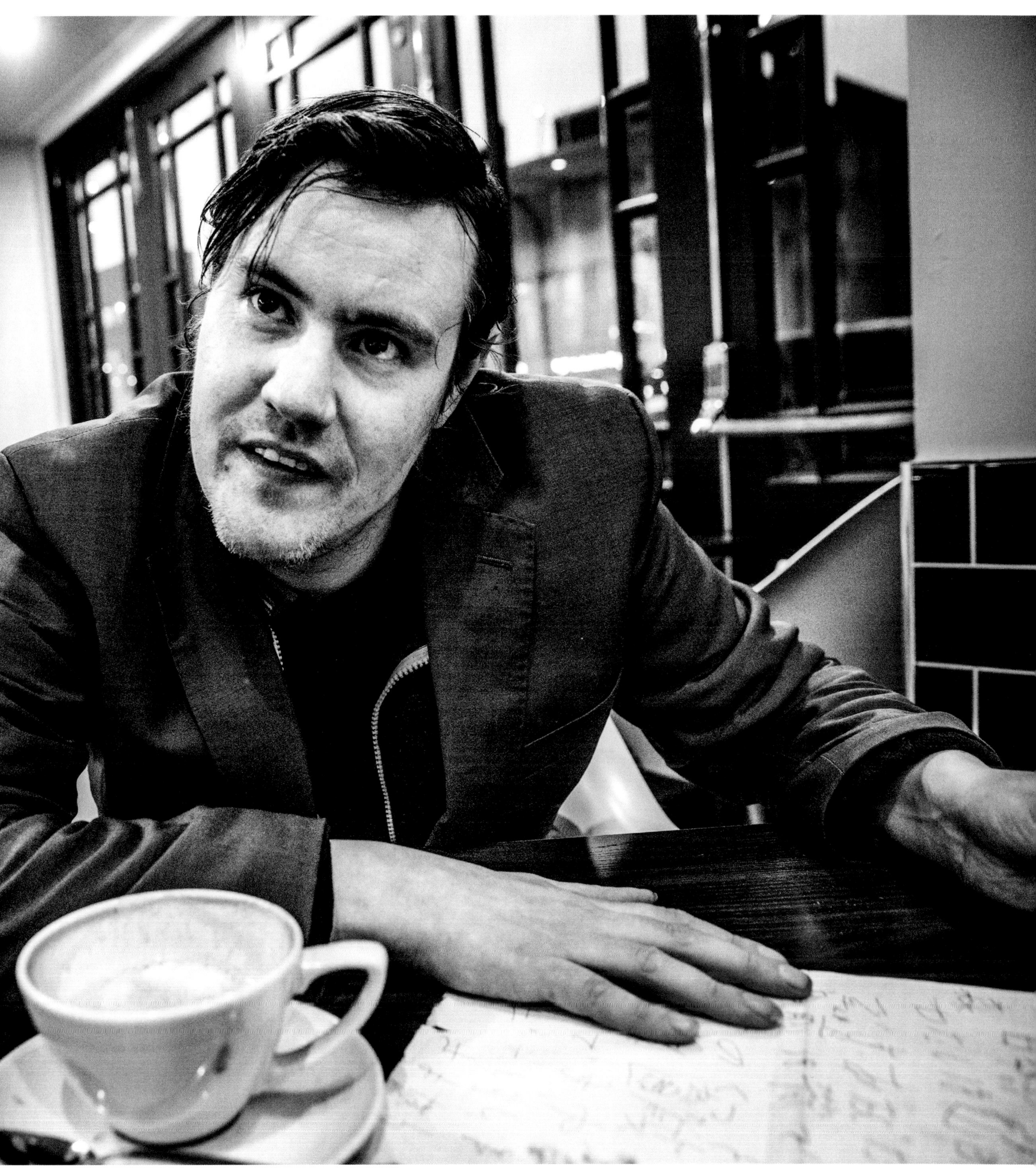

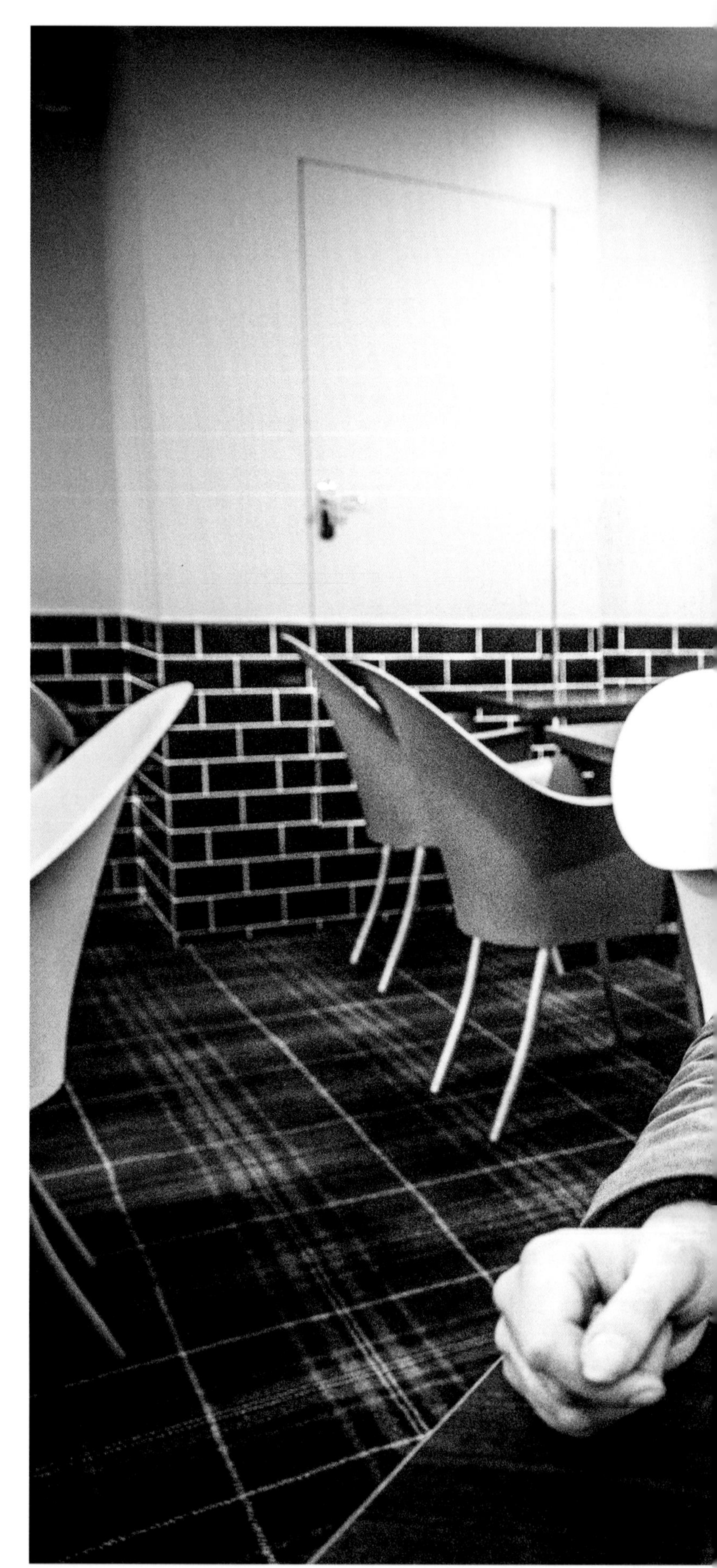

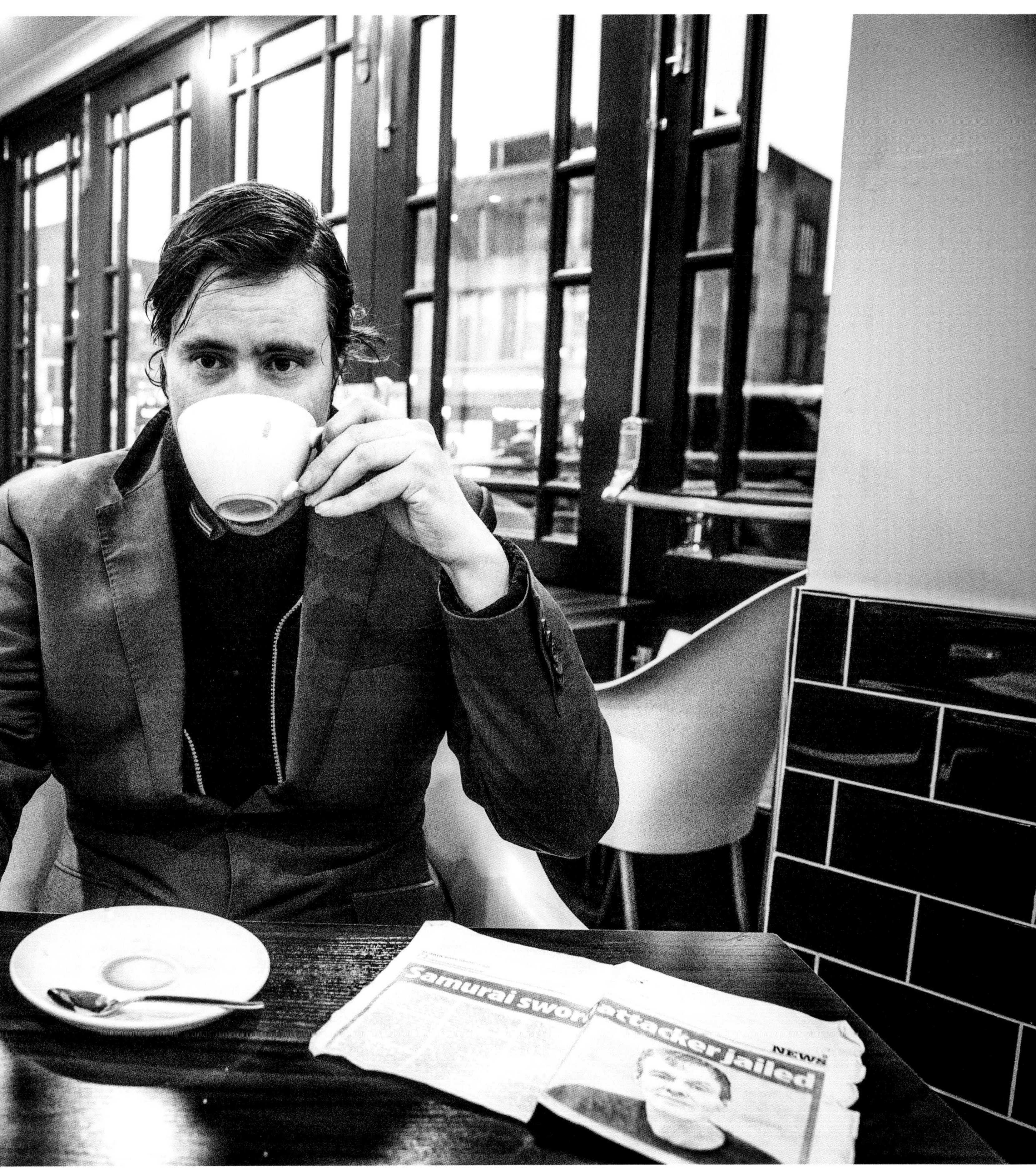
Samurai swor attacker jailed
NEWS

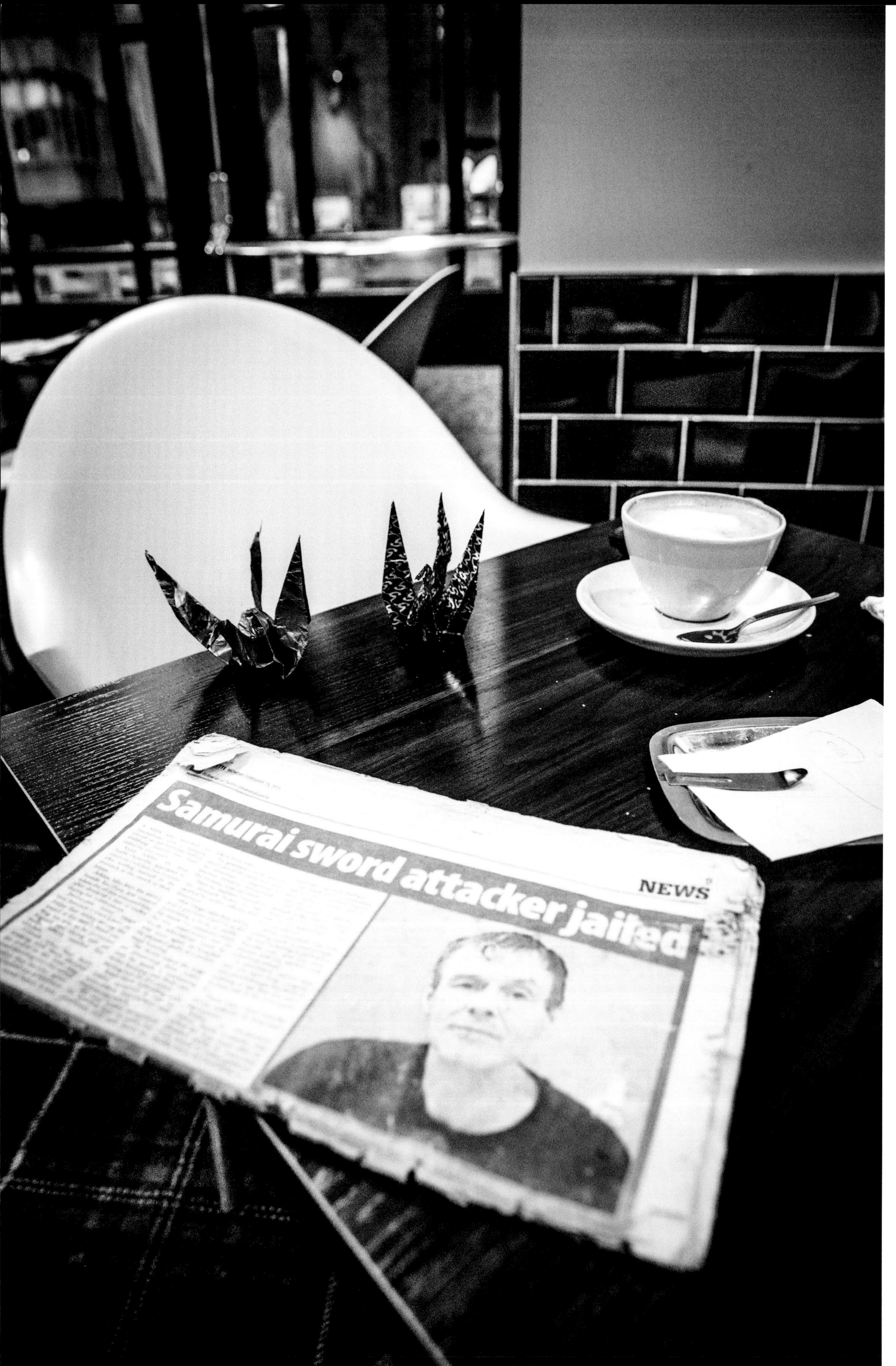
Samurai sword attacker jailed
NEWS

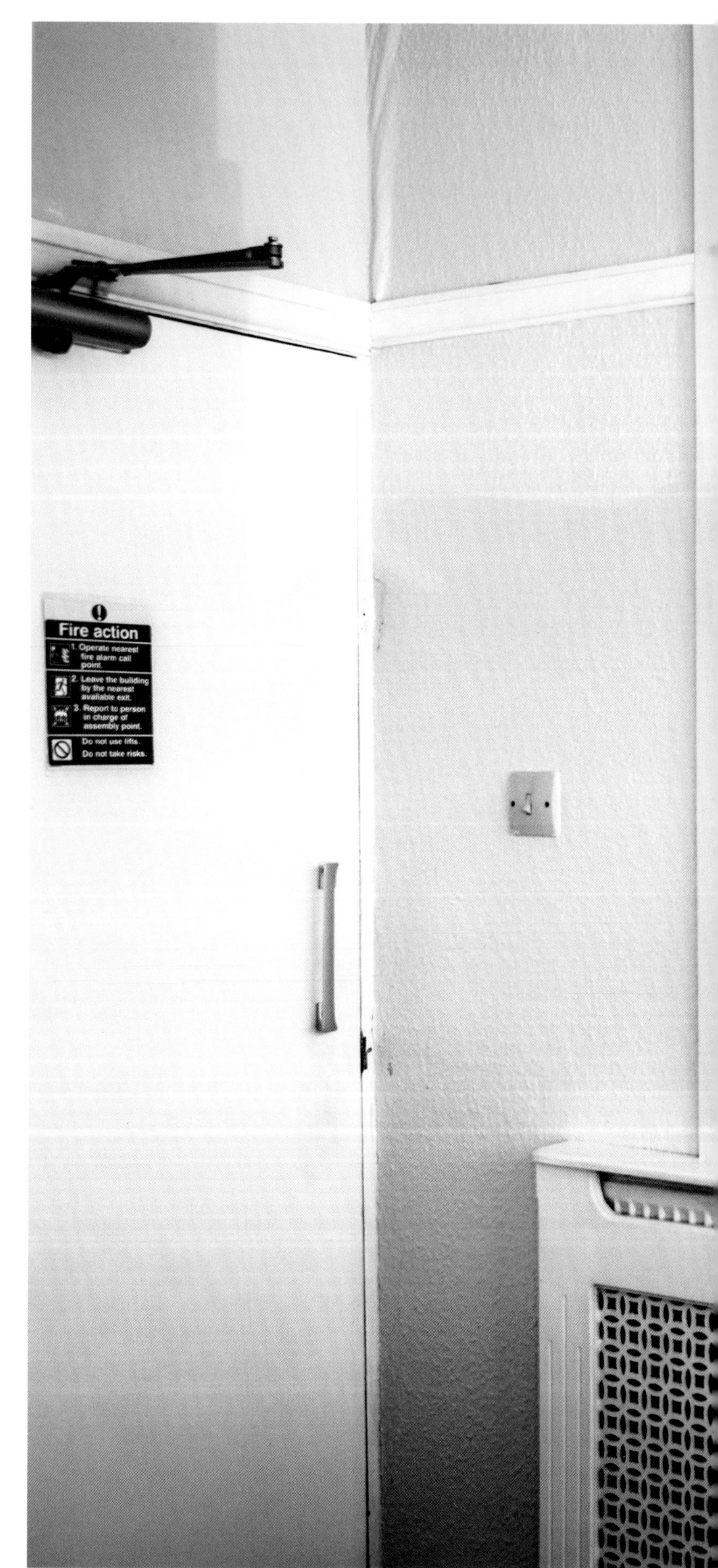

Fire action
1. Operate nearest fire alarm call point.
2. Leave the building by the nearest available exit.
3. Report to person in charge of assembly point.
Do not use lifts.
Do not take risks.

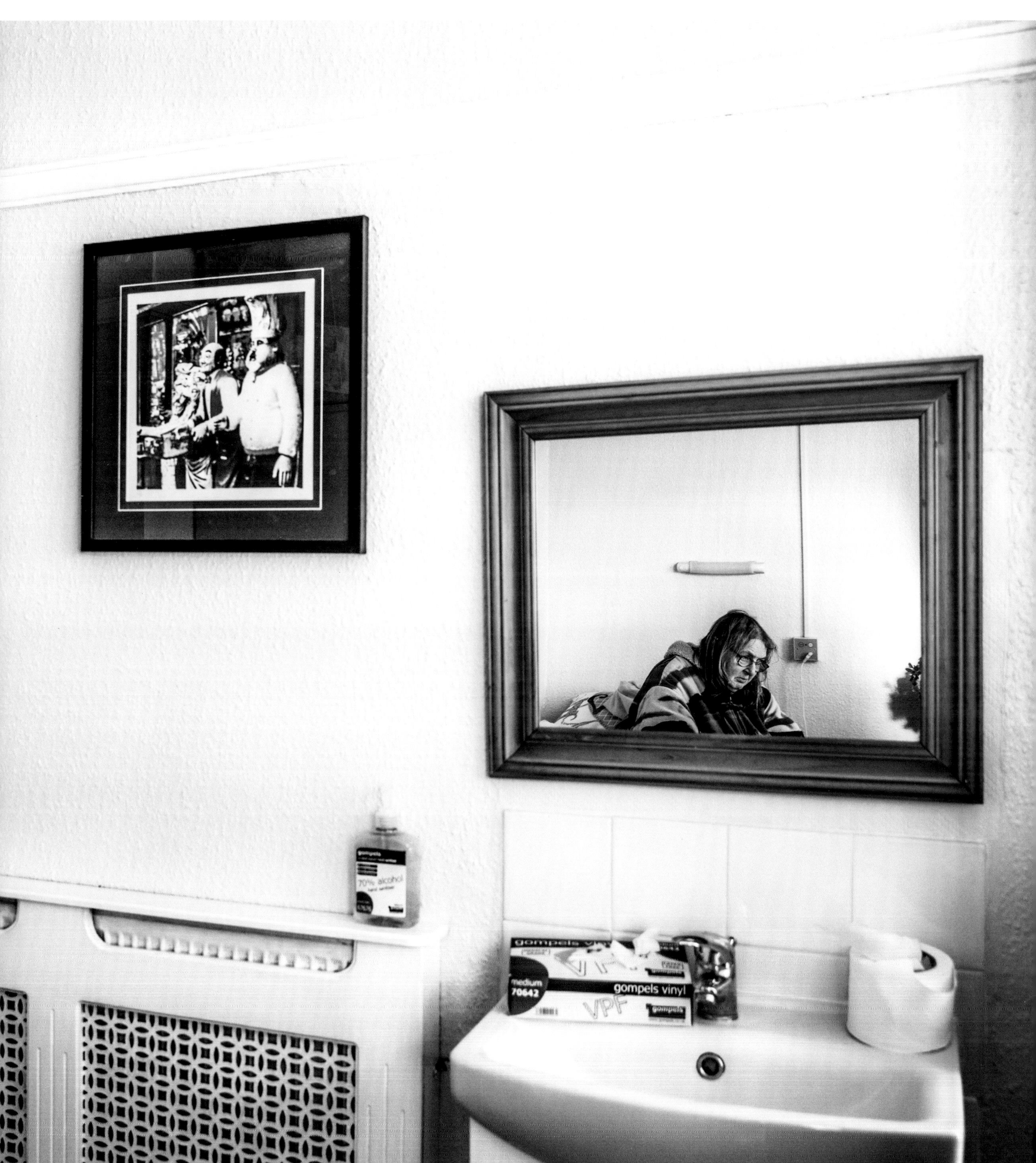

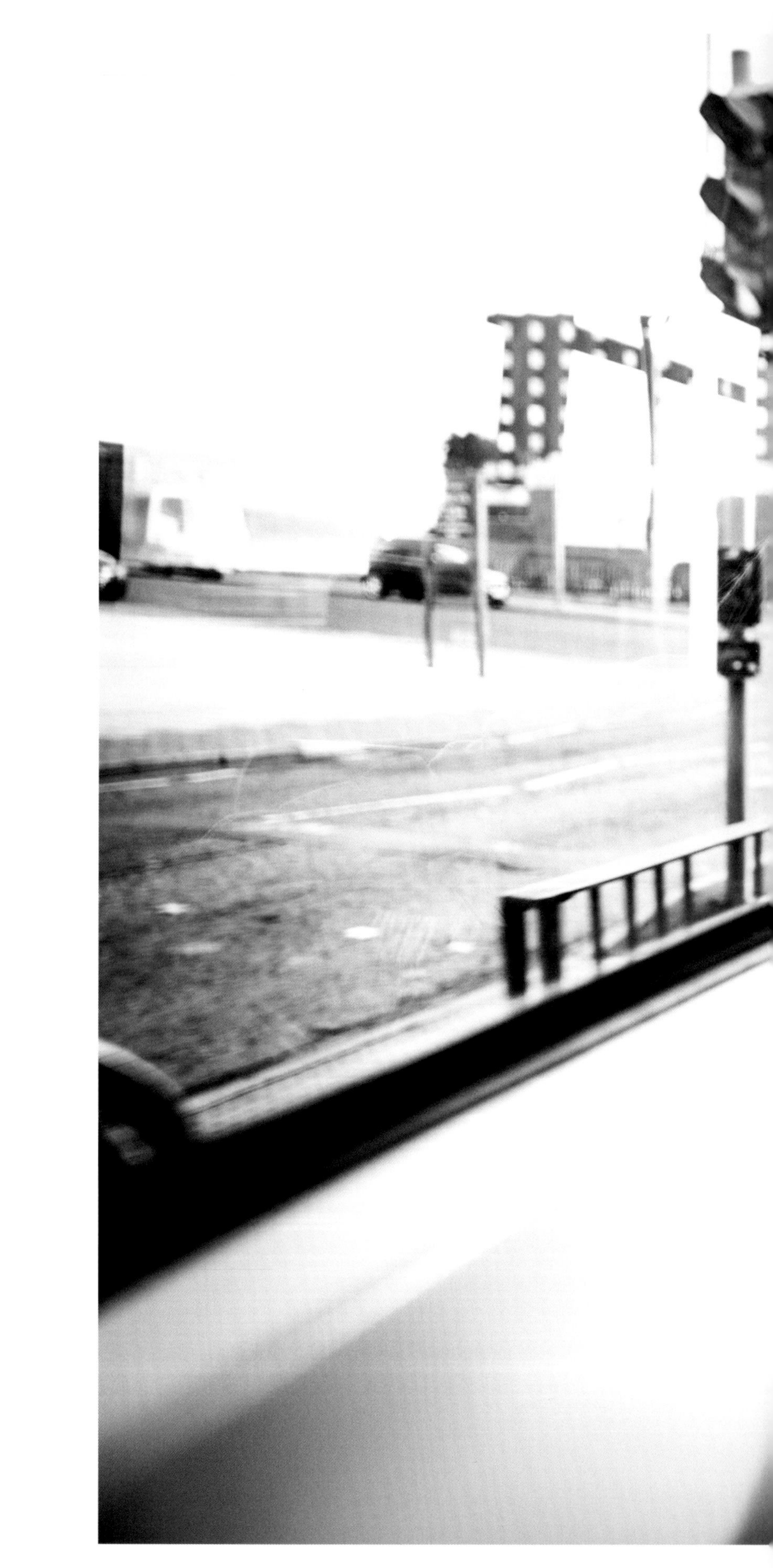

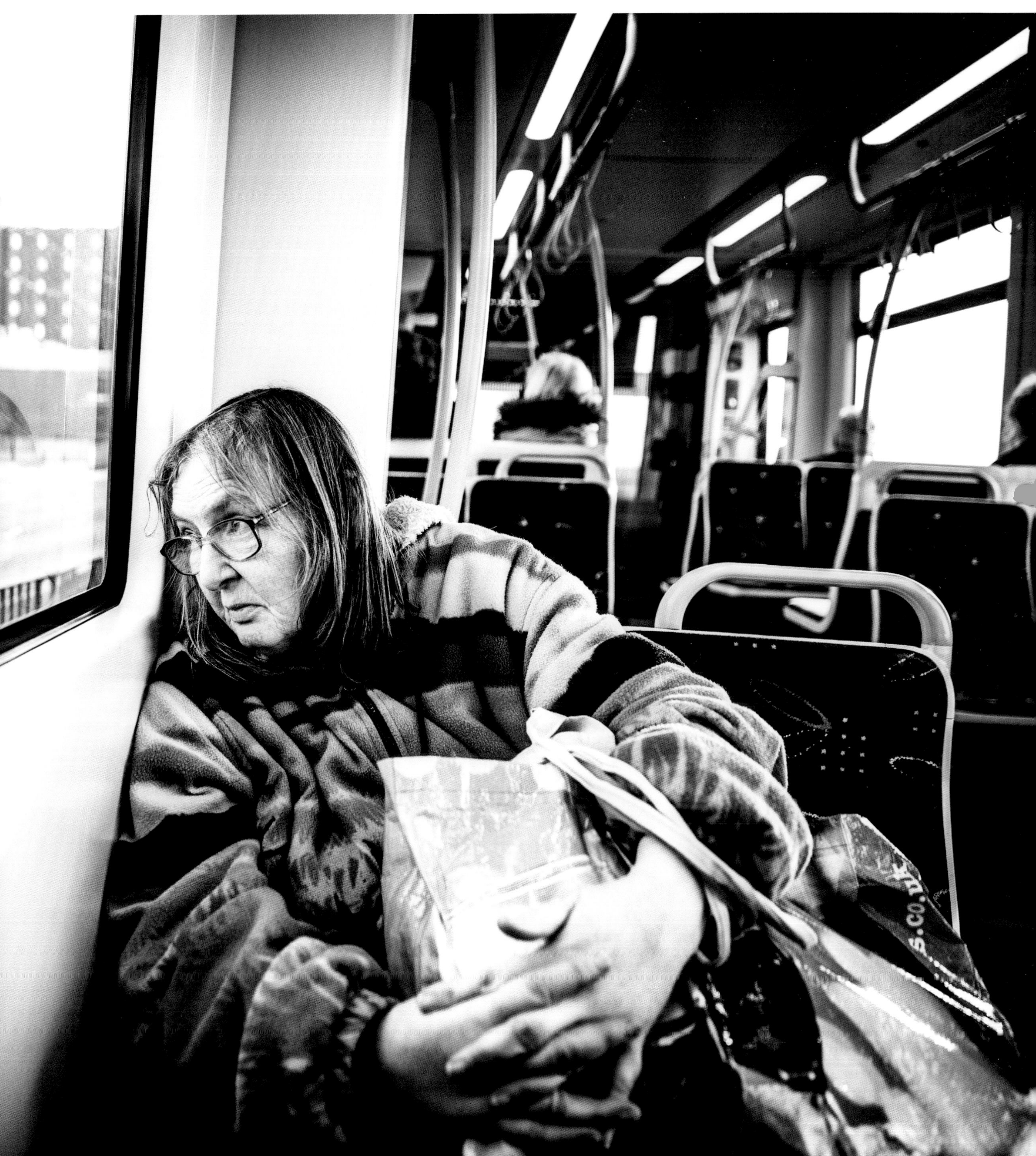

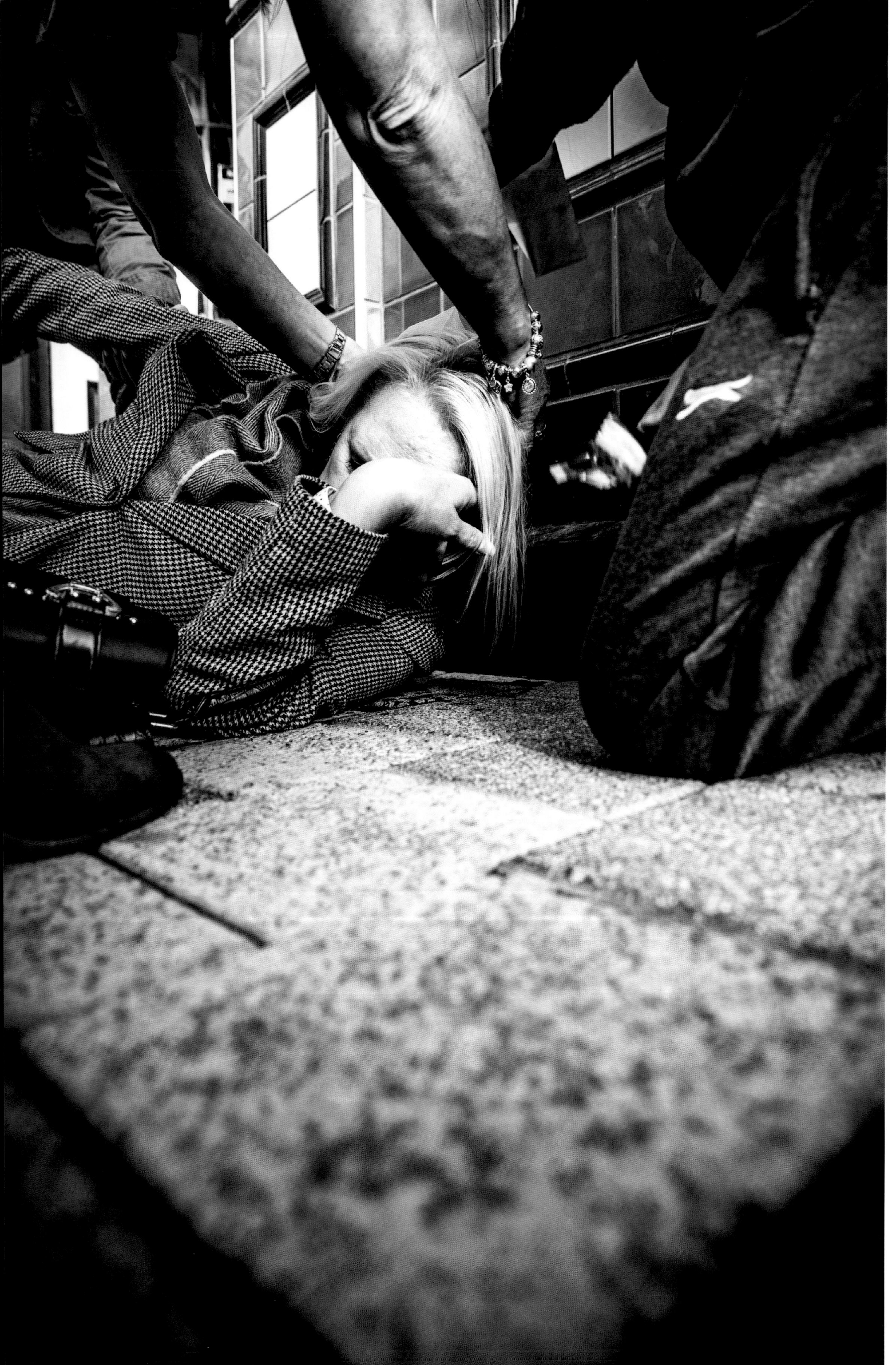

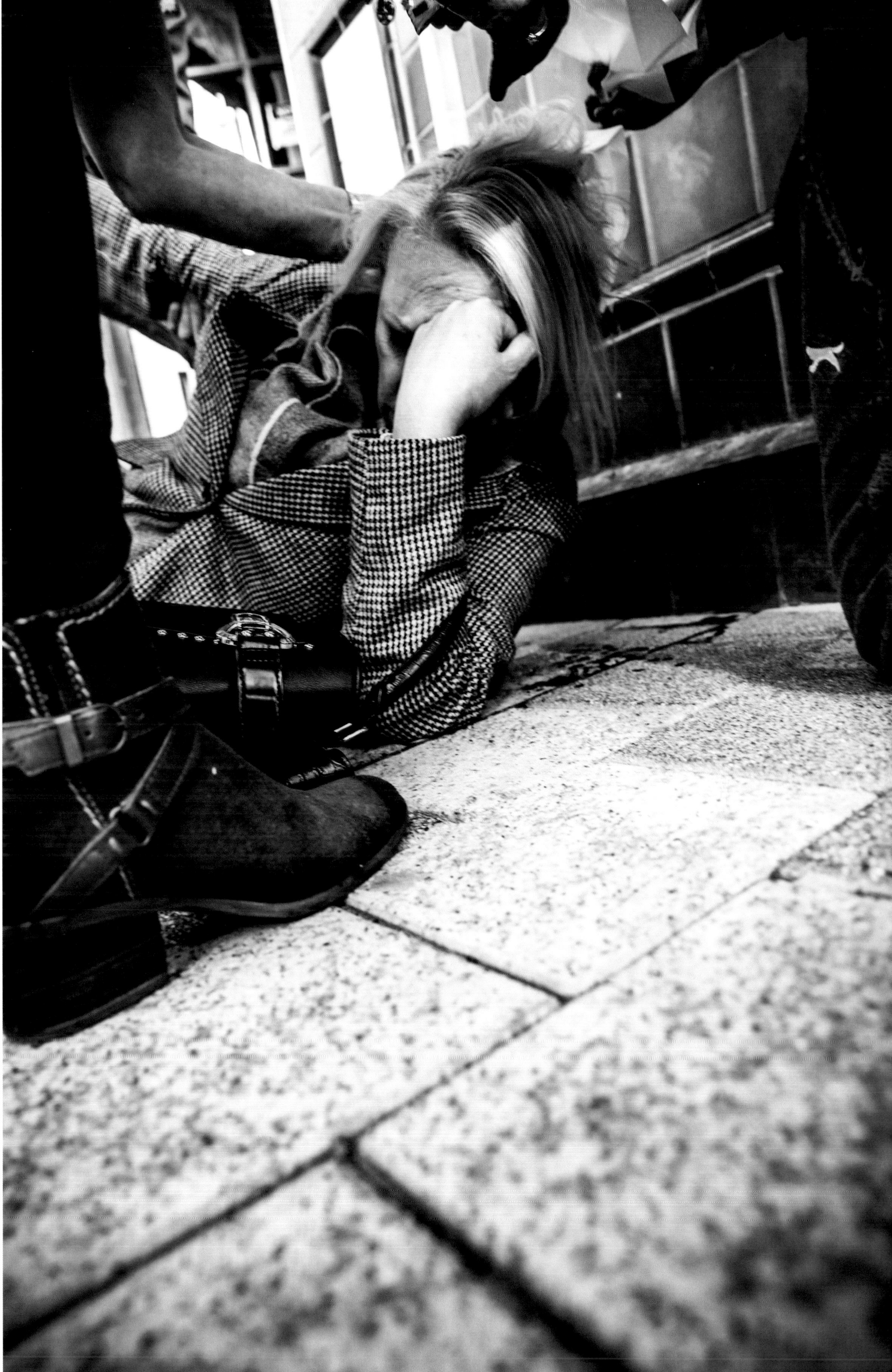

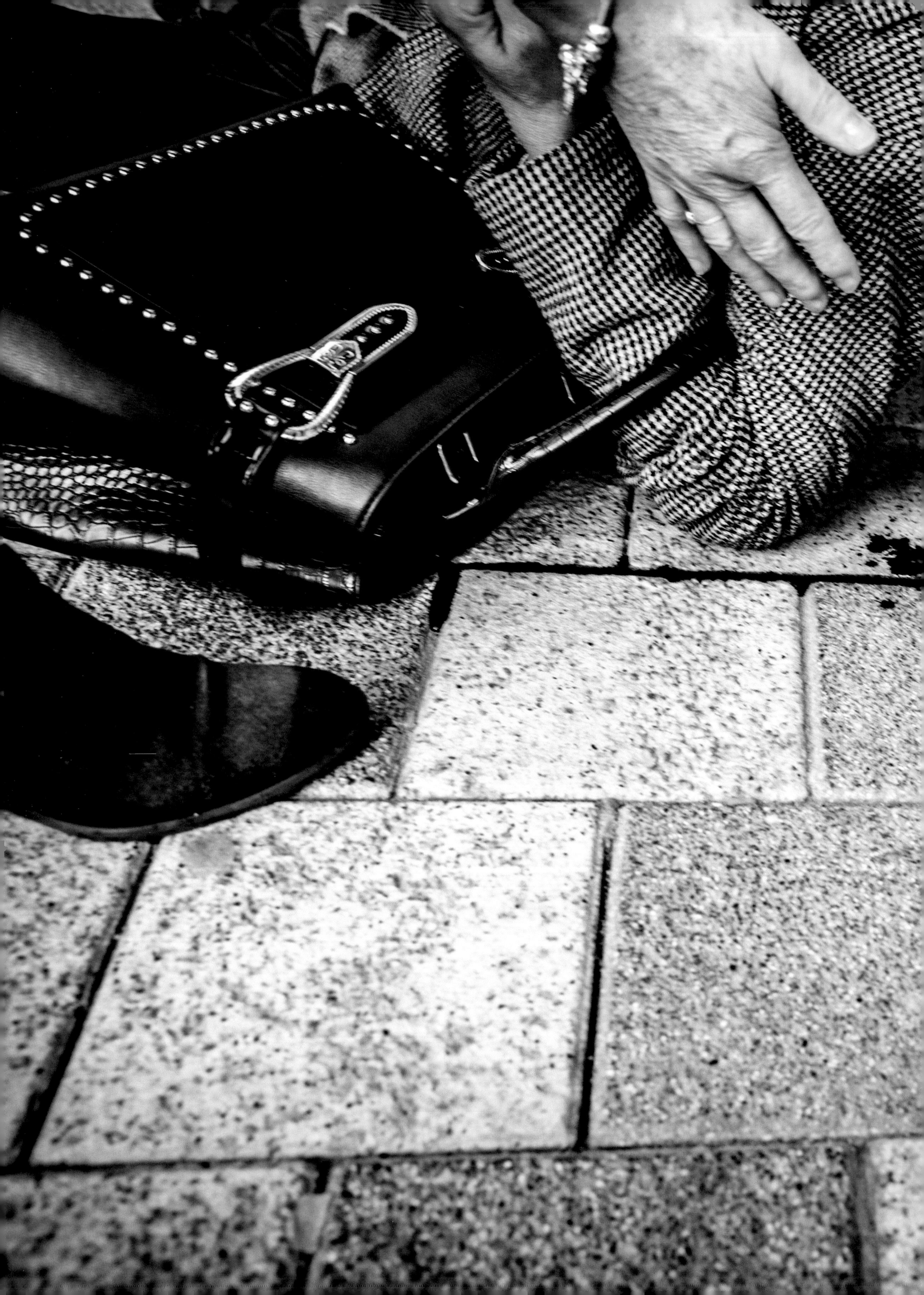

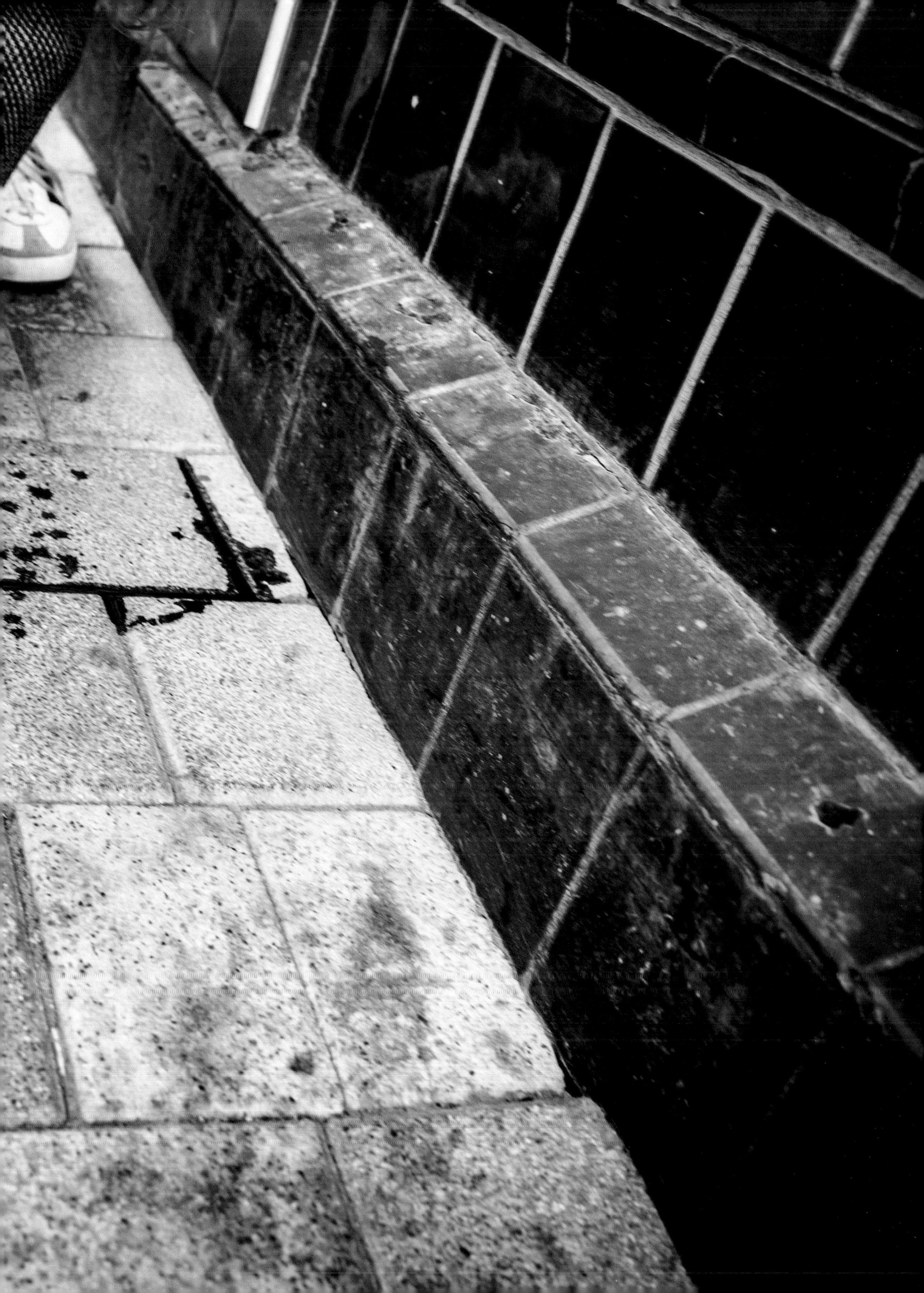

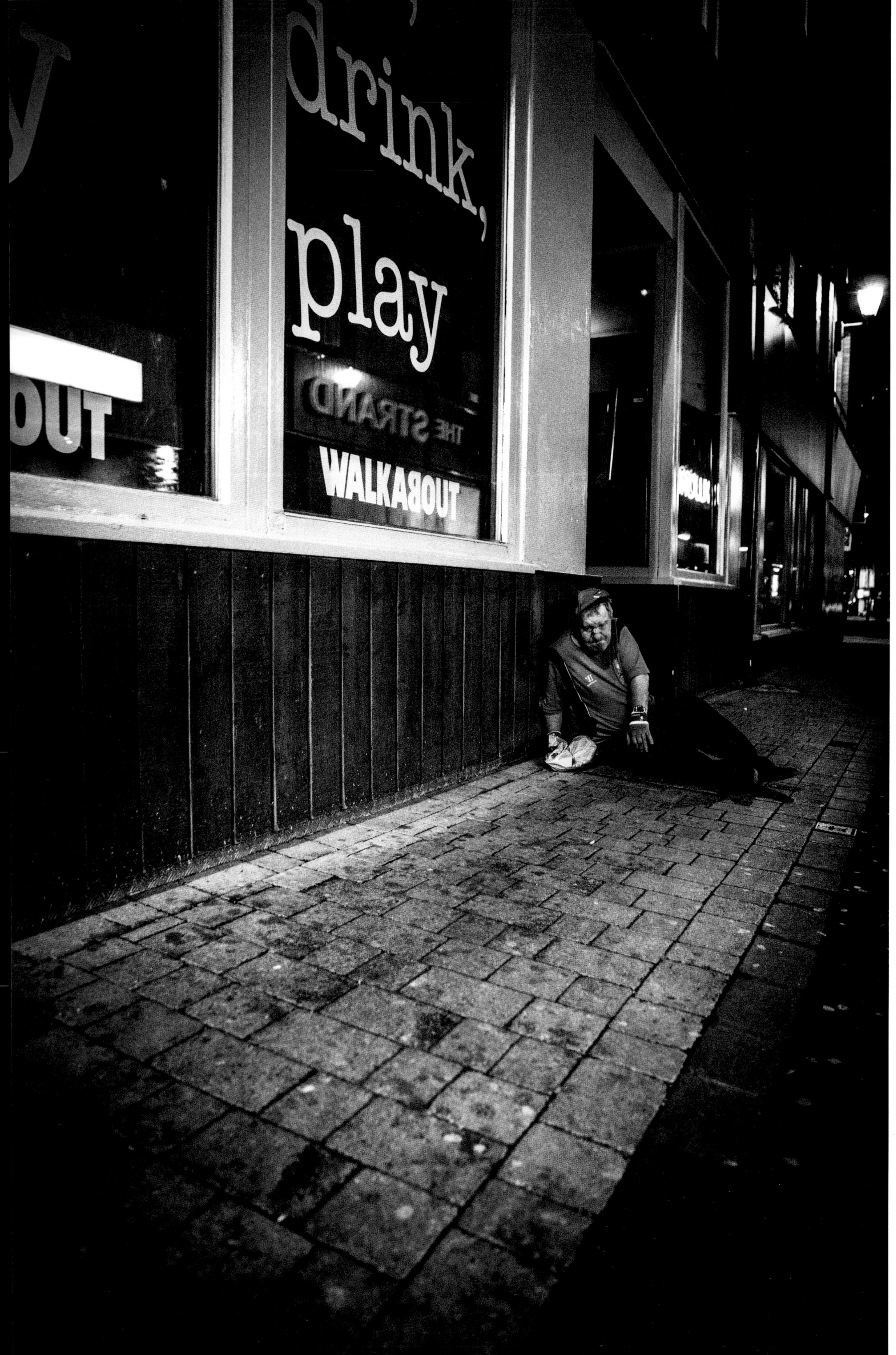

drink,
play
THE STRAND
WALKABOUT

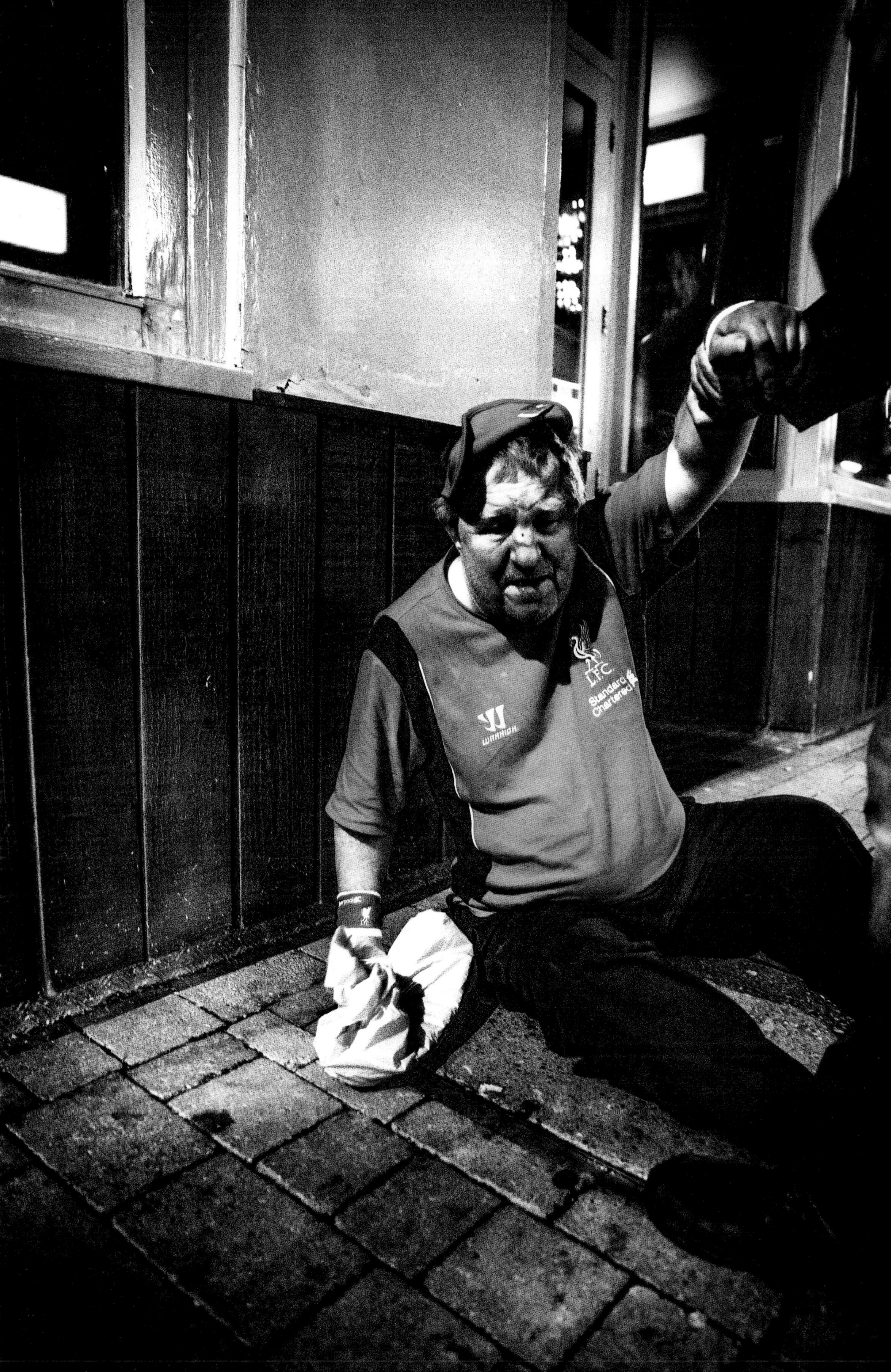

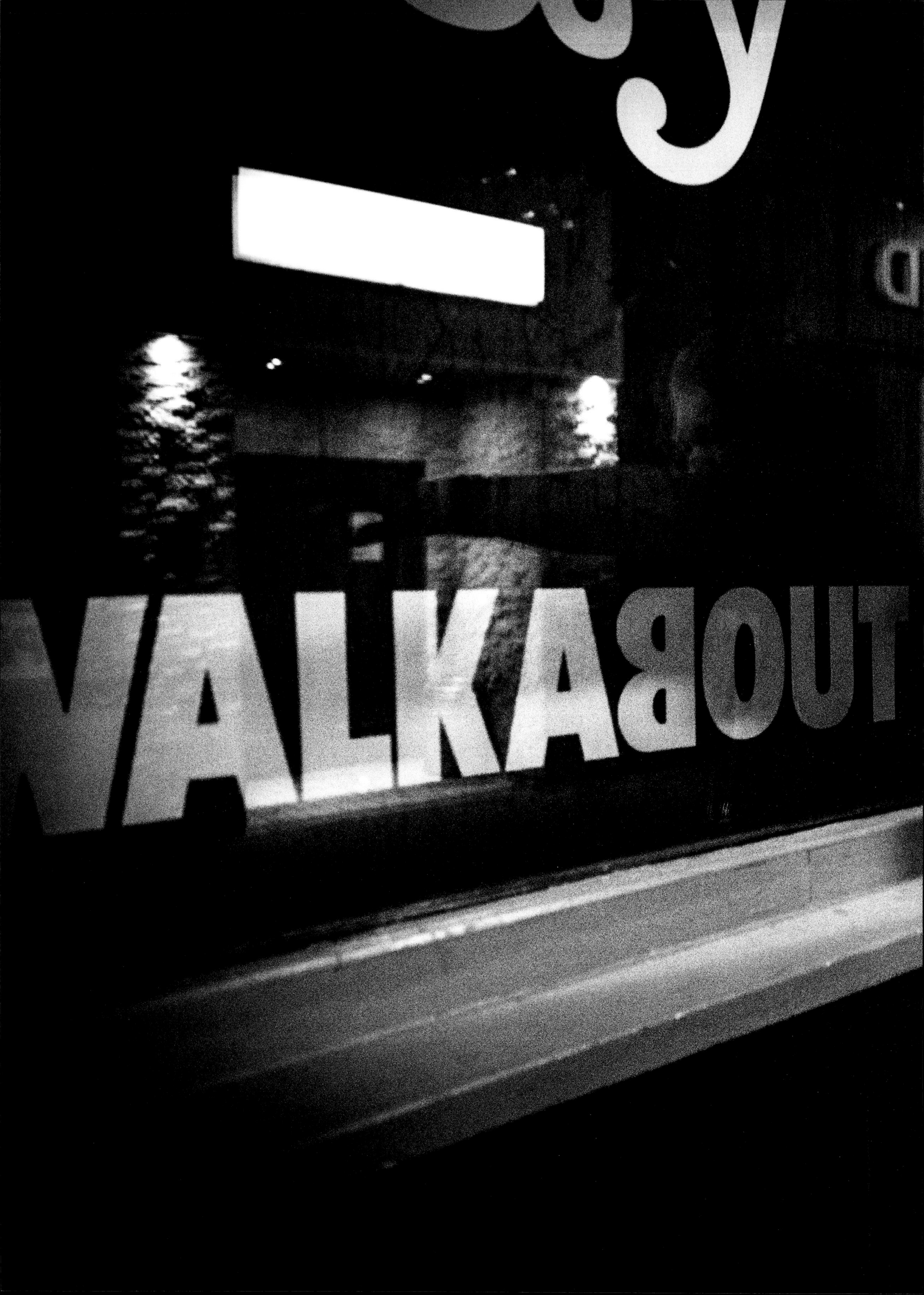

WALKABOUT

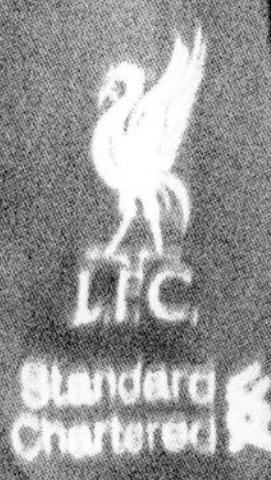

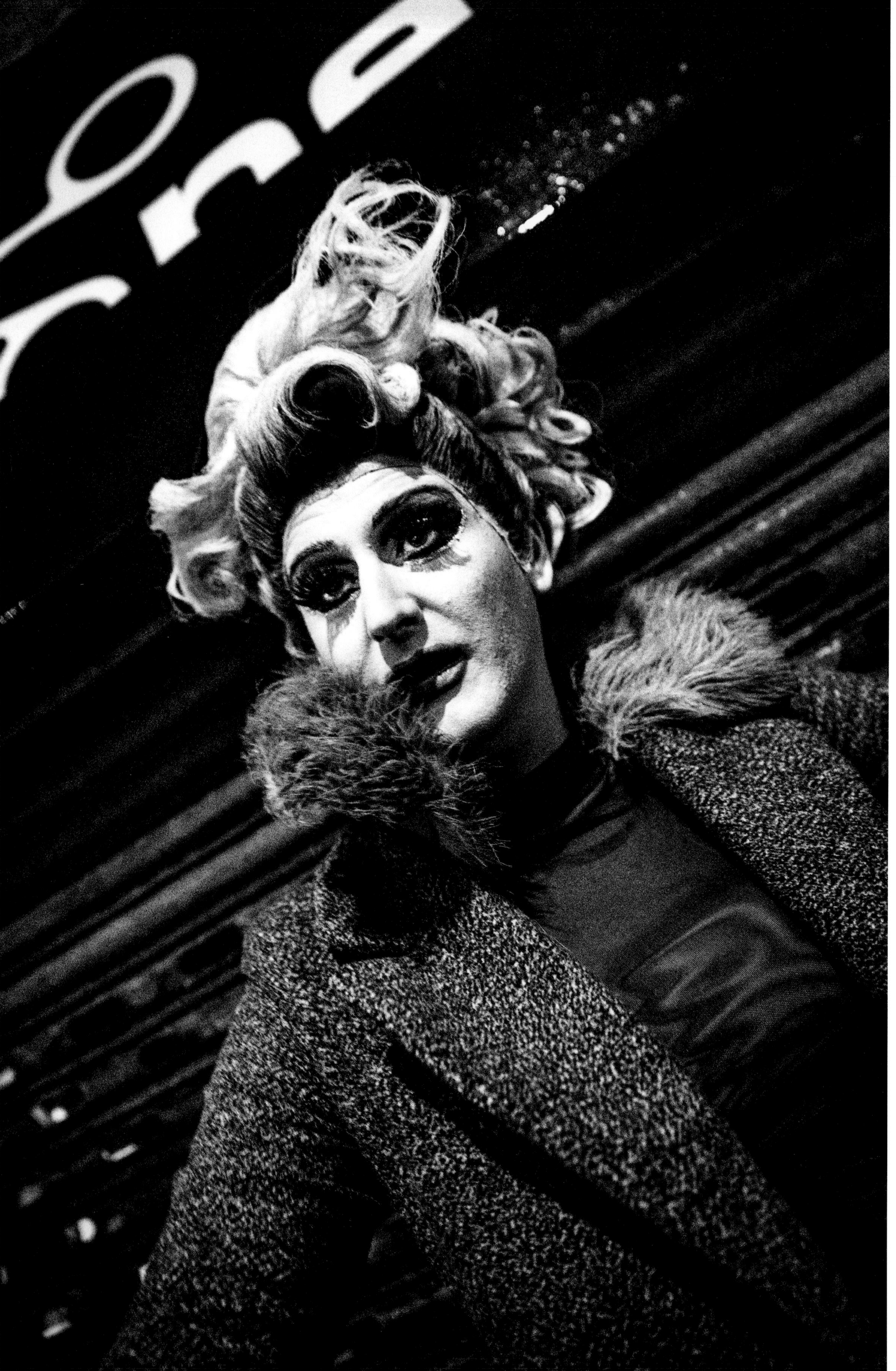

John A
TOWER SALON LTD

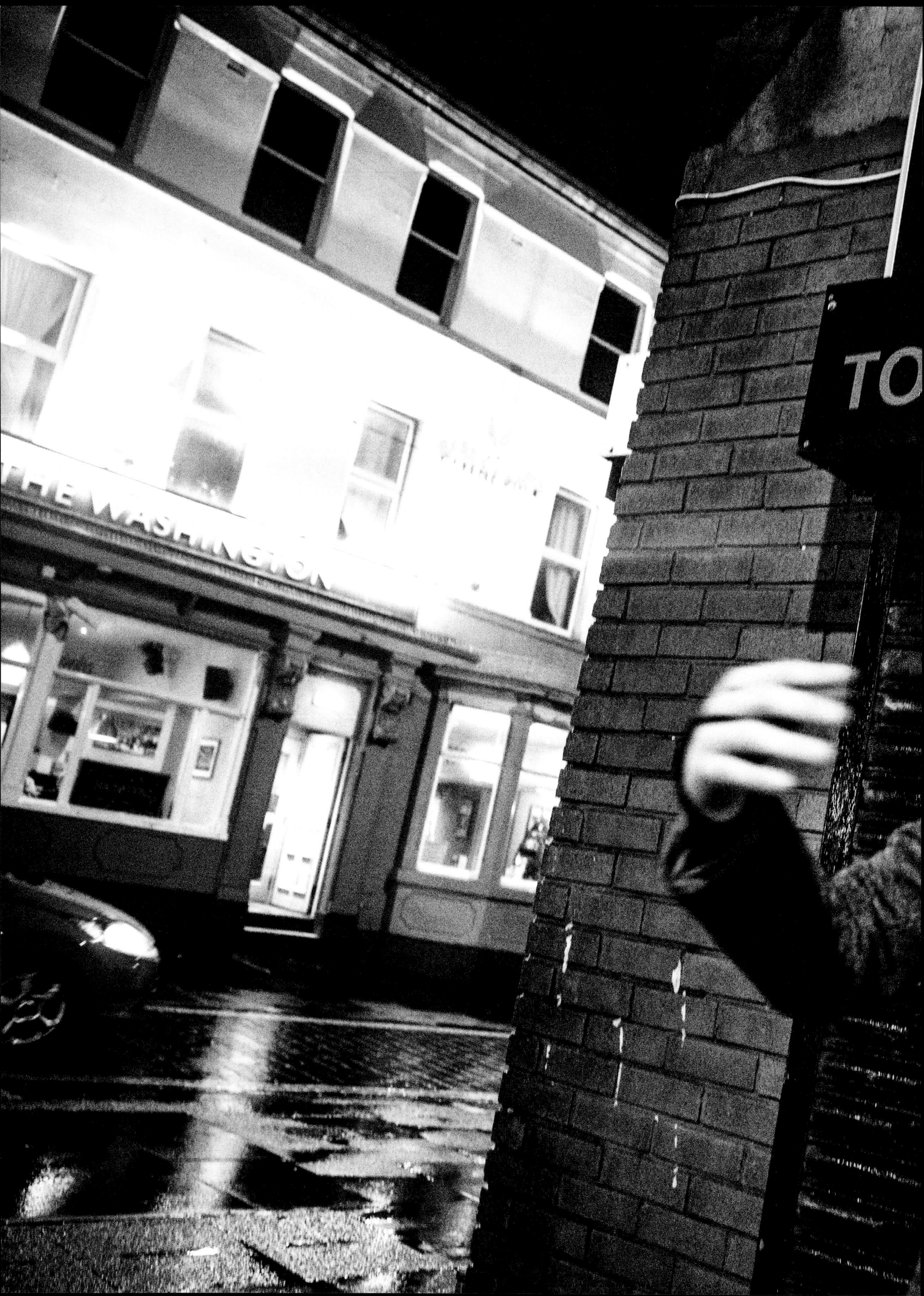

THE WASHINGTON
TO

John
ER S...N LTD

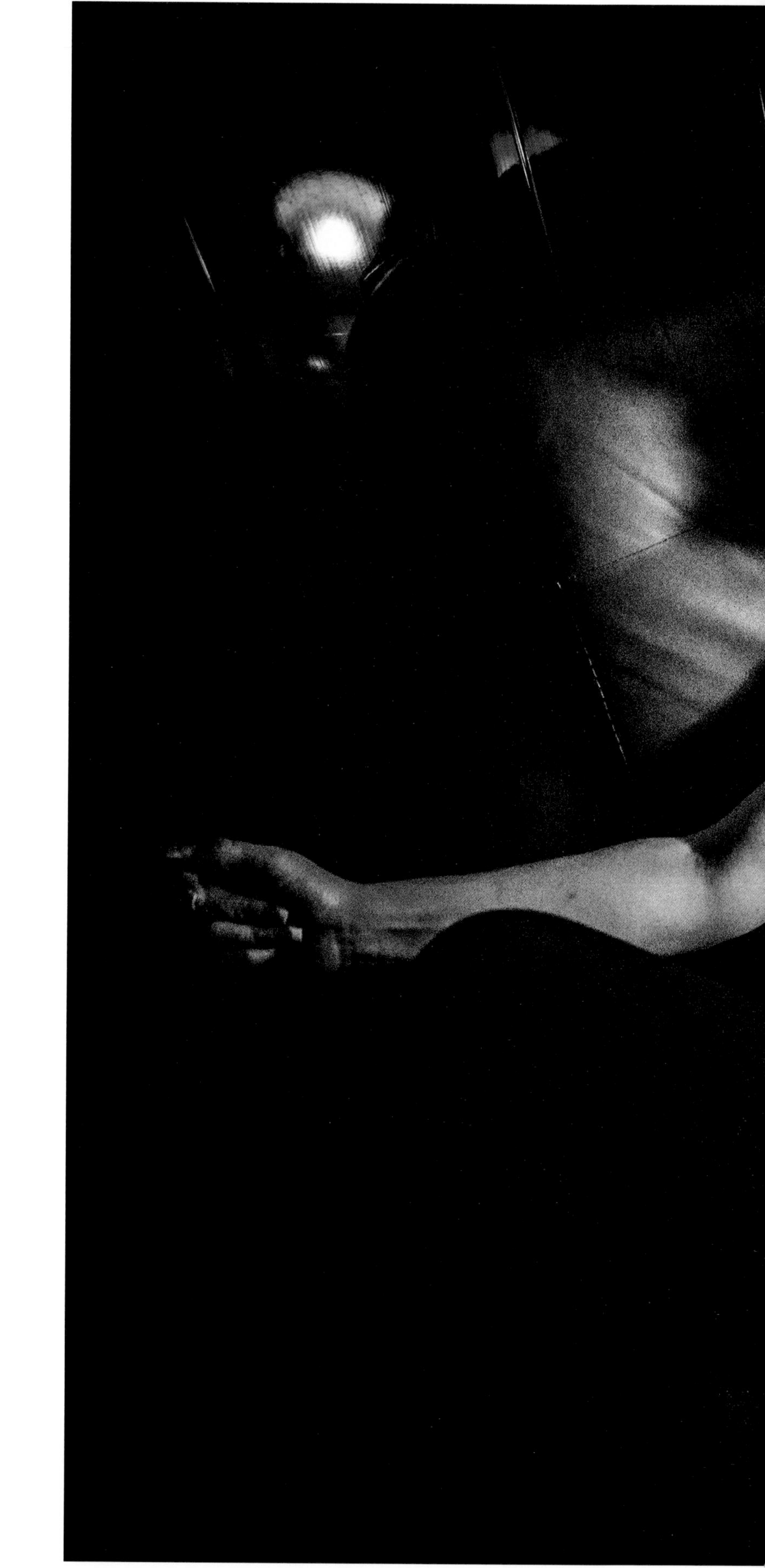

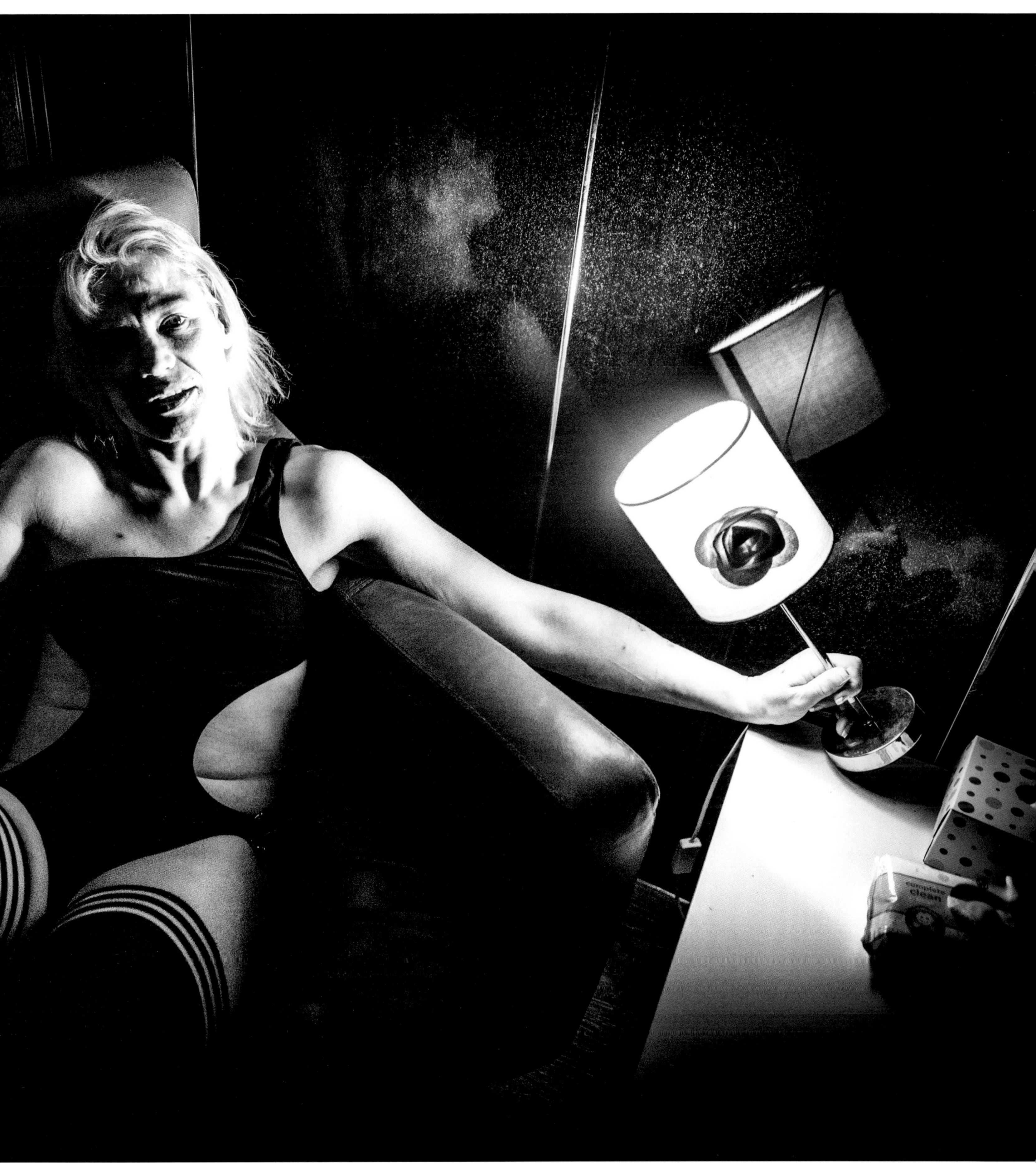

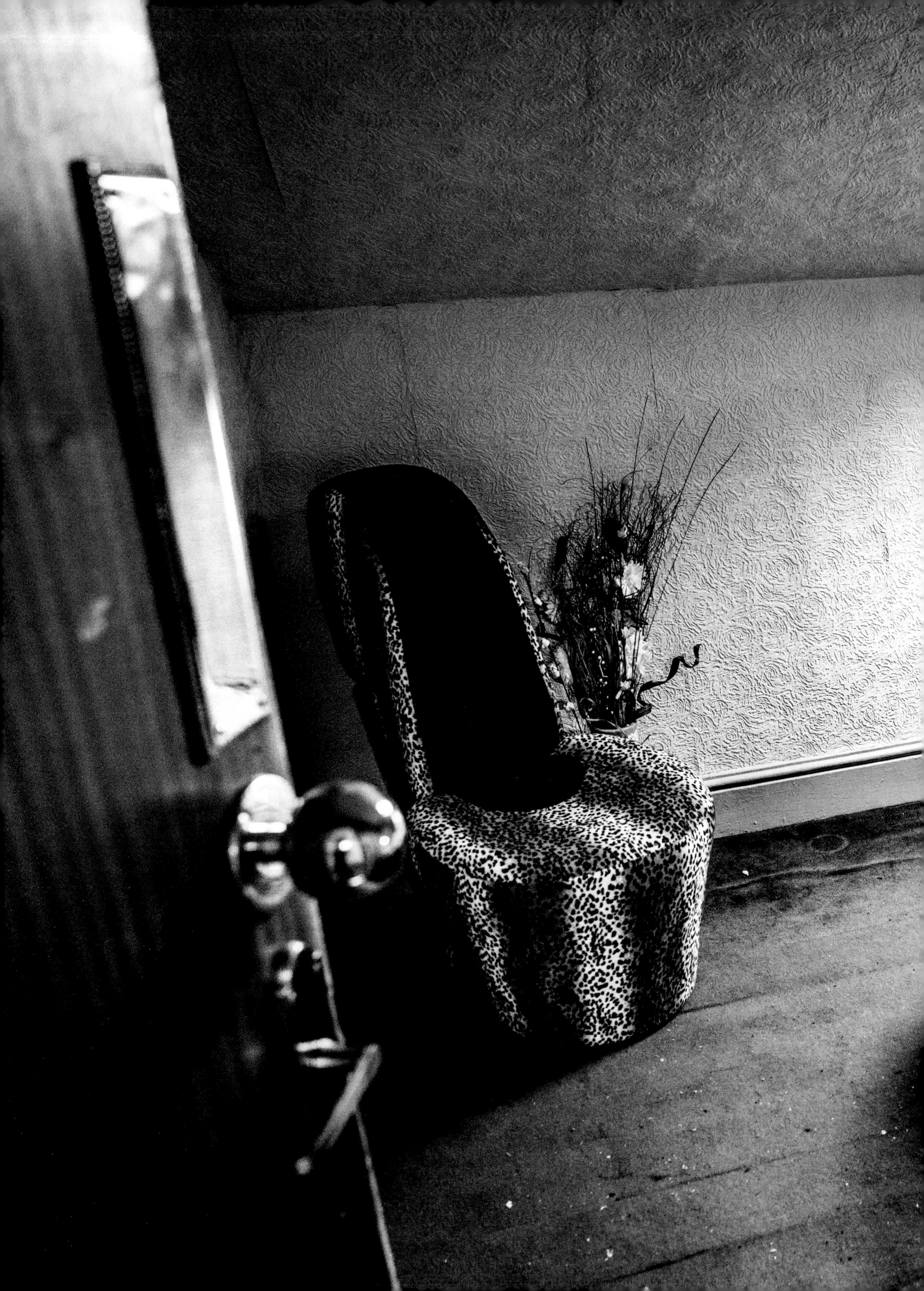

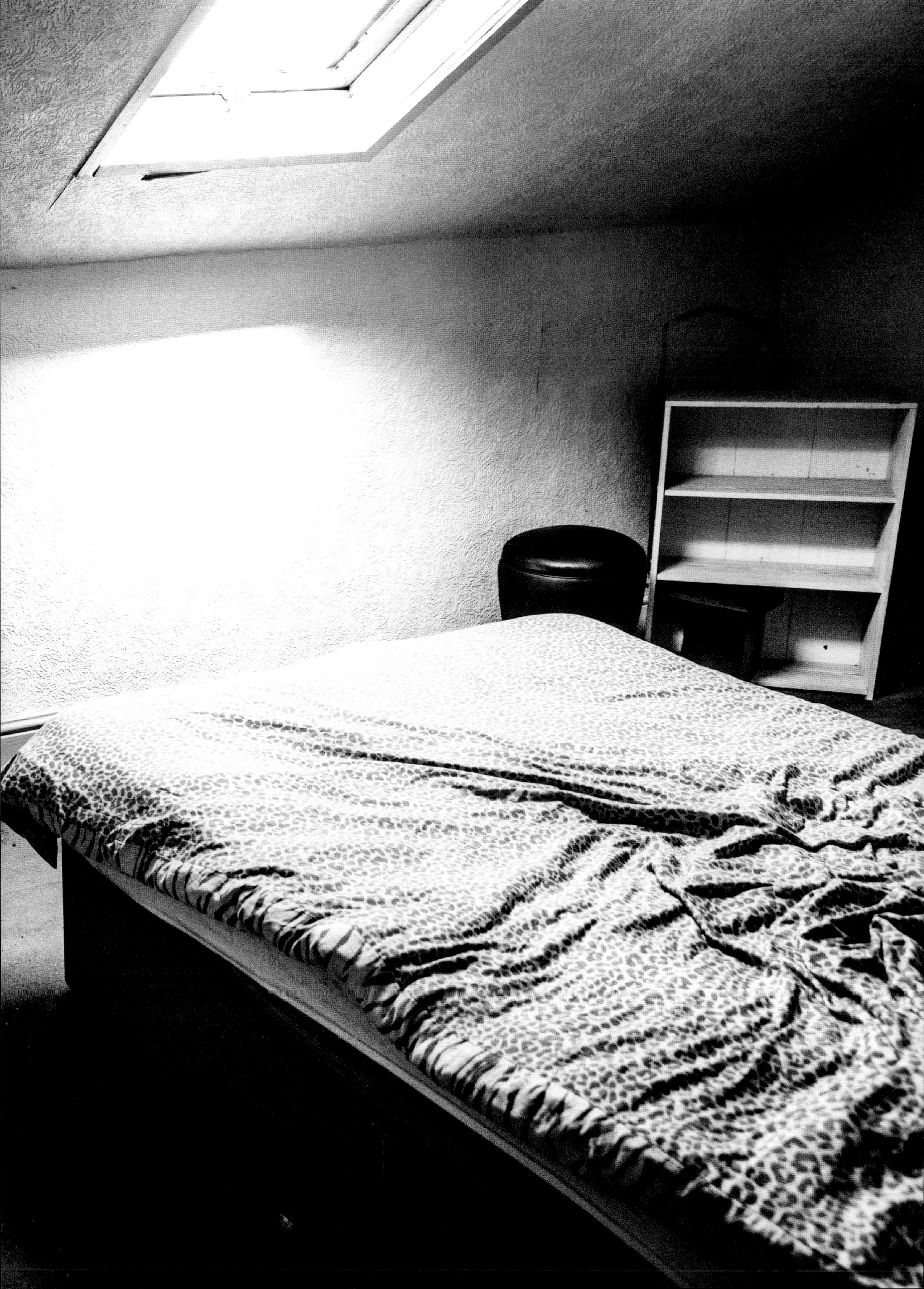

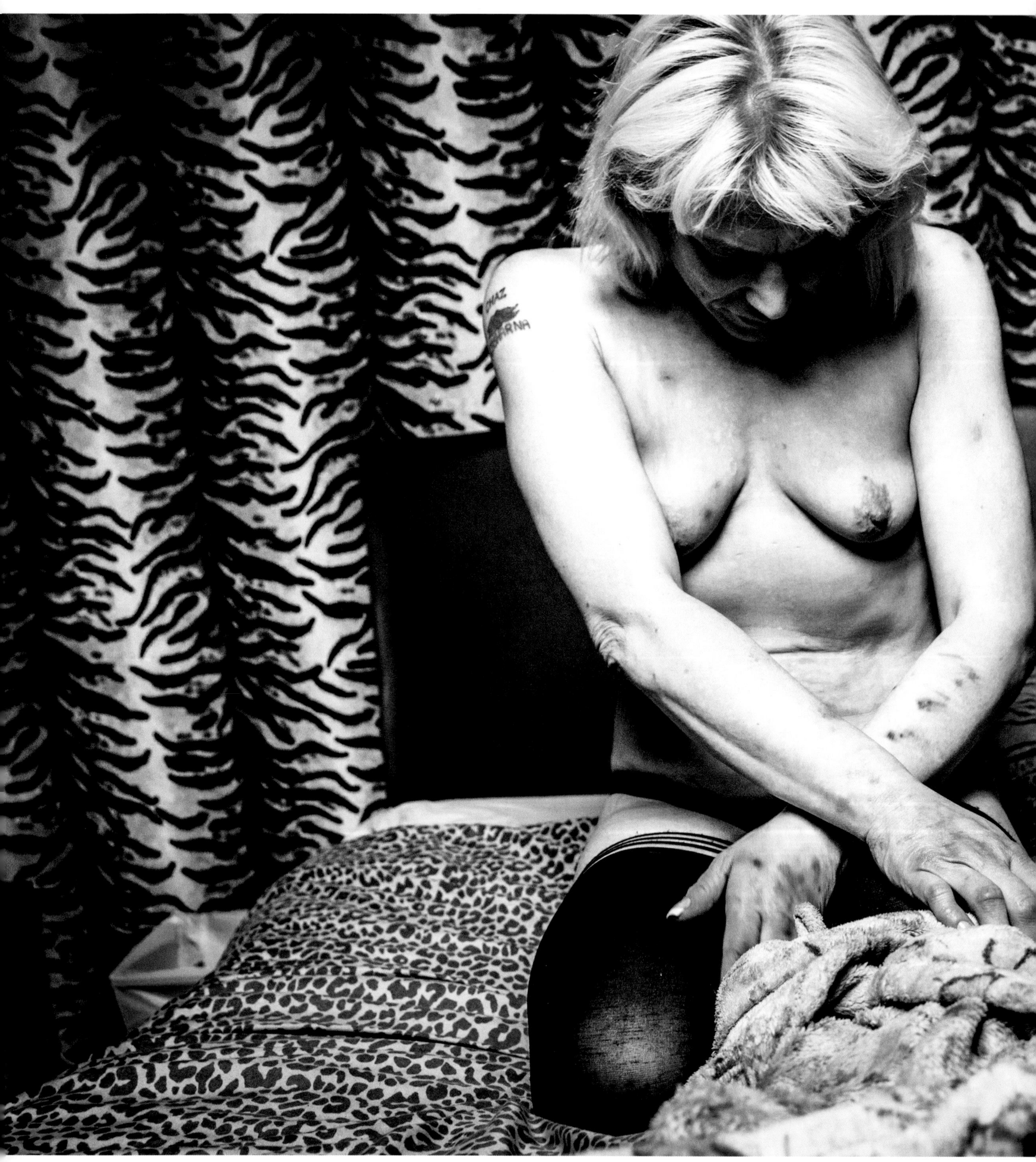

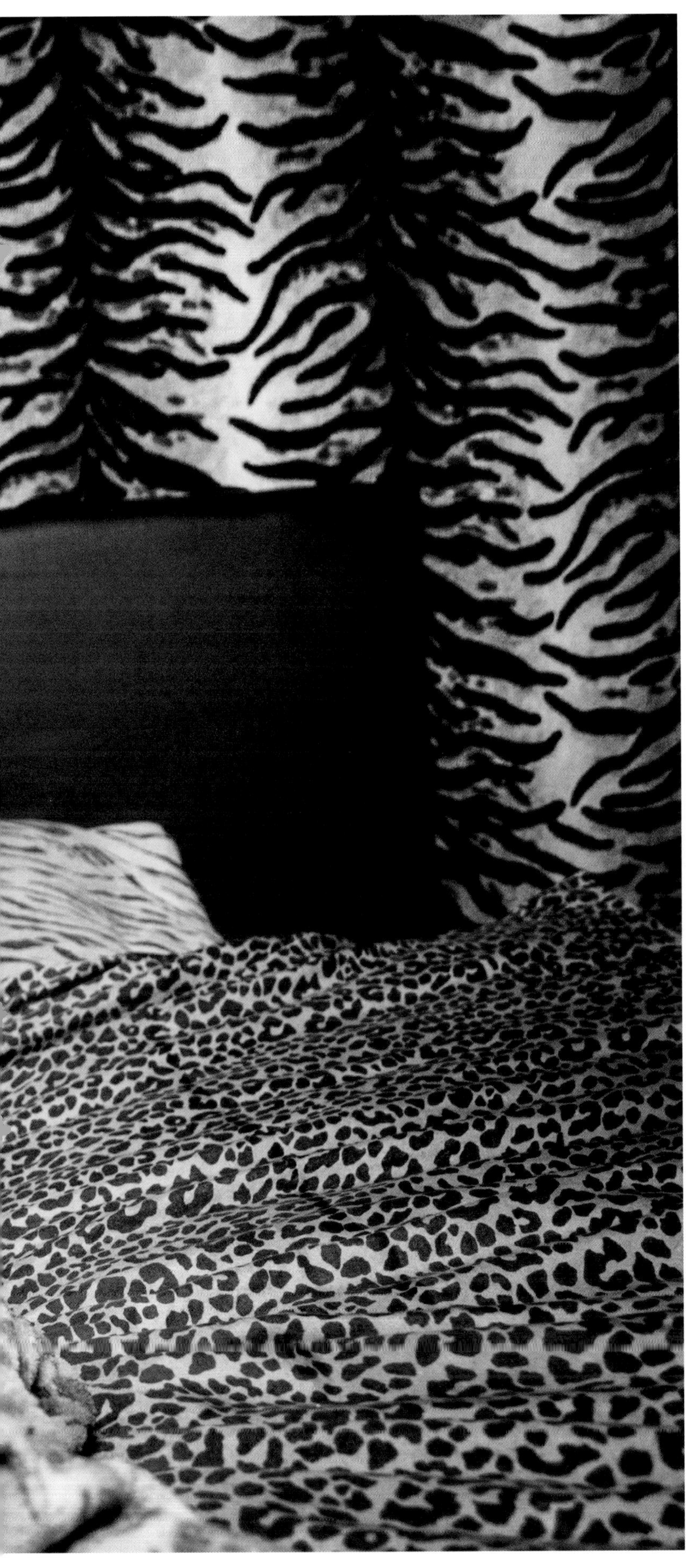

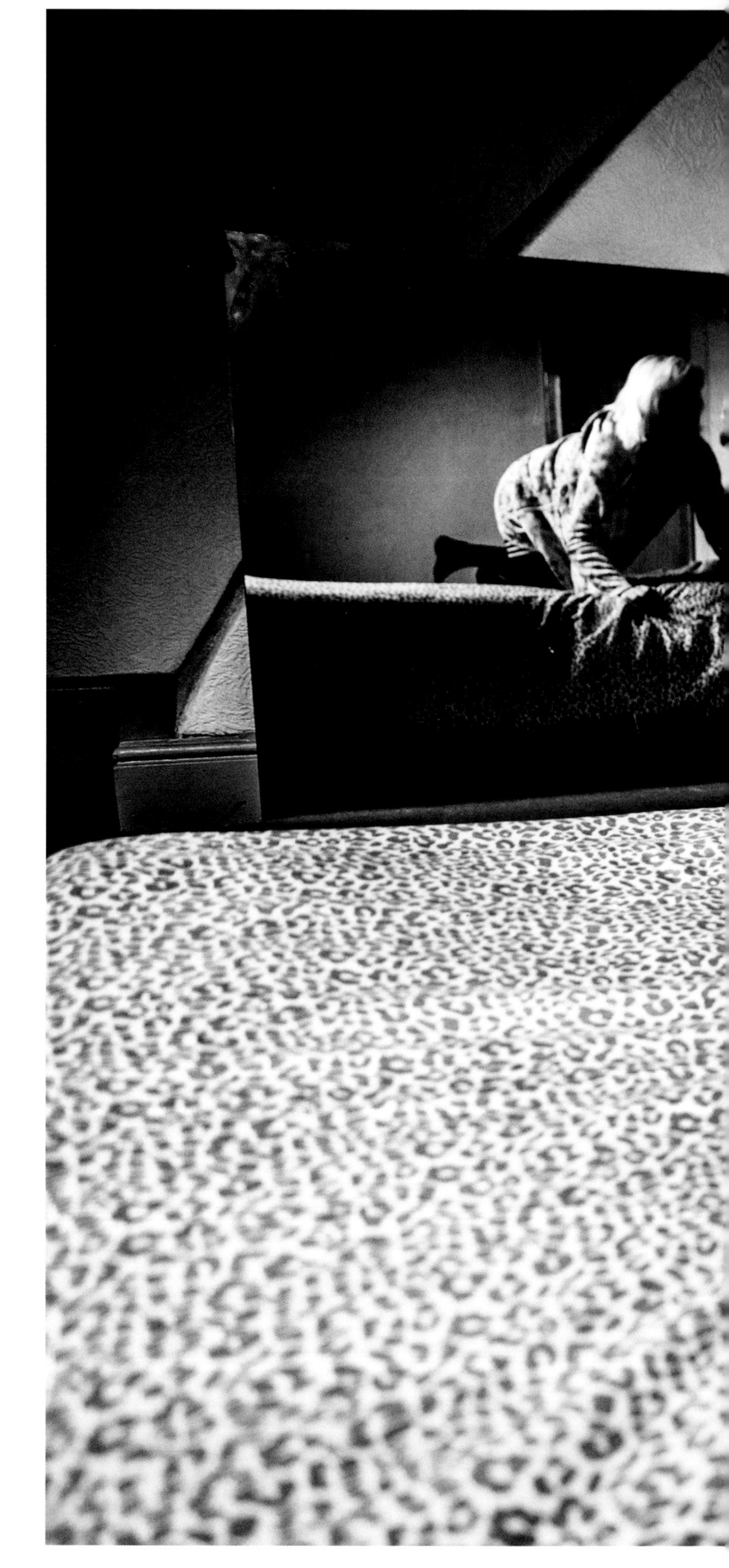

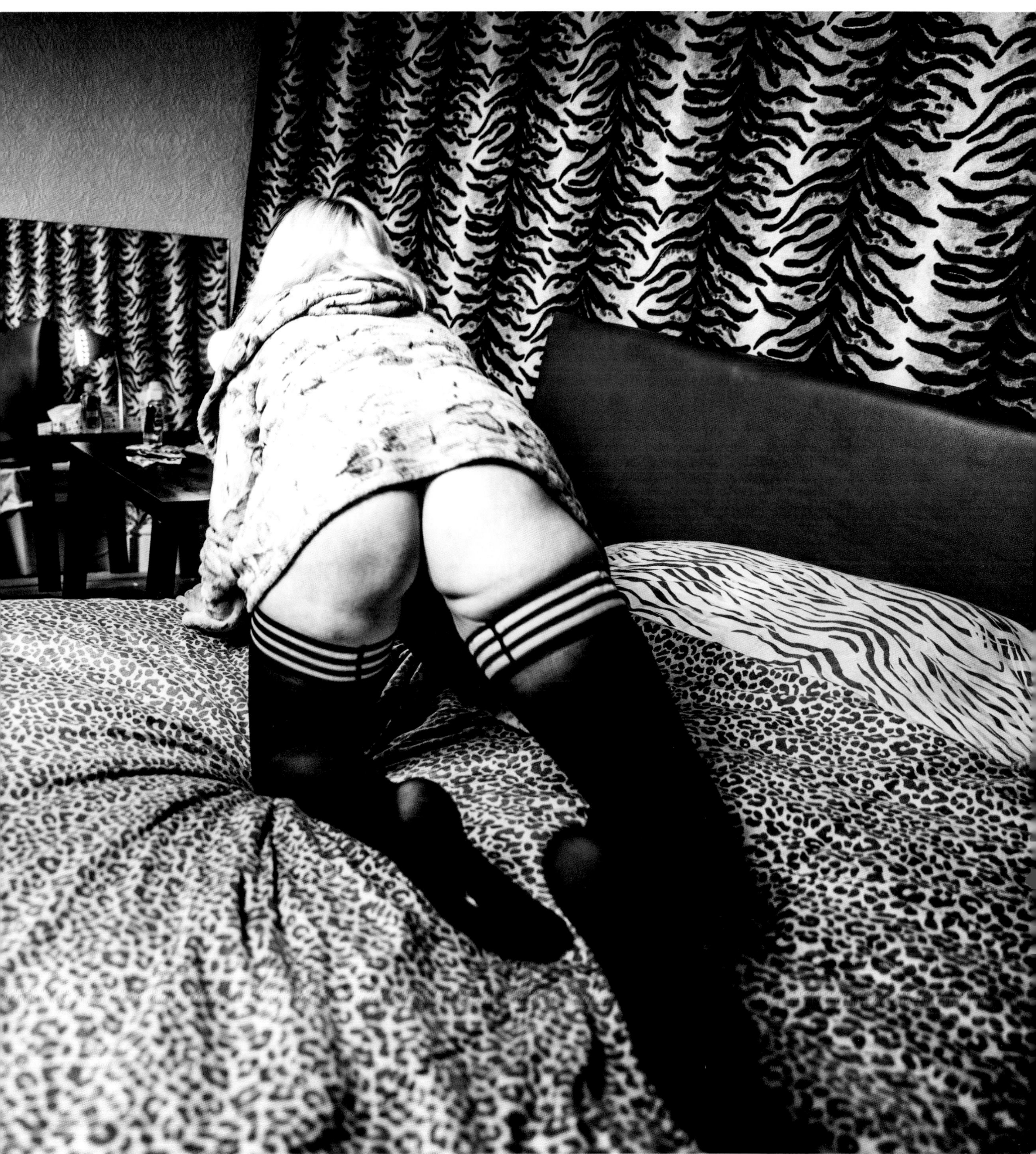

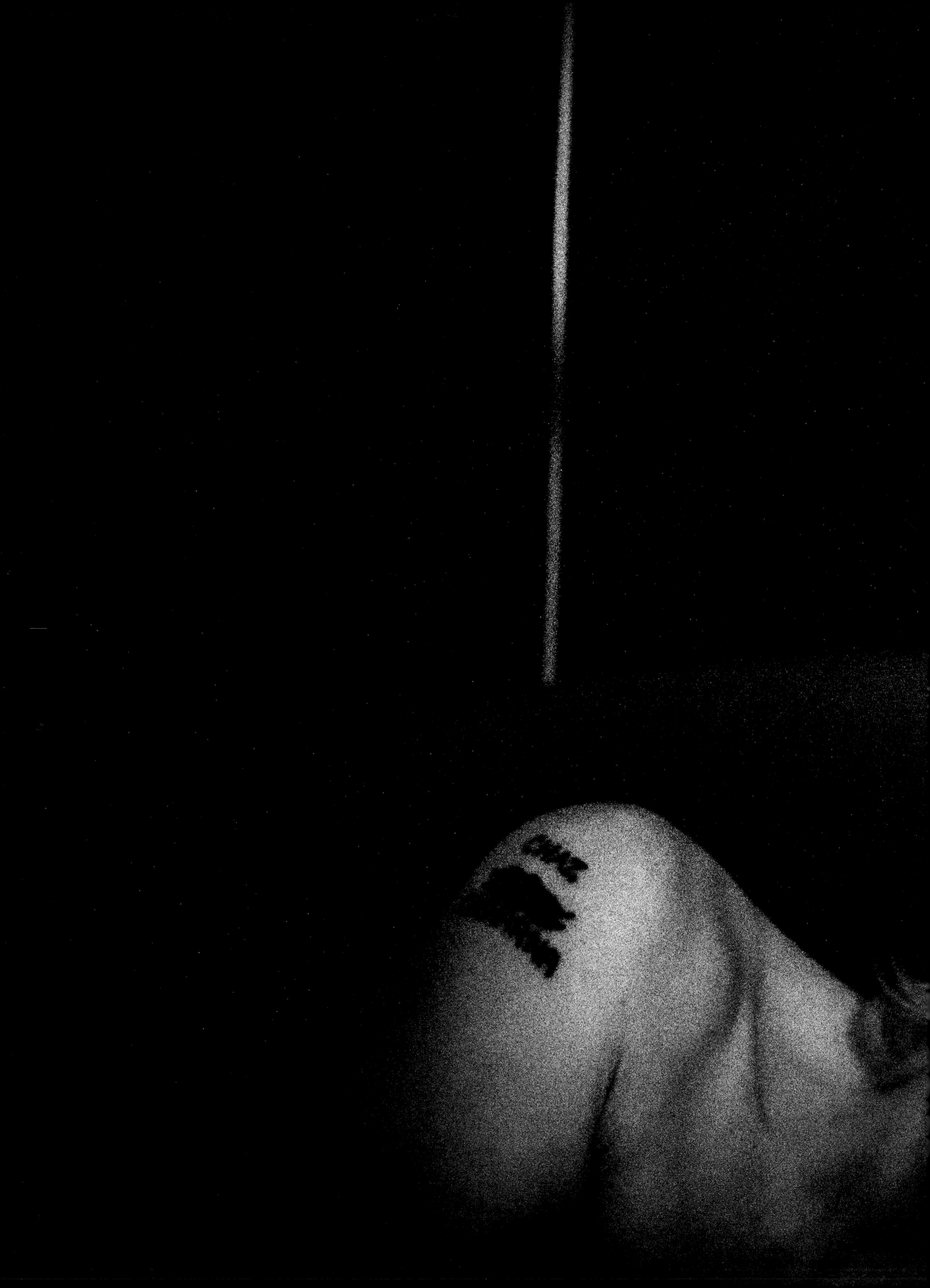

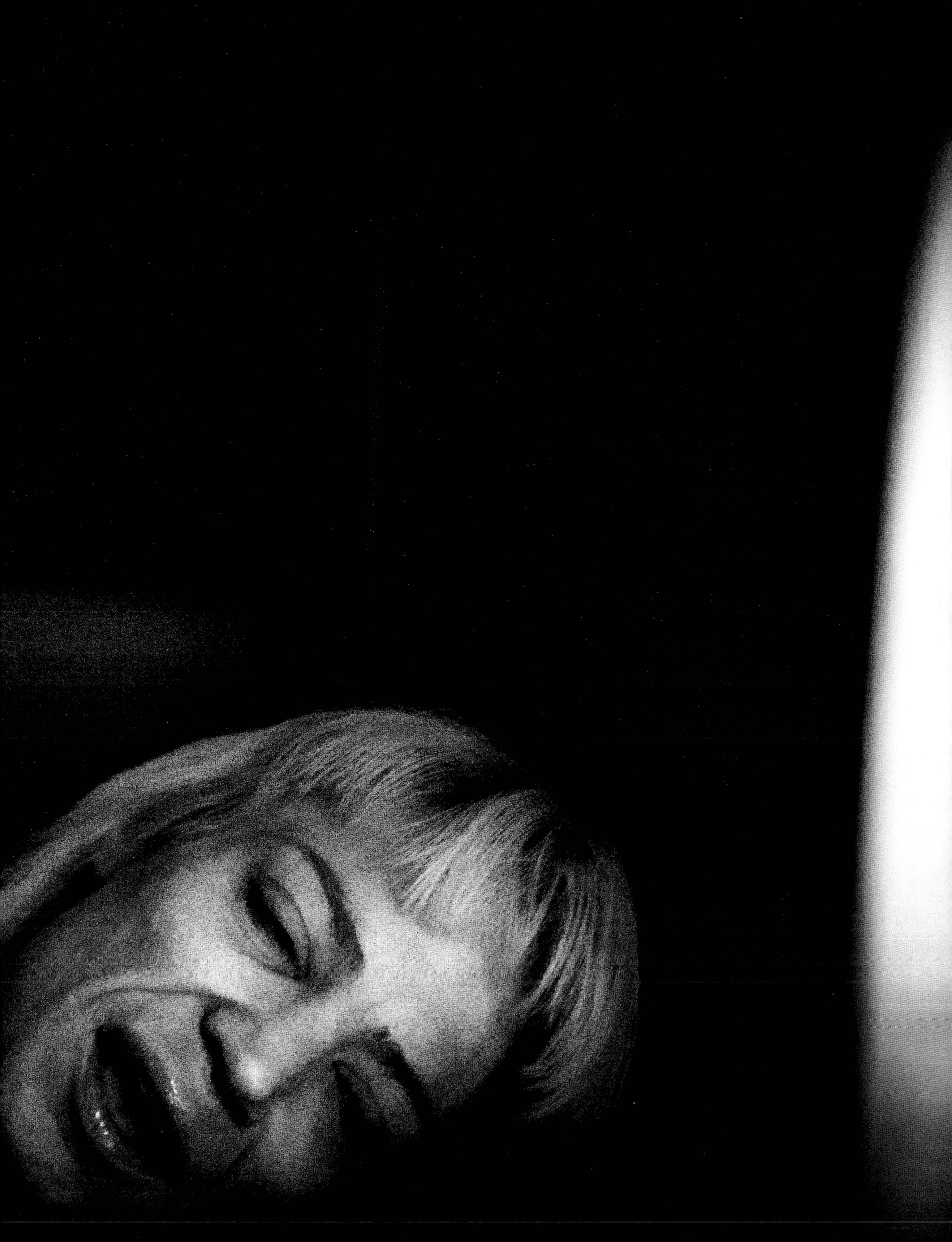

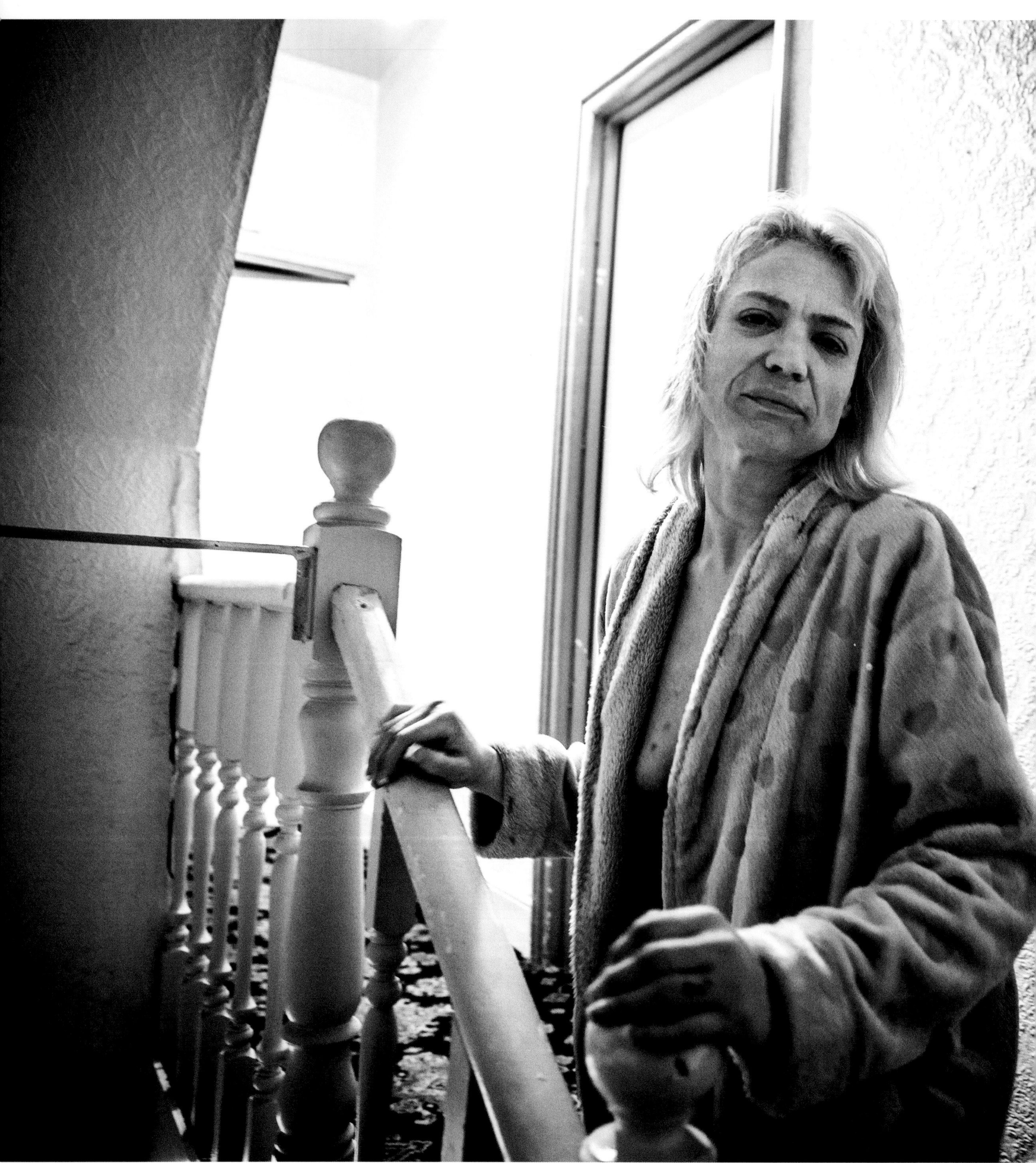

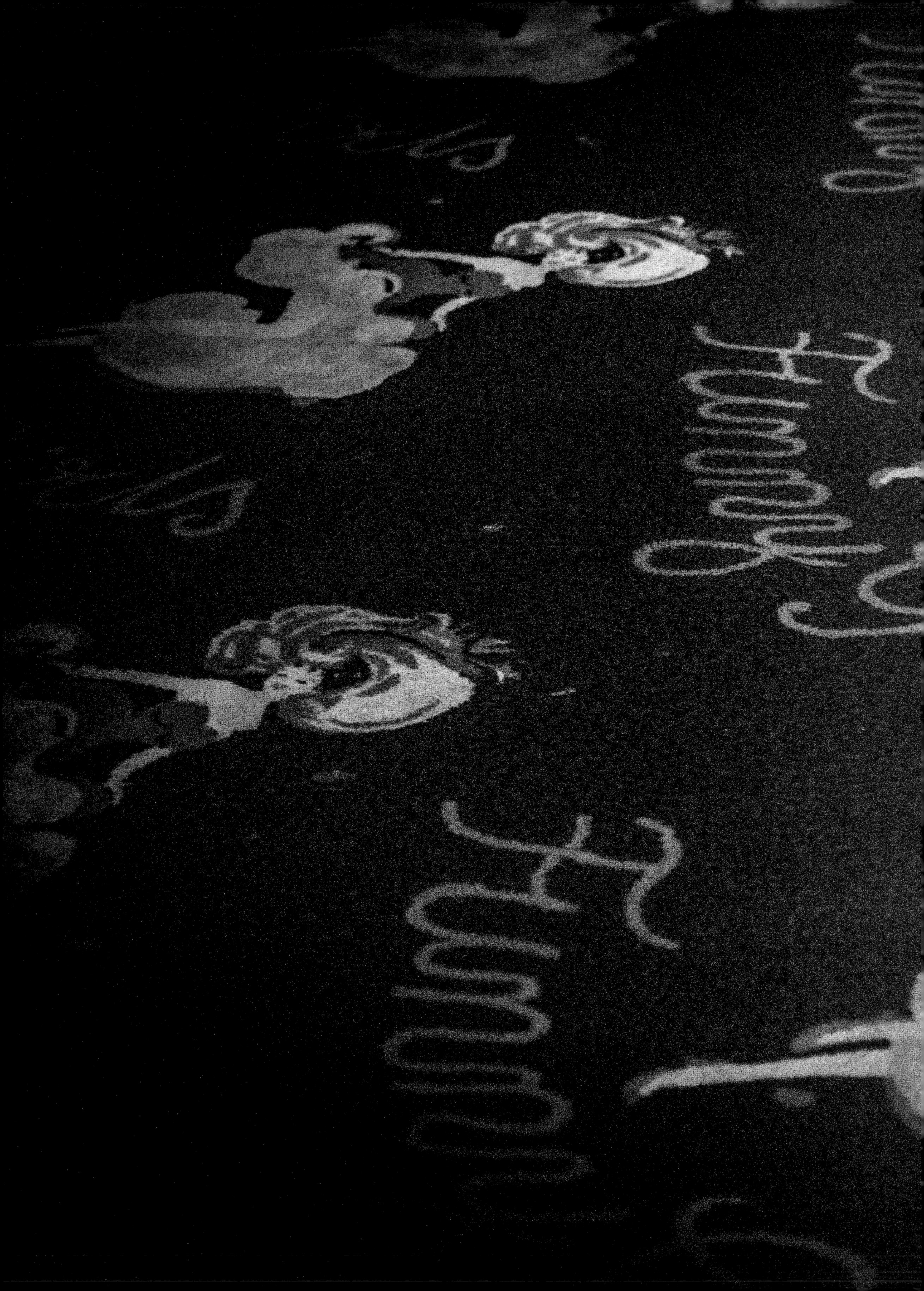

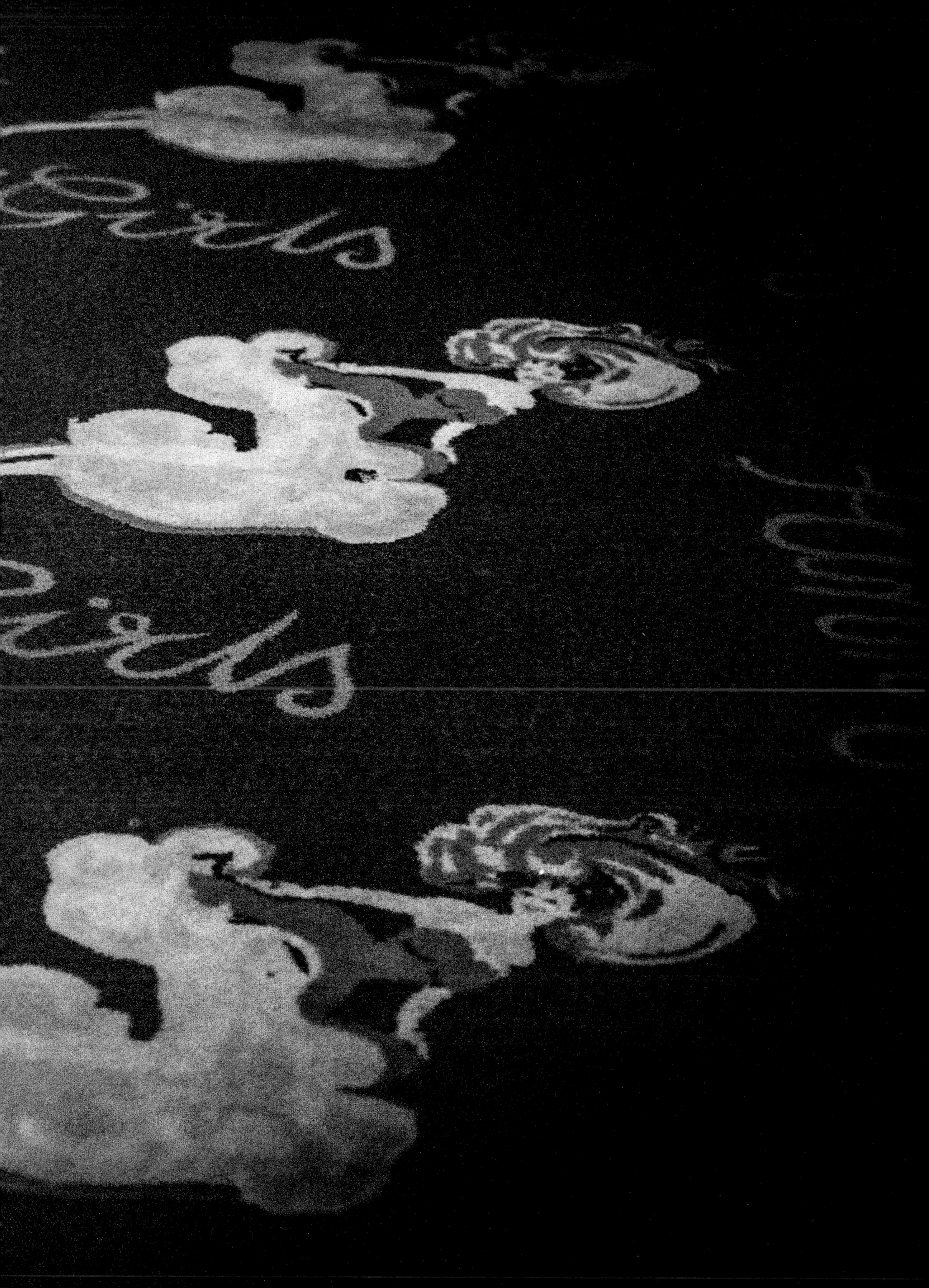
Girls
Girls

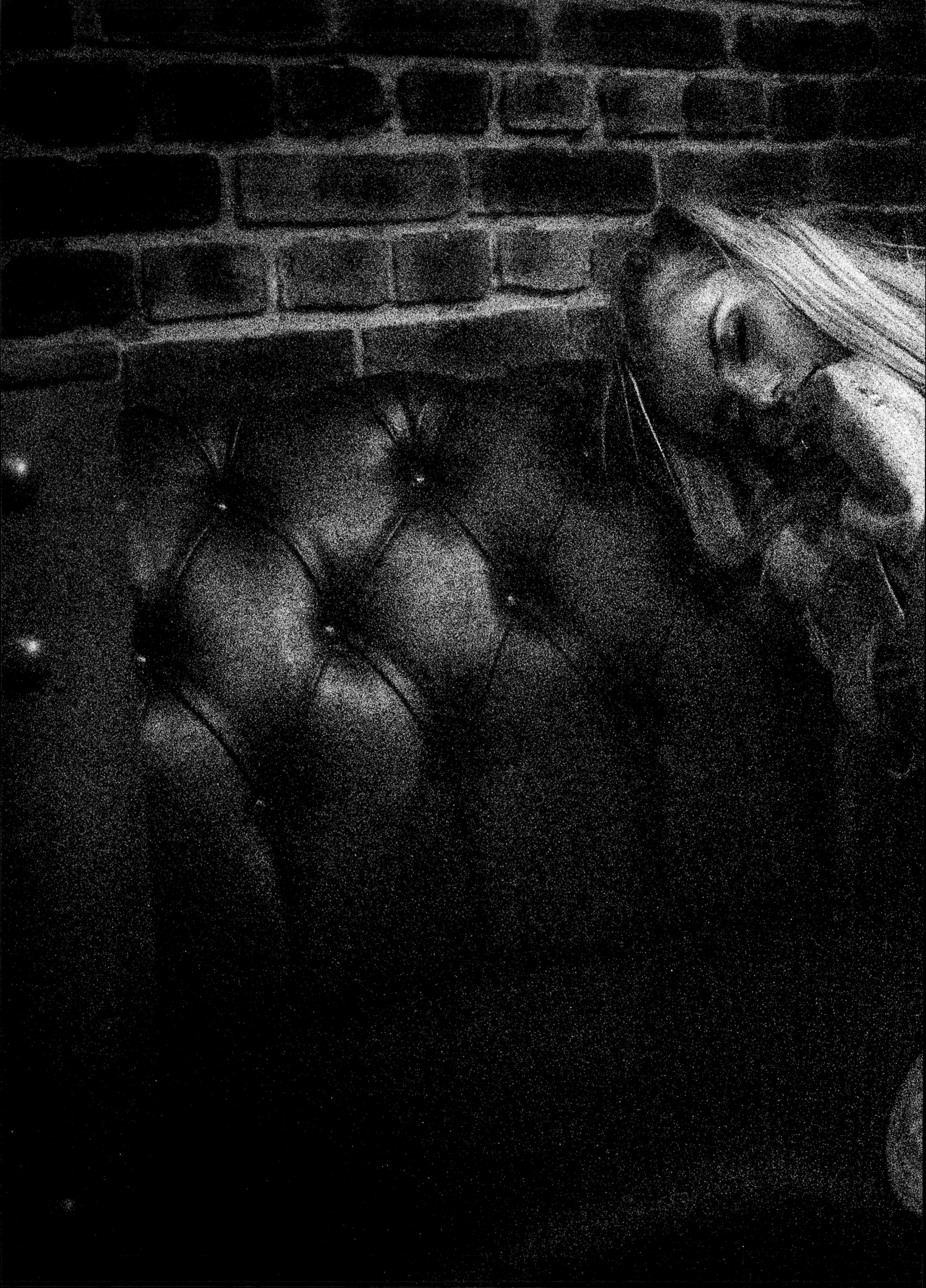

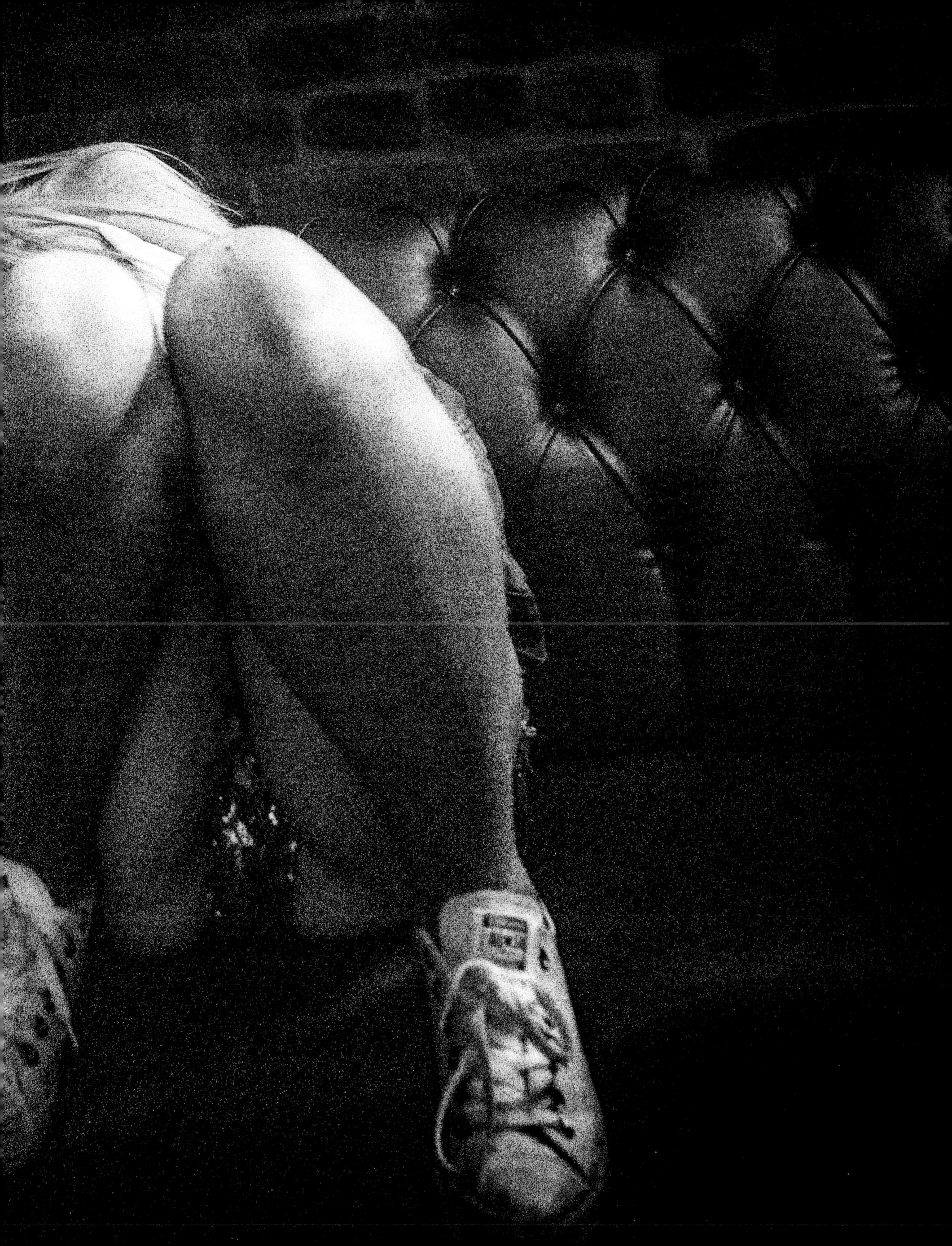

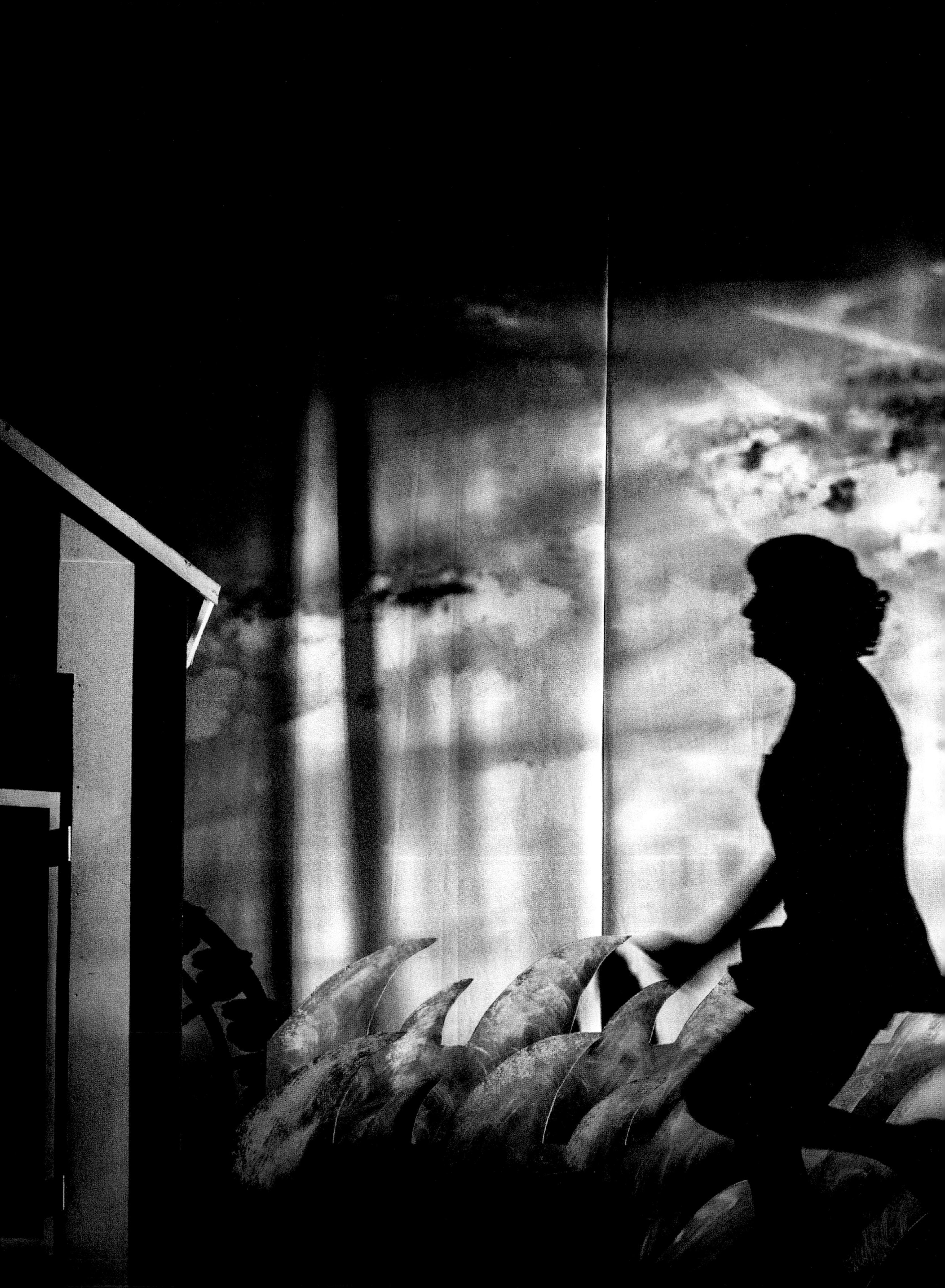

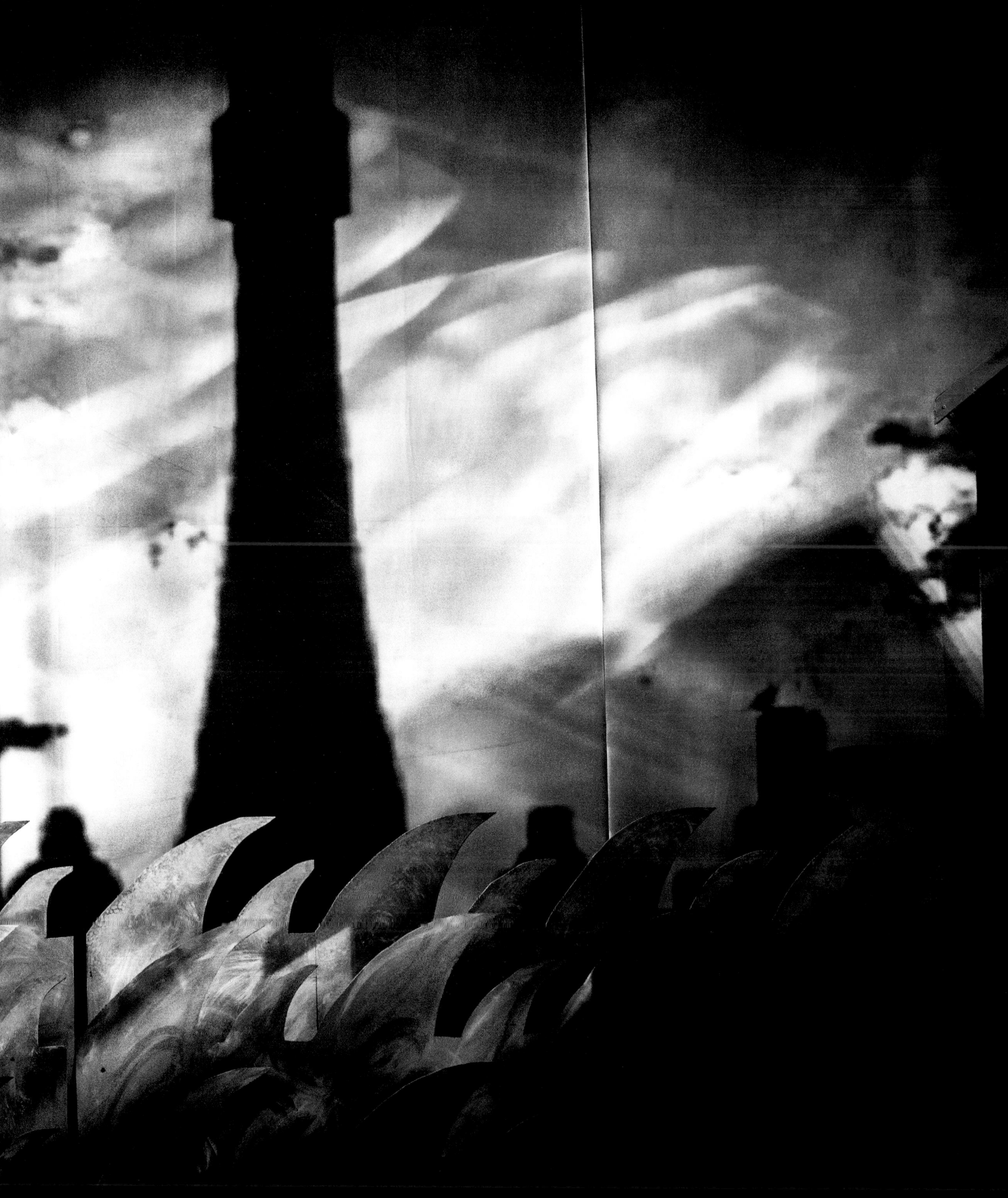

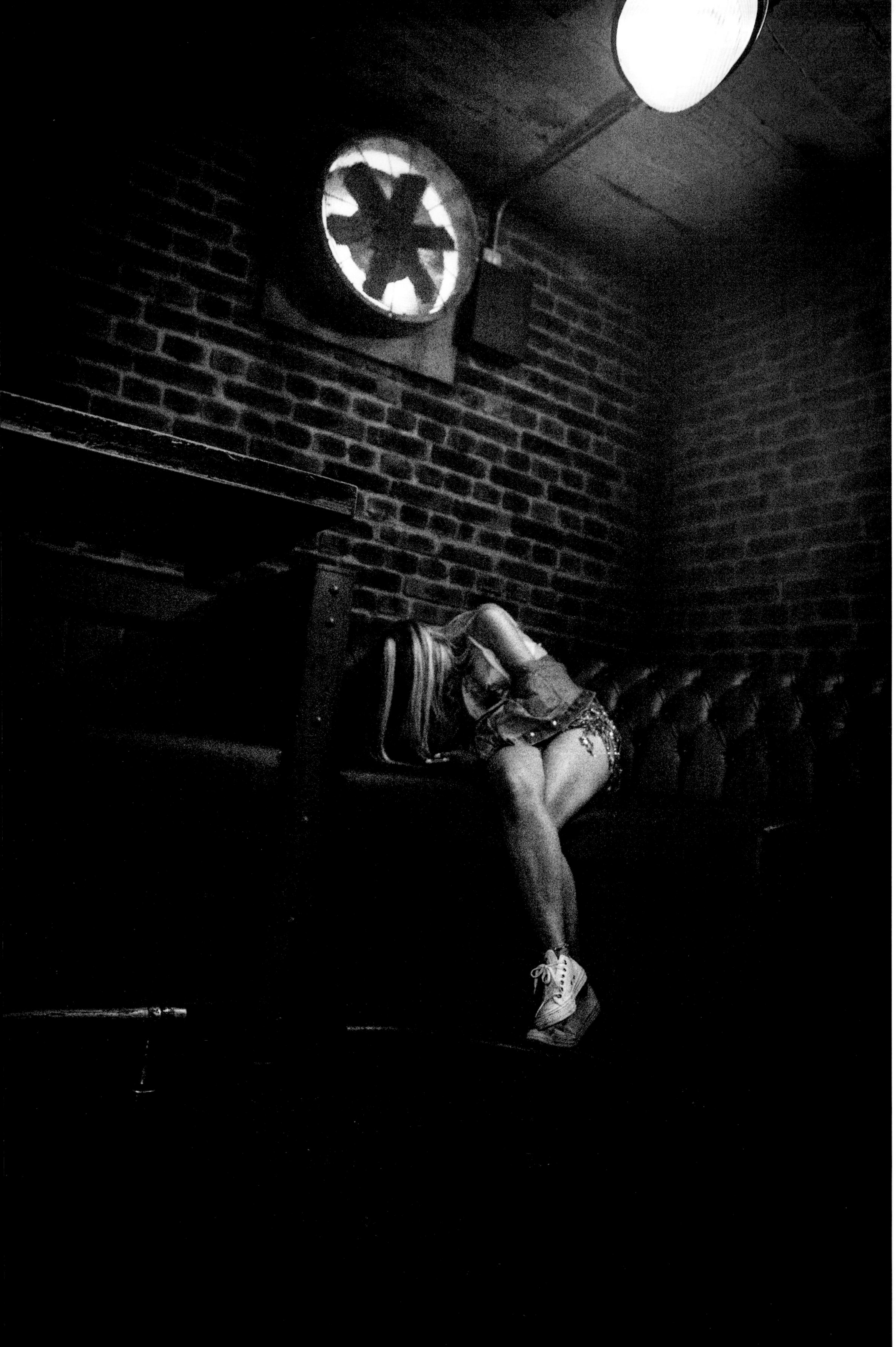

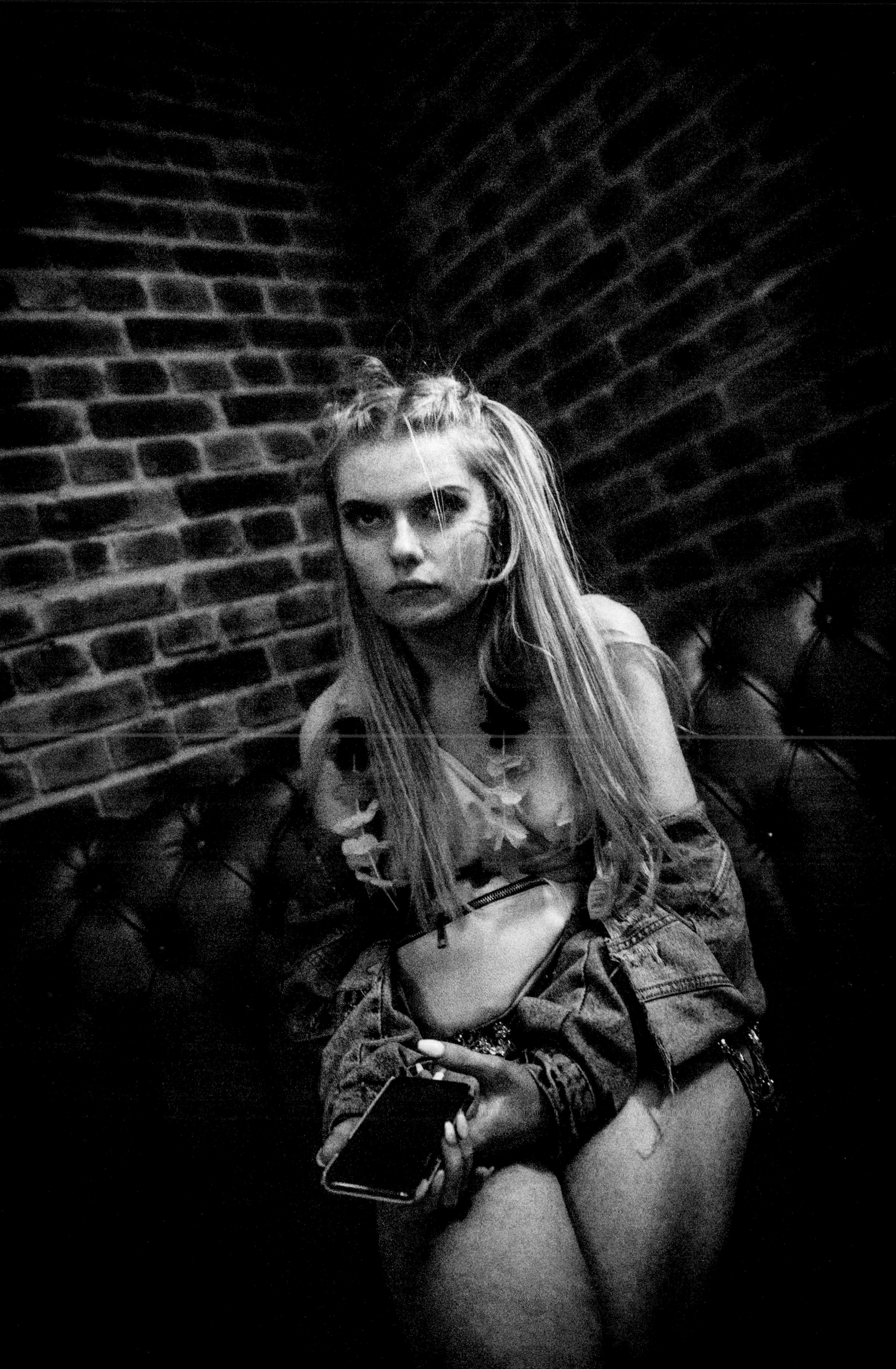

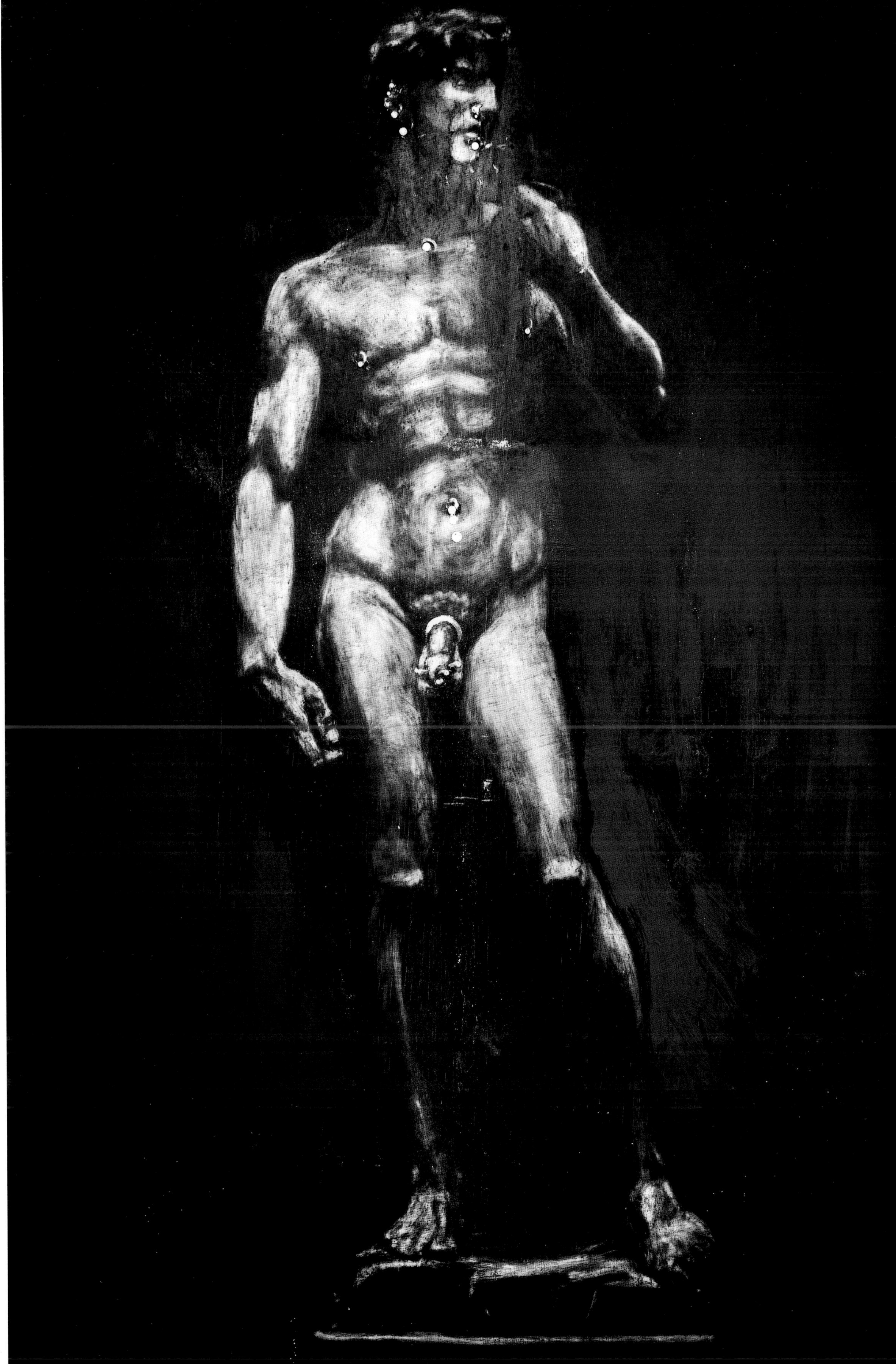

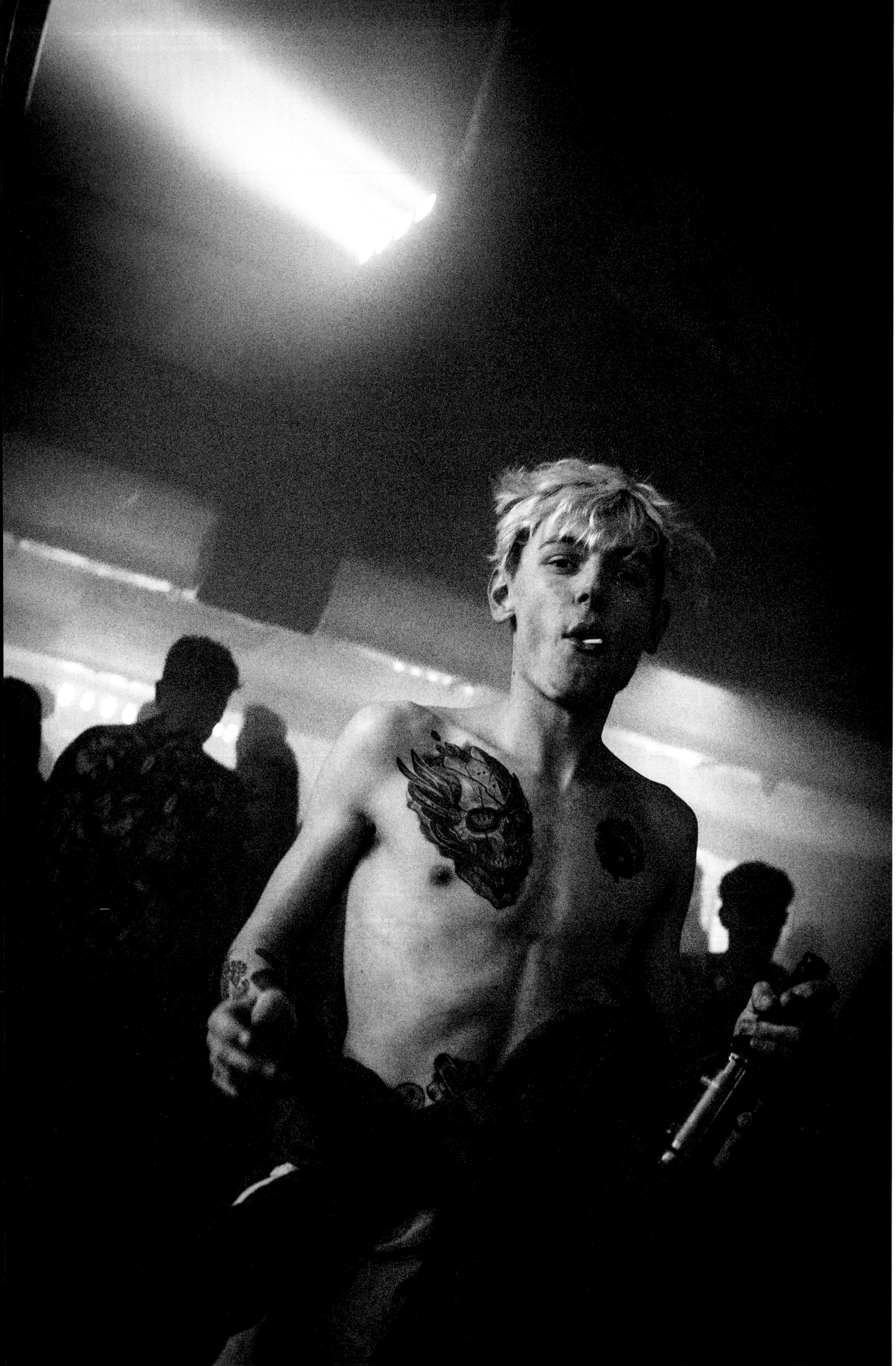

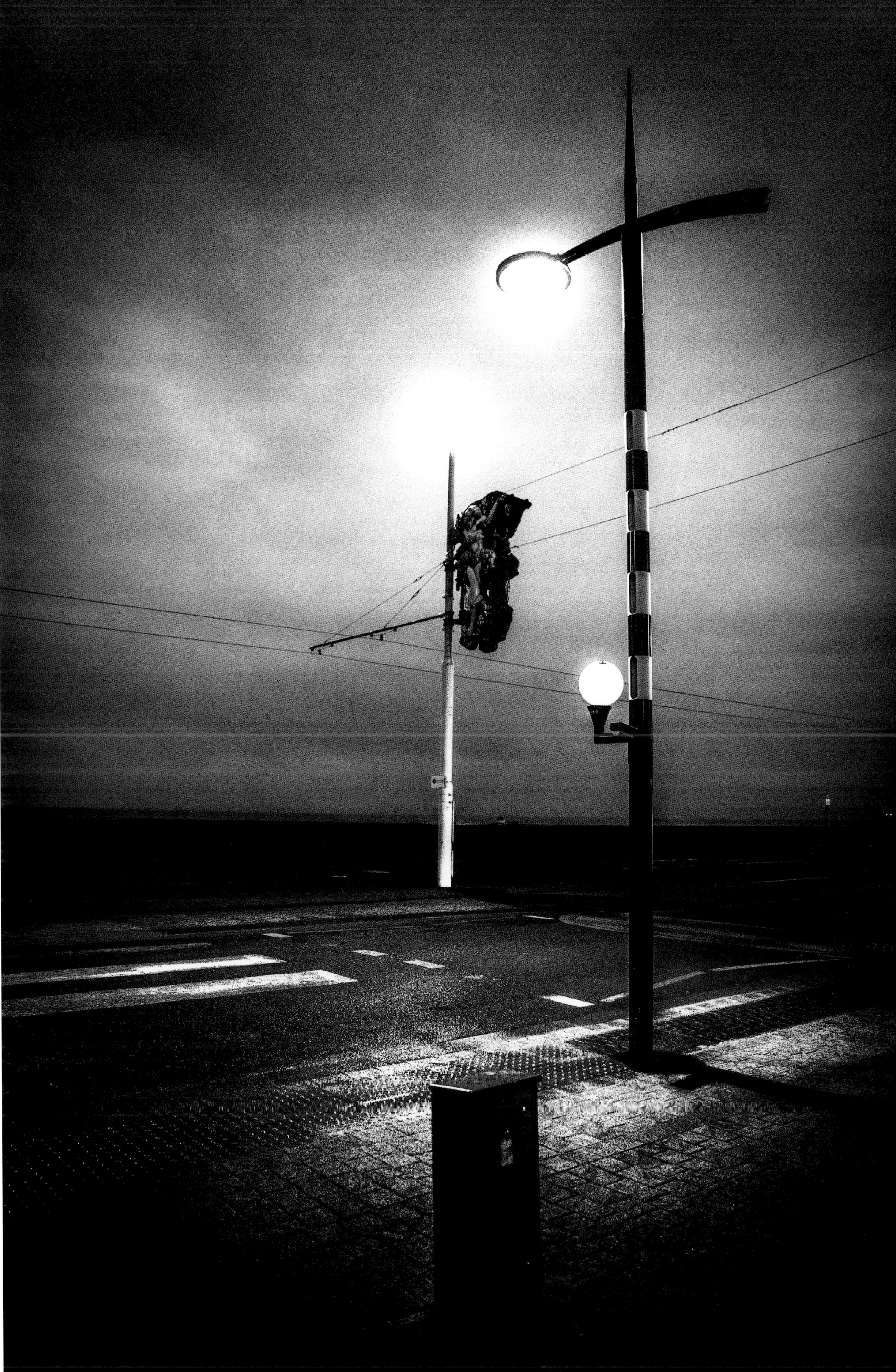

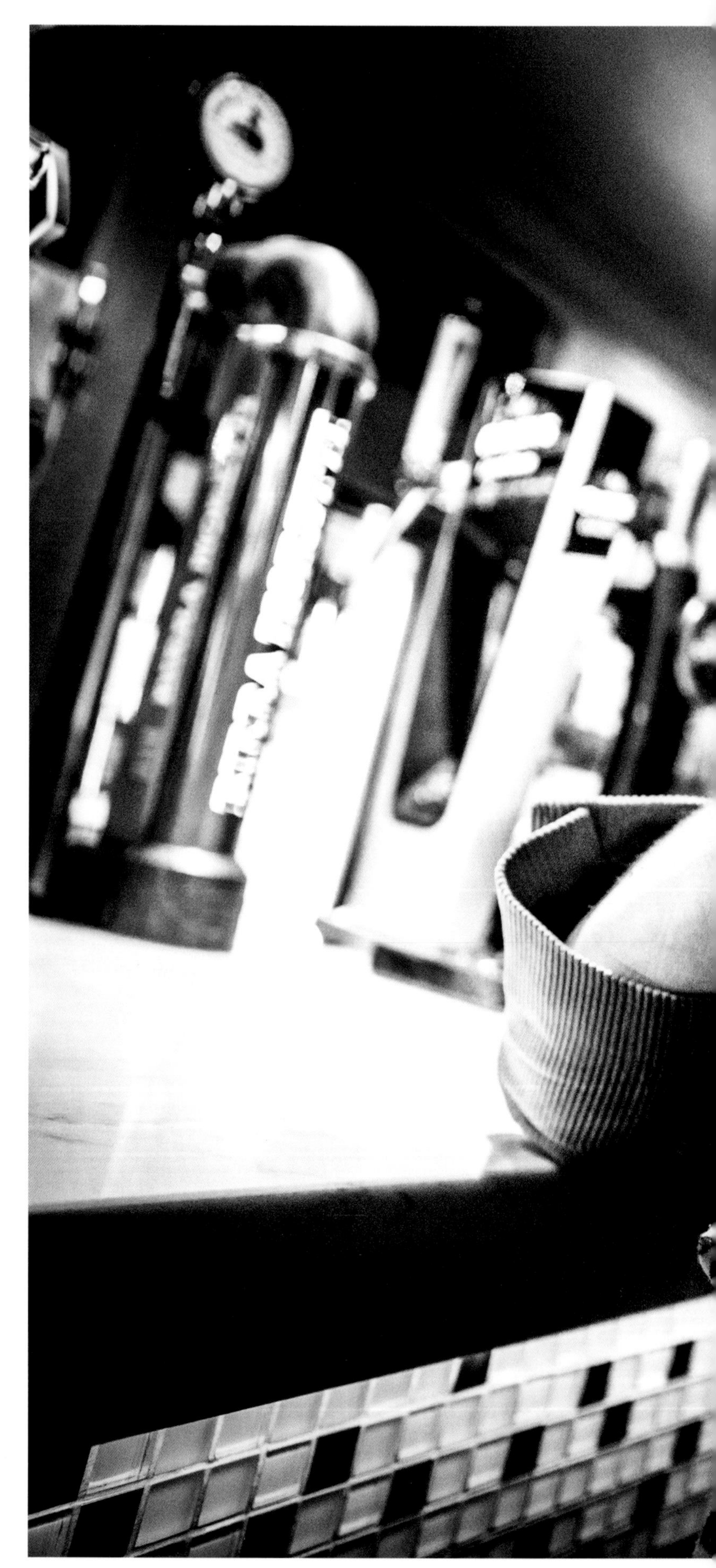

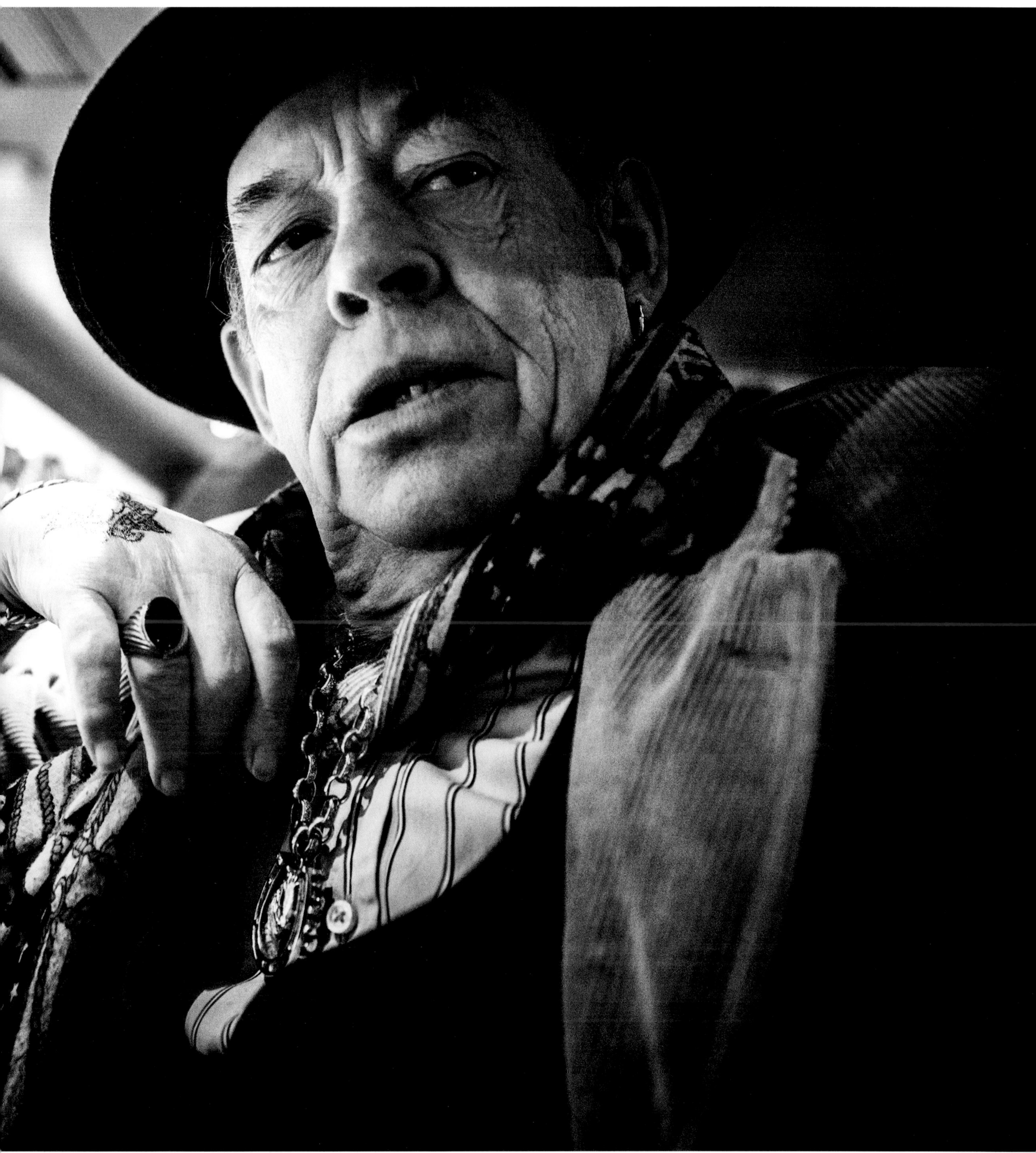

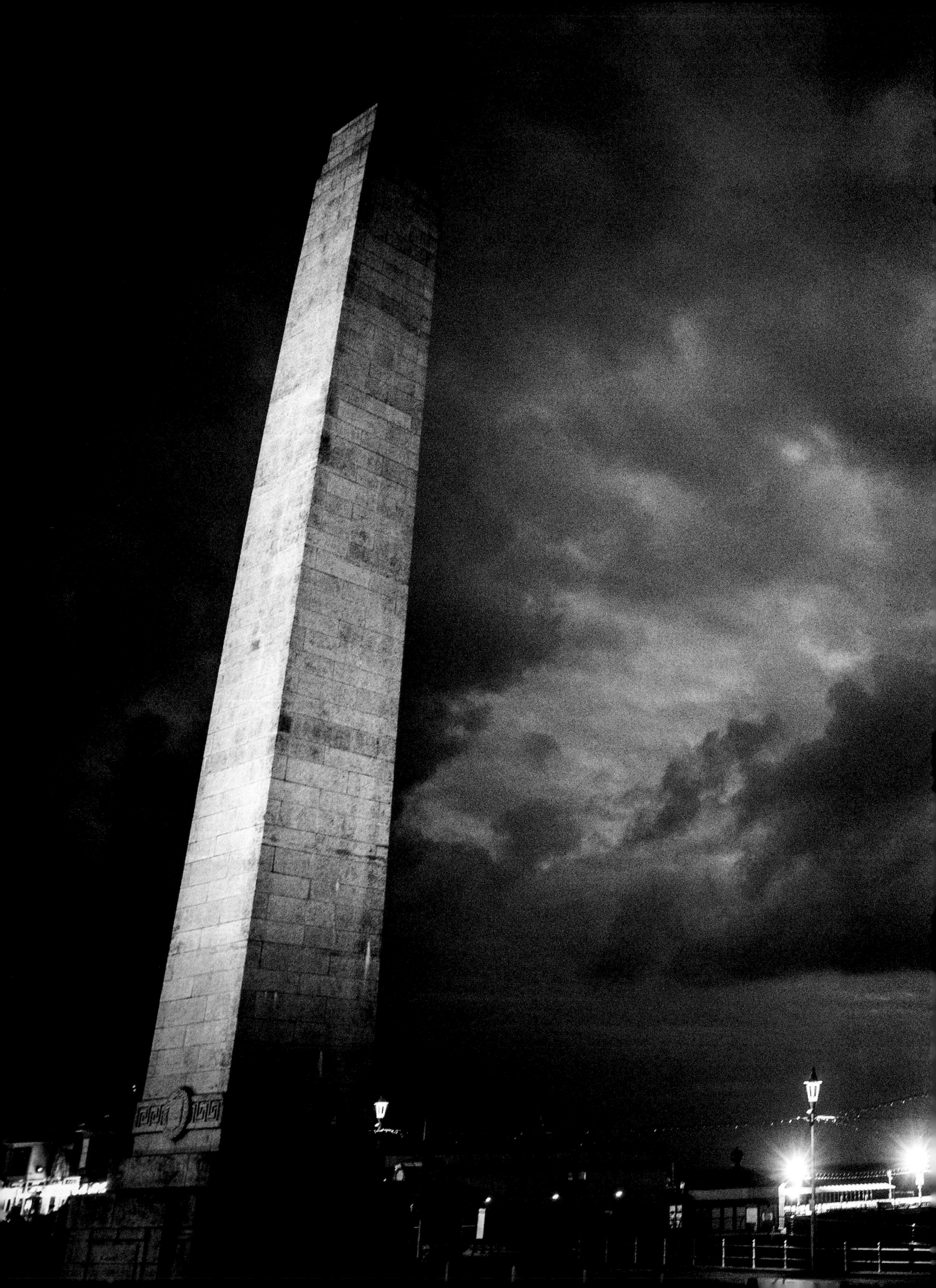

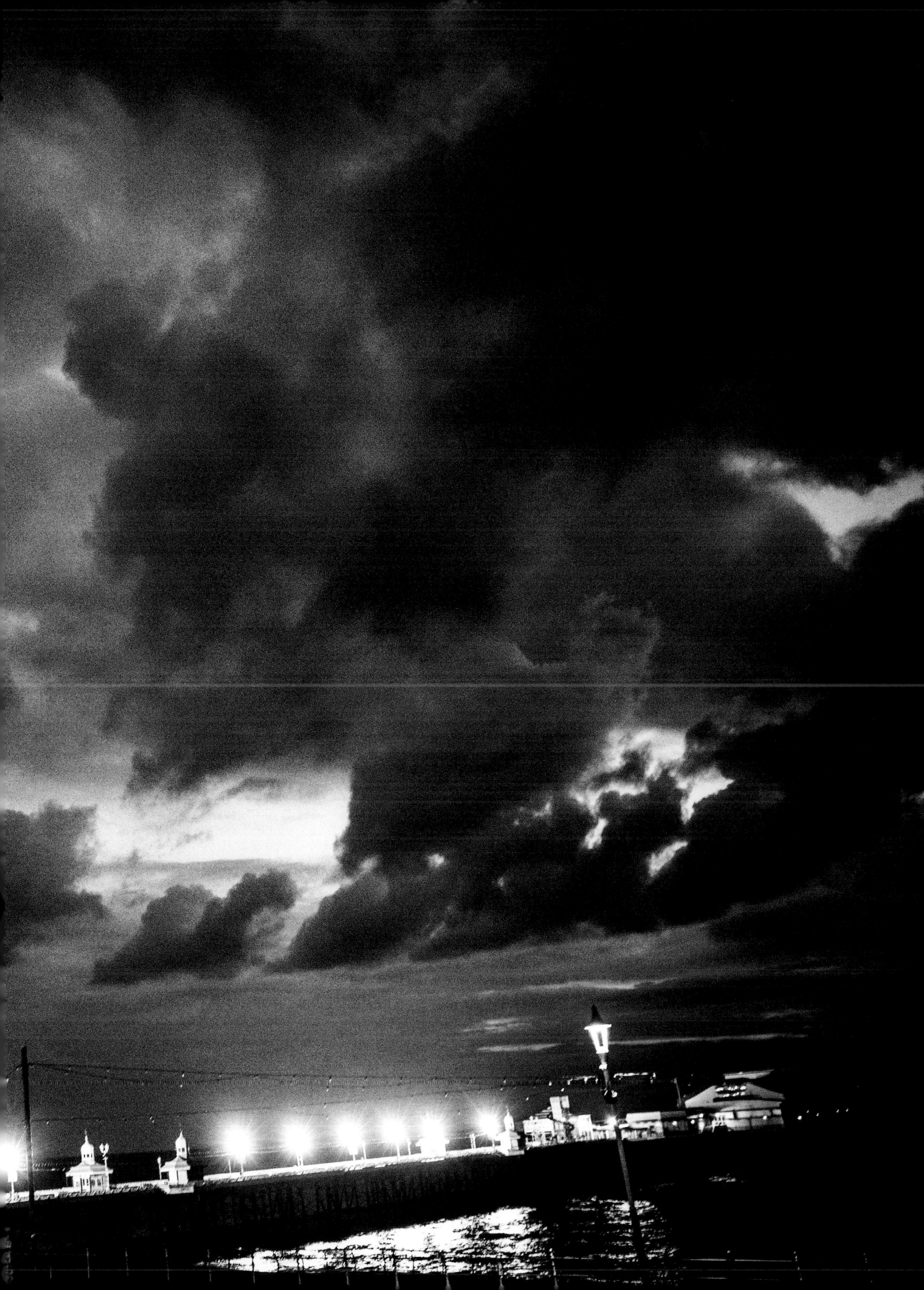

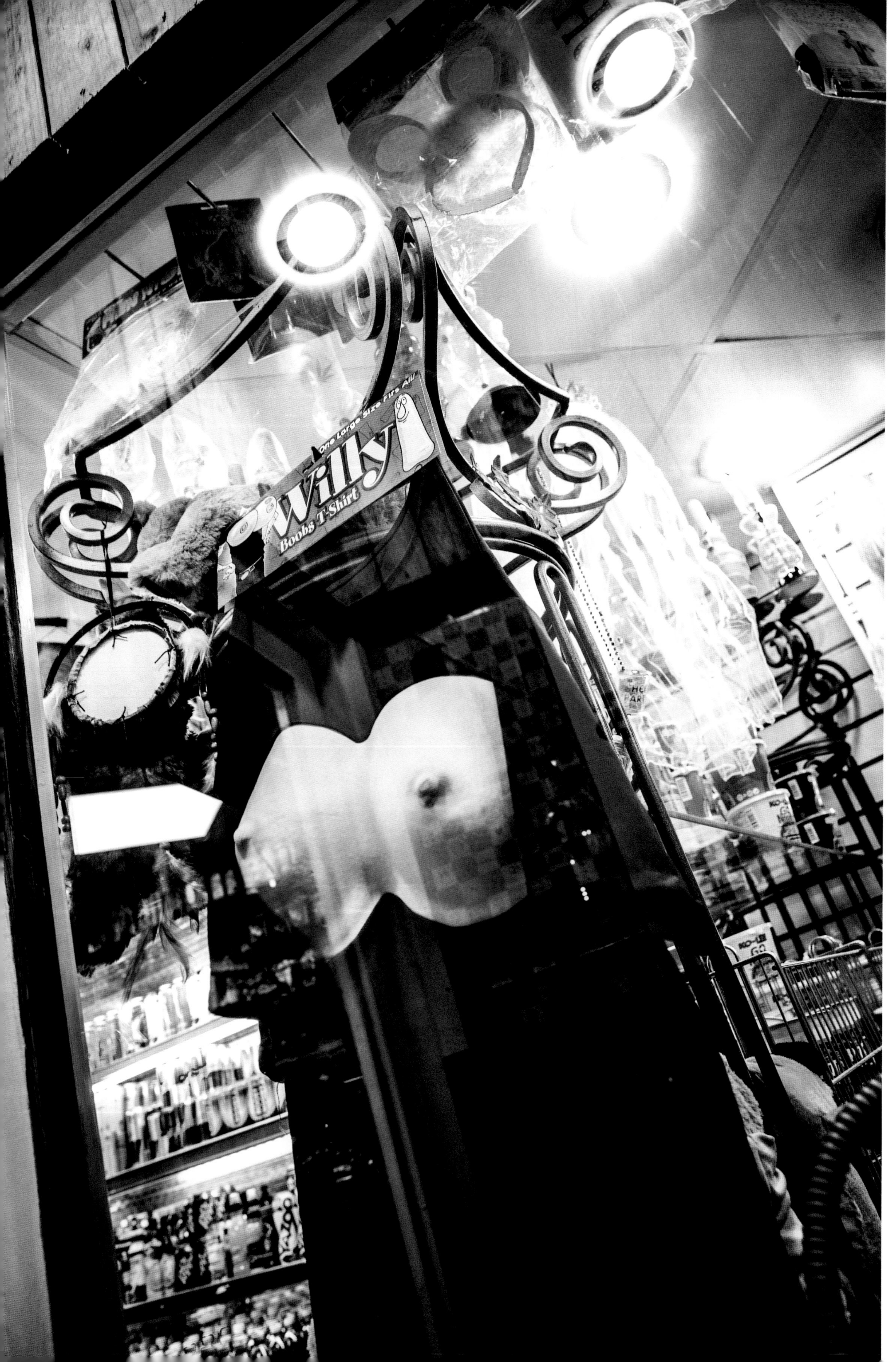

Willy
Boobs T-Shirt
One Large Size Fits All

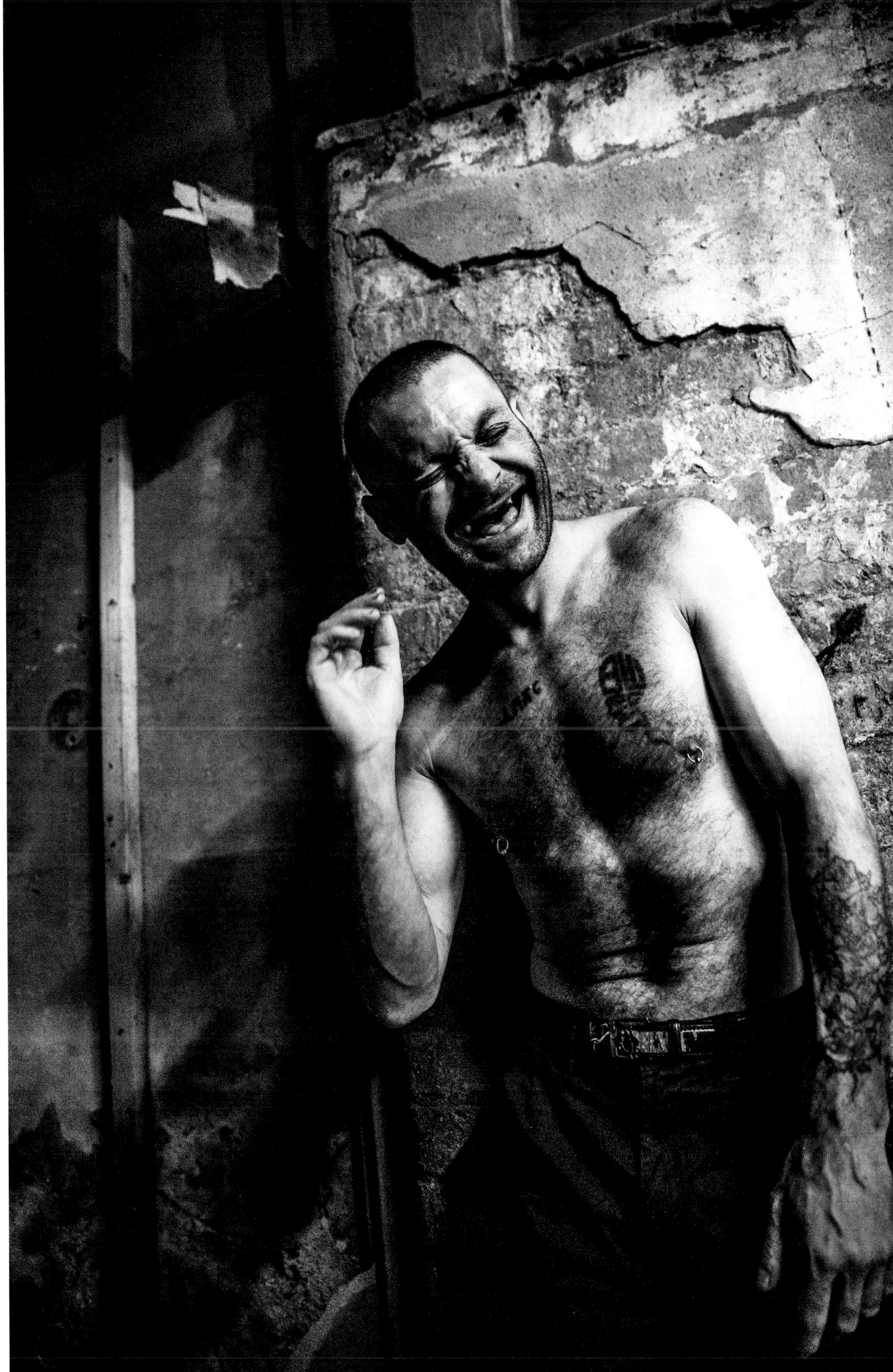

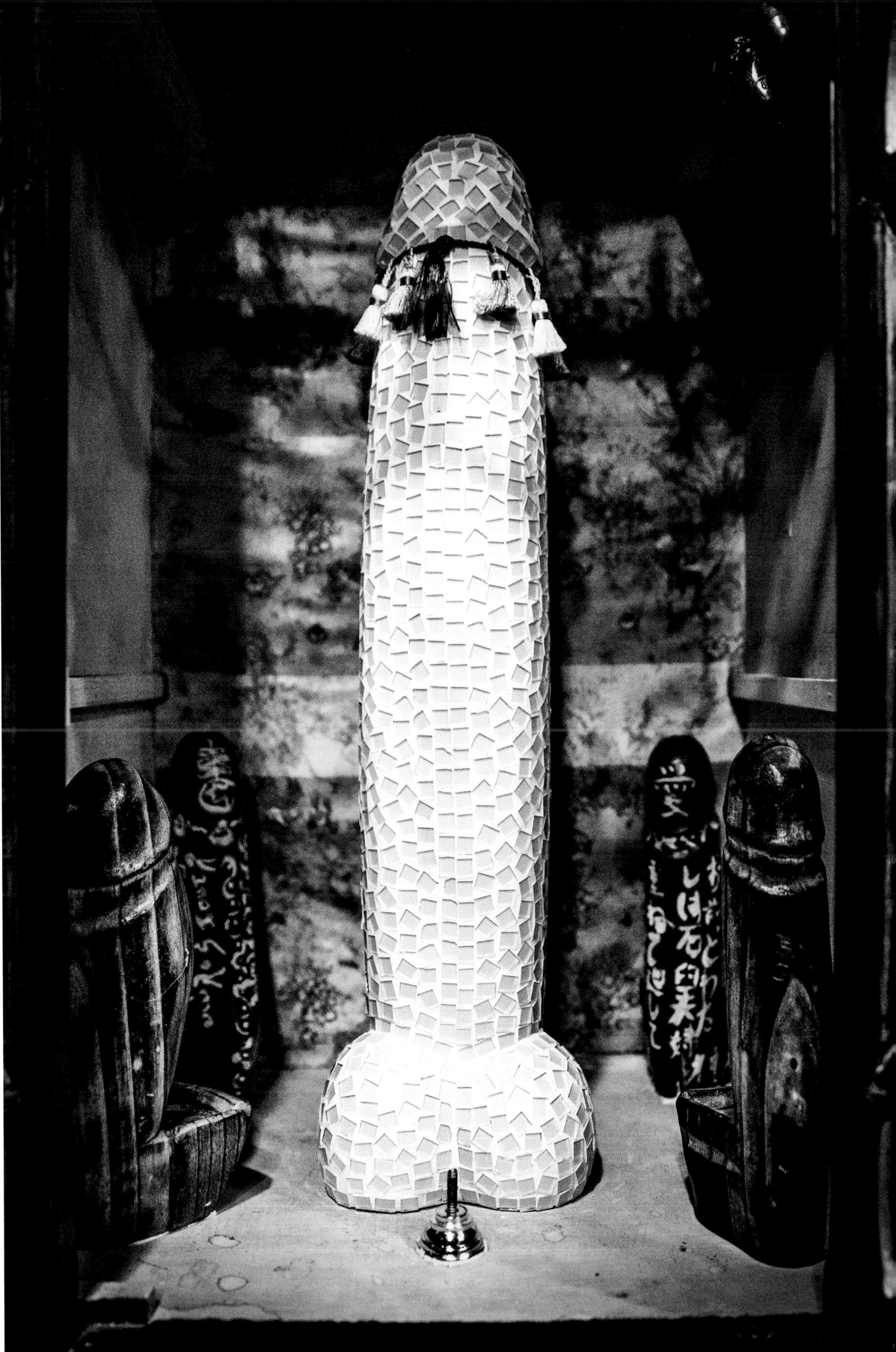

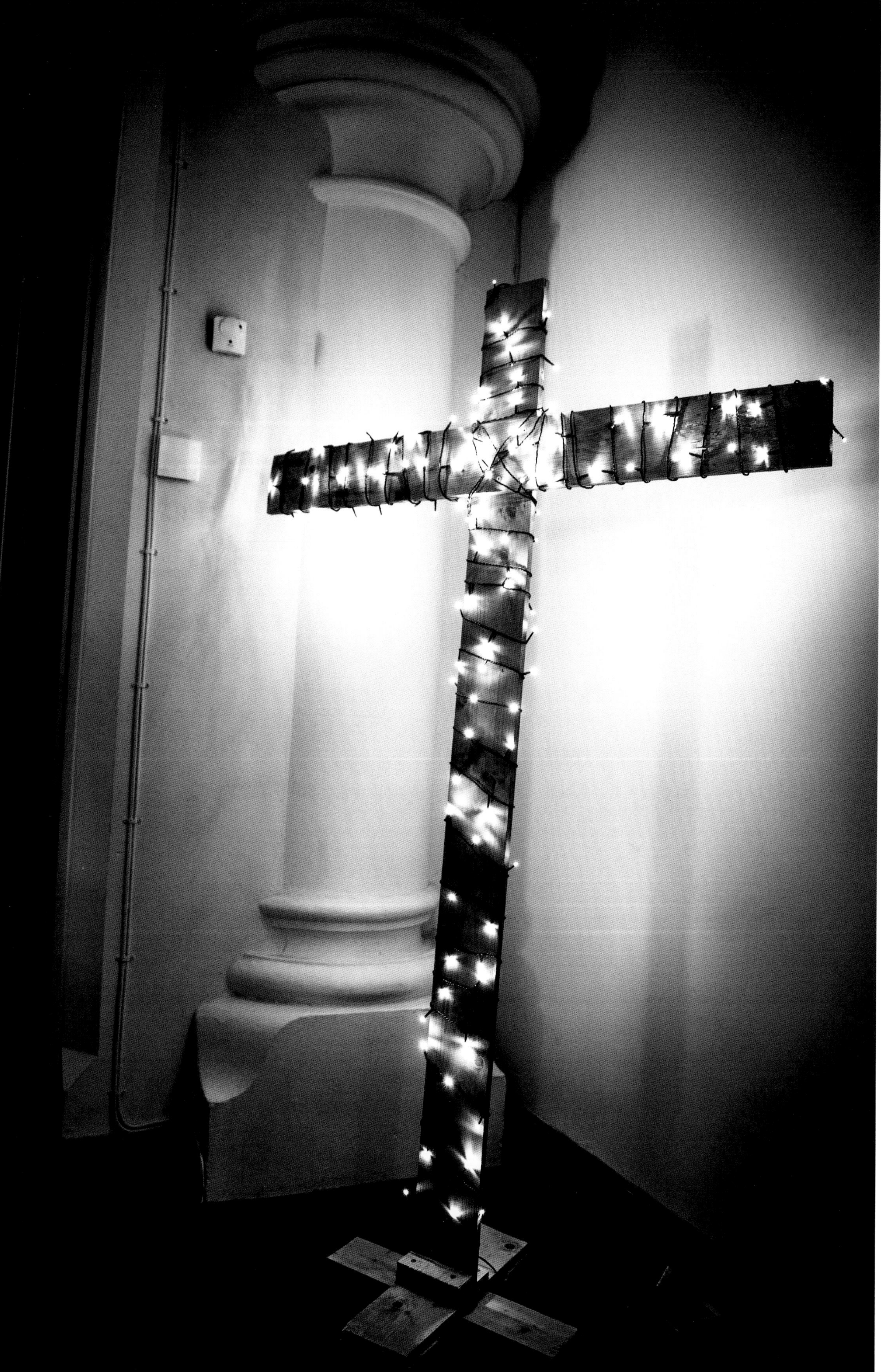

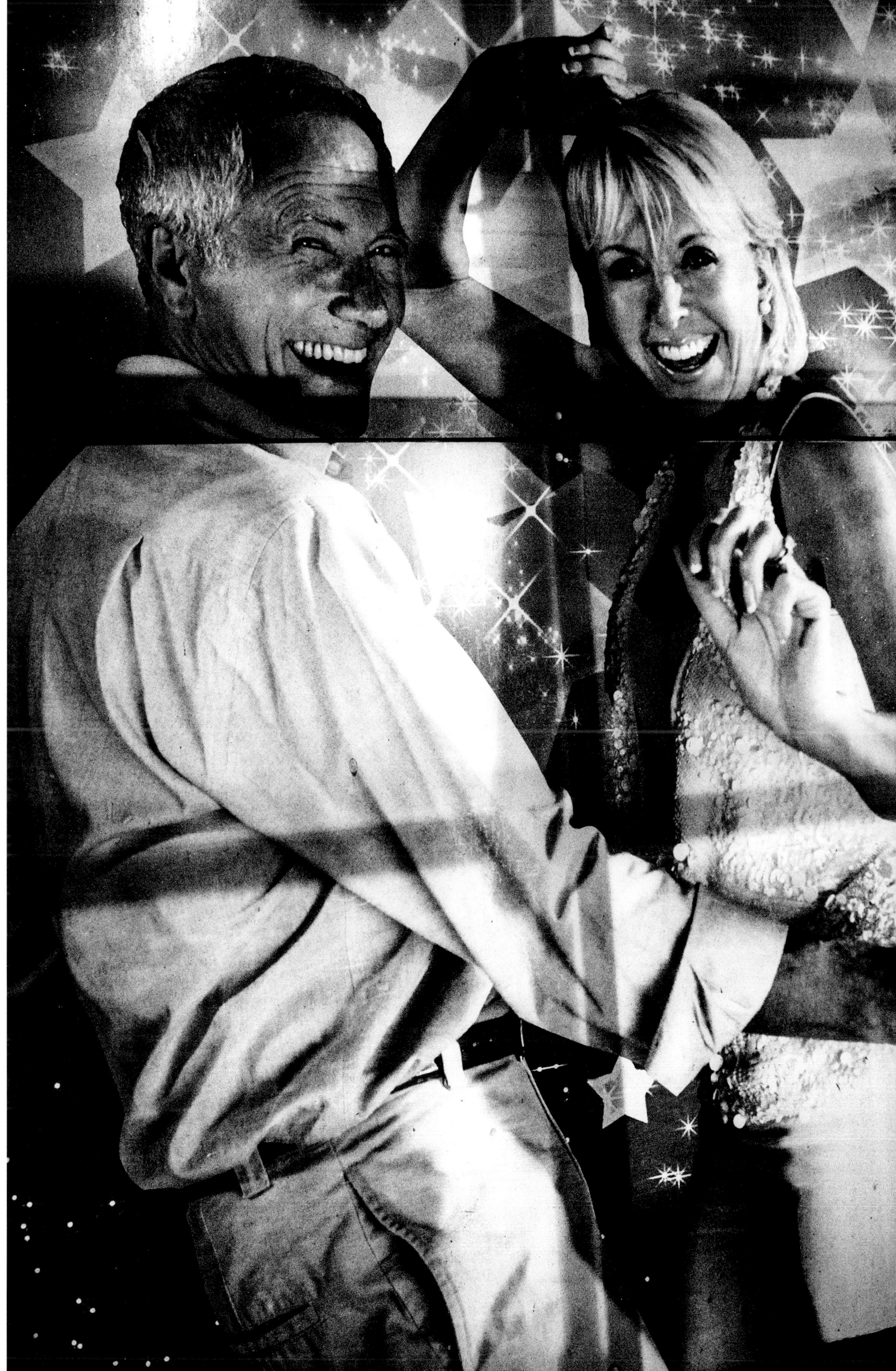

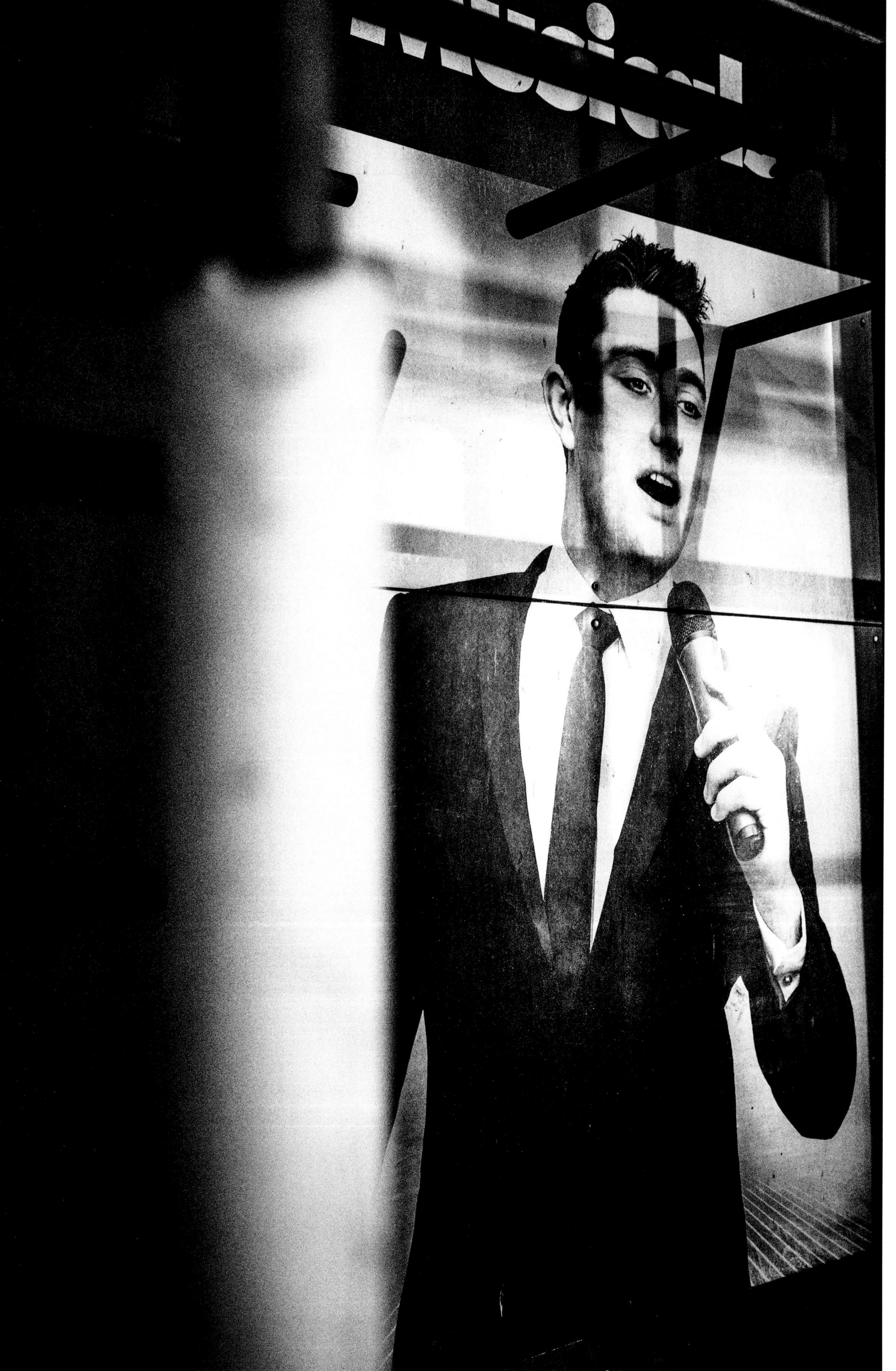
Musical

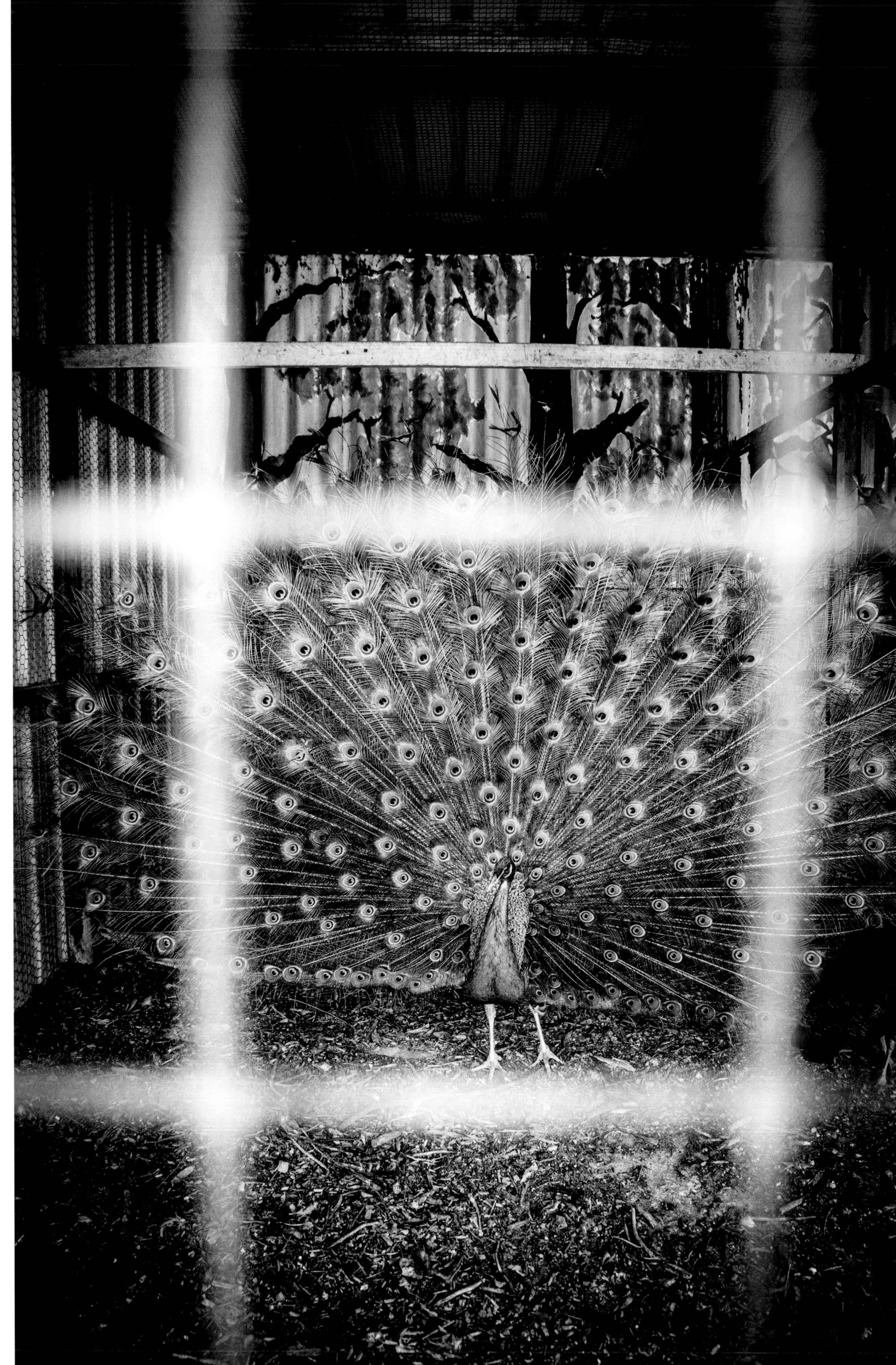

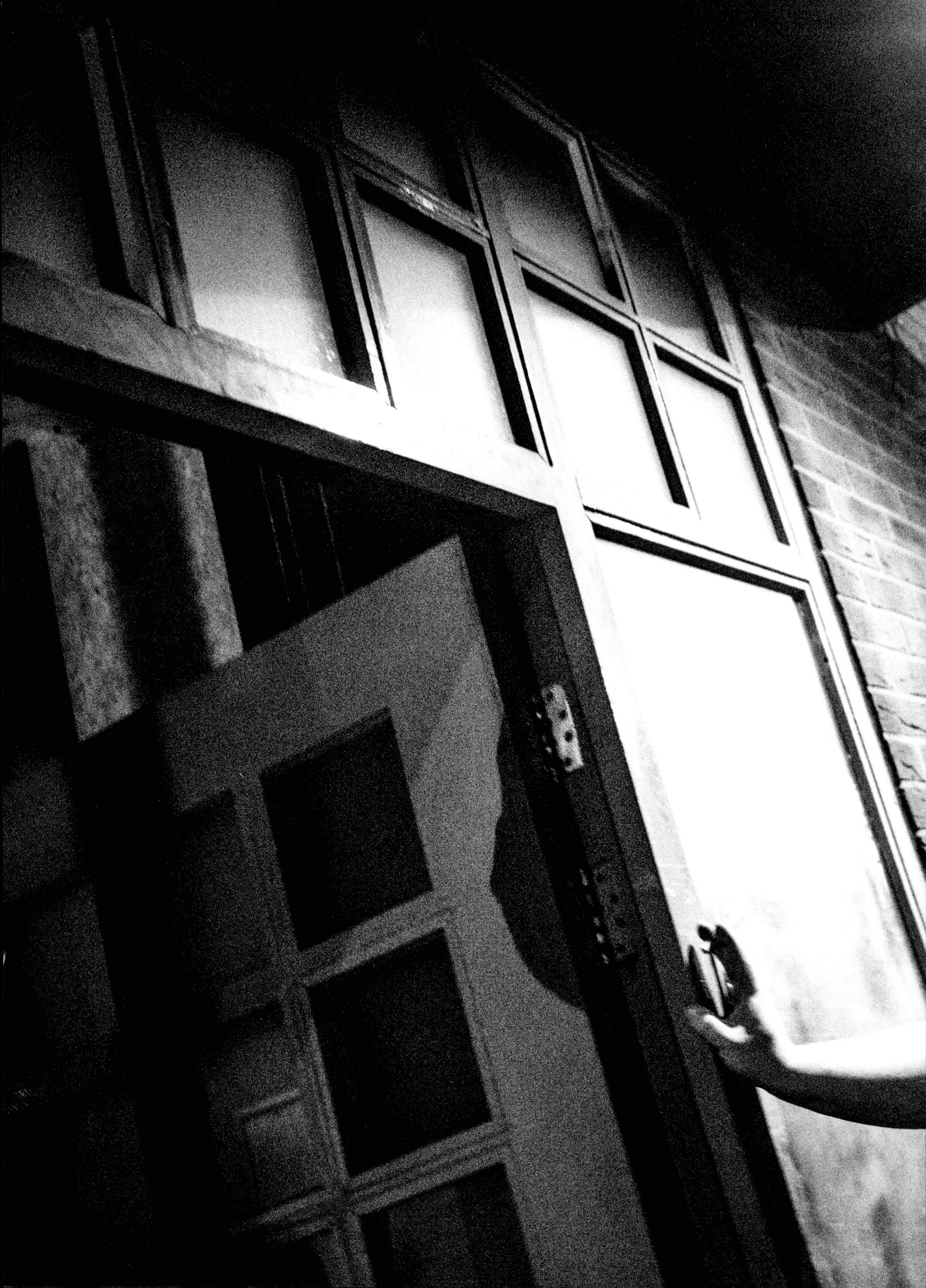

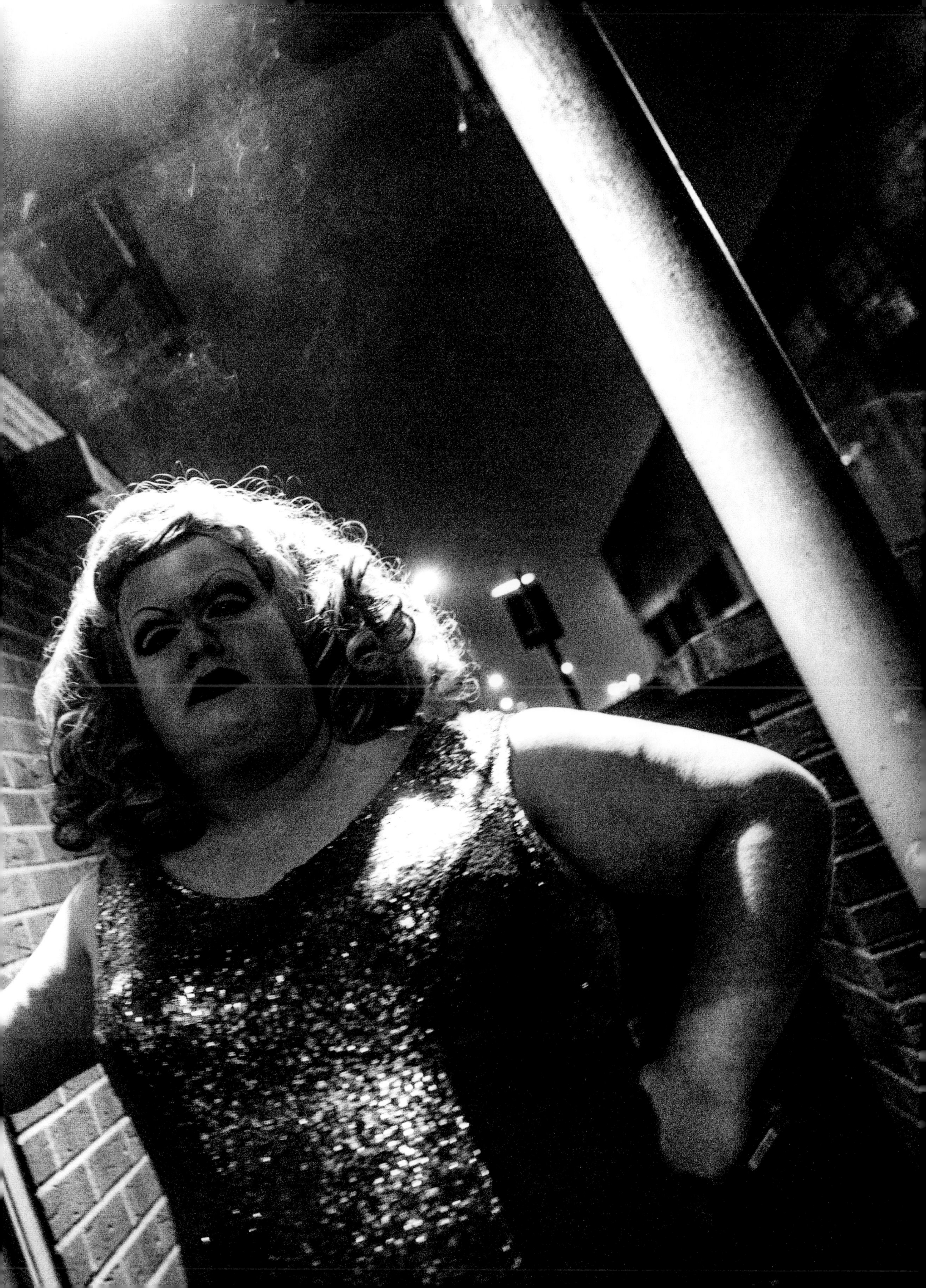

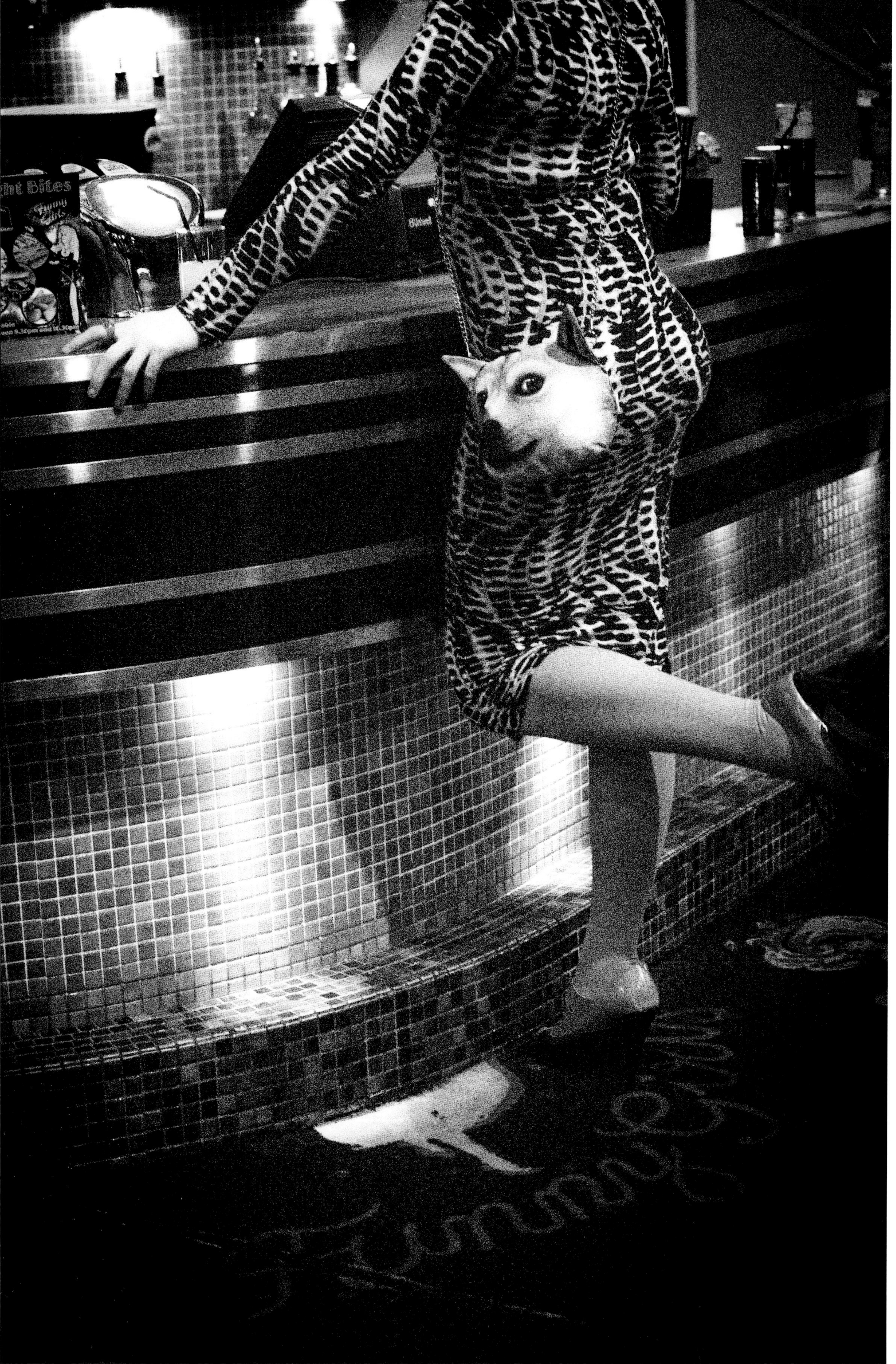

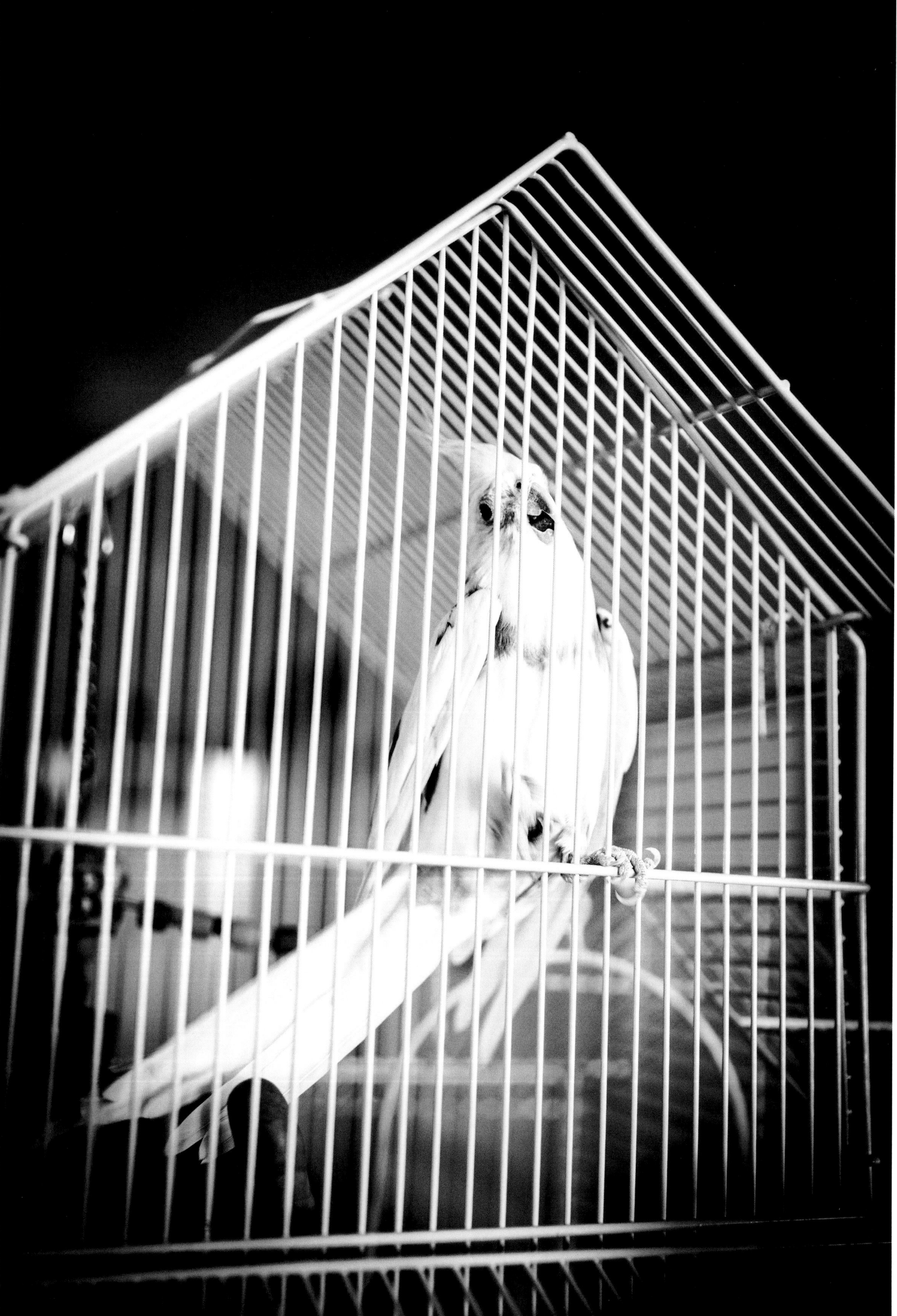

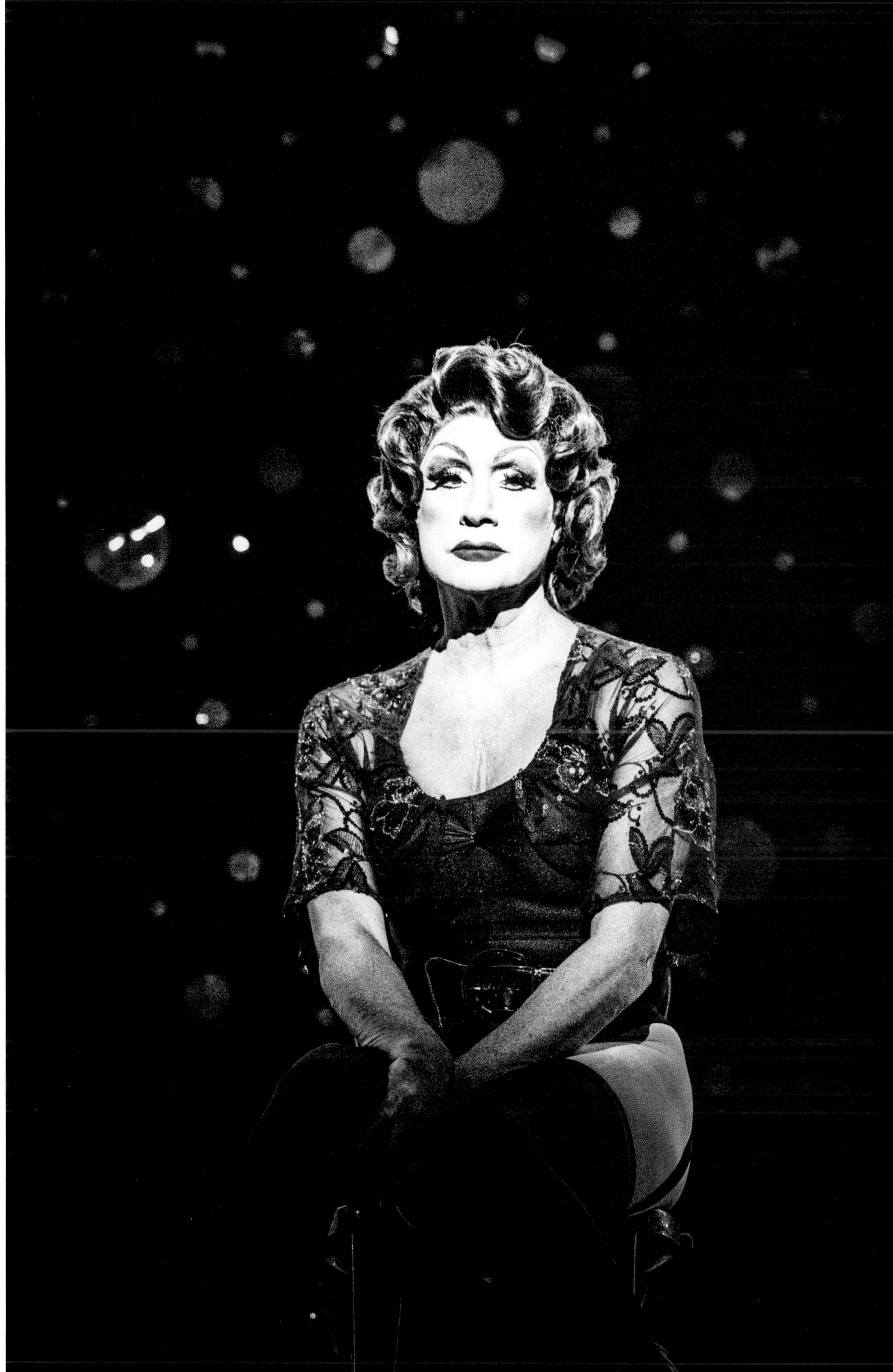

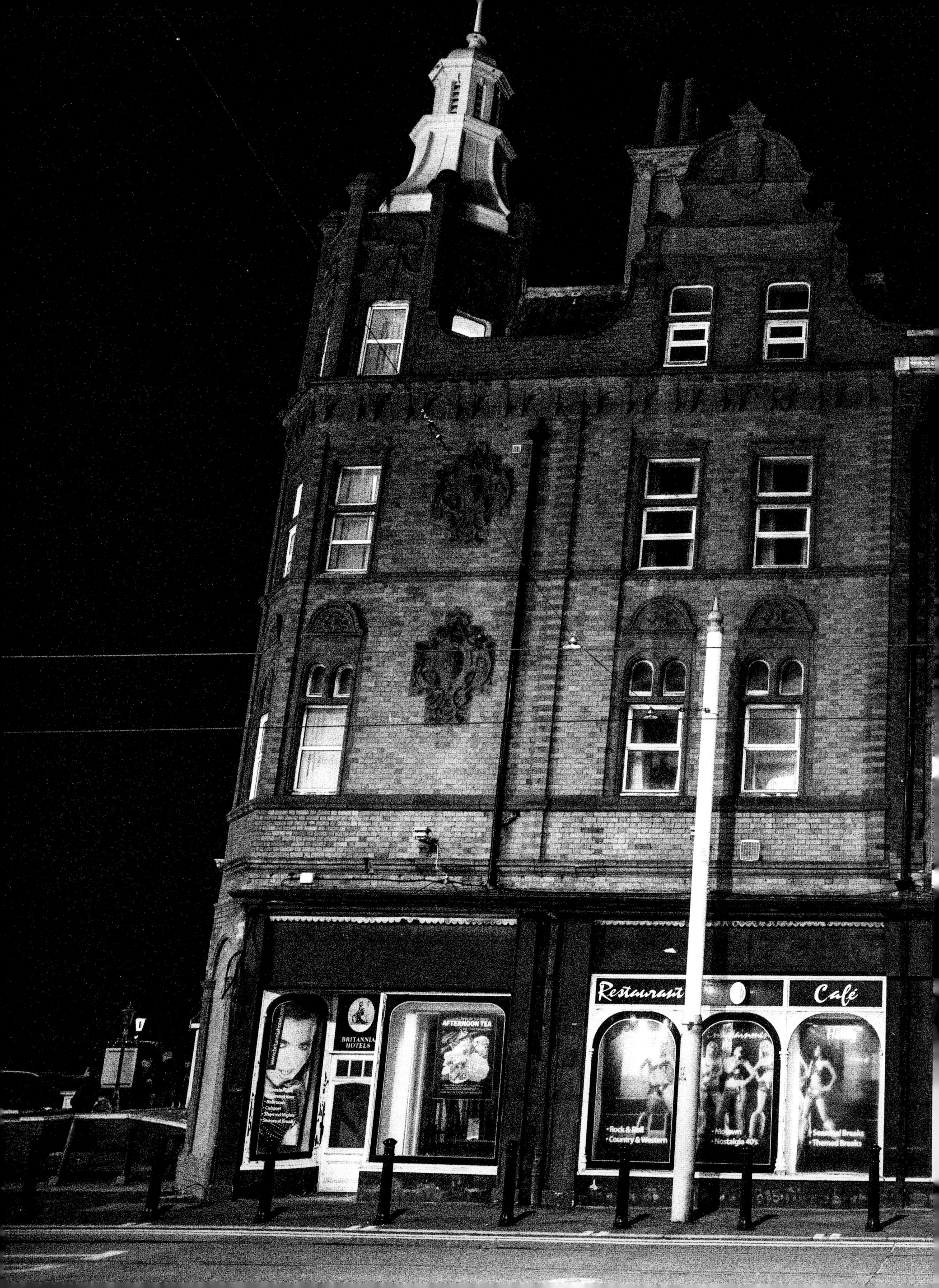

BRITANNIA HOTELS
AFTERNOON TEA
Restaurant
Café
Rock & Roll
Country & Western
Motown
Nostalgia 40's

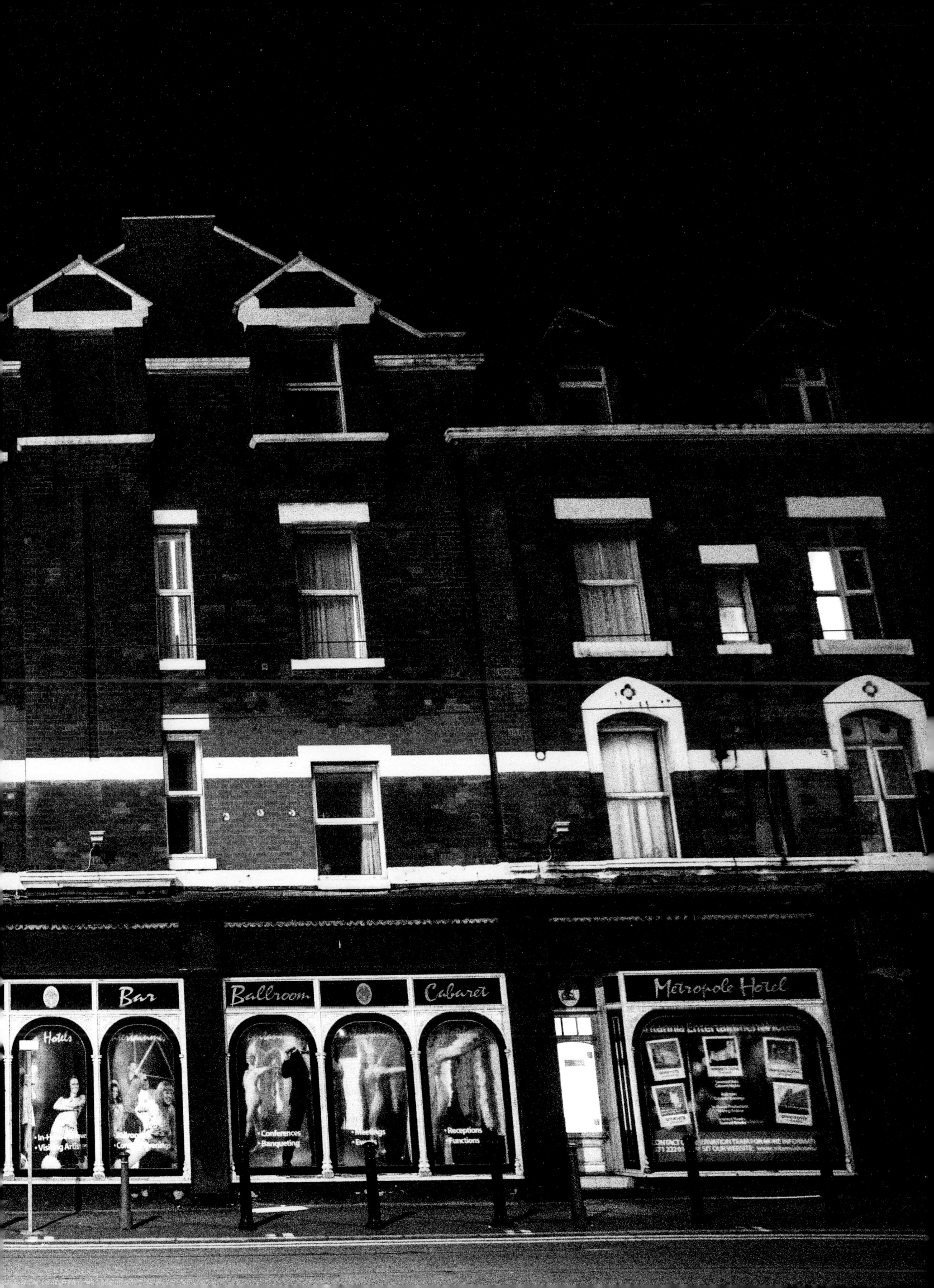

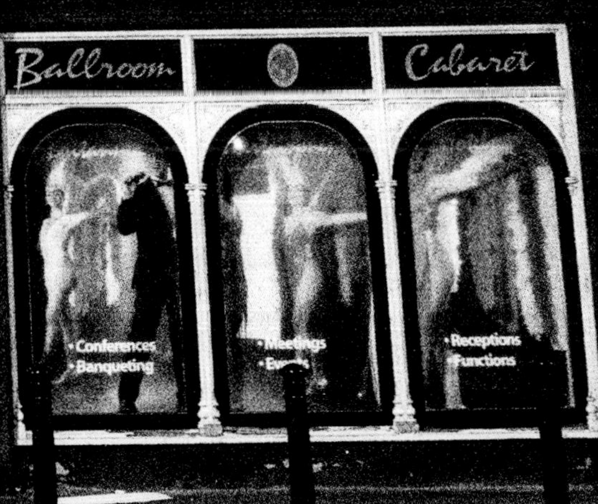

Bar
Ballroom
Cabaret
Hotels
Conferences
Banqueting
Meetings
Receptions
Functions

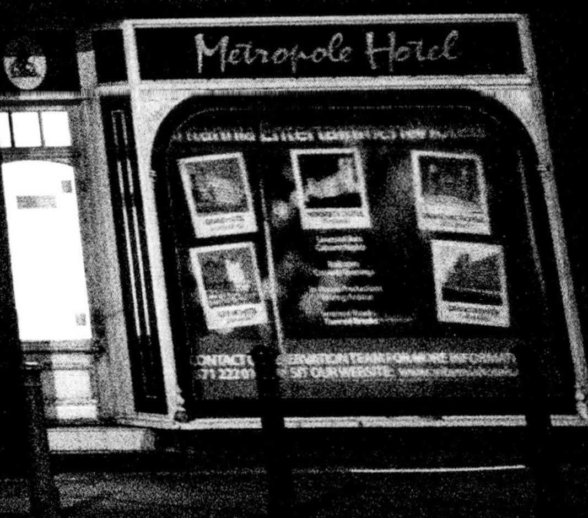

Metropole Hotel

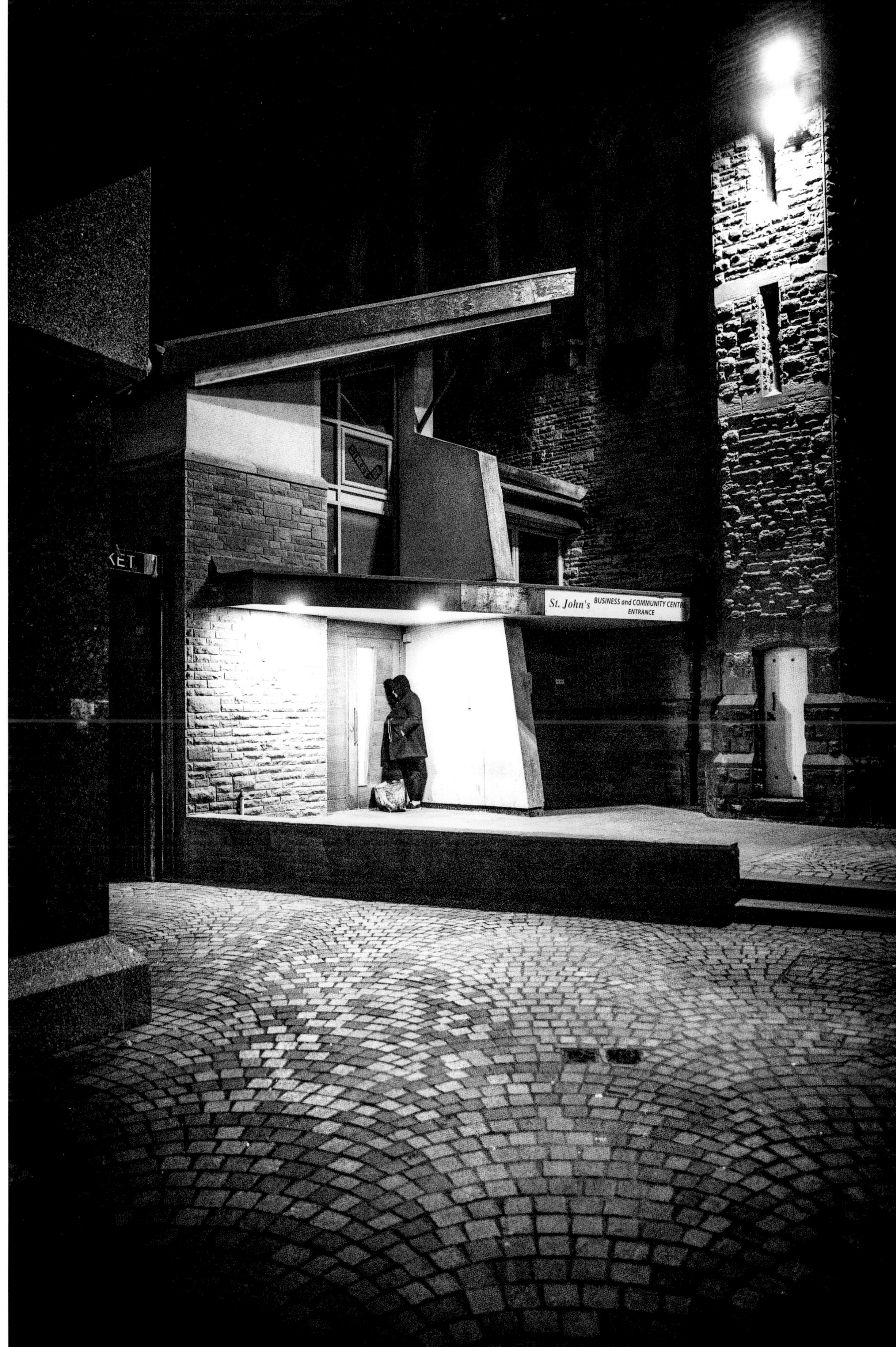
KET
St. John's BUSINESS and COMMUNITY CENTRE
ENTRANCE

Mark Gisbourne
Art historian, Critic, Curator /
Kunsthistoriker, Kritiker, Kurator

From Bathos to Pathos

(There and Back Again?)

Man is least himself when he talks in his own person.
Give him a mask, and he will tell the truth.

Oscar Wilde, *The Critic as Artist*[1]

There is a mysterious aspect of photography as direct pictorial experience, an unpredictability regarding an indicative personal and necessary aesthetic sense of visual reception. For the current ubiquity of photographs suggests there is sometimes a wafer-thin — yet nonetheless powerful — sensory space that exists between what is perceived as visual bathos or pathos, revocation or evocation, those qualities that Roland Barthes called the 'studium' and 'punctum' central to a photographic image.[2] For if the *studium* stimulates the intellectual visual interest of the viewer, it is the *punctum* that initiates the emotional evocative instinct of a spectator towards those small abstractive details that physicalise immediate feelings of affective sensation towards a photograph.[3] This sensory impulse towards what Vilém Flusser chose to call alternatively 'the symbolic and the improbable', could not be more relevant than when considering Benita Suchodrev's black-and-white photographs immediately at hand,[4] images that were taken during her second investigative foray into the cultural and visual schizophrenia of the summer and winter worlds of the famous Northern England seaside town of Blackpool. Long associated with the working class, and once known to the English as the 'Cloth-Cap Riviera', the town has proved a creatively fruitful and unique personal source of investigative engagement for this Russian-born artist-photographer over recent years.[5] Yet whereas her first publication tended to focus on instantaneity and the cacophonous impulses of the seaside summer season, its often expressive form of crass social vulgarity and gaudy consumption, the artist in her second series of photographs is more emotionally investigative and considered. In other words they reveal a darker psychical interiority of the town rather than that of summer surface appearance. Indeed, as the title *Of Lions and Lambs* suggests, we might think that we touch upon a blighted playground of the post-industrial age, where William Blake's satanic mills are no more, but whose residual aftermath bears the ugly urban scars of material displacement cast bereft.[6]

From the outset it is an error to consider these new and particular images of Blackpool as a mere follow-up investigation, or simply as a benign off-season winter account in immediate pursuit of a social commentary. To do so risks missing the complexity of pictorial-psychological ontology that is captured and intuitively revealed in this new series of Suchodrev photographs.[7] For the artist-photographer's at times gloomy images survey and bring a special timbre to what might otherwise seem an obscure view of the urban and cultural hidden world of a holiday coastal town in the vacated and locked-up hibernal period of the year. Nonetheless, we might also be tempted to see a pervasive Neo-Blakean psychical sense of the eschatological, a mortal uncanny sub-theme that runs throughout many of the photographs.[8] This being said, a remarkable pictorial insight is used to express not just various viewpoints and compositional tropes, but also to expand upon and develop a continuously inferred poetic narrative intention. These images were not just randomly realised simply as *ad hoc* incised moments of temporal instantaneity. For their visual truth exists not only in the material facts of record (the 'studium'), rather the images seek to reveal a 'hidden visible' or the permeating and omnipresent internal sense of an inferred indexical unseen — the seen-unseen. It is this that is intended by my chosen aphorism and epigraph, whereby the greater truth content lies masked within and behind the experiences wrought by these black-and-white representations. For the camera is an inevitable apparatus and instrumental mask, a spatial interloper and interface, while its aperture enacts the 'third eye' of displaced (in) sight.[9] The idea of functional and emotional displacement is a resonant subtext, a substrate to the process of image capture and realisation revealed in the photographs. They act as simile, for the town of Blackpool today exists in a state of perturbed social displacement, where even the cheapened jarring 'glitz' of former proletarian utility is now cast in the dreary garb of intermittent bourgeois parties and street derelicts.[10] Suchodrev presents a counter-intuitive juxtaposition, that is of images of interior events

and darkened exterior images of streets, alcoholics, dossers, various eccentrics, soup kitchens, alongside concom-
itant passing allusions to and homiletic claims of redemp-
tion and salvation. A powerful feeling of passage and the
transitory is made evident from the first instance as a congregation of starlings is shown massing in the sky above
the sea, the avian movement frozen and temporarily arrested from the frenetic impulse of aerial murmuration.
Thus a sense of human frangibility and illusive creatures of
passage, mortal life or post-mortem, become the extended pictorial metaphor that carries forward the contents
and visual presentation of the photographs.

The theatrical use of the party masquerade is one such
example of pictorial metaphor expanded into a type of
metonymy, which is to say where an object or event is
used to suggest a commensurate and deferred mental
state through an expanded allusion. In this instance the role
of a party mask operates as an afferent mechanism of social class and consciousness. In a series of chosen images
depicting a fancy dress party, or putative costume ball, the
participants are shown in random groups or pairings and
shot variously framed from low viewpoints. Well-heeled,
the partygoers are not photographed posed by Suchodrev,
rather they stand around or lounge against bars in a plush,
if somewhat mundane, hotel or club-room interior, made
vivacious by their Scaramouche masks and other sugges-
tive Commedia dell'Arte disguised characters of Carnival.[11]
Yet these seemingly unfazed and excised photographs
exude a straightforward sense of participatory affluence,
made distinct from the detached world of the catering
staff that give service to them. A singular example is the
image of the isolated waitress shown set apart with her tray
of hors d'oeuvres. This acknowledges that the artist's approach is markedly different from her earlier publication,
48 Hours Blackpool. Visiting in February 2019 and given
more discovery time, the town progressively unfolded and
became revealed to the artist. The eccentric characters she
met, the environment of peeling paint, hidden backspaces,
crumbling infrastructure, were free of obscurant now
locked arcades and funfairs and the blaring raucousness of
the summer months. As in all urban spaces the homeless
and social derelicts and street dwellers gather closer together, gravitate towards shelter and are drawn into the
towns and cities during the winter months. A depopulating
town that becomes free of tourists magnifies the otherwise hidden presence of its winter inhabitants. Summer
fantasies of desire and self-delusional escapism take on a
bleak and stark irony at this time of year. One image shows

the well-known Kensington Hotel pension and a nearby
'Welcome to Blackpool' sign. It appears somewhat counter-intuitive when photographed at this time of year. Close
by there is another letterset sign that refers to 'Donna's
Dream House', a local children's charity and holiday retreat.
These recognisable pictorial elements form a juxtaposition
of estranged image associations wedged at the oblique
corner of Barton Avenue. A fitful visual effect further
heightened when seen in the sullen and darkened post-
precipitation timbre of winter evening light. In fact the
evening and night images give a bleak sense of opaque
luminescence, back streets punctured by illuminated
shops and signage. A shoe shop with a Methodist Church
and illuminated cross at the upper floor level, expressive
of salvation and mammon in close proximity and in soul/
sole-gaining competition. Christian signage and illuminated tropes of salvation reinforce the message of a trans-
formative beyond, a post-mortem promise set against the
duress of a hard daily life. A photograph of a palmist and
clairvoyant outlet only furthers the paradox, resulting in
this instance in a vying trade between the cult and the oc-
cult. For even the most benign and seemingly obtuse image
can reveal an alternative inflection, there being a simul-
taneous yet indeterminate set of allusions, perhaps, as a
particular photograph shows a double garage entry, where
above one entrance we see the name 'Greenhill', the pre-
sumed occupier. This also becomes yet another unpredict-
able encounter with a deferred pseudo-spiritual sense of
resonance.[12] In this chance way many of the images evoke
hidden aspects and unintended inferences; a sort of dichot-
omous fantasy seems at times to prevail. There is no intention by Suchodrev to make specific religious inferences of
a personal nature, but simply to mirror the immediacy of
Blackpool winter life with referent signifiers of the afterlife
that seem to permeate the town, and which might otherwise go unnoticed in the full flood of the aestival season.

The town is stripped of a tinselled tackiness, the 'kiss-me-
quick' hats, souvenir stalls, seasonal toffee apples and candy-
floss, hot dogs and fish-and-chip stands are gone. As a
result there is something of a magnified sense of pictorial
realism, and as asserted a poetic visual clarity to these recent Suchodrev photographs. The images are noticeably
indicative and distinct, revealing quite another quality of
focus from the inferred nostalgia of an English colour photographer such as Martin Parr and his famous New Brighton seaside images. These are consciously made free of
arbitrary taxonomies that merely reproduce and categorise
simple material description and social class distinctions per

se.[13] The status of each sitter is literal and self-evident. Yet again in black-and-white they are also markedly different from the site-located and colour photograph studies of other celebrated photographers that have focussed on the British working class — photographic practitioners such as Tom Wood and Richard Billingham come to mind.[14] In this world of closed and nailed hoardings presented by the artist, we find the key and creative prompt to her meaningful intentions, a specific curiosity of enquiry responding to the circumstance of chance encounter and immediate suggestion. Things are less planned than happened upon, but revealed within a considered sense of temporal availability. In this way Benita Suchodrev made her chance encounters with 'the birdman' pigeon fancier, quested the errant world of soup kitchens and destitute homeless. It was with this clearly open-minded approach that she discovered urban invasions of animal life, apes, camels, rabbits and sheep, supplemented by a mixture of aggressive dogs and less ferocious pets. It is evident that the chosen Felliniesque ensemble acts as an optical compendium and a recitative litany of sorts, for they pervade and continuously syncopate the respective page flow of the present publication. The street disenchanted and the disenfranchised vie with the world of drag queens' burlesque and part-time 'hookers', a world where sex and abjection find an indeterminate if acceptable reprise. At times the visually depressed participants take on a sort of Ken Loach or Mike Leigh feeling of proletarian desperation. In fact we are tempted to see these photographs as arrested moments in terms of films or movies,[15] that is to say each image infers a sort of passing narrative moment, an extracted instant excised from an encompassing life. This metaphor is further extended to black-and-white English films of 1960s' social realism.[16]

The chosen title of the publication, *Of Lions and Lambs*, is also pregnant with metaphorical as well as biblical meaning.[17] While the lion is a symbolic animal identifiable with England, at the same time the lamb is also embedded and saturated in the Anglo-Saxon national psyche; not least the lion and the lamb are among the most common public house signs across the country. Yet the title also obviously refers to the predator and predated, the strong and the weak, the secure and the vulnerable, of which the contents of the book provide ample image examples of contrast. The title also plays with the seasonal qualification commonly used in regard to the weather, an English subject of preoccupation that fills much of the social and daily discourse of the nation.[18] But rather than just denotative contents (indicative signifiers), we find a connotative and expanded meaning at work in the photographs. For we sense an empathic quality that emerges between Suchodrev and the sitters that are represented, an intuitive affect that was able to emerge in the extended period that she spent in Blackpool. They are photographs of continuous counterpoint, showing the champagne excesses of the masquerade standing at variance to the performing poses of the transgender drag queens; the expensive and bourgeois couture of the former set in contradistinction to the self-beguiling and tacky simulacra of the latter. There is unquestionably a specific mirrored array of gender and non-gender juxtapositions, for it emerges in these photographs that poverty is a great leveller, and the male dossers and bedraggled female derelicts take on a shared state of human simile. This extends to the photographed environment of the town of Blackpool, and its famous late nineteenth-century tower. The structure homages the then recently completed Eiffel Tower in Paris five years earlier. It stands as witness to a confident and once expanding urban space that was considered among the most important political and cultural locations in the North of England.[19] An inanimate object, the tower acts as a non-sentient entity that also plays a pictorial role of experience and discovery in these photographs. Given the at times morose contents of the images, the edifice brings a certain presence of phallic dignity. In what is perhaps among the most charming of photographs, a young boy is shown with a club on the golf links, the tower is viewed on the left bridging the horizon. The photograph is shot from a foreshortened low viewpoint, in line with many of the images in the book; it irradiates an imagined sense of renewed and hopeful possibility for this depopulating seaside town of yesteryear. Shot on a day when the light favoured an optimism of potential, it represents the ultimate counterpoint of representative juxtaposition in this accomplished book of images. Hence the black-and-white photographs of Suchodrev reveal a continuous counterflow of moving sensibilities, which when set in polarity to her first chance summer sortie to Blackpool creates a different tone and deepened affection. In *48 Hours Blackpool* the contents were enacted at speed in Cartier-Bresson excised moments. On this second visit, while the compositional and editorial approach remained much the same, the recent images have an intense feeling of psychical immersion as against mere proximity. What results is both affective and arresting, and as an author I have experienced renewed a former set of life parameters with which I was once familiar. For this alone I must thank Benita Suchodrev for her acute intuition and visual insights.[20]

1   The epigraph is taken from a series of composed conversations by Wilde, *The Critic as Artist: With Some Remarks Upon the Importance of Doing Nothing* (1891). The text is available online at http:// rebels-library.org/files/the_critic_as_artist.pdf (accessed 15.6.19).

2   They constitute two states of emotional and aesthetic ambiguity. 'Bathos' is generally an effect of anticlimax created by a sudden unintentional lapse in mood from the sublime to the trivial or ridiculous. It is often indiscernibly distinct from 'pathos', which evokes pity or sadness.

3   While the 'studium' is invariably coded (culture, time, place and context) the sensed immediacy of the 'punctum' is not. See the distinction in Roland Barthes, *Camera Lucida*, trans., Richard Howard (London: Harper Collins, 1984), pp. 43–60.

4   An alternative usage of the symbolic ('studium') and improbable ('punctum') follows Vilém Flusser's serialised concept of 'image-apparatus-program-information' which serves as the basis for creating a philosophical understanding of photography. See 'Why a Philosophy of Photography is Necessary' in Vilém Flusser, *Towards a Philosophy of Photography* (London: Reaktion Books, 2000), pp. 76–82.

5   Formerly a location for summer industrial day-trippers, it is now well known for off-and-on seasonal 'hen' and 'stag' parties. See https://www.spectator.co.uk/2011/09/blackpools-ups-and-downs/ (accessed 15.6.19).

6   The neo-biblical allusion to 'dark satanic mills' comes from William Blake's preface to *Milton: A Poem in Two Books* (1804) entitled *Jerusalem*. It constitutes the commonly accepted national hymn of England.

7   Andrés Mario Zervigon, 'Ontology or Metaphor?' in Donna West Brett and Natalya Lusty (eds.), *Photography and Ontology: Unsettling Images* (London: Routledge, 2018), pp. 10–23.

8   See the symposium essays presented in David V. Erdman and John E. Grant (eds.), *Blake's Visionary Forms Dramatic* (Princeton: Princeton University Press, 2017).

9   The camera serves as a mask to the extent that it mediates the space between the human eye and the object or image of capture; when seen as apparatus (from *apparare*) it is 'to prepare'. The eye behind the mask is prepared to excise an image from the world. See 'Apparatus' in Flusser, *op cit.*, pp. 21–32.

10   Formerly an autonomous county borough, Blackpool is now a semi-unitary authority under the subsidiary scope of the county of Lancashire administration. It remains relatively undiversified and its primary resource is tourism, largely derived from the cities of East Lancashire and the West Riding of Yorkshire. It has seen a shrinking population since the turn of the millennium. It is a famed location for political and trade union conferences, and also referred to as the 'Gay Capital of the North'. See John Burke, *Blackpool Then & Now* (Stroud: The History Press, 2013).

11   Antonio Fava, *The Comic Mask in the Commedia dell'Arte* (Evanston: Northwestern University Press, 2006).

12   'Greenhill' is a common enough family name, but it is also an evocation for the English to the Hill of Golgotha, since it is the emblematic first line of a famous nineteenth-century hymn: 'There is a green hill far away, Without a city wall, Where our dear Lord was crucified; Who died to save us all…'. Text by Cecil Frances Alexander (1818–1895); music by John H. Gower (1855–1922).

13   Martin Parr (b. 1952) has been taking photographs primarily in colour since the 1980s, and his studies of the working class at seaside leisure in New Brighton, Wallasey, was developed in *The Last Resort* from 1982–85, published under that title in 1986 (repr. 1998, 2009).

14   Tom Wood (b. 1951), *Bus Odyssey*, published on the occasion of the exhibition *Tom Wood. Bus Odyssey: Photography 1976–1998*, Suermondt-Ludwig-Museum Aachen, et al. (Ostfildern-Ruit: Hatje Cantz, 2002). Also Richard Billingham (b. 1970) is known for his study of his alcoholic father Ray and obese mother Liz: *Ray's a Laugh* (1996), was recently realised by the artist as a biographical feature film, entitled *Ray and Liz* (2018).

15   See Mike Leigh, *All or Nothing* (London: Faber & Faber, 2003), and Anthony Hayward, *Which Side are You On? Ken Loach and His Films* (London: Bloomsbury, 2004).

16   For the British New Wave in film, 1959–63, see Michael O'Pray, *The British Avant-Garde Film, 1926 to 1995 – An Anthology of Writings* (London: University of Luton Press, 1996).

17   'No lion shall be there, nor any ravenous beast shall go up thereon, it shall not be found there; but the redeemed shall walk there', Isaiah 35:9.

18   Of relevance is this context, it is a proverbial usage referring to the transition from winter, through the month of March to the spring equinox: 'In like a Lion, Out like a Lamb'. There are any number of lion and lamb comparisons and contrasts in English literature.

19   The Blackpool Tower was begun in 1891 (Eiffel Tower, 1889), and completed in 1894. It stands 158 metres high (518 feet), see Peter Walton, *Blackpool Tower: A History* (Stroud: Amberley Publishing, 2016).

20   In an earlier life of pastoral postulant and Franciscan friar I lived with street alcoholics and derelicts in Kilburn, London. The photographs in this publication have led me to recall the profound immersion and complex sensibilities that were once part of my daily life.

Vom Bathos zum Pathos

(Hin und zurück?)

Der Mensch ist dann am wenigsten er selbst, wenn er im eigenen
Namen spricht. Gib ihm eine Maske, und er sagt die Wahrheit.

Oscar Wilde, *Der Kritiker als Künstler*[1]

Etwas Geheimnisvolles umgibt die direkte Bilderfahrung
der Fotografie, eine Art Unberechenbarkeit in Bezug auf
ein ebenso bezeichnendes persönliches wie notwendiges
ästhetisches Gespür für die visuelle Rezeption. Denn die
aktuelle Allgegenwart von fotografischen Bildern deutet auf einen mitunter hauchfeinen — aber doch mäch-
tigen — sensorischen Raum hin, der zwischen visuell
wahrgenommenem Bathos und Pathos existiert, zwischen
Revokation und Evokation, jenen Eigenschaften, die
Roland Barthes als zentrale Elemente einer Fotografie mit
studium und *punctum* bezeichnete.[2] Wo das *studium* das
verstandesgesteuerte visuelle Interesse des Betrachters
anregt, setzt das *punctum* den emotionalen, beschwören-
den Instinkt eines Zuschauers in Richtung auf jene kleinen abstraktiven Details in Gang, die beim Anblick einer
Fotografie unmittelbare Gefühlsempfindungen hervor-
rufen.[3] Diese Sinnesregung gegenüber dem, was Vilém
Flusser alternativ als „Symbol und Unwahrscheinlichkeit"
beschrieb, könnte nirgendwo passender sein als bei der
Betrachtung der hier vorliegenden Schwarz-Weiß-Foto-
grafien von Benita Suchodrev,[4] Bildern, die während des
zweiten investigativen Streifzugs dieser in Russland ge-
borenen Kunstfotografin durch die kulturell und visuell
schizophrene Sommer- und Winterwelt der berühmten
nordenglischen Küstenstadt Blackpool entstanden sind.
Die lange Zeit mit der Arbeiterklasse assoziierte Stadt,
unter Engländern einst als „Schiebermützen-Riviera" bekannt, erwies sich in den letzten Jahren als bildnerisch
ertragreiche und einzigartig persönliche Fundgrube für
Suchodrevs forschende fotografische Betätigung.[5] Doch
während sich ihr erstes Buch vorwiegend auf den spontanen Moment und die kakofonen Impulse einer Sommersaison am Meer konzentrierte, auf deren oft ausdrucks-
starke Formen von derber gesellschaftlicher Vulgarität
und grellem Konsum, geht die Künstlerin in ihrer zweiten
Fotoserie emotional tiefschürfender und überlegter vor.
Das heißt, ihre Aufnahmen enthüllen ein dunkleres see-
lisches Innenleben der Stadt als das der sommerlichen
Oberflächlichkeit. Tatsächlich könnte man meinen, wie

auch der Buchtitel *Of Lions and Lambs* (Von Löwen und
Lämmern) suggeriert, einen zerstörten Spielplatz des
nachindustriellen Zeitalters vor sich zu haben, von dem
William Blakes satanische Mühlen zwar verschwunden sind,
dessen Überreste jedoch die hässlichen urbanen Narben
der materiellen Entwurzelung eines Ortes tragen, der in
einen Zustand undefinierten Mangels versetzt wurde.[6]

Es wäre von vornherein ein Irrtum, diese neuen und beson-
deren Abbildungen von Blackpool als bloße Folgeunter-
suchung oder schlicht als wohlmeinenden Winterbericht
aufzufassen, der auf die Schnelle einen Sozialkommentar
außerhalb der Saison anstrebt. Wer die Aufnahmen den-
noch so begreift, läuft Gefahr, die Komplexität der bild-
lich-psychologischen Ontologie zu übersehen, die von
dieser neuen Fotoserie Suchodrevs eingefangen und
intuitiv offengelegt wird.[7] Denn die bisweilen düsteren
Aufnahmen der Kamerakünstlerin vermessen, was ande-
renfalls wie ein obskurer Anblick der versteckten Stadt-
und Kulturwelt eines am Meer gelegenen, während der
Winterzeit verlassenen und verriegelten Urlaubsorts
erscheinen könnte, und verleihen dem Gesehenen ein
spezielles Timbre. Man könnte jedoch auch versucht sein,
ein psychisch allgegenwärtiges, neoblakesches Endzeit-
gefühl auszumachen, ein so morbides wie unheimliches
Subthema, das viele der Fotografien durchdringt.[8] Davon
abgesehen bedient sich die Fotografin eines bemerkens-
werten Bildverständnisses, um nicht nur unterschiedli-
chen Blickwinkeln und kompositorischen Wendungen
Ausdruck zu verleihen, sondern auch eine durchgehend
erkennbare poetisch-erzählerische Absicht näher auszu-
führen und weiterzuentwickeln. Dass diese Aufnahmen
nicht als lediglich spontan inzidierte Momente zeitlicher
Sofortigkeit einfach wahllos realisiert wurden, ist daraus
abzuleiten, dass ihre visuelle Wahrhaftigkeit nicht nur in
den physisch dokumentierten Tatsachen (dem *studium*)
existiert, sondern sie vielmehr ein „verstecktes Sichtba-
res" oder das alles durchziehende und omnipräsente
inwendige Gefühl eines angedeuteten indexikalischen

Unsichtbaren — das Sichtbar-Unsichtbare — zum Vorschein bringen wollen. Genau darauf hinzuweisen, war die Absicht des hier vorangestellten Denkspruchs und Mottos, dem zufolge der größere Wahrheitsgehalt in und hinter der Maske der von diesen Schwarz-Weiß-Darstellungen erzeugten Erfahrungen verborgen liegt. Denn die Kamera ist sowohl unvermeidlicher Apparat als auch instrumentelle Maske, räumlicher Eindringling und Schnittstelle, während ihre Blende das „dritte Auge" des verschobenen (Ein-)Blicks spielt.[9] Die Idee einer funktionalen und emotionalen Verschiebung schwingt als Subtext mit, als Grundlage für den Vorgang der in den Fotografien offengelegten Erfassung und Realisation des Bildes. Weil sich Blackpool heute in einem Zustand gestörter sozialer Entwurzelung befindet, in dem sich selbst der billige, schrille „Glanz" früherer proletarischer Nützlichkeiten mittlerweile im trostlosen Gewand sporadisch abgehaltener bürgerlicher Feste oder auf der Straße lebender Obdachloser wiederfindet, fungieren die Aufnahmen als Gleichnisse.[10] Suchodrev präsentiert ein kontraintuitives Nebeneinander, indem sie Bildern von Veranstaltungen in Innenräumen dunkle Außenaufnahmen von Straßen, Alkoholikern, Tippelbrüdern, allerlei bunten Vögeln und Suppenküchen gegenüberstellt, Seite an Seite mit flüchtigen Anspielungen auf — und homiletischen Behauptungen von — Seelenrettung und Erlösung. Ein eindringliches Gefühl von Vorübergang und Vergänglichkeit wird vom ersten Moment an spürbar, wenn sich über dem Meer eine Ansammlung von Staren zusammenballt, ihre Bewegungen am Himmel eingefroren, ihr frenetischer Formationsflug vorübergehend gestoppt. Auf diese Weise werden die spürbare Zerbrechlichkeit des Menschen und unwirklich erscheinende Zugvogelschwärme, ob im irdischen Leben oder nach dem Tod, zu jener erweiterten bildhaften Metapher, über die sich die Inhalte und die visuelle Gestaltung der Fotografien transportieren.

Der theatralische Einsatz der festlichen Maskerade ist ein solches Beispiel einer bildhaften, zu einer Art Metonymie ausgebauten Metapher, bei der ein Gegenstand oder Ereignis genutzt wird, um mittels einer erweiterten Anspielung eine entsprechende und übertragene Geisteshaltung anzudeuten. In diesem Fall übernimmt eine Partymaske die Funktion eines sensiblen Mechanismus von sozialer Schicht und sozialem Bewusstsein. In einer Reihe von ausgewählten Aufnahmen, die ein Kostümfest oder einen vermeintlichen Maskenball wiedergeben, werden die in wechselnden Bildausschnitten in Untersicht abgelichteten Teilnehmer in zufälligen Gruppen oder Paarungen gezeigt.

Die gut betuchten Partygäste werden von Suchodrev nicht aufgestellt oder posieren für sie, sondern stehen in den vornehmen, wenn auch etwas profanen Räumlichkeiten eines Hotels oder Klubs herum oder lehnen an der Bar, temperamentvoll belebt durch ihre Skaramuz-Masken und andere Karnevalsverkleidungen nach Vorbildern der italienischen Commedia dell'Arte.[11] Doch die anscheinend unbeeindruckten Protagonisten dieser fotografischen Festausschnitte verströmen ein aufrichtiges Flair von Wohlstandsteilhabe, das sie von der separaten Welt des ihnen zu Diensten stehenden Bewirtungspersonals abhebt. Die Aufnahme einer einzelnen Serviererin, die mit ihrem Häppchentablett abseitssteht, verkörpert diesen Gegensatz auf einzigartige Weise. Damit ist klar, dass der Ansatz der Künstlerin sich deutlich von jenem ihrer vorangegangenen Publikation *48 Hours Blackpool* unterscheidet. Mit mehr Zeit für Entdeckungen während ihres zweiten Besuchs in Blackpool im Februar 2019 erlebte Suchodrev, wie sich die Stadt zunehmend entfaltete und ihr offenbarte. Die exzentrischen Gestalten, denen sie begegnete, das Umfeld von abblätternder Farbe, verborgenen Hinterhöfen, bröckelnder Infrastruktur, all dies war befreit von zweifelhaften, jetzt geschlossenen Spielhallen und Jahrmärkten und vom plärrenden Lärm der Sommermonate. Wie in jedem städtischen Raum rücken die Obdachlosen, Außenseiter und Landstreicher enger zusammen, suchen Unterkunft und streben während der Wintermonate in die kleineren und größeren Städte. In einer schrumpfenden Stadt ohne die üblichen Touristenströme zeigt sich die sonst verborgene Gegenwart ihrer Winterbewohner umso deutlicher. Sommerliche Sehnsuchtsfantasien und selbstbetrügerischer Eskapismus nehmen in dieser Zeit des Jahres eine ebenso nackte wie makabre Ironie an. Ein Bild zeigt eine Hinweistafel vor dem bekannten Kensington Hotel mit der Aufschrift „Willkommen in Blackpool", die um diese Jahreszeit der Intuition zu widersprechen scheint. Darunter wirbt ein Banner in großen Lettern für „Donna's Dream House", eine örtliche Wohltätigkeitsorganisation mit Ferienappartements für unheilbar kranke Kinder. Die im Dunkeln erkennbaren Elemente bilden an der abgeschrägten Ecke zur Barton Avenue ein Nebeneinander unverwandter Bildassoziationen. Dieser launenhafte visuelle Effekt wird zusätzlich verstärkt, wenn das Auge ihn in der trüben und verdüsterten Atmosphäre des abendlichen Winterlichts nach einem Regenguss wahrnimmt. Tatsächlich vermitteln Suchodrevs Abend- und Nachtaufnahmen einen freudlosen Eindruck von der matten Strahlkraft, mit der Geschäfte und Leuchtreklamen hier und da die Seitenstraßen erhellen. Ein Schuhgeschäft mit Methodistenkirche und angestrahltem Kreuz im ersten Stock zeugt von Erlösung und Mammon in engster Nachbarschaft und vom Wettstreit um Seelen und Sohlen. Christliche Schriftzüge und beleuchtete Erlösungsmetaphern untermauern die Botschaft vom transformativen Jenseits, der Härte des bitteren Alltags wird eine postmortale Verheißung entgegengesetzt. Eine andere Fotografie vom Stand einer Handleserin und Hellseherin treibt das Paradox nur weiter voran und läuft in diesem Fall auf einen Wettbewerb zwischen Religion und Okkultismus hinaus. Denn selbst die harmloseste und scheinbar banalste Aufnahme kann eine alternative Wendung preisgeben, wenn etwa eine einzelne Fotografie die Zufahrt zu einer Doppelgarage zeigt, über einem der Garagentore das Wort „Greenhill" prangt, der Name des mutmaßlichen Besitzers, und sich daraus womöglich eine Reihe simultaner, aber unbestimmter Anspielungen ergibt. So wird dieses Bild zu einer weiteren unvorhersehbaren Begegnung mit einem beiseitegeschobenen pseudospirituellen Resonanzgefühl.[12] Derart zufällig bringen viele der hier versammelten Fotografien verborgene Aspekte und unbeabsichtigte Schlüsse ans Licht; eine Art dichotome Fantasie scheint bisweilen den Ton anzugeben. Dabei geht es Suchodrev nicht darum, in ihren Aufnahmen bestimmte religiöse Schlussfolgerungen persönlicher Natur zu ziehen; vielmehr will sie mit referenziellen Hinweisen auf das Leben nach dem Tod, von denen die Stadt überzogen scheint und die im dichten Gewühl der Sommersaison untergehen könnten, lediglich die Direktheit des winterlichen Lebens in Blackpool widerspiegeln.

Die Stadt hat ihre kitschige Flitterhaftigkeit verloren, „Kiss me quick"-Hüte und Souvenirstände, kandierte Äpfel, Zuckerwatte, Hotdogs und Fish-and-Chips-Buden sind verschwunden. Dadurch haftet diesen neuesten Fotografien Suchodrevs nicht nur eine Art größerer Bildrealismus an, sondern, wie erklärt, zugleich eine poetisch-visuelle Klarheit. Die Bilder sind auffallend direkt und eindeutig, sie richten den Fokus gerade nicht auf die unterschwellige Nostalgie, für die der englische Farbfotograf Martin Parr mit seinen berühmten Aufnahmen des Badeorts New Brighton steht. Sie wurden bewusst von willkürlichen Einteilungen befreit, die einfache physische Darstellungen und Klassenunterschiede per se lediglich reproduzieren und kategorisieren.[13] Der Status aller Porträtierten ist buchstäblich zu nehmen und offensichtlich. Abermals in Schwarz-Weiß unterscheiden sie sich zudem merklich von den ortsgebundenen und farbigen Studien

anderer berühmter Fotografen, die ihr Augenmerk auf die britische Arbeiterklasse gerichtet haben — man denke etwa an Tom Wood oder Richard Billingham.[14] In dieser Welt der stillgelegten und vernagelten Plakatwände, wie die Künstlerin sie zeigt, liegt der Schlüssel und kreative Antrieb ihrer bedeutenden Intentionen verborgen, eine spezielle, forschende Neugier, die auf den Umstand der zufälligen Begegnung und spontanen Eingebung reagiert. Die Dinge werden weniger geplant als zufällig gefunden, dabei aber im Rahmen eines wohlüberlegten Gespürs für ihre zeitliche Verfügbarkeit gezeigt. Genau so verliefen Benita Suchodrevs zufällige Begegnungen mit dem „Vogelmann", der die Tauben liebt, genau so erforschte sie die fahrende Welt der Suppenküchen und verarmten Obdachlosen. Mit dieser sichtlich offenen Einstellung entdeckte sie auch tierische Invasionen von Affen, Kamelen, Kaninchen und Schafen mitten in der Stadt, ergänzt um eine Mischung aus aggressiven Hunden und weniger wilden Haustieren. Es ist nicht zu übersehen, dass dieses ausgewählte fellinieske Ensemble als optisches Kompendium und eine Art rezitativische Litanei auftritt, durchziehen und synkopieren seine Mitglieder doch kontinuierlich den jeweiligen Seitenfluss der vorliegenden Publikation. Die Desillusionierten und Entrechteten der Straße konkurrieren mit der Welt der Dragqueen-Varietés und „Teilzeithuren", einer Welt, in der Sex und Erniedrigung eine ungewisse, wiewohl hinnehmbare Wiederholung finden. Hin und wieder strahlen die sichtbar deprimierten Beteiligten eine proletarische Verzweiflung im Stil eines Ken Loach oder Mike Leigh aus. Tatsächlich ist die Versuchung groß, diese Fotografien als Standbilder von Fernseh- oder Kinofilmen zu sehen,[15] will heißen, jede Aufnahme deutet eine Art vorübergehenden Erzählmoment an, einen extrahierten Augenblick, exzidiert aus einem umfassenden Leben. Diese Metapher wird überdies erweitert auf Schwarz-Weiß-Filme des englischen Sozialrealismus der 1960er-Jahre.[16]

Der für die Publikation gewählte Titel, *Of Lions and Lambs* (Von Löwen und Lämmern), steckt ebenfalls voller metaphorischer und biblischer Bedeutungen.[17] Während der Löwe als Symboltier für England steht, ist auch das Lamm tief in der nationalen angelsächsischen Seele verwurzelt und von ihr durchtränkt; nicht zuletzt zählen der Löwe und das Lamm landesweit zu den gebräuchlichsten öffentlichen Hauszeichen. Doch der Titel bezieht sich offenkundig auch auf Jäger und Gejagte, Starke und Schwache, Sorglose und Schutzbedürftige, wofür der Inhalt des Buches zahlreiche kontrastierende Bildbeispiele liefert.

Darüber hinaus spielt der Titel mit landläufigen jahreszeitlichen Beschreibungen des Wetters, eines beherrschenden englischen Themas, das einen Großteil des gesellschaftlichen und täglichen Diskurses der Nation ausfüllt.[18] Doch anstelle bloßer denotativer Inhalte (bezeichnender Signifikanten) ist in den Fotografien ein konnotativer und erweiterter Sinngehalt am Werk. Man spürt die Empathie, die zwischen Suchodrev und den von ihr Porträtierten entsteht, eine intuitive Gefühlsregung, die sich während des längeren Aufenthalts der Künstlerin in Blackpool entwickeln konnte. Der stete Kontrapunkt kennzeichnet ihre Fotografien, etwa wenn den Champagnerexzessen der Maskenballbesucher die Bühnenposen der transsexuellen Dragqueens entgegengestellt werden und der teuren, bourgeoisen Couture der Ersteren die selbsttäuschenden, billigen Simulakren der Letzteren. Ohne Frage liegt hier eine präzise gespiegelte Reihe von geschlechtsspezifischen und nicht geschlechtsspezifischen Gegenüberstellungen vor, denn was diese Fotografien unmissverständlich demonstrieren, ist die Rolle der Armut als große Gleichmacherin, die männliche Stadtstreicher und verwahrloste weibliche Obdachlose gemeinsam das Stadium eines menschlichen Gleichnisses annehmen lässt. Dies gilt im erweiterten Sinne auch für die fotografierte Umwelt der Stadt Blackpool und ihren berühmten Turm aus dem 19. Jahrhundert. Die Konstruktion huldigt dem fünf Jahre früher fertiggestellten Pariser Eiffelturm und zeugt von einem selbstbewussten und ehemals wachsenden Stadtraum, der zu den wichtigsten politischen und kulturellen Schauplätzen im Norden Englands gezählt wurde.[19] Als unbelebtes Objekt übernimmt der Turm die Rolle einer nicht fühlenden Instanz, die in den vorliegenden Fotografien auch Werte wie Erfahrung und Entdeckergeist bildlich verkörpert. In Anbetracht der bisweilen verdrießlichen Bildinhalte sorgt das Bauwerk für die Präsenz einer gewissen phallische Würde. In einer der vielleicht bezauberndsten Aufnahmen geht ein Junge mit Schläger in der Hand über den Golfplatz, während links im Bild der Turm zu sehen ist, der vorsichtig über den Horizont ragt. Das Foto entstand wie zahlreiche Abbildungen in diesem Buch aus verkürzender Perspektive in Untersicht; es strahlt eine imaginierte Möglichkeit von Erneuerung und Hoffnung für diese schrumpfende Küstenstadt von vorgestern aus. Aufgenommen an einem Tag, an dem das Licht die Zuversicht in das Potenzial der Stadt bestärkte, symbolisiert es den ultimativen Kontrapunkt des fotografischen Nebeneinanders in diesem vollkommenen Bildband. Was Suchodrevs Schwarz-Weiß-Aufnahmen mithin zutage fördern, ist ein beständiger

Gegenstrom ergreifender Empfindungen, der gegenüber ihrem ersten zufälligen Abstecher nach Blackpool während des Sommers einen anderen Klang und eine tiefere Zuneigung erzeugt. In *48 Hours Blackpool* wurden die Bildinhalte in exzidierten Cartier-Bresson-Momenten mit hohem Tempo verfügt. Bei kompositorisch und redaktionell weitgehend unverändertem Ansatz während dieses zweiten Blackpoolbesuchs vermitteln die neueren Aufnahmen das intensive Gefühl eines tiefen seelischen Eintauchens anstelle einer bloßen Nähe. Das Ergebnis ist so emotional wie faszinierend, und als Autor habe ich ein früheres Sortiment von Lebensparametern neu durchlaufen, mit denen ich einmal vertraut war. Allein darum muss ich Benita Suchodrev für ihr feines Gespür und ihre visuellen Einblicke danken.[20]

1   Das Motto ist dem 1891 von Oscar Wilde verfassten, gleichsam sokratischen Dialog *Der Kritiker als Künstler* entnommen. Die deutsche Übersetzung von Joachim Bartholomae stammt aus dem Wilde-Bändchen *Die Wahrheit von Masken. Drei Essays*, Hamburg 2013, S. 83.

2   Bathos und Pathos sind zwei Zustände emotionaler und ästhetischer Ambiguität. Bathos bezeichnet gemeinhin einen antiklimaktischen Effekt, der durch ein plötzliches und unbeabsichtigtes Abgleiten des Tons vom Erhabenen ins Triviale oder Lächerliche erzeugt wird. Das Bathos unterscheidet sich oft nur unmerklich vom Pathos, welches Mitgefühl oder Traurigkeit hervorruft.

3   Während das *studium* immer codiert ist (durch Kultur, Zeit, Ort und Kontext), trifft dies auf die empfundene Unmittelbarkeit des *punctum* nicht zu; siehe die Unterscheidung in Roland Barthes, *Die helle Kammer. Bemerkungen zur Photographie* (1980), übers. von Dietrich Leube, Frankfurt am Main 2016, S. 33–70.

4   Eine alternative Verwendung des Symbolischen (*studium*) und des Unwahrscheinlichen (*punctum*) folgt Flussers Reihenkonzept von „Bild — Apparat — Programm — Information", das als Entwicklungsgrundlage für ein philosophisches Fotografieverständnis dient; siehe Vilém Flusser, „Die Notwendigkeit einer Philosophie der Fotografie", *Für eine Philosophie der Fotografie* (1983), Berlin 2018, S. 69–74.

5   Ehemals Schauplatz für sommerliche Tagesausflüge von Fabrikarbeitern ist Blackpool heute für ganzjährig stattfindende Junggesellinnen- und Junggesellenabschiede bekannt; siehe https://www.spectator.co.uk/2011/09/blackpools-ups-and-downs/ (aufgerufen am 27.6.2019).

6   Die neobiblische Anspielung auf die „dunklen satanischen Mühlen" entstammt dem Gedicht aus William Blakes Vorwort zu *Milton. Ein Gedicht* (1804). Das kurze lyrische Werk mit dem Titel *Jerusalem* ist heute allgemein als offizielle Nationalhymne Englands anerkannt.

7   Andrés Mario Zervigón, „Ontology or Metaphor?", in: Donna West Brett und Natalya Lusty (Hg.), *Photography and Ontology. Unsettling Images*, London 2018, S. 10–23.

8   Siehe die Tagungsbeiträge in: David V. Erdman und John E. Grant (Hg.), *Blake's Visionary Forms Dramatic*, Princeton 2017.

9   Die Kamera dient insofern als Maske, als sie das räumliche Bindeglied zwischen dem menschlichen Auge und dem zu erfassenden Bild oder Gegenstand darstellt; als Apparat (von lat. *apparare*) dient sie der „Vorbereitung": Das Auge hinter der Maske wird darauf vorbereitet, ein Bild aus der Welt herauszuschneiden; siehe Vilém Flusser, „Der Fotoapparat", op. cit., S. 20–30.

10   Die ehemals unabhängige kreisfreie Stadt ist heute eine quasi-autonome Einheitsgemeinde (*unitary authority*) im subsidiären Einflussbereich der Grafschaft Lancashire. Mit ihrer relativ undiversifizierten Wirtschaft ist die Seestadt hauptsächlich vom Tourismus abhängig, der sich überwiegend aus den Städten in East Lancashire und im West Riding of Yorkshire speist. Seit der Jahrtausendwende geht die Einwohnerzahl zurück. Blackpool ist als Schauplatz für Partei- und Gewerkschaftskongresse berühmt und wird auch als „schwule Hauptstadt des Nordens" bezeichnet; siehe John Burke, *Blackpool Then & Now*, Stroud 2013.

11   Antonio Fava, *La Maschera Comica nella Commedia dell'Arte*, Bologna 1999.

12   „Greenhill" ist als Familienname hinreichend verbreitet, beschwört jedoch als emblematische erste Zeile einer berühmten Hymne aus dem 19. Jahrhundert in England auch Bilder vom Berg Golgatha herauf: „There is a green hill far away, / Without a city wall, / Where the dear Lord was crucified, / Who died to save us all"; Text von Cecil Frances Alexander (1818–1895), Musik von John H. Gower (1855–1922).

13   Martin Parr (geb. 1952) fotografiert seit den 1980er-Jahren größtenteils in Farbe. Aus seinen Studien der urlaubenden Arbeiterklasse im Badeort New Brighton, Wallasey, entstand zwischen 1982 und 1985 die Fotoserie *The Last Resort*, die 1986 unter diesem Titel veröffentlicht wurde und 2009 bei Kehrer erstmals in einer deutschen Ausgabe erschien.

14   Tom Wood (geb. 1951), *Bus Odyssey*, hg. von Slyvia Böhmer, erschienen anlässlich der Ausstellung *Tom Wood. Bus Odyssey. Fotografien 1978 bis 1998*, Suermondt-Ludwig-Museum Aachen u. a., Ostfildern-Ruit 2002. Richard Billingham (geb. 1970) wurde mit *Ray's a Laugh* (1996) bekannt, einer fotografischen Studie seines alkoholabhängigen Vaters Ray und seiner übergewichtigen Mutter Liz. Erst kürzlich hat der Künstler den Stoff des Fotobands in einem biografischen Spielfilm mit dem Titel *Ray & Liz* (2018) erneut aufgegriffen.

15   Siehe Mike Leigh, *All or Nothing*, London 2002, und Anthony Hayward, *Which Side are You On? Ken Loach and His Films*, London 2004.

16   Zur New Wave des britischen Films von 1959 bis 1963 siehe Michael O'Pray, *The British Avant-Garde Film 1926 to 1995. An Anthology of Writings*, London 1996.

17   „Es wird da kein Löwe sein und kein reißendes Tier darauf gehen; sie sind dort nicht zu finden, sondern die Erlösten werden dort gehen" (Jesaja 35,9).

18   Bedeutsam ist in diesem Zusammenhang die Verwendung in einem Sprichwort, das sich auf den Übergang vom Winter über den Monat März hinweg bis zur Frühjahrs-Tagundnachtgleiche bezieht: „Der März kommt an wie ein Löwe und geht fort wie ein Lamm." In der englischen Literatur gibt es unzählige Vergleiche und Gegenüberstellungen von Löwen und Lämmern.

19   Der Blackpool Tower wurde 1891 begonnen (zwei Jahre nach der Einweihung des Eiffelturms) und 1894 fertiggestellt. Er ist 158 Meter hoch; siehe Peter Walton, *Blackpool Tower. A History*, Stroud 2016.

20   In einem früheren Leben als Postulant und Franziskanermönch habe ich mit Alkoholikern und Obdachlosen im Londoner Stadtteil Kilburn auf der Straße gelebt. Die Fotografien in diesem Buch haben mich veranlasst, mir das tiefe Eintauchen in diese Welt und die komplexen Empfindungen in Erinnerung zu rufen, die einmal Teil meines Alltags waren.

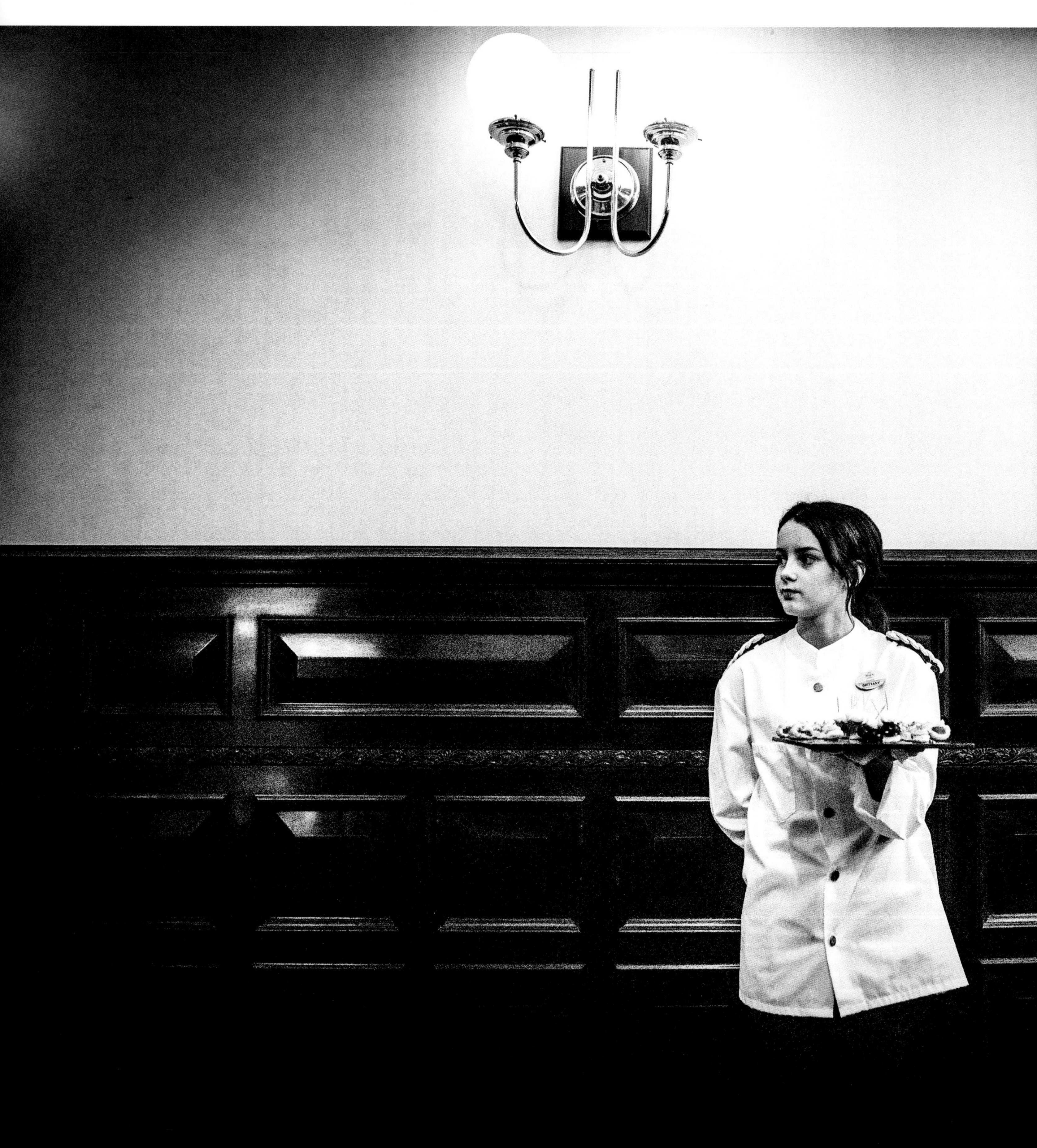

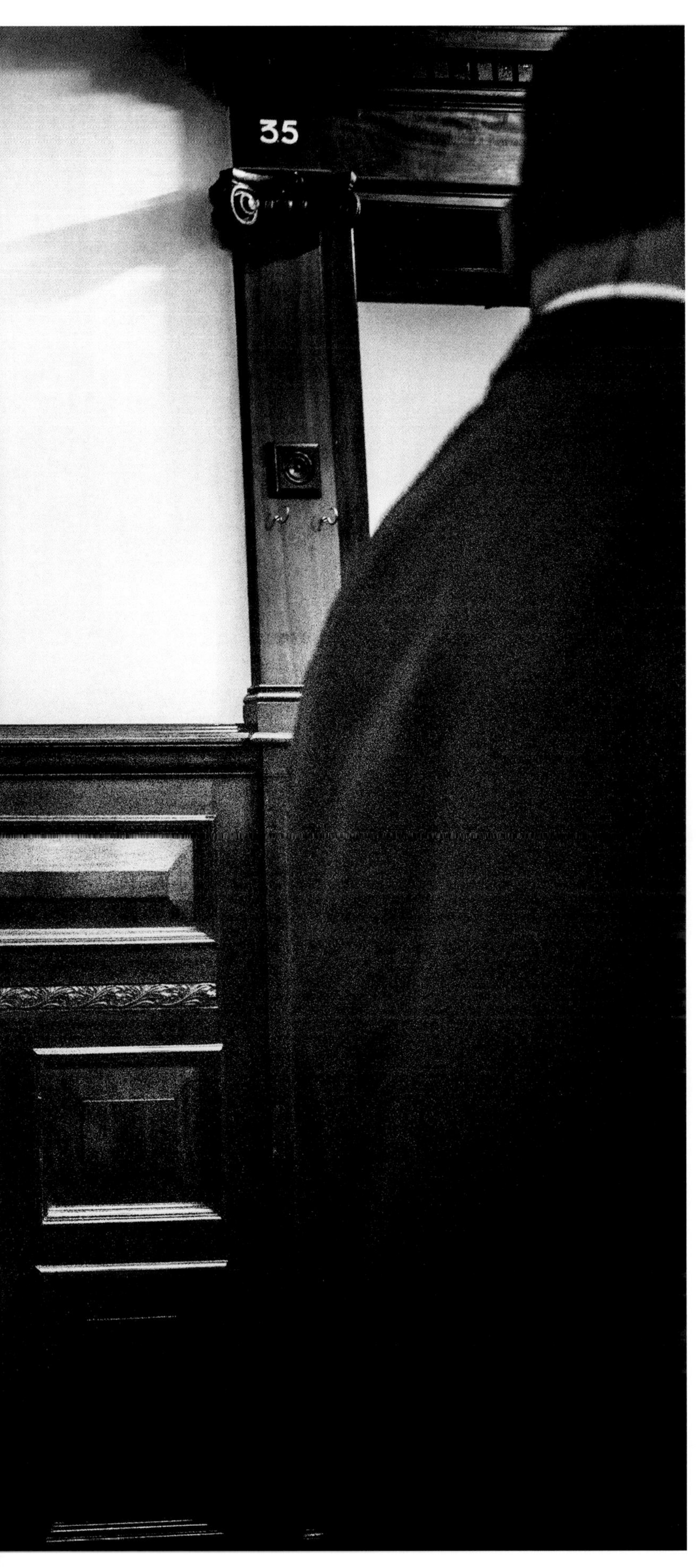

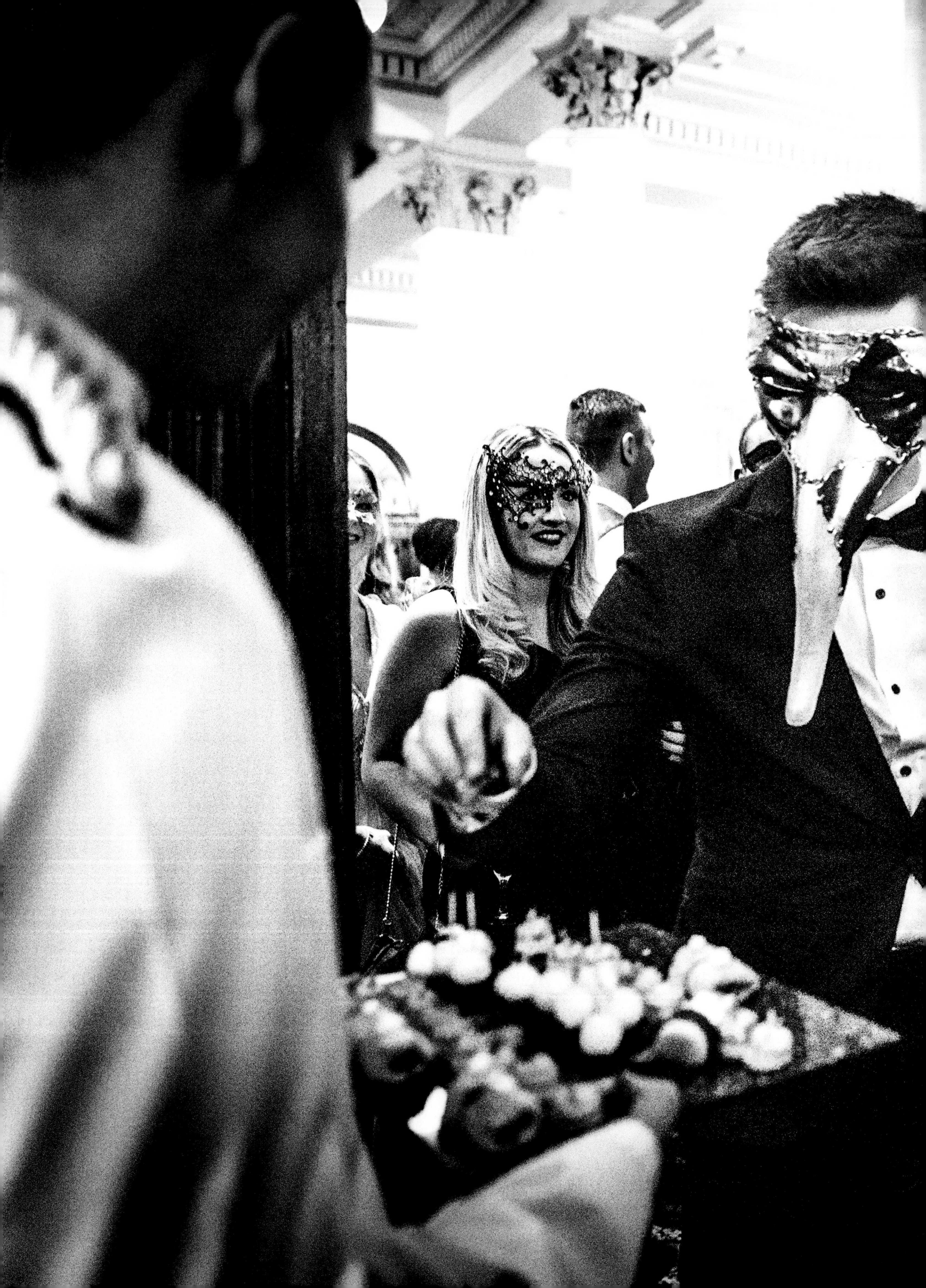

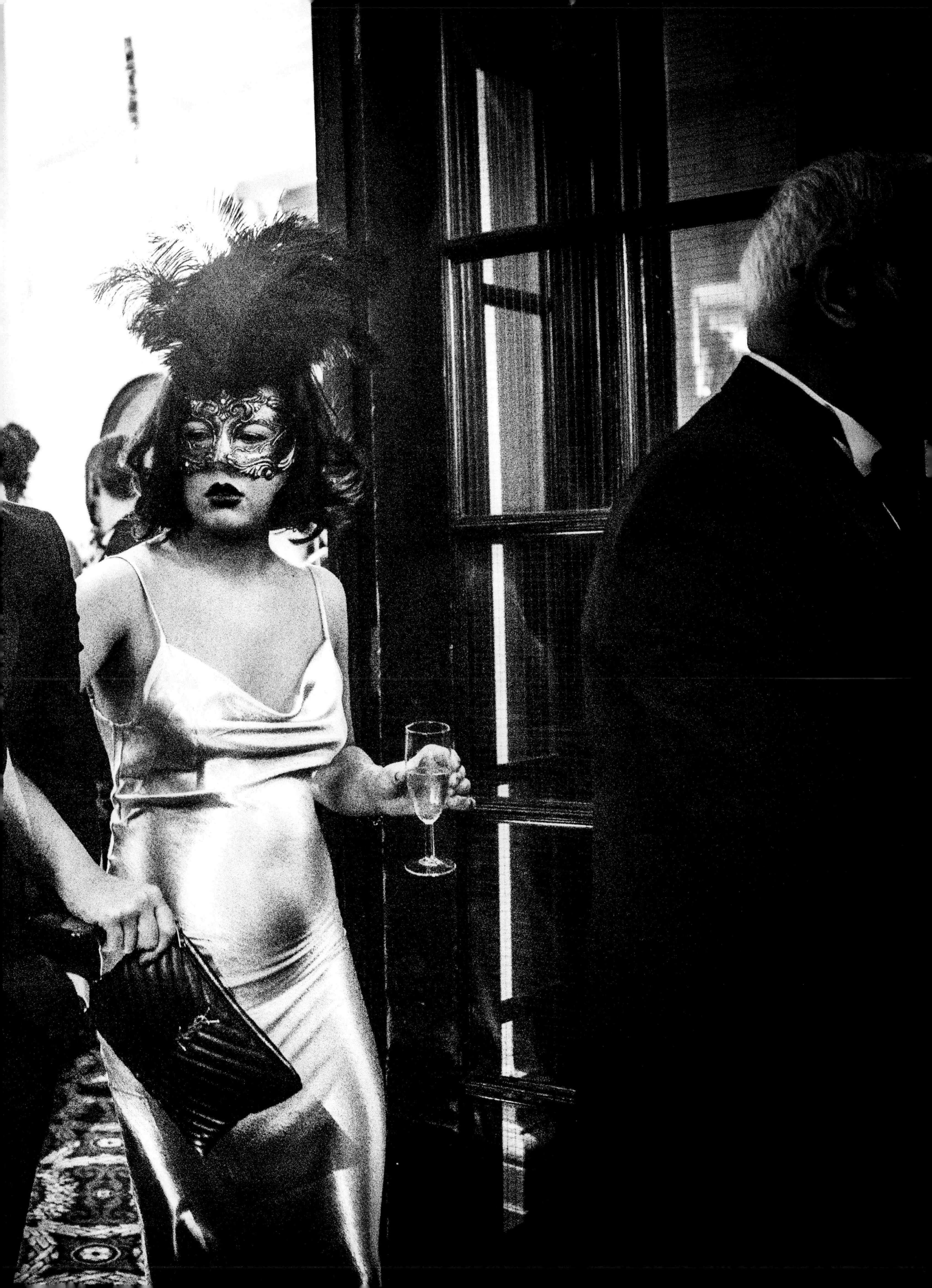

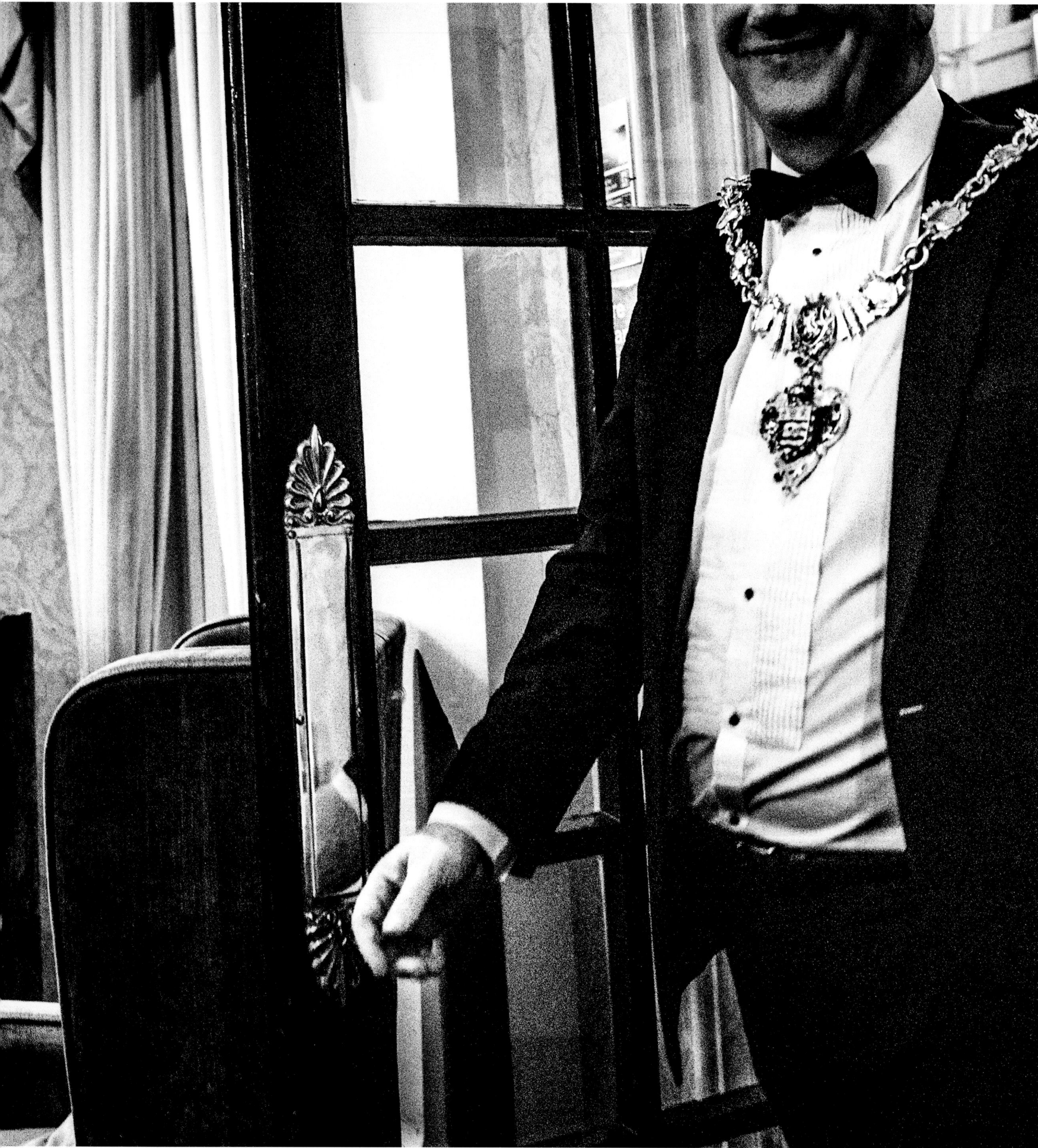

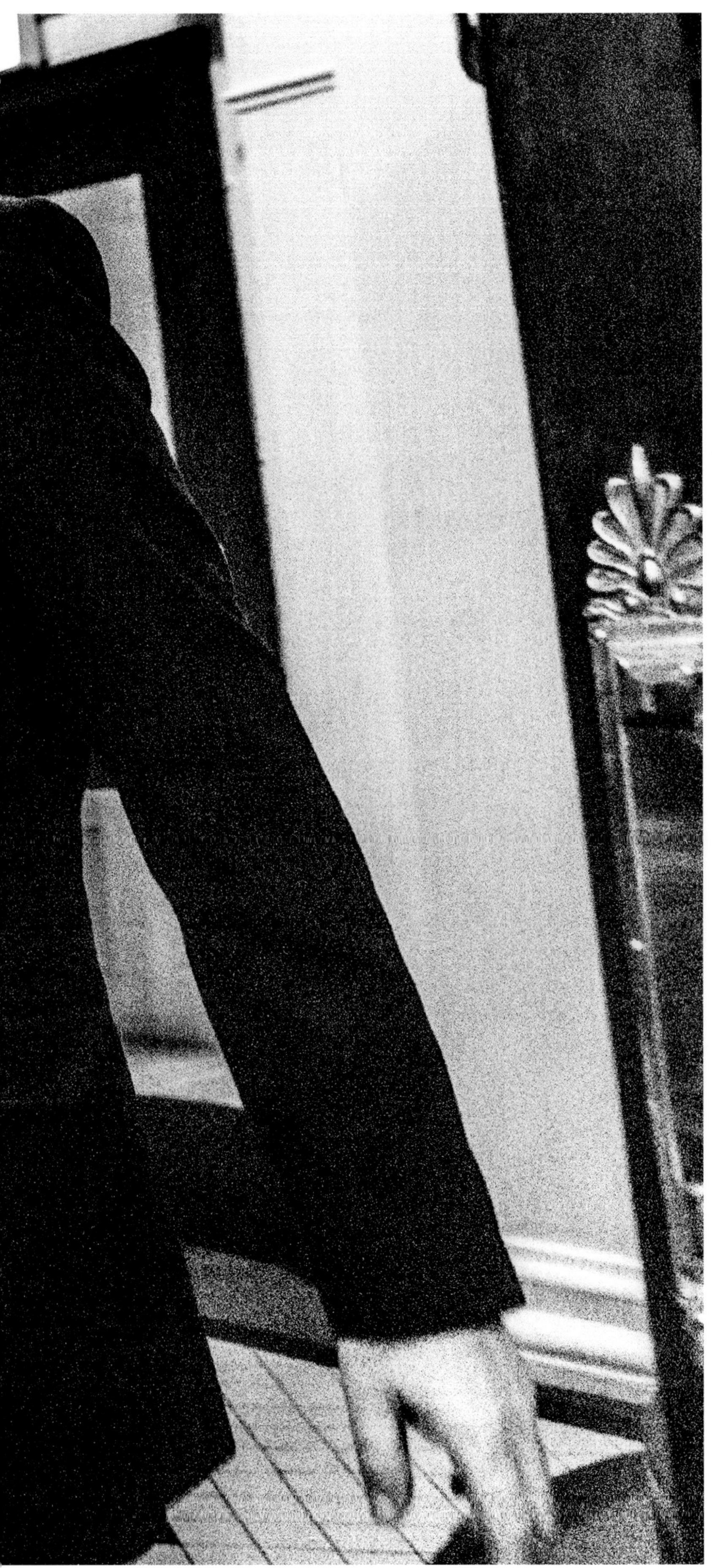

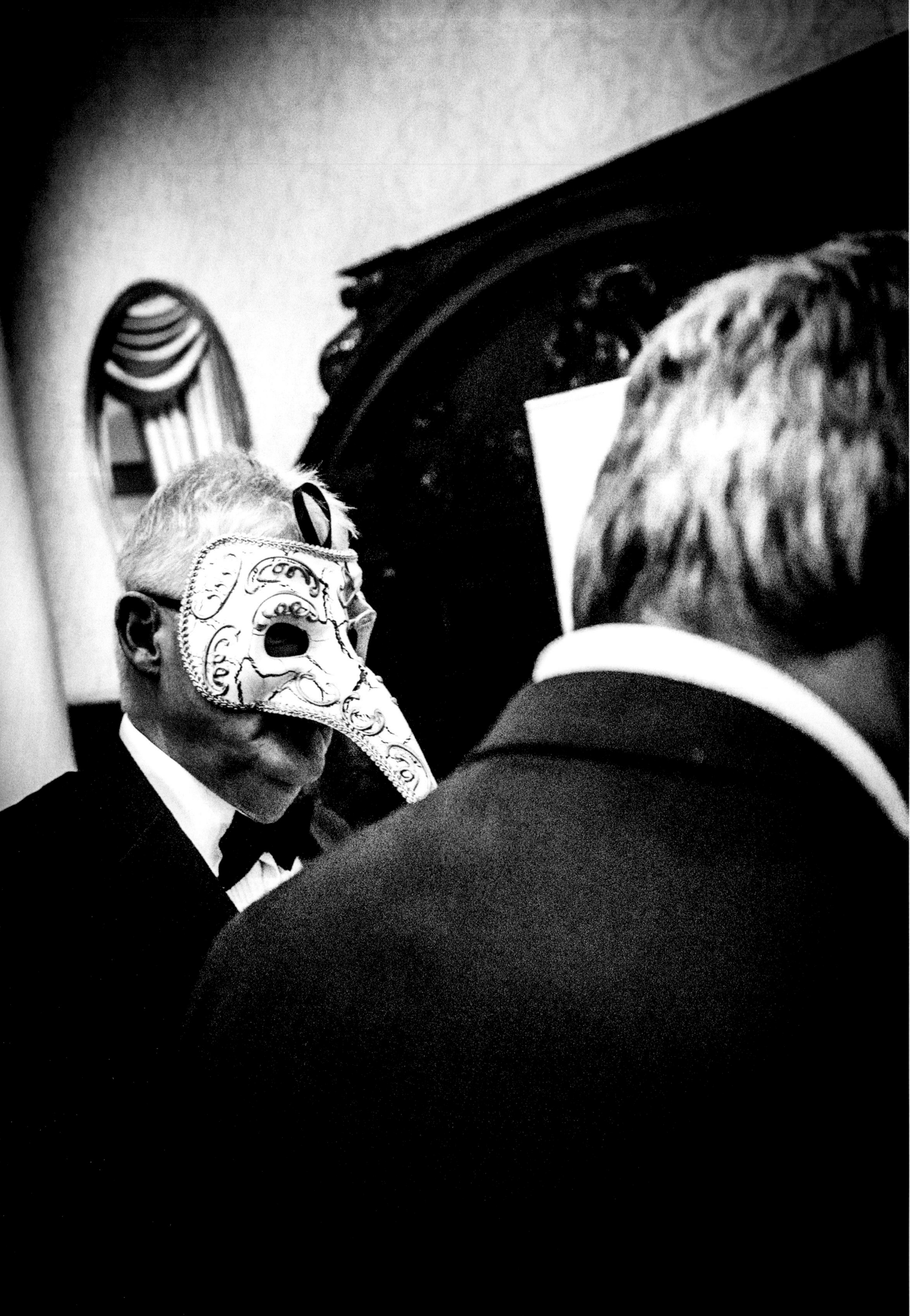

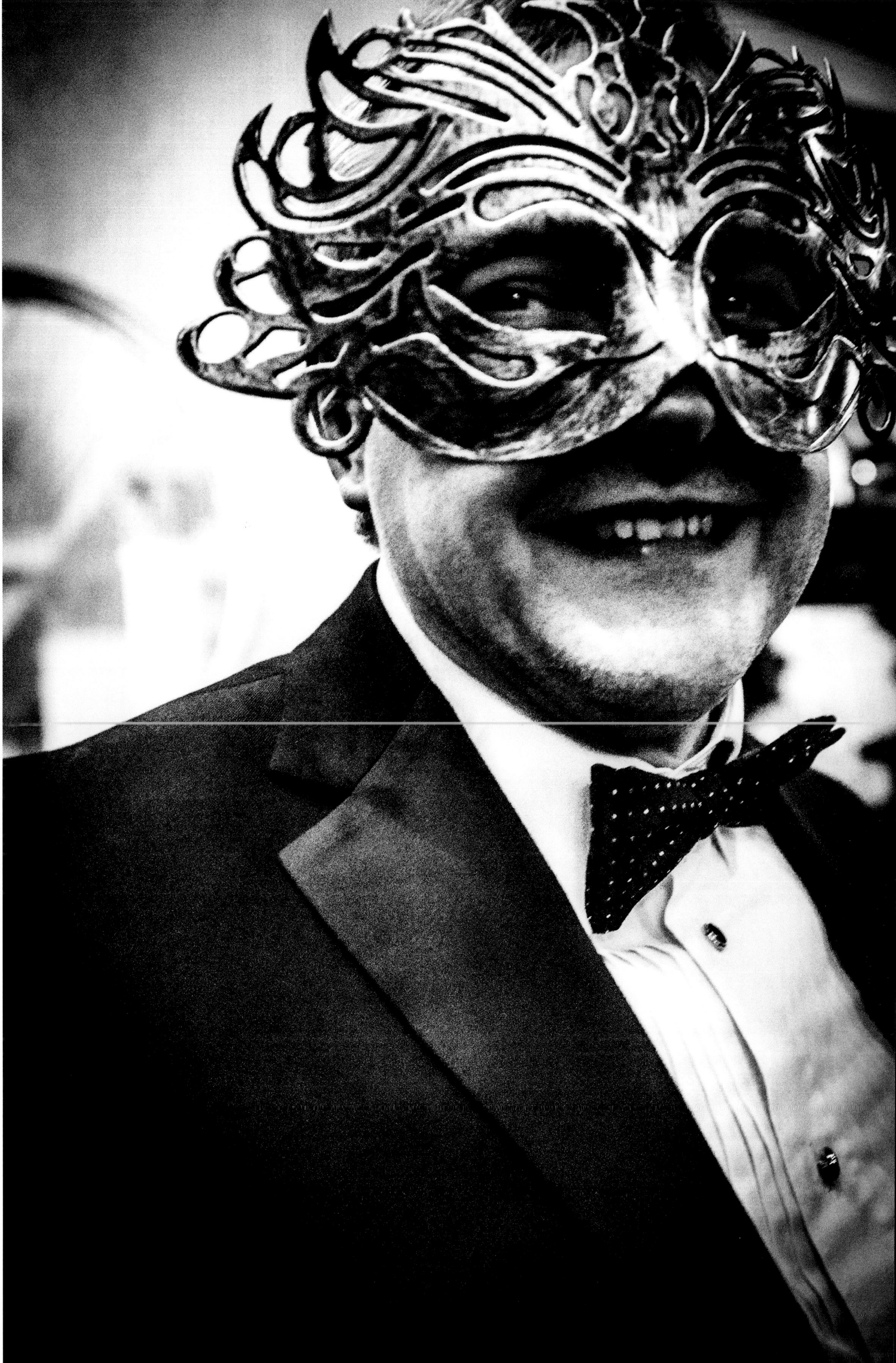

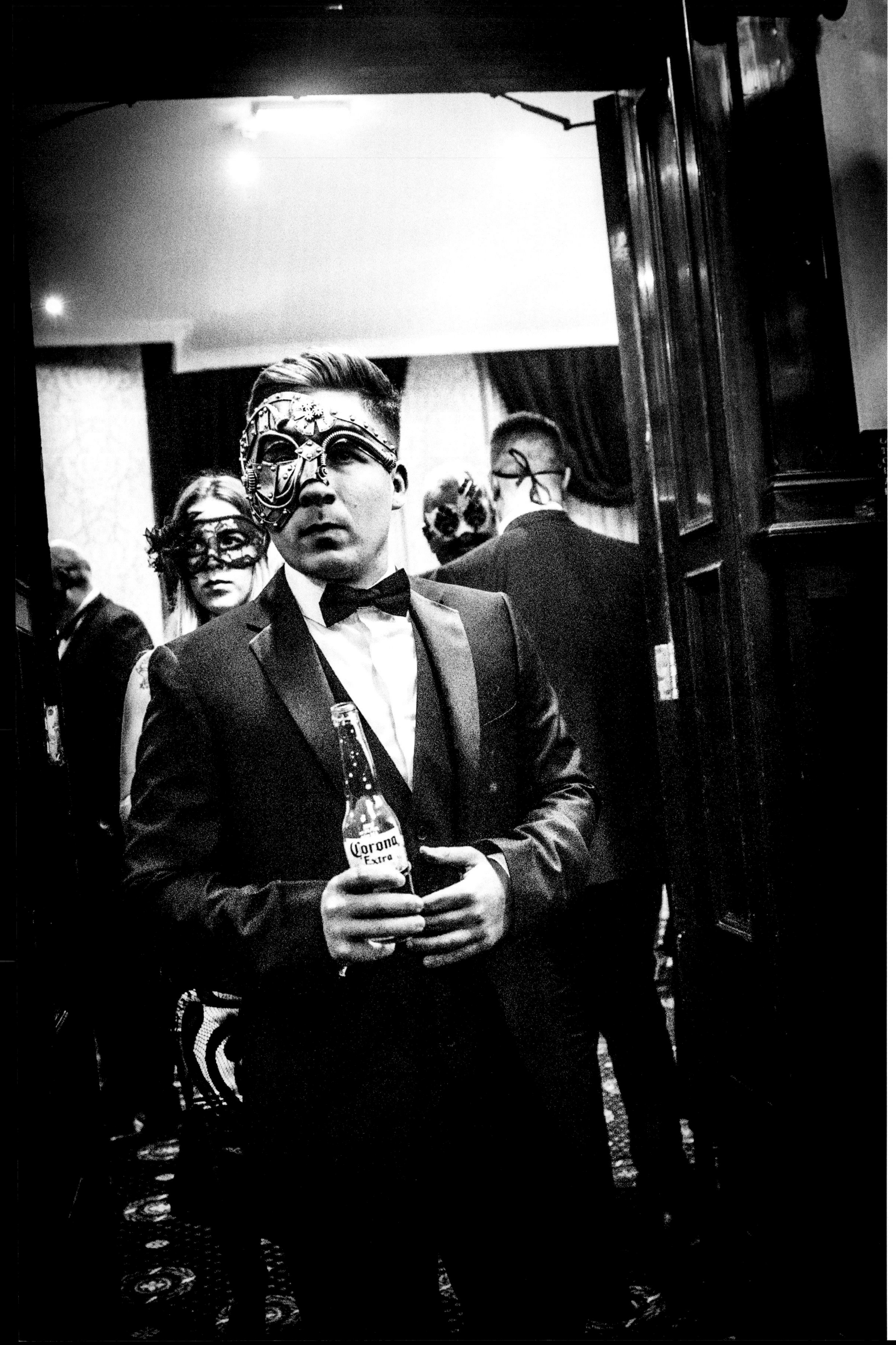

Corona
Extra

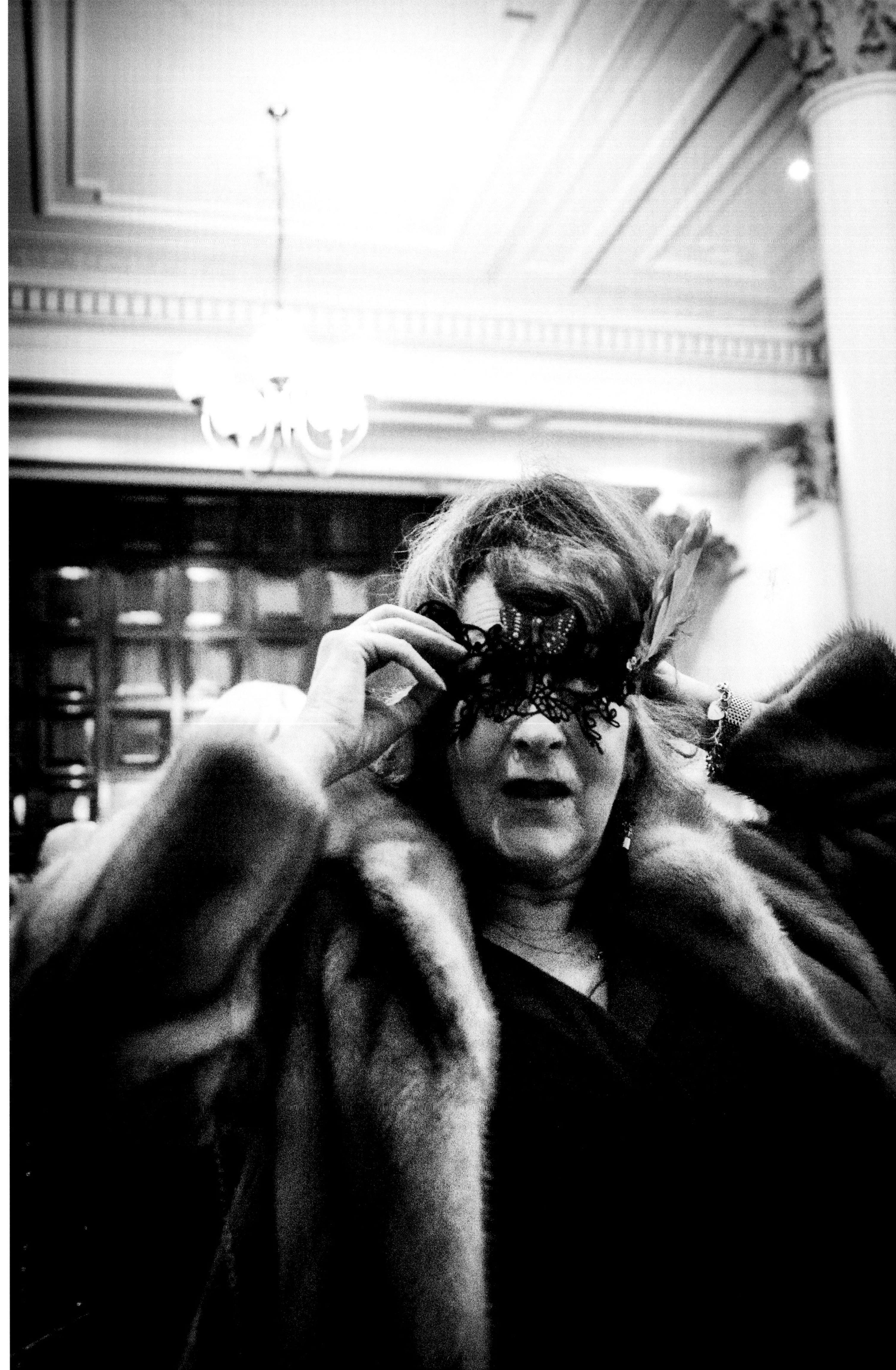

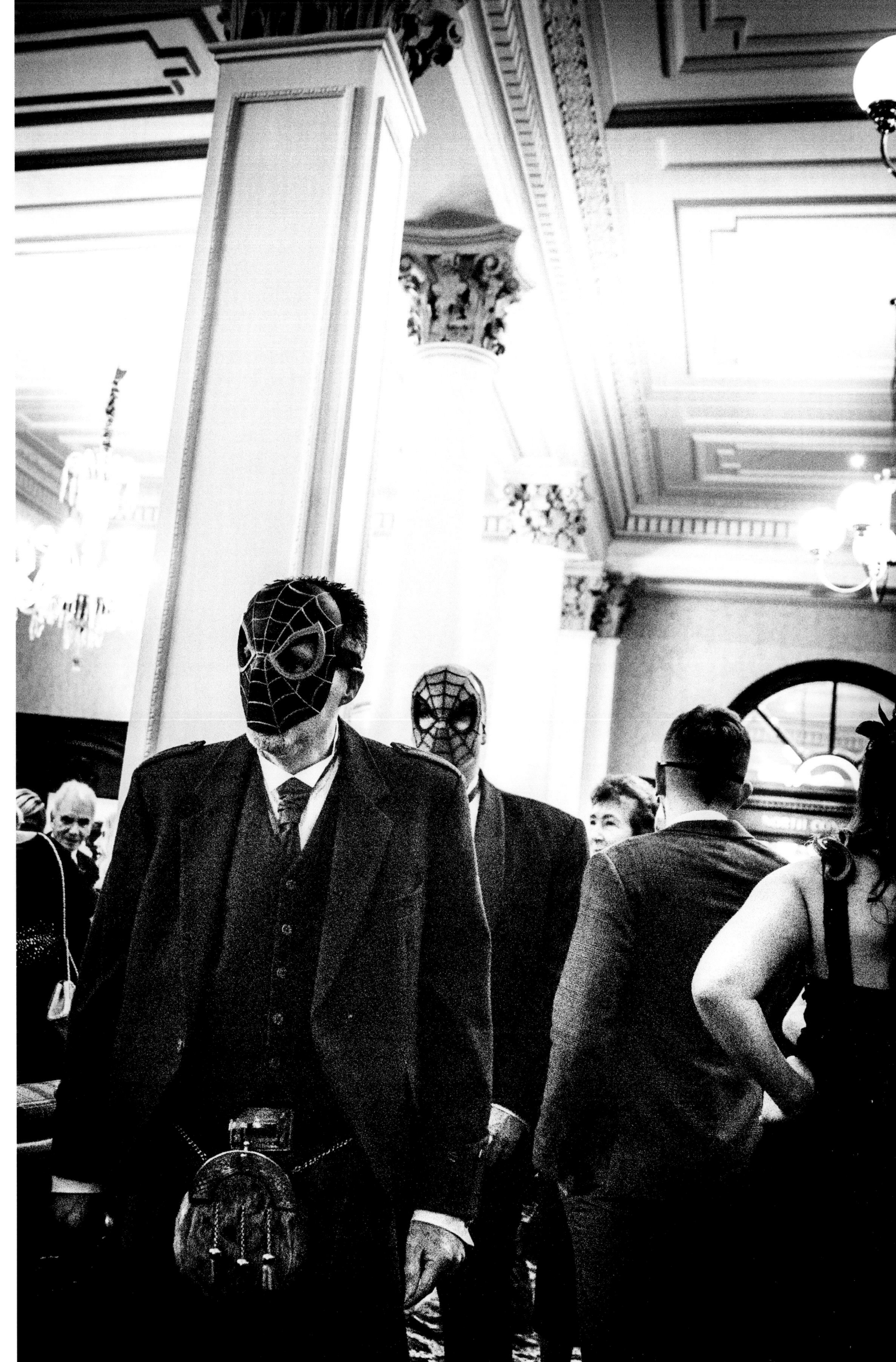

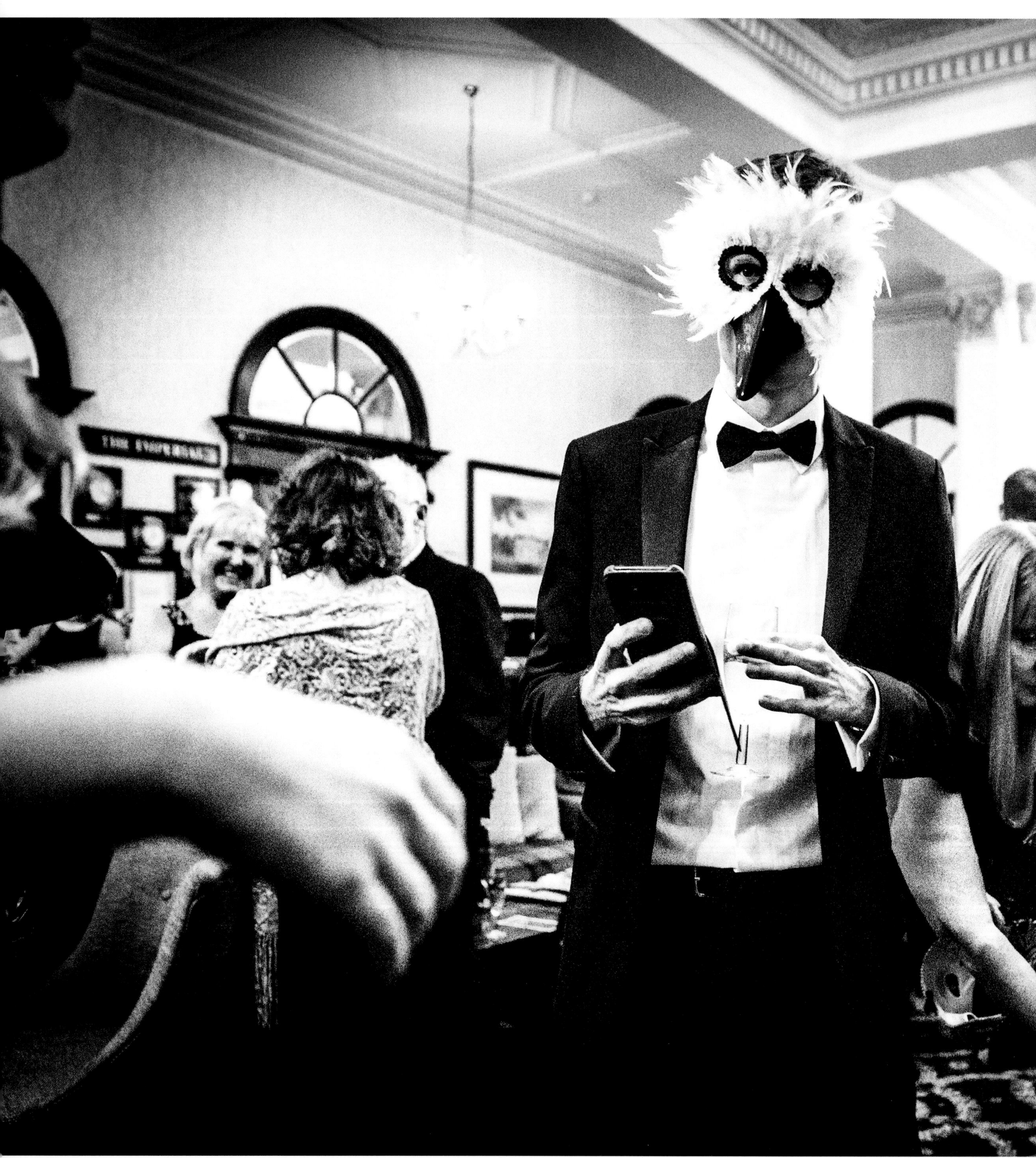

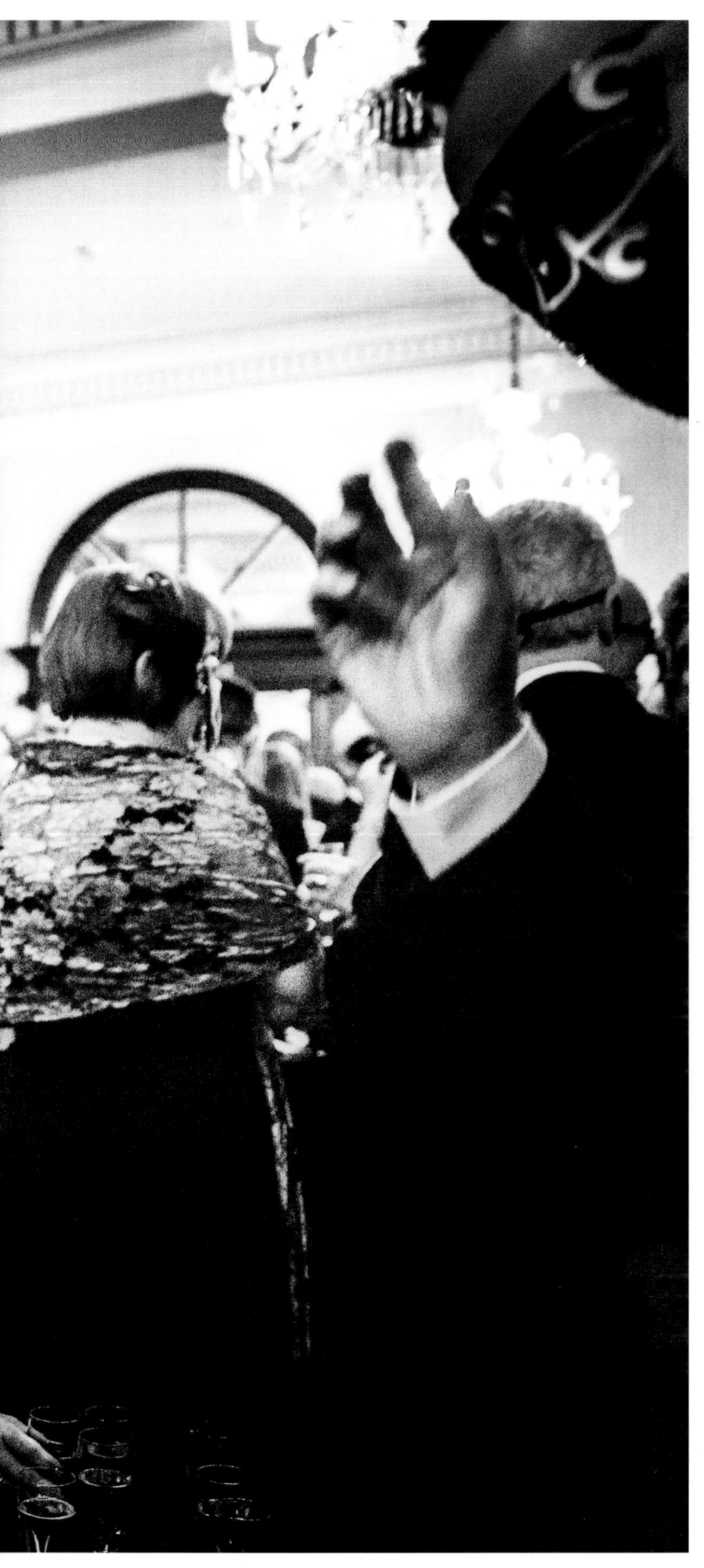

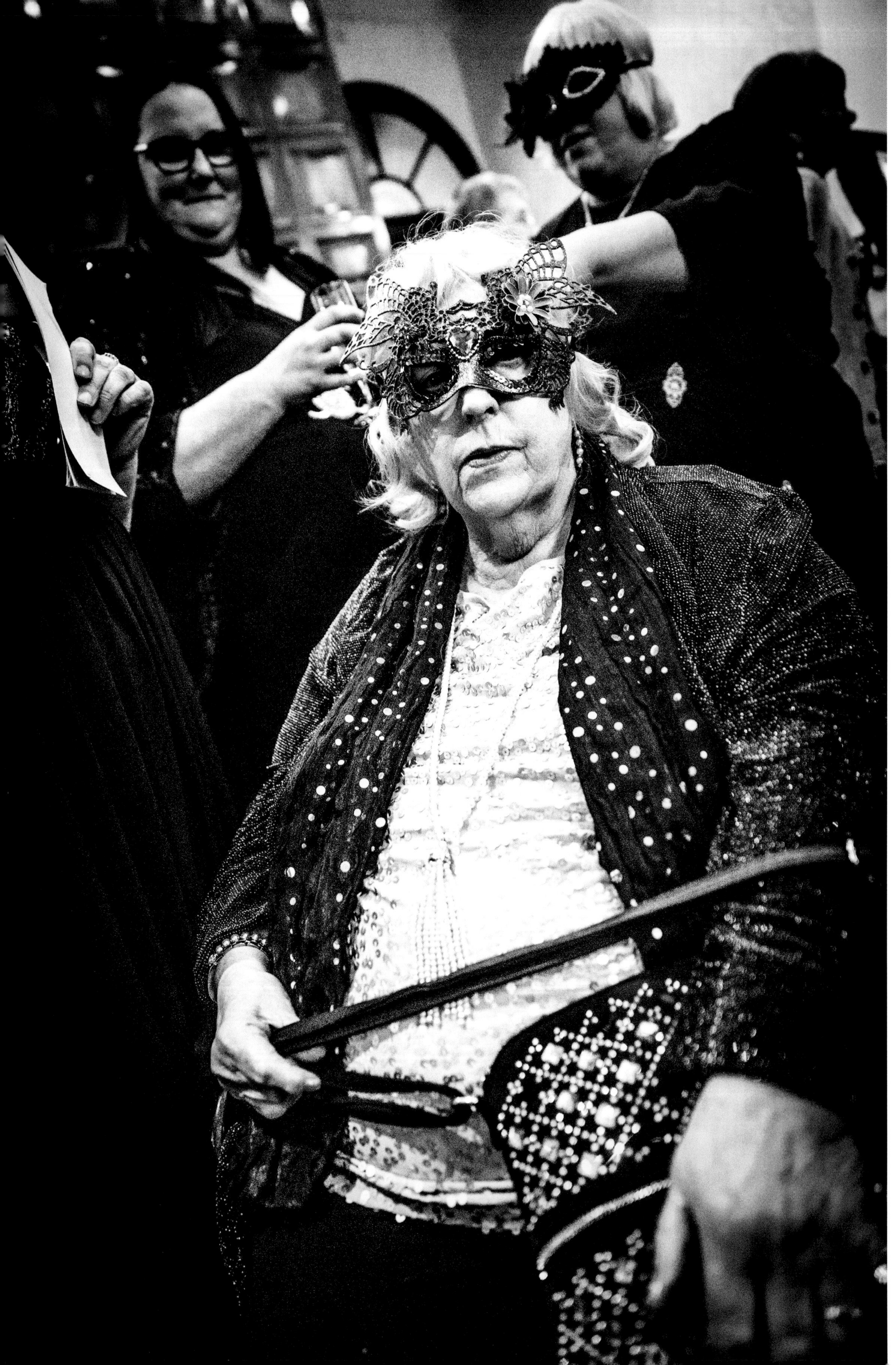

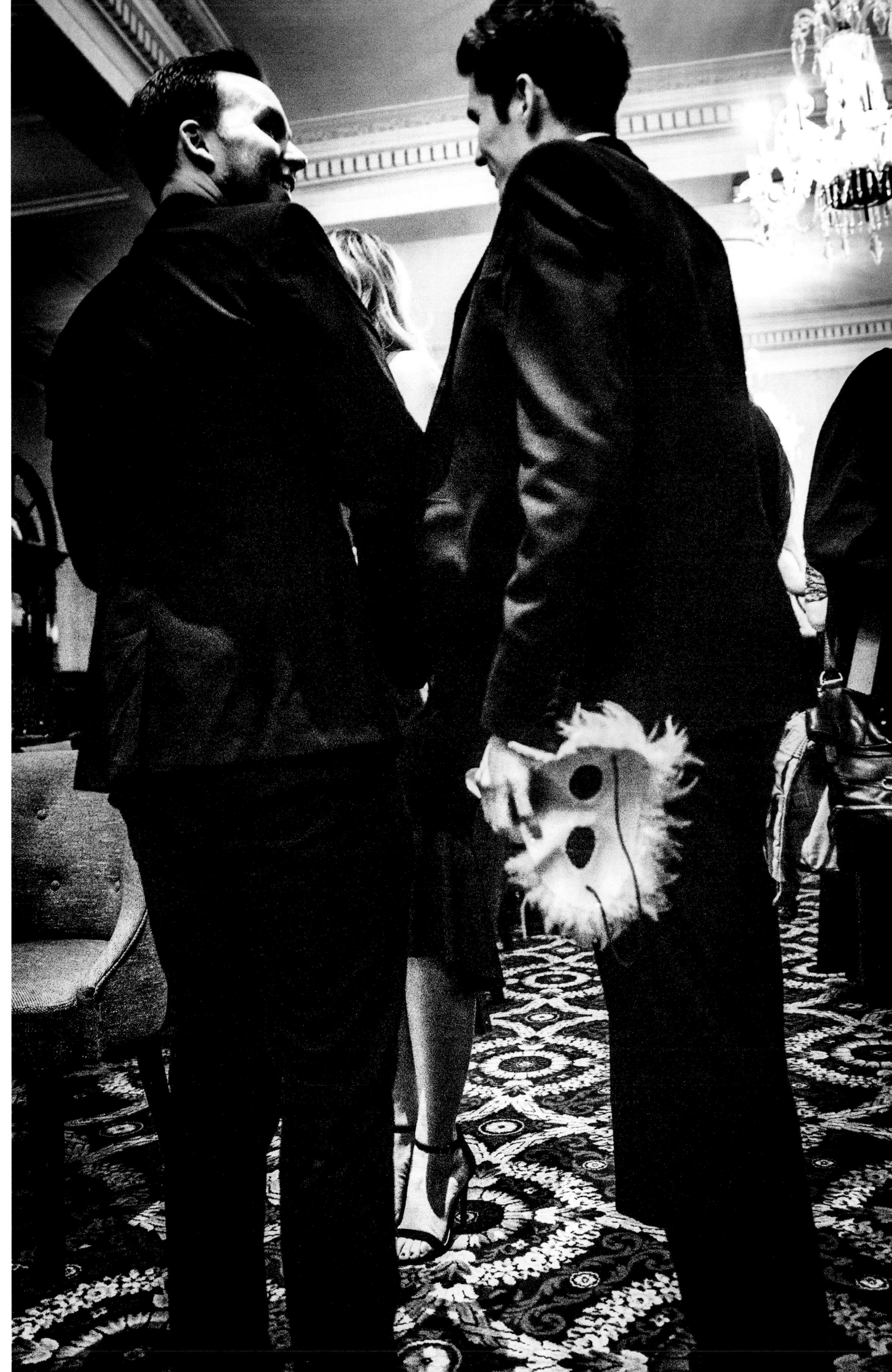

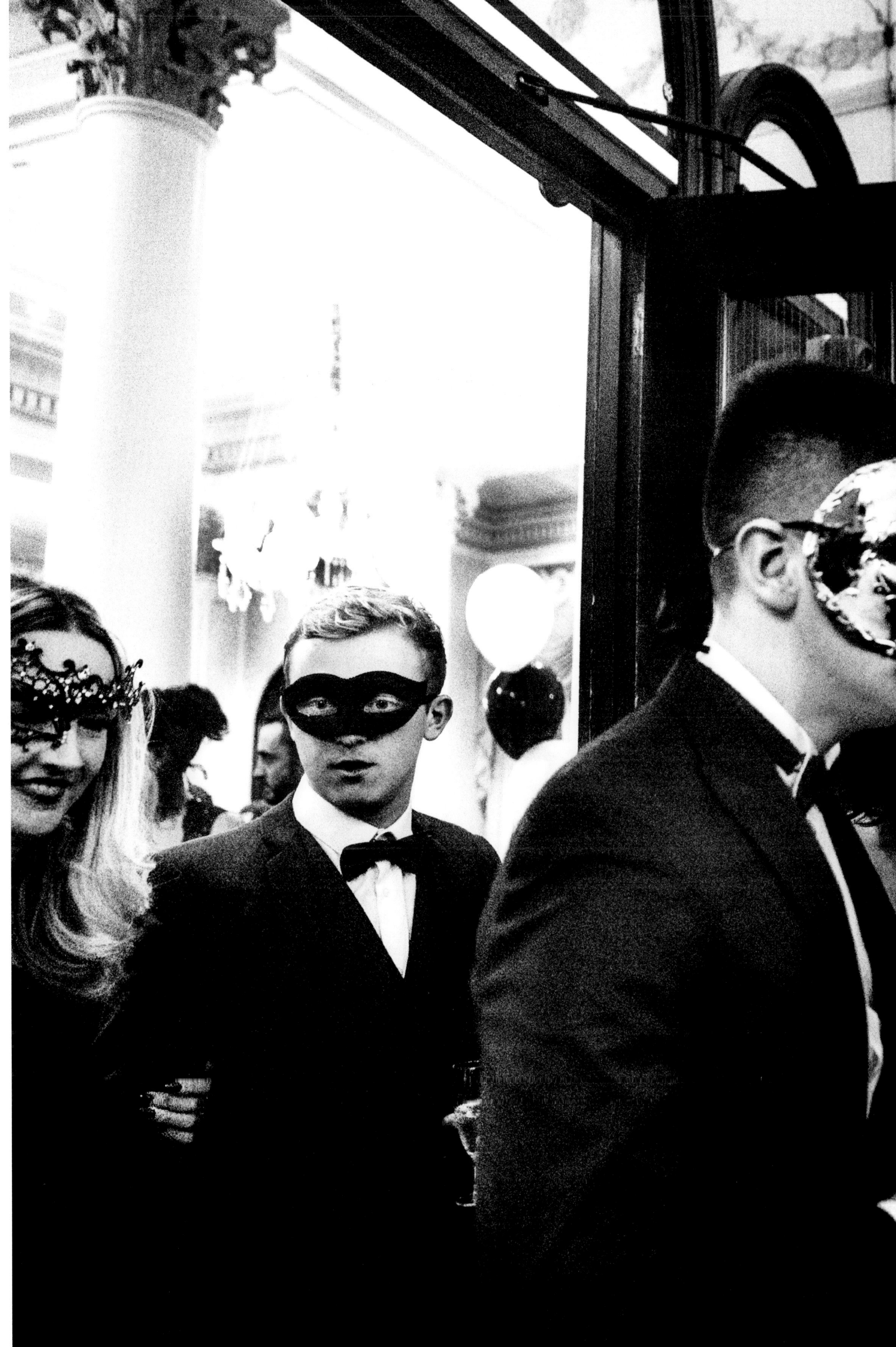

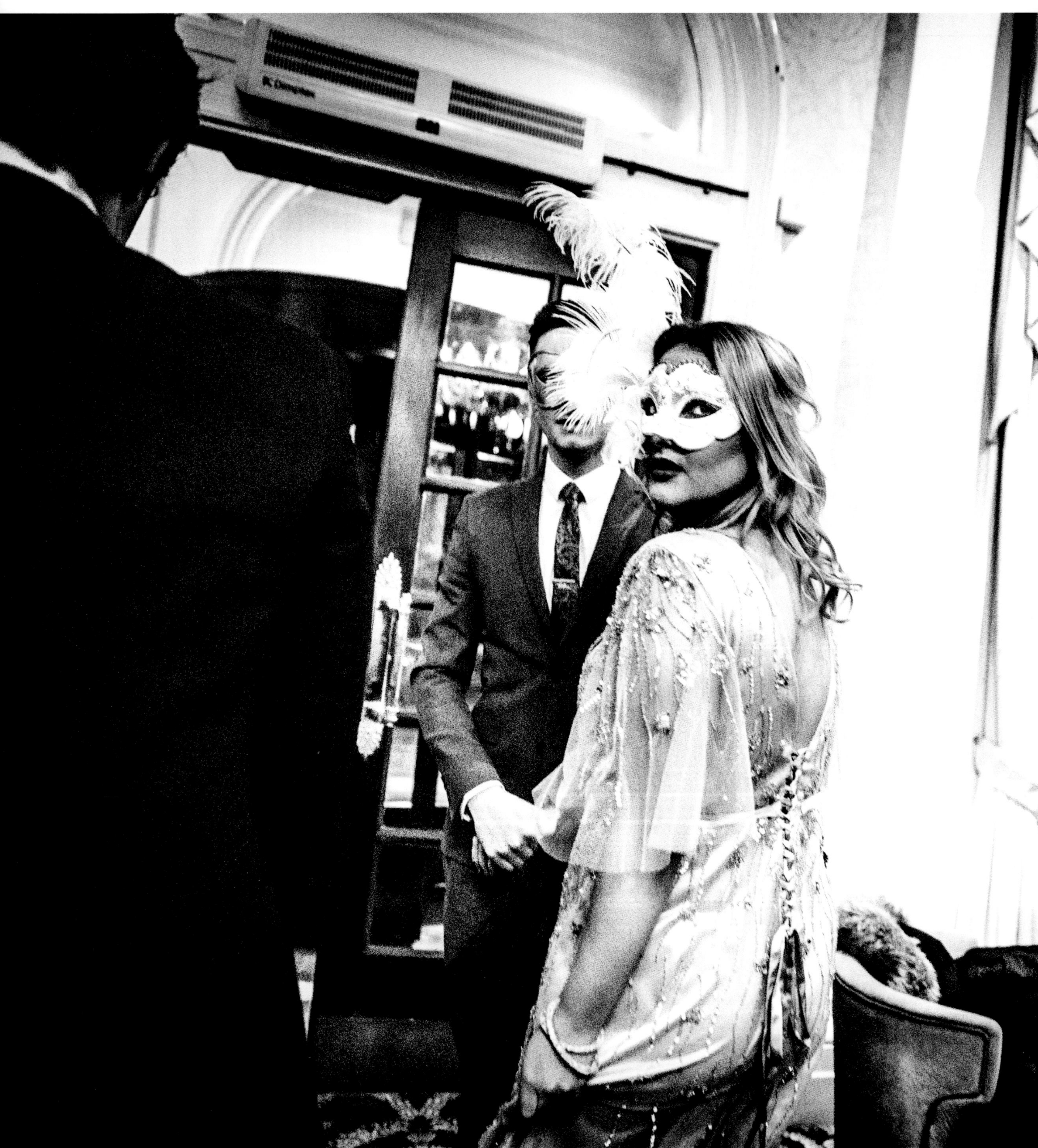

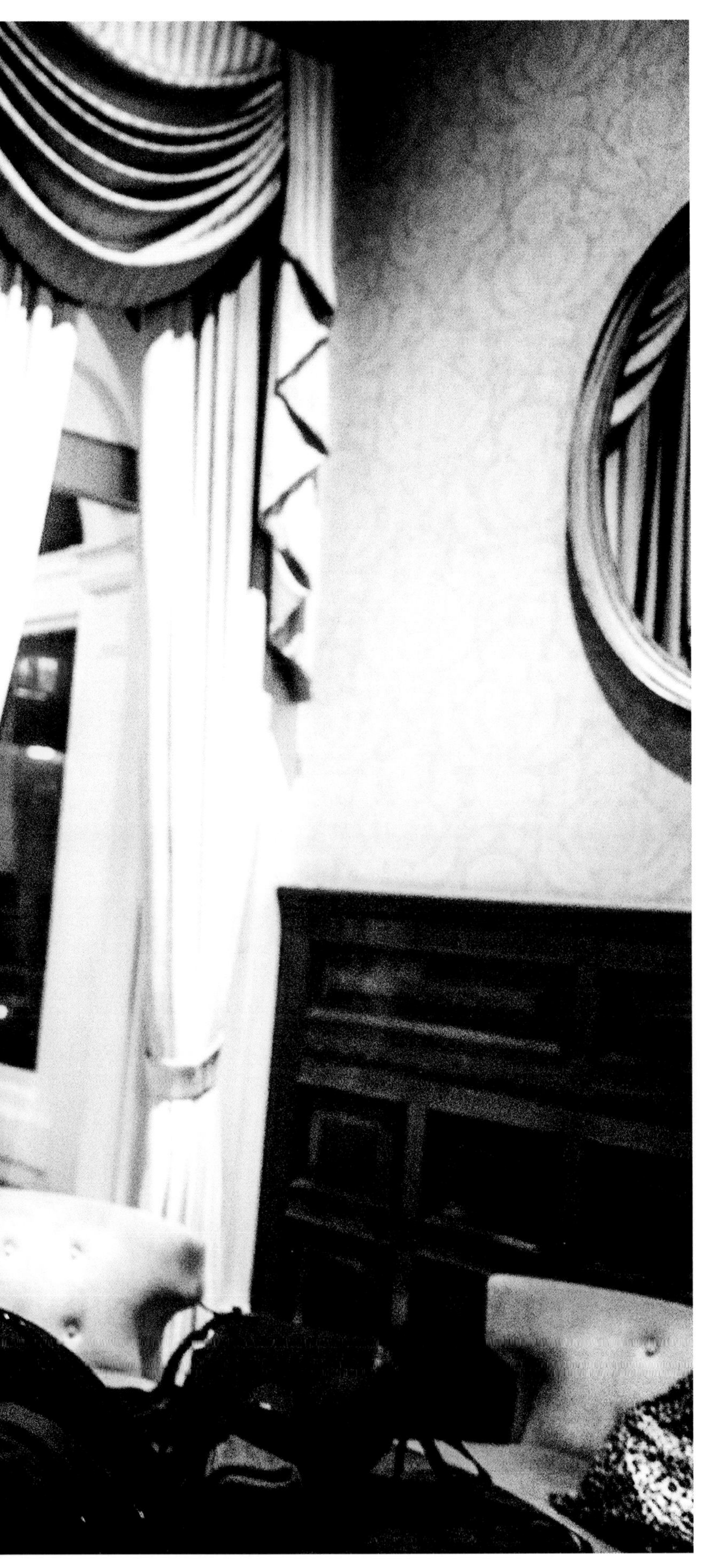

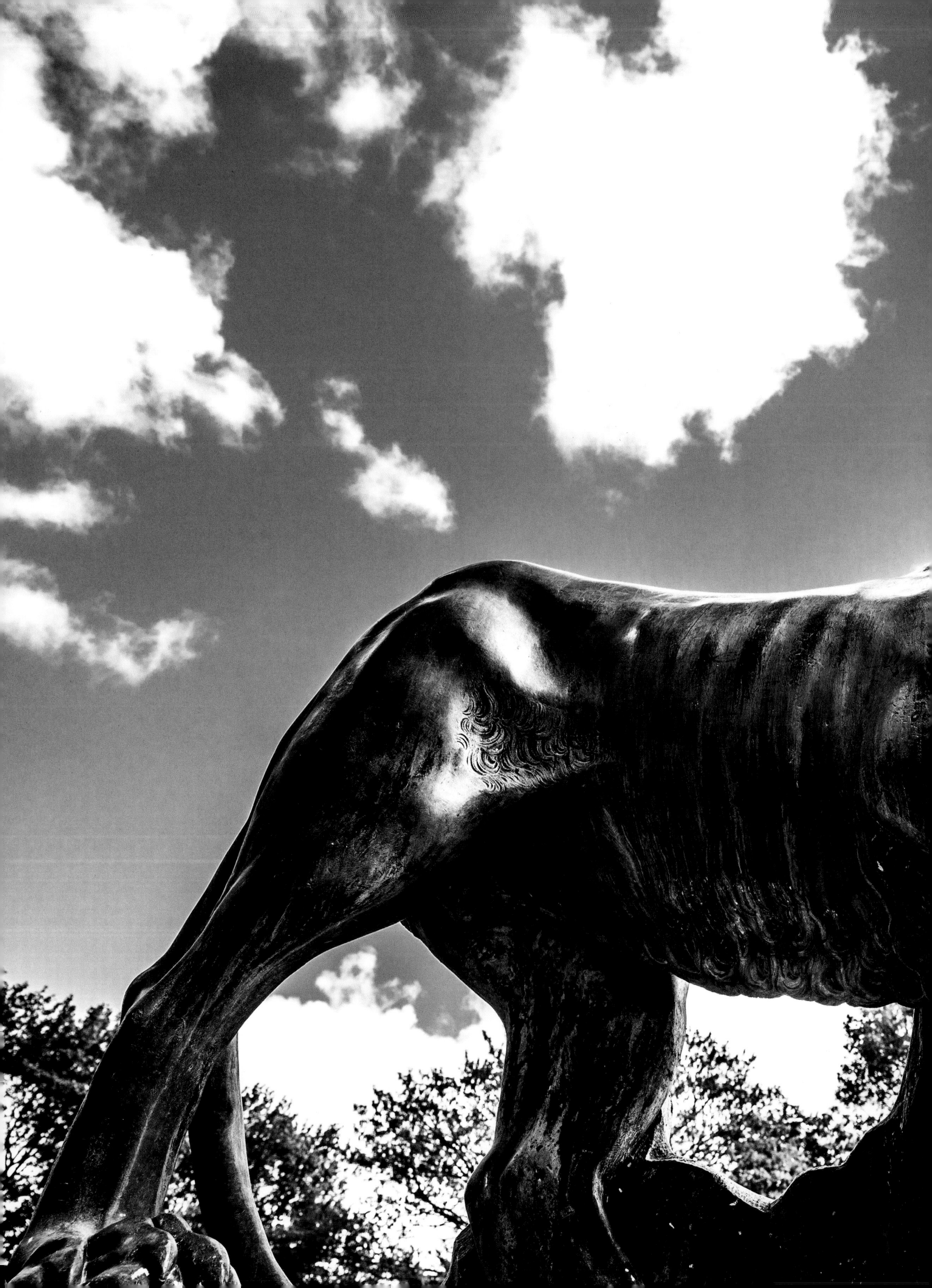

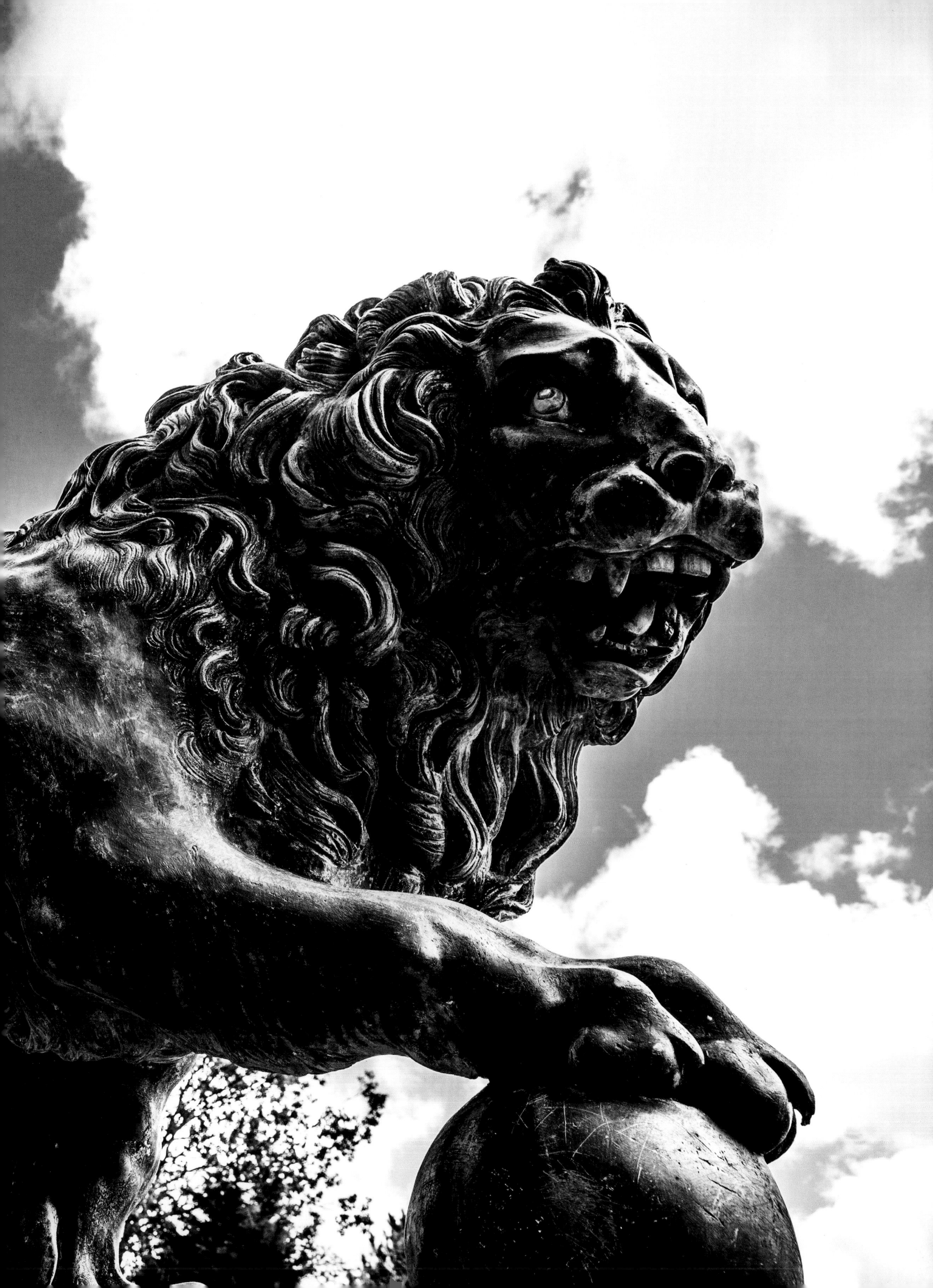

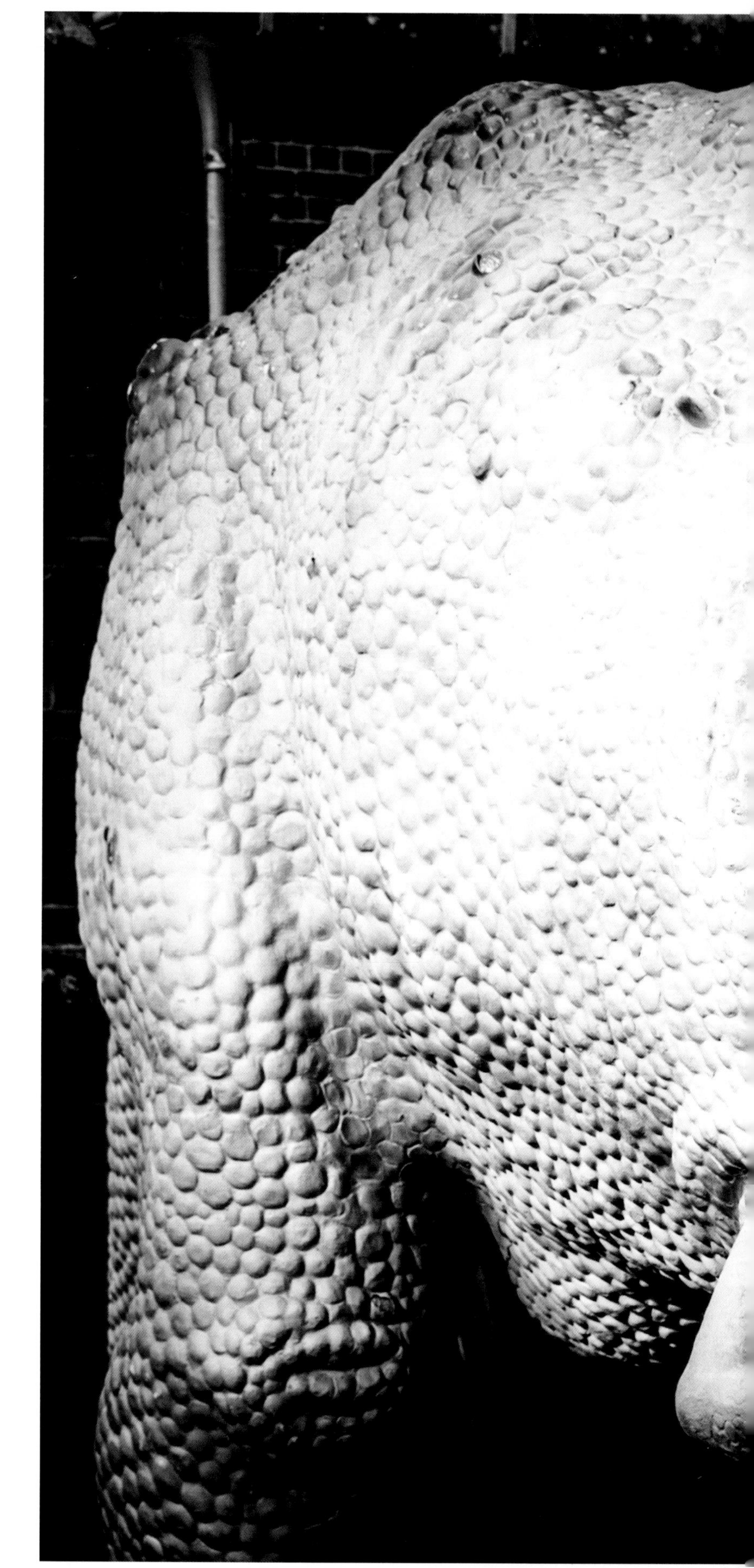

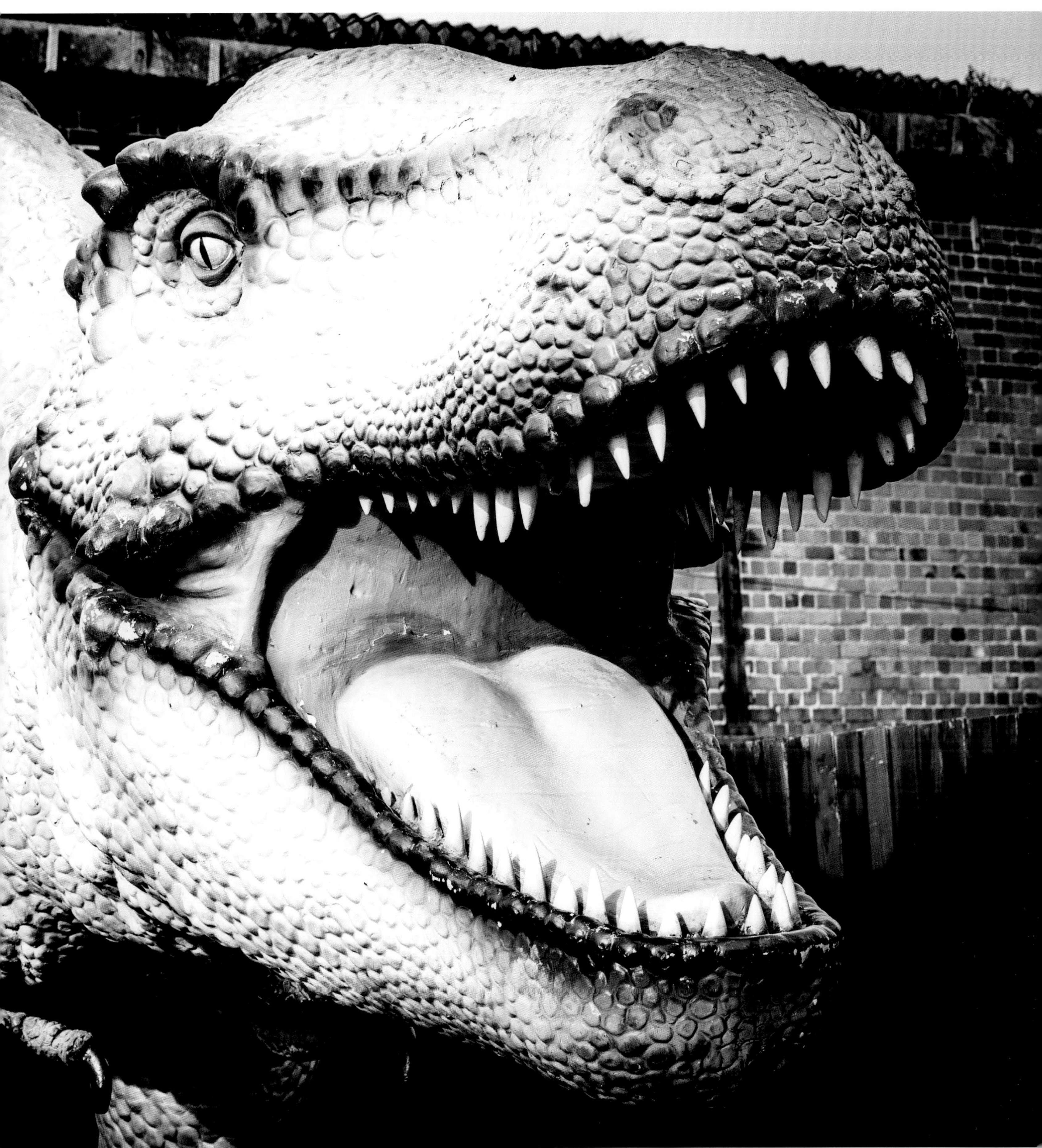

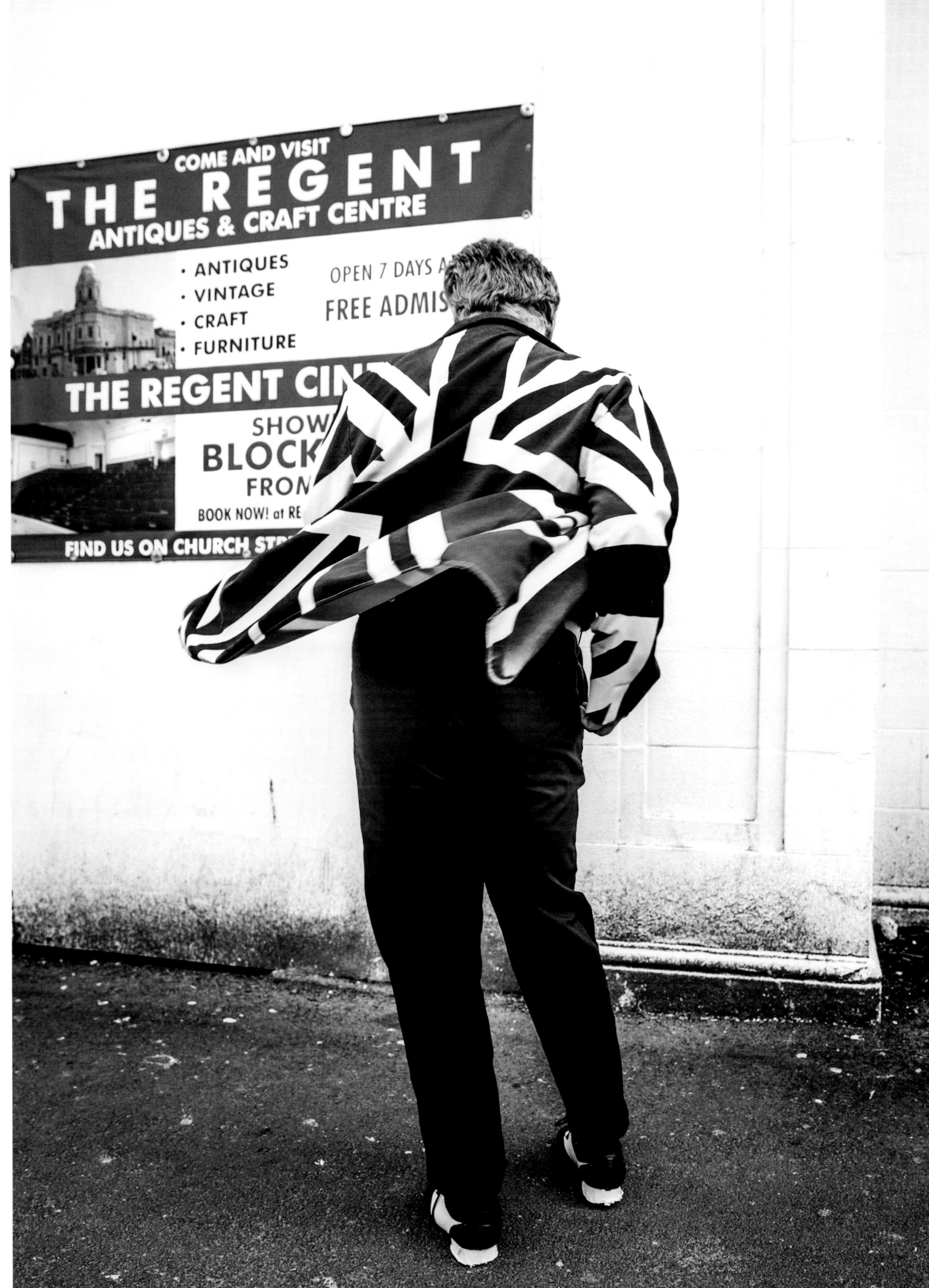

COME AND VISIT
THE REGENT
ANTIQUES & CRAFT CENTRE
• ANTIQUES
• VINTAGE
• CRAFT
• FURNITURE
OPEN 7 DAYS A
FREE ADMIS
THE REGENT CIN
SHOW
BLOCK
FROM
BOOK NOW! at RE
FIND US ON CHURCH STR

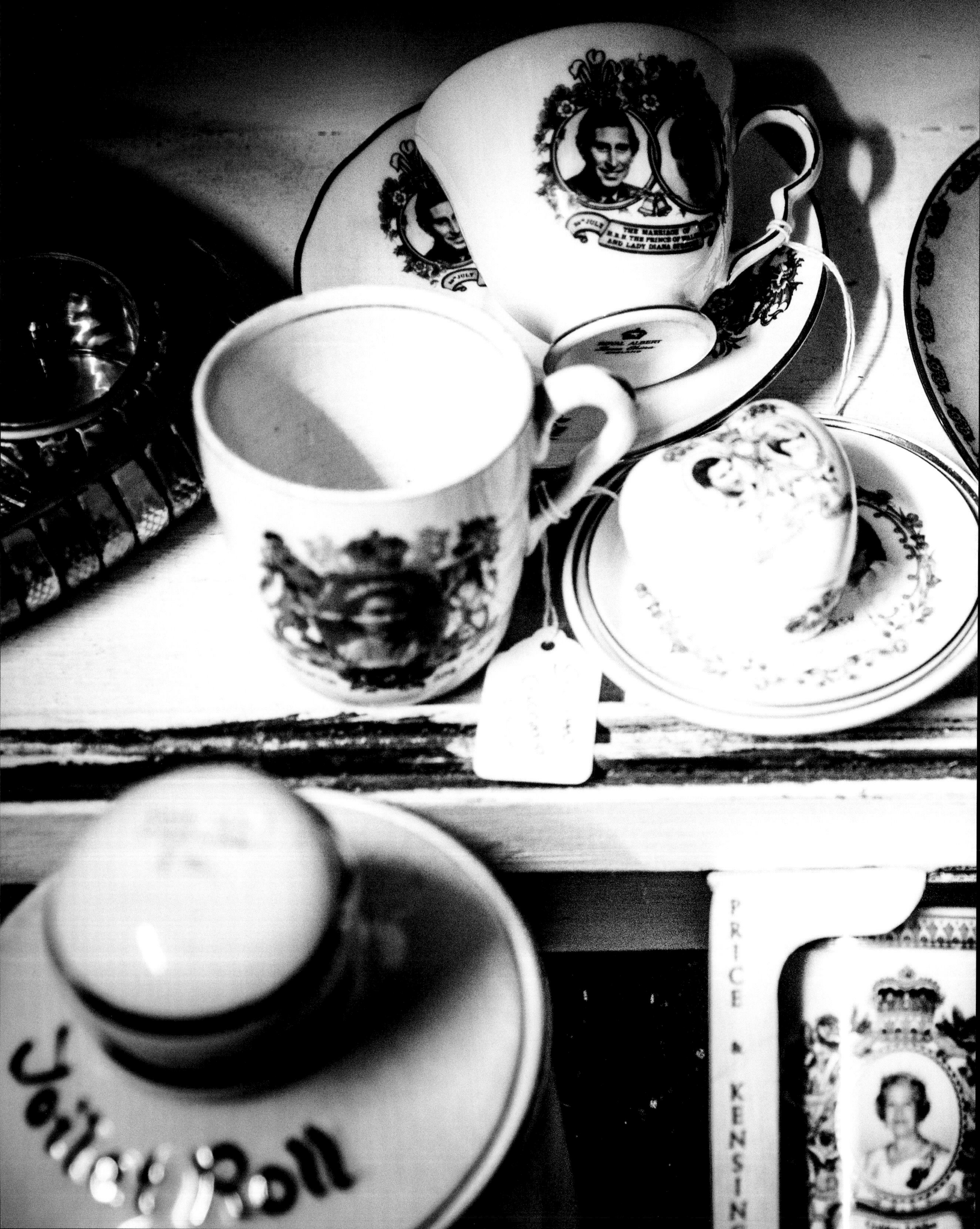

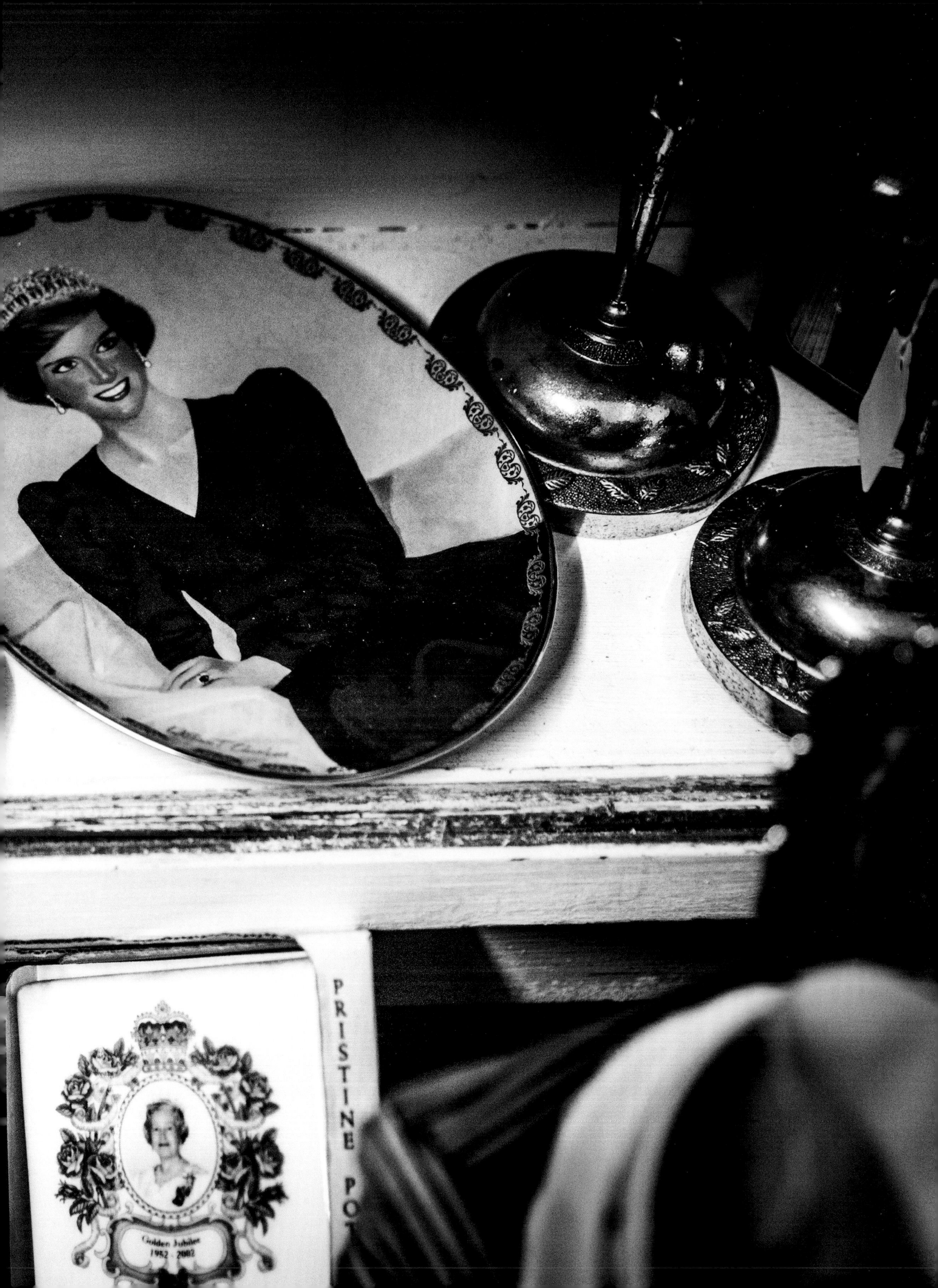

Golden Jubilee
1952 - 2002
PRISTINE PO

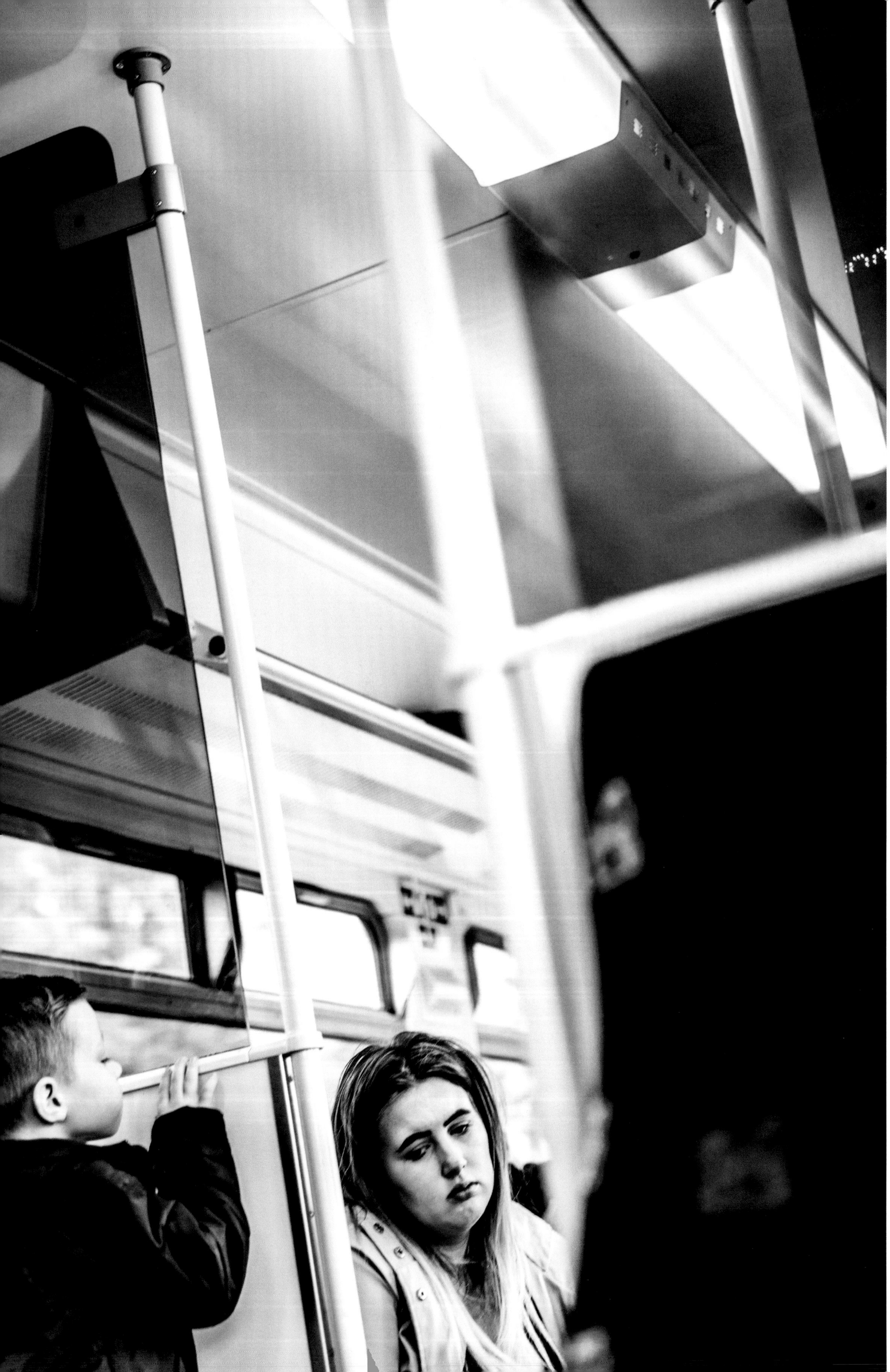

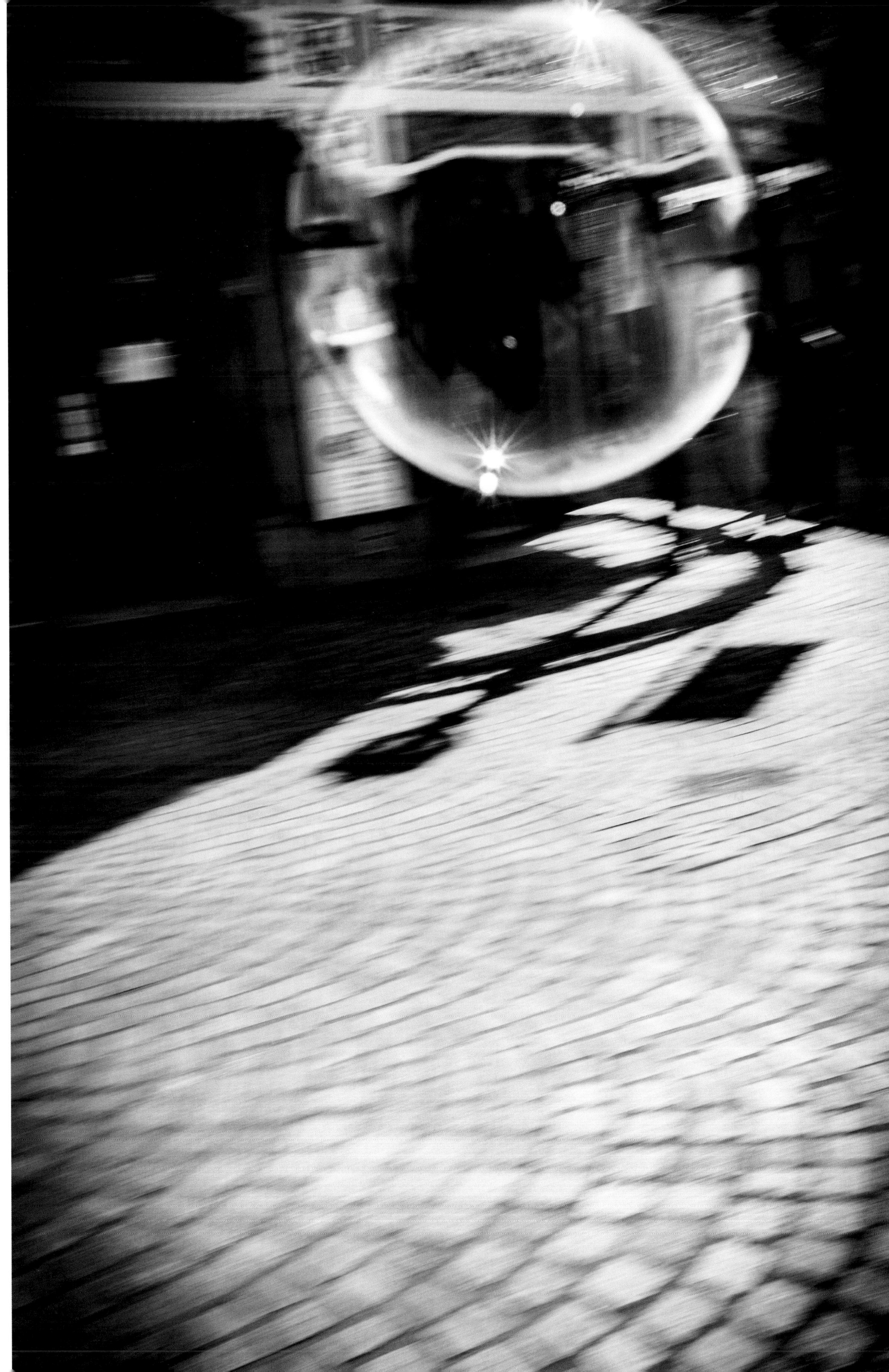

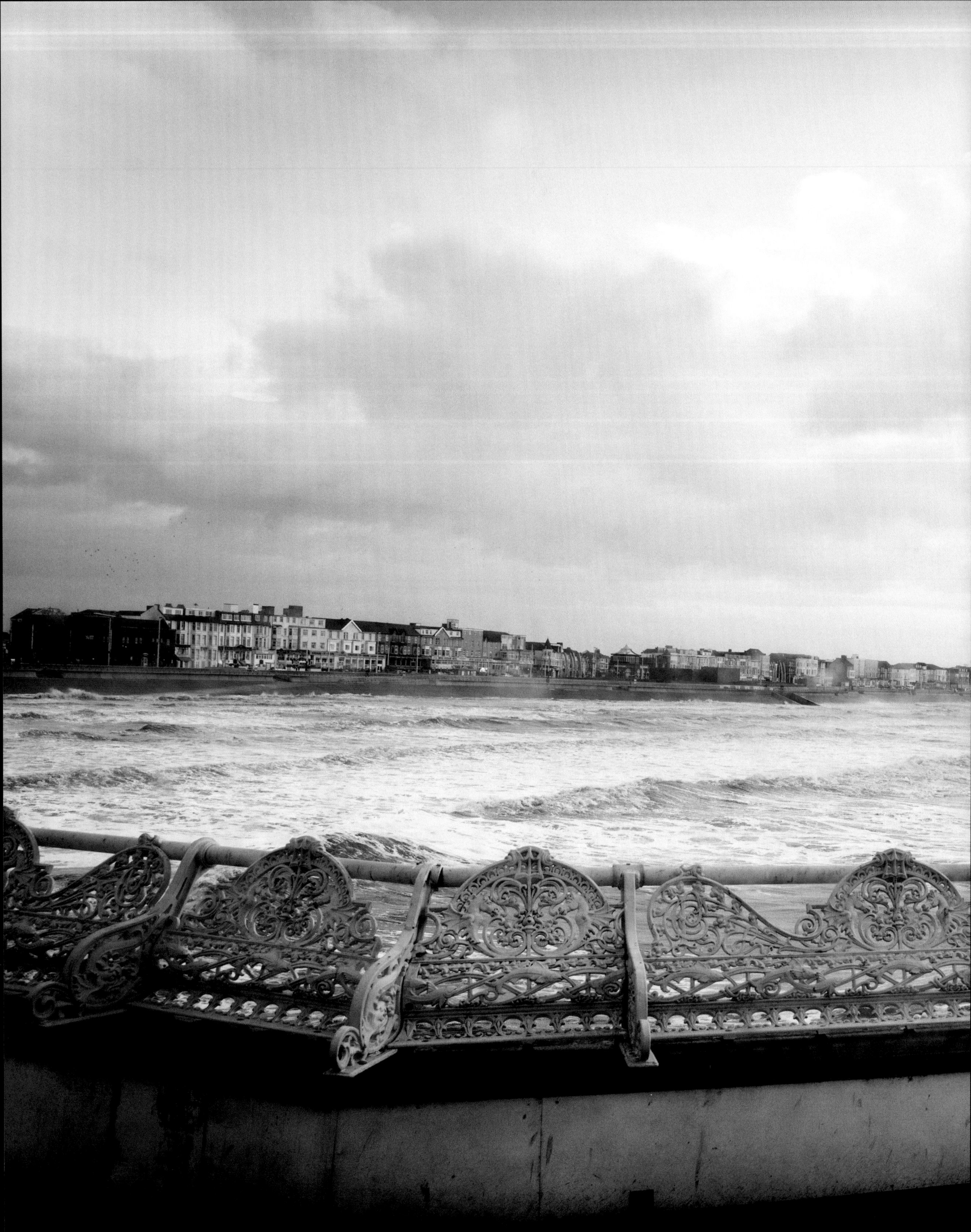

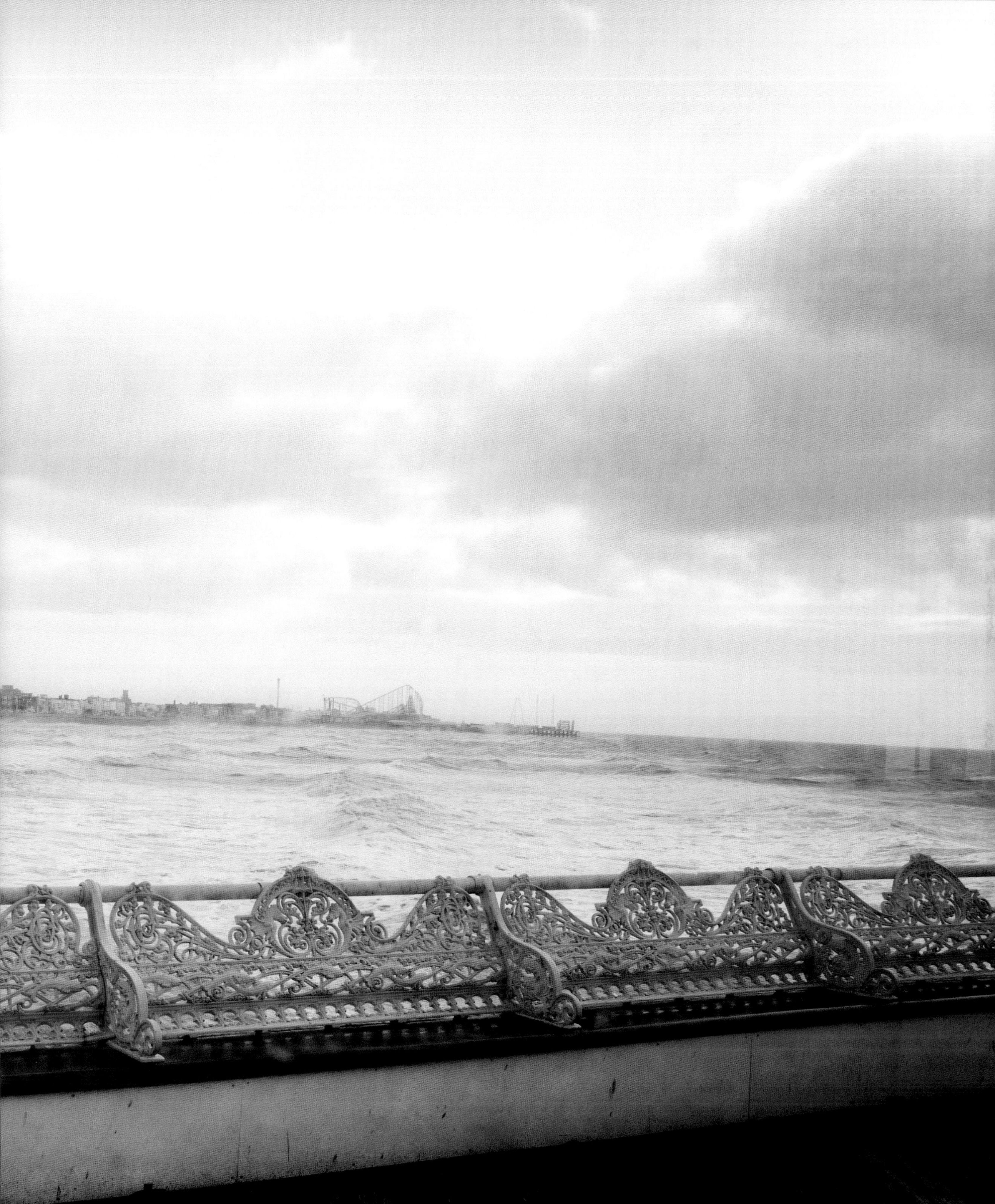

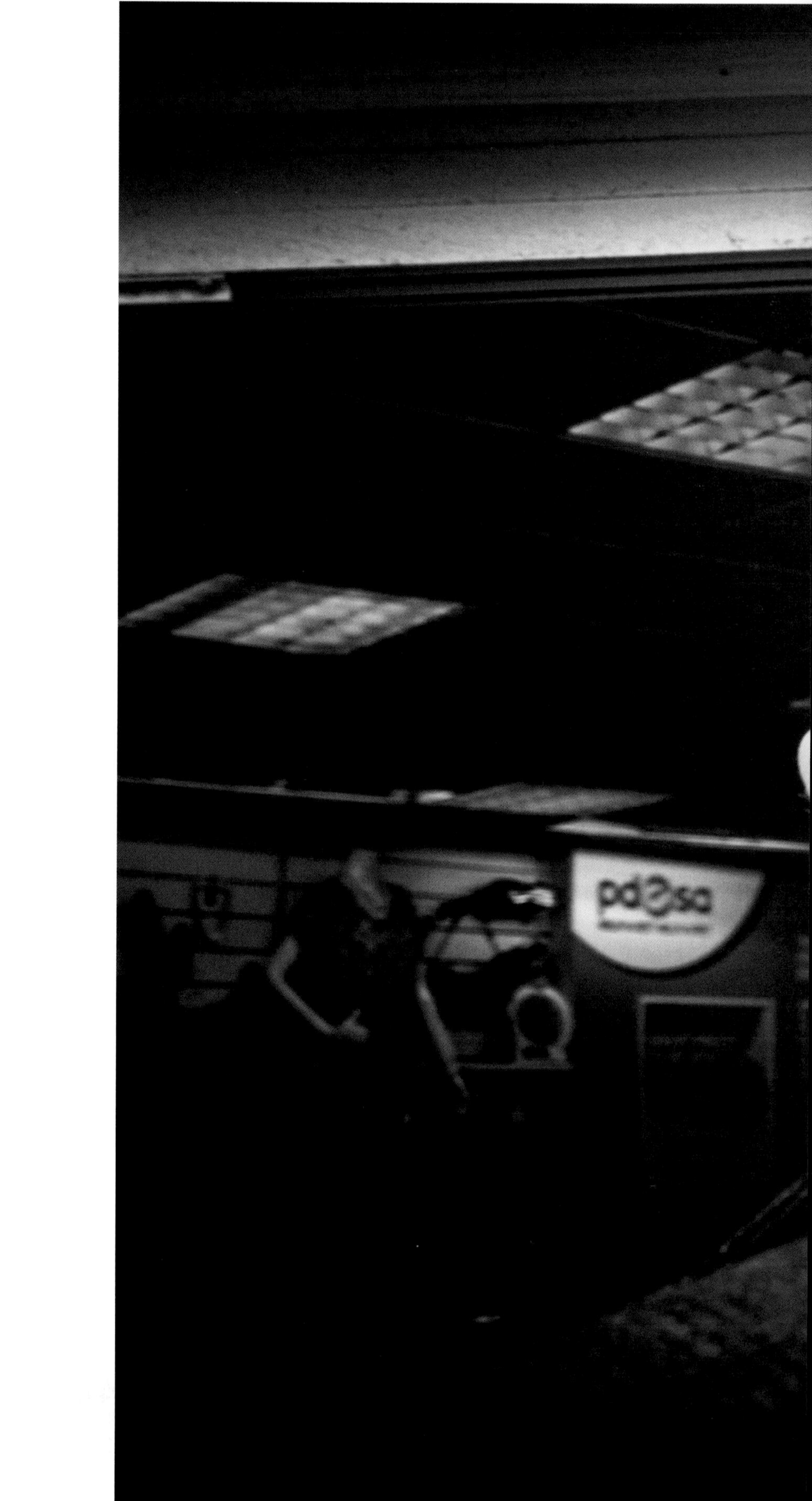

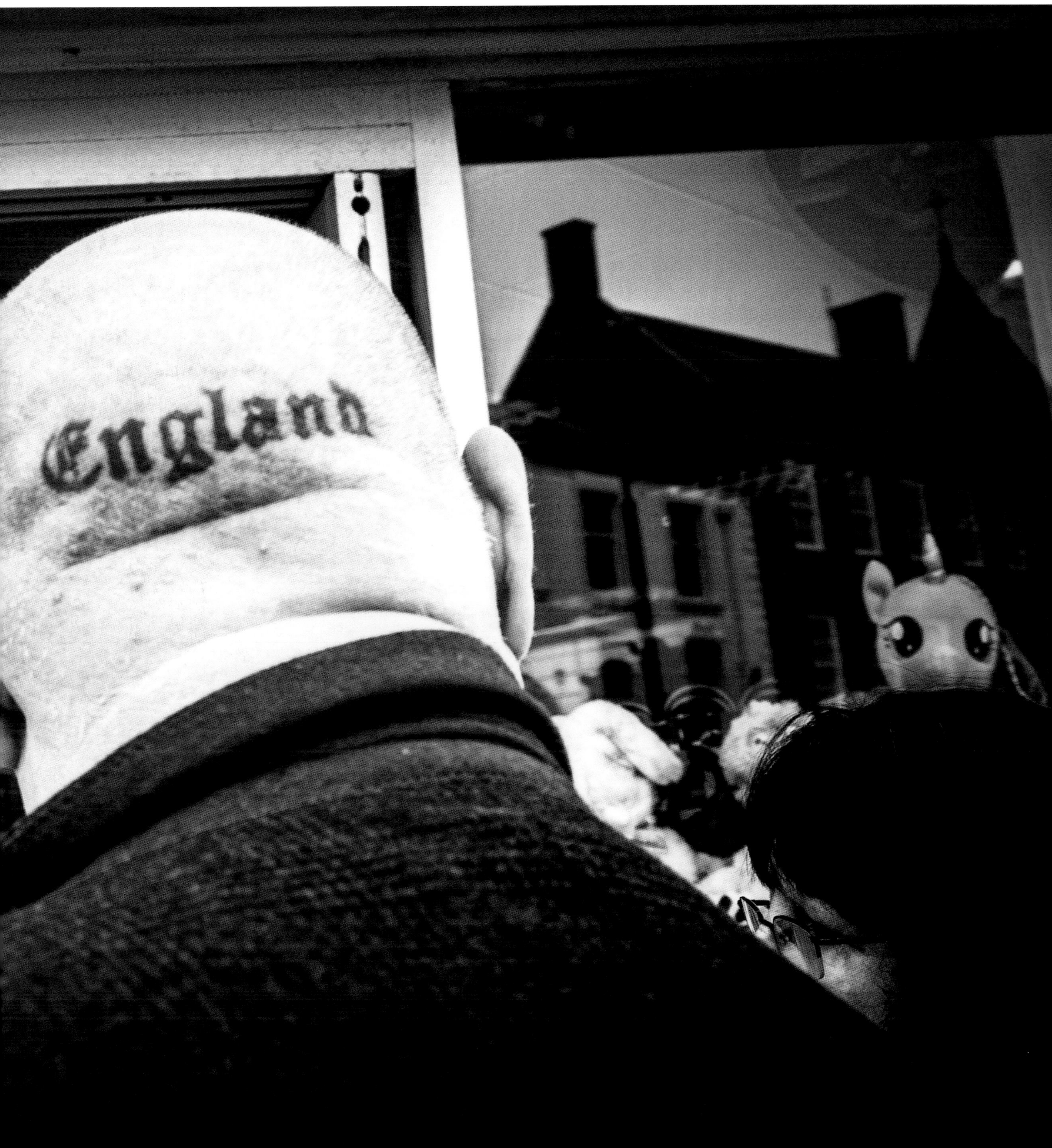

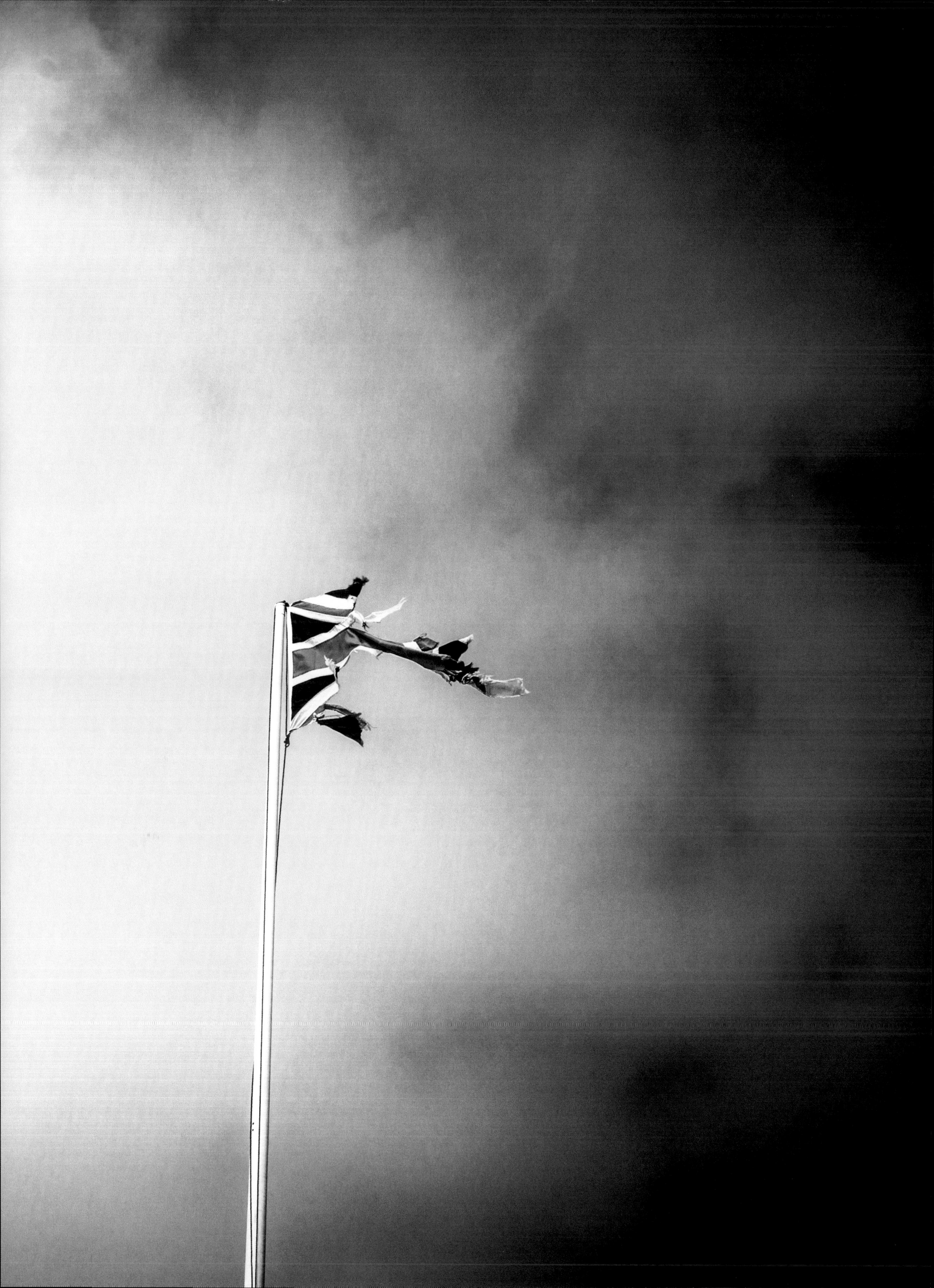

And the future is written in the stars /
Und die Zukunft steht in den Sternen

Benita Suchodrev was born in the former Soviet Union and immigrated to the United
States in 1990 where she received her Bachelor's degree in Liberal Arts with
a focus on Art History, followed by a Master's degree in English Literature, graduat-
ing with high honours. In 2008 Benita relocated to Berlin and began an extensive
documentation of the cosmopolitan city's multifaceted art scene while working on
diverse photographic projects, which have been exhibited in solo and group shows
nationally and internationally. Her portrait and documentary work is part of the
Rafael Tous Foundation for Contemporary Art in Barcelona, the Michael Horbach
Foundation in Cologne and private collections in Moscow, Berlin and New York.
Her photographs have appeared in *48 Hours Blackpool* (Kehrer Verlag, 2018),
Nachtleben Berlin: 1974 bis heute (Metrolit Verlag, 2013), *Berlin Now* (teNeues
Verlag, 2009) and have been covered by various print, radio and TV media including
The Guardian, *ZEIT ONLINE*, Stern.de, *Mare*, *Mind China*, *Amica Italy*, *Art*, *Frankfurter
Allgemeine Zeitung*, *Berliner Zeitung*, *Tagesspiegel*, *The Moscow Times*, Arte, ARD and
RBB Kulturradio, among others. Benita currently lives and works in Berlin.

Benita Suchodrev wurde in der ehemaligen Sowjetunion geboren und wanderte 1990
in die Vereinigten Staaten aus, wo sie ihren Bachelor-Abschluss in Geisteswissen-
schaften mit dem Schwerpunkt Kunstgeschichte gefolgt von einem Master-Abschluss
in englischer Literatur mit Auszeichnung bestand. Im Jahr 2008 zog Benita nach
Berlin und begann eine umfangreiche Dokumentation der facettenreichen Kunst-
szene der kosmopolitischen Stadt. Zeitgleich arbeitete sie an verschiedenen fotografischen Projekten, die in nationalen und internationalen Einzel- und Gruppenaus-
stellungen gezeigt wurden. Ihre Porträt- und Dokumentararbeiten sind Teil der
Rafael Tous Foundation for Contemporary Art in Barcelona, der Michael Horbach
Stiftung in Köln sowie von Privatsammlungen in Moskau, Berlin und New York. Ihre
Fotografien wurden in *48 Hours Blackpool* (Kehrer Verlag, 2018), *Nachtleben
Berlin: 1974 bis heute* (Metrolit Verlag, 2013) und *Berlin Now* (teNeues Verlag, 2009)
veröffentlicht und waren Gegenstand zahlreicher Berichte in TV, Hörfunk und
Druckmedien wie *The Guardian*, *ZEIT ONLINE*, Stern.de, *Mare*, *Mind China*, *Amica Italy*,
Art, *Frankfurter Allgemeine Zeitung*, *Berliner Zeitung*, *Tagesspiegel*, *The Moscow Times*,
Arte, ARD und RBB Kulturradio. Benita lebt und arbeitet derzeit in Berlin.

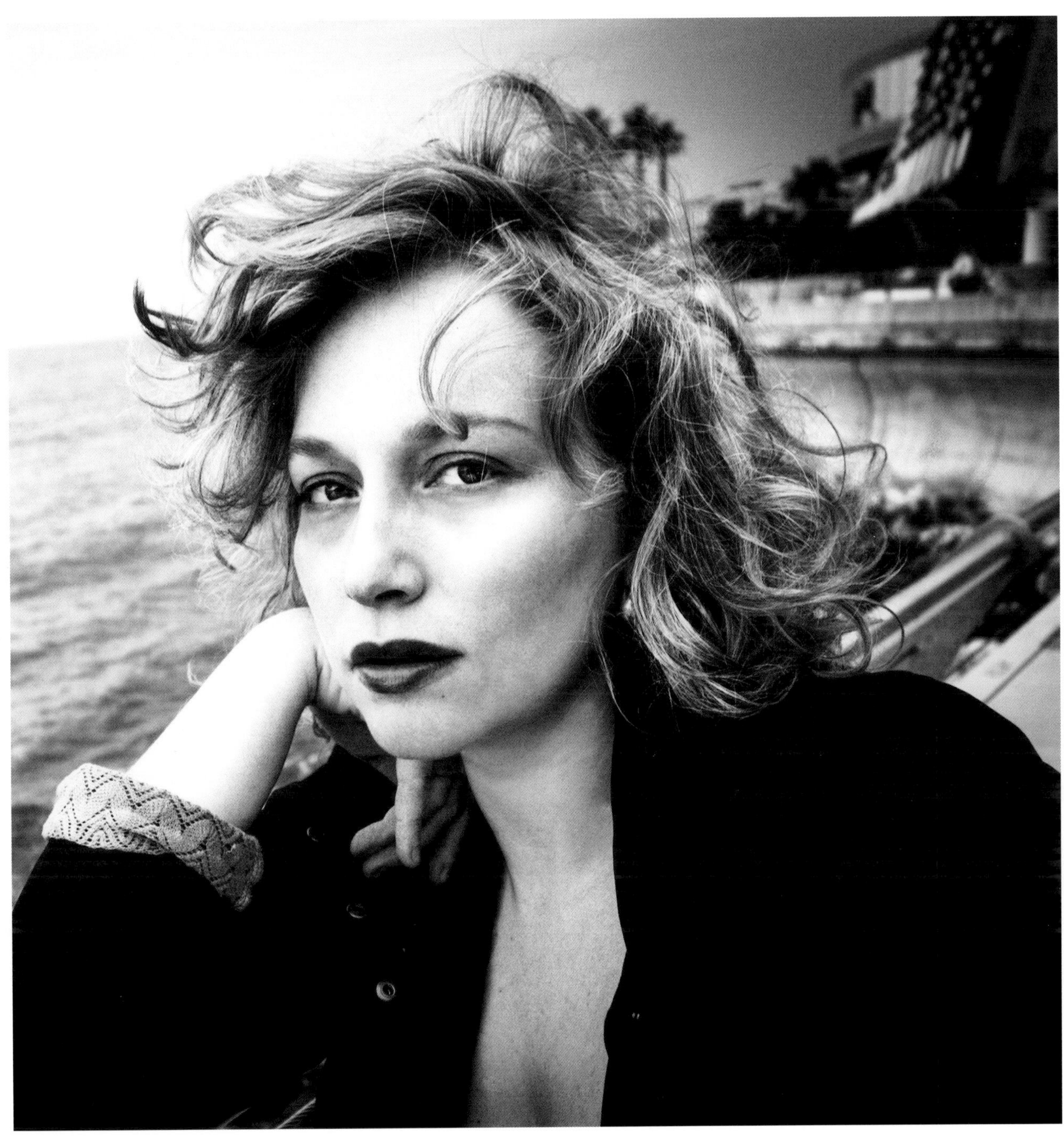

My special thanks to / Mein besonderer Dank an

Eva Bertram
For pulling me to shore when I was drowning in images. Her contribution as an
image editor was invaluable to the stories *Of Lions and Lambs* and its predecessor
48 Hours Blackpool /
Für ihre rettende Hand, als ich in der Flut der Bilder zu ertrinken drohte. Ihr Beitrag
zur Bildredaktion war für die Geschichte von *Of Lions and Lambs* und für deren Vor-
gänger *48 Hours Blackpool* von unschätzbarem Wert

Kurt Rehkopf
For translating the words and voices in this book with talent and accuracy /
Für die so gekonnte wie präzise Übersetzung der Worte und Stimmen in diesem Buch

Philippa Hurd
For her amiability and competence as editor and translator /
Für ihre Liebenswürdigkeit und Kompetenz als Lektorin und Übersetzerin

Katrin Günther
For her swift and effective editorial input /
Für ihren schnellen und effektiven redaktionellen Input

Matthias Harder
For his straightforward approach to photography /
Für seinen geradlinigen Blick auf die Fotografie

Mark Gisbourne
For his profound analysis of my work /
Für seine tiefgründige Analyse meiner Arbeit

Klaus Kehrer and his Team / Klaus Kehrer und sein Team
For their great support in the realization of this book /
Für ihre große Unterstützung beim Zustandekommen dieses Buches

All those who opened their doors, when I knocked, and their hearts when I asked /
All jene, die mir ihre Türen geöffnet haben, als ich bei ihnen anklopfte, und ihre
Herzen, als ich sie darum bat

Texts / Texte:
Mark Gisbourne, Matthias Harder, Benita Suchodrev

Editing, Proofreading / Lektorat, Korrektorat:
Philippa Hurd, Katrin Günther

Translations / Übersetzungen:
Kurt Rehkopf, Philippa Hurd

Design / Gestaltung:
Benita Suchodrev, Kehrer Design Heidelberg (July Mollik, Anja Aronska)

Image Editing / Bildredaktion:
Benita Suchodrev, Eva Bertram

Image Processing / Bildbearbeitung:
Benita Suchodrev, Kehrer Design Heidelberg (Patrick Horn)

Production / Gesamtherstellung:
Kehrer Design Heidelberg (Tom Streicher)

Bibliographic information published by the Deutsche National
bibliothek The Deutsche Nationalbibliothek lists this publication
in the Deutsche Nationalbibliografie; detailed bibliographic data
is available on the Internet at http://dnb.dnb.de. /
Bibliografische Information der Deutschen Nationalbibliothek
Die Deutsche Nationalbibliothek verzeichnet diese Publikation in
der Deutschen Nationalbibliografie; detaillierte bibliografische
Daten sind im Internet über http://dnb.dnb.de abrufbar.

Quotation p. 3 / Zitat S. 3:
Aesop, *The Kingdom of the Lion* / Äsop, *Königreich des Löwen*

www.benitasuchodrev.com

Printed and bound in Germany
ISBN 978-3-86828-949-7

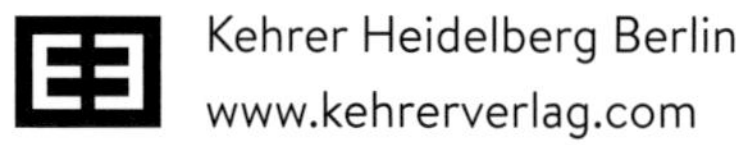

Kehrer Heidelberg Berlin
www.kehrerverlag.com